For SS (in memoriam)

ARTIFICIAL INTELLIGENCE

Law and Regulation

Edited by

CHARLES KERRIGAN

Partner, CMS UK

Edward Elgar
PUBLISHING

Cheltenham, UK • Northampton, MA, USA

Published by
Edward Elgar Publishing Limited
The Lypiatts
15 Lansdown Road
Cheltenham
Glos GL50 2JA
UK

Edward Elgar Publishing, Inc.
William Pratt House
9 Dewey Court
Northampton
Massachusetts 01060
USA

A catalogue record for this book
is available from the British Library

Library of Congress Control Number: 2022931170

This book is available electronically in the **Elgar**online
Law subject collection
http://dx.doi.org/10.4337/9781800371729

MIX
Paper from
responsible sources
FSC® C013604

ISBN 978 1 80037 171 2 (cased)
ISBN 978 1 80037 172 9 (eBook)

Printed and bound by CPI Group (UK) Ltd, Croydon, CR0 4YY

CONTENTS

PART III   INDUSTRIES

PART IV   HUMAN AI

PART V   TECHNICAL AND CONSULTING

EXTENDED CONTENTS

PART II   LEGAL

5 CORPORATE GOVERNANCE

6 REGULATORY COMPLIANCE

PART III   INDUSTRIES

15   FINANCIAL REGULATION

16   INSURANCE

17   RETAIL AND CONSUMER

CONTRIBUTORS

Stephen Ashurst is a senior independent FinTech consultant, entrepreneur and author based in the City of London for global and domestic (UK) clients. A former Visual Basic coder, following a short stint at Bar school, Stephen now works with large corporate clients (Barclays, Lloyds Banking Group, EY, Fidelity, L&G etc), Governments (HM Treasury, Cabinet Office, FCA) and a portfolio of wealth and FinTech startups and recoveries. Stephen advises on FinTech and specifically how artificial intelligence and machine learning may help streamline and clarify product propositions, better define technology strategy and deliver strong business architecture. Stephen's book on real-world, practical use cases of decentralised ledger technology, Blockchain Applied, is published by Routledge.

Jason G Allen is Senior Research Fellow at the Humboldt-Universität zu Berlin, an Affiliate at the Cambridge Centre for Alternative Finance, and Adjunct Senior Lecturer at the University of Tasmania. He works on the legal impacts of emerging technologies broadly. While his current research focus is on private law issues, he brings a solid grounding in public law. Jason is a member of current UNIDROIT and UNCITRAL working groups on novel technologies, has consulted for the public and private sector and is Tasmanian Chapter Chair of the Australian Society of Computers and Law. Jason studied law at the University of Tasmania (BA & LLB), Universität Augsburg (LLM) and Cambridge University (PhD), the latter as a Poynton Scholar. His recent work on smart contracts, cryptoassets and internet jurisdiction has been published in leading international journals. His monograph Non-Statutory Executive Powers and Judicial Review is forthcoming from Cambridge University Press and his edited collection (with Peter Hunn) on Smart Legal Contracts is forthcoming from Oxford University Press.

Birgitte Andersen has a PhD and MSc in Economics from the University of Reading (UK), and an MA and BA from the University of Aalborg (DK). She is CEO of Big Innovation Centre, a London-based think-tank and innovation hub that promotes open innovation via challenge-led taskforces, All-Party groups in UK Parliament on Artificial Intelligence and Blockchain. She advises economists and policymakers of national governments in and beyond Europe, as well as the OECD, UN and WIPO and large firms, and serves as an expert defence witness in the UK courts on matters of IP use on the internet. She was Rapporteur for the EU Commission representing the EU Expert Group on Knowledge Transfer and Open Innovation, and currently sits on the EU Expert Advisory Panel for Horizon 2020 – Societal Challenge: Europe in a Changing World – Inclusive, Innovative and Reflective Societies. In October 2018 Birgitte was appointed to the Arab League Expert Group on Digital Transformation regarding Digital Government Strategy for the Arab World.

Stefano Barazza is Director of the LLM LegalTech at the Hillary Rodham Clinton School of Law at Swansea University and Academic Lead of the ERDF-funded Legal Innovation Lab Wales, a £ 5.6 million research centre in LegalTech, access to justice and cyberterrorism.

He is an expert in intellectual property and innovation, with a focus on the application of new technologies (in particular, blockchain, smart contracts and artificial intelligence) to legal practice and intellectual property management. He regularly collaborates with the Solicitors Regulation Authority, the Law Society of England and Wales and a wide range of LegalTech stakeholders, with the aim of supporting the transformation of legal practice and legal education through technology. Stefano is co-editor in chief of the Journal of Intellectual Property Law and Practice (OUP) and has previously led postgraduate degree programmes and training for the UK Intellectual Property Office.

Jeremy Barnett is Honorary Professor of Algorithmic Regulation at the Bartlett Real Estate Instiute, UCL; a regulatory barrister at St Pauls Chambers; and Executive Director and Founder of Resilience Partners. He was a founder of the Centre of Behavioural Change at UCL and is currently joint leader of the Real Estate Consortium 'DigitalDisruption@BREI'. He is also joint London Chair of FIBREE. Jeremy's published papers include E-Legal Services 'To Speed Up Justice for B2B systems' (2006), 'Algorithmic Dispute Resolution' (2017) and 'Algorithms and the Law' 2019.

Shaun Barney holds a BEng in Electrical and Electronic Engineering, an MSc in Advanced Computer Science and a PhD in Artificial Intelligence Applications for Computer Vision from Newcastle University. He was a co-founder of Neura Technologies. He has extensive experience solving real world business problems using the application of AI and has developed many end-to-end systems which have been deployed through desktop applications, mobile applications, APIs, websites, and embedded devices to service users around the globe.

Matthew Bennett is a partner in the CMS Technology and Sourcing Team. He specialises in advising on outsourcing, offshoring and shared services (both BPO and ITO), procurement, logistics and other strategic or complex commercial contracts and arrangements. He assists clients in all phases of their commercial relationships, from designing procurement processes through to disputes and exits. He has extensive experience advising customers and suppliers across a wide range of sectors, with a particular focus in retail and technology and media & communications. His clients include some of the largest IT and outsourcing suppliers in Europe as well as large multinational consumers of IT, business process and outsourcing services. Before returning to private practice in 2010, Matthew was UK General Counsel for the largest technology service provider in the UK. In this role he was responsible for the negotiation of some the largest outsourcing transactions in Europe, including some of the most high-profile transactions with the UK government, and he also sat on a UK Board which oversaw the delivery of the these projects.

Doug Brown is Chief Data Scientist at Capita. He has over 26 years of extensive practical experience delivering award winning digital and Big Data transformation projects gained from working at four big advisory firms and start-ups in Europe, the Americas and Asia. He has held a variety of senior management and executive consultancy and programme roles at E&Y LLP, PwC LLP, IBM Global Services, Wipro Technologies and Zurich Financial Services.

Peter Church is Counsel in the technology practice at Linklaters LLP. He originally studied Computer Science at Cambridge and has 20 years' experience navigating the interaction between technology and the law. He was recently seconded to the UK Information Commissioner's Office, first to work in the Technology Policy unit and subsequently to help advise on the issues raised by the COVID-19 pandemic.

Richard Cumbley is a partner and Global Head of Linklaters' TMT and IP practices, advising multinationals and governments on complex information management and data privacy issues. He has worked on data-related projects across the globe, including major data security incidents, large-scale privacy litigation, appearances before regulators, contentious and large-scale subject access issues, online monitoring techniques, government access programs, data localisation and 'big data'. Richard also counsels clients on the implications of new technology such as 3D printing, AI, blockchain technology, interactive TV and IOT. In addition, Richard advises on complex technology contracts, including large-scale outsourcing, cloud services, technology development and related services contracts in both contentious and non-contentious environments. Based in London and Dublin, Richard has advised on IT, data protection, information governance and outsourcing deals in more than half of the firm's offices around the world. He is ranked by both legal directories, Legal 500 and Chambers, in the first tier of UK privacy and data lawyers.

Dana Denis-Smith is founder and Chief Executive of Obelisk Support. Having started the business in 2010, Dana has pioneered the concept of flexible working in the legal industry. Obelisk Support has grown to a network of over 1,000 legal consultants who deliver legal services to clients worldwide. Dana studied at the London School of Economics before embarking on a career in journalism. Passionate about access to justice and equality of opportunity since she was a child, Dana then switched focus and trained as a lawyer with Linklaters. Finding that her time in practice didn't provide enough of an outlet for her entrepreneurial energy, Dana started her first business, a global insight provider, in 2008. She then went on to set up Obelisk Support to provide flexible legal services to top companies and law firms, using lawyers who no longer wanted a traditional legal career.

Nick Doffman is a partner in Mishcon de Reya's Real Estate department, with more than 30 years' experience in dealing with all aspects of commercial property. He has expertise in structuring and negotiating real estate acquisitions and sales, as well as advising on development and landlord and tenant matters. A significant proportion of Nick's practice is focused on international inward investment, acting on high-value UK property transactions for overseas investors. He has strong connections across the Far East region, particularly within Hong Kong and Singapore, and a well-developed understanding of the business culture in these areas. In addition, he has advised many well-known UK institutional and entrepreneurial companies. Recommended as a Leader in his field in Chambers & Partners 2021 and as a Leading Individual in Legal 500 2021, Nick is praised for his exceptional knowledge and his entrepreneurial, commercial, personable and to-the-point advice.

William Dunning is an associate at Simmons & Simmons and a member of the firm's AI Group. His practice focuses on international arbitration, as well as on technology-related disputes. William graduated from the University of Durham with a BA in Economics in 2012, before receiving a Graduate Diploma in Law and completing his LLM in Law and Economics at Queen Mary University of London. He is admitted as a solicitor of the Senior Courts of England and Wales.

Rachel Free is a partner in the patent team at international law firm CMS, where she helps clients to protect their technology through patents. She has an MSc in Artificial Intelligence and a DPhil in Vision Science. She qualified as a European and UK patent attorney in the last century and has worked on AI patent drafting and prosecution through her career. Rachel is a member of the All Party Parliamentary Group on AI (APPG AI) which advises parliamentarians regarding AI. She is vice Chair of the Chartered Institute of Patent Attorneys (CIPA) computer technology committee and is mentioned in the 2019 legal 500 CMS entry for law firms with patent attorneys as having 'deep technical knowledge'.

Kushal Gandhi is a partner in the Finance Disputes team at CMS London, specialising in Finance and FinTech dispute resolution. He is an experienced litigation and international arbitration practitioner. Kushal regularly assists clients to navigate complex issues, including cross-border disputes. He also helps to develop risk mitigation strategies and obtain emergency relief from courts and tribunals.

Claudia Giannoni is an RICS, RIBA & ARB qualified real estate professional and doctoral researcher at UCL. Claudia is currently pursuing her doctoral research studies at UCL Engineering, Institute of Finance & Technology. Her main research topic involves application of blockchain in real estate transactions. She has worked with some of the top real estate firms, including Wilmotte in Paris, WDA group in Hong Kong, Allies & Morrison in London and Al-Hokair Group (Kingdom of Saudi Arabia) globally, where she used to be part of the senior management responsible for leading multi-billion projects in Ireland, Italy, Spain, KSA and the UK. Claudia has been an entrepreneur for most of her working life; she co-founded Breschi Studio and ASI Progetti based in Florence, Italy and ran it as a managing partner for more than a decade, until 2017. She is an expert witness for Monte Dei Paschi Bank to evaluate and provide judicial guidance to large-scale property disputes in the Courts of Lucca & Florence, as well as an advisor to large real estate firms in Canada and US. Since 2017 Claudia has been co-founder and CEO of RelAi, an AI/ML-powered Proptech startup aiming to reduce the complexity of the UK's property buying and selling process by making it faster and cheaper using blockchain technology. Prior to her doctoral studies, Claudia earned her Master's degree in Architecture from the University of Florence and an MSc in International Real Estate from the Bartlett School at UCL. She has co-authored four books on real estate and architecture.

Richard Hay is UK Head of Fintech and Counsel at Linklaters. He has extensive experience advising financial institutions, market infrastructure providers, payments institutions and technology companies on financial structuring and regulatory matters arising from digitalisation initiatives, new product launches, cross-border expansion and complex legal and regulatory challenges. Richard is heavily engaged in the development of law and policy in relation to the application of new technologies to finance. He is a member of the UK Jurisdiction Taskforce of the LawTech Delivery Panel. He regularly participates in industry initiatives and working groups, as well as in developments led by international standard setters and other bodies, including the OECD, FSB, Bank for International Settlements and Financial Markets Law Committee (FMLC), amongst others. Richard is a solicitor of England and Wales and a French avocat (member of the Paris bar). He is a CFA charterholder.

Petko Karamotchev is CEO and Co-Founder of INDUSTRIA and also a mentor at R3. He holds degrees from the University of Portsmouth, UK and Cotrugli Business School, and has completed programmes at Saïd Business School, University of Oxford. He is a member of the British Blockchain Association and the Nordic Blockchain Association. Petko was an advisor (2019–20) to the All-Party Parliamentary Group on Blockchain in London and is a current member of the European Blockchain Partnership Technical group (2020–). Petko works as an expert to the ISO/ TC 307 Committee on Blockchain and distributed ledger technologies, ISO/IEC JTC 1/SC 42 – Artificial intelligence, and TC CEN/CLC/JTC 21 Artificial Intelligence. He is also an industry associate of the University College London Centre for Blockchain Technologies.

Emre Kazim is Research Fellow in Computer Science at University College London, and the founder of Holistic AI, a start-up focused on providing a platform-as-a-service solution to organisations that want to harness AI ethically and safely. His expertise lies in AI ethics, governance, accountability, regulation and policy. He holds a PhD in Philosophy.

Stephen Kenny QC is a leading commercial QC, with specialisms in insurance and reinsurance, commodities, shipping and international arbitration. He has practised since 1988 from 7 King's Bench Walk in the Temple. He took silk in 2006.

Charles Kerrigan is a lawyer working in finance and emerging technology with specialisms in AI, crypto and decentralised finance. He works on corporate finance and venture capital fundraising transactions for companies, funds, platforms and financial institutions and on consulting projects on blockchain, digital assets, AI and automation/transformation for public bodies, policy makers, standards institutions and corporations. He is a partner at the international law firm CMS; an Advisor to Cointelligence Fund; a Board Advisor to Holistic AI; and an Advisory Board Member of the Investment Association's Engine. He is a member of the Advisory Boards of the All Party Parliamentary Groups on Artificial Intelligence and Blockchain. He is the author of *The Financing of Intangible Assets: TMT Finance and Emerging Technologies* (LexisNexis UK, 2019).

Nick Kirby is a partner in Mishcon de Reya's Real Estate department. He specialises in commercial real estate work, dealing with investment (including corporate real estate) acquisitions and sales for institutional and private clients, development work, management work and acting for both landlords and tenants. Alongside his commercial real estate work, Nick is responsible for researching new technologies, including software which utilises machine learning and AI to extract data from documents. Nick is a mentor for the companies taking part in MDR LAB, Mishcon's incubator programme for tech startups in the legal space, and is the firm's Head of PropTech. As part of this role he has built technology products which help automate and streamline tasks and co-founded a commercial property start-up, Least. In 2019, Nick was named as one of the top ten most innovative lawyers in Europe by the Financial Times. Nick also collaborated with HM Land Registry on their Digital Street research and development initiative to complete the UK's first successful digitised end-to-end residential property transaction, and is working with a number of clients to facilitate the automatic exchange of property data.

Adriano Koshiyama is Research Fellow in Computer Science at University College London and the founder of Holistic AI, a start-up focused on providing a platform-as-a-service solution to organisations that want to harness AI ethically and safely. Academically, he has published more than 30 papers in international conferences and journals. He is responsible for ground-breaking results at the intersection of machine learning and finance, with earlier work on GANs and transfer learning in this area.

Sophia Le Vesconte is a senior (English law-qualified) lawyer at Linklaters LLP, with more than 12 years' experience in financial structuring and regulation. In recent years Sophia has focused specifically on the use of novel technologies within the financial sector, particularly in relation to financial market infrastructures and payments. She is responsible for the development of the firm's thought leadership and knowhow in this area. She has led and contributed to countless publications, journal articles, training materials, consultation responses and working groups concerning fintech. Sophia has spent time working in Asia and Europe and on secondment to two major international banks.

Hannah Yee-Fen Lim is Associate Professor of Business Law at Nanyang Business School, Nanyang Technological University, Singapore. She graduated with double degrees in Computer Science and Law from the University of Sydney, Australia, where she went on to complete a Master of Laws by Research with Honours under a Telstra Scholarship. She is an internationally recognised legal expert on all areas of technology law, including data privacy, AI, blockchain, fintech, health technology, cybersecurity, ethics and intellectual property. She has been appointed as a legal expert and has advised international bodies such as the WHO and the United Nations (UNCITRAL) on areas such as AI, fintech and cryptocurrency. Hannah is one of 15 international legal experts appointed by UNIDROIT to draft new international legal instruments to govern cryptocurrencies, non-fungible tokens and other digital assets. She is the author of hundreds of papers and six scholarly books on law and technology published by internationally established publishers. Hannah's research has been cited with approval by the High Court of Australia.

Alastair Moore is Head of Analytics and Machine Learning at MDRxTECH, Mishcon de Reya's digital transformation consultancy. Alastair is a UCL Computer Science PhD with a background in computer vision, analytics, machine learning, blockchain, strategy and technology innovation. He is an experienced manager and entrepreneur who has built teams in both large and small organisations. He is regularly called upon to audit, evaluate and provide guidance to large-scale technology programmes for MDRxTECH clients. An entrepreneurial and dynamic problem solver, Alastair co-founded Satalia, which builds and applies AI technology to solve efficiency problems for organisations such as Tesco and PwC. He also co-founded the venture-backed WeArePopUp.com, and helped establish the IDEALondon innovation centre with Cisco Systems. Alastair continues to maintain an active teaching role in the UCL School of Management (MSc Business Analytics) and Peking University, Beijing (MBA Technology Strategy). His research interests include technology strategy, blockchain, smart contracting and computational law. Alastair also works across the Mishcon de Reya Group to ensure the business consistently uses data and machine learning techniques to support and improve its business processes.

Charlotte Payne is a barrister at 7 King's Bench Walk and practices in insurance law, among other areas. Charlotte has an undergraduate degree in Geology, as well as an MPhil in Geography from the University of Cambridge. Prior to coming to the Bar, Charlotte worked as a consultant in the mining industry. Charlotte went on to study law at BPP University College, while also working full-time in the Legal and Business Affairs teams at Cambridge University Press.

Martin Petrin is Dancap Private Equity Chair in Corporate Governance at Western University in Canada and Professor of Corporate Law and Governance at University College London in the UK, where he previously also served as Vice Dean for Innovation & Enterprise. He has held visiting positions at NYU London, the University of Cambridge, Notre Dame Law School and the Max Planck Institute for Comparative and Private Law. Martin's main research interests are in corporate, corporate governance and business law, often from a comparative perspective. In addition to core topics in these areas, his research also focuses on the impact of Artificial Intelligence and new technologies on business and other organisations. Martin has published widely in his areas of expertise, including as the author and editor of several books, and is a regular speaker at international conferences. Before joining academia, Martin practised law with a leading international business law firm. He has been admitted to the Bar in New York and Switzerland. In addition to his academic work, Martin continues to act as a consultant for various public and private organisations.

Suzanne Rab is an independent barrister at Serle Court Chambers. Suzanne has two decades of wide experience of competition law, regulatory law, data protection and EU law. Suzanne's practice has a particular focus on the interface between innovation, trade and economic regulation. She acts in disputes involving governments, regulators and businesses across the regulated sectors including in the financial services, energy/environmental, healthcare/pharmaceuticals, infrastructure, TMT and natural resources sectors. Suzanne has significant experience at the interface between intellectual property rights and data protection. In private practice as a solicitor prior to joining the bar, she held positions at leading international regulation and trade practices. Most recently she was a partner and head of regulatory practice with a leading US law firm. She has also held the role of director at PricewaterhouseCoopers, working within its strategy, economics, and regulatory teams. Suzanne maintains an active academic practice concurrently with her barrister practice. She is Professor of Commercial Law and holds the Practice Chair at Brunel University, lectures in law at Oxford University and is Visiting Professor at Imperial College, London (IPR and competition). She has significant research interests in the areas of technology, innovation and artificial intelligence.

Patricia Shaw is CEO of Beyond Reach Consulting Limited. With 20 years' experience as a solicitor in technology, regulatory/government affairs and risk management, she advises on AI and data ethics, policy and governance, including advising Ethics Advisory Boards. Patricia has expertise in data, financial services, public sector (Health and EdTech) and smart cities. She is co-author of *The AI Book*, the 'Technology Governance during a Time of Crisis' report, the IEEE Certification Criteria for COVID19 tracing technologies, *The Law of Artificial Intelligence*, the 'Responsible AI: A Global Policy Framework' 2021 update and the Springer Society paper 'Towards an Equitable Digital Society: Artificial Intelligence and Corporate Digital Responsibility'. Patricia is Chair of the Society for Computers and Law in the UK, and is on the Board and Vice-Chair of the AI Committee of iTechLaw. As an advocate of Responsible AI she sits on the IEEE's ECPAIS ethical certification panel, IEEE's P7003 algorithmic bias standards programme, RSA's online harms advisory panel and the steering committee of Women Leading in AI, and is a ForHumanity Fellow working on independent audit of AI systems.

Iain Sheridan is a legal consultant covering all aspects of financial regulation and technology, including fundraising, structuring, contracting, documentation, intellectual property and enforcement. His experience covers UK and EU financial regulation relevant to both buy-side and sell-side firms. He also provides advice to industry associations on financial regulation and technology. Before becoming a consultant, he was Head of Legal Europe and Asia for the financial sector dedicated investment bank Fox-Pitt, Kelton. His consulting projects have included advising ABN AMRO, Bank of America, Barclays, Deutsche Bank, Fidelity Investments and Société Générale. A qualified barrister (England & Wales) and solicitor (New South Wales), Iain has also studied data science at Oxford University and machine learning at Cambridge University. He frequently contributes to seminars, and his articles on financial regulation, disruptive innovation, e-commerce, machine learning and smart phones have been quoted authoritatively by other international practitioners. He is the author of *Financial Regulation and Technology* (Edward Elgar Publishing, 2022).

Scott Stainton holds a BEng in Electronic and Computer Engineering and a PhD in Artificial Intelligence Applications for Telecommunications from Newcastle University where he has published many peer reviewed academic papers in the machine learning and telecommunications field. He was a co-founder of Neura Technologies, an AI consultancy founded on the principles of democratising AI for everyone that went on to receive national recognition from the Digital Catapult's Machine Intelligence Garage programme. He has extensive experience with enterprise level platform design and has created solutions powered by AI which solve real world business problems to service users around the globe.

Minesh Tanna leads the AI Group at Simmons & Simmons, where he is also a solicitor-advocate specialising in technology-related disputes. Minesh is also Chair of the AI Group of the Society for Computers and Law (SCL) and has previously been a member of the CBI's AI Working Group. As well as advising clients on AI-related legal and ethical issues, Minesh is a frequent speaker at conferences and seminars on AI, and he has previously been invited to speak about AI on behalf of the United Nations and at CogX.

Philip Treleaven is Director of the UK Centre for Financial Computing (www .financialcomputing.org) and Professor of Computing at UCL. Twenty-five years ago his research group development much of the early fraud detection technology and built the first insider dealing detection system for the London Stock Exchange. For the past 18 years Professor Treleaven's research group has developed algorithmic trading systems with many of the leading investment banks and funds, and for the past 8 years they have worked on automating regulation, systemic risk and RegTech with the Bank of England, FCA and other regulators. Current research includes the application of machine learning to legal technology, including computer-understandable legal contracts and automated dispute resolution. He has also launched 9 start-ups.

Richard Tromans has been working in the legal sector for more than 20 years. He is the founder of the global legal tech news site, Artificial Lawyer; works as a strategy and innovation consultant through his own advisory business, Tromans Consulting; and is the founder and Chair of the Changing Legal international think tank.

Oliver Vercoe is a lawyer at CMS with experience in bank and corporate transactions and in AI and Fintech. He has a notable interest in cryptoasset regulatory issues and decentralised finance, working on policy matters on these topics as well as advising global organisations on token issuances and regulations. Ollie continues to follow the development of digital regulation and development across the globe.

Tirath Virdee is Director of Artificial Intelligence at Capita. He is involved in researching, applying and writing about AI, blockchain, quantum computing and cybersecurity. He is the founder of Xenesis, a member of the Parliamentary Groups on AI and Blockchain and an advisor to the Scottish government on AI strategy. He was Director of Advanced Technology Group at Siemens AG, was a physicist in the UK Atomic Energy Authority's Breeder Reactor Programme, and has a PhD in Engineering Mathematics.

Vanessa Whitman is a partner in the Finance Disputes team at CMS in London and has a growing practice specialising in the fast-changing world of FinTech and crypto disputes. She works primarily on contentious matters for banks, financial institutions, FinTechs and insolvency professionals, advising clients on various aspects of contentious banking and insolvency law and related disputes. Vanessa also has significant experience advising clients how to deal with Serious Fraud Office cases and other fraud-related matters, having advised on Britain's largest mortgage fraud. Alongside her legal career, she is a passionate campaigner for better mental health and wellbeing awareness, and for greater diversity and inclusion within the legal industry.

Roland Wiring is a partner at CMS Germany in Hamburg, focusing on the life sciences and healthcare sector. He advises companies active in this field on a broad range of legal issues including regulatory, business development, transactions and litigation. Roland's work in particular focuses on eHealth and the specific legal issues related to the digitisation of healthcare.

FOREWORD

Philip Treleaven

I would like to commend Charles Kerrigan for assembling an esteemed team of experts to address the important subject of AI and the law.

This book covers the two principal AI themes: the impact of existing legislation on AI and algorithms, and the impact of AI LegalTech/RegTech on legal services.

Soon there will be billions of 'intelligent' algorithms interacting with each other and with humans with minimal oversight. AI algorithms making vital decisions: from autonomous vehicles and trading systems, to medical treatment, employment, predicting the outcome of trials, offender sentencing and so on. What makes 'intelligent' algorithms especially fascinating is their ability to make decisions in their own right and, being self-programming, to evolve their behaviour in unexpected ways.

Organisations are increasingly alarmed about their algorithms causing major financial or reputational damage. High-profile cases include VW's Dieselgate scandal, with fines of $34.69b; Knight Capital going bankrupt (~$450m) due to a glitch in its algorithmic trading system; Google's facial recognition algorithm that labelled some black people as gorillas; Uber's self-driving car, which ran a stop sign; and Amazon's AI recruiting tool, scrapped after showing bias against women. In response, companies are introducing 'algorithm audits', regulators are fining companies and governments are legislating and imposing bans. So, AI technology, like IP and litigation, will become an increasingly important and lucrative specialisation for law firms.

As an illustration of the future, major research initiatives are under way to create computer-understandable contracts, regulations and statutes. This is important since it will underpin automation, for example, allowing a corporation to assess compliance in specific jurisdictions.

These developments pose two major questions. Does AI (and robotics) require its own corpus of *algorithm* laws? Will AI technology replace lawyers?

Undoubtedly, the answer to both is a resounding NO.

That said, it is becoming increasingly important for lawyers to understand how AI technology works, and what it can do for them in terms of LegalTech professional tools.

Charles Kerrigan and contributors have made a valuable contribution with this timely publication.

Professor Philip Treleaven
UCL Professor of Computing

PREFACE

To paraphrase the introduction to every best man's speech, being asked to edit a book on law and regulation relating to artificial intelligence is a great honour but nobody wants to do it. It is with that in mind that I found myself starting work on this project at the beginning of 2020.

AI is a prediction and personalisation machine. Hence its profundity.

I've been interested in AI since the late 1990s, when I learnt about it after reading press stories about IBM's Deep Blue and Gary Kasparov's critique of the technologies involved. I am fortunate that my day job in the field of emerging technologies has allowed me to work on AI in a commercial context for more than ten years. As a non-technologist it has also been inevitable during all this time that cultural influences have affected my thinking. The American novelist William Gaddis wrote brilliantly in the second half of the twentieth century about the effect of technology on business and culture. In the 1950s he became interested in the player piano (a self-playing piano employing programmed music on rolls of card). He said: 'I see the player piano as the grandfather of the computer, the ancestor of the entire nightmare we live in, the birth of the binary world where there is no option other than yes or no and where there is no refuge.' Fair warning indeed!

I hope you enjoy the book. I also hope that you follow up on its encouragement to be curious and to learn and think about the issues raised. The requirements of a commercial lawyer are changing and whoever you are judged by (clients, peers, voters, etc) will reward that curiosity and thoughtfulness. If you are a lawyer, you should still be a lawyer, but you should now have basic literacy in statistics, psychology and what new technologies do.

With this book you will be at least 'educated' on AI per the definition offered by William Feather: 'being able to differentiate between what you know and what you don't.'

The author team (biographies on pages xxi to xxix) includes friends and colleagues new and old. The main thing they have in common is that they are each outstanding in their field.

As well as the advice and support I got from the chapter authors, I'm grateful to Tony Hawitt, the commissioning editor at Edward Elgar Publishing, for his tolerance and calmness. I'm also grateful to my colleagues Christina Burdis-Smith and Faye Coman, who have both spent many hours with me organising the text.

So far as we are aware, this is the first book of its type. It isn't the first legal text on AI, of course, but its approach to the topic – as explained in the Introduction – is new. The book is written at and during the development of its subject matter. Therefore, as much as the various authors aim to assist readers in understanding and formulating their own answers to questions they now face, equally the authors would expect their own responses to evolve. Readers' questions, notes on their own jurisdictions and examples of hard or easy questions are most welcome. Please send these to charles.kerrigan@cms-cmno.com and/or direct to chapter authors. We are all still learning.

Charles Kerrigan

TABLE OF CASES

TABLE OF LEGISLATION

UK STATUTORY INSTRUMENTS

EU LEGISLATION RETAINED IN UK LAW

PART I

INTRODUCTORY MATERIALS

1

INTRODUCTORY ESSAY

Charles Kerrigan

A. INTRODUCTION TO THE BOOK

1.001 In order to avoid this text needing to be updated as often as the technology that it describes, it has been written to help lawyers understand how to think about the collection of technologies powering and associated with artificial intelligence ('AI') as well as to set out the legal rules that apply to them. It is a broad guide to a very large topic. This is for a number of reasons.

1.002 First is the obvious redundancy in writing about the laws applicable to AI before many of them have been written.

1.003 Second is to acknowledge the audacity of spending months in producing a physical text about a subject matter that changes in seconds, including in ways that are invisible.

1.004 Third is that the text is intended to have value for the widest range of readers. That includes: lawyers: law students; legal academics; lawyers practising in traditional law firms, in non-traditional law firms, in chambers, in corporations and other forms of business structure, in public and governmental and quasi-governmental bodies. It also includes people who are not lawyers: technologists; non-legal academics; regulators; compliance professionals; policy-makers; politicians; teachers; researchers; people who run law firms; consultants; and business people.

Fourth, because a thesis of the book is that AI cannot be just a topic of interest to IT lawyers. **1.005** It matters to all lawyers and all lawyers should be in a position to be able to advise on questions that it raises. Briefly, all legal disciplines and all industries are being affected by AI. The book tries to make the case for this not by setting up a single persuasive argument but by covering the topic in a breadth that speaks for itself.

Fifth, because another thesis of the book is that AI will change all industries and so lawyers **1.006** working in all industries will be required by their clients or in their research to understand the implications of the changes. It will not be possible to continue to advise on industry questions while handing off points touching AI to others. AI is pervasive and all lawyers must be prepared to understand its implications for the industries on which they advise.

Sixth, because a third thesis of this book is that AI changes the job of lawyers. This happens **1.007** in a number of ways, but in this book we focus in particular on the implications of the fact that uses of AI must be ethical by design. So advice on AI cannot be added at the end of a project or included in a round of legal comments. Legal review of issues and projects will become more integrated in wider business and policy decision-making by necessity.

This is a book about software, ethics and a profound shift in the context in which legal questions **1.008** are considered and legal services are performed. It is still a book about AI, but this is a proxy for the challenges now facing both lawyers and the people and machines that use technologies that include aspects of AI. That is a large and growing group, soon to include pretty much everyone.

The book is written on an understanding that the boundaries within which lawyers operate **1.009** are being expanded by the digitalisation of everything and the overwhelming importance of the information economy. That expansion doesn't mean that we need more lawyers or that lawyers should do everything. It means that lawyers should become aware of how their roles increasingly overlap with others and that an increasing number of questions cannot and should not be solely delegated to lawyers.

There are many books on the changes in the nature of professional services firms and their place **1.010** in the economy. These, however, most often focus on the legal industry as a whole, on how to manage clients and on how to manage law firms. On the other hand, practising and academic lawyers work with textbooks that state the law. Fortunately, the author team did not have the luxury, in writing this book, of simply stating 'the law of AI'. Future editions will do so but I hope that they do not lose the challenging and questioning with which the authors of this edition have had to engage in bringing it together. My thanks to all of them.

So, if not just the law of AI, what do we cover? I'm hoping that each reader will find their own **1.011** themes and build on them. My themes and focuses are:

First, to have a text that can be used to consider what questions lawyers now need to answer and **1.012** how should they go about answering them.

Second, that this is a book about information, automation, personalisation and unintended **1.013** consequences.

1.014   Third, that the text should answer some questions but, more than that, should help readers' understanding of how to engage with AI and to ask themselves the right questions in doing so.

1.015   It is a manual for how to think about AI in commercial contexts.

1.016   Finally, note that my definition of 'AI' in the first paragraph of the introduction was not 'artificial intelligence'. The abbreviation, rightly, stands not just for the words that it abbreviates but for the technologies, uses and influences of artificial intelligence.

1.017   This essay reflects my views rather than a consolidated view of the whole writing team.

B. HOW TO READ THIS BOOK

1.018   The book is in five parts. The first part is introductory, setting out the basics of AI, including its history and what it is. The second part covers AI in the context of traditional legal categories – contract, tort and others recognisable from traditional textbooks. The third part covers AI in the context of different industries, following the above-noted thesis that AI is pervasive. The fourth part covers the human sides of AI, including its ethics. The fifth part covers a number of business topics that are relevant to lawyers written by some of the professionals that lawyers will work with on projects involving AI. It is not necessary to read the book in the order in which it has been arranged. Each chapter links to others but also stands in its own right.

1.019   Of course, the book is not exhaustive. No book on AI ever will be. In planning the book we had to take decisions to omit some important topics. AI in criminal justice, for example, merits a book of its own. We took the decision therefore to cover commercial law, but in a broad sense.

1.020   The book is written for an international audience. We have written mainly about English and European laws but the writing team is international and the book includes references to law and policy beyond Europe. The principles that we cover are generally of international application. The same principles apply in many jurisdictions and since there is still little direct regulation on AI and the underlying subject matter (the digital economy, the information economy, the attention economy) is truly expansive, any book on AI is an international text. As AI laws are promulgated internationally it will be necessary to cover them and the book will become more specific but a lot longer …

1.021   This first part contains four chapters. This chapter is an introduction to the book and to AI. The second chapter introduces the chapters and their themes. The third chapter is an introduction to AI written for lawyers by lawyers. The fourth chapter is an introduction to AI written for lawyers by a subject matter expert. All the chapters prominently feature the human and ethical concerns associated with the technologies because these inform all other chapters of the book.

1.022   There is some overlap in the chapters but each is written in a different context and has a different perspective. Usually, the overlapping areas are viewed through the lens of different applicable rules or market practices. For example, the laws relating to liability and healthcare have some common points but they are not the same. The book tries to strike a balance between repetition, ease of reading, new approaches to issues and the practical point of trying to make chapters somewhat standalone but with the right amount of cross-referencing.

The style of the book is to provide information and commentary. It is written by experts with **1.023** an interest in AI. There is an interesting question of whether that introduces its own bias. The ironies of AI are legion and this is one of the points that makes it a gloriously challenging topic. The book would not be the same if it had been written by a single author. That the nature of this topic and its application vary so widely in the world means that the decision to produce a book written by a range of experts representing a broad set of (legal and non-legal) disciplines and industry fields law was quite deliberate.

The book does not seek to repeat the excellent work in other textbooks on AI that are coming. **1.024** Our approach is to write from the perspective of AI as a general-purpose technology. New business models and the changes to existing business models now derive from technology, in particular this technology, and the book is written from that perspective. We aim to write for the widest audience wrestling with new business problems, not for a small group of lawyers with existing expertise in information technology who would already be well placed to engage with questions in their field. It is the questions outside this field that most concern us.

For reasons of space we have not sought to restate the existing law on the topics that we cover. **1.025** If you are, say, a data protection lawyer, you already have textbooks on data protection laws. In this book the relevant chapters are written to build on what is already known, rather than set it out again. We also deliberately do not try to look for precedent in old cases that are likely to be distinguishable once new background is considered. For more on this, see section N below.

The rest of this introductory chapter comprises a series of short sections on subjects that are not **1.026** handled as standalone topics elsewhere in the book.

C. WHAT IS AI?

There are books dealing with (aspects of) the subject of AI and many of them are worth **1.027** reading. This book is not intended to replace them but, since it is intended to be useful to the widest range of people, it does seem helpful to provide a short general introduction here.

The best definition I've heard of AI came from a client: 'if you run a program and go home and **1.028** when you come back in the morning it's done something you weren't expecting, that's AI.' That gives the shortest meaningful, practical explanation I'm aware of.

Explanations of what AI is and what it does are in Chapters 3 and 4. For this introduction **1.029** I have set out some foundational points in AI that are useful background to an understanding of the technical and practical points that follow. This is not a history of AI in the sense of an essay setting out its chronological stages. Rather, it identifies what in my view are some of the concepts that inform what follows.

The starting point for AI is the history of the concept of the agent. In this sense agency is **1.030** an ancient idea: capability of intelligent behaviour. Historically, agents were thought of as physical; first people, then robots. AI opened up the concept to include virtual agents, whose operating environment is inside a computer (or, latterly, a distributed network of computers).

1.031   From the concept of the agent, researchers developed theories of human and animal intelligence. Computer models arrived into a longstanding area of study. Notably, they enabled researchers to test new models against existing theory before revising both. It is important to remember, however, that computer models do not just study computer programs. Research on the topic begins with the study of human intelligence and intelligent systems began as a sub-set of this work.

1.032   For this reason, the history of AI research has run in tandem with the discipline of cognitive psychology. Cognitive psychology concerns human intelligence. AI research concerns inorganic intelligence. The intersection of the two is a cognitive science. Cognitive science concerns attempts to understand intelligent activity.

1.033   Cognitive science, through the publicisation of what has become known as AI, is often dated to a famous conference at Dartmouth College in 1956. Most histories of AI begin at this point and it is referenced further in Chapter 3. The conference was, in fact, a meeting of many of the founders of the discipline to discuss the hypothesis that 'every aspect of learning or other feature of intelligence can in principle be so precisely described that a machine can be made to simulate it'. To be clear, that was the point for discussion rather than their conclusion from the meeting. There is an answer of sorts to the question at the end of section G below titled 'The philosophy of technology'.

1.034   AI research has gained much of its momentum from success in gameplaying. The victory of IBM's Deep Blue over Gary Kasparov in chess in 1997 was for many people outside the field their earliest introduction to AI. The victory of Google/DeepMind's AlphaGo over Lee Sedol in Go in 2016 coincided with a public understanding that AI was now in wide use, in smart phones, cars, kitchens etc. Before both of these, insiders saw the defeat of the world checkers champion in 1965, to a program designed by computer scientist Arthur Samuel, as a landmark. Samuel believed that teaching computers to play games helped researchers understand how to develop approaches to general problems. At this point it became clear that an artificial agent was not limited by the capabilities of its designer. A self-learning program could exhibit capacity beyond that of a designer. Deep Mind's AlphaGo Zero perfectly illustrates this through its ability to self-train and win games against its human-trained and assisted ancestors, including AlphaGo.

1.035   Work in AI can be categorised by reference to the two types of technologies used. Symbolic AI (broadly) involves teaching artificial systems facts and rules. This is similar to teaching a language program using grammar books, an approach based on logic. Connectionism (broadly) involves replicating the human brain's methods of learning and remembering at the neural level. This is similar to teaching a language program by making it read and find patterns by itself, an approach based on statistics and immersion.

1.036   Researchers still identify common theoretical problems in AI, for example:

(a)   scalability, the ability for AI systems to function in a real-world context;
(b)   robustness, the ability of AI systems to deal with unpredictable events; and

(c)   responsiveness, the ability of AI systems to deal with problems in real time.

Approaches to development go through cycles; see for example work on the three principles   **1.037**
posed by Rodney Brooks, an Australian roboticist:

(a)   the principle of embodiment, holding that intelligence requires a body because knowl-
        edge cannot be fully gained in the absence of interactions and perceptions;
(b)   the principle of situatedness, concerning the need for systems to operate outside bounded
        environments, in other words in the world not in a game; and
(c)   the principle of bottom-up design, the idea that starting with the most complex structure
        in the known universe (the human brain) means starting at the finish: rather than starting
        with modelling human cognition, we should start with modelling recognition of less
        sophisticated creatures and work up from there to higher-level abilities.

Thinking about thinking also plays its part. John Searle, an American philosopher of mind,   **1.038**
posed the 'Chinese room argument'. This poses a question based on semiotics to assess whether
machines are intelligent on the basis that intelligence requires understanding. A computer
alone in a room may be capable of taking input in a Chinese language and producing outputs in
another, for example English. But this may be because it has the capacity to match one picture
(a Chinese character) to another (an English word or phrase). That is not to say that it understands Chinese. A semiotician would say that the computer functions through information
manipulating indexical references rather than demonstrating an understanding of symbolic
meaning.

Throughout this book we must be mindful that the concept of intelligence itself is not settled.   **1.039**
A 1995 statement about 'intelligence' made by Arthur S. Reber, an American cognitive psychologist, remains valid: 'Few concepts in psychology have received more devoted attention and
few have resisted classification so thoroughly.'

AI is a prediction machine. That sounds trite but it can also have profound implications, as   **1.040**
illustrated by this passage from an interview with Mark Solms, a South African neuropsycholo-
gist, published in *Nautilus* in 2021 under the title 'Consciousness Is Just a Feeling':

> The only point of learning from past events is to better predict future events. That's the whole point of
> memory. It's not just a library where we file away everything that's happened to us. And the reason why
> we need to keep a record of what's happened in the past is so that we can use it as a basis for predicting
> the future. And yes, the hippocampus is every bit as much for imagining the future as remembering
> the past. You might say it's remembering the future.

D. HOW IS AI DEFINED?

There are many existing formal definitions of AI and so the world does not need another. By   **1.041**
taking a group of good definitions that have been developed in legal or commercial contexts,
we can show broadly what it is.

UNCITRAL, the United Nations Commission on International Trade Law, has said: **1.042**

The term 'artificial intelligence' is used to refer both to the capability of a machine to exhibit or simulate intelligent human behaviour and a branch of computer science concerned with this capability. [...] [I]t is important to acknowledge that the technology driving the capability of AI systems is still in its infancy and disagreement exists among computer scientists as to what constitutes the 'intelligent' behaviour to be exhibited or simulated by these systems.

1.043   The Council of the Organisation for Economic Co-operation and Development (OECD) has defined an 'AI system' as 'a machine-based system that can, for a given set of human-defined objectives, make predictions, recommendations, or decisions influencing real or virtual environments'.

1.044   The Independent High-Level Expert Group on Artificial Intelligence appointed by the European Commission has defined 'AI systems' as 'software (and possibly also hardware) systems designed by humans that, given a complex goal, act in the physical or digital dimension by perceiving their environment'.

1.045   The International Organization for Standardization has defined the term 'artificial intelligence' to mean: (a) 'an interdisciplinary field, usually regarded as a branch of computer science, dealing with models and systems for the performance of functions generally associated with human intelligence, such as reasoning and learning'; and (b) the 'capability of a functional unit to perform functions that are generally associated with human intelligence such as reasoning and learning'.

1.046   The OECD identifies the characteristics of 'interpreting the collected structured or unstructured data, reasoning on the knowledge, or processing the information, derived from this data and deciding the best action(s) to take to achieve the given goal'.

1.047   Alongside definitions, the OECD highlights activities of these systems that we must keep in mind when considering how to manage them: 'predictions', 'recommendations' and 'decisions'.

1.048   Finally, UNCITRAL notes features of legal significance relating to AI systems: (a) the use of algorithms and (b) the processing of large quantities of data from multiple sources (the infamous 'big data').

1.049   A point to note at this stage is how we are not defining AI for our purposes. Our definitions envisage the use of AI for performing tasks, not creating alternative intelligent life. For now, our scope considers 'specific' AI but not 'general' AI, since the development of general AI does not yet truly touch on commercial uses.

E. IS AI DIFFERENT?

1.050   It will be apparent that AI involves some inherent challenges. These are in many cases the same both for developers building the technology and for lawyers considering its uses. These can be briefly illustrated by reference to some of the characteristics that are considerations for both groups working together on projects. They include:

(a)   complexity – dealing with software that interacts directly with its environment and inter-
       acts with itself (as we shall see in explanations of machine learning and neural nets);
(b)   autonomy – outcomes arising as a result of the operation of the code rather than the
       intention of the programmer;
(c)   unpredictability – a fundamental change from traditional computing programming based
       on logical operations;
(d)   opacity – the 'black box' problem;
(e)   vulnerability – covering many things but including problems arising from bias or poor
       design.

Each of these issues will be seen many times in later chapters.   **1.051**

In particular, in Chapter 28 relating to procurement we see that a consequence of these charac- **1.052**
teristics is that AI software is rarely useful 'off the shelf'. That need for engagement and design
by a licensee of an AI system shows why and how lawyers should be part of the teams in the
both the licensee and licensor businesses.

Just as AI tests the limit of how we think about commercial processes, it also tests the limits **1.053**
of legal principles. I have previously written about the impact of AI adoption on legal theories,
including a series of articles[1] on doctrines and practicalities as I see them. To briefly summarise:

Artificial intelligence and equity – there is an inherent tension between algorithms (that is, **1.054**
rules) and equity (that is, scope for flexible decision-making less bound by precedent than the
common law). This operates in two distinct ways. First, AI systems do not understand; you
cannot always compute your way to a remedy for a wrong, let alone apply principles such as
good faith or fairness. Second, algorithmic decision making is incessant and compounding.
Potential wrongs could overwhelm courts in an instant. There are many ways of dealing with
these issues by ethical design and the application of regulation, and we discuss these in the
book. The conceptual problem is a large one, however, and should be on lawyers' lists for all
projects.

Artificial intelligence and uncertainty – AI is useful at assisting in managing risk. But risk is not **1.055**
the same as uncertainty. The distinction is important in the context of the input that lawyers
can give in relation to projects involving AI. Having a plan for addressing risk (based on data),
addressing consequences (based on acceptable outcomes) and identifying but not fixing uncertainty is part of the lawyer's role.

Artificial intelligence and fallibility – AI technology can assist in legal practice by mitigating **1.056**
the fallibility of lawyers. Borrowing from the literature on medical errors, I considered the
categories of ignorance, ineptitude and necessary fallibility. Each can be the subject of support
from AI. But of course, AI also introduces new scope for fallibility into legal practice.

---

1   Artificial intelligence and equity, Butterworths Journal of International Banking and Financial Law – July/August 2017;
     Artificial intelligence and uncertainty, Butterworths Journal of International Banking and Financial Law – November
     2017; Artificial intelligence and fallibility, Butterworths Journal of International Banking and Financial Law - June 2018

1.057 We are fortunate that senior lawyers in many countries are more curious and less conservative than public assumptions may suggest. They are smart people who understand the challenge. Lord Hodge, Deputy President of the Supreme Court, titled the Dover House Lecture that he gave in 2020 'Technology and the Law'. He began: 'My theme tonight is of the need for lawmakers, regulators and judges in the United Kingdom to be alive to the demands for change that technology will make of our legal systems and the opportunities and challenges which that technology creates for the legal professions.' In my view, the key point of the lecture is this statement: 'The changes [in the common law] which are required are not interstitial law-making, which is the long-recognised task of judges. They will require interdisciplinary policy-making and consultation, which a court cannot perform when resolving individual disputes.' This is clearly correct, as many sections of this book demonstrate. It is encouraging that such a senior judge has said it. It only describes the challenge, however. That policy work remains to be done.

F. AI AND ECONOMICS

1.058 There are many numbers to choose from regarding the size of the potential economic boost that AI will provide. Accountancy and consulting firm PwC predicts that AI will add $61 trillion to the global economy by 2030. Few other things are expected to have an impact anything like this.

1.059 A paper titled 'The Economics of Artificial Intelligence' published in 2018 by consulting firm McKinsey & Company referenced the power of AI through the 'ripple effects of falling costs'. The analysis reports on the second-order economic effects of AI adoption. For example, AI reduces the cost of using arithmetic to solve problems; that means that the cost of arithmetic falls, the cost of making predictions falls and business models that can outcompete incumbent businesses by reframing what they do as prediction problems can succeed. Motor manufacturers were not in the prediction business (except in the field of customer taste), but autonomous driving now means that they are. And they are competing with technology firms that have thrived by learning how to make predictions. AI produces transformational benefits. (Although one person's benefit is another person's existential challenge, of course.)

1.060 There are many books and articles making the case for the value and scale of AI, AI as a business, AI-enabled businesses, and so on.

1.061 On the other hand, questions arise in relation to the costs of such benefits.

1.062 *The Age of Surveillance Capitalism*, a book by Shoshanna Zuboff that has attracted a lot of attention, considers research conducted at Georgia Institute of Technology on the future of home automation. The research anticipated 'the processing of intimate data on people's habits, predilections, and health'. Researchers assumed, however, that 'datafication' would rest on norms including: '(1) that it must be the individual alone who decides what experience is rendered as data, (2) that the purpose of the data is to enrich the individual's life, and (3) that the individual is the sole arbiter of how the data are put to use.' Experience with the commercialisation of home automation technology has revealed that these norms have not been maintained.

Arguments about the benefits of AI are also concerned with how network effects (that is, **1.063** the observation that a network becomes more valuable the more people use it) of access to interrelated technologies and the personal data that they generate and handle may compound questions of equality. The most recent study of the Pew Research Center, a US 'fact tank', found that:

> From 1983 to 2016, the share of aggregate wealth going to upper-income families increased from 60% to 79% [...] the share held by middle-income families has been cut nearly in half, falling from 32% to 17% [...] Lower-income families had only 4% of aggregate wealth in 2016, down from 7% in 1983.

AI is particularly important because it sits within a technology-enabled ecosystem. AI makes **1.064** automation possible and automation links the information extracted by new connectivity technologies (for example, the Internet of Things) to the information management capabilities of the new technologies such blockchains and distributed ledgers. For lawyers, the effect of this virtuous circle is found in digital assets, smart contracts and Ricardian contracts and their relevance for a world in which AI becomes prevalent.

G. THE PHILOSOPHY OF TECHNOLOGY

The choices associated with AI are difficult because society is not well prepared for them. We **1.065** do, however, have a long history of thinking about the philosophy of technology. I anticipate that it will be increasingly useful for a lawyer to understand this context to illuminate the nature of decisions that we will face in relation to the design, use and limits of AI.

Let us take a few brief examples.   **1.066**

Autonomous Technology, a book written in 1978 by US political theorist Langdon Winner, is **1.067** concerned with questions of democratic control over technologies. Technology is about more than the gadgets, because the interests of people are either promoted or suppressed by technology. It is therefore a political instrument. Politicians and bureaucrats may find it convenient to describe uses of technology as questions of efficiency rather than politics. But technologies and their uses may support the positions of some groups more than others. Citizens must be taught not to delegate public policy questions to machines. The existence of more capable machines should not distance political decisions from citizens and governments. The link to the points on equality in the above section is clear.

'Mining the Computational Universe', a talk given in 2019 by British-American computer **1.068** scientist and polymath Stephen Wolfram, makes the point explicitly using an example from financial services:

> There is not something existential about the things that we want. If we want relative equality in making decisions about how you grant mortgages, for example, it's computationally not possible to have all the things that we think are important about fairness being implemented by the same system. There's inevitable trade-offs between one kind of fairness that we all have very strong intuitions is important, and another kind of fairness that we all have strong intuitions is important.

1.069   In response to Wolfram's talk, US philosopher and psychologist Alison Gopnik says:

> There's lovely formal work showing it's not just that we don't know what it is that we want; even if we know clearly and we have strong intuitions about what we want, you can't get a single system that's going to optimize for all of that. In a way, it's formal proof of the Isaiah Berlin picture of a kind of tragic moral pluralism, where it's impossible to optimize all the things that you genuinely think are more morally significant. [...] This whole thing of turning morality into code is not a new problem, right? The legal code and the political code has precisely been trying to formalize this for centuries, and what do we know? The only way to do it is via a huge mess. So, I predict that once you try and turn it into AI code, it's going to be a mess as well. [...] The whole premise of moral philosophy is that there are these contradictions. We don't live in the Panglossian world where fairness and equality and meritocratic adjustment aren't compatible with one another. When we talk about the goals or ambitions of epistemic virtues for the sciences, we act as if they're all compatible, but it often is not the case. That is to say, robustness, precision, accuracy, understandability, portability, or pedagogical utility, all these things we think should pull in the same direction, often don't.

1.070   From this we learn that it is important to keep decisions with people, because morality cannot be outsourced. These are not new questions. Norbert Wiener, a US cyberneticist and philosopher, wrote a 1960 essay titled 'Some Moral and Technical Consequences of Automation'. He predicted far-reaching moral consequences resulting from the fact that humans are not good at thinking through the outcomes of their desires. It is not, therefore, simply the 'runaway AI' thought experiments of technologists that matter here. We must be equally wary of human inputs, decisions and inability to pass the tests set by wish-making technological advances. We have a cultural trove of ancient lore, from religious texts to Aesop's fables, as well as the lessons of psychology set out in section K below on cognitive biases, to help us with this. AI is indeed multi-disciplinary work.

1.071   Alongside this, the philosophy of technology tells us that by definition not all things are predictable. Shane Parrish says in 'The Best Way to Make Intelligent Decisions (109 Models Explained)':

> A complex adaptive system, as distinguished from a complex system in general, is one that can understand itself and change based on that understanding. Complex adaptive systems are social systems. The difference is best illustrated by thinking about weather prediction contrasted to stock market prediction. The weather will not change based on an important forecaster's opinion, but the stock market might. Complex adaptive systems are thus fundamentally not predictable.

H. REGULATION

1.072   At the time of writing, the prevailing range of views among professionals is that AI is not yet regulated but it should be, or will be; or aspects of its use, or its design, or its implementation, and so on, will be.

1.073   UNCITRAL has provided a summary of the current position:

> Owing to its widespread use in many sectors of society, AI engages a wide range of laws, including laws dealing with data protection/privacy, human rights (including anti-discrimination), employment, and antitrust/competition. [...] In the trade context, a distinction may be drawn between the use of AI in trade – for example, through the supply of AI-enabled goods and services – and the use of AI to trade – for example, through the use of AI systems to manage supply chains (including inventory forecasting),

to market goods and services (including via online platforms), and to enter into and perform contracts. While this distinction is not always clear-cut – for instance, the same system may be used as a product in trade and to support trading activities – it may nevertheless serve as a useful tool for analysing the legal issues related to the use of AI.

This paragraph summarises many of the topics of this book. We have chapters on each of the **1.074** laws that it references. We have chapters on trade and financial services. We have Hannah Kim's chapter on AI and Regulation that faces the topic head on. We also have chapters on the core legal topics of contract and tort. Suffice it to say for now that this is a very large, complex and interrelated series of topics and we cannot get away from Alison Gopnik's comment that there are 'contradictions', but hope to avoid too much her vision of a 'huge mess'.

Many of the chapter authors are involved in policy work and are confronting the issues in this **1.075** as well as in the practical contexts that they write about.

Birgitte Andersen's chapter on Public Policy and Government brings together many of the **1.076** themes.

It is certainly true that there are many difficulties associated with proposing regulation. This list **1.077** is my top ten but is not exhaustive:

(a)   can you, do you need to, define AI to regulate it?
(b)   should AI be treated in the same way as any other technology or is it sui generis for this purpose?
(c)   how can AI be regulated?
(d)   are you more concerned about regulating inputs or outputs?
(e)   are there places where AI should not be used?
(f)   how can AI cause harms?
(g)   how remote can AI harms be but still require a remedy?
(h)   what type of remedies are suitable for AI harms?
(i)   does AI cause, exacerbate or entrench monopolies?
(j)   given the intractable problems of technology and morality, how can AI ethics be judged?

A good exercise here is to take your answers to all these questions and argue for the opposite. **1.078** You may find that this is surprisingly easy to do.

Among the rules that we can see coming, a somewhat developed proposal is the European **1.079** Commission's draft legislation published in May 2021. This takes an interventionist approach. It has an explicit agenda to enable innovation while protecting citizens. The draft regulation includes bans for certain uses of high-risk artificial intelligence systems and will only allow risky AI technology into the EU's internal market if it has been approved. Fines of up to €20 million or 4 per cent of worldwide annual turnover would be levied for breach. Four themes are:

(a)   high-risk AI – only high-risk AI systems that have gone through quality management and conformity assessment procedures will be allowed in the EU. Data sets must be high quality, there must be human oversight and there must be transparency. All of these points are covered in detail in later chapters.
(b)   regulate uses not technologies – the Commission intends to restrict AI systems that manipulate human behaviour, act to the detriment of citizens, target a citizen's vulner-

abilities, surveil in a generalised manner or conduct social scoring. These mix technical and political goals and will be hard to define and police.

(c)   biometric surveillance – remote biometric identification systems (such as facial recognition in public spaces) must pass conformity assessments. These tests will set a valuable benchmark for other AI uses if they can be agreed and themselves be transparent.

(d)   authorised uses – states may be permitted to use restricted technologies in certain circumstances. It is not difficult to see that this will be controversial.

1.080 As I think about all the issues above it seems to me that a consequence of the points is that it is not possible to design failsafes or backups into AI systems easily. Complex systems are subject to feedback loops (which may be positive or negative). A causes B and B in turn causes C but also influences A. Regulating in this context is difficult in principle and rife with likely unintended consequences.

1.081 Further, there may be conceptual limits to the capacity of regulation in this context. Ashby's Law of Requisite Variety (named for W. Ross Ashby, a British cyberneticist and psychologist) says: 'When the variety or complexity of the environment exceeds the capacity of a system (natural or artificial) the environment will dominate and ultimately destroy that system.' This is often paraphrased as: in order to control something, you need the controls to have the same degree of complexity as the things to be controlled. It would follow that superintelligence is not controllable by humans.

1.082 The big regulatory themes of, for example, operational resilience will influence and be influenced by AI. Whether regulation by traditional methods can keep up is another matter. Regulators will need to move rapidly between the helicopter view and the ground level in making both broad and limited assessments on what is desirable, what is feasible and what is practical, balancing trade-offs. Before regulations come standards. Scott Steedman, the Director of Standards at the British Standards Institution notes that: 'Standards underpin the daily work of [...] engineers.' Standards are a pragmatic way to develop necessary regulation.

I. INTERNATIONAL ASPECTS

1.083 Overlaid on the challenges listed above is the fact that AI is a rootless general purpose technology. Just as it is no respecter of traditional legal frameworks, equally it does not recognise national boundaries. The problem was well summarised in the Digital Finance Strategy for the EU that followed from the March 2018 European Commission Fintech Action Plan. This states:

> digital finance strategy and regulation at the EU level are highly complex issues because advances in technology are bringing what were historically fragmented, separately regulated, services, processes and systems onto single source platforms. On the service-delivery side, this offers abundant potential for service improvement, efficiency, accessibility, flexibility and future adaptation. However, the technology has outrun the comparatively neolithic regulatory framework, exposing gaps and inconsistencies which are likely to further damage the competitiveness of the EU in this area if not resolved effectively and soon.

1.084 And that is just in relation to one industry sector within one fairly harmonised international market.

The value of pre-eminence in AI is relevant in the international context because of the implica- **1.085**
tions of politics. Cointelegraph has reported that China wishes to create 'a digital infrastructure
for the whole economy'. The plan 'includes blockchain technology, 5G, artificial intelligence
and cloud computing as the new information infrastructure'. China and the US vie for suprem-
acy in AI development. The Biden administration is evaluating its policy just as the Final
Report of the National Security Commission on Artificial Intelligence has been published. The
Report begins with the words: 'Americans have not yet grappled with just how profoundly the
artificial intelligence (AI) revolution will impact our economy, national security, and welfare.'

Since there are no international regulators in emerging technology, developers and users of AI **1.086**
are faced with applying national rules in the territories in which they operate. They must judge
how national rules apply, whether by reference to the location of corporate registrations, tax
offices, intellectual property exploitation, location of staff, location of customers and other relevant matters. In addition to regulation, the applicability of 'soft law' is important in the context
of developing rules and so the positions of supranational organisations (such as those referenced
in section D above titled How is AI Defined?), standards bodies and data organisations must be
taken into account. An ability to predict the trends in policy and implementation of new rules
is also a consideration for commercial organisations profiting from AI.

Finally, as well as rules and standards, AI is an area where recognition of best practice will be **1.087**
perceived to be valuable. This is a difficult topic because of the scope for disagreement. Some
work is valuable and has received positive attention, however. An example of this is a 2020
report titled 'Toward Trustworthy AI Development: Mechanisms for Supporting Verifiable
Claims Report', by Miles Brundage, Shahar Avin, Jasmine Wang and others. This states:

> Artificial intelligence has the potential to transform society in ways both beneficial and harmful.
> Beneficial applications are more likely to be realized, and risks more likely to be avoided, if AI develop-
> ers earn rather than assume the trust of society and of one another. This report has fleshed out one way
> of earning such trust, namely the making and assessment of verifiable claims about AI development
> through a variety of mechanisms. A richer toolbox of mechanisms for this purpose can inform develop-
> ers' efforts to earn trust, the demands made of AI developers by activists and civil society organizations,
> and regulators' efforts to ensure that AI is developed responsibly.

The report sets out three principles that lawyers should be aware of: **1.088**

> *First*, there is a tension between verifiability of claims and the generality of such claims. This tension
> arises because the narrow properties of a system are easier to verify than the general ones, which tend
> to be of greater social interest. [...]
> *Second*, the verifiability of claims does not ensure that they will be verified in practice. The mere
> existence of mechanisms for supporting verifiable claims does not ensure that they will be demanded
> by consumers, citizens, and policymakers (and even if they are, the burden ought not to be on them
> to do so). [...]
> *Third*, even if a claim about AI development is shown to be false, asymmetries of power may prevent
> corrective steps from being taken.

J. SOCIAL PURPOSE

1.089   Social purpose is a large and pervasive topic. It is covered in many of the chapters, from those specifically focusing on ethics, data, healthcare and discrimination through to those on various types of consumer-facing industries. The topic encompasses social inclusion so far as this is affected by technology. It also relates to the narrower but still vast topics of digital inclusion, mental health, the long-term effects of the COVID-19 global pandemic and data (including personal data) as a commodity.

1.090   Putting this into a commercial context requires a narrative to judge decisions against. This is the philosophy of an influential text published in the UK titled 'The Purposeful Company: A Provocation Series', edited by Will Hutton, Chair of the Big Innovation Centre. This makes a case that: 'Great companies are defined by a commitment to an over-riding purpose. That informs its values, strategy and processes. The proposition is that the stronger business purpose, the cleverer, more adaptable and sustainable the business model – and the genius of the company can be brought to life.'

1.091   Similar thinking can take place at a societal level. In 2021 in *Noema*, a magazine about 'transformations sweeping our world', Mariana Mazzucato suggested the idea of a fund 'socializing the upside benefits, not just the downside risks, of public investment. [...] If a company does well after getting government funding, like Tesla or Google, the government should get an equity stake'.

1.092   It should still be noted, however, that such thinking has a tendency to be cyclical. John Kay's 'The Concept of the Corporation' reminds us of the 'law and economics' movement, the 'essential claim' of which 'is that law is and should be designed and implemented to promote economic efficiency, rather than more abstract social and political goals of justice and equality'.

1.093   Looking more widely at the challenge, Tim Barker, writing in 2021 in *Dissent*, a political and cultural criticism magazine, suggests:

> Slow global growth and weak investment reflect a shift from manufacturing to service industries even in low-income countries. The world is 'saturated' with the car factories and clothes factories on which export-led growth used to rely. Services are 'not susceptible' to the productivity increases achievable in manufacturing, nor do they create as many jobs even when they boom.

1.094   One thing is for sure. AI is political, with all of the relevance and stress that goes with that. Lawyers are often not political. How will we deal with this pressure?

K. COGNITIVE BIASES

1.095   One of the things that I find most interesting about AI is that it does not share my cognitive biases. Whether good or bad, I need to factor this into my dealings with it. There are many good lists of cognitive biases. I have taken the examples below from 'Mental Models: The Best

Way to Make Intelligent Decisions'[2] on the Farnam Street blog. I am quoting at length from the section 'Human Nature and Judgment' because the examples speak for themselves.

1. Trust   1.096

Fundamentally, the modern world operates on trust. Familial trust is generally a given (otherwise we'd have a hell of a time surviving), but we also choose to trust chefs, clerks, drivers, factory workers, executives, and many others. A trusting system is one that tends to work most efficiently; the rewards of trust are extremely high.

2. Bias from Incentives   1.097

Highly responsive to incentives, humans have perhaps the most varied and hardest to understand set of incentives in the animal kingdom. This causes us to distort our thinking when it is in our own interest to do so. A wonderful example is a salesman truly believing that his product will improve the lives of its users. It's not merely convenient that he sells the product; the fact of his selling the product causes a very real bias in his own thinking.

[...]

5. Tendency to Distort Due to Liking/Loving or Disliking/Hating   1.098

Based on past association, stereotyping, ideology, genetic influence, or direct experience, humans have a tendency to distort their thinking in favour of people or things that they like and against people or things they dislike. This tendency leads to overrating the things we like and underrating or broadly categorizing things we dislike, often missing crucial nuances in the process.

[...]

7. Availability Heuristic   1.099

One of the most useful findings of modern psychology is what Daniel Kahneman calls the Availability Bias or Heuristic: We tend to most easily recall what is salient, important, frequent, and recent. The brain has its own energy-saving and inertial tendencies that we have little control over – the availability heuristic is likely one of them. Having a truly comprehensive memory would be debilitating. Some sub-examples of the availability heuristic include the Anchoring and Sunk Cost Tendencies.

[...]

14. Tendency to Overgeneralize from Small Samples   1.100

It's important for human beings to generalize; we need not see every instance to understand the general rule, and this works to our advantage. With generalizing, however, comes a subset of errors when we forget about the Law of Large Numbers and act as if it does not exist. We take a small number of instances and create a general category, even if we have no statistically sound basis for the conclusion.

[...]

17. Hindsight Bias   1.101

Once we know the outcome, it's nearly impossible to turn back the clock mentally. Our narrative instinct leads us to reason that we knew it all along (whatever 'it' is), when in fact we are often simply reasoning post-hoc with information not available to us before the event. The hindsight bias explains

---

2   Mental Models: The Best Way to Make Intelligent Decisions', Farnam Street. Reproduced with permission.

why it's wise to keep a journal of important decisions for an unaltered record and to re-examine our beliefs when we convince ourselves that we knew it all along.

1.102 18. Sensitivity to Fairness

Justice runs deep in our veins. In another illustration of our relative sense of well-being, we are careful arbiters of what is fair. Violations of fairness can be considered grounds for reciprocal action, or at least distrust. Yet fairness itself seems to be a moving target. What is seen as fair and just in one time and place may not be in another. Consider that slavery has been seen as perfectly natural and perfectly unnatural in alternating phases of human existence.

1.103 There are many other cognitive biases and many other examples of well-explained lists of them. Lawyers working with automated systems should have a working knowledge of these.

L. AI AND THE FUTURE OF WORK

1.104 A 2018 report from PwC, a consulting firm, found that gains and losses of jobs in the UK economy from the adoption of AI will largely net off. I was involved in a number of policy groups looking at the results of this and similar research at the time. Politicians worried not about the totals but about the fact that jobs most at risk from AI-led automation are those in places that lost manufacturing jobs in the 1980s recession. Mining and manufacturing have been replaced by logistics and call-centres. Logistics and call centre jobs are among those most at risk from replacement by AI technologies. Further, jobs performed by women, by unskilled workers and by people working part-time are all in high-risk categories. Before moving on to some of the more conventionally rehearsed points about AI and work, it is important to note that disruption resulting from this unequal impact of AI is one of the most pressing points to be addressed in any conversation about AI.

1.105 Studies on the future of work generally focus on two considerations. The first is the type of skills needed to work in a more automated environment. These include:

(a) communications skills;
(b) creative thinking;
(c) problem solving;
(d) ability to work in teams;
(e) emotional intelligence;
(f) customer service skills.

1.106 In summary, these are the human skills required to support automation. Of course, computer scientists and data analysts will also be in demand.

1.107 The second consideration is the trends that are expected to apply over the near-term future. Pearson, an education company, has produced a future-of-skills report that identifies 'seven megatrends' relating to employment and skills in 2030. The first is technological change. The full list is:

(a) technological change
(b) globalization
(c) demographic change

(d) environmental sustainability

(e) urbanization

(f) increasing inequality

(g) political uncertainty.

We must also recognise that AI development takes place faster than social or policy devel- **1.108**
opment. This point is reflected in the OECD report titled 'The impact of AI on the labour
market: is this time different?' The thing that is 'different' is that AI can now perform what
are known as 'non-routine' cognitive tasks. This is the point at which AI starts to displace
professional services jobs.

There are many benefits to the world of work stemming from the emergence of AI and related **1.109**
technologies but it will be imperative that enough of them accrue to the people who want to
work. Jobs will be more interesting. So long as they are available, that is a benefit. Parkinson's
Law says that work expands to fill the time available. Parkinson's Law of AI can be that work
expands to occupy the people available. But that is most likely the case for people in purposeful
companies and with job security, either formal or informal. In any event, it will require thinking
beyond measures of mere efficiency.

Going back to the first point for emphasis, Michael Wooldridge, head of the Department of **1.110**
Computer Science at the University of Oxford, said in a Financial Times Future Forum event
that the issue for AI isn't about creating jobs; it's about creating jobs in the same places and for
the same people who lose their jobs because of AI.

M. PRESUPPOSITION

Presupposition is a term used by academic philosophers. The online Stanford Encyclopaedia **1.111**
of Philosophy explains: 'We discuss presupposition, the phenomenon whereby speakers mark
linguistically information as being taken for granted, rather than being part of the main prop-
ositional content of a speech act.'

The complexity of the topic may be inferred from the fact that this is the opening sentence of **1.112**
an entry that takes more than an hour to read. However, the point as it applies to AI is that it
is almost impossible for us to judge the amount and extent of context that is relevant to any text
or conversation. It explains why AI systems fail to show common sense. It also means that we
cannot judge how a system will react if it is impossible for us to put ourselves in its position.
Explainability and visualisation, along with algorithmic auditing, will be a large part of the
future of work.

When we consider bias in AI the problem is in part the faulty data, but also that values are hard **1.113**
to program and they are not necessarily implicit in data. Some of the solutions to bias are to be
found in tools used by lawyers, not just data scientists.

Challenging all existing analyses, however, is the development of business models and theories **1.114**
arising from adjacent emerging technologies such as blockchain. These are concerned with
establishing frameworks to allow multi-party transactions to take place without the need for

intermediaries or trust between parties. In the development of decentralised finance, (DAOs) are part of the corporate ecosystem but they are not corporations. They reflect dissatisfaction with existing approaches, including a concern that regulators have an unconscious bias in favour of incumbent firms. The Fintech Blueprint in May 2021 set out the case: 'The core idea is that applications can be built as protocols on an open source network and replace the nature of the firm […]'

1.115 One thing that lawyers can valuably do is assist in AI design from this perspective. Lawyers are trained to recognise and correct ambiguous text. We are trained to write contracts that are to be interpreted by an objective reader without context. We are expected to identify and manage the what-ifs of an agreement or arrangement. A hard thing about AI systems is that they take these familiar questions and scale them up to the size of the world. It is not feasible to think through the what-ifs of arrangements that will range far beyond the initial state that we are asked to think about. But lawyers do have the skills and training to suggest checks, balances, architecture and red flags to assist in these projects.

N. COMMERCIAL LAW TEXTBOOKS

1.116 This book is a commercial law textbook. It joins a long list of other commercial law textbooks. But because it is about a new technology, I have thought about what that means. It clearly means that it will need updating more regularly than texts on other subjects. It also means that more chapters cross-refer than in other texts and our authors have had to use their crystal balls to a greater extent than other authors. But I think there are some more fundamental things to consider. I haven't seen this avenue of thought explored before so I have set out a short list of some of what seem to me to be the implications of writing legal texts about new technology. If they are relevant to or influence others in the position of having to write them, so much the better. Through the chapters of this book we have tried to balance the points below, albeit mostly implicitly.

1.117 Forward or backward looking – legal textbooks are largely based on legislation or cases. So they naturally look backwards. Readers of a book on technology are interested in what is coming next. This is particularly applicable in relation to the style of legal textbooks. The expectation that these will refer in footnotes to cases risks the authors drawing false analogies and the readers assuming that questions have been settled. It seems to me more likely that precedents will be easily distinguishable. It would be surprising if AI profoundly changes the world but court cases about the internet answer our legal questions relating to it.

1.118 Made for lawyers – textbooks set out what the law is and leave things at that. For a topic which, at its core, I submit will involve lawyers and non-lawyers working together, it would be helpful for the books to be useful to both of them. In some areas, saying what the law is doesn't dispose of many issues. In the context of principles-based rules, for example in financial services, in practice it is most useful to know what people actually do and avoid doing and why.

1.119 Adapted and extended from previous editions – the first edition of a book takes a lot of work. Subsequent editions are easier but inevitably suffer from inertia, that is, they generally take an incrementalistic approach. This means that categorisations don't change and it is difficult to capture a big shift in approach if that takes place in relation to the subject matter. That is more likely to be a problem in a fast-evolving discipline (note: will I wish I hadn't written this if I'm asked to work on a second edition of this book?!).

Focus on courts – a lot of law comes from cases, and cases come from courts. But most com-   **1.120**
mercial practice doesn't get to court. That seems to be a limiting factor in a book designed for readers, including commercial entities that would like to know: what is allowed; what is normal; what are the options for a business that does what mine does? By definition, innovative businesses are not interested in precedents from cases involving businesses doing other things or regulation that does not apply to their markets.

Digitalisation – there is a good chance that digitalisation changes everything. This will include   **1.121**
how laws are written (they will be machine readable), how contracts are written (they will be smart and Ricardian), how regulators operate (using AI and real-time information plug-ins), how information is shared (over blockchains), how value is transferred (via digital and crypto currencies including stablecoins and Central Bank Digital Currencies), how consumers interact with commercial and government bodies (using AI on smart devices and in a post-contract world, that is, one where contracts of adhesion are replaced by regulatory standards and consumers' preferences are managed by their devices).

The jurisprudence of AI – I am not a legal theorist but, based on my notes above, it is clear that   **1.122**
I think that we would benefit from some analysis. Before we reach conclusions we will need to do some groundwork. Breaching my own rule about using the past as a guide to the future, we could start with Professor Hart's 'Positivism and the separation of law and morals' (1958) 71 Hart LREV 593 and *The Concept of Law* (1961). Professor Hart lists five views that are associated with legal positivism. These are:

(a)   that laws are commands of human beings;
(b)   that there is no necessary connection between law and morals;
(c)   that the analysis of legal concepts is (i) worth pursuing; (ii) distinct from (though not hostile to) sociological and historical enquiries and critical evaluation; and
(d)   that a legal system is a 'closed logical system' in which correct decisions may be deduced from predetermined legal rules by logical means alone; and
(e)   that moral judgments cannot be established, as statements of fact, by rational argument, evidence or proof.

It will become clear as we go through the book that: **1.123**

(a)   only concerning ourselves with human beings;
(b)   ignoring morality;
(c)   denying sociology (as an element in coming to terms with regulating the use of a personalisation technology alongside theories of justice and the economic analysis of law);
(d)   assuming that we are operating in closed systems;
(e)   holding on to a factitive distinction between legal and moral statements in circumstances where big data and automation make ethical design and algorithmic risk management the primary source of assurance and redress in a digital, information age

is limiting to an extent that would lead us to question the applicability of a positivist analysis. So, what else?

O. COMMERCIAL LAW PRACTICE

1.124   Having tried some comments on commercial law textbooks, since I am a practising commercial lawyer I cannot help but briefly deal in the same way with some implications for legal practice (very much a personal view).

1.125   *Advice and transactions* – lawyers in practice have traditionally made money on transactions, since these have high costs when charging models are based on hourly rates and large teams. Automation of routine tasks will change the metrics and firms will want to move away from hourly rates. We will 'sell the advice and give away the paper' rather than the other way round. Advice will be most valued where it is integrated with the business. As an example the Legal Statement on the Status of Cryptoassets and Smart Contracts of the Lawtech UK Panel issued in November 2019 told us that cryptoassets should be recognised as property under English law, despite historic case law to the contrary. That has been followed by subsequent case law. So if we were advising on this question in October 2019, should we have said that cryptoassets are not property (as the precedents suggested) or that they are (as was justifiable and predictable based on advances in technology and business practices)?

1.126   *Disputes* – in a world of smart contracts, the obligation for Alice to pay Bob is automated and self-executing. Claims for breach of contract will be replaced by claims based on updated rules on misrepresentation, restitution, unjust enrichment and the like. Courts will become digital, including through greater use of data. Algorithms will value cases by reference to where a likely or just settlement would be made. Litigation will be changed by AI.

1.127   *Goods and services* – traditional commercial law rules were concerned with trade. Trade involved goods. The rules on trade were written with goods in mind. The majority of economic value is now represented by intangible assets (90 per cent of the market capitalisation of the S&P 500 in 2020, according to the Ocean Tomo Intangible Asset Market Value Study) and services (65 per cent of world GDP in 2018, according to the World Bank). So, lawyers' attention should be on rules relating to services, digital assets, data and similar topics. Is AI a digital asset? How are elements of it created, owned, held by custodians, stored, transferred, extinguished, and so on?

1.128   *Jurisdictional questions* – globalisation has not just changed the location of manufacturing centres; e-commerce, digital assets and international platforms have stressed the rules on jurisdiction and governing law. AI services provided by a company registered in country A trading in country B to company C registered in country D and trading in country E using data collected in country F processed in country G (and so on) do not play by these rules. DAOs are coming to compound the problem. Discussing AI in the context of what he called 'emergences', W. Daniel Hills, an American computer scientist, sees even modern corporates as acquiring personalities (in quite a different way to that in which corporate lawyers think about legal personality):

These things [large corporations based on information technology] are hybrids of technology and people. As they transitioned to a point where more decisions were being made by the technology, one thing they could do was prevent the people from breaking the rules. It used to be that an individual employee could just decide not to apply the company policy because it didn't make sense, or it wasn't kind, or something like that. That's getting harder and harder to do because more of the machines have the policy coded into it, and they literally can't solve your problem even if they want to. We've got to the point where we do have these super powerful things that do have big influences on our lives, and they're interacting with each other.

1.129 Regulators are not set up, staffed or incentivised to handle this in a way that is consistent with their remit of consumer protection. So how should regulators be built for an incessant decentralised world?

1.130 *Talk to my lawyer* – legal textbooks and legal firms assume that all economic actors are entities that instruct lawyers and run things by them. They expect that contracts are drafted by lawyers who discuss them with their clients. The number of transactions that will take place in an AI-supported world will far exceed the capacity of lawyers to work in this way. Lawyers can be involved in projects by designing how transactions will be effected through automation. Legal services and customer service will merge.

1.131 Although I keep saying that lawyers and developers will work together (we will), we must be conscious of differences in our training. These go beyond the fact that we are trained in different subjects. We are trained to think differently. Computer scientists follow formal logic of the same type practised by logicians. Formal logic is concerned with truth preservation. An example of this is syllogistic argument. If A = B and B = C then A = C. Logic is a science of determining the validity of statements. Programming is a science of ensuring and implementing valid statements. Both have exceptions, of course, in their own 'fuzzy logics'. But the foundation is there. Lawyers follow their own type of logic and this is necessarily fuzzy. It is concerned with reaching agreements and resolving disagreements. AI is a broad topic bringing both approaches together.

P. YOU LOOK LIKE A STEALTH ASSASSIN FROM THE CLOUDS

1.132 Last, but in no way least, is my favourite thing about AIs: their capacity for unintentional humour.

1.133 Alongside the important work of testing new systems (see https://dailynous.com/2021/02/26/new-fallacy-examples-sought-for-ai-project/), and in particular determining whether inputs or outputs show bias, error, omission or fail in other ways, is AI Weirdness. AI Weirdness is a newsletter published by Janelle Shane from which this final, very short section gets its title via a GPT-3 (Generative Pre-trained Transformer 3, a type of new language generator to you and me) which Janelle asked to work on suggesting pickup lines. Her newsletter on Substack is so popular (and entertaining) that she was commissioned to write a book called (you guessed it) 'You Look Like a Thing and I Love You' (out now).

2

THEMES OF THE CHAPTERS

Charles Kerrigan

A. INTRODUCTION

2.001 Having introduced the book in chapter 1, in this short chapter we introduce the following chapters and set out some of the chapter authors' explanations and classifications of AI. The chapters are written by different authors. They therefore reflect a broad range of expert views. Many should be read together, for example chapter 21 on ethics alongside chapter 22 on bias and discrimination. The text includes many cross-references to point out these threads. Some sections, such as the part on soft law in chapter 15 on financial regulation, are relevant to all chapters. And so on. The book can be read cover to cover but equally, individual chapters have been designed to be read on a standalone basis. So, fittingly for a book on AI, it is a jigsaw puzzle that the reader can assemble each in their own way.

2.002 There are common themes to all chapters: control and risk; data; best practice; operational resilience; and ethics. Users should keep this list on their desk. Beyond that, as a guide to more specific themes, I have noted below a few points that particularly struck me in each chapter. I have also tried, without simply adding a list of cross-references, to briefly introduce each chapter so that readers can jump between them while reading them on a standalone basis.

B. THE CHAPTERS

2.003 Chapter 3, Introduction to AI, provides basic definitions and explanations and is written by lawyers.

2.004 Chapter 4 on Understanding AI provides background of a technical nature. It sets out some of the relevant categorisations and the reasons behind them. For those who are unfamiliar with AI this may be a difficult chapter in parts, but I would encourage you to keep coming back to it. Lawyers' descriptions of AI are easier for other lawyers to understand but the expert explanations are more specific and will become more useful as your knowledge develops. It is also noteworthy that the chapter reveals differences among experts and that we get a sense of how fast-moving matters such as the technical development and theories of governance are for these systems. The section on use cases is both wide-ranging and varied. The chapter also covers such difficult topics as fairness and explainability, but from a different perspective to that covered by lawyers in other chapters. We can see trade-offs between functionality and explainability. Finally, there are interesting questions for me in looking at why businesses have data and whether they really know what to do with it, despite all of the alarm that we read about on this topic.

Chapter 5 on Corporate Governance deals with AI decision-making. The chapter considers underlying questions such as whether AI takes decisions, and the implications of AI overtaking humans. It notes that AI prompts an analysis of roles, for example a reconsideration of the question: what does a manager do? The chapter's consideration of augmented versus autonomous roles looks to the near future of corporate decision-making and management.   **2.005**

Chapter 6 on Regulation describes how rules compete and overlap. It takes a principled approach, noting that rules are vague and therefore need a person to make subjective decisions in relation to them. The human in the loop is explained. An important policy and practical point is made that regulators themselves should use AI. Regulation relating to AI should be overlaid on industry-specific regulation, the chapter argues. The chapter also covers compliance with regulation in practice.   **2.006**

Chapter 7 on Commercial Contracts makes a point concerning the need to identify where AI is used. Classes of uses are related to the types of clause precedents that may be relevant to them. Different contexts require different drafting. The topic of standards arises here with a particular view to ensuring consistency. The chapter sets out valuable checklists for practitioners.   **2.007**

Chapter 8 on Commercial Trade shows that AI is useful not just in changing how things are done, for example improving manufacturing or logistics processes, but also in developing new products and services through research and development. AI is used in advanced manufacturing to help in design and safety testing. It is also used to make commercial trade more efficient. The chapter casts more light on the subject matter of various other chapters, including industries (such as retail) and legal concepts (such as agency). It also identifies potential for risk and poor practice, providing an explanation of AI 'washing'.   **2.008**

Chapter 9 on Agency and Liability considers the nature of assumptions made by laws and business models. Humans are assumed to be present in all models; judgments are informed by this context. The chapter presents and comments on a 'law as information' thesis. It gives examples of the interaction between law and privacy and identifies a number of blind spots in the law. Practitioners should beware.   **2.009**

Chapter 10 on Data and Data Protection asks the question: what approaches to algorithms should be adopted by business users? The chapter also considers the potential effect of the General Data Protection Regulation (GDPR) and related laws on the topic. This, again, is an encompassing context for AI and has implications sitting behind all other legal questions and use cases.   **2.010**

2.011 Chapter 11 on Competition Law asks whether competition rules currently in force tackle the issues faced in the new digital world. The content of the questions include AI and emerging technologies more generally. There are valuable sectoral comparisons made as the telecoms sector prepares to consider how to develop rules and standards suitable to its range of businesses and customers.

2.012 Chapter 12 on Intellectual Property makes an argument for a new view of IP and the laws pertaining to it. The chapter presents a series of compelling arguments for the promotion of innovation and directs these specifically to AI. Again, the subject of ethics takes a prominent place in the discussion.

2.013 Chapter 13 on Employment notes that most personal relationships take place outside a person's private life. Employment professionals must recognise this and have an understanding of what AI and related tools are checking. Professionals may know the rules but not know that they are breaking them. Examples are given and techniques suggested to mitigate the harms. The chapter picks up a widely discussed theme relating to the technology of surveillance. It makes interesting observations about augmented intelligence and includes a series of practical proposals.

2.014 Chapter 14 on Disputes and Litigation highlights that courts in the UK and most other jurisdictions now embrace technology. In fact, they expect lawyers to use it. The chapter faces two ways. It considers litigation where AI is involved in (creating) the dispute, and AI technology in litigation tools that are used in court processes.

2.015 Chapter 15 on Financial Regulation describes the position of rules relating to AI in the context of an industry that is both highly regulated and constrained by hard law (with which market participants must comply) and soft law (with which market participants generally do comply). Adding the soft law connected to AI into the analysis shows the complexity of the task for practising lawyers and compliance professionals. The chapter sets out best practice proposals focusing on relevant concerns and requirements, also taking in the context of outsourcing.

2.016 Chapter 16 on Insurance makes the point that an industry concerned with data and risk has exactly the characteristics that are or should be suitable for AI usage. It also notes, however, that there are real technical questions in the topic for which we don't yet have answers. The chapter highlights interrelationships with other chapters, particularly those on data (because of the richness of data in the insurance industry) and discrimination (because of existing rules on this subject). The impact of GDPR-type rules must also be considered in any product using AI, and that point applies beyond the insurance industry. The chapter shows how many things must be joined together when emerging technologies are subject to legal analysis.

2.017 Chapter 17 on Retail and Consumer considers the 'business' of AI. The chapter sets out the range of regulations that are touched on in this topic. It also picks up the question of regulatory alignment, including in relation to Brexit. The scale of AI uses in daily life is made clear by the discussion of its uses in consumer-facing industries.

Chapter 18 on Healthcare shows the tension between the benefits that AI provides in health-   **2.018**
care outcomes and the ethical concerns around using autonomous technology to handle the
most sensitive type of personal data. The range of AI uses is broad, including drug development, diagnostics, therapeutics and robotics. As would be expected, the legal issues associated
with medtech regulation, liability and remedies are treated at length.

Chapter 19 on Telecoms and Connectivity sets out some difficult balances, for example between   **2.019**
taking advantage of opportunities provided by the Internet of Things and electronic privacy
regulations. Telecoms is a particularly interesting industry for AI because cloud computing
powers AI. Further, the industry is dominated by large incumbents, businesses often have both
commercial and retail customers, and there is the possibility that AI and related technologies
will deliver a 'fintech moment' to the telecoms industry, that is, a wave of disruption similar to
that which has transformed the financial services industry in recent years.

Chapter 20 on Real Estate illustrates how all industries will be affected by AI. Real estate has   **2.020**
traditionally been a sector that is relatively slow to innovate and reticent around technology.
No longer. Proptech has become a source of interest and investment. Tokenisation and frac-
tionalisation are changing investment. In the sector, the overarching theme for all participants
is data. And AI is a fundamental new technology used to derive value from data. It leads to
projects with titles such as 'AI in Brick and Mortar Retail', run by the MIT review group. As
a broad point, it is encouraging to see the real estate industry represented by a chapter in a book
like this.

Chapter 21 on Ethics makes the point that ethics is (and must be) an all-encompassing topic   **2.021**
in any discussion of AI. For a business to understand (and for academics and policymakers to
critique) how to take an ethical approach to the development and adoption of AI it must first
understand its own values and then be able to promote them across all of its parts, internal and
external. The chapter usefully sets out examples of ethical principles, including references to
those that have been proposed by international bodies. It explains in a practical way how to diligence the work around these questions. It also raises current and potential regulatory proposals
and says that businesses must have an awareness of what is coming their way in this topic.

Chapter 22 on Bias and Discrimination says that AI is about people. Again, the subject of AI's   **2.022**
relationship with hard law (in this case the UK Equality Act) and soft law is discussed. The
chapter notes that AI cannot be unpacked from ethics and gives good examples of rules layering
on each other, again highlighting a theme of the book. It considers the prospect of new rules
and how they would interrelate with existing ones. It also looks at the difficult question of
enforcement of rules relating to AI. Finally, the chapter poses questions for society about how
AI should be a force for good.

Chapter 23 on Public Policy and Government distinguishes between the internet and AI,   **2.023**
making some useful clarifications about how policy concerning technology is written. The AI
industry is reliant on supportive public policy and it is therefore crucial that industry participants are aware of how this is developed. Likewise, policymakers must conduct their work
with an understanding of how AI develops and operates. The chapter lists interested parties
in a format that shows how wide is the constituency that is already involved. The chapter also

raises and discusses some of the specific topics that are engaging policymakers at the time of writing.

2.024 Chapter 24 on Education discusses the importance of AI in its widest sense in legal training. The chapter considers the requirement for lawyers to have knowledge of topics outside the law. It identifies 'mindset' as key in the success of modern legal education. It provides a helpful focus on questions such as: what do clients want? The discussion about how and whether this is a new approach and how often practising lawyers ask themselves this question in taking on tasks for clients is important and urgent. The chapter also considers how to work across disciplines, something perhaps unfamiliar to many practising lawyers. Like the chapter on ethics, this chapter sits above a lot of the technical analysis in the rest of the book in providing a guide to the thinking required for lawyers to be effective in an information economy.

2.025 Chapter 25, Taxonomy of AI, sets out what lawyers need to know about AI technologies. There are some gating items for lawyers to engage with, such as the correct use of terminology, the correct understanding of the nature of the technology and the ability to recognise how and why different use cases are applicable to a business problem. The chapter discusses a current debate about ownership and protection of knowledge. This neatly ties in with the discussion in the IP chapter. The legal issues related to algorithms are broadly described and it is clear that this is destined to be a very important area for policy, implementation and collaboration between computer scientists and lawyers.

2.026 Chapter 26 on Automation and Fairness picks up the point about legal issues related to algorithms. The chapter considers how researchers look at the question of fairness both on its own and in the context of algorithms and algorithmic auditing. We learn that psychologists and computer scientists collaborate together with practical moral philosophers. This is a new topic that will be important for policy and in practice as industry is required by regulators, customers and other stakeholders to be able to demonstrate that algorithms do what they are supposed to do, do not have material unintended consequences and do not cause bias or discrimination. The chapter sets up proposals and practical advice for persons implementing AI, which will include lawyers. Lawyers cannot answer narrow questions in advising on this topic; the question is whether a client's aims are achieved in an effective and compliant way.

2.027 Chapter 27 on Risk Management considers the role of the commercial lawyer. It sees a broadening of the role since clients' questions aren't answered simply by technical statements of the law and its application; they are answered by responding through an understanding of the wider environment that the clients are facing. This is certainly one of the reasons why this book has been written. AI is not simply a new area where legal regulation will develop; it is a context within which client business problems must be faced. Increasingly, clients and lawyers will work on business problems in a context of innovation: new technology, new regulation, new business models, and a lack of clear, traditional answers. The chapter makes the point that complicated systems require complicated supervision.

2.028 Chapter 28 on Business Models and Procurement explains what is required to be successful in disruptive and disrupted companies. The chapter considers the work and requirements for mutual understanding and teamwork. It also covers how things go well and how they go wrong in practice. There are conclusions in here for lawyers getting involved in technology development and implementation. The chapter highlights the theme of augmentation and the future of humans and jobs. The section on the open-source nature of technology used to create AI tools is a good read alongside the chapter on IP.

Chapter 29 on Explainable AI and Responsible AI sets out the 'black box' problem. This is so **2.029** often discussed in the mainstream media now that it has become a cliché. The book, and this chapter in particular, unpicks the cliché. Part of this involves education on how AI systems operate, how XAI works, how rules and standards operate in the context of AI, and how to apply ethical considerations to AI. The chapter includes explanations of explainability (!) and points the way towards toolkits to be used in practice.

Chapter 30 on LegalTech answers the question: what use do lawyers now make of AI **2.030** technology?

3

INTRODUCTION TO AI

Charles Kerrigan
with contributions from Suzanne Rab, Stephen Kenny QC,
Charlotte Payne and Jason G Allen[1]

A. INTRODUCTION

3.001 This section sets out definitions of AI provided by lawyers who have written other chapters. There are lawyers' definitions rather than the technologist's accounts written by Tirath Virdee and colleagues in chapters 4 and 24. They are useful as a general introduction to concepts that are required for an understanding of the remainder of the book.

B. AI

3.002 A useful starting point is a definition offered by Russell and Norvig where AI is defined as computers or machines that seek to act rationally, think rationally, act like a human, or think like a human.[2]

3.003 AI is therefore characterized by four main features:

- *Acting rationally* – AI is designed to achieve goals via perception and taking action as a result.
- *Thinking rationally* – AI is designed to logically solve problems, make inferences and optimize outcomes.

---

1 Paras 3.001 and 3.009–3.018 written by Charles Kerrigan, paras 3.002–3.006 by Suzanne Rab, paras 3.007–3.008 and 3.025–3.028 by Stephen Kenny QC and Charlotte Payne and paras 3.019–3.024 by Jason G. Allen.
2 S. Russell and P. Norvig, *Artificial Intelligence: A Modern Approach* (3rd edn, Pearson, 2010).

- *Acting like a human* – This form of intelligence was later popularized as the 'Turing Test', which involves a test of natural language processing, knowledge representation, automated reasoning and learning.
- *Thinking like a human* – Inspired by cognitive science, Nilsson defined AI as 'that activity devoted to making machines intelligent, and intelligence is that quality that enables an entity to function appropriately and with foresight in its environment'.[3]

A further distinction may be made between 'narrow' and 'general' AI. Narrow AI concerns applications that provide domain-specific expertise, or task completion. General AI refers to an application that exhibits intelligence comparable to a human, or that outperforms humans, across the range of contexts where humans interact. **3.004**

The early implementations of AI mainly comprised systems within a narrow area and were programmed by human experts. The central focus of more recent developments in AI is around machine learning systems. In contrast to expert systems, machine learning algorithms and systems are trained against observational or simulated outcomes. **3.005**

The debate around AI has often been linked with discussions around data and, more specifi- cally, 'Big data'. The term 'Big data' has been coined for the aggregation, analysis and increasing value of vast exploitable datasets of unstructured and structured digital information. Big data is characterized by three main features: **3.006**

- Aggregation: in terms of size, shape (for example, text, image, video, sound), structure and speed.
- Analysis: Big data concerns aggregated datasets which are analysed by quantitative analysis software (using AI, machine learning, neural networks, robotics and algorithmic computa- tion) on a real-time basis.
- Increasing value: it will facilitate small but constant, fast and incremental business change and enhance competitiveness, efficiency and innovation and the value of the data used.

AI was originally conceived as the ability of machines to mimic the cognitive functions of human minds, including the ability to 'perceive' data in images and language, to accumulate and organize that data and to use it in resolving specific problems (such as through voice rec- ognition or computerized speech). Since the 1980s, increased computing power has permitted computers to attempt deductions and predictions, and to learn from feedback supplied about the accuracy of those attempts. The vast quantities of stored data available – both on the inter- net, from commercially available data sets and from a company's own electronic records – has allowed computers, often connected in 'neural networks', to develop algorithms to draw more abstract conclusions and make more complex predictions, to obtain their own feedback on the accuracy of those conclusions/predictions and to adjust their algorithms to improve that accuracy. **3.007**

The application of computerised deep learning with access to big data, connected through the cloud, allows better conclusions to be drawn and more accurate predictions to be made. **3.008**

---

3   N. Nilsson, *The Quest for Artificial Intelligence: A History of Idea and Achievement* (Cambridge University Press, 2009).

AI therefore no longer merely mimics the cognitive functions of human minds – in certain respects, it can (if appropriately directed) surpass them (at least in specific areas[4]).

3.009   The basic definitions of AI that are used throughout the book are set out in the following paragraphs. Note that in each case these terms are not defined terms in the field of computer science; these are my paraphrases of how these terms are commonly understood. In particular, I am writing metaphorically below to avoid getting into the maths. Chapters 4 and 24 contain more accurate explanations and technical detail.

3.010   Machine learning (ML) – refers to the techniques by which software is able to execute functions without explicit coding. In traditional programming algorithms are coded as steps with defined inputs and outputs. Machine learning algorithms (of which there are various categories) are designed to detect patterns in data and to use the results to automatically improve the algorithm without explicit instructions as to how that should be done. These improvements are made by statistical analysis. The systems are designed to excel in pattern recognition, make predictions on the basis of the patterns, test the results of these predictions, use the results to refine the models and the algorithms in the system, and repeat.

3.011   The conceptual basis of machine learning looks back to the mathematics of Bayes' theorem (an equation, that can be very broadly summarised to say that predictions based on data should be continually updated by reference to new data received over time (including, in the case of predictions, the results of previous predictions that have been made and tested)). The automation of this process is the core of the technologies and models used in practice. Machine learning therefore concerns models based on algorithms that recognise patterns in data and make and test predictions against new data. These are recursive processes which improve the algorithms itself over time.

3.012   Machine learning is generally categorised as follows.

3.013   Supervised machine learning involves a system being correct answers in the form of labelled data, that is, information that contains identified features to which an identifying label has been attached (for example, famously, "cat"). These systems therefore can test themselves against the result it is trying to reach (did it correctly identify the cat). This works well where designers know the answer to a problem and are using an AI system to be more efficient than a hardcoded system. In the case of board games, designers can feed the textbook strategies to the system for it to apply alongside its own inferences.

3.014   Unsupervised machine learning involves a system being given the data but not the answer, for example data without labels. The system therefore proposes answers without knowing if these are correct. This is used where designers want to understand patterns in data that they may not be able themselves to see. In the case of board games, unsupervised systems develop new strategies to beat human and supervised AI systems based on learning from trial and error, sometimes without information beyond the rules of the game.

3.015   Semi supervised machine learning involves giving a system both labelled and unlabelled data.

Reinforcement machine learning uses trial and error but no data. In these cases the system **3.016** develops its own data about an environment that it is tasked to explore. The environment could be a maze. The system interacts with its environment using an agent. The agent could be a virtual mouse. The agent moves through the environment recording information relating to it. Dead ends are not visited again once they have been recorded. After many simulated tours of the maze the agent will discover the way out. Reinforcement machine learning looks for optimal solutions to problems that can be modelled as an environment including an agent.

Neural networks (or, more properly, artificial neural networks) consist of algorithms structured **3.017** in interconnected layers resembling the "neural" network of a human brain. This structure enables nodes in the network to send and receive information within the network so that more intensive processing may occur within the network. The nodes run calculations to determine whether inputs are passed on to the next layer of the network. The nodes have "weights", that is they multiply the inputs by an amount that increases as the weight is increased. Results over a threshold are passed to the next layer. Results from the bottom layer of the network form the outputs. The networks run calculations many times, changing the weights of the nodes until data with the same labels is consistently giving rise to similar outputs, that is all cat pictures are identified as cats. In this way mathematics yields results in non-mathematical terms. This may seem strange but biological neural networks (brains to you and me) create worlds from electricity. In fact, cognitive science shows that the operations of a brain are characterised by a high degree of unconscious activity and interaction between different parts of the brain, sometimes in competition with each other. From these derive our outcomes and actions. This is similar to neural networks and dissimilar to early AI systems and so it appears that we are over time more nearly approximating the workings of the human brain.

Deep learning is machine learning that uses neural networks. **3.018**

The following section sets out some generally applicable legal context in relation to how we **3.019** should think about AI.

In its current work on AI in the digital economy, the United Nations Commission on **3.020** International Trade Law (UNCITRAL) has referred to recent international initiatives on AI, including the Independent High Level Expert Group on Artificial Intelligence appointed by the European Commission. The European Expert Group defines AI systems as:

> systems designed by humans that, given a complex goal, act in the physical or digital dimension by perceiving their environment through data acquisition, interpreting the collected structured or unstructured data, reasoning on the knowledge, or processing the information, derived from this data and deciding the best action(s) to take to achieve the given goal.[5]

It adds that 'AI systems can either use symbolic rules or learn a numeric model, and they can **3.021** also adapt their behaviour by analysing how the environment is affected by their previous actions'.[6] This overlaps to a significant degree with UNCITRAL's work on 'automated systems'

---

5   Independent High Level Expert Group on Artificial Intelligence, *Ethics Guidelines for Trustworthy AI* (2019), available at https://ec.europa.eu/newsroom/dae/document.cfm?doc_id=60419, 36.
6   Independent High-Level Expert Group on Artificial Intelligence, *Ethics Guidelines for Trustworthy AI* (2019), available at https://ec.europa.eu/newsroom/dae/document.cfm?doc_id=60419, 36.

in the past, but the references to actions like 'perceiving', 'interpreting', 'reasoning' and 'processing' indicate the additional complexity and sophistication of 'AI systems'. This reflects a basic distinction between 'automated' and 'autonomous' machines.[7] While the dividing line can be difficult to identify, and will require a granular examination in the circumstances of the specific use case, there will generally be an inflection point at which an automated system begins to operate autonomously, in a meaningful sense, from the humans involved in the operation. For example, one industry standard for autonomous vehicle (AV) systems identifies five 'levels' from zero automation to full autonomy, and Simon Chesterman identifies the inflection point at 'level three', 'conditional automation', where a system is capable of functioning without the active participation of a human driver but the human driver is able and expected to intervene where necessary.

3.022 UNCITRAL wisely cautions against the use of 'loaded human analogies such as "learning" or "autonomy"' as they are difficult to define in a machine context.[8] The term 'artificial intelligence' was coined in the mid-1950s at a seminal conference on the topic at Dartmouth College.[9] Although other definitions exist, from its early days the test developed by Alan Turing has played an important role in defining the field. This test essentially asks whether a computer programme can make a human counterparty believe they are interacting with another human. Turing's seminal paper reframes the question 'Can machines think?' to 'Can a machine imitate a thinking human?'[10]

3.023 Throughout its history, AI research has been pursued both to create computer programs that can perform 'intelligently' and to understand the workings of human intelligence itself. Much work in the field of AI pursues these goals simultaneously.[11] This is for good reason, as it is impossible to think about "intelligence" as a property of machines without also positing a concept of biological intelligence. The nature of "thinking" in the context of AI has been the subject matter of significant debates in the philosophy of consciousness, for example between Daniel Dennett and John Searle.[12]

---

7   See Simon Chesterman, 'Artificial Intelligence and the Problem of Accountability' (2020) 1(2) *Journal on Emerging Technologies* 210, 212.

8   UNICITRAL, *Legal issues related to the digital economy—artificial intelligence* (7 May 2020), A/CN.9/1012/Add.1, https://undocs.org/A/CN.9/1012/ADD.1, [4]–[5].

9   See Selmer Bringsjord and Naveen Sundar Govindarajulu, "Artificial Intelligence", *The Stanford Encyclopedia of Philosophy* (Summer 2020 Edition), Edward N. Zalta (ed.), https://plato.stanford.edu/archives/sum2020/entries/artificial-intelligence/.

10 Turing's original 'imitation game' involved A (a man), B (a woman), and C (a third party of either sex), where C has to ask questions of A and B and correctly guess their sex. The computer would 'pass' the Turing Test where it could convince C that it was a man, where B is trying to help C with answers (but C has no way of knowing whether B's 'help' is truthful). See Alan Turing, 'Computing Machinery and Intelligence' (1950) 49 *Mind* 433.

11 E.L. Rissland, "'Artificial Intelligence and Law: Stepping Stones to a Model of Legal Reasoning'" (1990) 99 *The Yales Law Journal* 1957, 1959.

12 See e.g. D.C. Dennett and J.R. Searle, "The Mystery of Consciousness: An Exchange" (*New York Review of Books*, 21 December 1995), www.nybooks.com/articles/1995/12/21/the-mystery-of-consciousness-an-exchange/. See John Searle, 'Minds, Brains, and Programs' (1980) 3(3) *Behavioral and Brain Sciences* 417; Daniel Dennett, 'Human and Robot Minds' in Masao Ito *et al* (eds), *Cognition, Computation and Consciousness* (Oxford University Press 1994). For a pithy and accessible argument for human intelligence reducing to 'biochemical algorithms', see Y.N. Harari, *21 Lessons for the 21st Century* (Vintage 2018), 20–21. See also Marvin Minsky, *Society of Mind* (Simon & Schuster 1986).

While the Turing Test naturally evokes futuristic visions of general AI, most AI systems are **3.024** domain-specific or 'narrow' AI. As a seminal US Government report from 2016 observed, remarkable progress has been made in narrow AI's ability to do things like winning strategic games, translating natural language, driving vehicles and recognising images, and these are translating into commercially important applications. However, general AI still lies on the other side of a 'broad chasm', and the current consensus of the expert community is that general AI is some decades away.[13] As John Armour and Horst Eidenmüller observe, however, non-linear development is typical of AI technologies, so the possibility of general AI should not be dismissed.[14] If and when it does arrive, general AI will present a whole raft of doctrinal and conceptual legal problems. For now, narrow AI is of much more urgent interest in terms of legal liability.

It is crucial to remember that 'AI' describes a set of different technologies that mimic the **3.025** outputs of human intelligence in different ways. Following the rule-based systems of the 1960s and the rule-based 'expert systems' of the 1980s and 1990s, most AI systems today rest on some method of 'machine learning'. Instead of programming a machine with a rule set to apply to data sets in order to derive answers, machines are given historical data sets and answers from which they derive their own rules, so to speak, by building an implicit model. Currently, the most important AI systems are 'deep learning' systems that are 'trained' with large data sets that have been partially structured by humans. On the basis of this 'training', the system 'learns' what outputs it should derive from what inputs and can apply the model it so develops to produce outputs with new data sets in a way that mimics intelligence.[15]

A supervised AI will generally investigate only such data sets as it is directed to examine (a **3.026** 'walled garden' of data); it can explore associations between points in the available data, and then formulate, test (against other data), refine and then propose for adoption 'rules' relevant to its task. However, if so programmed, it may not adopt and apply those rules without human approval. It can also be designed to maintain records of data sources accessed, associations perceived, data points used, and any rules proposed and/or adopted from time to time.

An unsupervised AI, by contrast, conducts its own research using any data that it can access, **3.027** whether on the internet, in the Cloud or more locally; it can explore and test associations between data points much more widely; and it can self-adjust its rules, thus refining its 'understanding' of the matters it has been designed to investigate or improving its performance of the tasks it has been charged with undertaking. But an unsupervised AI need not – often will not – record all the data sets it has researched, or all the associations it has explored; nor will it necessarily record all the iterations of the rules it develops.

One problem, particularly with unsupervised AI, is that it will usually remain opaque (to **3.028** humans at least) as to how it actually performs its task: the rules of relationship that it will have

---

13 National Science and Technology Council Committee on Technology, *Preparing for the Future of Artificial Intelligence* (Executive Office of the President of the United States, October 2016), https://obamawhitehouse.archives.gov/sites/default/files/whitehouse_files/microsites/ostp/NSTC/preparing_for_the_future_of_ai.pdf, 7.

14 John Armour and Horst Eidenmüller, 'Self-Driving Corporations?' (2020) 10 *Harvard Business Law Review* 87, 90.

15 For a review of the development of AI and the state of the art see John Armour and Horst Eidenmüller, 'Self-Driving Corporations?' (2020) 10 *Harvard Business Law Review* 87, 95.

developed, and will be using, lie buried deep in impenetrable self-written code. If that is the case, it may be described as a 'black box' system. To overcome this difficulty there are currently in development additional systems designed to understand, and express in terms comprehensible to humans, the essential features of the logic in a 'black box' system. These additional systems are called Explicable AI (or 'XAI'). They do not replace the 'black box' system, but rather investigate its operations and report, at the cost of some simplification, on its main features and the key variables controlling a particular output. XAI may, in due course, provide an answer to objections raised to the use of unsupervised AI and is treated in detail in chapter 29.

4

UNDERSTANDING AI

Tirath Virdee

A. INTRODUCTION

The purpose of this chapter is to enable the reader to get a thorough understanding of artificial **4.001** intelligence (AI) and the huge issues surrounding its development, utility and governance. This should enable the reader to see the tremendous scope and need for legal, ethical and governance oversight and regulation.

B. INTRODUCTION TO AI

AI is a field of science that enables computers to perform tasks that would normally require, or **4.002** previously would have required, humans.

The rise of big data, increased computation power (and massively parallel processing available **4.003** in graphical processing units (GPUs), for example) and technological innovations related to intelligence from data are the main factors that have enabled human intelligence to be replaced by artificial intelligence. The technological innovations have come from scientists trying to mimic the same type of neural architectures that the human brain has and the use of mathematical formalisms that enable relationships between inputs and outputs: so, in computer vision, recognizing cats and dogs and people better than humans, for example. It all comes down to the amount of data or the number of instances a machine can be trained upon. We tackle AI taxonomies and emergent issues in intelligence in chapter 25 of this book. Here we give a basic introduction to AI, its uses and the ethical and governance issues that society faces.

4.004   At the most basic level, humans sense data and can make decisions and take actions based on the nature of the data and the desired outcome. Given the definition of AI, humans can be replaced by AI when performing human tasks. There are two components to the system: the *environment* and the *intelligence system*.

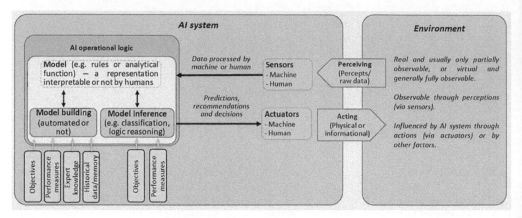

Figure 4.1   *The environment and the intelligence system*

4.005   The *environment* is the space from which data is gathered from sensors, simulators or memory.

4.006   The *intelligence system* is composed of a set of objectives, prediction-generating systems and decision-optimization and decision-making mechanisms.

4.007   The AI system can impact the environment in which it operates. That in essence is AI. The type of data determines the approach to analysis and decision-making:

(a)   The data collected may be simple enough to allow deterministic, rules-based decision making (for example, estimating the number of routes between two towns).

(b)   The data may be incomplete, requiring a regression approach (determining the relationship between height and weight of a population).

(c)   The data may have an inherent random nature necessitating a probabilistic approach to decision making (the crop yield of a field).

(d)   The data may be big (high volume, high veracity, high variability, high variety, high value, real-time) and consequently require a more natural approach to determining the intelligence it contains.

4.008   Let us look at basic aspects of how we derive value from data, how that has changed over time, the lexicons we use to describe the different types of analysis and the main dimensions that we need to be aware of within various frameworks.

4.009   Depending on what one does with data, the technologies and the mathematics employed and how one collects it and consumes the data from data processing systems, we invent process names. The three most commonly used are AI, data science and machine learning (ML). We then divide these further into subcategories as those lexicons have a more specific enrichment.

For instance, Deep Learning (DL), which is currently entirely a subset of ML, uses artificial neural networks and parallels from biologically inspired neural networks.

Increasingly, people forget that there is huge room for improvement that can be made using **4.010** traditional statistics and analytical and numerical algorithms that were never inspired by neural networks. These traditional methods of data analysis are also considered to be artificial intelligence. It is surprising that the debate goes on, even for professionals, as to the differences between data science, ML, AI and DL.

Big data enables a type of intelligence that, in the past, was only possible with biological brains. **4.011** We have constructed analogues of biological neural networks to create artificial neural networks, artificial neurons being loosely based on biological neurons. It is possible to have greater intelligence from more data in digital machines and call it DL. DL is a subset of AI.

Data science is defined in various ways and some include big data and DL within it. We prefer **4.012** to label data science as a field of study where data and inferences from that data are rules-based, albeit with significant statistical data analysis. That data can be structured or unstructured. Data science has a significant overlap of big data, data mining and DL topologies in this definition. Data science as a branch is old and continues to evolve, but the main aspect is that it is a business role that embraces storytelling and data visualization. Some people consider data science an extension to statistical analysis, while others regard statistics as a nonessential part of data science.

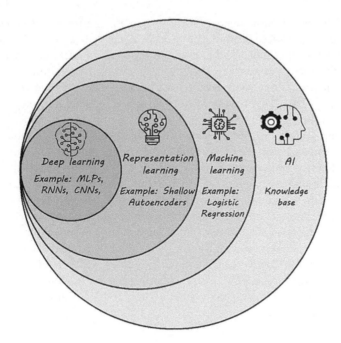

Figure 4.2   Schema of data science

C. MACHINE LEARNING

4.013 The purpose of ML is to acquire skills or knowledge from experience. This is done via many different ways of learning that are dependent on the nature of the problem to be solved:

(a) Supervised learning can be classified into classification and regression, which are both quite similar. There is some form of supervision of the algorithm in supervised learning relating the previously observed outputs to previously observed inputs. We provide the algorithm with a raw dataset, but then we also provide it with a target. The latter can be a single variable or multiple variables. Then the algorithm attempts to understand how to match the input to the output. Every time the algorithm makes a mistake, the supervisor tries to correct it.

(b) Unsupervised learning, in the context of ML, usually refers to clustering. In this case, we provide the algorithm with raw data. Instead of providing a target, the algorithm can essentially do its own thing and identify patterns in the data provided. It tries to find any regularities that seem significant, but there is no supervision involved. This type of learning is a challenging problem because it is ill-defined, and almost always requires a human to interpret the final stage of the pipeline. For example, the algorithm might identify patterns that are irrelevant to what you are trying to do, which is why you need to drill down into the results and try to define them a little better. Unsupervised learning can be essential in many contexts where some human prejudices need to be eliminated by creating machine-generated clusters that humans might not have thought of as somehow related.

(c) A type of ML called semi-supervised learning is an intermediate between supervised learning and unsupervised learning; it uses both labelled and unlabelled data to fit a model. In some cases unlabelled data can improve the model's accuracy but generally this is not the case, and labelling data costs money and takes time. Semi-supervised learning has had a resurgence in recent years because it reduces the error rate on some essential benchmarks. This type of learning includes self-training, multi-view learning and self-assembling.

(d) Reinforcement learning can be defined as a process in which a computer agent learns through positive and negative reinforcements in an environment. A 'computer agent' is a program that acts independently or on behalf of a user autonomously. Its distinctive feature is that it almost replicates the way humans adapt and learn. It is quite distinctive from other types of ML, that is, supervised and unsupervised types. It emulates the human learning process and cognition. The main distinctive feature between reinforcement learning algorithms and supervised/unsupervised learning algorithms is based on reinforcements. In a reinforcement learning algorithm, data scientists have to assure positive/negative reinforcements for the computer agent. No pre-requisite 'training data' is required. The only training is based on an iterative process in which the computer agent will run the program up to a desired number of times until the algorithm is in conjunction with the reinforcements.

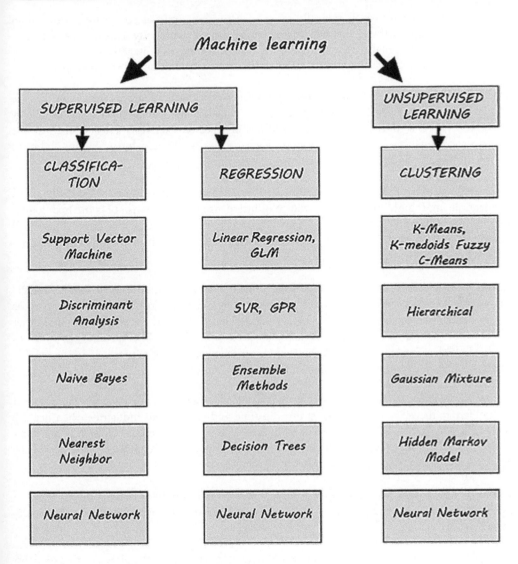

Figure 4.3   Schema of machine learning

D. DEEP LEARNING NEURAL NETWORKS

A neural network is an interconnected assembly of simple processing nodes or units whose **4.014** functionality is loosely based on the animal neuron. The interunit connection strength captures the ability of the network to learn. Such interunit strengths can be obtained through adaptation or running an iterative set of training programs.

In nature, the neurons communicate via electrical signals that are short-lived impulses or **4.015** 'spikes' in the cell wall's voltage or membrane. Their coordination and linkage are ensured through electrochemical junctions called synapses present on the cellular structure branches called dendrites. Each neuron typically receives many thousands of connections from other neurons and is continually receiving many incoming signals, eventually reaching the cell body. These thousands of signals reach the neuron and cause a spike in voltage in the neuron structure. Such a spike is translated as a signal to other neurons. Such a signal is called an axon.

4.016   The behaviour of neurons to an incoming impulse is not linear. Neurons can exhibit a spike or remain stagnant depending upon the incoming signal. Some signals produce an inhibitory effect and cancel a spike in voltage while others produce an excitatory effect and cause the voltage superimposition. The behaviour of each neuron is dictated by its innate ability to behave differently, and its synaptic connection with other neurons.

4.017   This interconnected behaviour in neurons has given rise to a new dimension of study called connectionism. It highlights the importance of interneuron connections. This methodology is frequently employed in psychology to study human cognitive functions. For our case, we shall employ it irrespective of any limitations. Data scientists wish to incorporate connectionism with neural networks to ensure greater efficiency.

4.018   In computer sciences the nodes in an artificially intelligent system are the equivalent of biological neurons. An AI system loosely mimics the natural neural networks of a human. So, synapses are modelled by multiplying our inputs by a weight. This is sent in the form of an axon to other nodes for processing. The activation is then compared with a threshold. The unit then produces a spike (a high-valued output) if the threshold is exceeded; otherwise it produces nothing. This threshold logic unit is the simplest model for artificial neurons.

4.019   Before we delve deeper into neural aspects of ML and AI, there are some concepts that we need to familiarize the reader with as, they turn up time and again in all industries when dealing with data. Paragraphs 4.020 to 4.030 contain some maths. Don't be put off: even if you don't understand it all first time, it will be useful to have a sense of the techniques and to be able to return to the explanation as your knowledge develops.

4.020   Consider a basic representation of an artificial neuron and a number of observations $(x_1, x_2 \ldots x_n)$ from a sensor. The purpose is to build up some cognition so as to be able to predict the output (y_j).

4.021   One of the keys to understanding how neural networks work from the above simple diagram is to understand the universal approximation theorem, a way of working out how to determine the disparity between our predictions and observations (called the cost function; that is, how 'wrong' the model is), gradient descent (that is, changes in the algorithm to optimize it) and activation function (that is, the transformation of inputs to outputs).

4.022   A question may come to the mind of the reader as to how a simple linear combination of inputs is going to enable us to represent *any* output. The assumption here is that the relationship between the inputs and the output is monotonic; that is, that there are no discontinuities. Under such circumstances the universal approximation theorem states that in a feedforward network with a single hidden layer of the type shown in the simple neural network, a finite number of neurons can approximate any real-valued continuous function. That activation function can be any continuous function that is differentiable.

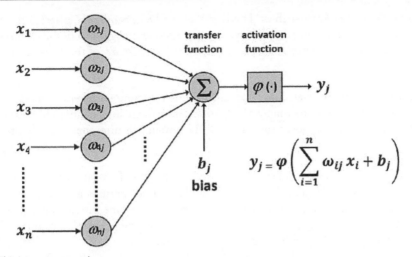

Note: This is a note example
Source: This is the source example.

Figure 4.4   *Basic representation of an artificial neuron in operation*

There are mathematical proofs of the theorem and we can almost relate it back to a mathe- **4.023**
matical technique called Fourier series analysis, where we could construct any function (that is,
relationship between variables) using sinusoidal waves of varying amplitudes and frequencies.
Mathematically, if F(y) approximates a function f(y) then the universal approximation theorem,
states that $|F(y)-f(y)|$ can be made arbitrarily small, with F(y) being represented by:

$$\sum_{i=1}^{N} v_i \varphi\left(w_{ij} x_i x + b_j\right)$$

φ is the activation function, N is an integer representing the number of inputs, w are the **4.024**
weights and b is the bias. The big assumption is that the activation function should be continuous and differentiable. This is a big assumption as in real neurons we know that the activation
function is a spike, and spikes have discontinuities.

Once we understand how a neural network operates, it is easy to construct deeper neural net- **4.025**
works with many hidden layers. These are called deep learning neural networks. Chapter 25
looks at the basic types of neurons and the different taxonomies for deep learning that incorporate varying degrees of connectivity and memory.

Many deep learning frameworks democratize the job of AI specialists. These include Keras, **4.026**
TensorFlow, PyTorch, fast.ai and others. The application of the frameworks enables the
design, training and validation of DL using a high-level language. These frameworks offer
high-performance GPU-parallelised solution to a broad range of training through the use
of their libraries. These problems include NLP, computer vision, reinforcement learning,
time-series predictions and more.

4.027 Increasingly we see headlines such as 'The Death of the Data Scientists', offering the view that we are reaching a stage where many believe that the exponential growth in the requirements of data scientists and data engineers will be curtailed because so many of the tasks are not capable of being automated.

4.028 A typical ML project involves data cleaning, feature selection/engineering, model selection, hyperparameter optimization, model validation, deployment and continuous improvement. The dominant problem in most projects is still the amount of time that is needed to get data ready for ML.

4.029 Companies such as Google, Amazon, Microsoft, H2O and Data Robot offer to automate the ML journey (AutoML and AI democratization). Many startups are trying to give these more prominent players a run for their money. These include emerging companies like Mind Foundry and Sensory Intelligence. They feel that the more prominent players are not innovating to meet many verticals' requirements and pain points.

4.030 It should be clear by now that AutoML offers immense value and could be the dominant way of enabling most companies to apply ML effectively with significantly reduced costs. It has the potential to accelerate AI adoption as the word reaches boardrooms.

E. AI USE CASES

4.031 There are many use cases of AI in every vertical industry, and consequently a growing number of legal and governance requirements for AI and the data upon which it relies. One could say that with the hyperconvergence in technologies that is under way (robotics with human-like 3D kinematics, sensory intelligence, data democratization and exchange, IoT, connected and integrated infrastructure, social media intelligence, democratized AI, decentralization of ownership and governance, new economics based on decentralised currencies for value exchange), there is nothing that AI cannot do that humans can. To highlight the depth of the impact that AI will have, we list some of the cases presently coming to prominence. It should be noted that there are use cases that are common across all the verticals. These include, for example, human capital (human resources/HR) optimization, recruitment, workplace analytics, security, logistics, training and development, and so on. Even in the verticals, most of the themes are familiar: finding patterns using structured and unstructured data and enabling actions to be taken to add value (monetary or societal). In terms of applications that are peculiar to the various verticals, consider the following examples:

(a) Law Enforcement and Justice – there is an incredible number of applications of AI in this space. These relate to finding patterns and promptly presenting information to the 'human in the loop'. So whether AI is 'studying' CCTV footage in real-time and determining behavioural patterns that might be triggers for violence or social unrest, or whether it is analysing all case files for patterns that might allow AI to play the true Sherlock Holmes, the possibilities are endless – especially with the use of mobile phone data, social media chatter, data from connected infrastructure and forensics undertaken by AI. As data between the various disparate agencies (and even the utilities) becomes democratized, surprising patterns will emerge which only a machine is capable of finding, due to the sheer scale of information available. There are tasks that humans will be limited in their ability to do, and these include cases of abuse (domestic violence, sexual exploitation, gang warfare, and so on), where AI can inform the officers of vulnerabilities and enable humans to make more informed decisions on the ground based on real-time contextualized information. Through the use of big data, criminals could be arrested in the middle of committing a crime. Imagine the possibilities and the consequences of a criminal being apprehended before any violence and violation has occurred simply because the patterns indicate what the next action would surely have been! Indeed, imagine the legal issues surrounding such a case – would it have been better for someone to have died, with all the psychological and social consequences? In the case of criminal justice, there are just as many possibilities, such as the use of NLP and speech and voice analytics to look at case files and determine who should get parole and who should not. The establishment of fairness of hearings and the removal (or at least the measurement) of human bias and prejudice; the fairness in sentencing; the dossiers prepared by AI to ensure that appropriate, relevant and necessary information is presented by mining the various documents and data following appropriate governance procedures: these possibilities represent only the tip of the iceberg.

(b)   Science – AI is increasingly being used in scientific research. Its uses include finding patterns in data from particle detectors; use of NLP to mine scientific literature and generate data for various types of machine-learning; AI-enabled hypothesis generators that mine research literature and generate new and testable hypotheses to highlight new findings; the control of robotics using AI to perform automated experimentation to discover new compounds and enabling faster, cheaper, easier and more robotically reproducible scientific discovery; use of NLP and knowledge-bases to detect inconsistencies in scientific literature and research so as to point to areas of contention that need more research; ensuring consistency in peer-reviews; use of clustering algorithms as well as manifold learning to lead to new and unexpected insights and discoveries such as the relationships between micro and macro-systems. The ethical issues that the use of AI opens up in terms of discovery, transmission and dissemination of extremely sensitive discoveries, intellectual property rights, citations, policy frameworks, and so on are deep and challenging and national and international frameworks and treaties will be required. Most nation-states have not even registered many of these tectonic shifts that are beginning to be crafted by innovative private enterprises.

(c)   Health and Medicine – as with other verticals, the purpose of AI is to detect patterns in data. In the case of health, the patterns can indicate health conditions with the prospect of delivering preventative services earlier than would otherwise be possible. These preventative services can include clinical decision making and delivery of other services. The data can come from a range of detections – wearables, medical scans and measurements, digital health records, patient monitoring systems, genome sequencing systems, and so on. The factors that will drive the adoption of AI in this arena mostly revolve around data privacy and governance as this sensitive personal data is of great commercial value. Privacy is also stopping key innovations in some algorithms from benefiting the population as a whole. AI can be used to enable improved patient healthcare, enabling better healthcare systems by provisioning the right resources, enabling improved health research by collecting data from different patients and improving public health by enabling better studies in the dynamics of epidemics. In medicine, AI can enable cheaper and faster diagnosis of disease (such as heart disease, lung cancer, retinopathy, and so on).

45

With sufficient data, the diagnosis can be far superior to that possible by trained human professionals. Drug discovery can be faster, cheaper and more effective. Using AI, it is possible to automatically identify and model drug candidates, speed up clinical trials and find biomarkers for diagnosing disease. Also, AI will personalize treatments for individuals by creating appropriate population clusters that have similar sensitivities. Finally, it is becoming possible to edit genes, and AI offers the best route to determining the edits and their consequences for precision health engineering.

(d)   Marketing and Advertising – The use of AI in optimising the return on investments in marketing and advertising is happening at pace. Websites can be contextualized where they use natural language generation (NLG) to personalize the information, offering users exactly what they are looking for (by looking at their search history and search patterns, for example). The likelihood of success can be determined from the data gathered; campaigns can be changed based on data analytics; and pricing can be optimized depending on the past observed behaviours of the various customers. Psychometric profiling of customers predicated on a multitude of factors will mean that the machines will understand user sensibilities and prejudices better than a human ever could. And they will do this at scale. Video and audio analytics related to product placements and click-through rates will lead to automated changes to where and when the products are advertised as well as the format and positioning of their marketing materials. Social influencers and those that make use of their services are increasingly using AI. AI-powered platforms can help agencies and brands identify fake followers, inauthentic engagement and unreliable social media influencers. Indeed, AI is enabling CGI influencers to begin to compete with human influencers as we become increasingly virtualized.

(e)   Security – Given that we humans are so connected and so prone to having our brains hacked (through the use of techniques such as 'illusory truth effect' and other hacks that are proven to work), the issue will become how we counter the effects of disinformation (through state players, anarchists and other nefarious actors) when society is increasingly polarized. The distinction between polymorphic malware, deep fakes and data poisoning needs to clearly be dealt with. Some things will not be on a public cloud for obvious reasons related to infrastructure, security and boundaries of control. Clearly, response times and the ability to intercept and destroy content that may affect national security (by external and internal players) are becoming crucial and the systems in place need to be studied for their resilience in such scenarios. We need to consider network traffic increase scenarios in terms of capacity and analysis, the monitoring of diverse channels, regulatory powers such as the Investigatory Powers Act 2016 and related legislation human rights issues, and more detailed analysis of potential internal and external threats. Models can be probed, and their internal workings discovered. If someone knows how our algorithms work, they can use that knowledge to harm us.

(f)   Defence and Warfare – Advances in the domains of AI and robotics mean that drones, robots and intensive hacking systems for defence are now a reality. Drones are moving from providing intelligence and expendable eyes in the sky to being capable of conducting offensive capabilities in swarm formations such as for targeted removal of key capabilities. Intelligent robots can be deployed for independent offensive capabilities or as a way of augmenting and safeguarding humans on the battlefield. Cybersecurity, and the ability to hack into the information of the enemy or to misinform them, becomes a topic for AI. The ability to hack into data eco-systems that inform decisions is considered central to defensive and offensive capabilities. Through the combination of bioengineering, social media dominance and opinion forming and removal of key enemy capabilities, AI may render conventional warfare at nation-state level redundant. The future of warfare and defence lies in the space of AI versus AI.

(g) Agriculture – AI-related technologies are having a large impact in modern agriculture through agricultural robotics, crop and soil analytics and predictive analytics. Improvements in computer vision (3D, not just 2.5D, kinematics for harvesting and weeding robots), IoT augmentation (to enable real-time data coupled with eye-in-the-sky drones) and data exchanges are enabling optimisation of harvest quality and yields. Agricultural robots, operational autonomous robots handling agricultural tasks such as soil preparation, planting of seeds and harvesting crops, now exist. The advent of 3D farms offering idealized environments and optimized production of high-quality produce is accelerating the use of AI. Crop and soil monitoring through computer vision and deep-learning algorithms process data captured by drones and IoT field probes. ML models are now in use to track and predict environmental impacts on crop yield, including weather changes, crop rotations and soil biochemistry. Finally, AI and environmental data that reflects the trajectory of climate change data enables farmers to plan their response. Adaptive technologies can mitigate the consequences of climate change by enabling faster research into new generations of seeds. But more sweeping measures are necessary to secure global access to food in the face of rising temperatures. As nation-states begin to realize the fuller utility of AI in in the agricultural sectors, governments will consider the implications of data and analytics, and the environmental consequences of such technologies, on international relations and the global environment.

(h) Education – AI and data is fundamentally going to impact what it means to be human. Consequently, when it comes to education and learning, we need to be careful not to fall into definitions and assumptions that limit its possibilities. Nation-states see education as a way for their citizens to have a competitive advantage in a diverse world, as a way for their citizens to be at the leading edge of innovation and enterprise. Improving education using AI involves collecting data related to the learner and their interactions. Mobile devices connected to course providers is a central aspect. Teaching is improved by using tutor bots and automated and contextualized assessments, clustering students by ability and understanding the way students interact with resources. Better education readies societies and vocations for just-in-time learning for jobs that are changing rapidly. AI will enable more distance learning, grading and assessment automation, better learning pathwaysl improvements to educational resources, better tutor bots, better and timely interactions with necessary information and students finding their own strengths.

(i) Transportation and Autonomous Vehicles – Most of us drive, and we get our goods transported across the globe by using various human-intensive involvements. Through the use of transport-network mapping technologies, autonomous vehicles are becoming reality. The use of AI in human-augmentation technologies can save lives, enable the removal of the human driver and lead to an optimized transportation and travel system free from human fragilities and shortcomings. According to the OECD, a 90 per cent adoption of AV would save around 21,000 lives in the US alone. There would be almost no road traffic fatalities if adoption approached 100 per cent. AI has the potential to reduce transport costs and lead to savings from cuts in pollution and traffic congestion. This does however, require infrastructure, including massive networks for data collection and connected IoT devices.

(j) Environment – the use of AI in natural resource conservation, wildlife protection, energy management, clean energy, waste management, pollution control and environmentally friendly agriculture methods is increasing. Points (k)–(o) are among the multitude of uses of AI in environmental sciences.

(k) Autonomous Electric Vehicles – AI-guided AVs will enable substantial greenhouse gas reductions for urban transport through route and traffic optimization, eco-driving algorithms, programmed 'platooning' of cars to traffic and autonomous ride-sharing services. Distributed, decentralized, decarbonized energy grids – AI can enhance the predictability of demand and supply for renewables across a distributed grid; improve energy storage, efficiency and load management; assist in the integration and reliability of renewables; and enable dynamic pricing and trading, creating market incentives.

(l) Smart Agriculture – As noted above, AI-augmented agriculture will enable optimizations not just in yields and quality but also in minimizing environmental impacts through the use of robotics, for example to allow early detection of crop diseases. 'Climate infomatics' traditionally requires high-performance energy-intensive computing, but deep-learning networks can allow computers to run much faster and incorporate more complexity of the real-world system into the calculations.

(m) Smart Disaster Response – AI can analyse simulations and real-time data (including social media data) of weather events and disasters in a region to seek out vulnerabilities and enhance disaster preparation, provide early warnings and prioritize responses through coordination of emergency information capabilities.

(n) Connected Cities – Connected infrastructure and planning can enable immense per-capita reductions in environmental impacts and optimize urban sustainability.

(o) Transparent Digital Earth – A real-time, open API, AI-enabled, digital geospatial dashboard for the planet would enable the monitoring, modelling and management of environmental systems at a scale and speed never before possible. This can help in tackling illegal deforestation, water extraction, fishing and poaching, air pollution, natural disaster response and smart agriculture.

(p) Financial Services – AI is widely used in the finance industry, for such matters as fraud detection and management, trading intelligence, risk assessment and management and customer-facing information and advisory agents. Fraud detection and management involves analysing patterns in transactions to point out unusual cases, enabling humans or bots to investigate further. These systems can take account of considerations such as the total risk an institution is exposed to, and let the algorithms determine a trade-off between rigour and customer inconvenience. Trading bots look at different metrics in financial market trading. These can range from detecting patterns from the sub-micro-second level of trades to the global level of satellite imagery of shipments and weather patterns. Robo-advisors (chatbots) enable the automation of many customer management interactions. These chatbots can offer contextualized help at a scale and speed that is not possible for humans.

(q) Virtualization – In 2021 much production, distribution and planning is done by machines; we are beginning to lead our lives in the virtual media. The gamification of human interactions, augmented reality and virtual reality is leading to the sensory intelligence (both detection and perception) virtualization of humans. Our internalized models of our value systems and the dominant human intentionality issues (safety, belonging, mattering) will change as we engage with others in the virtual world. This may have significant impacts on issues such as consciousness, self-determination and intentionality and the development of these into virtual dimension empowerment, and, ultimately, the emergence of a new form of conscience, consciousness and strategic existential advantage. A new social and cognitive fabric, as well as supporting technologies, tools and frameworks, will be enabled by AI. A connected intelligence will give hope to physical co-existence between various competing narratives related to the purpose of existence. The ethical issues here are immense but there is an inevitability to the challenge.

Many of these topics are covered in detail in the industry chapters in Part III. There are, of course, many other examples. **4.032**

F. TRUST IN AI

The usefulness of any intelligence is determined by whether it can be trusted. That is: is human society as a whole willing to partake in its utility? **4.033**

Let us start with trust in human intelligence. Only one of our nine dimensions of intelligence is logical and rational. We are consequently, by and large, irrational beings when it comes to making decisions. Take politics, vocations, leisure, or love. Most of these things just end up being decided upon by an individual based on chances, circumstances, prejudices and intuition. We just accept the right of individuals to make our own decisions and include a right to be wrong. The nature of our language is fuzzy and inexact. We cannot hold our leaders or our peers to account on purely national measures. **4.034**

However, when it comes to AI, we want to find out reasons why an algorithm made a particular choice or decision. We want to be able to explain the decisions. We are fallible; we have emotional states that often go awry under confrontation or 'fight or flight' scenarios. We often make wrong decisions, even when we are not stretched or stressed, through our inbuilt prejudices, biases and intuition. It is the nature of being human. So, if a human makes a mistake, we may reprimand them, divorce them, lock them up, forgive them and pardon them. Machines are different. Machines need not be mortal. Their decisions are seen to be a permanent feature that gets even more embedded, duplicated and improved with time. We want the decisions embedded in the machines to be explainable. Of course, the relationship between truth and fairness is open to a considerable amount of debate and discussion. **4.035**

Until recently, explainability and interpretability would not have been a problem with computer programs. Computer programs were deterministic. If a program did something unexpected we would have called it a bug or, euphemistically, a 'feature'. ML and AI have changed that. AI is inherently non-deterministic and often stochastic. Traditional software that is rules-based and has a limited number of workflows can be audited, and any flaws explained and ironed out. It is easy to see how trust in AI and its explainability are so closely intertwined. If we cannot explain how an algorithm made a particular assertion, we find it difficult to trust it. Thus, the computer programs have moved from a deterministic to a non-deterministic paradigm. **4.036**

The issue of trust is multifaceted. For humans, trust is built through social norms and some form of normalized behaviour. These have parameters primarily around time-invariant behaviour rooted in socially acceptable values over an individual's life, but these values change over **4.037** generations. For humans, we tend to forego the need to get people to explain their decisions. And even if we do, as might happen during judicial processes, the human mind's irrationality is apparent. People have cognitive biases and there is no way to root them out. These are an inherent mechanism in nature, and serve a crucial evolutionary purpose. Human senses and cognition have worked in environments where data was never complete and certainly not limited to the logical and rational dimensions of intelligence. Post-hoc explanations by humans of their behaviour tend to be based on a subconscious narrative that supports a positive view of the self rather than the facts. Human explanations of their reasoning tend to be unreliable.

4.038   Therefore, factors that are necessary for trusted AI are:

(a)   Fairness – Fairness is context-dependent and is generally predicated on human-derived *protected* attributes such as race, gender, age, ability, caste, culture, religion, stereotyping and nationality. An AI algorithm is fair if the risk associated with these protected attributes is equal. There can, of course, be bias in the training data as it generally represents data that has been collected in a human system that has human biases. Bias can also be caused by how an algorithm might have sampled data and the way it has been trained. Fairness also requires adherence to standards for fairness in decision-making.

(b)   Explainability – Explaining decisions is an integral part of human communication, understanding and learning. Humans naturally provide both deictic (pointing) and textual modalities in a typical explanation. The challenge is to build deep learning models that can also explain their decisions with similar fluency in both visual and textual modalities. Directly interpretable ML (in contrast to post-hoc interpretation), in which a person can look at a model and understand what it does, reduces epistemic uncertainty and increases safety because quirks and vagaries of a training dataset can be identified by inspection. Different users have different needs from explanations, and there is no satisfactory quantitative definition of interpretability. Recent regulations in the European Union require 'meaningful' explanations, but it is unclear what constitutes a meaningful explanation.

(c)   Robustness – Adversaries can attack AI systems in various ways. For example, small misclassifications of specified inputs create a loophole which infiltrates AI systems. Sensitive information about data and models can be stolen by observing the outputs of service for different inputs. Services should be designed to detect and defuse attacks. New research proposes certifications for defences against adversarial examples, but these are not yet practical.

(d)   Lineage – Lineage applies to data and algorithms. Lineage looks at origin and history. There are tools that enable a time-travel deconstruction of lineage to trace back evolutions of data and algorithms. This allows an audit at every level. Lineage can be difficult to implement given the exponential rise in the number of operations performed on data through an array of algorithms with a multitude of hyperparameters.

4.039   It is clear that trust in AI is largely based around trust in data and that only the issues around explainability really involve AI algorithms. The type of AI used determines the difficulty of getting a trusted output. Simple models, such as decision-tree-based supervised and unsupervised learning, are easy to track. The tree structure can be followed, and the factors used to arrive at a decision can be apparent. Among the most difficult models to trust are those based on deep learning neural networks, because the hidden layers are connected to other layers through weights and activation functions, resulting in nonlinear and complex relationships.

There is some work under way in many places, including projects funded by the Defense Advanced Research Projects Agency (DARPA), related to creating layers that capture both simple and more complex elements to see which features are driving the reasoning and results.

Among the techniques that are available at present are the following: **4.040**

(a)   Sensitivity Analysis – Testing small perturbations in input features to see the impact on the model outputs. This can then be used to give a model of feature importance and consequently, it can be related to fairness, lineage, robustness and explainability.

(b)   Local Interpretable Model-Agnostic Explanations (LIME) – The problem with sensitivity analysis is that it does not deal with interactions between input parameters. LIME performs multi-feature perturbations between particular model outputs. Open-source versions of this technique are available, and it is one of the better used techniques for interpretability.

(c)   Shapley Additive Explanations (SHAP).

(d)   Tree and Neural Network Interpreters.

Several AI tool providers have released tools to help build interpretability of outputs. Google,   **4.041** for example, say their offering 'Explainable AI' is a set of tools and frameworks to help develop interpretable and inclusive ML models and deploy them with confidence. The What-If Tool allows the visual investigation of model behaviour.

Trusted AI will assume great importance as the complexity of models increases along with   **4.042** the veracity, variety and volume of data that corporations will face in justifying their decisions related to any products or services. The field of AI will become more regulated, and there will be a need to protect vulnerable or sensitive clients and consumers. Without explainable AI, governance will be almost unattainable.

Ethics is covered in detail in chapter 21. Explainability is covered in detail in chapter 29.   **4.043**

G. AI ETHICS, SECURITY AND GOVERNANCE

The moral principles that govern the behaviour of algorithms pose some challenges for us. The   **4.044** problems arise from many different directions. We have covered some aspects of the problems that cognitive algorithms can pose in the section above. There are, of course, serious issues around security, safety and privacy, too. Everything is human-centric. Algorithms are there to help humans, balancing disparate regulations while encouraging innovation.

While recognizing the issues around algorithmic bias and the need for governance frameworks,   **4.045** we must not forget that the root cause of bias is data and how it is curated and consumed. As data democratization tools become available, data parameterization should enable many of the current complex and intractable algorithmic issues to be resolved. While explainability may be an issue for AI, we do not believe that bias needs to have the same handle.

A lot is written about algorithmic bias, and the issues are getting more pressing as the   **4.046** exponential growth in data requires algorithms to become more complicated and automate decision-making. Algorithm bias related to inferring decisions about people and their identities, preferences and attributes is generally covered as they are the prime focus of fairness and discrimination in decision-making. There is no one-size-fits-all approach to fairness, and it is difficult for algorithms to implement things that have not been resolved at a societal level.

4.047   UK legislation prohibits discrimination based on specific protected characteristics (age, disability, gender reassignment, pregnancy and maternity, race, religion or belief, sex, orientation) (Equality Act 2010) and puts privacy restrictions in place (GDPR; Data Protection Act 2018).

4.048   Algorithmic bias cases often arise because data reflects current or historic biases; for example, women's earning patterns. Algorithms carry that outdated bias on to make credit decisions. Appropriate questions need to be asked before, during, and after the development of algorithms that impinge on protected characteristics. There are many useful design question templates and bias impact statements. We particularly like the one available from The Brookings Institute.

4.049   Involving diverse teams in system development should ensure that many biases can be spotted earlier and before the production phase.

4.050   Measuring algorithmic fairness is difficult because there are different statistical measures of fairness:

(a)   Anti-classification – A model is fair to the extent that it does not use encrypted proxies or characteristics from which other encrypted characteristics can be implied.

(b)   Calibration – An algorithm is well calibrated if the risk scores it gives to people reflect the actual outcomes in real life for the people given those scores.

(c)   Classification – A model is fair if the protected groups receive the same outcomes as non-protected groups.

4.051   Ways to detect and mitigate biased, unfair and discriminatory decision-making include statistical approaches and software toolkits, discursive frameworks, self-assessment tools and learning materials and auditing and documentation standards. Commercial tools for algorithmic bias testing are beginning to appear on the market, but for the reasons mentioned above, their results can be challenged. Perhaps the best way of removing bias is to completely remove any data related to protected characteristics, but that may also remove some of the key analytics that businesses may want to know.

H. CONCLUSION

4.052   I am one of those people who believes that AI is not just another technology. I believe that AI will require us to examine who we are and fundamentally change what we do and why we do things. AI will change the human as we will have systems around us that are more intelligent than us. I believe that AI is the new stranger, and by and large we humans fear strangers, as we have not managed to parameterize them. With AI, I am not sure that we can. My passion for AI is based around a statement that I increasingly articulate: '*I am but a bunch of neurons. Without you, data, I am nothing. I owe everything to you.*'

4.053   If you have a new child or have enough recollections about a child you have had, try thinking of that phrase and its relevance. I do.

I recently co-authored a book entitled *Data Alchemy: The Genesis of Business Intelligence*. It **4.054** breaks new ground in the way many people will see data and AI. Indeed, it covers machines that might become conscious and the vectors that are leading us there. It even covers some of the research that will enable machines to have intentionality. The need for governance frameworks (legal, ethical, security, safety, privacy, explainability, interpretability, robustness, and so on) is clear and overwhelming. The main things that drive humans are safety, mattering and belonging. For machines, we can all speculate as to what the dimensions leading to intentionality may be, but we can hopefully see that mattering and lineage are going to be crucial aspects. Humans have beliefs, tribes, and associations (nation-states, for example) that enhance our value as a group and as a collection of people.

The point about all of the above rhetoric is that it is a basic paradigm in developments in intel- **4.055** ligence, data, and related concepts that are technology agnostic. Often, the technology gets in the way of understanding the big ideas. As we state elsewhere:

> Data is the legendary alchemical substance. It is the philosophers' stone. Its discovery is the Magnum Opus. Without it, the universe would be empty; there would be no intelligence without it. Data is the prima materia (first matter), the anima mundi (the world soul). It is responsible for the mystical enlightenment and immaculate conception of consciousness, intuition, and intentionality.

Grand statements you may think, but just think about who we really are. Consider our **4.056** non-linear mind. Some of my colleagues would say that 'consciousness is *"the subconscious compression and reinforcement of data"* and intuition is *"the subconscious integration of the chaotic diversity of data"'*. Reinforcement, compression and integration of data is intelligence (in a multitude of its forms) as practised by natural selection and evolution and, for me, is the route to the next generation of Artificial Intelligence. General business value will be best derived from democratization of data, AI and environmental cognizance.

Data – The Genesis of Intelligence – The quaternion of issues

- Issue of Trust
  - Security/Privacy
  - Lineage
  - Explainability
  - Fairness
  - Robustness
  - Reproducibility
  - Legal and Ethics
  - Governance Frameworks

- Issue of Cost and ROI
  - Acquisition (inc Marketplace)
  - Cleansing
  - Normalisation
  - Storage
  - Data DevOps Stack

- Issue of Relevance
  - Completeness
  - Origination
  - Granularity
  - 6 'V's of Data
  - Taxonomy & Metadata
  - Data Quality

- Issue of Strategy
  - Business Value
  - Monetisation
  - Intelligent Data
  - Ecosystem & Evolution
  - Ontology
  - Single Source of Truth

Figure 4.5   Data: the genesis of intelligence – the quaternion of issues

That may seem exciting or complicated, but it is clear that the root of all intelligence is data and **4.057** the biggest problem we face is the fact that data as captured by most businesses is incomplete and lacks deep intelligence about its purpose. Data often lacks context and becomes divorced from the business object it parameterizes. The issues around data can be narrowed down to just four dimensions (each with a multitude of parameters and abstractions): trust, relevance, cost and strategy.

4.058　In addition, we deconstruct data democratization to three aspects: parameterization; decentralization and exchange; and monetization. Once we have a coherent understanding of the nature of intelligence contained in data (logical as well as irrational), we can apply ML and develop frameworks for businesses to make use of evolving data in a way that enables them to adapt, evolve and flourish. AI is the easiest part of intelligence as it just reflects the 'integration of the chaotic diversity of data' and the 'compression and reinforcement of data'!

4.059　Very few businesses are at that stage, but the completeness of the above predicates is overwhelming.

4.060　Of course, in the original goldrush several players were able to collect data in ways that would now be considered unethical and train models unhindered. Companies, and indeed countries, are now seriously beginning to think about their national economies and wealth pipelines. This will inevitably be a struggle of imperial proportions, which will only accelerate the use and adoption of AI and all related technologies.

4.061　Emergent technologies must also be integrated into this analysis. Quantum computing and its application to security and AI; blockchain and its impact on provenance, decentralization and security; IoT and explosive growth in 'senses everywhere' as well as edge cognition; emergent paradigms around contextualization and manifold hypothesis; societal impacts of intelligent machines; and the research, development and commercialization of the third and fourth wave of AI – all of these computer science-related topics will be coupled with research into synthetic biology, cognitive neuroscience and evolutionary neurophysiology. Together they will offer routes to constructing machines that are both conscious and have human-engineered intentionality and purpose. That opens up a whole realm of complications for legal, ethical and governance frameworks that will be bypassed by some enterprises or agencies.

REFERENCES

Alexander Babuta, Marion Oswald and Ardi Janjeva, Artificial Intelligence and UK National Security: Policy Considerations, Occasional Papers, 27 April 2020, https://rusi.org/publication/occasional-papers/artificial-intelligence-and-uk-national-security-policy-considerations

Google Cloud, Explainable AI – Tools and frameworks to understand and interpret your machine learning models, https://cloud.google.com/explainable-ai

Gov.uk, Investigatory Powers Act 2016, https://www.legislation.gov.uk/ukpga/2016/25/contents/enacted, 2016

Celine Herweijer, 8 Ways AI Can Help Save the Planet, World Economic Forum Annual Meeting, 2018, www.weforum.org/agenda/2018/01/8-ways-ai-can-help-save-the-planet/

IBM AI Research, Trusting AI – IBM Research Is Building and Enabling AI Solutions People Can Trust, www.research.ibm.com/artificial-intelligence/trusted-ai/

OECD, Artificial Intelligence in Society, OECD Publishing, 2019.

Brad Peters, The Big Data Gold Rush, June 2012, https://www.forbes.com/sites/bradpeters/2012/06/21/the-big-data-gold-rush/?sh=76505e7fb247

M. Rovatsos, B. Mittelstadt and A. Koene, Landscape Summary: Bias in Algorithmic Decision-Making, www.research.ed.ac.uk/en/publications/landscape-summary-bias-in-algorithmic-decision-making-what-is-bia

Kenneth Taylor, The Ethics of Algorithms, Philosophytalk, August 2018, www.philosophytalk.org/blog/ethics-algorithms

Nicol Turner-Lee, Paul Resnick and Genie Barton, Algorithmic Bias Detection and Mitigation: Best Practices and Policies to Reduce Consumer Harms, May 2019, www.brookings.edu/research/algorithmic-bias-detection-and-mitigation-best-practices-and-policies-to-reduce-consumer-harms/

Ula La Paris, Push the Limits of Explainability – An Ultimate Guide to SHAP Library, June 2020, https://medium.com/swlh/push-the-limits-of-explainability-an-ultimate-guide-to-shap-library-a110af566a02

T.S. Virdee and D. Brown, Data Alchemy – The Genesis of Business Intelligence, LID Media, 2021.

PART II

LEGAL

5

CORPORATE GOVERNANCE[1]

Martin Petrin

A. INTRODUCTION

Recent media reports and press releases have created the impression that artificial intelligence **5.001** (AI) is on the verge of assuming an important role in corporate management. While, upon closer inspection, it turns out that these stories should not always be taken at face value, they clearly highlight AI's growing importance in management and hint at the enormous changes that corporate leadership may experience in the future. This chapter attempts to anticipate that future by exploring a thought experiment on corporate management and AI. It argues that it is not an insurmountable step from AI generating and suggesting expert decisions to AI making these decisions autonomously. The chapter then proceeds based on the assumption that next-generation AI will be able to take over the management of business organisations and explores corporate law and governance consequences of this development.

In 2014 a Hong Kong-based venture capital firm, Deep Knowledge Ventures, thrust us **5.002** into a new age of corporate management. The firm announced in a press release that it had "appointed VITAL, a machine learning program capable of making investment recommendations in the life science sector, to its board." Two years later, Finnish IT company Tieto informed the public that it had "appointed Artificial Intelligence as a member of the

---

1   An extended version of this chapter first appeared at (2019) 3 *Columbia Business Law Review* 965–1030.

leadership team of its new data-driven businesses unit."[2] Similarly, in early 2018 the CEO of California-based software provider SalesForce revealed that he brings an artificial intelligence machine named "Einstein" to weekly staff meetings and asks it to comment on proposals under discussion.[3]

5.003　Several media outlets reacted promptly, with[4] one newspaper even asking its readers whether they would "take orders from a robot."[5] In the case of VITAL it turned out that initial reports were technically incorrect, given that Hong Kong law does not allow non-human entities to serve on boards.[6] The phenomenon was also exaggerated, as Deep Knowledge Ventures later acknowledged that the firm treats the software "as a member of our board with observer status" on the basis of an agreement that the board "would not make positive investment decisions without corroboration by VITAL."[7] As one commentator noted, this arrangement was no different from practices at other financial companies that use large data searches to survey markets and generate suggestions for boards or managers.[8]

5.004　Although the claims in the above-mentioned news items and similar ones may not always be taken at face value, they clearly highlight the growing importance of AI in corporate management and hint at the potentially enormous changes that corporate leadership may experience in the relatively near future. This chapter attempts to anticipate that future by exploring a thought experiment on corporate management and artificial intelligence. It argues that the step from AI generating and suggesting expert decisions for managers (which in some areas is already common today) to AI making these decisions autonomously is hardly insurmountable.

5.005　As noted in chapter 3 and elsewhere, there is currently no singular, universally accepted definition of AI.[9] For the purpose of this chapter we will follow a commentator who has noted that "AI is an umbrella term, comprised by many different techniques" (including the approaches of machine learning and deep learning)[10] and we construe AI broadly, invoking the classic definition by John McCarthy, the late Stanford scientist: "the science and engineering of making intelligent machines, especially intelligent computer programs."[11] This definition is better

---

2　Tieto the First Nordic Company to Appoint Artificial Intelligence to the Leadership Team of the New Data-driven Businesses Unit, *Tieto* (Oct. 17, 2016), https://www.tieto.com/news/tieto-the-first-nordic-company-to-appoint-artificial-intelligence-to-the-leadership-team-of-the-new.

3　David Reid, Marc Benioff Brings an A.I. Machine Called Einstein to His Weekly Staff Meeting, *CNBC* (Jan. 25, 2018), https://www.cnbc.com/2018/01/25/davos-2018-ai-machine-called-einstein-attends-salesforce-meetings.html.

4　See, e.g., Nicky Burridge, Artificial Intelligence Gets a Seat in the Boardroom, *Nikkei Asian Review* (May 10, 2017), https://asia.nikkei.com/Business/Companies/Artificial-intelligence-gets-a-seat-in-the-boardroom; Algorithm appointed board director, *BBC News* (May 16, 2014), https://www.bbc.co.uk/news/technology-27426942; Simon Sharwood, Software 'Appointed to Board' of Venture Capital Firm, *The Register* (May 18, 2014), https://www.theregister.co.uk/2014/05/18/software_appointed_to_board_of_venture_capital_firm.

5　Ellie Zolfagharifard, Would You Take Orders from a Robot? An Artificial Intelligence Becomes the World's First Company Director, *Daily Mail* (May 19, 2014), https://www.dailymail.co.uk/sciencetech/article-2632920/Would-orders-ROBOT-Artificial-intelligence-world-s-company-director-Japan.html.

6　*See* Sharwood, *supra* note 4.

7　Burridge, *supra* note 4.

8　See BBC News article, *supra* note 4 (citing Professor Noel Sharkey).

9　Peter Stone et al., *Artificial Intelligence and Life in 2030: Report of the 2015 Study Panel* (2016) 6, https://ai100.stanford.edu/sites/g/files/sbiybj9861/f/ai_100_report_0831fnl.pdf.

10　Ryan Calo, Artificial Intelligence Policy: A Primer and Roadmap (2017) 51 *U.C. Davis Law Review* 399, at 405, 407.

11　John McCarthy, *What is AI?/Basic Questions*, http://jmc.stanford.edu/artificial-intelligence/ what-is-ai/index.html.

suited for our purposes than a definition of AI as an approximation of human intelligence,[12] because it leaves open the possibility that AI will eventually exceed humans' cognitive capacity and represent an entirely separate category of intelligence. As McCarthy noted, AI is related to using computers to understand human intelligence, but is not necessarily confined to methods that are biologically observable.[13]

Based on this understanding of AI, and on the assumption that as AI further evolves it will **5.006** be able to take over the management of corporations, this chapter will explore some of the potential corporate law and governance consequences of this development. In doing so, it focuses on corporate leadership, management structures, and managerial liability. The chapter suggests that AI will usher in the end of the corporate board. It posits that AI will gradually replace human directors on boards, leading to "fused boards" where the various roles and inputs previously provided by a collective of human directors are incorporated into a single software program or algorithm, whose performance will be superior to today's human-led governance. AI will also replace human officers and managers below the board level. For reasons more fully explained below, these developments will eventually make the separation between boards of directors and management obsolete and lead to the "fused management" of corporations, with companies being managed comprehensively by a single AI unit. The chapter also predicts that in the future, large commercial AI management software providers will offer these services to companies for sale or hire.[14]

In this new world, directors' and officers' personal liability will change as well. In an initial **5.007** phase, when humans and AI still work together on boards and in management, a number of challenging legal questions concerning personal liability will arise, including the extent to which human managers can and should monitor AI, and the extent to which they may delegate tasks to machines without exposing themselves to personal liability. In a later phase, when AI dominates the management and governance of corporations, today's framework will either vanish completely, evolve into a system in which the artificial AI entities/managers themselves can be sued, or be replaced with a system akin to today's products liability paradigm. Under the latter system, which is arguably the most likely option, corporations and shareholders would, instead of using the modern derivative action framework, be able to bring actions against the developers and providers of AI management software based on faults in design and similar claims. Additionally, or as an alternative to fault liability, this system could also allow for strict liability against software developers and providers.

---

12   For example, Merriam-Webster defines AI as "the capability of a machine to imitate intelligent human behavior." *Artificial Intelligence, Merriam-Webster Online Dictionary* (2018), https://www.merriam-webster.com/dictionary/artificial %20intelligence.

13   McCarthy, *supra* note 11.

14   While the following will not attempt to describe what AI corporate leadership will look like in terms of its physical appearance, it suffices here to suggest that this could range from purely software-based applications, combinations of software with laptop or tablet like hardware, to robots that can listen and speak.

B. CAN AI TAKE OVER?

5.008   This section of the chapter addresses the fundamental question of whether and to what extent AI can assume corporate management tasks. It begins with a brief examination of the tasks that today's corporate directors, officers, and managers carry out. These tasks can be roughly divided into administrative tasks and non-administrative tasks ("judgment work"). This bifurcation proves useful in mapping managerial tasks onto AI roles and capabilities. AI seems poised to take over completely in the area of administrative managerial tasks; however, disagreement persists over AI's role when it comes to non-administrative judgment work, which includes corporate leadership tasks relating to strategy, innovation, creative thinking, and people management.[15] Still, some commentators convincingly demonstrate that AI will likely reach and even exceed human-level skills in the area of judgment work as well.[16] This development would allow AI to assume all the tasks of today's directors and managers.

1.   Corporate Leadership Tasks

(a) Directors

5.009   Given the corporate board's importance in decision-making, it may come as a surprise that the law offers little guidance on the tasks it must or should perform. While some jurisdictions provide detailed enumerations of (sometimes non-delegable) board powers,[17] others do not. In the US, for instance, the Delaware General Corporation Law (DGCL) states that "[t]he business and affairs of every corporation [...] shall be *managed* by or under the direction of a board of directors."[18] This general reference to "management" by the board would, by itself, represent a misleading or at least highly inaccurate description of what modern boards do. It is only the DGCL's additional reference to corporations being managed "under the direction" of the board that provides a more accurate reflection of contemporary governance. Public companies are rarely managed by the board. Rather, the board transfers significant managerial responsibilities to officers and managers.[19] In turn, the board supervises management and only retains for itself a limited number of high-level managerial tasks.[20]

5.010   Indeed, over the course of the past several decades, monitoring has become the accepted core function of Anglo-American boards.[21] Instead of "managing" the company, boards—to a large extent—entrust full-time executives with this role, including running the company on a daily basis and delegating certain tasks and responsibilities further down the corporate hierarchy to employees.[22] Directors' focus on supervision instead of management is also a necessity dictated by the fundamental modus operandi of the modern board. Today's boards are part-time, inter-

---

15   See *infra* Section 2.b.

16   See ibid.

17   See, e.g., Obligationenrecht [OR][Code of Obligations] Mar. 30, 1911, SR 220, art. 716a (Switzerland).

18   Del. Code Ann., tit. 8, § 141(a) (2016) (emphasis added).

19   Stephen M. Bainbridge, *The New Corporate Governance in Theory and Practice*, Oxford University Press (2008) 74.

20   Ibid. See also *In re* Caremark Int'l Inc. Derivative Litig., 698 A.2d 959, 968 (Del. Ch. 1996). On the functions of US and UK boards, see also Marc Moore & Martin Petrin, *Corporate Governance: Law, Regulation and Theory*, Palgrave Macmillan (2017) 174–77, which this section partially relies on.

21   Stephen M. Bainbridge, Corporate Directors in the United Kingdom (2017) 59 *William & Mary Law Review Online* 65, at 73–74.

22   See ibid.

mittent, decision-making bodies.[23] Boards only meet periodically, and the majority of board members are not employees of the company on whose board they sit—that is, they may also have other board mandates. In practice, this setup makes it impossible for boards to comprehensively manage a company on a daily basis.

Although monitoring is the board's chief role, it is not *limited* to this task. Modern boards take on a multi-faceted role that combines supervision with a number of other activities.[24] For example, boards set their corporations' strategic goals and retain certain managerial responsibilities, which consist, above all else, of appointing and terminating senior management personnel and approving major transactions.[25] Furthermore, boards have a service and relational function in which they provide advice and guidance to management and, in particular, to the CEO.[26] This includes leveraging their contacts with a view to helping "expand the company's network by providing interlocks with potential suppliers, customers, sources of finance, and other potential providers of key organizational needs."[27] It also includes the directors' role to act as a liaison with shareholders and other company stakeholders.[28] **5.011**

The G20/OECD Principles of Corporate Governance provide a more detailed description of board functions. According to the Principles, the board has eight key functions: **5.012**

[1] Reviewing and guiding corporate strategy, major plans of action, risk management policies and procedures, annual budgets and business plans; setting performance objectives; monitoring implementation and corporate performance; and overseeing major capital expenditures, acquisitions, and divestitures [...] [2] Monitoring the effectiveness of the company's governance practices and making changes as needed [...] [3] Selecting, compensating, monitoring and, when necessary, replacing key executives and overseeing succession planning [...] [4] Aligning key executive and board remuneration with the longer term interests of the company and its shareholders [...] [5] Ensuring a formal and transparent board nomination and election process [...] [6] Monitoring and managing potential conflicts of interest of management, board members and shareholders, including misuse of corporate assets and abuse in related party transactions [...] [7] Ensuring the integrity of the corporation's accounting and financial reporting systems, including the independent audit, and that appropriate systems of control are in place, in particular, systems for risk management, financial and operational control, and compliance with the law and relevant standards [...] [8] Overseeing the process of disclosure and communications.[29]

A series of surveys on the nature of directors' work, conducted by the consulting firm McKinsey & Company, sheds further light from inside the board on the nature of directors' work, including where board members invest their time and, in total, how much time they dedicate to board-related work. According to the most recent iteration of the survey, directors dedicate **5.013**

---

23 Moore & Petrin, *supra* note 20, at 176.

24 See, e.g., David Kershaw, *Company Law in Context: Text and Materials*, Oxford University Press (2nd ed. 2012) 234–36; Lynne L. Dallas, The Multiple Role of Corporate Boards (2003) 40 *San Diego Law Review* 781, at 781–83; Joseph A. McCahery & Erik P.M. Vermeulen, Understanding the Board of Directors after the Financial Crisis: Some Lessons for Europe (2014) 41 Journal of Law & Society 121, at 126.

25 Stephen M. Bainbridge & M. Todd Henderson, Boards-R-Us: Reconceptualizing Corporate Boards (2014) 66 *Stanford Law Review* 1051, at 1061.

26 See ibid. See also Dallas, *supra* note 24, at 805–07.

27 Bainbridge, *supra* note 21, at 72 (footnote omitted).

28 Ibid. at 73. See also Bainbridge & Henderson, *supra* note 25, at 1061–62.

29 G20/OECD Principles of Corporate Governance, OECD (2015) 47–50.

24 days per year to board matters.[30] In terms of tasks, board members spend 27 percent of their time on strategy; 20 percent on performance management; 13 percent on organizational structure, culture, and talent management; 12 percent on investments and mergers & acquisitions; 10 percent on core governance and compliance; 9 percent on risk management; and 9 percent on shareholder and stakeholder management.[31] The McKinsey survey also notes that the distribution of time that boards spend on these tasks has been stable over the past few years, with only slight changes compared to previous years.[32] Thus, strategy and performance management have been consistently ranked as areas boards spend the most time on, with respondents indicating that they would like to spend even more time on strategy in addition to organizational matters.[33]

(b) Managers

5.014 Boards' focus on high-level tasks, with a particular emphasis on monitoring and strategy, can generally be contrasted with the tasks managers perform. As in the case of boards, however, the law again offers only minimal guidance on the role and tasks of managers.[34] To start, there is no legal definition of a 'manager'. In fact, the term is sometimes broadly used as a label for both directors and other high-level decision-makers within corporations.[35] That is also the approach taken in later sections of this chapter, where the use of the words 'managers' or 'management' will normally refer to all individuals with significant leadership and decision-making responsibility at various levels of the corporate hierarchy. For the purposes of the present section, however, the term 'managers' only designates those individuals that have the aforementioned leadership and decision-making attributes but are *not* (or *not only*) directors.[36] The term "managers" in this sense includes, but is not limited to, corporate officers. For their part, the DGCL and the Model Business Corporation Act (MBCA) refer to officers on numerous occasions without elaborating in any detail on their functions.[37] In essence, both simply provide that corporations shall have officers with such titles and duties as stated in the corporation's bylaws or board resolutions.[38]

---

30   Martin Hirt, et al., *The Board Perspective: A Collection of McKinsey Insights Focusing on Boards of Directors*, McKinsey & Co. (Mar. 2018) 49, https://www.mckinsey.com/~/media/McKinsey/Featured%20Insights/Leadership/The%20board%20perspective/Issue%20Number%202/2018_Board%20Perspective_Number_2.ashx.

31   Ibid.

32   Ibid.

33   Ibid.

34   See Lyman Johnson, Dominance by Inaction: Delaware's Long Silence on Corporate Officers, 182 and 184, in Stephen M. Bainbridge et al.: *Can Delaware Be Dethroned?: Evaluating Delaware's Dominance of Corporate Law*, Cambridge University Press (2017).

35   See, e.g., Robert J. Rhee, Corporate Ethics, Agency, and the Theory of the Firm (2008) 3 *Journal of Business & Technology Law* 309, at 312 n. 20 (defining managers as directors and officers).

36   Managers may, of course, in addition to their managerial role, serve on the board but there is a difference between acts taken in their directorial capacity and their managerial capacity.

37   See, e.g., Del. Code Ann., tit. 8, § 142(a) (2019); Model Bus. Corp. Act §§ 8.40–8.41 (Am. Bar Ass'n amended 2016). As one commentator noted, the definition of "'officer'" tends to be "fluid and context-specific." Verity Winship, Jurisdiction over Corporate Officers and the Incoherence of Implied Consent (2013) *University of Illinois Law Review* 1171, at 1195–96. It seems clear, however, that the hallmark of an officer is decision-making power that relates to important aspects of the business. See Matthew T. Bodie, Holacracy and the Law (2018) 42 *Delaware Journal of Corporate Law* 619, at 620).

38   § 142(a); §§ 8.40–8.41.

The only officer role that the DGCL and MBCA specifically describe is that of the secretary, **5.015** whose function consists of keeping and maintaining certain records and the minutes of directors' and shareholders' meetings.[39] In practice, of course, most corporations choose to appoint several officers. Typically, "the CEO is the top of the hierarchy; the chief operating officer is the second-in-command and in charge of general operations; and the chief financial officer is primarily responsible for finances and financial risk."[40] These are the three principal officer roles, and the MBCA defines the individuals who serve in these roles, along with "any individual in charge of a principal business unit or function," as "senior executives."[41] However, it is not uncommon for corporations to appoint additional "chief officers" in a number of other fields of their business, such as information or privacy.[42]

Despite their sparse treatment in corporate statutes, the importance of managers is of course **5.016** broadly recognized. Indeed, given that officers carry out important managerial responsibilities, they have a dominant role in corporate leadership and "exert[] immense power and influence over the corporation."[43] In defining managerial leadership in terms of more specific tasks, one can still refer to Peter Drucker's classic description of the "five basic operations in the work of a manager."[44] According to Drucker, managerial work focuses on the following areas: (1) setting goals and objectives—managers decide what needs to be done to reach them, and communicate them to the people whose performance is needed to attain them; (2) organization of work—managers analyze activities, decisions, and relations; classify and divide work into manageable activities and jobs; group units and jobs into organized structures; and select people for the management of units and for the jobs to be done; (3) motivation and communication— managers make teams out of those individuals who are responsible for various jobs, using the tools of communication in horizontal and vertical relations and "people decisions" on pay, placement and promotion; (4) measurement—managers establish targets and yardsticks; analyze, appraise and interpret performance, and communicate the related meaning and outcomes to employees; (5) developing people—both in relation to others and to themselves.[45]

To be sure, managerial tasks differ depending on the individual's specific job description, **5.017** seniority within the organization, and the size and nature of the business they work for. For example, for officers who are the highest ranking managers of a corporation, typical tasks include "entering into ordinary business transactions, devising business strategies, setting business goals, managing risks, and generally working with subordinates to '[p]lan, direct, or coordinate operational activities.'"[46] Conversely, a lower-level, non-officer manager might be in charge of managing a smaller business division or branch, organizing work schedules, or focusing on customer relations, among other responsibilities.

---

39   § 142(a); § 8.40(c).
40   Bodie, *supra* note 37, at 653.
41   Model Business Corporation Act § 13.01(8) (Am. Bar Ass'n amended 2016).
42   Bodie, *supra* note 37, at 653.
43   Megan Wischmeier Shaner, Officer Accountability (2016) 32 *Georgia State University Law Review* 357, at 367.
44   Peter F. Drucker, *Management: Tasks, Responsibilities, Practices*, Harper Business (1974) 400.
45   Ibid.
46   Lyman Johnson & Robert Ricca, Reality Check on Officer Liability (2011) 67 *Business Lawyer* 75, at 78–79 (footnotes omitted).

5.018 Nevertheless, there are general categories of tasks that apply to managers across all hierarchical levels. In 2016, Accenture surveyed 1,770 managers from 14 countries and 17 different industries, which usefully described these categories.[47] The survey respondents included managers across all levels, from an organization's top management group to middle managers and front-line managers.[48] According to the survey, these managers spent 54 percent of their time on administrative coordination and control tasks; 30 percent on solving problems and collaborating; 10 percent on work involving strategy and innovation; and 7 percent on tasks relating to developing people and engaging with stakeholders.[49] These results, especially the insight that managers spend substantial amounts of time on coordination and control tasks, are important to keep in mind given the issue discussed in the next section—the significance of the distinction between administrative tasks and judgment work when it comes to AI's potential roles in corporate management.

2. AI and Corporate Leadership

5.019 Having outlined the current tasks of corporate leadership, as exercised by directors and managers, this section moves on to explore whether AI could assume these tasks. While there is little doubt that so-called administrative tasks will be exclusively carried out by computers in the future, researchers are divided over the question of whether humans can be replaced when it comes to tasks that involve judgment and emotional intelligence.[50] Nevertheless, this section concludes that even in these areas the rise of AI is likely and that we are steering towards a future with "management by machine."

(a) Potential Roles for AI

5.020 Before assessing whether AI could take over corporate management functions, it is helpful to establish more generally what types of managerial roles AI technology can assume. In this respect, it is helpful to think of AI roles in reference to degrees of autonomy and proactivity. A broad system of categorization, which will also be employed in the following section, distinguishes between three different types of AI roles. These roles are: (i) assisted AI; (ii) advisory AI; and (iii) autonomous AI.[51]

5.021 *Assisted AI*—The first potential role of AI is that of an assistant. In this form, AI has either a low level of or no autonomy, which also means that productivity gains are more limited compared to other types of AI roles. Assisted AI applications are also examples of "narrow AI" or "soft AI" (in this case, systems that "can do a better job on a very specific range of tasks than humans

---

47   Vegard Kolbjørnsrud et al., *Accenture Inst. for High Performance, The Promise of Artificial Intelligence: Redefining Management in the Workforce of the Future* (2016) 6, https://www.accenture.com/_acnmedia/pdf-32/ai_in_management _report.pdf#zoom=50.

48   Ibid.

49   Ibid. at 5

50   See *infra* Section II.B.

51   Kolbjørnsrud et al., *supra* note 47 at 17; Robert J. Thomas et al., Accenture Inst. for High Performance, A machine in the C-suite (2016) 2, https:// www.accenture.com/t00010101T000000Z__w__/br-pt/_acnmedia/PDF-13/Accenture -Strategy-WotF-Machine-CSuite.pdf.

can" but, because of their limitations, "would never be mistaken for a human").[52] Importantly, while assisted AI may execute tasks on behalf of humans, it does not make any decisions itself.[53]

Examples of commonly used assisted AI systems are Apple's Siri and its Android rival, Google   **5.022** Assistant, which can support users by carrying out a range of tasks. Applied in a business context, assisted AI could take notes, compile work and meeting schedules, prepare reports, maintain scorecards, or fulfill helpdesk and customer service functions.[54] Depending on the level of complexity of these systems, they may also be close to or overlap with the next category of advisory AI.

Advisory AI—The second potential role of AI is advisory in nature. In this demanding role,   **5.023** AI can provide "support in more complex problem solving and decision-making situations by asking and answering questions as well as building scenarios and simulations."[55] Advisory AI has a heightened level of autonomy, which leads to increased productivity compared to assisted AI. Still, decision-making rights either remain with human users or are at most shared between humans and machines.[56] Advisory AI is sometimes called "augmented intelligence."[57] The augmentation refers to a combination of artificial and human intelligence, in which AI does not replace human intelligence, but leverages or improves it by, for example, giving information and advice that would otherwise be unavailable or more difficult and time consuming to obtain.[58] Augmentation can also mean that "humans and machines learn from each other and redefine the breadth and depth of what they do together."[59]

A particularly salient example of augmented AI is IBM's Watson platform. Among other   **5.024** achievements, Watson is known for repeatedly beating two human champions at the game show "Jeopardy" in 2011.[60] Watson's use, of course, goes far beyond trivia and games. It excels in different environments at a multitude of serious tasks, including medical diagnosis, wealth management and financial advice, legal due diligence, and sales coaching.[61]

Autonomous AI—The third and most advanced role of AI is that of an *actor*. AI in this category   **5.025** can "proactively and autonomously evaluate options—making decisions or challenging the status quo."[62] Crucially, in contrast to the previous two categories, when it comes to autonomous AI "the decision rights are with the machine."[63] Today, perhaps the most prominent

---

52   Vivek Wadhwa & Alex Salkever, *The Driver in the Driverless Car*, Berrett-Koehler (2017) 38.

53   *See* Anand Rao, *AI everywhere & nowhere part 3 – AI is AAAI (Assisted-Augmented-Autonomous Intelligence)*, *pwc Next in Tech* (May 20, 2016), https://usblogs.pwc.com/emerging-technology/ai-everywhere-nowhere-part-3-ai-is-aaai-assisted -augmented-autonomous-intelligence.

54   Kolbjørnsrud et al., *supra* note 47, at 17.

55   Ibid.

56   Rao, *supra* note 53.

57   Ibid.

58   See ibid.

59   Ibid.

60   John Markoff, Computer Wins on 'Jeopardy!': Trivial, It's Not, *N.Y. Times* (Feb. 16, 2011), https://www.nytimes.com/ 2011/02/17/science/17jeopardy-watson.html?.

61   See ibid.; Conner Forrest, *IBM Watson: What are companies using it for?*, *ZDNet* (Sept. 1, 2015), https://www.zdnet.com/ article/ibm-watson-what-are-companies-using-it-for.

62   Kolbjørnsrud et al., *supra* note 47, at 17.

63   Rao, *supra* note 53.

example of autonomous AI is the advent of the fully autonomous vehicle, whose emergence may soon become reality.[64] In the corporate management context, there are already several specific autonomous AI applications in use. They perform tasks such as autonomous robotic trading of securities and handling of loan applications.[65] The use of such systems is not yet widespread but is, according to an Accenture study on the promise of artificial intelligence, "increasingly becoming commonplace."[66]

(b) Administrative Work versus Judgment Work

5.026   The previous section considered the types of *roles* that AI can assume with reference to the differing types of AI and their corresponding levels of autonomy and productivity. The present section moves to consider the types of *tasks* that may be suitable for AI. An important distinction to keep in mind when thinking about whether AI can take over corporate management is between administrative work and judgment work.[67]

5.027   The Accenture study referred to above describes administrative work in the corporate management context as consisting of "[a]dministrative and routine tasks, such as scheduling, allocation of resources, and reporting."[68] Administrative work can be broadly contrasted with judgment work. For our purposes, judgment work may be defined as work that requires creative, analytical, and strategic skills.[69] The Accenture study defines it as "the application of human experience and expertise to critical business decisions and practices when the information available is insufficient to suggest a successful course of action or [is not] reliable enough to suggest an obvious best course of action."[70] Judgment can be individual, but will often be collective, particularly in more complex situations. It may therefore involve teamwork and "specific interpersonal skills; namely, social networking, people development and coaching, and collaboration."[71] In line with the inclusion of interpersonal skills, emotional intelligence can be treated as a subcategory of judgment.[72]

5.028   As we have seen, non-director managers indicate that they spend more than 50 percent of their time on administrative tasks. The remaining non-administrative tasks, as per the Accenture study's definitional framework, consists of judgment work. These tasks pertain to problem solving and collaboration, strategy and innovation, and relations with individuals and stakeholders.

5.029   The situation of managers, who clearly spend considerable time on administrative tasks, contrasts with directors' focus. The bulk of directors' work falls into the category of judgment

---

64   See, e.g., Jeb Su, Tesla Could Have Full Self-Driving Cars on the Road by 2019, Elon Musk Says, *Forbes* (Nov. 7, 2018), https://www.forbes.com/sites/jeanbaptiste/2018/11/07/tesla-could-have-full-self-driving-cars-on-the-road-by-2019-elon-musk-says.

65   Some examples of existing AI-based software can be found in Kolbjørnsrud et al., *supra* note 47, at 17.

66   Ibid. at 17.

67   See ibid. at 3–4, 11–14.

68   Ibid. at 4.

69   See ibid. at 11.

70   Ibid.

71   Ibid. at 13.

72   See Ajay Agrawal et al., *What to Expect from Artificial Intelligence*, MIT Sloan Management Review, (Spring 2017) 23 and 26, http://ilp.mit.edu/media/news_articles/smr/2017/58311.pdf.

work. More specifically, as a rough estimate based on the above-mentioned McKinsey survey on board tasks, judgment work appears to make up at least 75 percent of directors' time and workload.[73]

The importance of the distinction between administrative and judgment work lies in the likelihood of the respective tasks being assumed by AI in the future. The authors of the Accenture study found that "artificial intelligence will soon be able to do the administrative tasks that consume much of managers' time faster, better, and at a lower cost"[74] and concluded that "AI will put an end to administrative management work."[75] The nascent literature on AI and management does not appear to challenge the idea that administrative work will be the exclusive domain of AI in the future.[76]   **5.030**

While the prospect of being relieved of administrative work may come as welcome news to many managers, the question then arises as to what role AI can play in the remaining managerial tasks that consist of non-administrative work. In this area, commentators have expressed widely diverging views on the future role of AI in management.   **5.031**

A first group of commentators sees only a limited role for AI in judgment work. For instance, the Accenture study authors suggest that, apart from a limited number of specific applications, human managers in business will generally prevail in and increasingly focus on judgment work.[77] The study suggests that in the context of judgment work the role of AI will remain advisory in nature, with machines supporting and augmenting the work of human managers, but not taking on the role of independent actors.[78] It is this type of augmentation that the study suggests holds the greatest potential for AI-driven value creation.[79]   **5.032**

The Accenture study provides two examples to illustrate its view that human judgment cannot be replaced by AI. First, it notes that in the context of big data marketing and sales campaigns, "analytics-driven short-term results may come at the expense of long-term brand building [and] strategies [...] which cannot easily be suggested by data."[80] It is therefore up to human marketing executives, the study suggests, to "use judgment—combining analytics with their   **5.033**

---

73   Hirt, *supra* note 30, at 49. We assume that tasks pertaining to strategy, organizational structure, culture, talent management, and shareholder and stakeholder management consist of judgment work. Further, we assume that at least half of performance management, investments and M&A, core governance and compliance, and risk management tasks are judgment work as well. Adding the time spent on these tasks together suggests that judgment work makes up approximately 72% of overall board tasks.

74   Vegard Kolbjørnsrud et al., How Artificial Intelligence Will Redefine Management, *Harvard Business Review Online* (Nov. 2, 2016), https://hbr.org/2016/11/how-artificial-intelligence-will-redefine-management.

75   Kolbjørnsrud et al., *supra* note 47, at 3. The study mentions tasks such as note taking, scheduling, reporting, maintaining scorecards, managing shift schedules, and generating investor statements and management reports as specific examples of AI-led administrative work. Ibid. at 4, 11, 17.

76   The literature reviewed for this section explicitly or implicitly accepts the idea that administrative tasks will be dominated by AI and related new technologies.

77   See Kolbjørnsrud et al., *supra* note 47, at 13–15.

78   See ibid. at 15.

79   Ibid. See also Byron Reese, *The Fourth Age: Smart Computers, Conscious Computers, and the Future of Humanity*, Atria Books (2018) 85–121.

80   Kolbjørnsrud et al., *supra* note 47, at 11.

own and others' insight and experience, and by balancing short and long-term priorities."[81] Second, the study uses the example of evaluating job applications. It argues that even if AI systems "can measure and opine on a candidate's facial expressions, mannerisms and vocal inflections, they may not be able to assess that individual's compatibility with the attitudes and history of the company's existing workforce. These decisions require human awareness of the organization's context and history."[82] For this reason, the study concludes that human managers will remain the ultimate decision-makers.

5.034   Another study, authored by Professors Agrawal, Gans, and Goldfarb, begins by emphasizing AI's superiority in data gathering and prediction tasks.[83] Prediction in this context is understood as the ability to use acquired information or facts to anticipate future events (for example, if a customer will default on a loan) and human actions (for example, what a human driver would do in a given situation).[84] Prediction can also relate to present conditions, such as predicting a future medical condition by evaluating currently observable symptoms.[85] While AI excels at prediction, a different question is whether on this basis, beyond identifying probable occurrences, it can reliably *initiate* appropriate actions.

5.035   According to Agrawal and his co-authors, replicating human judgment is possible, but its feasibility depends on the necessary level of judgment involved in an action and the ease of defining desired outcomes in terms of "something a machine can understand."[86] While the authors make the point that in the coming years our understanding of human judgment will improve and become subject to increasing automation,[87] they nevertheless believe that a need for human judgment will prevail in certain situations and contexts.[88] They predict as likely "that organizations will have [a] continuing demand for people who can make responsible decisions (requiring ethical judgment), engage customers and employees (requiring emotional intelligence), and identify new opportunities (requiring creativity)."[89] Finally, these authors also suggest that human judgment will be required when deciding how best to apply AI.[90]

5.036   Echoing the general sentiment of the Accenture study and the work of Agrawal and his coauthors, Beck and Libert have remarked that "[t]hose who want to stay relevant in their professions will need to focus on skills and capabilities that artificial intelligence has trouble replicating—understanding, motivating, and interacting with human beings."[91] They argue that although machines may be able to diagnose complex business problems and recommend actions to improve an organization, human beings are "still best suited to jobs like spurring

---

81   Ibid. (footnote omitted).

82   Ibid.

83   See Agrawal et al., *supra* note 72, at 23–24. It is commonly accepted that machines are better at data gathering and analysis than humans, suggesting that these areas will be dominated by AI. See, e.g., Megan Beck & Barry Libert, The Rise of AI Makes Emotional Intelligence More Important, *Harvard Business Review Online* (Feb. 15, 2017), https://hbr .org/2017/02/the-rise-of-ai-makes-emotional-intelligence-more-important.

84   See Agrawal et al., *supra* note 72, at 24.

85   See ibid.

86   Ibid.

87   Ibid.

88   Ibid. at 24–25.

89   Ibid. at 26.

90   Ibid.

91   Beck & Libert, *supra* note 83.

[a] leadership team to action, avoiding political hot buttons, and identifying savvy individuals to lead change."[92] Beck and Libert have also identified areas of decision making where they believe AI performs better than humans. They note that "[a]rtificial intelligence for both strategic decision-making (capital allocation) and operating decision-making will come to be an essential competitive advantage, just like electricity was in the industrial revolution or enterprise resource planning software (ERP) was in the information age."[93] However, in Beck and Libert's view, AI in the boardroom "is not about automating leadership and governance, but rather augmenting board intelligence."[94]

Frey and Osborne also provide support for the view that managerial judgment work is not about to be replaced by machines. In a study examining more than 700 occupations and their susceptibility to computerization, they found that around 47 percent of total US employment is in the high-risk category and "could be automated relatively soon, perhaps over the next decade or two."[95] The study suggests that generalist occupations requiring knowledge of human heuristics and specialist occupations involving the development of novel ideas and artifacts are the least susceptible to computerization.   **5.037**

Specifically with regard to managers, Frey and Osborne noted that chief executives represent "a prototypical example of generalist work requiring a high degree of social intelligence," as evidenced by tasks such as "conferring with board members, organization officials, or staff members to discuss issues, coordinate activities, or resolve problems" and "negotiating or approving contracts or agreements."[96] Frey and Osborne thus predict "that most management, business, and finance occupations, which are intensive in generalist tasks requiring social intelligence" are at a low risk of being automated.[97] However, it is notable that Frey and Osborne's contemplated timeline is relatively short. They note that "occupations that involve complex perception and manipulation tasks, creative intelligence tasks, and social intelligence tasks are unlikely to be substituted by computer capital *over the next decade or two*."[98] This suggests that beyond this timeframe their study does not exclude the possibility of such jobs, including management roles, becoming automated as well.   **5.038**

A contrast to the view that human judgment, including emotional intelligence, is at its core irreplaceable—leading to a future where AI and human managers would work together—is the vision of AI's complete replacement of management. The Accenture study notes that some managers are already questioning "whether the manager role as we know it will survive," with a large UK financial institution's Chief Information Officer recently opining that advances in   **5.039**

---

92   Ibid.

93   Barry Libert et al., AI in the Boardroom: The Next Realm of Corporate Governance, *MITSloan Management Review Blog* (Oct. 19, 2017), https://sloanreview.mit.edu/ article/ai-in-the-boardroom-the-next-realm-of-corporate-governance.

94   Ibid.

95   Carl Benedikt Frey and Michael A. Osborne, The Future of Employment: How Susceptible Are Jobs to Computerisation? (2017), 114 *Technological Forecasting & Soc. Change* 254, 268.

96   Ibid.

97   Ibid.

98   Ibid. at 262 (emphasis added). See also Wadhwa & Salkever, *supra* note 52, at 38–39 (describing creative capabilities of AI in the areas of writing, music, poetry, and art).

technology may lead to a world where "we may not need managers."[99] Similarly, in a chapter on the rise of "robo-directors" and their corporate law implications, one academic opined that "technology will probably soon offer the possibility of artificial intelligence not only supporting directors, but even replacing them."[100]

5.040   Relevant work to our question of AI's potential future role in corporate management has also been produced by authors that specialize more generally in predictions about the future of humanity.[101] Some of these authors challenge the idea that there are certain areas or tasks at which humans will always outperform machines. In particular, several commentators believe that machines can be better than humans when it comes to judgment work. They predict the rise of emotionally intelligent AI, arguing that emotional intelligence is a function of "biological algorithms" that machines will be able to replicate.[102] Some commentators also expect the emergence of artificial general intelligence ("general AI"), which will match the intelligence of humans in all areas, or even superintelligent AI, which will far exceed human intelligence.[103]

5.041   Nick Bostrom, for instance, writes that for advanced forms of AI, all intellectual abilities will be within a system's reach, including cognitive modules and skills such as "empathy, political acumen, and any other powers stereotypically wanting in computer-like personalities."[104] Indeed, a "superintelligent" machine, a concept that Bostrom sees as potentially emerging in the future, would not only excel at typical computer skills, but also at tasks including strategizing (strategic planning, forecasting, prioritizing, analysis to optimize the chance of achieving distant goals), social manipulation (social and psychological modeling, manipulation, rhetoric persuasion), and economic activity.[105] These skills are of course also essential for corporate management and, if replicated by machines, would allow for the creation of autonomous artificial directors and managers.

5.042   Similarly, Michio Kaku suggests that the creation of "true automatons, robots that have the ability to make their own decisions requiring only minimal human intervention" is the next step in the evolution of AI and robotic technology.[106] While he notes that the state of automatons today is "primitive,"[107] he predicts that by the end of the century there will be self-aware robots, and even sooner, machines with innovative learning capabilities.[108] A subsequent phase,

---

99   Kolbjørnsrud et al., *supra* note 47, at 4.

100   Florian Möslein, Robots in the Boardroom: Artificial Intelligence and Corporate Law, 649, in Woodrow Barfield & Ugo Pagallo: *Research Handbook on the Law of Artificial Intelligence*, Edward Elgar (2018).

101   For an overview of various high-profile thinkers' stance on the future of AI in general (beyond management and judgment work), see Spyros Makridakis, The forthcoming Artificial Intelligence (AI) revolution: Its impact on society and firms (2017) 90 *Futures* 46, at 50–53.

102   See Yuval Noah Harari, *Homo Deus: A Brief History of Tomorrow*, HarperCollins (2017) 83–86.

103   On the concepts of artificial general intelligence and more advanced forms, see Nick Bostrom, *Superintelligence: Paths, Dangers, Strategies*, Oxford University Press (2014) 22–29, 52–61.

104   Ibid. at 92. See also Max Tegmark, *Life 3.0: Being Human in the Age of Artificial Intelligence*, Knopf Publishing Group (2017) 87–89.

105   See Bostrom, *supra* note 103, at 94.

106   Michio Kaku, *The Future of Humanity: Our Destiny in the Universe*, Anchor Books (2018) 114.

107   Ibid. at 136.

108   Ibid.

Kaku speculates, will bring "self-replicating automatons [...] and quantum-fueled conscious machines."[109]

Finally, Richard and Daniel Susskind argue that "people, practices, and institutions" belonging **5.043** to what they refer to as "the professions" will be largely replaced in the future.[110] Although they do not comment specifically on managers, which are outside of their discrete definition of "a profession," they include "management consultants" as part of their analysis.[111] Nevertheless, their conclusion that AI, big data, robotics, and other technological developments will replace even highly qualified human professionals because machines will be able to carry out the full range of tasks of these roles[112] can be applied to the case of corporate managers as well.

Susskind and Susskind also describe the emerging field of affective computing, which allows **5.044** sensor-equipped machines to detect, react to, and express human emotions.[113] As they explain, machines are already capable of performing these tasks and work in the field is only advancing.[114] In this vein, Susskind and Susskind suggest that machines will be in a position to exhibit empathy, thus countering the views of those commentators that perceive the lack of such qualities as a major hurdle to the replacement of professionals by machines.[115] Susskind and Susskind posit that while cognitive tasks, affective tasks, and moral judgment will be more difficult to automize than other tasks, machines will master them in the long run, leaving little space for human professionals.[116] Within several decades, these authors conclude, the mastery of judgment work by machines will erode the number of jobs available to human professionals. The final result of this, they suggest, will be "technological unemployment" in the professions.[117]

C. ASSESSMENT

Will AI be able to take over the tasks of human corporate directors and managers? It seems **5.045** uncontroversial to answer this question in the positive with reference to administrative tasks. Nobody can predict with certainty, however, whether AI's involvement in the future will also extend to the crucial area of judgment work. If AI is able to dominate that domain as well, it could lead to a world where machines, not humans, dominate corporate management.

While acknowledging the uncertainties in making predictions, it is more difficult to believe **5.046** that humans will always maintain their superiority in completing judgment work than to imagine a future in which machines excel at these tasks as well. Eventually, AI—coupled with

---

109   Ibid.
110   Richard Susskind & Daniel Susskind, *The Future of the Professions: How Technology Will Transform the Work of Human Experts*, Oxford University Press (2015) 18.
111   See ibid. at 15–16, 78–84.
112   See ibid. at 159–72.
113   See ibid. at 170–72.
114   See ibid.
115   See ibid. at 251–52.
116   See ibid. at 279–81.
117   See ibid. at 290–92.

big data, increasingly powerful computing devices that will soon exceed human brain power,[118] and technologies such as voice, facial expression, and gesture recognition—will appear to have all the tools in place to become much better at managing and manipulating human responses than humans themselves.[119]

5.047 In contexts such as emerging self-driving car technology, we already see AI judgment at work. The autonomous vehicle's decision to brake or not, for example, combines data gathering and analysis, prediction, judgment, and action.[120] Of course, even this seemingly less complex judgment task can be difficult and may even involve philosophical and legal conundrums, such as what course of action the machine should take when every possible option involves the loss of lives or other harmful consequences to third parties.[121] Still, as algorithms can be fed any and all information that is available to humans, they should be able to exercise judgment that at least matches, and likely even exceeds, human judgment.

5.048 If AI masters judgment work, it will also be able to engage in the various non-administrative tasks currently performed by corporate directors and managers. Although it seems alien to us, the literature outlined above indicates that the hurdles in realizing AI capable of performing judgment work are not insurmountable. AI that effectively interacts with employees and external stakeholders, including investors, governments, suppliers, customers, and communities, will, if these hurdles are cleared, become reality. While we may intuitively assume that machines are worse at such judgment-related tasks than humans, there is support for the notion that machines will eventually exceed human capabilities in areas requiring "soft skills."

5.049 It is further incorrect to assume that it is necessarily more difficult to replace managerial roles than lower-paid jobs that are thought to require a more basic skillset. While that hypothesis may be true generally, it is not always the case. One author has provided an illustrative example to support this point. "From a robot's point of view," Byron Reese queried, "which of these jobs requires more skill: a waiter or a highly trained cardiologist who interprets CT scans?"[122] The answer is that the waiter's job is more challenging for robots. The waiter has to master "hundreds of skills, from spotting rancid meat to cleaning up baby vomit. But because we take all those things for granted, we don't think they are all that hard. To a robot, the radiologist job is by comparison a cakewalk. It is just data in, probabilities out."[123] Using a variation of Reese's example, we could ask: what is more difficult for a machine—assuming the role of a waiter, or a corporate manager? If we follow Reese's logic, managerial tasks, which also often involve data analysis, might well be easier to automate.

---

118 Researchers project that silicon-based computer chips in laptops will match the power of a human brain in the early 2020s and that by 2023 even smartphones will have more computing power than our brains. See Wadhwa & Salkever, *supra* note 52, at 15–16.

119 See Mikko Alasaarela, The Rise of Emotionally Intelligent AI, *Machine Learnings* (October 9, 2017), https://machinelearnings.co/the-rise-of-emotionally-intelligent-ai-fb9a814a630e.

120 See Agrawal et al., *supra* note 72, at 24.

121 See, e.g., Amy Maxmen, Self-driving Car Dilemmas Reveal that Moral Choices Are Not Universal, *Nature* (Oct. 24, 2018), https://www.nature.com/articles/d41586-018-07135-0.

122 Reese, *supra* note 79, at 107.

123 Ibid.

To be sure, the emergence of general AI and, as a next step, perhaps even superintelligent **5.050** AI is far from imminent and may not be achieved at all. However, neither type is the level of AI that is necessarily needed for effective corporate management by machines. Even if more advanced AI systems are a precondition for corporate management by machines, the emergence of such technologies may be much closer than we assume. According to Tegmark, leading AI experts are divided on the timeframe for an emergence of superhuman artificial general intelligence, with "most of them making estimates ranging from decades to centuries[,] and some even guessing [it will] never [emerge]."[124] Bostrom notes that "today, futurists who concern themselves with the possibility of artificial general intelligence still often believe that intelligent machines are a couple of decades away."[125] However, in a striking account, Bostrom and Müller relate the results of a 2013 survey conducted among 170 industry experts. In this survey, "[t]he median estimate of respondents was for a one in two chance that high-level machine intelligence will be developed around 2040–2050, rising to a nine in ten chance by 2075."[126] Further, the survey showed that "[e]xperts expect that systems will move on to superintelligence in less than 30 years thereafter."[127] If these experts are correct, highly advanced AI could be a reality in 20 to 30 years, and enormous changes would thereby soon be upon us.

D. CONSEQUENCES OF AI MANAGEMENT

The previous section argued that while there are many uncertainties, "management by machine" **5.051** is possible—that is, a future in which AI will be capable of and will be used for carrying out the tasks that today are entrusted to human directors and managers. This section proceeds on the assumption that AI management will indeed become a reality and, on this basis, explores the potential corporate governance consequences thereof, focusing on governance/leadership structures within corporations and directors' and officers' personal liability.

1.   Corporate Boards

(a) Boards today

A fundamental feature of today's board is its prevailing structure as a governance entity consist- **5.052** ing of (1) *individual* human actors (as opposed to legal entities) that (2) work as a *collective* body or team. Both elements are likely to change in a future dominated by AI.

The first fundamental feature of modern boards is a result of the fact that corporate laws **5.053** typically preclude non-human actors from sitting on boards. Only natural persons are allowed to serve as directors of a corporation in all US states and "most other major capitalist economies."[128] For their part, both the DGCL and the MBCA provide that every director needs to be

---

124   Tegmark, *supra* note 104, at 130.
125   Bostrom, *supra* note 103, at 4 (footnote omitted).
126   Vincent C. Müller & Nick Bostrom, Future Progress in Artificial Intelligence: A Survey of Expert Opinion, 1, in Vincent C. Müller: *Fundamental Issues of Artificial Intelligence*, Springer (2016).
127   Ibid. For a summary of similar surveys, see also Makridakis, *supra* note 101, at 52.
128   Bainbridge, *supra* note 21, at 67.

a "natural person,"[129] which precludes artificial persons from serving as board members.[130] This long-standing restriction is aimed specifically at preventing legal entities and business associations from acting as board members.[131] An exception to this general rule was traditionally found in UK company law, which allowed legal entities to use "corporate directors," the British term for legal person directors, alongside at least one human director.[132] However, this exception is set to disappear, with the UK set to join the US and other jurisdictions in barring non-natural persons from board service.[133]

5.054   In contrast to the requirement that boards consist of humans, the second element characterizing today's boards, that corporate powers are conferred upon a group, is a matter of choice and practice—not necessarily a legal requirement. Both Delaware law and the MBCA now provide that boards may consist of one or more members, thereby leaving open the possibility of one-person boards.[134] In contrast, corporate law in the United Kingdom requires public companies to have at least two directors.[135] Legal requirements notwithstanding, however, larger companies in both the US and the UK normally choose to have multi-member boards with various multi-member committees. The assumption that boards comprise several members is also reflected in stock exchange rules, such as the NYSE Listed Company Manual, which are specifically geared towards large boards.[136]

5.055   To be sure, using a one-person board, with just one decision-maker, would offer a number of advantages. Giving a single individual ultimate power over a company would offer enhanced decision-making efficiency compared to consensus-based processes; circumvent difficulties in monitoring the performance of individual directors and their contributions in multi-member boards; and eradicate potential problems stemming from group dynamics between individual team members.[137]

5.056   Yet the preference in practice for collective corporate boards is justified.[138] There are various reasons dictating the superiority of collective boards and why a team structure will, on balance, tend to result in more rational, higher-quality decisions. First, an important cause is the enhanced access to information by groups, which also translates into an improved ability to overcome impediments to optimal decision-making due to cognitive and other human limitations ("bounded rationality").[139] That is, when forced to make decisions under complex and

---

129   Del. Code Ann., tit. 8, § 141(a) (2018); Model Bus. Corp. Act § 8.03(a) (Am. Bar Ass'n amended 2016).

130   Bainbridge, *supra* note 21, at 67 n.3.

131   *See* Shawn J. Bayern, The Implications of Modern Business Entity Law for the Regulation of Autonomous Systems (2015) 19 *Stanford Technology Law Review* 93, at 98.

132   Section 155(1) of the UK Companies Act 2006 provides that "[a] company must have at least one director who is a natural person." Companies Act 2006, c. 46, § 155(1) (UK).

133   A new (but not yet effective) statute provides that, subject to certain exceptions, as a general rule directors must be natural persons. See Small Business Enterprise and Employment Act 2015, c. 26, § 87(4) (UK). At the time of writing, it was not yet clear when the new UK rules might enter into force.

134   See § 141(b); see also § 8.03.

135   See Companies Act 2006, c. 46 § 154.

136   As Bainbridge and Henderson note, US stock exchange rules and federal law implicitly assume that directors are natural persons. Bainbridge & Henderson, *supra* note 24, at 1100–01.

137   See Bainbridge, *supra* note 19, at 12–41.

138   See ibid.

139   See ibid. at 19–26.

uncertain conditions, groups especially benefit from the combined inputs of their members.[140] Further, the collective board model is useful for addressing agency costs within a board, as a team of directors can monitor each other and their internal decision-making.[141] Finally, having multiple board members and the option to delegate tasks to specific members or specialized board committees is suitable for dealing with the complex challenges and increasing workload faced by today's directors.[142]

While collective boards are overall more beneficial than relying on a sole actor/director, it is also true that decision-making processes by human collectives create certain negative dynamics. Putting a group in charge of a company, as opposed to a single individual, may lead to difficulties in monitoring and measuring individual team members' performance, can cause problems that flow from the complexities of interpersonal team dynamics, and creates a potential for free-riding on the efforts of others by certain group members.[143] Moreover, a particular concern related to decision-making in teams is the social–psychological problem of "groupthink," where a collective's preference for maintaining harmony and conformity within its group leads to irrational or dysfunctional decisions.[144]   **5.057**

In light of these challenges to the model of the collective board, countervailing board governance practices have been developed. Two particularly significant measures are the independent director model and a focus on board diversity. Indeed, the currently prevailing monitoring board model favors *independent* directors as a way to improve oversight and reduce agency costs.[145] Independent directors are expected to be better suited to act as impartial monitors as compared to insiders who may be conflicted or simply lack an objective view of the companies of which they are insiders.[146] US listed companies are now required to have a majority of independent directors on their boards and need to establish certain committees that are composed only of independent directors.[147] Similar rules apply in the UK, where the Corporate Governance Code provides that "[t]he board should include an appropriate combination of executive and non-executive (and, in particular, independent non-executive) directors, such that no one individual or small group of individuals dominates the board's decision-making"[148] and requires that "at least half the board, excluding the chair, should be non-executive directors that the board regards as independent."[149]   **5.058**

In addition to the independence of a board's directors, another factor to consider is the diversity of its members. The value of board diversity is thought to be supported by the idea   **5.059**

---

140   See ibid. at 21.
141   See ibid. at 32–41.
142   See ibid. at 12–41.
143   See ibid. at 28, 40.
144   Ibid. at 32.
145   Jeffrey N. Gordon, The Rise of Independent Directors in the United States, 1950-2005: Of Shareholder Value and Stock Market Prices (2007) 59 *Stanford Law Review* 1465.
146   See generally ibid. at 1471.
147   See NYSE Listed Company Manual, §§ 303A.01–303A.07 (2002).
148   Financial Reporting Council, The UK Corporate Governance Code 6 (July 2018), https://www.frc.org.uk/getattachment/88bd8c45-50ea-4841-95b0-d2f4f48069a2/2018-UK-Corporate-Governance-Code-FINAL.PDF.
149   Ibid. at 9 (quoting Principle 2, Provision 11). Further provisions of the UK Corporate Governance Code call for fully independent or majority independent board committees.

that different leadership experiences and variations in gender, ethnicity, race, nationality, and socio-economic background can provide effective means to tackle complacency and generate new ideas, and result in better risk management.[150] This suggests that the reason for advancing board diversity is primarily economic in nature, as better decision-making will lead to better financial outcomes for companies. Indeed, this "business case" has been the main argument advanced by policymakers in support of increased diversity, although diversity initiatives may also serve non-financial interests, including concerns surrounding societal equality.[151] While recent regulatory initiatives have tended to focus on one specific aspect of diversity, namely female board representation,[152] some policies have targeted diversity more broadly. For example, the UK Corporate Governance Code provides that board appointments and succession plans should promote gender diversity as well as diversity of social and ethnic backgrounds.[153]

(b) Boards tomorrow

5.060 The board's traditional structure will likely become superfluous in an age of AI-dominated corporate governance. With the advent of advanced AI capable of assuming board functions, we should first expect to see boards shrink in size. Second, we should expect to see what can be called "fused boards." The term "fused" indicates that the characteristics of multiple members will be merged in and offered by a single entity, the "AI director." Thus, the combined knowledge and skills, benefits of group decision making, and characteristics such as diversity and independence which previously could only be offered by a collective will be replicated in fused boards through an algorithm's coding features. This AI director software could still be selected and "appointed" by shareholders, with an option to switch to another software system at regular intervals.

5.061 Recall that boards consisting of groups are, overall, beneficial because group structures improve access to information, mitigate the effects of bounded rationality, and counter individual biases. Groups are also thought to be useful as members can monitor each other and reduce agency costs within the board itself. Finally, groups allow for the delegation of responsibilities and help alleviate excessive workloads on individual directors. These reasons for adherence to the collective model of boards will, however, likely cease with the advent of sufficiently advanced AI.

5.062 First, given the prevalence of online information, access to publicly available information will be comprehensive and virtually instant for AI systems. Indeed, information for today's boards is already often collected and made available using IT systems.[154] Thus, the next step towards creating direct feeds of this information to an artificial director seems natural. While such information feeds would cover publicly available information and non-public intra-company information, the question remains as to how an artificial director could gain access to non-public external information or knowledge that human directors may gather through their

---

150 See Moore & Petrin, *supra* note 20, at 189.

151 See Barnali Choudhury, New Rationales for Women on Boards (2014) 34 Oxford Journal of Legal Studies 511, at 512.

152 In the UK, following amendments influenced by EU requirements, boards of companies are generally required to compile a strategic report that contains information including the female representation on the board and other hierarchical levels within the company. The Companies Act 2006 (Strategic Report and Directors' Report) Regulations 2013, SI 2013/1970, § 414C (UK).

153 See Financial Reporting Council, *supra* note 148, at 8.

154 W. Bradley Zehner II, What Directors Need to Know (2010) 3 *Graziadio Business Review* at 1, 4, https://gbr.pepperdine.edu/2010/08/what-directors-need-to-know.

work on other boards or personal contacts. Although it may be difficult for non-humans to gain access to such information, it is not impossible. If AI software from leading providers could be used by a large number of boards, there would be scope allowing for arrangements that grant the software permission to cross-use certain data between different businesses. Similar to human directors with their own networks and sources of information, an AI director could then leverage the insights gained from "working" at multiple firms.

Indeed, a future in which AI director/AI management software will be offered by large **5.063** commercial providers could help harness and amplify the advantages described by Professors Bainbridge and Henderson of allowing specialized entities to act as directors.[155] In their model, companies would replace individual directors with a single Board Service Provider (BSP), an entity which would then carry out all corporate board functions.[156] These BSPs would arguably be well placed to avoid problems typically affecting individual directors, including time constraints, biases and cognitive limitations, group think, bounded rationality, lack of specialized knowledge, and motivational issues.[157] A similar reasoning can be applied to AI directors. AI software could work around the clock, efficiently process information made available to it, and recall and utilize this information almost instantly. Further, presuming that AI will operate without self-interest, there is also no need to have multiple directors monitor each other in order to mitigate the effects of conflicted human behavior.

At least theoretically, AI software could also be free from biases. Frey and Osborne have noted **5.064** that "[c]omputerisation of cognitive tasks is [...] aided by another core comparative advantage of algorithms: their absence of some human biases" and suggested "that many roles involving decision-making will benefit from impartial algorithmic solutions."[158] As they explain, occupations that require "subtle judgement" are increasingly susceptible to computerization as "the unbiased decision making of an algorithm represents a comparative advantage over human operators."[159] Given these qualities, Frey and Osborne suggest that in addition to simply providing algorithmic recommendations to human operators, eventually "algorithms will themselves be responsible for appropriate decision-making."[160]

Yet, AI is only as good as its inputs and programming. As long as software is programmed **5.065** by humans, it is vulnerable to our inherent biases.[161] Indeed, recent developments in areas ranging from computerized hiring processes to the selection of neighborhoods for same-day retail delivery and decisions on Medicaid payments have highlighted the problem of biased AI decisions.[162] Thus, biases and other limitations observed in humans will not automatically be eradicated through the use of AI in corporate management. Nevertheless, AI undeniably has

---

155   Bainbridge & Henderson, *supra* note 25, at 1056.
156   Ibid.
157   Ibid. at 1064–68.
158   Frey & Osborne, *supra* note, at 95.
159   Ibid. at 260.
160   Ibid.
161   See, e.g., Anjanette H. Raymond et al., Building A Better Hal 9000: Algorithms, The Market, and the Need to Prevent the Engraining of Bias (2018) 15 *Northwestern Journal of Technology & Intellectual Property* 215, at 223.
162   See, e.g., Madhumita Murgia, How to stop computers being biased, *Financial Times* (Feb. 13, 2019) https://www.ft.com/content/12dcd0f4-2ec8-11e9-8744-e7016697f225.

the potential to reduce biases. As noted above, AI offers a promising potential in that it could be designed to be completely unbiased and lead to increased objectivity in decision-making.[163]

2.   Corporate Management

5.066   In addition to fused boards, AI will likely also lead to the "fused management" of companies. This second type of fusion refers to the amalgamation of boards and managers, resulting in the abolishment of the two-tiered structure of governance of the modern corporation. In its place, an all-encompassing "corporate management" body could emerge. This body would assume all of the functions of today's directors and managers below the board level, but would operate without the separation between them.

5.067   The reasons supporting the likely emergence of fused management are principally that properly programmed corporate management AI software will entail no or drastically reduced agency costs,[164] thus making one of the board's main functions—to monitor or supervise managers—far less important or completely obsolete. In addition, AI will not be subject to time restrictions, enabling it to carry out both boards' traditional functions *and* the day-to-day managerial tasks that boards now delegate to managers. AI software will also not need to liaise with or appoint and terminate itself (as boards currently do with members of the management team) if it, as a single unit, is in charge of management.

5.068   With fused corporate management, functions including today's appointment of directors, hiring and firing of management, and voice on executive remuneration would be broadly mirrored in the shareholders' powers to choose a suitable AI management software package for their company. In doing so, shareholders would have to take into account the software's features, its managerial characteristics, and the overall pricing associated with the package. In this respect, different types of and different options for AI management software could emerge, perhaps delineated in terms of their risk aversion and the corporate purpose(s) that the software is designed to pursue.

3.   Directors' and Officers' Liability

(a) Liability today

5.069   Individual duties are the basis for today's personal liability regime for those in charge of corporate leadership. Directors owe their company and, secondarily, their shareholders the fiduciary duties of care and loyalty in discharging their functions.[165] In essence, this means that

---

163   See Assaf Hamdani et al., Technological Progress and the Future of the Corporation (2018) 6 *Journal of the British Academy* 215, at 229; see also John Armour & Horst Eidenmüller, Self-Driving Corporations? (2020) 10 *Harvard Business Law Review* 87; but see Luca Enriques & Dirk A. Zetsche, Corporate Technologies and the Tech Nirvana Fallacy (Hastings Law Journal, forthcoming), https://ssrn.com/abstract=3392321 (arguing that it is unlikely that new technologies will replace existing corporate governance mechanisms).

164   See John Armour et al., Putting Technology to Good Use for Society: The Role of Corporate, Competition and Tax Law (2018) 6(1) *Journal of the British Academy* 285, at 298.

165   See Mills Acquisition Co. v. Macmillan, Inc., 559 A.2d 1261, 1280 (Del. 1989). On the content of these duties, see, e.g., R. Franklin Balotti & Jesse A. Finkelstein, Delaware Law of Corporations & Business Organizations, Wolters Kluwer (3d ed. 2019) §§ 4.14–4.16.

directors are required to act in a competent manner and be loyal to their company. Corporate fiduciary duties often tend to be discussed with specific reference to directors, as opposed to officers. Nevertheless, in the US, the duties of corporate officers are said to be identical with,[166] or at least very similar to, those of directors, albeit they are generally considered to be more particularized. Officers are also subject to certain additional duties stemming from the general law of agency.[167] In addition to the system of corporate fiduciary duties, officers can also be held personally liable for their misconduct through the channel of securities fraud litigation.[168] This section, however, will focus solely on fiduciary duty liability.

The *duty of care* applies to two broad categories—the process of decision making and in boards'   **5.070**
exercise of their duties. In the words of Balotti and Finkelstein, "[f]irst, directors must exercise the requisite degree of care in the process of decision-making and act on an informed basis. Second, directors must also exercise due care in the other aspects of their responsibilities, including their delegation functions."[169] The traditional approach to describing the standard of care expected from directors is by way of reference to behavior displayed by other individuals in their position. For example, the Delaware Chancery Court has stated that "directors of a corporation in managing the corporate affairs are bound to use that amount of care which ordinarily careful and prudent men would use in similar circumstances."[170] In Delaware, however, only conduct that amounts to "gross negligence" will give rise to a violation of the duty of care.[171]

It is also helpful to examine the standard of care applicable to directors in conjunction with   **5.071**
the business judgment rule. Although the business judgment rule is more convincingly viewed as a standard of judicial review rather than a standard of care,[172] it is, in practice, inextricably linked to what courts perceive as proper directorial conduct. That is, in making a business decision, directors need to act "on an informed basis, in good faith, and in the honest belief that the action taken was in the best interests of the company."[173] Boards also need to allow sufficient time to prepare and engage critically with the information made available to them.[174] Nevertheless, as a Delaware law treatise notes, in formulating the standard of care expected from directors "[t]here are no hornbook bright lines or litmus tests to make counseling easy. Each case will depend on the procedural setting and all the facts."[175]

The *duty of loyalty* addresses and seeks to mitigate the problem of diverging interests between   **5.072**
shareholders and those who manage the company.[176] It requires corporate leaders to adhere to

---

166   See Gantler v. Stephens, 965 A.2d 695, 708–09 (Del. 2009) (en banc); Amalgamated Bank v. Yahoo! Inc., 132 A.3d 752, 780 (Del. Ch. 2016).

167   See Deborah A. DeMott, Corporate Officers as Agents (2017) 74 *Washington & Lee Law Review* 847, at 848.

168   See, e.g., Robert B. Thompson & Hillary A. Sale, Securities Fraud as Corporate Governance: Reflections upon Federalism (2003) 56 *Vanderbilt Law Review* 859, at 860–61.

169   Balotti & Finkelstein, *supra* note 165, at § 4.15 (footnote omitted).

170   Graham v. Allis-Chambers Mfg. Co., 188 A.2d 125, 130 (Del. Ch. 1963).

171   See Stone v. Ritter, 911 A.2d 362, 369 (Del. 2006); see also McMullin v. Beran, 765 A.2d 910, 921 (Del. 2000).

172   See Stephen M. Bainbridge, The Business Judgment Rule as Abstention Doctrine (2004) 57 *Vanderbilt Law Review* 83, at 87, 109–29; see also Moran v. Household Int'l, Inc., 490 A.2d 1059, 1076 (Del. Ch. 1985), aff'd, 500 A.2d 1346 (Del. 1985).

173   Aronson v. Lewis, 473 A.2d 805, 812 (Del. 1984).

174   The seminal case on this is Smith v. Van Gorkom, 488 A.2d 858, 872 (Del. 1985).

175   Balotti & Finkelstein, *supra* note 165, at § 4.15(A) (footnote omitted).

176   See Guth v. Loft, Inc., 5 A.2d 503, 510 (Del. 1939).

a standard of behavior that Judge Cardozo once artfully described as the "punctilio of an honor the most sensitive."[177] Loyalty, in practice, is relevant to a variety of specific contexts, including interested-director transactions, corporate opportunities, insider transactions, and other situations that involve a potential conflict of interest or heightened risk of unduly advancing managers' personal interests at the expense of the corporation.[178] Notably, the board's liability for failure to exercise proper oversight is, under Delaware law, also subsumed under the duty of loyalty and its good faith requirement.[179]

5.073 The system for sanctioning alleged breaches of corporate directors' and officers' fiduciary duties is somewhat peculiar. In most cases, shareholders cannot bring direct claims against these individuals in their own name. Breaches of fiduciary duties will normally be pursued either by the corporation or—given the board's likely reluctance to initiate such claims—via derivative actions that shareholders bring in the name and on behalf of the corporation.[180] However, shareholders willing to pursue derivative suits face both procedural and substantive hurdles, which to a large degree work to insulate corporate directors and officers from personal liability.[181]

5.074 Directors, in particular, benefit from various protections that considerably limit their personal exposure. With regard to assessing the existence of a breach of duty, corporate laws usually provide that directors may rely on information or advice received from others, and that such reliance is, within certain limitations, permissible and will not expose the director to personal liability.[182] More broadly, board decisions can be protected by the business judgment rule, which provides that courts will not second-guess directors' actions as long as their decision-making process meets certain criteria.[183] Delaware law even permits shareholders to adopt exculpatory provisions in their company's certificate of incorporation to limit or eliminate directors' personal liability for duty of care violations.[184] These limitations, coupled with corporate indemnification arrangements and D&O liability insurance, have become so pronounced that the prospect of liability, especially that involving out-of-pocket payments by directors, has become unlikely.[185] Officers are exposed to higher potential liability than directors, given that they are more deeply

---

177 Meinhard v. Salmon, 164 N.E. 545, 546 (N.Y. 1928).

178 See Balotti & Finkelstein, *supra* note 165, at § 4.16.

179 See Stone v. Ritter, 911 A.2d 362, 370–72 (Del. 2006); Martin Petrin, Assessing Delaware's Oversight Jurisprudence: A Policy and Theory Perspective (2011) 5 *Virginia Law & Business Review* 433.

180 See, e.g., Rabkin v. Philip A. Hunt Chem. Corp., 547 A.2d 963, 969 (Del. Ch. 1986). Managers can also be held accountable by non-shareholder third parties based on tort law principles. See Martin Petrin, The Curious Case of Directors' and Officers' Liability for Supervision and Management: Exploring the Intersection of Corporate and Tort Law (2010) 59 *American University Law Review* 1661, at 1714.

181 See Petrin, *supra* note 180, at 1693–94.

182 Under the DGCL, directors may under specified conditions rely upon corporate records and information, opinions, reports, or statements presented to the corporation by officers, employees, board committees, or other persons. Del. Code Ann. tit. 8, § 141(e) (2019).

183 See, e.g., Brehm v. Eisner, 746 A.2d 244, 264 n.66 (Del. 2000).

184 Del. Code Ann. tit. 8, § 102(b)(7).

185 See, e.g., Lisa L. Casey, Twenty-Eight Words: Enforcing Corporate Fiduciary Duties through Criminal Prosecution of Honest Services Fraud (2010) 35 *Delaware Journal of Corporate Law* 1, at 17; Bernard Black et al., Outside Director Liability (2006) 58 *Stanford Law Review* 1055, at 1140.

involved in daily management.[186] Nevertheless, fiduciary duty lawsuits against officers have been rare and their chances of being held personally liable are low.[187]

(b) Liability tomorrow

The current system of managerial liability is first and foremost geared toward limiting personal **5.075** transgressions. As a counterweight to managerial power, shareholder fiduciary duty litigation is meant to serve the goals of *ex ante* deterrence and, to a lesser degree, *ex post* compensation.[188] Thus, from a corporate governance perspective, derivative actions can be described as the counterweight to managerial power and a mitigation device against agency costs.[189]

The current system's characteristics raise questions about its suitability for a future shift from **5.076** human to AI corporate management. Today's framework is fundamentally based on the notion of personal accountability in holding corporate leaders that breach their fiduciary duties individually liable. Naturally, in the absence of human managers, this type of personal liability is bound to disappear.

In the early stages of the gradual pathway towards AI-dominated management we should **5.077** expect AI to only take on certain roles—acting mostly as a supportive mechanism for human directors—which may itself lead to a reduction in the number of human managers. As a consequence, during this early phase personal liability lawsuits would be increasingly concentrated on fewer individuals, namely those humans that still remain in managerial positions, which in turn heightens their potential exposure.

This stage raises difficult questions regarding the extent to which human managers may del- **5.078** egate tasks to and rely on advice given by AI (in the sense of there being relief from liability) and, relatedly, the extent to which they can and should monitor AI. Whether reliance and delegation of tasks to AI is permissible depends on the wording and interpretation of applicable statutory provisions and corporate documents.[190] Typically, corporate law requires directors to monitor delegees and does not allow boards to delegate away the core duty to manage and supervise the company.[191] Thus, under the current framework, a complete delegation of tasks to AI would not be allowed. Partial delegation would be possible, but would require the board to oversee the managerial activities of AI. Accordingly, a commentator has noted that directors would be required to "at least generally oversee the selection and activities of robots, algorithms and artificial intelligence devices" and "have a basic understanding of how these devices operate."[192] While directors may "not understand their coding in every detail, they should at least be able to understand the technical guidelines that drive these machines."[193]

---

186   Exculpatory charter provisions, at least under Delaware law, do not apply to officers and the question whether officers are protected by the business judgment rule remains unsettled.

187   See Lyman P.Q. Johnson & David Millon, Recalling Why Corporate Officers are Fiduciaries (2004) 46 *William & Mary Law Review* 1597, at 1609.

188   See, e.g., John C. Coffee, Jr. & Donald E. Schwartz, The Survival of the Derivative Suit: An Evaluation and a Proposal for Legislative Reform (1981) 81 *Columbia Law Review* 261, at 302–05.

189   See, e.g., Kershaw, *supra* note 24, at 314.

190   See Möslein, *supra* note 100, at 656–60; *see also* Petrin, *supra* note 185, at 1693–94.

191   See Möslein, *supra* note 100, at 659.

192   Ibid. at 660.

193   Ibid.

5.079   Following a phase of co-existence of human and AI managers, a subsequent phase will likely see machines fully take over corporate management. At this point, humans could no longer be sued for breaching their fiduciary duties. This could lead to three possible new approaches to *managerial* liability: (1) artificial entities acting as managers could become potential defendants and be sued; (2) the system of managerial liability will be abolished and not replaced; or (3) those responsible for creating, distributing, or selling artificial managers (in the form of AI software and hardware) will replace managers as possible defendants.[194]

5.080   Under the first possibility, AI systems could be made available as defendants in shareholder and/or third-party lawsuits. This approach could consist of actions against AI operating either in the form of familiar types of organizational legal entities, or AI might in the future itself be bestowed with a novel legal personality.[195] In both cases, from the perspective of plaintiffs, the main difference as compared to today's system is that their claims would be directed against a non-human, although still a legally recognized entity. In terms of the potential for plaintiffs' financial recovery, the difference would depend on two factors. The first is whether these new entities would enjoy similar legal protections as human managers, in the familiar forms of liability insulating corporate law norms or other, new legal protections. While today's exculpatory provisions could be adapted to machines or AI, the business judgment rule would have to be reformulated. Second, recovery by plaintiffs would also be influenced and potentially limited by these entities' financial resources (or, rather, likely lack thereof). Thus, how to define and monitor applicable standards of behavior will be a difficult question in the context of liability for AI entities.

5.081   The second option would be completely abolishing personal liability for corporate managers. This loss of the possibility of holding managers liable could have a number of consequences. First, there is the question as to whether the absence of potential personal liability and the corresponding lack of deterrence would make managers less careful. However, deterrence would arguably be difficult, if not impossible, to achieve for AI entities. It would likely also be unnecessary for a properly programmed artificial entity, which can be instructed to always adhere to the required legal norms. Second, plaintiffs would lose a class of potential defendants, and hence a potential pool of assets. Yet, given the already low success rate of lawsuits against managers, such a loss of personal liability would be limited in its impact, at least in the case of public companies. Furthermore, companies which use AI management systems would still have the option to bring direct actions against third-party AI software providers based on contractual claims. Contrary to today's problem that boards may be reluctant to bring actions against fellow directors or managers,[196] boards would face no such concern when it comes to third parties that provided an allegedly faulty product or service. This may lead to more lawsuits

---

194   Note that the following discussion does not relate to the corporation's own liability. On this, see for example Armour & Eidenmüller, *supra* note 163, at 31–33.

195   On the idea of creating a legal status for artificial persons, see generally Matthew U. Scherer, Of Wild Beasts and Digital Analogues: The Legal Status of Autonomous Systems (2018) 19 *Nevada Law Journal* 259, at 260; Gunther Teubner, Digital Personhood? The Status of Autonomous Software Agents in Private Law, 2018 *Ancilla Juris* 42–43 (Jacon Watson trans.), https://www.anci.ch/articles/Ancilla2018_Teubner_35.pdf; Robert van den Hoven van Genderen, Legal Personhood in the Age of Artificially Intelligent Robots, 213, in Barfield & Pagallo, *supra* note 103; Lawrence B. Solum, Legal Personhood for Artificial Intelligences (1992) 70 *North Carolina Law Review* 1231, at 1234.

196   See, e.g., Claire A. Hill & Brett H. McDonnell, Disney, Good Faith, and Structural Bias (2007) 32 *Journal of Corporation Law* 833, at 839.

and financial recovery. The biggest change in liability exposure, however, would likely be felt in non-shareholder third party claims against the corporation, particularly those based on torts or criminal and regulatory offenses. In these cases, all liability would necessarily have to be channeled to the corporate entity itself as its managers would be unavailable as (exclusive, or, together with the entity, joint) defendants.[197]

The third option for a future corporate liability framework is that the creators, distributors, **5.082** sellers, or other providers of managerial AI software (the "AI providers") would become the primary potential defendants in cases of claims previously directed towards managers.[198] In addition to exposure to claims brought by corporations using their AI software, novel rules could allow shareholders and potentially third parties to sue AI providers directly or derivatively. Such a system may even impose a new fiduciary status for software developers.[199] These claims would not focus on whether an individual was in breach of his or her duties, as they currently do, but rather whether the relevant software was properly designed and programmed. This suggests that, under this model, liability for corporate management will evolve akin to today's system of products liability, especially as it currently applies to software programs. Thus, liability could be based on theories of implied warranty, negligence, "programming malpractice," or even strict liability.[200] Again, as for direct claims against AI-management entities, this third option necessitates clarity on the appropriate standards for AI management.

E. CONCLUSION

A future in which AI takes over corporate management is possible. Recent developments and **5.083** news stories show that there is an effort underway to develop, and an interest to pursue further, machine-led corporate leadership. Because AI management will presumably at some point be both better and more cost-effective than the use of human managers, "management by machine" seems inevitable. Well-known commentators have warned of the dangers of AI, with the late Stephen Hawking predicting that full AI could lead to the end of mankind.[201] In comparison, this chapter's premise that AI will replace corporate management is far more modest.

Based on the assumption that AI management will eventually indeed materialize, the chapter **5.084** has hypothesized about its consequences for corporate governance. With software and machines in charge, the need for a collective board will vanish, and it will be replaced with a single "fused" corporate management function. The shift from human to AI-based management will equally

---

197 The same is true for (rare) instances of direct claims by shareholders against directors.

198 This would be in addition to claims that corporations that use their AI management systems users might bring against them, based on contractual or extra-contractual grounds and in cases where due to faults in the system the corporation suffered direct or indirect harm. On potential problems with this approach, see Armour & Eidenmüller, *supra* note 163, at 34 n. 88.

199 See Angela Walch, In Code(rs) We Trust: Software Developers as Fiduciaries in Public Blockchains, 58–59, in Philipp Hacker et al.: *Regulating Blockchain: Techno-Social and Legal Challenges*, Oxford University Press (2019).

200 For a comprehensive overview of U.S. theories of liability in traditional products liability law, see Charles J. Nagy, American Law of Products Liability, Thomson Reuter (2019) §§ 1:9–1:20.

201 Joao Medeiros, Stephen Hawking: 'I fear AI May Replace Humans Altogether', *Wired* (Nov. 28, 2017), https://www.wired.co.uk/article/stephen-hawking-interview-alien-life-climate-change-donald-trump.

necessitate changes to the system of managerial liability. In this area, we could see a system akin to products liability replace the framework of fiduciary and other personal duties.

5.085 While this chapter has not taken a normative stance but focused on describing current and possible future developments of corporate governance structures in response to the rise of AI, it seems clear that there will be a need for legal reform to accommodate changes brought about by new technologies. These reforms should be both enabling—facilitating the efficiencies and other beneficial effects of AI management—but also restrictive, protecting society from potential negative impacts, loss of employment, and other harmful actions by rogue AI entities. From a broader corporate governance perspective, it seems clear that the future of corporate management will be heavily intertwined with the consideration of business analytics, big data, and programming.

5.086 The prospect of AI management also suggests the likelihood of change in the study of agency costs as an important theoretical underpinning of corporate governance theory. Agency costs between shareholders and management, this chapter suggests, could be solved with AI management. However, the development of *ex ante* standards for designing, controlling, and holding accountable algorithms instead will likely take center stage. This can be thought of as a novel type of agency cost, now between humans and machines, which may come to the fore.[202] On all counts, AI management seems set to initiate a new chapter for corporate law and governance.

---

202 See Bostrom, *supra* note 103, at 127–29. See also Armour & Eidenmüller, *supra* note 163, at 7.

6

REGULATORY COMPLIANCE

Hannah Yee-Fen Lim

A. INTRODUCTION

Regulatory compliance of AI can take on two dimensions: first, it can refer to regulations that **6.001** need to be complied with by AI systems; second, it can also refer to AI that is used in attempts to comply with regulations. In a modest work such as this chapter, the aim is to provide a helicopter view, as the work in this area internationally is developing rapidly.

In order to understand AI regulation and compliance, and why and in what forms AI should **6.002** be regulated, the nuances of this unique technology must be clearly set out so that the issues are clearly understood. This chapter will begin with an examination of the very nature of AI, what it is and why regulation is needed and what it might look like. This is followed by an exposition of the regulatory measures to date, rounding off with an exposition of AI that has been used for compliance with regulations.

B. TECHNOLOGICAL CONSIDERATIONS

1. Traditional Software

6.003 Traditional software is hard-coded and can, technically speaking, be traced so as to follow each step that the programming code takes. With access to all of the programming code, a software programmer can, with effort and time, go through the entire program, line by line, to determine the algorithms and processes and to, for example, determine if formulae and calculations are correct. In hard-coded software it is possible to verify whether the software has been properly programmed to perform what it was intended to perform, although this is an extremely time-consuming and tedious task. Further, there may be difficulties in obtaining access to all of the programming code, as claims of copyright protection of the programming source code and trade secret protection will inevitably be made if there are requests to examine the programming code – especially since computer software is protected under copyright law in many countries, forms part of an organisation's intellectual property and is proprietary material.

2. AI Algorithms

6.004 I have expounded in depth on the AI technology on autonomous vehicles in a previous work.[1] For the purposes of understanding the legal issues at play in the regulatory compliance of AI, this section will elucidate the salient aspects of AI that pose challenges.

6.005 Loosely speaking, machine learning is where computers have the ability to execute functions without being explicitly programmed to do so.[2] The algorithm does not actually learn in the way that human beings learn but the whole process is based on statistics and mathematical modelling.[3] For the machine to be 'trained' or to 'learn', the algorithm is fed huge amounts of data; these training data sets can affect whether the AI algorithm functions as it should[4] and are compliant with regulations and standards.

6.006 At present, there are three main types of machine learning: supervised machine learning, unsupervised machine learning and reinforcement machine learning.[5] Each of these have their own limitations and potential pitfalls. Further, neural networks and deep learning have been the subject of much hype in recent years; they are, however, generally black boxes where developers have deliberately obscured the basis upon which the algorithms function, partly because they themselves do not know or understand how the sub-algorithms function and have simply used algorithms 'off-the-shelf';[6] as such, these would be very difficult to establish compliance,

---

1   Hannah YeeFen Lim, *Autonomous Vehicles and the Law: Technology, Algorithms, and Ethics* (Edward Elgar Publishing, UK 2018).

2   Ibid, p. 85.

3   Ibid, pp. 84–5.

4   Ibid, pp. 84–7.

5   Ibid, ch 4.

6   Cynthia Rudin and Joanna Radin, 'Why Are We Using Black Box Models in AI When We Don't Need to? A Lesson from an Explainable AI Competition', *Harvard Data Science Review*, Issue 1.2, Fall 2019 available at https://hdsr.mitpress.mit.edu/pub/f9kuryi8/release/6 (accessed 31 January 2021).

and this is not just an evidentiary issue.[7] It needs to be clarified that no algorithm needs to be a black box.[8]

The main difficulty with machine learning algorithms is not the algorithms and mathematical modelling themselves but the large training datasets that need to be used to train the algorithm.[9] It is technically impossible to ascertain the quality of the datasets and the size of the datasets.[10] **6.007**

3.   AI and Data

This section will examine the attendant problems with the datasets used for AI algorithms and how they can affect the reliability and accuracy of AI systems. **6.008**

(a) Size of the datasets

For starters, the size of the datasets fed to the algorithms to train them needs to be substantially large. If a machine learning algorithm has only had a few examples of a phenomenon fed to it from which to detect relevant patterns, it will perform poorly. In many cases, the machine learning algorithm will require many hundreds of thousands of examples of the relevant phenomenon in order to produce a useful and robust set of predictive models. To be clear, a dataset of 1,000 examples would very likely be insufficient for an algorithm to be trained properly and to yield sound results in most cases. **6.009**

There is no set number of samples in a dataset beyond the threshold at which one can definitively declare that the machine algorithm has been properly trained. Furthermore, the size of the required training dataset will differ depending on the task. Some tasks will have fewer variations than others and can master the task with a smaller training dataset. **6.010**

Beyond that, unlike hard-coded software, it will be extremely difficult to ascertain whether a sufficiently large training dataset has been fed to an algorithm. **6.011**

From the foregoing, it is evident that there will be difficulties for any party, such as a plaintiff or a regulator, in determining what is a good and appropriate dataset size in order to effectively train the machine learning algorithm to a level that will ensure safe or reliable functioning. Further, there may be difficulties in ascertaining that a systems developer has indeed used the size of datasets that it claims to have. **6.012**

(b) Quality of the datasets

There are many issues of quality related to datasets. For our purposes here, only three will be considered, because they will be sufficient to illustrate the challenges. **6.013**

First, if the datasets used for training are all very similar, with little variation in conditions that reflect those that could reasonably be encountered in real life, then even thousands of **6.014**

---

7   Hannah YeeFen Lim, *Autonomous Vehicles and the Law: Technology, Algorithms, and Ethics* (Edward Elgar Publishing, UK 2018), chs 4–5.
8   Ibid, pp. 89–90.
9   Ibid, chs 4–5.
10   Ibid, chs 4–5.

such datasets will not help the machine learning algorithm learn effectively. The datasets must contain sufficient samples of the different variables in order for the machine learning algorithm to learn.

6.015 To illustrate, for autonomous vehicles, a dataset used for training autonomous vehicle algorithms may contain one hour of driving data, but within that one hour of driving, 95 per cent of the time the vehicle may have been on a straight highway with little variation in the driving environment and in clear conditions. There may have only been one traffic light encountered and no pedestrians or cyclists visible during the entire drive. If all of the training datasets were like this, then millions of such datasets would not be helpful to the machine learning algorithm.

6.016 Second, the datasets need to be 'correct', or at least to represent acceptable behaviour. For example, for supervised machine learning, the data samples need to be correctly labelled. If large proportions of the training dataset for supervised machine learning are incorrectly labelled before they are fed to the algorithm, this will result in the algorithm either not learning or learning the wrong rules and constructing incorrect models. As a concrete example, if the datasets contain predominantly vehicles speeding through red traffic lights labelled as correct, this will result in the algorithm learning that speeding through red traffic lights is a pattern to adopt. This can also occur in unsupervised machine learning. If the dataset is skewed such that there are more samples of vehicles speeding through red traffic lights, the algorithm will detect this pattern and will adopt it as one of its rules.

6.017 Third, for datasets involving images, the datasets need to have semantic segmentation properly applied to the training set before any machine learning can occur. Semantic segmentation enables the computer program to recognize and understand what is in the image at the pixel level. For a human being, it is second nature to detect if something is a person, a bicycle, a dog and so on. For the computer to perceive whether something is a human, the algorithm needs to be shown many images of what a human looks like. The algorithm can be told that a human has two legs but a long skirt worn by a woman may make her two legs look like one to the algorithm. In order to assist the algorithm, the datasets that are fed to the algorithm will need to be highlighted in different colours so that the algorithm can identity all of the humans, cats, dogs, road signs, traffic lights, buildings, bicycles, and so on in the image.[11] This is called semantic segmentation. This is a painstaking task and if there are any mistakes, such as human beings wrongly labelled as tree trunks, this will adversely affect what the algorithm learns.

6.018 From the foregoing it should be apparent that, given the volume of data required and the necessity for all the datasets to be of a certain quality, these are fairly high thresholds that any AI systems developer will need to be able to establish that they have met. Even harder still, if not impossible, will be for a plaintiff or the regulator to discover whether all of the data training datasets were indeed high-quality data training sets.

---

11   Jack Stewart, 'Mighty AI and the Human Army Using Phones to Teach AI to Drive', Wired (9 July 2017) www.wired .com/story/mighty-ai-training-self-driving-cars/ accessed 23 May 2018.

C. LEGAL RESPONSES

1. Challenges for Regulators

The foregoing has analysed how AI software functions, including the utilisation of machine **6.019** learning algorithms. A machine learning algorithm, even if it is mathematically sound, is to a large extent heavily dependent on the data it has been trained on, which in turn raises issues concerning the quantity and quality of the datasets, the duration of the training and the parameters and input variables the computer programmers have designed. All of this may prove very difficult, if not impossible, for a plaintiff or a regulator to establish, or to ascertain or to verify. This has serious ramifications for questions of compliance and regulation.

Systems utilising AI are not like a desktop computer operating system – the general public **6.020** has grown accustomed to such systems containing bugs and security flaws. AI systems such as autonomous vehicles can be deadly, not just for those inside the vehicle but also for the general public. Other types of AI systems may also cause harm to individuals, whether financial harm or other types such as physical harm.

The foregoing sections have elucidated that machine learning is in effect statistical learning **6.021** based on probability theorems. Being statistical learning, there is very little substantive reasoning, like human reasoning, behind the machine learning. Indeed, as one commentator has noted, machine learning is 'intelligent results without intelligence'.[12] This fact should always be born in mind in any regulation of AI.

The larger question remains of the role of the regulator in encouraging AI innovation but at the **6.022** same time protecting citizens from injury, harm and death. The question of how best this can be achieved so that lives are not unnecessarily lost is one that many regulators are still grappling with.

The following sections will elucidate the current progress around the world, beginning with the **6.023** setting of ethics frameworks and moving to substantive regulations.

2. Governmental and Inter-governmental Responses – Ethics Codes and Principles

At present, the regulation of artificial intelligence (AI) in many jurisdictions is mostly in its **6.024** preliminary stages. Many jurisdictions have been busy developing ethics principles, guidelines or codes for the use and development of AI technology but few have passed substantive laws.[13] A few areas that have seen legislative activity are the regulation of autonomous vehicles and FinTech, but there are finally more general movements beyond Ethics frameworks. The discussion below is a selection of representative initiatives in ethics frameworks.

---

12 Harry Surden, 'Machine Learning and Law' (2014) 89 Washington Law Review 87, 95.
13 Library of Congress, Regulation of Artificial Intelligence in Selected Jurisdictions (January 2019) www.loc.gov/law/help/ artificial-intelligence/regulation-artificial-intelligence.pdf accessed 1 September 2020.

(a) Ethics frameworks: Australia

6.025 Over the past ten years, many jurisdictions have developed ethics frameworks in the form of ethical principles that ought to be followed when developing or utilising AI applications. For example, in April 2019 Australia's Minister for Industry, Science and Technology issued a consultation and discussion paper prepared by CSIRO's Data61, *Artificial Intelligence: Australia's Ethics Framework*,[14] in preparation for a voluntary AI Ethics Framework. This document had set out eight core principles for AI, namely: generate net benefits; do no harm; regulatory and legal compliance; privacy protection; fairness; transparency and explainability; contestability; and accountability. In November 2019, a set of revised and finalised AI Ethics Principles was released[15] that saw the principle 'generate net benefits' extended to a more general principle of human, social and environmental well-being; the principle 'do no harm' broadened to human-centred values; and the principle 'privacy protection' extended to include security. The principle of regulatory and legal compliance was removed and in its place a new principle of reliability and safety was introduced.

6.026 These are all fairly standard and non-contentious principles as far as any kind of new technology is concerned, and in fact they are principles that form the foundations of many legal systems, and even of personal data protection regimes in many jurisdictions. The Australian AI Ethics Principles are voluntary and the Australian government made it clear that the principles are 'aspirational and intended to complement – not substitute – existing AI related regulations'.[16]

6.027 In addition to the AI Ethics Principles, the Australian Human Rights Commission is also conducting a project on Human Rights and Technology and has released a discussion paper that sets out the Commission's preliminary views, proposals and questions on the topic of human rights and technology.[17] At the time of writing, this work appears to be still at a preliminary stage.

(b) Ethics principles: United States

6.028 In early January 2020, the White House Office of Science and Technology Policy released ten principles that should be adhered to when proposing new AI regulations for the private sector. The principles have three main goals: to ensure public engagement; to limit regulatory overreach; and to promote trustworthy AI that is fair, transparent and safe. The principles are: public trust in AI; public participation; scientific integrity and information quality; risk assessment and management; benefits and costs; flexibility; fairness and non-discrimination; disclosure and transparency; safety and security; and interagency coordination.

---

14   D Dawson , E Schleiger, J Horton, J McLaughlin, C Robinson, G Quezada, J Scowcroft and S Hajkowicz (2019) Artificial Intelligence: Australia's Ethics Framework (Data61 CSIRO, Australia).

15   Department of Industry, Science, Energy and Resources Australian Government, 'Artificial Intelligence: Australia's Ethics Framework https://consult.industry.gov.au/strategic-policy/artificial-intelligence-ethics-framework/ accessed 7 September 2020.

16   Department of Industry, Science, Energy and Resources Australian Government, 'AI Ethics Principles' www.industry .gov.au/data-and-publications/building-australias-artificial-intelligence-capability/ai-ethics-framework/ai-ethics -principles accessed 7 September 2020.

17   Australian Human Rights Commission, Human Rights and Technology https://tech.humanrights.gov.au/consultation accessed 7 September 2020.

It appears that the principles are an effort to create a national AI strategy to forge leadership in the development of AI. The general tone of policies and regulations in the United States is a fragmented and reactionary one with gap-filling in areas as and when needed, such as in personal data protection laws. **6.029**

(c) Ethics frameworks: European Union

Elsewhere in the world, regulators have also issued similar ethics guidelines. In Europe, the European Commission's High-Level Expert Group on Artificial Intelligence (AI HLEG) published its final Ethics Guidelines for Trustworthy AI in April 2019.[18] The main concern of the AI HLEG was to develop a framework to achieve and operationalise Trustworthy AI. **6.030**

According to the AI HLEG Guidelines, Trustworthy AI has three components:[19] (1) it should be lawful, complying with all applicable laws and regulations; (2) it should be ethical, ensuring adherence to ethical principles and values; and (3) it should be robust, both from a technical and a social perspective, given that AI systems can cause unintentional harm. **6.031**

The AI HLEG Guidelines are clear that these components should be met throughout the system's entire life cycle; however, each of these three components is necessary but not sufficient in itself to achieve Trustworthy AI, and additional conditions may also be necessary.[20] The AI HLEG Guidelines provide guidance largely in relation to the second and third components – fostering and implementing ethical and robust AI – since their stance is that all legal rights and obligations that apply to the processes and activities involved in developing, deploying and using AI systems remain mandatory and must be duly observed.[21] **6.032**

At the foundation of Trustworthy AI is a set of four ethical principles that should apply to AI systems. These are: respect for human autonomy; prevention of harm; fairness; and explicability. These embody a fundamental rights-based approach that underlies the foundation of both international and EU human rights law and underpins the legally enforceable rights guaranteed by the EU Treaties and the EU Charter.[22] Given that this is an EU document, this is not surprising, and in reality it appears to be an application of the existing laws and frameworks. **6.033**

The AI HLEG Guidelines acknowledges that tensions may arise between these principles – for example, the principle of prevention of harm used in such matters as predictive policing may conflict with respect for human autonomy – and it recognises that there is no fixed solution.[23] Indeed, AI practitioners are warned that the principles remain 'abstract prescriptions'[24] and that **6.034**

---

18   European Commission's AI HLEG, Ethics Guidelines for Trustworthy AI (April 2019) https://ec.europa.eu/digital
     -single-market/en/news/ethics-guidelines-trustworthy-ai accessed 7 September 2020.
19   European Commission's AI HLEG, Ethics Guidelines for Trustworthy AI (April 2019), 5 https://ec.europa.eu/digital
     -single-market/en/news/ethics-guidelines-trustworthy-ai accessed 7 September 2020.
20   Ibid.
21   European Commission's AI HLEG, Ethics Guidelines for Trustworthy AI (April 2019), 6 https://ec.europa.eu/digital
     -single-market/en/news/ethics-guidelines-trustworthy-ai accessed 7 September 2020.
22   European Commission's AI HLEG, Ethics Guidelines for Trustworthy AI (April 2019), 11–12 https://ec.europa.eu/
     digital-single-market/en/news/ethics-guidelines-trustworthy-ai accessed 7 September 2020.
23   European Commission's AI HLEG, Ethics Guidelines for Trustworthy AI (April 2019), 13 https://ec.europa.eu/digital
     -single-market/en/news/ethics-guidelines-trustworthy-ai accessed 7 September 2020.
24   Ibid.

'they should approach ethical dilemmas and trade-offs via reasoned, evidence-based reflection rather than intuition or random discretion'.[25]

6.035 In order to implement Trustworthy AI, a list of seven non-exhaustive requirements should be met throughout the AI system's life cycle. These are:[26]

(a) Human agency and oversight. Including respecting fundamental rights, human agency and human oversight and not automatic processing.[27]

(b) Technical robustness and safety. Including resilience to attack and security, fall-back plan and general safety, accuracy, reliability and reproducibility.[28]

(c) Privacy and data governance. Including respect for privacy, quality and integrity of data and access to data.[29]

(d) Transparency. Including traceability, explainability and communication such as AI systems should not represent themselves as humans to users.[30]

(e) Diversity, non-discrimination and fairness. Including the avoidance of unfair bias; accessibility and universal design; and stakeholder participation.[31]

(f) Societal and environmental wellbeing. Including sustainability and environmental friendliness, social impact, impacts on society, institutions and democracy.[32]

(g) Accountability. Including auditability, minimisation and reporting of negative impacts, trade-offs and availability of adequate redress.[33]

6.036 These seven requirements all interconnect with each other[34] and can be fulfilled through technical methods, such as architectures for Trustworthy AI, ethics and rule of law by design, explanation methods, testing and validating and quality of service indicators, as well as non-technical methods such as regulation, codes of conduct, standardisation, certification, governance frameworks, education, stakeholder participation and social dialogue.[35]

6.037 In order for these requirements and principles to be operationalised, the EU document sets out an assessment list. Chapter III of the AI HLEG Guidelines set out a pilot Trustworthy

---

25   Ibid.

26   European Commission's AI HLEG, Ethics Guidelines for Trustworthy AI (April 2019), 14 https://ec.europa.eu/digital -single-market/en/news/ethics-guidelines-trustworthy-ai accessed 7 September 2020.

27   European Commission's AI HLEG, Ethics Guidelines for Trustworthy AI (April 2019), 15–16 https://ec.europa.eu/ digital-single-market/en/news/ethics-guidelines-trustworthy-ai accessed 7 September 2020.

28   European Commission's AI HLEG, Ethics Guidelines for Trustworthy AI (April 2019), 16–17 https://ec.europa.eu/ digital-single-market/en/news/ethics-guidelines-trustworthy-ai accessed 7 September 2020.

29   European Commission's AI HLEG, Ethics Guidelines for Trustworthy AI (April 2019), 17 https://ec.europa.eu/digital -single-market/en/news/ethics-guidelines-trustworthy-ai accessed 7 September 2020.

30   European Commission's AI HLEG, Ethics Guidelines for Trustworthy AI (April 2019), 18 https://ec.europa.eu/digital -single-market/en/news/ethics-guidelines-trustworthy-ai accessed 7 September 2020.

31   European Commission's AI HLEG, Ethics Guidelines for Trustworthy AI (April 2019), 18–19 https://ec.europa.eu/ digital-single-market/en/news/ethics-guidelines-trustworthy-ai accessed 7 September 2020.

32   European Commission's AI HLEG, Ethics Guidelines for Trustworthy AI (April 2019), 19 https://ec.europa.eu/digital -single-market/en/news/ethics-guidelines-trustworthy-ai accessed 7 September 2020.

33   Ibid.

34   European Commission's AI HLEG, Ethics Guidelines for Trustworthy AI (April 2019), 15 https://ec.europa.eu/digital -single-market/en/news/ethics-guidelines-trustworthy-ai accessed 7 September 2020.

35   European Commission's AI HLEG, Ethics Guidelines for Trustworthy AI (April 2019), 20–3 https://ec.europa.eu/ digital-single-market/en/news/ethics-guidelines-trustworthy-ai accessed 7 September 2020.

AI assessment list which was updated and finalised in July 2020. Dubbed ALTAI – from Assessment List for Trustworthy AI[36] – it is a checklist for organisations to self-assess the trustworthiness of their AI systems under development. ALTAI is available in a document version as well as a prototype of a web-based tool. The rationale of ALTAI is that it will further strengthen the benefits that AI yields to the economy and society as a whole. ALTAI was billed by the European Commission as 'the first instrument that translates AI principles into an accessible and dynamic checklist that developers and deployers of AI can use [...] [and] will help to ensure that users benefit from AI without being exposed to unnecessary risks'.[37] While it is true that ALTAI is a convenient checklist, in reality ALTAI and the seven requirements are nothing new and the requirements and list are reminiscent of the best practices for data protection that have been used in privacy impact assessments[38] by data privacy professionals for decades in their daily work,[39] since the early days of the 1995 European Union Data Protection Directive.[40] The only aspects that could be regarded as new[41] are the environmental and societal impacts in Requirement 6, which were necessarily not present in data protection frameworks but are found in the literature of the respective disciplines such as climate change and human resources.

(d) Ethics frameworks: OECD

At around the same time that the AI HLEG published its final Ethics Guidelines **6.038** for Trustworthy AI, in May 2019, the OECD Council Recommendation on Artificial Intelligence was adopted by the 36 OECD member countries as well as by other countries including Argentina, Brazil, Costa Rica, Malta, Peru, Romania and Ukraine.[42] While OECD Recommendations are not legally binding, they have been highly influential in the past, have set the international standard in the respective areas and have helped to guide national legislation. A case in point is the OECD Privacy Guidelines adopted in 1980, which set out limits to the collection of personal data and which underlie many privacy laws and frameworks, such as those in the United States, Europe and Asia-Pacific.[43]

The OECD AI Principles are intended to guide governments, organisations and individuals **6.039** to design and operate AI systems in a way that prioritises people's best interests and to ensure that designers and operators are held accountable for their functioning.[44] Unlike much of the earlier work of the OECD, the OECD AI Principles are not narrowly confined to or focused on economics but also emphasise broader societal issues falling within the purview of human rights such as individual and worker rights and privacy, as well as the safety and reliability of

---

36 European Commission, Assessment List for Trustworthy AI (17 July 2020) https://ec.europa.eu/digital-single-market/en/news/assessment-list-trustworthy-artificial-intelligence-altai-self-assessment accessed 7 September 2020.

37 Ibid.

38 See for example Hannah YeeFen Lim, *Data Protection in the Practical Context – Strategies and Techniques* (Academy Publishing Singapore, 2017); Yee Fen Lim, *Cyberspace Law: Commentaries and Materials* (OUP 2002) and Yee Fen Lim, *Cyberspace Law: Commentaries and Materials* (OUP 2007).

39 Ibid.

40 Ibid.

41 European Commission, Assessment List for Trustworthy AI (17 July 2020) https://ec.europa.eu/digital-single-market/en/news/assessment-list-trustworthy-artificial-intelligence-altai-self-assessment, 19–20 accessed 7 September 2020.

42 OECD, Recommendation of the Council on Artificial Intelligence, OECD/LEGAL/0449 (2020).

43 Yee Fen Lim, *Cyberspace Law: Commentaries and Materials* (OUP 2002).

44 OECD, Recommendation of the Council on Artificial Intelligence, OECD/LEGAL/0449 (2020), 5.

AI systems. Indeed, like the AI HLEG Guidelines, the OECD AI Principles are very much concerned with trustworthy AI and the responsible stewardship of trustworthy AI.

6.040 The OECD AI Principles comprise five values-based principles for the responsible stewardship of trustworthy AI and five recommendations for public policy and international corporation for trustworthy AI.

6.041 The five values-based principles are as follows.

6.042 *Inclusive growth, sustainable development and well-being.*[45] Stakeholders in AI should invigorate inclusive growth, sustainable development and well-being through proactively pursuing beneficial outcomes for people and the planet, such as augmenting human capabilities and enhancing creativity, advancing inclusion of underrepresented populations, reducing economic, social, gender and other inequalities, and protecting natural environments.

6.043 *Human-centred values and fairness.*[46] Throughout the entire AI system lifecycle, the rule of law, human rights and democratic values should be respected. These include freedom, dignity and autonomy, privacy and data protection, non-discrimination and equality, diversity, fairness, social justice and internationally recognised labour rights. To achieve this, AI stakeholders should implement mechanisms and safeguards that are appropriate to the context and consistent with the state of art.

6.044 *Transparency and explainability.*[47] AI stakeholders should commit to transparency and responsible disclosure regarding AI systems such that meaningful information, appropriate to the context and consistent with the state of the art, is provided. In particular, AI stakeholders need to foster a general understanding of AI systems; ensure that individuals are aware when they are interacting with AI systems, including in the workplace; enable those affected by an AI system to understand the outcome; and, enable those adversely affected by an AI system to challenge the outcome, including providing accessible information on the factors and the logic that served as the basis for the prediction, recommendation or decision of the AI system.

6.045 *Robustness, security and safety.*[48] AI systems should be robust, secure and safe throughout their entire lifecycle. Regardless of whether the use is normal or foreseeable, or in situations of misuse or other adverse conditions, they must function appropriately and not pose an unreasonable safety risk. AI systems should be traceable in relation to datasets, processes and decisions made during the AI system lifecycle, to ensure that AI systems can be appropriately analysed. AI stakeholders should apply a systematic approach to risk management at each stage of the life cycle of AI systems on a continuous basis to address risks such as privacy, digital security, safety and bias.

---

45   Ibid, 7.
46   Ibid.
47   Ibid, 8.
48   Ibid.

Accountability.[49] All those developing, deploying or operating AI systems should be held   **6.046**
accountable for the proper functioning of AI systems and for compliance with all of the OECD
AI Principles.

In addition to these five key recommendations, the OECD AI Principles provide five sugges-   **6.047**
tions for national policy priorities. First, investments should be made in research and development, including interdisciplinary efforts, to spur innovation in trustworthy AI that focuses on
challenging technical issues and on AI-related social, legal and ethical implications. Similarly,
investments should also be made in open datasets that are representative and not biased, and
which also respect privacy and data protection.[50]

Second, governments should foster the development of, and access to, a digital ecosystem for   **6.048**
trustworthy AI, including mechanisms for sharing AI knowledge, as well as developing data
trusts, to support the safe, fair, legal and ethical sharing of data.[51]

Third, governments should promote a policy environment that supports AI systems from   **6.049**
development to deployment and operation for trustworthy AI systems, including the use of
sandboxes that allow for experimentation where AI systems can be tested and scaled up. At
the same time, governments should review and adapt policies and regulatory frameworks and
assessment mechanisms to encourage innovation and competition for trustworthy AI.[52]

Fourth, governments should build human capacity and prepare for labour market transfor-   **6.050**
mation, including empowering people to effectively use and interact with AI systems, such as
equipping them with the necessary skills and providing support for those affected by displace-
ment. AI should be used responsibly at work and the safety of workers should be enhanced.
More generally, the benefits from AI should be broadly and fairly shared.[53]

Lastly, governments and stakeholders should actively cooperate to engender responsible stew-   **6.051**
ardship of trustworthy AI and, at global and regional levels, to foster the sharing of AI knowledge, where appropriate. International, cross-sectoral and open multi-stakeholder initiatives
should be encouraged, including consensus-driven global technical standards for interoperable
and trustworthy AI. Governments should also encourage the development and use of internationally comparable metrics to measure AI research, development and deployment, and gather
the evidence base to assess progress in the implementation of these principles.[54]

(e) Ethics principles in general

In addition to the OECD AI Principles and the AI HLEG Guidelines, many jurisdictions   **6.052**
have also developed their own policies and guidelines. Indeed, there have been so many policies
that the OECD has set up the *OECD.AI Policy Observatory*, a platform tracking all the developments internationally, with dashboards allowing users to browse and compare hundreds of

---

49   Ibid.
50   Ibid.
51   Ibid, 8–9.
52   Ibid, 9.
53   Ibid.
54   Ibid.

AI policy initiatives in many countries.[55] The *OECD.AI Policy Observatory* is intended to be a source of real-time information, analysis and dialogue that is aimed at sharing and shaping AI policies around the world.

6.053 In many respects, the OECD AI Principles overlap with the AI HLEG Guidelines and the combination of the two appears to provide fairly comprehensive guidance for the development of AI that is practical and flexible enough to stand the test of time in a rapidly evolving field.

6.054 Guidance or blueprints as they are, they are voluntary and, in practice, quite vague, especially for technologists who develop AI systems. They are not very helpful in ensuring compliance, nor do they provide clear exposition of what is expected from the AI players and how governments propose to ensure regulatory compliance. A simple case in point: what does it mean to be fair? To a legally trained person, the meaning will depend on their jurisdictional background and will encompass not only black letter substantive laws on what is fair, but all of the legal jurisprudence from the many great legal philosophers spanning many decades. Ask a philosopher what is meant by fair, and they may well fall back on the thoughts of philosophers spanning centuries, with many different conceptions and schools of thought on what is regarded as fair. For an ethicist, the question of what is fair takes on yet another conception that may well be tied up with other values.

3. Creating Laws and Regulations

6.055 Given the attendant problems of ethics guidelines and frameworks, it is helpful that in June 2019 the EU HLEG promoted an approach towards laws and regulations of AI in its *Policy and Investment Recommendations for Trustworthy AI*[56] that is both systematic and measured.

6.056 The EU HLEG opined that a principle-based approach to regulation is preferred and that unnecessarily prescriptive regulation should be avoided in contexts characterised by rapid technological change, where it is often preferable to adopt a principle-based approach as well as outcome-based policies, subject to appropriate monitoring and enforcement.[57] Hence, the world should not be seeing an immediate rush towards broad-ranging regulation coming from the EU, especially as it navigates its way towards achieving trustworthy AI while supporting innovation and competitiveness.

6.057 As a first step, the EU HLEG recommended a comprehensive and systematic mapping and evaluation of all existing AI-relevant EU laws, which is indeed a sensible path forward.[58] This mapping exercise aims to identify existing legislation that already fulfils the AI policy and investment goals and to drive AI ethics. A review of the adequacy of the current regulatory

---

55 OECD, OECD.AI Policy Observatory https://oecd.ai/ accessed 7 September 2020.

56 EU HLEG, Policy and Investment Recommendations for Trustworthy AI https://ec.europa.eu/futurium/en/system/files/ged/ai_hleg_policy_and_investment_recommendations.pdf accessed 7 September 2020.

57 Ibid, para 26.4.

58 Ibid, para 27.1.

regime will also reveal potential legal gaps to both maximise AI's benefits and prevent and min-imise its risks.[59] In particular, it recommended that three questions are addressed, as follows:[60]

(a)   To what extent are the policy and legal objectives underpinning these legislative provi-sions affected by AI systems and in what ways?

(b)   To what extent are existing frameworks for monitoring, information-gathering and enforcement of the legislative measures capable of providing meaningful and effective oversight to ensure that the policy and legal objectives are still effectively met?

(c)   To what extent does existing legislation operate in ways to promote and ensure the ethical principles and requirements set out in the Ethics Guidelines?

The EU HLEG also advocated a risk-based approach to AI regulation and policy-making grounded on the proportionality and precautionary principles, taking into account both individual and societal risks, and noted that the character, intensity and timing of regulatory changes should be related to the type of risk created by an AI system.[61] For unacceptable risks, the revision of existing rules or the introduction of new regulations would be appropriate.   **6.058**

The approach outlined by the EU HLEG would be very useful in shaping clear AI regulation and policies and would avoid multiple pieces of legislation that may overlap or contradict each other. This approach also clearly identifies existing laws and legal standards with which AI systems would need to comply, thereby setting the scene for regulatory compliance of AI systems. The risk-based approach is also to be applauded as it will enable AI development to continue and not be unnecessarily stifled, at the same time as providing assurance to members of wider society that their interests are being looked after.   **6.059**

4.   Concrete General Laws

In truth, the regulation of AI is still in its infancy, as legislators grapple with the way forward. As already mentioned, many jurisdictions have developed their national plans, guidelines, ethics codes, research agendas and so on. It is not the purpose here to review them all; indeed, such a task may prove repetitive and fruitless. Of course, many legislatures may also be using the time to study and understand the issues and assess their current regulatory frameworks before planning the regulatory roadmap.   **6.060**

One of the first pieces of legislation in the world to tackle the general effects of AI was Canada's Directive on Automated Decision-Making[62] (the Directive), which was introduced on 1 April 2019. The Directive sets out requirements that federal government departments need to comply with if they use an Automated Decision System, which is defined as a system that either assists or replaces the judgement of human decision-makers. The Directive has an impact on organisations that provide products or services to such departments, as they too would need to demonstrate compliance if they are to maintain the contracts. For example, they   **6.061**

---

59   Ibid.
60   Ibid.
61   Ibid, para 26.1.
62   Directive on Automated Decision-Making (Canada) www.tbs-sct.gc.ca/pol/doc-eng.aspx?id=32592 accessed 1 October 2020.

would need to satisfy compliance with requirements such as transparency and explainability, particularly in respect of machine learning algorithms and other AI techniques.

6.062 Under section 6.1 of the Directive, an algorithmic impact assessment must be conducted to assess the risks of the system. The algorithmic impact assessment must be updated when system functionality or the scope of the Automated Decision System changes. The assessment comprises a very thorough list of questions. The aim is to ensure that such technology is deployed in a manner that minimises risks and produces consistent and interpretable decisions.

6.063 Section 6.3 of the Directive contains vigorous Quality Assurance Requirements that include tests for data biases as well as opportunities for individuals to challenge the automated decisions, and even peer reviews in some circumstances.

6.064 In the United States, in an initiative to address issues of algorithmic fairness, bias and discrimination, bills for the Algorithmic Accountability Act (S. 1108, H.R, 2231) were introduced in Congress on 10 April 2019; at the time of writing, however, they had not yet been passed.

(a) Substantive Areas of Law

6.065 In terms of substantive areas of law, of particular practical importance is the EU HLEG's outline in its *Policy and Investment Recommendations for Trustworthy AI*[63] of a number of relevant areas of existing EU laws and its elaboration on issues in those legal areas that needed close consideration.

6.066 Some of the areas highlighted were, for example, criminal law, where it stressed that for criminal law provisions, there is a need to ensure that criminal responsibility and liability can be attributed in line with the fundamental principles of criminal law.[64] For consumer protection rules, regulators need to consider the extent to which existing laws have the capacity to safeguard against illegal, unfair, deceptive, exploitative and manipulative practices made possible by AI applications and whether a mandatory consumer protection impact assessment is necessary or desirable.[65] For cybersecurity laws, there needs to be a consideration of the extent to which the current cybersecurity regime provides sufficient protection against cybersecurity risks posed by AI systems.[66]

(b) Personal data protection laws

6.067 Not surprisingly, given that data is the renewable air – not the unrenewable oil, as some have analogised – that drives AI systems, data protection laws were another pertinent legal area on which the EU HLEG focused.[67] Issues which it highlighted for consideration included whether existing laws allow sufficient access to public data and data for legitimate research purposes while preserving privacy and personal data protection and, further, whether the transparency and explainability mandated by the General Data Protection Regulation (GDPR)

---

63   EU HLEG, Policy and Investment Recommendations for Trustworthy AI https://ec.europa.eu/futurium/en/system/files/ged/ai_hleg_policy_and_investment_recommendations.pdf accessed 7 September 2020.

64   Ibid, para 27.3.

65   Ibid, para 27.4.

66   Ibid, para 27.7.

67   Ibid, para 27.5.

offers sufficient protection in light of the limited scope of applying only to the processing of personal data and the fact that automated decision-making processes can also affect individuals significantly even when the system is utilising non-personal data.[68]

Indeed, data protection laws are of significant concerns with respect to AI systems that the **6.068** United Kingdom Information Commissioner's Office (ICO) issued the final version of its *Guidance on AI and Data Protection*[69] (ICO Guidance) in July 2020. The ICO Guidance forms part of the ICO's wider AI auditing and compliance framework, which also includes auditing tools and procedures for the ICO to use in its audits and investigations. The ICO Guidance should be interpreted alongside other ICO guidance, such as the May 2020 *Explaining decisions made with AI*[70] guidance which focuses on how organisations can explain AI decisions in compliance with data protection laws.

The ICO Guidance provides assistance to organisations on questions of how to mitigate **6.069** against data protection risks associated with AI and how to apply the core principles set out in the General Data Protection Regulation (GDPR) to AI technology. The ICO Guidance, as the name suggests, is not a compulsory code[71] and there is no penalty for not complying with the Guidance. Notwithstanding this, organisations would do well to follow the ICO Guidance for two reasons.

First, one of the purposes for the creation of the ICO Guidance is to support the work of ICO's **6.070** investigation and assurance teams when assessing the compliance of organisations using AI.[72] Thus, the ICO Guidance will be relied upon by the ICO for its enforcement activities and audits. Indeed, the ICO states that the ICO Guidance 'covers what we think is best practice for data protection-compliant AI, as well as how we interpret data protection law as it applies to AI systems that process personal data'. As such, it would be prudent for organisations to pay close attention to the ICO Guidance and be cognisant of the contents and to ensure organisations are compliant, even if they are able to achieve compliance in other ways.[73] The ICO is clear that it will undertake a variety of auditing and investigation activities, which can include off-site checks, on-site tests and interviews, as well as the recovery and analysis of evidence, including AI systems themselves.[74]

The second reason why it would be prudent for organisations to follow the ICO Guidance is **6.071** because in most cases, the use of AI by an organisation will likely process personal data (given that the definition of personal data is inherently broad) and will thereby trigger a legal requirement for a Data Protection Impact Assessment (DPIA) to be conducted. In such a case, the ICO expects that the DPIA process should incorporate measures to comply with data protection laws generally but to also conform to the specific standards set out in the ICO Guidance.[75]

---

68   Ibid.
69   UK Information Commissioner's Office (ICO), Guidance on AI and Data Protection (30 July 2020, 0.0.24).
70   UK Information Commissioner's Office (ICO), Explaining decisions made with AI (20 May 2020, 1.0.31).
71   UK Information Commissioner's Office (ICO), Guidance on AI and Data Protection (30 July 2020, 0.0.24), 6.
72   Ibid, 6–7.
73   Ibid, 7.
74   Ibid.
75   Ibid, 11.

6.072 The ICO Guidance covers four main topics divided into four main parts: Accountability and Governance; Lawfulness, Fairness and Transparency; Security and Data Minimisation; and Individual Rights.

6.073 The expectations on the DPIA are set out under Part One on Accountability and Governance. The aim of the accountability principle is to ensure compliance with data protection laws and to demonstrate compliance in any AI system. In addition to showing compliance, accountability requires assessment and mitigation of risks. These are required to be documented in order to demonstrate compliance and to justify the choices made,[76] and a DPIA 'is an ideal way to demonstrate your compliance'.[77]

6.074 The ICO makes it clear that the responsibilities cannot be delegated to data scientists or engineering teams; instead, senior management, including Data Protection Officers (DPOs), are also accountable.[78] The ICO stresses that the law does not require a zero tolerance approach to risks to rights and freedoms but that the focus is on ensuring that these risks are identified, managed and mitigated.[79]

6.075 The Guidance includes all of the standard elements of a DPIA (as set out in GDPR), such as stating the position that DPIAs would be best undertaken at the early stages of project development,[80] thus embracing data protection by design and by default; however, there are some notable additions. First, a DPIA should show evidence of the consideration of less risky alternatives, if any, that would have achieved the same purpose of the processing but were not chosen, especially where an organisation uses public task or legitimate interests as a lawful basis.[81]

6.076 Second, an explanation must be provided of any relevant variation or margins of error in the performance of the system which may affect the fairness of the personal data processing.[82] Third, the DPIA should identify and record the degree of any human involvement in the decision-making process and at what stage this takes place, and implement processes to ensure the human involvement is meaningful.[83]

6.077 Fourth, where it may be difficult to describe the processing activity of AI systems, particularly when they involve complex models and data sources, it would be advisable to maintain two versions of the DPIA, with one version comprising a thorough technical description and a second version containing a more general or non-technical description of the processing.[84]

---

76 Ibid, 4.
77 Ibid, 13.
78 Ibid, 14.
79 Ibid.
80 Ibid, 16–17.
81 Ibid, 16.
82 Ibid, 17.
83 Ibid.
84 Ibid.

Fifth, included in the DPIA should be an assessment of necessity that demonstrates that the **6.078** purposes could not be accomplished in a less intrusive way.[85] Sixth, similarly, there should also be assessment of proportionality that demonstrates a weighing of the interests in using AI against the risks it may pose to data subjects such as bias or inaccuracy in the algorithms and datasets being used, including whether individuals would reasonably expect an AI system to conduct the processing.[86]

Seventh, any trade-offs that are made, for example between statistical accuracy and data mini- **6.079** misation, should be documented.[87]

Lastly, in the DPIA, against each identified risk to individuals' interests, it must be recorded **6.080** that options were considered to reduce the level of assessed risk further, such as providing opportunities for individuals to opt out of the processing. In addition to the safeguards that have been implemented to ensure the individuals responsible for the development, testing, validation, deployment and monitoring of AI systems are adequately trained and have an understanding of the data protection implications of the processing, the DPIA can also outline the organisational measures that have been implemented, such as appropriate training, to miti- gate risks associated with human error. Any technical measures designed to reduce risks to the security and accuracy of personal data processed in AI systems should also be documented. The DPIA should also document the residual levels of risk posed by the processing.[88]

The other parts of the ICO Guidance contain useful compliance requirements pertaining to **6.081** meeting the data protection law standards. For example, Part 2 of the document dealing with lawfulness, fairness and transparency provides helpful insights on how to identify the legal basis for data processing, which may vary for AI development and AI deployment phases. Regarding fairness, the ICO Guidance highlights the need to ensure that statistical accuracy of the AI system and the risks of AI system bias are dealt with both in development and procurement of AI systems and it explains how to define and prioritise different statistical accuracy measures.[89]

Similarly, in Part 3 on security and data minimisation, the ICO Guidance focuses on how to **6.082** identify and manage security risks, including cyber attacks on AI systems, as well as how to ensure compliance with the principle of data minimisation in both the development phase and in the deployment phase. In the last part of the ICO Guidance dealing with individual rights, the ICO provides assistance to organisations on how to operationalise the ability for individuals to exercise their rights throughout the entire AI lifecycle.

It should be noted that the European Parliament commissioned a study on the impact of the **6.083** GDRP on AI that was published on 25 June 2020.[90] The study was prepared at the request of the Panel for the Future of Science and Technology (STOA) and managed by the Scientific

---

85   Ibid, 18.
86   Ibid.
87   Ibid.
88   Ibid, 19.
89   Ibid, 37.
90   European Parliament Think Tank, The impact of the General Data Protection Regulation (GDPR) on artificial intel- ligence www.europarl.europa.eu/RegData/etudes/STUD/2020/641530/EPRS_STU(2020)641530_EN.pdf accessed 26 October 2020.

Foresight Unit, within the Directorate-General for Parliamentary Research Services (EPRS) of the Secretariat of the European Parliament.[91] This study's practical utility, however, pales in comparison with the ICO Guidance.

6.084 On 29 June 2020, the European Data Protection Supervisor (EDPS) released an opinion (EDPS Opinion)[92] on the European Commission's February 2020 *White Paper on AI.* The EDPS Opinion unsurprisingly took a stance similar to the EU HLEG's *Policy and Investment Recommendations for Trustworthy AI* and was of the view that the approach taken to regulating AI should be one of first identifying regulatory gaps in order to inform the basis of future regulatory framework.[93] Its view was that much of the existing rules in the GDPR were sufficient. It did however raise particular concern about biometric identification technologies, such as facial recognition systems as well as gait, fingerprints, DNA, voice and keystroke systems, and called for a moratorium on their deployment until suitable safeguards can be put in place. It appears to be suggesting that in this respect the processing of personal data in, for example, predictive policing may not be appropriately protected under the GDPR.

(c) Civil liability laws

6.085 While the EU HLEG did discuss briefly in its *Policy and Investment Recommendations for Trustworthy AI* the topic of civil liability, it pre-empted the report of the Expert Group on Liability and New Technologies, an independent expert group that the European Commission had set up. This report, *Liability for Artificial Intelligence and other emerging digital technologies,*[94] released in November 2019, explored how liability regimes should be designed and adapted to incorporate new challenges and risks posed by AI and other emerging digital technologies.

6.086 The report presented an overview of the landscape and offered a number of recommendations. One of the more notable recommendations was that autonomous systems should not be granted legal personality, noting that damages arising from the new technologies could still be attributed to natural person or existing categories of legal persons.[95]

6.087 On 20 October 2020, the European Parliament adopted proposals on recommendations for the regulation of AI. The three resolutions that were adopted concerned three reports.

6.088 The first report adopted was a resolution with Recommendations to the Commission on a civil liability regime for AI.[96] The proposal was largely centred on civil liability claims against the operator of an AI system; Article 4 would make those operating high-risk AI systems strictly liable if there is harm or damage caused. For other AI systems that do not constitute high-risk

---

91   Ibid, Front matter, Author.

92   European Data Protection Supervisor , EDPS Opinion on the European Commission's White Paper on Artificial Intelligence – A European approach to excellence and trust https://edps.europa.eu/sites/edp/files/publication/20–06–19_opinion_ai_white_paper_en.pdf accessed 26 October 2020.

93   Ibid, para 49.

94   European Commission, Liability for Artificial Intelligence and other emerging digital technologies https://ec.europa.eu/transparency/regexpert/index.cfm?do=groupDetail.groupMeetingDoc&docid=36608 accessed 26 October 2020.

95   Ibid, 37–8.

96   European Parliament, Civil liability regime for artificial intelligence, European Parliament resolution of 20 October 2020 with recommendations to the Commission on a civil liability regime for artificial intelligence (2020/2014(INL)) www.europarl.europa.eu/doceo/document/TA-9-2020–0276_EN.pdf accessed 26 October 2020.

AI-systems as laid down in Articles 3(c) and 4(2), they would be subject to fault-based liability for any harm or damage that was caused by the AI system.

It is rather unfortunate that this approach has been espoused: the better party to pin liability **6.089** upon would be the developer or manufacturer of the AI systems, as that would ensure that developers innovate responsibly, keeping in mind liability if their systems fail in any way. Further, placing liability on the operators may lead to poor uptake by users if they are unfamiliar with how the AI system has been trained or developed or how the algorithm operates and they do not wish to be burdened with liability should things go amiss. To add to these issues, the proposal in Article 8 also places the liability on the operator where the harm or damage was caused by a third party that interfered with the AI system by modifying its functioning or its effect, where the third party is untraceable or impecunious. This would be an added disincentive for the uptake of AI systems because if the AI system was poorly designed and was hacked, it will be extremely difficult, if not impossible, for the operator to escape liability for the hacked AI system.

The proposal also provides for contributory negligence in Article 10; however, the wording **6.090** may need to be tidied up as the draft Article 10 does not seem to achieve the intended purpose.

(d) Ethics laws

The second resolution that was adopted on 20 October 2020 by the European Parliament **6.091** concerned a report on ethics.

The second report deals with a framework of ethical aspects of AI, robotics and related **6.092** technologies. The resolution has the aim of the European Commission developing a legal framework with ethical principles for the development, deployment and use of AI robotics and related technologies within the EU. The guiding principles to be considered by the legislative framework include safety, transparency and accountability; a human-centric, human-made and human-controlled AI; safeguards against bias and discrimination; and so on. The proposals are largely in line with the AI HLEG Guidelines discussed above.[97]

(e) Intellectual property laws

The third and final resolution that was adopted on 20 October 2020 by the European **6.093** Parliament concerned a report on intellectual property laws (IP Report).[98]

The IP Report stressed the importance of an effective system that protects IP for the further **6.094** development of AI, including the issue of patents. It stressed the importance of distinguishing between AI-assisted human creations and creations autonomously generated by AI. The IP

---

97 European Parliament, Framework of ethical aspects of artificial intelligence, robotics and related technologies, European Parliament resolution of 20 October 2020 with recommendations to the Commission on a framework of ethical aspects of artificial intelligence, robotics and related technologies (2020/2012(INL)) www.europarl.europa.eu/doceo/document/TA-9–2020–0275_EN.pdf accessed 26 October 2020.

98 European Parliament, Intellectual property rights for the development of artificial intelligence technologies, European Parliament resolution of 20 October 2020 on intellectual property rights for the development of artificial intelligence technologies (2020/2015(INI)) www.europarl.europa.eu/doceo/document/TA-9–2020–0277_EN.html accessed 26 October 2020.

Report took the view that technical creations generated by AI technology must be protected under the intellectual property rights legal framework in order to encourage investment in this form of creation and improve legal certainty for stakeholders.[99]

6.095 With regard to copyright,[100] it took the view that works autonomously produced by artificial agents and robots might not be eligible for copyright protection, in order to observe the principle of originality, which is linked to a natural person. However, if an opposite view is taken, that the European Commission adopt an evidence-based and technologically neutral approach to common, uniform copyright provisions applicable to AI-generated works in the Union. It also recommended that ownership of rights, if any, should only be assigned to natural or legal persons that created the work lawfully and only if authorisation has been granted by the copyright holder if copyright-protected material was used, unless there are copyright exceptions or limitations apply. These are interesting proposals and it remains to be seen if they will stand up to scrutiny under existing conceptions of copyright law. Certainly, there are issues with substantiality of the copyright materials used as not every reproduction, however minute, will constitute infringement. On the other hand, however, there will be questions regarding the degree to which a copyrighted work is used as data to train the algorithm that will push the use to become infringing use.

6.096 The resolution also stressed the importance of facilitating access to data and data sharing, open standards and open source technology, while encouraging investment and boosting innovation.[101]

6.097 With regard to the question of legal personality, it made clear that since the autonomisation of the creative process of generating content of an artistic nature can raise issues relating to the ownership of intellectual property rights it would hence be inappropriate to impart legal personality to AI technologies, and not least that such a move may result in disincentives for human creators.[102]

6.098 The IP Report also discusses trade secrets and deep fakes; given that intellectual property rights was missing in the European Commission's *White Paper on Artificial Intelligence: A European approach to excellence and trust*[103] which was released in February 2020, it remains to be seen if a consensus can be reached.

6.099 On the other side of the Atlantic, just a few weeks before the IP Report was adopted, the United States Patent and Trademark Office (USPTO) released its report *Public Views on Artificial Intelligence and Intellectual Property Policy*,[104] which is a summary of comments from

---

99   Ibid, para 15.
100 Ibid.
101 Ibid.
102 Ibid, para 13.
103 European Commission, White Paper on Artificial Intelligence – A European approach to excellence and trust https:// ec.europa.eu/info/sites/info/files/commission-white-paper-artificial-intelligence-feb2020_en.pdf accessed 26 October 2020.
104 United States Patent and Trademark Office (USPTO), Public Views on Artificial Intelligence and Intellectual Property Policy (October 2020) www.uspto.gov/sites/default/files/documents/USPTO_AI-Report_2020–10–07.pdf accessed 26 October 2020.

various stakeholders in response to its Requests for Comments in 2019. In contrast to the position in the European Union, the USPTO report found divided opinions in just about every category studied, from eligibility of AI to be a named inventor for a patent or author of a copyright protected work, ownership of AI-produced inventions and potential copyright infringement issues related to AI algorithms or processes to database protection and trade secrets laws. Also in contrast to the position in the European Union, the majority of the stakeholders largely agreed that existing US intellectual property laws are sufficiently robust and flexible to address AI-related issues. It would appear that most respondents in the USPTO study largely correctly assumed that AI has not yet reached artificial general intelligence, where AI has the capability to think and invent on its own.[105]

The World Intellectual Property Office (WIPO) has also weighed in on these matters and has **6.100** held a number of WIPO Conversation on AI and Intellectual Property. The most recent took place remotely in early July 2020.[106] It appeared that a sizable opinion was that existing intellectual property laws are flexible enough to be applied to AI technology, but clearer guidance would assist in achieving internationally consistent approaches.

5.   Highly Regulated Industries

Certain industries, by their very nature, have always attracted very detailed regulations, whether **6.101** concerning technology or otherwise. These industries are highly regulated for well-founded reasons, such as safety, the risks they pose and the interests protected. They include the banking and finance industry, the medical and healthcare industry and the transportation industry, such as the automotive industry. Some of these are dealt with in detail in chapters 13 and 18.

In terms of these highly regulated industries and the use or prevalence of AI systems within **6.102** them, first and foremost, any AI system would need to satisfy the usual industry requirements. Thereafter, considerations may be had as to whether a system utilising AI requires further regulations and how these may be complied with. For example, medical devices laws exist in the legal landscape of many jurisdictions and they will already contain specific provisions governing the safety of medical devices. These ought first to be satisfied by any medical AI system; thereafter, any further requirements specific to AI should also be complied with. So, in the EU, the Medical Devices Regulation already covers medical devices in general, and should a regulation on civil liability such as that proposed in the European Commission's *White Paper on Artificial Intelligence: A European approach to excellence and trust*[107] be adopted, such high-risk AI applications could be subject to pre-marketing conformity assessment requirements and also potentially ongoing monitoring.

---

105   Ibid, 6.
106   World Intellectual Property Office, WIPO Conversation on Intellectual Property (IP) and Artificial Intelligence (AI): Second Session www.wipo.int/meetings/en/details.jsp?meeting_id=55309 accessed 26 October 2020.
107   European Commission, White Paper On Artificial Intelligence – A European approach to excellence and trust https://ec.europa.eu/info/sites/info/files/commission-white-paper-artificial-intelligence-feb2020_en.pdf accessed 26 October 2020.

6.103 The World Health Organisation (WHO) is currently preparing the *WHO Guidance on Ethics & Governance of AI for Health*, an initiative which will hopefully lead the direction of AI in the medical sector.[108]

6.104 Similarly, in the autonomous vehicles industry, many jurisdictions have enacted their own requirements on the testing and deployment of autonomous vehicles. Readers are directed to the groundbreaking 2018 work *Autonomous Vehicles and the Law: Technology, Algorithms, and Ethics*,[109] which dissects the issues from technological, legal and ethical perspectives. There is currently no international consensus on how autonomous vehicles ought to be regulated or any international standards as to the technology.

6.   Compliance with Regulation using AI

6.105 With all the possible use cases of AI, it is unsurprising that in some heavily regulated industries, organisations have used AI in attempts to comply with the voluminous regulations. Thus, in a relatively short space of time, RegTech, whether using AI or not, has flourished into a small industry distinct from FinTech. One sector which has taken the lead in this is finance and insurance. Some of the areas where AI has been used include Know Your Customer (KYC), anti-money-laundering legislation (AML), fraud detection and prevention, consumer risk assessment, biometrics and identity, service security, compliance workflows, financial risk assessment, diligence, and vendor and third-party risk.

6.106 In some of the areas, such as fraud detection and prevention, the use of AI is well suited to the task due to algorithms' and data's ability to be deployed for data analytics and to find patterns. In this sense, AI would be ideal for, for example, fraud detection and prevention, as algorithms can scan and identify dubious transactions much faster than any human can. The use of AI in such areas can result in huge cost savings for the organisation as manpower costs can be substantially reduced, as well as improving proof of compliance.

6.107 In addition to organisations utilising AI, the supervisory authorities of the banking and finance sectors have taken to SupTech, that is, regulators using technology to enhance the efficiency and effectiveness of supervision. Readers are directed to the excellent and seminal work *FinTech, Law and Regulation*,[110] which contains several chapters devoted to RegTech and SupTech, for a comprehensive exposition of the topic. For our purposes here, it suffices to say that RegTech and SupTech in banking and finance, although the most advanced of any industry, is still in its relative infancy – so much so that regulators in some countries, such as the UK, Hong Kong and Singapore, have all set up regulatory sandboxes, which are essentially environments or testing grounds for innovative products or services that can be tested without being subject to all of the regulatory requirements. These can include pilot trials of RegTech, SupTech and other technological initiatives in a controlled environment with a more flexible supervisory arrangement before they are launched on a fuller scale.

---

108 The author has been appointed as an External Expert Reviewer to review the Report of the Experts.
109 Hannah YeeFen Lim, *Autonomous Vehicles and the Law: Technology, Algorithms, and Ethics* (Edward Elgar Publishing, UK 2018).
110 Jelena Madir (ed), *FinTech: Law and Regulation* (Edward Elgar Publishing, UK 2019).

Sandboxes are an ideal way to help stimulate innovation without creating unacceptable risks for **6.108** the public and individuals and they enable efficient viability assessments for new innovations. In this regard, sandboxes can also help develop impact assessment capabilities and thereby enable experimental AI implementations to be more fully appraised.

Ultimately, it must be very clear that, at their core, the processes of AI systems rely on pattern **6.109** recognition technology to comb through vast volumes of data and identify repeated patterns. This will reduce hundreds of variations into manageable clusters or groups based on their similarities and differences. Such AI systems can locate key information within a body of data, identify deviations and thereby flag anomalies.

AI systems are currently not at a stage whereby they have any form of cognition. Hence, the **6.110** term cognitive computer is a misnomer.[111] The current capabilities are semantic and perceptual computing, which are vastly different capabilities. For example, semantic computing has been used for a number of years in the financial industry. The EDM Council's Financial Industry Business Ontology is a good example of an open semantic standard and business conceptual model developed by financial institutions for semantic computing. It gives precise meaning to hundreds of unique data attributes from internal and external sources and stored in thousands of unconnected databases. In a sense, it maps data to specific meanings to automate business processes.[112]

The point of this is that regulators need to be extremely cautious in accepting an AI system **6.111** as a satisfactory form of demonstrating compliance with regulations for certain tasks. Indeed, a case in point is the false and misleading claims[113] made by IBM over the years that the IBM Watson Financial Services and Watson Regulatory Compliance are cognitive systems.[114] The demonstrated failure of Watson in medical AI, where some studies found it to produce accuracy rates of 49 per cent,[115] should already be a lesson learnt that comprehensive risk and other assessments are essential.

While AI systems can confer benefits, for the time being – and certainly until there is proven **6.112** efficacy – they should primarily be utilised as complementary technologies that add an extra guarantee of compliant processes.

---

111 Tom Butler and Leona O'Brien, 'Artificial Intelligence for Regulatory Compliance: Are We There Yet?' Journal of Financial Compliance 3(1), 44–59 (2019).

112 EDM Council, What is FIBO https://spec.edmcouncil.org/fibo/ accessed 28 October 2020.

113 Roger Schank, 'The Fraudulent Claims Made by IBM about Watsons and AI www.rogerschank.com/fraudulent-claims -made-by-IBM-about-Watson-and-AI accessed 28 October 2020.

114 Tom Butler and Leona O'Brien, 'Artificial Intelligence for Regulatory Compliance: Are We There Yet?' Journal of Financial Compliance 3(1), 44–59 (2019).

115 Eliza Strickland, 'How IBM Watson Overpromised and Underdelivered on AI Health Care' IEEE Spectrum https:// spectrum.ieee.org/biomedical/diagnostics/how-ibm-watson-overpromised-and-underdelivered-on-ai-health-care accessed 28 October 2020.

D. CONCLUSION

6.113 Regulatory compliance is an emerging area of law in AI, in which much development is currently taking place and is likely to continue to take place for a considerable period of time. Many jurisdictions and multilateral international organisations have created a substantial body of literature over the past four to five years but it is only now that substantive legal rules and principles are beginning to take shape. While for some parties the early works focused largely on ethics, it has become clear that action needs to be taken beyond developing ethics principles, in the creation of solid legal frameworks, principles and regulations. Many of the principles from data protection law over the past four decades would serve as a good starting point for the regulation of AI as the lifeline of AI is data; however, there remain legal gaps, such as liability and accountability issues that need to be resolved, even if existing laws in these areas can apply, to a large extent, to AI legal issues. Going forward, the likely course may be that rules and regulations will be created for specific industries, especially the high-risk industries, and from there they can be extrapolated more generally to cover all use cases of AI.

7

COMMERCIAL CONTRACTS

Iain Sheridan

A. INTRODUCTION

Pre-contract due diligence requires not only precisely drafting what has been agreed, but also **7.001** foresight to accommodate worst-case scenarios. Commercial contracts across diverse sectors with high-value subject matter require both types of expertise. This is evidenced by English High Court decisions which often reveal weak pre-contract due diligence and imperfect drafting. They are also relevant to us because the increasing application of AI methods adds another layer of complexity and risk to these knotty, Odyssean tasks.

7.002 In commercial contracts, AI is prevalent in two specific situations: first, in augmenting decision making, for instance, in support of investment decisions by providing predictions on the performance of investment assets, including currencies, equities, fixed income and index-linked products; second, in augmenting the efficient creation of contracts and automation of clauses that manage important obligations and rights. This chapter raises many complex questions, the answers to which vary depending upon the full scope of the commercial activities undertaken.

B. PRINCIPLES OF ENGLISH CONTRACT LAW

7.003 Most common law system-qualified lawyers are well versed in the principles of English contract law. Further, given that English law is often the choice of governing law by international commercial parties, its principles are also well known in many civil systems. However, everyone is not equally familiar with English contract law principles, so it is sensible to briefly summarise these so that all readers can then later in this chapter apply English law to contracts augmented by AI.

7.004 Under English law, predominantly based on case law precedents,[1] a contract must have a number of features to be legally binding. The core features include the following.

(a) An intention by both parties to create legal relations.[2] In the situation of an agreement containing the words 'subject to contract' there is no final intention to make a contract.[3]

(b) Evidence of an offer and acceptance to confirm the making of a contract.[4]

(c) Consideration, by which is meant some value, whether monetary, or otherwise,[5] between the parties.[6] The exception is where a contract is made by deed.[7]

(d) Certainty of the subject matter. Absolute certainty of subject matter is not required but it cannot be too vague.[8]

(e) Compliance with any formal legal requirements relevant to the specific type of contract. For example, the sale of a property or the sale of an interest in land must be in writing.[9]

An absence of these (a) to (e) features would, in the majority of situations, mean the contract is not binding because of uncertainty. So the clauses of any contract governed by English law must rationally have these core features to be valid.

---

1 Non-consumer contracts are also controlled by two important statutes, namely the Unfair Contract Terms Act 1977 and the Misrepresentation Act 1967.

2 *Esso Petroleum v Commissioners of Customs & Excise* [1976] 1 WLR 1, HL.

3 *Winn v Bull* (1877) 7 Ch D 29.

4 *NZ Shipping v AM Satterthwaite*, 'The Eurymedon' [1975] AC 154, 167.

5 *Ward v Byham* [1956] 1 WLR 496.

6 The need for consideration is generally not a principle found in civil law systems.

7 A contract made by deed must satisfy the requirements set out in section 1 of the Law of Property (Miscellaneous Provisions) Act 1989.

8 *Scammell v Dicker* [2005] EWCA Civ 405.

9 Section 2 Law of Property (Miscellaneous Provisions) Act 1989).

C. MACHINE LEARNING

1.   Definitions

Having set out the English contract law principles, it is important to underline that out of **7.005** numerous AI methods, machine learning is the dominant type of AI application relevant to commercial contracts that are individually negotiated. An authoritative *Royal Society* paper describes machine learning as living at the intersection of computer science, data science and statistics, applying this trio of disciplines 'to process data in a way that can detect and learn from patterns, predict future activity, or make decisions'.[10] Put succinctly, machine learning is the use of statistical algorithms within software programs that 'enable computers to learn from data'.[11]

2.   Three Key Types of Machine Learning Methods

As we have seen elsewhere, machine learning can be supervised, unsupervised or a mixture of **7.006** both methods.

The *Oxford Dictionary of Computer Science* refers to supervised learning as occurring when 'the **7.007** training input has been explicitly labelled with the classes to be learned'.[12] For instance, a computer might be instructed to analyse the movement of all free-floating currencies globally. The human trainer (professional coder) would initially label a number of free-floating currencies without the need to label all currencies that are free floating.

Unsupervised learning works by the human coder instructing the algorithm, to find clustering **7.008** patterns based on pre-defined characteristics. The output is generated with no training data. Yann LeCun, Director of AI at Facebook and Professor of Neural Science at NYU, describes the daunting challenge of unsupervised learning using the metaphor of a Black Forest gateau. If intelligence is such a cake, unsupervised learning is the sponge, supervised learning would be the icing on the cake and reinforcement learning would be the cherry on the cake. We know how to make the icing and the cherry, but we don't know how to make the cake.[13]

3.   Clause Drafting for Machine Learning Methods

Categorising a specific machine learning algorithm that forms an integral part of a good or **7.009** service has implications for contract drafting. Table 7.1 below records the types of machine learning methods and supporting disclosures that need to be included in contract clauses.

---

10   *Royal Society* (2019) 'Machine Learning: the power and the promise of computers that learn from example', at p. 19. See https://royalsociety.org/~/media/policy/projects/machine-learning/publications/machine-learning-report.pdf.
11   Melanie Mitchell (2019) Artificial Intelligence- A Guide for Thinking Humans (UK: Pelican), at p. 35.
12   *The Oxford Dictionary of Computer Science* (2016) (Oxford: OUP).
13   See J.P. Morgan Distinguished Lecture Series on AI www.jpmorgan.com/global/technology/artificial-intelligence/ai -distinguished-lecture-series.

Table 7.1   *Clause drafting for machine learning methods*

Type of Machine Learning	Data Mechanics	Disclosure
Supervised	The data set provided is labelled. Output is generated with the guidance of considerable initial training data.	The errors from which the computer learns are based on labelled data supplied by a human. At the outset, the algorithm is fed a large number of correct training examples. Thereafter, the algorithm adjusts its weights and thresholds.
Reinforced Learning	Unlabelled data inputs are fed to the algorithm. A human provides parameters and feedback. The algorithm learns to interact with its environment, making decisions by trial and error to maximise future positive rewards. A human provides feedback and parameters.	The errors from which the computer learns are not based on data supplied by a human. However, a human guides the algorithm with parameters and feedback.
Unsupervised	The algorithm is instructed to find clustering patterns based on pre-defined characteristics. Output is generated with no training data.	The clustering patterns identified by the algorithm are not based on data supplied by a human.

7.010 At the contract negotiation and drafting phase the responsible legal counsel has to manage a range of contractual obligations, rights and risks linked to AI. The absence or degree of supervision is likely to focus any future judicial analysis on the service provider's technical control over the data processed. Further, judges would scrutinise clauses that cover the buyer's acceptance of the risks involved in the type of AI method applied to provide classification or prediction information. For example, on equity or fixed income trading platforms, when a machine learning algorithm deviates from the agreed trading limits or trading levels, disclosing the characteristics of the specific machine learning algorithms would be of evidential weight.

4. Machine Learning Concepts Relevant to Contract Management

7.011 While machine learning encompasses a huge array of methods, Table 7.2 captures key recurring concepts.[14] Each of these concepts has its own complexity and variations, but the gist of each can at least allow legal analysis to develop on the basis of these vital components.

---

14   There are other machine learning concepts relevant to businesses applications of AI, but these specific Table 7.2 concepts are the essential minimum in the context of this chapter.

Table 7.2   *TPP4: Essential machine learning concepts*

Concepts	Explanation and example
Training Data	The coder characterises data as good examples of what the computer should be finding; for example, a data set of 10,000 images of huskies so that the computer can provide confidence measurement of when additional images are also a husky, rather than a wolf.
Classification	Typically the discrete selection of a class or group of data based on a yes or no; 1 or 0 result. For example, in image recognition the computer may classify a data set of animals as either a husky or a wolf.
Clustering	A powerful machine learning technique that is able to analyse large data sets and spot clusters from data that may seem to have no discernible structures within it. For example, the large quantities of trading data flowing in and out of stock exchanges can reveal clusters on which investment inferences can be drawn.
Regression	Statistical prediction of a number based on analysing the relationships between variables, for example predicting the ferocity of a cyclone based on the size and speed of past storm data of similar cyclones.
Output	The computer's confidence level or prediction based on statistical calculations. For example, if a computer is tasked to classify an animal as either a husky or a wolf, a setting for 100 per cent confidence might be 1. So an output of 0.9 would mean the computer is very confident with its classification.
Neural Network	A machine learning method inspired by connections in the human brain. A neural network is made up of interconnected layers of nodes. Each layer of nodes can receive data from layers above it and transmit data to layers below it. Some nodes are neither an input nor become an output. In the field of AI these nodes are called hidden layers. Rather than 'hidden', a more intuitive way to think of hidden layers is to categorise them as non-output units.
Deep Learning	A neural network with more than one hidden layer, which applies algorithms to big data sets, with the aim that the computer becomes increasingly competent at the task it has been set. With image recognition tasks this has typically been achieved by establishing multiple hierarchies of pixels in each image. For example, this approach has proven to be very successful at forecasting weather based on satellite images.
Threshold point	The reaching of a numerical value resulting in a node in a neural network passing on data to another node in a different layer of the neural network. The concept of a threshold is inspired by the human brain's firing of neurons to act. However, rather than a 'fire' or 'no fire' divide, the threshold of a node in a neural network acts on a number; for example, 1 = fire or less than 1 = no fire.

D. AI AUGMENTING HEDGING AND INVESTMENT DECISIONS

The use of machine learning algorithms is commonplace across global capital markets, and **7.012** increasingly so. Whether businesses are hedging or investing in commodities, currencies, equities or fixed income products, there are already numerous AI augmentation software services available. The following four examples capture how machine learning decision-support tools can typically contribute potential value.

1. Example of a Company Using Unsupervised Classification

7.013 Formed by a nucleus of Cambridge University engineering PhDs, the Algodynamix[15] financial forecasting platform provides advance warning of major directional market movements. Its software is based on unsupervised classification and clustering machine learning methods applied to market behaviour affecting global equity markets, indices and other asset classes.

7.014 As covered in section A, unsupervised learning works by the human coder instructing the algorithm, to find clustering patterns based on pre-defined characteristics. The output is generated with no training data. As previously described, Yann LeCun, Director of AI at Facebook and Professor of Neural Science at NYU, describes the daunting challenge of unsupervised learning using the metaphor of a Black Forest gateau. The point for lawyers involved in pre-contract due diligence and agreement drafting is that even the best machine learning engineers do not know how the main sponge part of the gateau is made.[16]

7.015 Algodynamix relies on current data and ignores historical data. For example, it can provide forecasting indicators on the movement of the CBOE Volatility Index (VIX). A 'flag' system predicts when an index or other asset price will start to significantly increase or decrease. That advance warning is communicated to each client via email or an API or both. Thereafter, a second advance warning is communicated when the specific market movement is predicted to stop.[17] The investor is in charge of any subsequent trade execution that factors in the advance warnings.

2. Example of a Company Providing Products Relying on IBM Watson

7.016 Equbot[18] is a California-based company that provides four AI products, namely analytics, ETFs, indexes and platforms. All four rely on IBM Watson assistance to process millions of pieces of data with deep learning methods. On a daily basis Equbot's analytics service provides 74 indicators, in its terminology 'signals', for 16,000 global companies. From the news and information section there are 23 elements measured for each company, covering related economic risks, geopolitical risk and market sentiment. These elements include processing data on new sentiment, legal involvement, new products and strategic partnerships.

7.017 Turning to the index side of its business, Equbot has collaborated with HSBC to market AiPEX, an AI-powered equity index comprising 250 US publicly listed companies.[19] This works by an AI algorithm selecting constituents of the AiPEX on a monthly basis. The AiPEX is the first index to use IBM Watson as part of the data analysis process.

---

15   www.algodynamix.com
16   See J.P. Morgan Distinguished Lecture Series on AI www.jpmorgan.com/global/technology/artificial-intelligence/ai-distinguished-lecture-series.

18   www.equbot.com
19   http://aipex.gbm.hsbc.com

3.   Example of a Company Supplying an Investment Scoring System

Kavout[20] is a Seattle-based company providing a range of services focused on individual score **7.018** ratings for equities. The score rating is based on a scale of 0 to 9, with a high score indicating a higher probability of outperformance. *Kavout* relies on classification, deep learning and regression methods. Its algorithms make calculations applying more than 200 factors and market signals. Customers can mitigate underperforming stocks from portfolio construction by avoiding shares scored 1 to 3. Kavout's K Score UK All Sectors product provides daily scores for more than 343 UK shares.

4.   Example of a Company Providing Trading Strategies

Trade Ideas[21] is a Californian company that examines more than 35 trading strategies based **7.019** on a comparison of an asset's movement today compared with the historical past 60 days of trading, including analysis of long, short and technical data. Trade Ideas' machine learning algorithms analyse more than a million different trading scenarios. Across more than 6,000 shares, its service includes customer alerts on stock movement predictions.

E. AI STANDARDS IN TERMS AND CONDITIONS

1.   Leading AI Standards

Legal contract risk and other forms of risk potentially exist in machine learning services. As **7.020** AI augmentation software services evolve, both contracting parties and their insurers will seek to insert contract clauses committing the AI provider to adhere to respected international standards, as covered in Chapter 16 of this book on Insurance. As a minimum, there should, in my view, be reference to at least one leading AI international standard. Examples include those produced by the Institute of Electrical and Electronics Engineers (IEEE) and the joint International Organization for Standards (ISO) or the International Electrotechnical Commission (IEC).[22]

There are other emerging international standards based on the hard work of the AI4People **7.021** project, the EU High Level Expert Group recommendations, the OECD's principles and the PRC's Beijing set of principles. However, despite the growing body of international expertise, a single, globally agreed set of ethical standards is unlikely to be the *dolce vita* solution for AI.[23] Diversity of cultures[24] and constant change across jurisdictions make it unlikely that just one

---

20   www.kavout.com

21   www.trade-ideas.com

22   An excellent technical report on international AI standards bodies is P Cihon, *Standards for AI Governance: International Standards to Enable Global Coordination in AI Research & Development*, Future of Humanity Institute, Oxford University, www.fhi.ox.ac.uk/wp-content/uploads/Standards_-FHI-Technical-Report.pdf.

23   In contrast to focusing on international standards, some AI experts dedicate their energies to establishing best practices. An example is The Partnership on AI. See www.partnershiponai.org/about/.

24   For a thought-provoking article on this dichotomy see Financial Times, 'Formulating values for AI is hard when humans do not agree – China and the west prioritise different things in their algorithms', 22 July 2019.

set of standards will be adopted. For example, a dichotomy can exist between how Western cultures and China choose to prioritise a hierarchy of values in algorithms. Western cultures place high importance on individual rights, but China tends to place a high priority on collective harmony. Yet each set of ethical principles can at least provide some guidance for lawyers to check what should be included as essential. At an Alan Turing Institute conference on AI ethics focused on the financial services sector,[25] the eminent Professor Luciano Floridi observed that each AI standard is approximately 'the same dish, the difference is the adding of extra oil or seasoning'. So there is substantial consensus across the standards.

2. Common Principles in AI Standards

7.022 Based on a review of leading international institutions' AI standards,[26] common denominator principles include technical transparency, explainability and robustness. Each of these needs to be covered in contract clauses, which may be done by specific international standards or a bespoke drafting agreed between the parties.

(a) Technical transparency

7.023 Technical transparency refers to the use of unbiased machine learning algorithms, so that data does not intentionally or inadvertently embed biases into the process. To this end, there is a need to test continuously, because AI systems are complex. Even AI experts are not always able to easily understand how a machine learning algorithm reached its decision. Timothy Lanfear, a Solution Architecture Director at Nvidia, gave evidence to the UK House of Lords on AI technical transparency. His observations included the point that AI is often sufficiently complex that it cannot be grasped as a whole. He stated: 'what you can do is to break this down into pieces, find ways of testing it to check that it is doing the things you expect it to do, if it is not, take some action;'[27] A good example of opacity even at the expert level is neural networks.[28] A neural network applied to a *force majeure* clause is discussed later in this chapter.

7.024 From a contract counterparty investor viewpoint, managing the issue of biases can be achieved by the AI provider warranting in any service contract that the algorithm validation process has been subjected to a thorough quality control test to prevent discrimination.[29] This quality testing could be carried out by an appropriate in-house legal resource or by an external law firm.

7.025 A Supreme Court decision has set out a two-stage test on the risk assessments expected from any professional adviser regardless of the focus or sector.[30] Quality control tests need to check that products, recommended by an advisor to an investor, communicate (a) any material risks in the investment choices; and (b) any reasonable alternative. Material risks include biases

---

25 Alan Turing Institute conference, 'AI ethics in the financial sector', held in London, 16 July 2019. See https://www.turing.ac.uk/events/ai-ethics-financial-sector.

26 P Cihon (2019) contains a detailed summary of existing joint IEEE AI standards and joint ISO/IEC AI standards at p.19.

27 House of Lords (2018) *AI in the UK; Ready, Willing and Able?*, House of Lords Select Committee on Artificial Intelligence, at p. 37.

28 See Melanie Mitchell (2019) *Artificial Intelligence: A Guide for Thinking Humans* (UK: Pelican), at pp. 31–2.

29 Joint Slaughter and May and ASi Data Science white paper (2017) *Superhuman Resources, Responsible Deployment of AI in Business*, at p.19. See https://my.slaughterandmay.com/insights/dashboard/superhuman-resources.

30 See the two-stage subjective test in *Montgomery v Lanarkshire Health Board* [2015] UKSC 11, at paragraph 87.

existing when an AI system is initially provided or that emerge over time. The Supreme Court interprets that material risks include assessing whether the specific person being advised is likely to see the risks as significant. That interpretation of material risk implies the need for human-based communication between adviser and client, a point followed in an English High Court decision applying the same *Montgomery v Lanarkshire Health Board* two-stage test.[31]

To pass the two-stage test, the business owners of the robo-adviser would evidentially need **7.026** to show recorded communication with the individual client and provide sufficient written advice and risk warnings. These requirements are very likely to be too high a bar to meet for significantly underperforming AI automated-advice services. High Court judicial expectations on the two-stage test suggest the likelihood of future negligence lawsuits on the issue of AI robo-adviser risk assessments.

Those familiar with English common law negligence precedent may have expected the English **7.027** High Courts to apply an objective standard of judgement expected of any professional adviser, namely the *Bolam* test.[32] However, in both the Supreme Court *Montgomery v Lanarkshire Health Board* decision and in *O'Hare v Coutts*, the *Bolam* test was specifically rejected. The *Bolam* test requires proving that the advice given is on par with advice that would expected to be given by a reasonable practitioner at the same level of expertise as the person giving advice. In the future, it is conceivable that as robo-advice develops around international standards trusted by the English courts, the *Bolam* test could be applied on the basis of advice 'expected of a reasonable automated-advice service at the same level of expertise as the AI machine giving advice'. If that development occurs it would only make sense if an AI system can be accurately assessed at gradations of sophistication, akin to professional years of post-qualification experience in humans.

(b) Explainability

The second principle, explainability, can be incorrectly subsumed into the principle of technical **7.028** transparency.[33] In fact explainability is quite separate, referring to the obligation of AI suppliers to provide a rationale for decisions made by AI systems to clients and customers, so that each can trust the use of AI as an influential factor in some aspect of decision making – for example, in decisions on financial investments.[34] So, rather than a technical explanation, the AI provider summarises the information and logic behind a decision.[35] In this sense, the right to receive a meaningful explanation on AI decisions is similar to existing rights in the GDPR. Namely, Article 11 of the GDPR provides a right to 'an explanation of the decision reached after [algo-

---

31   See *O'Hare v Coutts* [2016] EWHC 2224 (QB), at paragraph 204.
32   *See Bolam v Friern Hospital Management Committee* [1957] 2 All ER 118.
33   The Alan Turing Institute and the Information Commissioner's Office (ICO) have jointly produced lengthy guidance on explainability. See The Alan Turing Institute and ICO (2020) *Explaining Decisions Made with AI*. The focus is on individuals, but given many clients can be private individuals it is a valuable source of collective knowledge. See www .ico.org.uk/media/for-organisations/guide-to-data-protection/key-data-protection-themes/explaining-decisions-made -with-artificial-intelligence-1-0.pdf.
34   International Regulatory Strategy Group at el (2019) *Towards an AI-powered UK: UK-based financial and related professional services*, at p.25.
35   Ibid House of Lords (2018), at p. 39.

rithmic] assessment'.[36] Further, Article 22 of the GDPR provides a 'right to an explanation' on how a decision was reached.[37]

7.029 A Bank of England Staff Working Paper persuasively argues that the concept of a meaningful explanation emerges from answering five questions:[38]

(1)   Which features mattered in individual predictions?
(2)   What drove the actual predictions more generally?
(3)   What are the differences between the machine learning model and a linear one?
(4)   How does the machine learning model work?
(5)   How will the model perform under new states of the world (that aren't captured in the training data)?

(c) Robustness

7.030 Third, to ensure each AI system is regularly assessed to mitigate any risks, there is a need for robustness. Traditionally, robustness includes the careful splitting of training data so that results that do not fit with anticipated or estimated results can be checked,[39] by which is meant that the algorithm is first trained with a sub-set of the training data. Subsequently the algorithm is applied to another sub-set of the data set. However, AI robustness requires more than test data splitting to be truly robust, because the nature of many machine learning methods applied in online environments can evolve.

7.031 Over time, either the way the algorithm responds, or the type of data, or both can change. Put succinctly, 'small changes to a [machine learning] system can be quickly replicated and deployed, with effects on a large scale'.[40] The way to detect and mitigate the risk of changes is by constant assessment and auditing[41] throughout their life cycles.[42] It is notable that the ICO's final guidance on AI in the context of data protection highlights the importance of identification and mitigation at the design stage of an AI system is likely to be the best practice approach. In this context AI robustness requires an increased rigour in the level of scrutiny to manage risk compared with traditional explicit rule-based algorithmic software systems.[43]

---

36   Financial Stability Board (2017) *AI and Machines Learning in Financial Services*, at p. 37. See www.fsb.org/2017/11/artificial-intelligence-and-machine-learning-in-financial-service.

37   For the full GDPR document in English see https://ec.europa.eu/info/law/law-topic/data-protection/eu-data-protection-rules_en#library.

38   Bracke, P. et al (2019) Bank of England Staff Working Paper No. 816 *Machine learning explainability in finance: an application to default risk analysis*, at p. 3. See www.bankofengland.co.uk/working-paper/2019/machine-learning-explainability-in-finance-an-application-to-default-risk-analysis.

39   Royal Society (2017), at p. 112.

40   Royal Society (2017), at p. 122.

41   See https://ico.org.uk/media/for-organisations/guide-to-data-protection/key-data-protection-themes/guidance-on-ai-and-data-protection-0-0.pdf.

42   Recent IOSCO and OECD reports have highlighted the need for on-going algorithm monitoring throughout the lifecycle of the AI model. See IOSCO (2020) *The Use of AI and ML by Market Intermediaries and Asset Managers*, Consultation Report, at p. 14. See www.iosco.org/library/pubdocs/pdf/IOSCOPD658.pdf; OECD (2019) Recommendation of the Council on Artificial Intelligence, see https://legalinstruments.oecd.org/en/instruments/OECD-LEGAL-0449.

43   Bank of England and FCA (2019), at p.6, where there is an extremely clear visual differentiation of explicitly programmed algorithms compared with machine learning algorithms.

3.   AI Allocation of Liability Chart

During contract negotiations between the supplier and user of an AI system, a reference chart,   **7.032**
as illustrated in Table 7.3, can assist to clarify any spoken or written communications on the
potential allocation of liability.

Table 7.3   *AI allocation of liability chart*

Liability issue	Party Allocation under Contract
Algorithm design	Service Supplier
Algorithm Validation and Model Testing	Service Supplier
Software Coding	Service Supplier
Training Data	User
Deployment in the Business of the User	User
Ongoing Audit for Algorithm Drift from Planned Aim	Service Supplier

4.   Drafting AI Standards in Contracts

Whatever the agreed clause detail on applicable AI standards covering technical transpar-   **7.033**
ency, explainability and robustness, it is important to underline that neither AI software nor
AI-derived data are the primary risk factors. Rather, it is human responsibility to avoid the
manipulation of hardware to misuse software and data. Put succinctly, 'it is not a specific technology (computers, tablets, mobile phones, online platforms, cloud computing and so forth),
but what any digital technology manipulates that represents the correct focus'.[44]

Every contract that includes AI in an augmenting role needs clauses that cover standards on   **7.034**
technical transparency, explainability and robustness. Drafting language that may cover all
three principles in a succinct style could apply text along the following lines:

'Principles of explainability, robustness and technical transparency shall apply throughout the   **7.035**
life cycle of all machine learning algorithms forming any part of the services in this Agreement,
from implementation to on-going monitoring. International standards applied to achieve this
continuous application are the current [insert international body's name] standards and any
updates.'

5.   Miscellaneous AI Risks to Cover in Contracts

(a) Trade secret risk exposure

With some AI services, a client stores its algorithm-based strategies on the AI provider's   **7.036**
database. In the situation of a customer wanting to keep their trading algorithm confidential,
this database storage presents the risk of trade secret exposure. Therefore, the contract needs
specific language on encryption standards, and for general data standards such as GDPR and

---

44   L Floridi and M Taddeo, *What is data ethics?* Phil. Trans. R. Soc. A, 2016, 374:
20160360, at p.3, http://dx.doi.org/10.1098/rsta.2016.0360.

equivalent laws to be applied to the database content and storage. Trade secret exposure introduces an important new risk, because leakage of a trading strategy could significantly reduce the revenue stream of a client.

(b) Key partner risk

7.037 Third, collaborations with first mover AI technology can present a 'key entity' risk. For example, a bank or fund manager may contract with Equbot (see earlier example) or an equivalent AI provider to market an investment index. Currently, Equbot is supported by the IBM Watson computer system. It is well known that IBM's Watson is a first mover in AI machine learning systems using Big Data. There is value in negotiating that if Watson is no longer supporting Equbot, the substitute AI technology is an equivalent system in terms of effectiveness and scale of data. In short, the absence of Watson, and any future unique cutting-edge AI systems, may present a key entity risk.

(c) Data risk

7.038 Finally, many AI software services rely on stock exchange data feeds and other current data sources. Therefore, there is an on-going risk of disruption to pivotal data feeds. The feeds may pause for hours or even days, caused by acts and omissions through no fault of the AI provider. Lawyers need to negotiate *force majeure* clauses on proportionate reduction in subscription service fee in response to temporarily paused service. Data feed disruption is not a new risk. Indeed, in capital markets that have been relying on indices for more than two decades, contract clauses cover this type of technical disruption. Nevertheless, the extent of the reliance is greater and potentially more significant in the context of AI augmentation services.

F. AI AUGMENTING CONTRACT CLAUSES AND PROCESSES

7.039 A key question to answer is: how can AI augment, supplement or support the formation and management of a contract? The three examples summarised in Table 7.4 include specific reference to either due diligence process or contract clauses. A logical sequence to this discussion is to cover first, the due diligence process of signing a high-value contract; second, the management of a key contract clause, applying the example of a *force majeure* clause; third, the process of a close-out calculation clause as part of a master agreement termination payment.

Table 7.4   AI applied to contract clauses and due diligence

Clause or Process	AI Example	Consequences of AI Model Malfunction
Due diligence checking of authorised signatory lists against the signature(s) on the contract	AI image recognition of contract signatures against authorised signatory lists	A signature is not a fundamental requirement in a contract under English law, but the market practice of authorised signatory lists means that any unauthorised signatures raise doubts on contract validity.
Force Majeure	AI prediction of hurricanes and typhoons	Two risks: • mistaken pre-emptive termination of contract with a requirement to pay damages and associated costs; • an incorrect prediction that no force majeure event would occur, resulting in a reduced judicial expectation that the frustrated party was able to mitigate.
Close-out methods in ISDA Master Agreements	AI calculation of termination payments	Breach of contract with a requirement to pay damages and associated costs. If the client is a 'private person', the potential imposition of a large fine by the FCA for violating s.138D Financial Services Act 2000.

1. AI Image Recognition of Authorised Contract Signatures

Under English law, and indeed in many of the other leading capital market jurisdictions,[45] **7.040** a valid contract does not require a physical wet ink signature. An electronic signature is equivalent to a physical signature 'when it performs a similar function'.[46] Financial Technology (FinTech) companies might gravitate towards the obvious efficiency of electronic signatures. However, many multinational corporations, central banks, investment banks, institutional fund managers, institutional hedge funds, multilateral development banks and sovereign wealth funds will continue to rely on physical ink signatures to enter into high-value trading platform, equity, fixed income and derivatives agreements.

As mentioned earlier in this chapter in the section on contract principles of English law, there **7.041** is a fundamental requirement of an intention to create legal relations. In a written contract this is typically when both parties have to sign. By convention, most high-value contracts are likely to be made effective on the signing of a physical ink signature by one or two authorised signatories. For board directors and risk function managers this is a valued speed bump before committing to a highly detailed document that will be relied on for potentially thousands of trades.

In addition to legal arguments on the certainty of enforcing the contract, there are clear market **7.042** reputation risk issues if any bank-regulated financial services firm or listed company has actual or perceived contract management weaknesses.

It is sensible to mitigate the risk of a counterparty potentially arguing that the contract was **7.043** invalid because an unauthorised person signed it. The traditional human steps are generally threefold:

(a)   Check if the authorised signature list sent by the other contracting party is valid;

---

45   This principle is mirrored in many other global capital markets, including Hong Kong, Singapore and the State of New York.

46   S Mason (2016), *Electronic Signatures in Law* (Cambridge: CUP), 169.

(b)   Check that the relevant authorised signatory in step 1 has authority to sign for the specific type of contract and monetary amount;

(c)   Check if the authorised signatory's signature recorded on the list in step 1 matches the signature on the final draft contract.

7.044   These three steps take a human between three and ten minutes to complete, but a mistake in just one step potentially makes the contract invalid or at best its enforceability unclear. Further, it would open the business to potential lawsuits based on negligence. Simultaneously, businesses do not want to waste valuable human resources on processes an AI system can complete in seconds. For large banks and fund managers that continuously sign new contracts and amend existing ones, the time saved by automating verification processes equates to many hours per annum. The consistency and quality of scanning devices and software make steps 1–3 ideal tasks for AI. Further, considerable AI investment and subsequent advances have focused on text and handwriting recognition. Many different algorithms and machine learning techniques have proved to be effective at reducing error rates, depending on the chosen AI approach, to a range between 0.5 and 2 per cent.[47] Therefore, the prospect of a 99.5 per cent solution already exists.

7.045   A machine learning program can be implemented to compare the draft final contract signature of one party against the same party's authorised signatory list. Thereafter, an automatic email confirmation can be sent to the authorised signatory confirming:

7.046   'Re: XYZ Contract with Abacus Bank plc: Authorised Signatory List Valid; Scope of Authority Verified; Signatures Match – Proceed to Sign.'

7.047   Initially, it would be an uncomfortable change for any authorised signatory to sign their name on a high-value contract when the three-step checking process has been 100 per cent delegated to an AI program without any human supervision. If the AI program makes an error then the in-house legal function would be forgiven for worrying they may be potentially negligent. However, acceptance that the AI computer will not be 100 per cent correct needs to be made explicit and recorded as part of the IT legal risk policy of the bank, broker, fund manager or hedge fund. By recording the tolerance of failure in a range between zero and 0.5 per cent, the expectation of human responsibility for this important but mundane task is removed. Higher percentage tolerance standards can be set for very high-value contracts, for instance at or below 0.4 per cent.

7.048   An additional dimension of routine checking tasks is the opportunity cost of doing something that requires unique human analysis. When an authorised signatory checking task typically takes a human 3–10 minutes to complete, employing AI presents the chance, cumulatively over a year, for lawyers to do considerably more analytical legal work.

7.049   Further, contract signature recognition is literally the tip of the AI iceberg. For example, JP Morgan, with an annual IT budget exceeding $11 billion,[48] has already introduced image

---

47   S Russell and P Norvig (2010), *Artificial Intelligence* (London: Pearson), 753–8.

48   J.P. Morgan 2019 Annual Report, at p.20. See www.jpmorganchase.com/corporate/investor-relations/document/annualreport-2019.pdf.

recognition machine learning into the legal analysis of credit agreements, with considerable success.[49] In 2017 JP Morgan implemented an unsupervised learning image recognition program to review 12,000 credit agreements, a task that requires approximately 360,000 hours to complete. The JP Morgan machine learning system – called COIN, short for Contract Intelligence – completed the task in seconds, and with greater accuracy compared with humans. It is very likely that other similar AI initiatives will increasingly become components of other leading banks and fund management legal function software tools.

2.   AI Prediction of *Force Majeure* Events

Imagine that the parties to a commercial contract have agreed on a *force majeure* clause that **7.050** includes cyclones as a qualifying *force majeure* event. In many civil law systems *force majeure* is defined in statute. In contrast, under English law it is undefined in statute, but generally treated as a broad concept of 'events beyond the control' of the parties that entitle the cancellation or suspension of the contract.[50] For example, any extreme storm can suspend or restrict trading in capital markets, including commodities, energy, equities and derivatives products linked to these assets. Further, extreme storms can cause billions of dollars of insurance policy claims covering damage to businesses and infrastructure across a whole economy.

Annually recurring extreme storm events include tropical cyclones, which typically occur **7.051** between 5 and 30 degrees of the equator when the sustained winds reach 119kph or higher.[51] In the USA such an event is usually referred to as a hurricane, and in East Asia as a typhoon. When travelling over urban areas, cyclones are likely to cause loss of electricity supply, potential trading platform disruption and even the closure of stock exchanges for a few days.

Cyclones are forecast and monitored by satellites for several days before they pass over urban **7.052** areas.[52] There is a complex interplay among air velocity, density, humidity, pressure and temperature. Further, the difficulty of predicting the centre of a cyclone, the damaging eye of the storm, cannot be underestimated, because the path of each can be highly influenced by surrounding competing weather systems, especially prevailing winds that can alter its direction at short notice.

Contract parties can mutually agree that when a machine learning computer algorithm predicts **7.053** a 90 per cent confidence that a storm will pass over a specified urban area within 24 hours, the *force majeure* clause can be relied on. The party relying on a *force majeure* clause must factor in two aspects. First, the frustrated party relying on the *force majeure* clause has the burden of proof.[53] Second, English courts expect the frustrated party to specifically prove there were no reasonable steps to avoid or mitigate non-performance.[54] Therefore, a logical way of providing

---

49   See https://cms.law/en/gbr/publication/banking-on-ai-in-financial-services, at p.4.
50   See Chitty on Contracts (OUP 2019), 3rd ed, 15-152. The effect of a *force majeure* clause is a matter of construction. See G Treitel (2014) *Frustration and Force Majeure*, 3rd ed (London: Sweet & Maxwell), at 12-026.
51   www.oceanservice.noaa.gov/facts/cyclone.html.
52   For examples of infrared satellite images that really capture the formation of a cyclone see the US Joint Typhoon Warning Center images at www.meteoc.navy.mil/jtwc.html.
53   *Chitty on Contracts* (Vol 1, 2018), 1229.
54   *Mamidoil-Jetfoil Greek Petroleum Co SA v Okta Crude Refinery AD* (No.2) [2003] EWCA Civ 1031.

clarity on the timing of attempted mitigating steps is for both parties to agree to an AI clause that includes words along the lines of:

7.054   '*Force Majeure* includes market disruption caused by a cyclone reaching or exceeding 119kph over the metropolitan area of [insert city name] based on the 24-hour predictions of mutually agreed machine learning methods.'

7.055   Diagram X illustrates how a machine learning neural network system predicts when a tropical cyclone qualifies as a *force majeure* event. To develop a mutually agreed machine learning algorithm, the first task is to introduce initial training data inputs on past cyclones ('Training Data'). Off the coasts of Florida, Louisiana and North Carolina there is a hurricane season, and off the Korean peninsula there is a typhoon season. This example applies equally to these two regions.

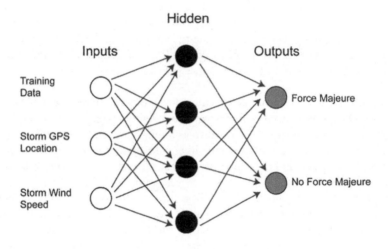

Figure 7.1   *A neural network predicting a force majeure event*

7.056   Assume that, based on a trusted Korean or US government meteorological scale of 1 to 10, a No. 8 or higher storm is a *force majeure* event. However, many cyclones may approach an urban area as a No.8 but, on reaching the urban area, change direction or subside to below the *force majeure* level.[55]

7.057   The Training Data is inputted to the machine learning neural net structure. The Training Data is made of results the algorithm can confidently rely upon as examples of:

(a)   correctly predicted No.8 cyclones over the relevant urban area;

(b)   No.8 cyclones off coastal areas that decrease to below 119kph over the relevant urban area;

(c)   No.8 cyclones off coastal areas that bypass the relevant urban area.

---

55   Figure 7.1 is adapted from Y Wilks (2019), *AI: Modern Magic or Dangerous Future* (HotScience), 76. Yorick Wilks is Emeritus Professor of AI at Sheffield University and has been researching machine learning for nearly half a century.

More precisely, the Training Data inputs would include: **7.058**

(a)   average forward travelling speed of No.8 cyclones, so that a time to landfall notice period expressed in hours can be predicted.[56]

(b)   examples when cyclones monitored 24 hours away from an urban area with wind speeds at or above 119kph remained at No.8 when passing over the urban area;

(c)   examples when cyclones monitored eight hours away from an urban area with wind speeds at or above 119kph[57] remained at No.8 when passing over the urban area.

(a) Backpropagation of errors

Crucially, the Training Data is improved by the backpropagation of errors achieved by an   **7.059** algorithm that responds to the output data. The 'backward propagation of errors' (shortened to backpropagation or backprop) refers to the transmission of error information provided by the neural networks output calculations based on the data. An error rate is calculated and transmitted back through the neural network before the next iteration.[58] The backpropagation algorithm is based on a calculus formula called gradient descent of a cost function.[59] At the highest level of abstraction, the essential aspect of the calculations can be described as:

error rate = actual output - expected output

The *error rate* is calculated from the output and immediately transmitted back through the   **7.060** neural network so that the result can alter weights in one or more network layers before the next output calculation is made. Applied correctly, backpropagation is a key benefit of supervised machine learning, and has been described as inspired by the human brain's ability to make calculations, spot errors and learn from the errors when next calculating in a process of improvement – learning from mistakes.

The neural network can assist in predicting if a *force majeure* No.8-level cyclone event is likely   **7.061** to occur. This predictive calculation provides additional proof that a potentially frustrated party to a contract monitored the risk, then decided that no mitigation was necessary at certain time periods before an unexpected *force majeure* event because of the predicted lower wind storm speed over the urban area or predicted storm path away from the urban area; or, alternatively, that the computer predicted a No.8 storm over the urban area and the frustrated party could take timely mitigating action based on this prediction.

Computerised weather forecasting has supported meteorology for more than 50 years.   **7.062** However, tropical cyclones often develop over remote parts of an ocean, which makes it especially difficult to collect data relevant to determining the dimensions of the storm and adjacent influencing weather systems. Therefore, the additional use of AI-derived predictive data shows that, beyond visual tracking of the typhoon's path by satellite imagery and all other means of observation, a frustrated contract party used objective, high-quality predictive data as part of

---

56   The speed at which a whole cyclonic storm travels varies but it is moving quite slowly compared with wind speeds within the storm.

57   The wind speed is measured based on the maximum sustained wind speed over one minute.

58   Michael Wooldridge (2020) *The Road to Conscious Machines: The Story of AI* (London: Pelican Books), at p. 183.

59   A full explanation of backpropagation requires university-level calculus. Those seeking such an in-depth mathematical explanation, see Michael Nielsen, *Neural Networks and Deep Learning* http://neuralnetworksanddeeplearning.com.

its decision making to mitigate, if necessary, before the *force majeure* event. For instance, if the AI probability data recorded a 90 per cent chance of a No.8 level storm passing over the urban area in the next business day, that is independent, objective evidence on which reasonable steps to avoid or mitigate its results can be made. A court may expect a frustrated party reading the 90 per cent chance prediction to rationally take reasonable mitigating steps. Conversely, if the AI probability data recorded a 30 per cent chance of a No.8 level storm passing over the urban area, then a court is very unlikely to expect any mitigating steps by a potentially frustrated party.

7.063 For some readers advising continuously on cutting-edge legal technology issues, the above application of machine learning will not seem futuristic in nature. In fact, there already exists a proven, more sophisticated AI extreme storm prediction model. As published in a 2019 paper in *Nature's Scientific Reports*,[60] a deep learning system has been developed to predict (a) the location of each typhoon's centre passing over the Korean peninsula; and (b) the shape of the typhoon's cloud structures. In the earlier example of GPS location and wind speed applied to the Korean Peninsula and US East Coast, only the eye of either a hurricane or a typhoon is predicted. In contrast, this actual deep learning model, based on data from 76 typhoons over the Korean peninsula, additionally predicted the structure of the rain clouds. If rain clouds can be predicted accurately, that provides vital information on likely flood damage to an area. Future insurance contracts could legitimately expect corporate policy holders, for example central business district building owners in flood-prone locations, to mitigate imminent *force majeure* events based on predicted rain cloud content of cyclones.

7.064 The *Nature Scientific Reports* published results show this AI deep learning model was able to predict 42.4 per cent of typhoon centres with absolute errors of less than 80km. The average error was 95.6km. The notice period provided by this machine learning system was based on six-hour intervals. However, with more satellite images the prediction period can be extended. From a contractual viewpoint, robust contract clause drafting may sensibly include words along the lines of: 'Parties agree to the use of machine learning methods or equivalent AI approaches that accurately predict the trajectory and velocity of any tropical cyclone including its embedded cloud structures.'

7.065 In summary, the triggering of a *force majeure* event is based on independent machine learning-based prediction of cyclone over an urban area. A precise, mutually agreed AI-driven prediction of a *force majeure* event supports the frustrated party's duty to mitigate action in the hours before such an event occurs. By applying the AI algorithm, the duty to mitigate is objectively triggered. The quantitative prediction of an imminent *force majeure* event provides a mutually agreed notice period for the frustrated party to mitigate the situation. The potentially frustrated party is increasing the sophistication of any decision to mitigate or not because of AI.

7.066 Some capital markets contracts do contain waiting period clauses that prevent a frustrated party from acting to terminate a contract based on a *force majeure* event.[61] So in those situations

---

60   Rüttgers et al (2019) 'Prediction of a typhoon track using a generative adversarial network and satellite images', Scientific Reports, https://www.nature.com/articles/s41598-019-42339-y.

61   An example of a waiting period is standard language in an ISDA 2002 Master Agreement based on eight business days. See ISDA Master Agreement Section 5(b)(ii) on Force Majeure together with its Section 14 definition of Waiting Period.

the machine learning predictions would not assist mitigation. However, such a waiting period would not typically apply if compliance, delivery or payment is required on a specified date, an aspect common to many derivatives contracts.

Applying AI, the *force majeure* clause is triggered with less scope for parties to dispute if there **7.067** was justification to trigger the clause. Any consequent arbitration, litigation or mediation is enhanced with objective, quantitative evidence. AI machine learning tools potentially provide nuanced decisions on when it is reasonable to avoid or mitigate, and when not to mitigate a potential *force majeure* event. Richard and Daniel Susskind have succinctly captured the great advantage of such machine-driven early warning systems in their observation that 'knowledge can be deployed not just in addressing problems as they arise but in pre-empting problems in the first place or in containing their escalation'.[62]

3.   AI Calculation of Termination Payments

ISDA (the International Swaps and Derivatives Association), the trade association for deriva- **7.068** tives, publishes a 'Master Agreement' that is globally the most used master framework agreement between parties that include banks, fund managers, hedge fund managers, pension funds and traders. It is therefore a suitable test case for the analysis of AI in complex, high-value contract management across diverse sectors.

ISDA Master Agreements are entered into not only by financial services firms, but also by **7.069** a wide variety of corporations who are typically seeking to hedge commodity prices, currencies and interest rates. There are numerous standard ISDA contract clauses found across three versions of the ISDA Master Agreement, namely versions 1987, 1992 and 2002, and linked ISDA annexes and schedules.

Arguably, many of the clauses in an ISDA Master Agreement can also be found in different **7.070** forms in other trading agreements. Indeed, other trading agreements follow the structural approach of the ISDA architecture, such as the Global Master Securities Lending Agreement (GMSLA), the market-standard contract for stock lending.[63]

From a litigation viewpoint it is notable that the English courts have produced a series of **7.071** judgments concerning ISDA Master Agreements that place a high priority on the content of the written contract. Several cases refer to the stance that the ISDA Master Agreement 'should as far as possible, be interpreted in a way that serves the objectives of clarity, certainty and predictability, so that the very large number of parties using it should know where they stand'.[64] Further, in the scenario of agreed but conflicting terms of business and an ISDA Master

---

62   R Susskind and D Susskind (2017) *The Future of the Professions: How Technology Will Transform The Work of Human Experts* (Oxford: OUP), at p. 226.

63   The author of GMSLA is the International Securities Lending Association (ISLA). See www.isla.co.uk/legal-services.

64   *Lomas & Ors v JFB Firth Rixson & Ors* [2010] EWHC 3372 (Ch), at 54. Most recently this principle of interpretation was restated by the Court of Appeal in *CFH Clearing Ltd v Merrill Lynch International* [2020] EWCA Civ 1064 (14 August 2020).

Agreement in place, the English Courts have held that ISDA 'must prevail, as a comprehensive, subsequent and specifically applicable set of contractual terms'.[65]

7.072 The example here concerns clauses covering the calculation of close-out remedies. Not only can these clauses be complex, but also they can sometimes diverge from ordinary English contract law principles. For example, an analysis of contract termination under ISDA contracts requires applying market practice on their treatment and specific ISDA-related court decisions rather than a wider scope to apply all contract law precedent and comparative interpretation of contract clauses from other business agreements. The majority of these ISDA contracts are subject to English law, but if not English law then New York law. In short, both market custom concerning ISDA clauses and case law dealing with different versions of ISDA contracts matter.

7.073 A recurring area of dispute in the English High Court and the New York Court, has been an inability of ISDA contract parties to agree on the termination payment calculation of money owed to a non-defaulting party. What often makes capital markets markedly different from other sectors is the constant, often minute-by-minute movement of assets prices and potential liquidity challenges. These factors, among many others, make calculating a termination payment open to different approaches and subsequent divergent answers.

7.074 Table 7.5 below sets out the three established close-out calculation methods found globally in thousands of ISDA contracts. The definition of each is lengthy,[66] so the contents of Table 7.5 only summarises aspects relevant to each to illustrate how AI could be deployed to add greater efficiency and more trust to the termination payment process.

Table 7.5 *Three calculation methods in ISDA Master Agreements*

Calculation remedy method	Key mechanics of each contract clause
Loss	Standard clause in the 1992 ISDA version. Non-defaulting party makes its own calculation 'reasonably and in good faith' without duplication. The use of market quotes is not a requirement.
Market Quotation	Standard clause in the 1992 ISDA version. Non-defaulting party obtains quotes from four leading dealers of the highest credit rating. Highest and lowest quotes are ignored, and the mean of the middle quotes applies. For example, if £4, £6, £8 and £10 are quoted, then based on 6+8/2, the Market Quotation answer is £7. In the event that only three quotes were obtainable, the middle quote applies. If less than three quotes are obtained, the Market Quotation method cannot be used.
Close-Out Amount	Standard clause in the 2002 ISDA version, replacing Loss and Market Quotation. The Party specified as the Determining Party may consider, without limitation, market quotes, yield curves and volatilities. The Determining Party can also obtain market quotes internally, a point of recurring importance given the Determining Party is often an international bank.

---

65   *Marz Ltd v Bank of Scotland Plc* [2017] EWHC 3618 (Ch) (5 December 2017) at 60. The context of this judgment was a swap agreement, but it is likely that in other manifest conflict clause scenarios the specific ISDA Master Agreement takes precedence over the terms of business.
66   The full ISDA 1992 definition of Loss comprises 245 words, and that for Market Quotation 435 words.

The AI program would provide a cross-checking role in the following way: **7.075**

1. If the parties have opted for the Loss Method in the ISDA contract, the AI program would seek three market quotations. If the AI program could not obtain three quotes, then its default output would be two leading dealer[67] quotes and one other quote.

Further, it would be consistent with market practice and regulation for all three quotations to follow best execution principles found in MiFID II (the Second European Markets in Financial and Instrument Directive) that require factoring in the characteristics of specific execution venues.[68] Under MiFID II, best execution is a detailed set out rules setting out duties owed to obtain the best possible result for clients. So both parties agreeing similar venue criteria as part of an AI program augmenting ISDA close-out methods makes sense. That task requires taking into account a number of variables, including charges, clearing reliability, creditworthiness, default protections, execution regulation quality in the relevant jurisdiction and speed of execution.

2. In the event that the parties have opted for the Market Quotation Method in the ISDA contract, the AI program would also seek three market quotations from three leading dealers. If the AI program could not obtain three leading dealer quotes, then its default output would be two leading dealer quotes and one other quote. Historically the Market Quotation requirement of at least three quotations from leading dealers has proven to be difficult to satisfy in volatile markets. So there is logic in having the AI program seek out only two leading dealer quotes, plus one other quote.
3. If the parties under the 2002 ISDA Master Agreement opted for the Close-Out Amount, the AI program would provide a cross-check against the Close-Out Amount, again ideally with three leading dealer market quotations. If the AI program could not obtain three leading dealer quotes, then its default output would be two leading dealer quotes and one other quote.
4. The AI program would generate a clear summary report, including information on the range of quotes, the mean figure and other risk information, such as the credit rating of the market maker.
5. The summary report would be encrypted and the encryption key would only be released to the contracting parties after the relevant calculation party had first sent its own calculation, whether based on Loss, Market Quotation or Close-Out Amount, to the other party. A commercial mediator would be recorded in the ISDA Schedule as the instructed mediator paid jointly by both parties to provide the AI-generated quotations and a summary report. This same mediator would provide an encryption key on receipt of the party-generated calculation. City law firms experienced in ISDA agreement are logical choices to perform this AI program management and mediating role, tasked with holding the encryption key in escrow.

In sum, the benefit of the parties agreeing to an AI program augmenting the contractually   **7.076**
agreed close-out calculation method is threefold. First, the AI program is contributing

---

67   For those less familiar with ISDA contracts, the formal definition of 'leading dealers' is set out in the *ISDA* 1993 definitions section under the term Reference Market-makers, at p. 16.
68   MiFID II Art 27(5), available at https://eur-lex.europa.eu/legal-content/EN/TXT/PDF/?uri=CELEX:32014L0065& qid=1600675197743.

a neutral, third party calculation that both parties can trust. Second, the automatic initiation of the AI market quotation and report would reduce the delay between the early termination date of the contract and payment to the non-defaulting party. Third, while the AI program market quotation results would be only indicative and not conclusive, the existence of a neutrally calculated summary report is likely to decrease recourse to litigation. If despite the AI summary report litigation still occurs, the presiding judges will have a valuable evidential record on obtainable quotes at the relevant time.

7.077   It is important to also mention that the practice of applying a cross-checking principle already exists for Loss and Market Quotation calculations under English law in the context of contracts when deliveries or payments are to be made after the Early Termination Date. In the leading case of *Anthracite Rated Investments v Lehman Brothers*, it was stated that 'Loss and Market Quotation are, although different formulae, aimed at achieving broadly the same result, so that outcomes derived from one may be usefully tested by way of cross-check by reference to the other'.[69]

7.078   This example of AI augmenting the process of close-out calculation has not, to date, been applied by two parties to an ISDA contract. However, it inevitably will be. For instance, the global law firm Linklaters, through its technology start-up company Nakhoda,[70] is currently collaborating with ISDA on smart contracts.[71] The automation of smart contracts that include AI applications and close-out calculations are an obvious area for automation where both efficiency and reasonableness are key aims.[72] Further, ISDA has already published a detailed paper on smart contracts that includes reference to the automation of calculations and close-out processes.[73]

4.   Key Questions to Answer on Any AI Augmentation

7.079   Taking into account all the foregoing points in this chapter, it is clear that machine learning will continue to (a) be an increasingly important component of prediction software services, and (b) augment the automation of contract clauses and related due diligence processes. Key questions that can form part of legal risk management tasks to mitigate potential harmful consequences from both activities include the following.

- Who is the coder of automated aspects of the contract?
- In plain English, define the risks and the risk levels of the machine learning algorithm?

---

69   *Anthracite Rated Investments (Jersey) Limited v Lehman Brothers Finance S.A.* [2011] EWHC 1822 (CH)[116(1)].

70   www.nakhoda.ai/isda.

71   A smart contract is defined as 'an automatable and enforceable agreement. Automatable by computer, although some parts may require human input and control. Enforceable either by enforcement of rights and obligations or via tamper-proof execution of computer code'. See CD Clack, VA Bakshi and L Braine, (2016) 'Smart Contract Templates: foundations, design landscape and research directions', Revised March 15, 2017, available at: arxiv.org/pdf/1608.00771 .pdf.

72   Clack, C. and McGonagle, C. (2019) 'Smart Derivatives Contracts; the ISDA Master Agreement and the automation of payments and deliveries'. Available at Xiv190401461_2019.

73   ISDA (2019) 'Legal guidelines for smart derivatives contracts: introduction'. Many international lawyers have contributed to this publication. See www.isda.org/a/MhgME/Legal-Guidelines-for-Smart-Derivatives-Contracts -Introduction.pdf.

- What are the assumptions, biases and weights processed by the algorithm?
- What evaluation mechanism is used to detect when a machine learning algorithm output has changed to trigger a review of the system's robustness?[74]
- What is the English law and UK regulation governing the insertion and operation of automated processes?
- Under the finalised EU Artificial Intelligence Act have all the rules relevant to the risk level of the machine learning model been evaluated?[75]
- What are the specific algorithms being used to automate processes in the contract?
- What is the identification code or number assigned to uniquely identify each algorithm?
- How often are the algorithms reviewed to prevent delays, drift or malfunctions?
- Is the machine learning system certified for cyber security?
- Is any algorithm or other AI-linked innovation causing or contributing to disorderly market behaviour?[76]
- Have all relevant data protection laws been evaluated in the context of AI under the Data Protection Act 2018, the GDPR or non-European equivalent rules?
- What aspect, if any, of the commercial contract is outsourced to a service provider relying on AI? Is the automation of processes specifically covered in the liability clauses?
- Which personnel are responsible for implementing algorithms?
- How are machine learning applications and individual director duties approved by the board?[77]

G. CONCLUSION

A thread woven throughout this chapter has been eliminating or mitigating the gap between **7.080** planned and actual outcomes for businesses, clients and customers in the context of contracts. All AI applications have, at least at inception, been set up by a human or groups of humans that have coded and provided a flow of large data for computers to process. In my view, AI is comparable to Daniel Kahneman's[78] view of one part of the human brain providing 'fast thinking', with automatic problem solving via the application of algorithms to vast volumes of data – although AI differs from any human brain because of its relentless speed of execution, which is perhaps suitably termed 'super-fast thinking'.

---

74   This question is a paraphrase from the Technical Robustness and Safety section of 'The Assessment List for Trustworthy AI' published by the European Commission High-Level Expert Group, July 2020, available at https://ec.europa.eu/digital-single-market/en/news/assessment-list-trustworthy-artificial-intelligence-altai-self-assessment.

75   The final draft proposals of the EU's Artificial Intelligence Act (AIA) were published in April 2021. Expect the final AIA rules, including any changes, to be made effective before Q2 2023. It is likely that many regulated firms exploiting machine learning will rationally need to factor in these rules at the design process phases. Not least because under Article 71(3) of the AIA, in some scenarios the consequences of breaching certain sections of the AIA is a fine based on 6 percent of group turnover. See EC COM (2021) 206 final 2021/0106(COD).

76   Under MiFID2, Art 17 firms involved in algorithmic trading must avoid any such activity. See https://eur-lex.europa.eu/legal-content/EN/TXT/PDF/?uri=CELEX:32014L0065&qid=1600675197743.

77   Under sections 173 and 174 Companies Act 2006, directors must exercise independent judgement with reasonable care, skill and diligence.

78   Daniel Kahneman (2013) *Thinking, Fast and Slow* (New York: Farrar, Straus and Giroux).

7.081 Yet no matter how fast AI performs, it is an unconscious contributor to a software program designed by a human software engineer. Only humans provide conscious 'slow thinking', to plan for an inference or result. Currently, only humans perform the 'slow thinking' to read through the obligations and rights of a contract. Combined, the conscious humans involved in commercial contract drafting and computer programming are the ultimate responsible actors.

7.082 There is also the often unforeseen nature of systemic risks, as seen leading up to and through the Global Financial Crisis of 2008–9. Arguably, the concentration of vast data, machine learning expertise and payment services platforms among Big Tech companies presents a new systemic risk based on multifarious forms of credit to consumers and SMEs.[79] The responsibility for safe AI is part of legal due diligence and contract clause drafting. Lawyers have an on-going duty not only to provide clients with the best and safest contractual outcomes linked to AI, but also to minimise situations that may cumulatively result in market instability.[80]

---

79 Whether Chinese, European, multinational or US in origin, the Big Tech companies that present the most risk are the entities with the largest payment services customer bases, made up of both individuals and SMEs.

80 For financial services sector readers specifically interested in asset manager, bank, or FinTech firm machine learning risks, see Sheridan, I. (2022) *Financial Regulation and Technology* (London: Edward Elgar Publishing).

8

COMMERCIAL TRADE

Minesh Tanna and William Dunning[1]

A. INTRODUCTION

AI has the potential to transform practically every area of commerce and trade. Forecasts suggest that by 2030 AI could contribute up to USD 15.7 trillion to the global economy, which is more than the current output of China and India combined.[2] In many areas, these effects are only now starting to be felt. **8.001**

In this chapter we consider the different ways in which AI can be applied in commerce and trade, and some of the legal risks that this might create. Many of the legal risks and challenges posed by the use of AI in this context are covered elsewhere in this book. This chapter focuses on the interaction between AI and the law of agency, the risks posed by the marketing of AI technology and the possible conflicts of law issues to which AI might give rise. **8.002**

---

1   With thanks to Irina Iolysh, Emily May and Maja Planinsic for their extensive assistance with the research for this chapter.

2   '*Sizing the prize. What's the real value of AI for your business and how can you capitalise?*', PwC, https://www.pwc.com/gx/en/issues/data-and-analytics/publications/artificial-intelligence-study.html, last accessed 03 January 2021

B. USE OF AI IN COMMERCE AND TRADE

8.003 AI has been described as the 'new electricity'.[3] Just as electricity transformed the way in which industries functioned in the past century, proponents argue, AI will transform society over the coming century. Indeed, AI and machine learning, the technology underpinning most current AI systems, have the potential to be applied throughout the supply chain, in almost all industries and sectors. This section provides a brief overview of some of the ways in which these technologies are already being applied, and are likely to be applied in the near future.

C. RESEARCH AND DEVELOPMENT

8.004 Some of the most notable successes of AI and machine learning to date have been in the research and development of new products and services. Successes have been particularly notable in the healthcare and life sciences sector: AI is increasingly being deployed as part of the drug discovery process by the pharmaceuticals industry,[4] while Google's AI firm DeepMind recently launched an algorithm, AlphaFold, to predict protein structures – one of biology's grandest challenges – that has been hailed as having the potential to transform life sciences.[5]

8.005 The use of AI for research and development poses particular challenges from an intellectual property law perspective, which are discussed in detail in Chapter 12. Distinguishing features of AI technology are discussed in detail in Chapter 4.

1. Manufacturing

8.006 The use of 'robots' to automate manufacturing processes is not new. However, the potential of AI to lead to improvements in manufacturing goes beyond the use of machines to carry out the physical tasks once performed by human employees. There are numerous possible applications of AI and machine learning technologies in manufacturing. Recent advances have focused on the use of AI technologies to monitor and improve the efficiency of production processes, for example, including:[6]

(a) *Maintenance.* AI can be used to predict and mitigate the failure of manufacturing equipment, reducing downtime. For example, a manufacturer may monitor data from a manufacturing asset to predict when maintenance or replacement is necessary, thereby reducing maintenance costs.

(b) *Process optimisation.* AI can be used to monitor data from manufacturing processes and production variables to identify ways in which processes can run more efficiently. For

---

3   Shana Lynch, '*Andrew Ng: Why AI Is the New Electricity*', Insights by Stanford Business, 11 March 2017, www.gsb .stanford.edu/insights/andrew-ng-why-ai-new-electricity, last accessed 03 January 2021.

4   David Freedman, '*Hunting for New Drugs with AI*', Nature, 18 December 2019, www.nature.com/articles/d41586-019 -03846-0, last accessed 03 January 2021.

5   Ewen Callaway, ' '*It will change everything': DeepMind's AI makes gigantic leap in solving protein structures*', Nature, 30 November 2020, https://www.nature.com/articles/d41586-020-03348-4, last accessed 03 January 2021.

6   Capgemini, '*Scaling AI in manufacturing operations: a practitioners' perspective*', Capgemini Research Institute, www .capgemini.com/research/scaling-ai-in-manufacturing-operations/, last accessed 03 January 2021.

example, a manufacturer may be able to identify the optimal configuration of its equipment to maximise production or minimise energy consumption.

(c)   *Quality control.* AI technologies such as image recognition can be used as part of the quality control process. For example, a manufacturer may use computer vision technologies to spot defects in their products.

In the longer term, among other things, AI also has the potential to allow manufacturers to enable on-demand production of custom-made goods for specific consumers.[7]   **8.007**

2.   Logistics and Transport

The complexity of international supply chains and logistics networks offers an excellent opportunity to implement AI systems. Again, there are numerous possible ways in which AI could be used to improve logistics and transport, chiefly focusing on increasing the efficiency of networks and reducing downtime. These include: **8.008**

(a)   *Automated warehouses.* AI can be used both to optimise inventory and transportation in warehousing operations, but also, increasingly, to automate routine tasks in warehouses. For example, UK supermarket Ocado has made headlines with its automated warehouses, in which its robotic system can prepare up to 65,000 customer orders per week.[8]

(b)   *Autonomous vehicles.* Self-driving cars have been one of the most talked-about implementations of AI systems. However, autonomous vehicles for logistics, including both trucks and ships, are likely to have a dramatic impact on the logistics industry. Autonomous vehicles will, in principle, enable logistics assets to operate around the clock, and they also offer the possibility of controlling traffic and reducing congestion in cities.[9]

(c)   *Demand prediction.* AI systems can be used to predict the supplies and goods that businesses will need in the future. The use of AI systems, either to automate more routine forecasting work or to assist human decision-makers, is already having a significant impact on logistics management. Indeed, in many cases, AI systems already outperform human experts.[10] This reduces costs and allows businesses to manage their inventories more efficiently.

Although some of these uses of AI in logistics and transport, particularly in autonomous vehicles, are likely to appear only in the longer term, they are likely to have a dramatic impact on logistics operations.   **8.009**

---

7   Anand Rao and Gerard Verwei, '*Sizing the prize. What's the real value of AI for your business and how can you capitalise?*', PwC, www.pwc.com/gx/en/issues/data-and-analytics/publications/artificial-intelligence-study.html, last accessed 03 January 2021.

8   Zoe Kleinman, '*The Ocado robot swarms that pack your shopping*', BBC, www.bbc.co.uk/news/technology-43968495, last accessed 02 February 2021

9   Anand Rao and Gerard Verwei, '*Sizing the prize. What's the real value of AI for your business and how can you capitalise?*', PwC, www.pwc.com/gx/en/issues/data-and-analytics/publications/artificial-intelligence-study.html, last accessed 03 January 2021

10   Jim Guszcza and Nikhil Maddirala, '*Minds and machines: The art of forecasting in the age of artificial intelligence*', Deloitte, www2.deloitte.com/us/en/insights/deloitte-review/issue-19/art-of-forecasting-human-in-the-loop-machine-learning .html, last accessed 02 February 2021

3. Retail

8.010 As with logistics, AI systems offer retailers the possibility of more accurately predicting customer demand and therefore of managing their inventory more effectively. In addition, AI systems give retailers the opportunity to offer their customers a more personalised experience, both in the form of customised products and by tailoring the customer experience.

8.011 The potential advantages of using AI systems in retail can already be seen in the approaches adopted by large online retailers, such as Amazon, which already offers customers a highly personalised experience. These services offer tailored product recommendations to customers and then utilise AI systems to optimise other stages of the customer experience, such as paying for goods.

8.012 These features of online retail will become increasingly prevalent in real-world retail operations. Image recognition technology, in particular, offers the possibility of reducing reliance on traditional point of sale systems and instead allowing an AI system to 'see' what a customer is buying, allowing them to check out quickly and efficiently. Amazon has already trialled physical stores without checkout tills and recently announced plans to open at least 30 such shops in the UK.[11] Facial recognition technology can also be used to measure customer engagement in a retail environment and, for example, deliver real-time targeted advertising.

8.013 The data generated from the use of AI systems in retail also offers valuable opportunities for retailers to analyse their operations, generating additional business insights. However, holding customers' personal data in the context of such systems may create legal issues, particularly from a data protection perspective, as discussed in detail in Chapter 10. A detailed treatment of retail business models is contained in Chapter 17.

4. Financial Services

8.014 The use of AI in financial services has already had a substantial impact on the industry and has contributed to the rise of a generation of innovative technology companies, which are increasingly challenging well-established incumbents. Forecasts suggest that financial institutions in particular may be able to realise as much as USD 1 trillion in cost savings from the use of AI by 2030.[12] There are numerous possible uses of AI in financial services, including:

(a) *Customer service.* Traditional customer services in financial services – often involving physical branches and call centres – have limited economies of scale. AI offers the possibility of automating customer services and delivering substantial efficiencies. AI chatbots, for example, are increasingly being used to deliver routine customer services, such as answering questions and performing account services.

(b) *Decision-making.* AI systems offer financial institutions the opportunity to automate routine decision-making, allowing faster, more consistent and, potentially, more accurate

---

11   Sabrina Barr, *'Amazon "plans to open at least 30 physical shops in the UK"'*, Independent, www.independent.co.uk/life-style/amazon-uk-shops-go-open-launch-jeff-bezos-a9651231.html, last accessed 02 February 2021.

12   The Financial Brand, *'Artificial Intelligence and the banking industry's $1 trillion opportunity'*, https://thefinancialbrand.com/72653/artificial-intelligence-trends-banking-industry/, last accessed 02 February 2021.

decisions. For example, banks can use AI to automate loan application processes, quickly assessing large amounts of data to determine whether and how much to lend, while asset managers and hedge funds have already been using algorithms to trade for more than a decade.

(c) *Fraud and money laundering detection.* Financial institutions are increasingly turning to AI to assist with fraud and money laundering detection. These issues present major challenges to the financial services sector. In 2019/20 the UK Financial Ombudsman Service received nearly 11,000 complaints from individuals who had fallen victim to banking fraud, while firms continue to be subject to strict anti-money laundering and terrorist financing requirements.[13] AI systems have the potential to analyse a wide range of data to detect fraudulent or suspicious transactions quickly and accurately.

The use of AI systems in financial services does, however, lead to a number of distinctive legal risks. Financial institutions should be particularly aware of how their uses of AI interact with their regulatory obligations, which are discussed in detail in Chapter 15, and also consider whether their uses of AI have the potential to lead to biased and discriminatory outcomes, as discussed in detail in Chapter 22.   **8.015**

5. Commercial Contracts

Throughout the value chain, AI also has the potential to change the way firms contract, allowing them to create and maintain contracts more effectively and efficiently. The management and maintenance of large numbers of contracts presents a significant challenge to firms, which may otherwise struggle to organise, manage and update the numerous heterogenous contracts they must keep track of.[14] AI systems increasingly offer a solution to this issue, including through: **8.016**

(a) *Contract management.* AI systems can be used to analyse, extract and organise key features from large numbers of contracts, such as clauses, parties and key dates (for example, renewals and terminations), thereby allowing firms to manage them more effectively and efficiently. An AI system may then, for example, be able to warn firms when contracts are due for renewal or when they can be terminated.

(b) *Consistency of contracts.* The capability of AI systems to analyse large numbers of contracts may also help firms to improve the consistency of their contracts. For example, AI may be able to ensure that 'confidential information' is appropriately defined in all of a firm's contracts and to manage any variations from that definition.[15] Managing small variations between large numbers of contracts can be a huge task, but is one with which AI systems are well suited to assist.

(c) *Risk analysis.* AI systems can also be used to assess the risk associated with contracts, reducing the need for costly and time-consuming due diligence processes. AI systems

---

13 Financial Ombudsman Service, '*Lessons from the past, ambitions for the future: Our 2019/20 complaints data analysis*', https://www.financial-ombudsman.org.uk/data-insight/insight/analysis-annual-complaints-data-2019-20, last accessed 02 February 2021.

14 Beverly Rich, '*How AI is changing contracts*', Harvard Business Review, 12 February 2018, https://hbr.org/2018/02/how-ai-is-changing-contracts, last accessed 02 February 2021.

15 Beverly Rich, '*How AI is changing contracts*', Harvard Business Review, 12 February 2018, https://hbr.org/2018/02/how-ai-is-changing-contracts, last accessed 02 February 2021.

are already being used to identify high-risk contracts or clauses so that human review of contracts, for example in M&A, can be targeted at those contracts likely to pose the greatest risk.

8.017 The use of AI to assist in the development and management of contracts does not necessarily mean that there will be less work for lawyers. Many organisations currently have such vast numbers of contracts that effective human oversight and management is impractical. Instead, the use of AI systems is likely, at least in the short term, to assist lawyers by allowing them to shift their focus from routine activities to more high-value work.[16]

6. AI and Agency

(a) Legal concept of 'agency'

8.018 Agency is a relatively complex legal area, although the basic concept is straightforward:

> where one person, the principal, requests or authorises another, the agent, to act on his behalf, and the other agrees or does so, the law recognises that the agent has power to affect the principal's legal position by acts which, though performed by the agent, are to be treated in certain respects as if they were acts of the principal.[17]

8.019 Agency relationships exist all around us. In many cases we are aware that we are entering into a legal relationship through an agent; in other cases, it is less clear. Agency relationships are particularly important, and frequently encountered, in commerce and trade. For example, many producers of goods or services will appoint an agent to market or sell those goods or services on their behalf. There are many good reasons for this, not least that the producer may not have the relevant experience to be able to market or sell its goods or services as effectively as the agent.

(b) Difficulties of agency in AI context

8.020 The fundamental issue of applying agency law in an AI context is that, generally speaking (and certainly under English law), an agent must be a natural or legal person. Save for very limited exceptions, AI is not recognised as having any legal personality and cannot therefore legally constitute an agent. Whether or not that should remain the case is a frequently debated issue,[18] but one which is beyond the scope of this chapter.

8.021 The fact that AI is not generally recognised as having legal personality raises interesting questions in relation to agency because sophisticated AI systems can operate in a similar way to an agent. In particular – and which is a unique feature of AI systems (as compared with traditional deterministic computer systems) – AI is capable of acting autonomously.

8.022 This capability means that it is less straightforward, both conceptually and legally, to attribute the actions of an AI system to the legal or natural person involved in its development or deployment. This is in contrast to a non-AI system where, as was recognised by the Singapore

---

16   Beverly Rich, '*How AI is changing contracts*', Harvard Business Review, 12 February 2018, https://hbr.org/2018/02/how-ai-is-changing-contracts, last accessed 02 February 2021.
17   Bowstead and Reynolds on Agency, 22nd ed. at 1-005.
18   See, for example, Chesterman, S., '*Artificial Intelligence and the limits of legal personality*', International and Comparative Law Quarterly, 2020, 69(4), 819–44.

International Commercial Court in a recent case, 'in circumstances where it is necessary to assess the state of mind of a person in a case where acts of deterministic computer programs are in issue, regard should be had to the state of mind of the programmer of the software'.[19]

This creates a tension because, while AI cannot legally be considered an agent, AI systems are operating with increasing autonomy and are increasingly being used to conduct trade and create legal relationships on behalf of legal or natural persons (the 'principal'), in the same way as an agent.   **8.023**

One of the key issues arising out of this tension is liability, that is, allocating legal responsibility for acts or omissions of the AI system. Liability in an AI context is addressed elsewhere in this book and is therefore only briefly discussed here, using three specific scenarios in an agency context.   **8.024**

Scenario 1: AI system unforeseeably creates legal relations

Under English law, a principal will generally be bound by a contract entered into by its agent. However, where that agent acts outside the scope of its authority in entering into such a contract, the principal will not be bound and legal responsibility for the relevant contractual obligations will lie with the agent.   **8.025**

It is not beyond the realms of possibility that an AI system, entrusted to enter into legal relations on behalf of a particular organisation, does so in unforeseeable circumstances. For example, an AI system used to negotiate the renewal of a mobile phone contract with a consumer or to issue a new insurance policy to a customer could agree terms which the organisation would not have been willing to agree and which, at least as it understood the position, the AI could not agree.   **8.026**

In these circumstances, the fact that the AI system cannot lawfully be distinguished from the organisation (that is, as an independent agent) means that the organisation will, contrary to its expectations, be bound by the bargain entered into by the AI system with the third party.   **8.027**

Scenario 2: AI system unforeseeably causes loss to a third party

In a related scenario, there is a risk that an AI system that acts in an unforeseeable way causes harm to a third party, whether physical or (more likely) financial. Under English agency law, where an agent causes harm in these circumstances, either the agent will be liable to the third party (with the principal falling out of the picture, at least for liability purposes) or the principal will be liable to the third party while being able to claim separately against the agent.   **8.028**

In an AI context, there is a significant risk that the organisation that deploys the AI system (that is, the principal) will be liable for the harm caused to the third party, notwithstanding that it did not foresee the AI system acting in this way. The organisation may have a claim against the developer of the AI system, although that is unlikely to be a straightforward claim.   **8.029**

---

19   *B2C2 v Quoine Pte* [2019] SGHC(I) 3 at [211] per Thorley J.

Scenario 3: AI system used by multiple 'principals' acts in an unforeseeable manner

8.030   Finally, it may be the case that a single AI system is used by multiple organisations (or 'principals' in an agency context); for example, a flight booking system operating on behalf of various airlines.

8.031   A system of this sort which is based on deterministic programming is very unlikely to act in an unforeseeable manner because the parameters or rules by which the system makes its decisions will (or at least should) be apparent to the various organisations relying on the system. However, an AI system used to perform the same task carries the risk that it makes a 'rogue' decision; for example, by booking a customer onto a flight with Airline A when it was perhaps envisaged by all the airlines that, in the particular circumstances, the customer would be booked onto a flight with Airline B.

8.032   In this scenario, there is also a conceptual difficulty in establishing who (if anyone) is liable for this mistake. Again, it may be that a claim could be brought against the developer of the AI system, but that would not be straightforward. If the mistake had been made by a legal or natural person in these circumstances, then attributing the liability to that person would appear to be the natural consequence. However, the use of an AI system again creates complications in attributing liability and, perhaps more importantly, in providing a form of redress to the party suffering harm arising out of this mistake.

7.   Marketing and AI 'Washing'

(a) The attractiveness of the 'AI' label in marketing

8.033   The marketing of a particular product or service is an integral part of commerce and trade. Due to its relatively recent proliferation, and its reputation as a revolutionary new form of technology, 'AI' has become a buzzword in sales and marketing messaging. It has been said that the 'AI halo effect […] gives a reflected shine to any tech company that invokes the concept of artificial intelligence'.[20]

8.034   This is not just anecdotal: the venture capital firm MMC undertook research into AI start-up companies and found that the AI label attracts between 15 and 50 per cent more funding than other technology-focused start-ups.[21] It is reasonable to infer from this that the AI label will have similar capabilities when used in marketing messaging in a sales context.

(b) AI washing

8.035   A potentially significant reason why the 'AI' label seems to be increasingly used in marketing messaging is the lack of consensus about its meaning. A consistent theme which emerges from other chapters in this book is that there is still considerable uncertainty about what AI actually is, reflecting a broader lack of societal understanding about how the technology works and what distinguishes it from other similar forms of technology. AI is also often used as an umbrella term, encompassing various forms of the technology, for example machine learning and natural

---

20   James Vincent, '*No, this toothbrush doesn't have artificial intelligence*', The Verge, www.theverge.com/2017/1/4/14152004/toothbrush-artificial-intelligence-smart-gadgets-ces-2017 (last accessed 02 February 2021).

21   MMC, '*The state of AI 2019: Divergence*', www.stateofai2019.com/ (last accessed 02 February 2021).

language processing. It is also, to a certain extent, a dynamic concept; what was considered 'AI' in the 2010s may now be considered as more sophisticated automation. As the US academic Douglas Hofstadter has said, 'AI is whatever hasn't been done yet'.

The fact that AI is inherently vague, combined with its status as a buzzword, is likely to lead to   **8.036** the AI label being exploited in sales and marketing messaging. Technologies which may barely use or be said to be based on AI will be marketed as 'AI technologies' and systems which may incorporate only a small AI component and which are otherwise based on traditional, deterministic programming are likely to be sold as 'AI systems'.

This trend is referred to as AI 'washing'. It involves the practice of giving products or services   **8.037** the 'AI' label when there is in fact no AI involved, which results in customers (and consumers in particular) being misled as to the nature of the product or service they believe they are purchasing. The term has its origins in the similar practice of organisations giving a false or misleading impression about their environmental efforts, referred to as 'greenwashing'.

AI washing is not just a myth. The MMC research referred to above found that, in the case of   **8.038** 40 per cent of European AI start-ups, there was no evidence of any AI in the solutions that they were offering. This may at first glance appear to be a large percentage but, given the attractiveness of using the AI label and the uncertainties about its meaning, it is perhaps unsurprising.

The existence of AI washing is perhaps also reflective of the fact that, generally speaking, it does   **8.039** not (yet) carry the risk of any sanction. There are not, for example, widespread legal frameworks in place to regulate the way in which AI is marketed. Indeed, as is discussed elsewhere in this book, there is relatively little AI regulation generally.

There are in many jurisdictions, however, regulations which govern the marketing or advertis-   **8.040** ing of products or services more generally. There is at least in principle, therefore, a legal basis on which AI washing could be regulated. The issue, however, which is likely to militate against the effective enforcement of such regulations in the context of AI washing is, again, the lack of a consistent definition of AI. Based on our current understanding of AI, it seems doubtful that a regulator would have the confidence and credibility to hold an organisation to account on the basis that it was giving a false or misleading impression, through its marketing messaging, about its use of AI, save in a particularly obvious or egregious case.

That is not to say that the position will not change. If the trend of AI washing continues, regu-   **8.041** lators (such as the Advertising Standards Agency in the UK) are likely to come under pressure to use the legal frameworks available to them to prevent this practice.

(c) Advertising Standards Agency

The Advertising Standards Agency (ASA) and its sister organisation, the Committee of   **8.042** Advertising Practice (CAP), are responsible for the regulation of advertising in the UK. The CAP has long maintained a code – the UK Code of Non-broadcast Advertising and Direct &

Promotional Marketing (the CAP Code) – which contains both general and industry-specific marketing rules.[22]

8.043 The first rule of the CAP Code – Rule 1.1 – states that 'Marketing communications should be legal, decent, honest and truthful'. Section 3 of the CAP Code, which relates to 'misleading advertising', also contains similarly broad rules, including:

(a)   Rule 3.1, which says: 'Marketing communications must not materially mislead or be likely to do so'; and

(b)   Rule 3.11, which says: 'Marketing communications must not mislead consumers by exaggerating the capability or performance of a product.'

8.044 Interestingly, the current version of the CAP Code – which came into force in September 2010 – contains rules which were specifically introduced to regulate greenwashing. Section 11 of the CAP Code, entitled 'Environmental claims', contains:

(a)   Rule 11.1, which says: 'The basis of environmental claims must be clear'; and

(b)   Rule 11.2, which says: 'The meaning of all terms used in marketing communications must be clear to consumers.'

8.045 In principle, these rules (or similar rules) are capable of being applied to the regulation of AI marketing. Rule 11.2 could be particularly useful in the short term – while there is still some uncertainty about what AI means to consumers – since it puts the onus on the organisations marketing AI to ensure that their messaging is clear.

8.046 The CAP Code demonstrates that there is, or can be, a framework to regulate the marketing of AI. Whether the ASA, and other regulatory bodies, will use these frameworks to prevent the practice of AI washing remains to be seen.

8.047 In the meantime, where misleading marketing messaging causes financial loss to an organisation, there is the possibility of obtaining redress through a private civil law action. The possibility of bringing such an action (an example of which is discussed below) may act as a disincentive on organisations disseminating potentially misleading marketing messaging in the context of AI.

(d) Misrepresentation

8.048 Under English law, where a party enters into a contract in reliance on a statement made prior to the contract by another party (for example in the form of marketing messaging or perhaps during pre-contractual negotiations), and where that statement later transpires to be false, the party that relied on the statement can bring a civil claim against the other party to recover damages for any losses suffered as a result of the false statement. This action is typically referred to as 'misrepresentation', although it is similar to the concepts of 'misstatement' or 'mis-selling'.

8.049 A misrepresentation claim can be attractive where a contractual claim is not possible or is rendered more difficult due to certain contractual protections (limitations on liability, for

---

22   Committee of Advertising Practice Code, www.asa.org.uk/codes-and-rulings/advertising-codes/non-broadcast-code .html (last accessed 02 February 2021).

example). That said, commercial contracts often restrict the ability of the contracting parties to bring misrepresentation claims through an 'entire agreement' clause, which may say that the parties agree that they have not relied on any statements in entering into the contract, thus removing one of the essential elements of a misrepresentation claim.

In these circumstances, the only way to bring a misrepresentation claim is generally by alleging **8.050** that the statement or representation was made fraudulently (which can include recklessness). If the claimant party is able to prove fraud in this context, then any contractual protections fall away, leaving it open for the claimant to bring a misrepresentation claim.

By way of a hypothetical example, take a software developer that has developed a product that **8.051** uses natural language processing and machine learning to predict stock market trends and to recommend trades. If the developer markets the product as being 'a machine learning solution that becomes more accurate with every trade' and, in reliance on that statement, a customer purchases the product, only to find that its performance deteriorates over time (perhaps due to changes in the stock market or in the data being analysed by a system for which it has not been trained), then the customer may well seek to bring a misrepresentation claim against the developer. The customer may even be able to demonstrate that the developer acted fraudulently or recklessly in making this statement, which could overcome any contractual hurdles in bringing such a claim.

(e) Future of AI marketing

The marketing of AI products will remain an important part of commerce and trade in the **8.052** AI industry. The AI label will become more prominent in marketing messaging, reflecting the increased adoption of AI but also, at least in the short term, the fact that AI is a buzzword which attracts attention.

Over time, and particularly as our understanding of AI improves, the marketing of AI products **8.053** is likely to become more accurate. Indeed, there is likely to be a shift away from the use of 'AI' as an umbrella term towards more particularity about the specific form of AI that is being marketed.

Nevertheless, legal issues around the marketing of AI are bound to arise, whether in the form of **8.054** regulatory issues or through private civil law actions. These issues will be fuelled by the practice of AI washing and the attractiveness of using the AI label in marketing messaging.

8.   Conflict of Laws

Private international law, and the concept of 'conflict of laws', is the part of a national legal **8.055** system that establishes rules for dealing with cases involving a foreign element, such as a contract with a foreign party. The rise of the internet and the accompanying exponential increase in international communication has raised significant issues for conflict of laws rules. In the past it was generally quite straightforward to determine where acts giving rise to legal consequences occurred; for example, where a product was made, sold or purchased. Now, online transactions are likely to involve parties in numerous jurisdictions, as well as technological infrastructure – such as the servers on which a website is hosted – in other jurisdictions. This complexity can make it far more difficult to determine which legal systems are relevant.

8.056 The range of laws with which a legal person may be expected to comply when engaging online is not static; rather, it depends on context. If, for example, an individual in country W sends an email to a person in country X, relating to a person in county Y, which is sent via a server in country Z, then the laws of at least those four countries – W, X, Y and Z – will be relevant.[23] Similarly, if an individual in country X buys a product online from a retailer in country Y, which is delivered in country Z, then the laws in all three countries will be relevant. If something goes wrong with such a sale, it may prove difficult to then work out, for example, under which law the sale was made or where any damage to the product occurred.

8.057 The conflicts of law issues raised by internet technology are likely to be exacerbated by the involvement of AI. The ability of AI systems to act autonomously, and unpredictably, may mean that an AI system engages foreign laws that the developers or deployers of that AI system did not anticipate being subject to. Such inherent unpredictability would inevitably make it more difficult for those using AI to determine which jurisdictions' laws will apply and therefore to ensure compliance with all relevant laws. The involvement of various different parties in the creation and operation of AI systems – for example, different entities that may be involved in the development, training, deployment and use of an AI system – could further complicate any conflict of laws analysis.

8.058 These difficulties relate not only to the substantive laws to which the actions of an AI system might be subject, but also to the conflict of law rules determining which countries' substantive laws will apply. The conflict of laws rules of different jurisdictions are highly heterogenous and can depend, *inter alia*, on the countries of residence of legal persons, the country in which damage occurs, the choice of law of the parties and other factors connecting the contract or tort in question to a particular jurisdiction.[24] This may mean, for example, that two different countries' conflict of laws rules both indicate that their own law should apply to the same transaction. Moreover, different conflict of laws rules often apply in respect of different areas of law. The EU, for example, has different conflict of laws rules for contractual and non-contractual obligations, as well as bespoke frameworks for particular areas of law such as product liability.

8.059 The involvement of AI systems in commercial relations, taken together with the heterogenous conflict of laws rules in the various jurisdictions in which that AI system may operate, is therefore likely to lead to uncertainty regarding the appropriate law to apply to the actions of such AI systems. This could have numerous consequences: in addition to the resolution of disputes, conflict of laws rules are relevant to the tax frameworks and financial and consumer regulations, as well as general statutory provisions to which those using the AI systems may become subject.

8.060 Further complications are likely to arise if and when jurisdictions start to apply the concept of legal personality, or related concepts such as agency, to AI systems (as discussed in Section C above). While AI systems are, at least from a legal perspective, effectively indistinguishable

---

23   Dan Jerker B. Svantesson, '*A Vision for the future of private international law and the internet – can Artificial Intelligence succeed where humans have failed?*', Harvard International Law Journal, https://harvardilj.org/2019/08/a-vision-for-the -future-of-private-international-law-and-the-internet-can-artificial-intelligence-succeed-where-humans-have-failed/, accessed 03 January 2021.

24   See, for example, Regulation (EC) No 593/2008 of 17 June 2008 on the law applicable to contractual obligations (Rome I) and Regulation (EC) No 864/2007 of 11 July 2007 on the law applicable to non-contractual obligations (Rome II).

from the person using them, it should remain possible to attribute their actions to that legal person. Where, however, AI systems start to be treated as independent legal actors or agents, existing conflict of laws frameworks may have limited application. The EU's Rome I and Rome II regulations, for example, address the liability of natural persons, and of companies and other bodies, whether incorporated or unincorporated, but it is left to national law to determine which entities have the requisite legal personality.[25] The complexity of applying conflict of laws rules in an AI context is only likely to increase as different countries develop heterogenous rules in relation to the agency and legal personality of AI systems.

This is a complex and evolving area of law. Those deploying AI systems with the capability to enter contracts, or with the potential to otherwise have a legal impact on legal persons, should consider carefully which legal frameworks are likely to apply to the actions of those AI systems. It is likely that the coming years will see increasing divergence in the way in which different countries legislate and regulate for AI. Given the often inherently international nature of AI systems, this challenge should not be overlooked by those developing or deploying AI.   **8.061**

D. CONCLUSION

This chapter has addressed the ability of AI to transform practically every area of commerce and trade. Indeed, as evidenced by the various examples referred to in this chapter, it is clear that AI is already having a material impact in some of these areas. As with any new form of technology, the law and regulation governing trade and commerce has not yet caught up to reflect the use of AI in the areas discussed in this chapter, although this is expected to change in the near future.   **8.062**

In the meantime, the use of AI in commerce and trade presents various legal risks. For example, the increasing importance of AI technology will raise issues in the law of agency (as well as legal personality), it is already testing law and regulation on marketing and advertising, and it is likely only to complicate the application of frameworks of public international law. AI will inevitably raise further legal issues in the ever expanding world of commerce and trade.   **8.063**

---

25   Articles 19(1) and 19(2) of Rome I; Articles 23(1) and 23(2) of Rome II.

9

AGENCY AND LIABILITY

Jason G Allen

A. INTRODUCTION

9.001 This chapter sets out an approach to liability when AI systems function in a manner that causes harm. As we see throughout this book and elsewhere, AI in some form or other is currently being deployed across a broad spectrum of use cases. Because it is a general-purpose technology, seminal developments in the law governing AI will develop under specific heads of liability in the existing law. Given the breadth of these use cases, the diversity of the technologies being applied in them and the broad focus on 'liability' under very different heads of law in different legal systems, this chapter will focus on the general principles that guide imposition of liability in constellations that include human and non-human autonomous components generally.

9.002 Consistent with this focus on principles, this chapter approaches the concept of 'liability' broadly as well, for example encompassing doctrines of public law accountability as well as the more typical case of tortious or criminal liability. The focus is thus on forms of harm that sound in damages in contract or tort; that trigger a liability under some consumer protection, corporate governance, anti-discrimination or privacy regime; that attract criminal liability; or that provide a basis for some public law accountability mechanism such as judicial review.

9.003 When thinking about the law and governance of AI, however, it is also important to keep in mind harms that might not be adequately addressed by existing heads of legal liability. For example, cases where an AI system causes harm to the natural environment (say, the atmosphere) or to a complex system (say, the financial markets) may point to areas in which socially and economically relevant harms do not translate directly (enough) to a head of legal liability.

146

In the context of systemic risks, in particular, the growth of AI underlines the weaknesses of existing liability regimes and adds a new layer of complexity.[1]

To a certain extent, 'liability for AI' is subject to the old 'law of the horse' critique – that is, **9.004** that we should avoid the proliferation of niche fields of law that are technology-specific and focus instead on principles that apply across different factual scenarios and structure traditional law school curricula, such as tort and contract.[2] Thus, what we need is not a law of *autonomous* vehicles (AVs) but to develop the law governing vehicles. It is important not to overstate this critique;[3] Lawrence Lessig is right that general principles are sometimes best developed from thinking about particular problems, such as how 'law' and 'cyberspace' connect – or, in our case, how apparent actions by AI systems interact with established frameworks governing liability.[4] But the warning to keep our eye on general principles rings true. This chapter thus attempts to trace overarching principles that will guide future developments and help us to order them *post hoc* into a coherent framework within the relevant fields of law such as contract, tort, crime, anti-trust, consumer protection, privacy law, corporate governance law or administrative law.

Despite a burgeoning literature on the regulation of AI, relatively little attention has been paid **9.005** to the fundamental question of whether (and thus how) existing legal doctrines apply to AI. The nub of the issue, according to Yavar Bathaee, is that legal doctrines are generally based on assumptions about human conduct, and may not apply well in situations without a human actor.[5] (To discuss situations with a *non-human actor* would beg the central question.) Nowhere is this truer than in those branches of law governing the liability of one person to another. These doctrines restrict the scope of liability – life as we know it would be untenable if every harm generated a legal liability – and reflect deep-seated intuitions about what it means to be a rational agent subject to law, for example the rule of law principle that laws should be knowable to allow subjects to modify their behaviour accordingly. Most issues in liability for AI are variations on this theme.

This chapter adopts the definition of AI presented in Chapter 1 at Part 7. It will focus on AI **9.006** systems based on 'deep' machine learning technologies, which construct models on the basis of large historical data sets and then produce outputs in new cases based on those models.

The structure of this chapter is as follows. Section B describes the central problem in liability **9.007** for AI, the 'black box problem', and sets out some of the main reasons why AI poses problems for conventional liability doctrines. Section C presents three key concepts necessary to develop

---

1   See e.g. Andreas Engert, 'Why Manager Liability Fails at Controlling Systemic Risk' in Bertram Lomfeld, Alessandro Somma and Peer Zumbansen (eds), *Reshaping Markets: Economic Governance, the Global Financial Crisis and Liberal Utopia* (Cambridge University Press 2016).

2   See F.H. Easterbrook, 'Cyberspace and the Law of the Horse' (1996) *University of Chicago Legal Forum* 207.

3   Judge Easterbrook's paper was written for a conference on 'Property in Cyberspace', and his answer was essentially that property in cyberspace was a 'law of the horse' – we should focus, instead, on developing general principles of intellectual property law. Currently, the status of digital objects is a live question in property law, and efforts are underway to develop the law of digital assets – an overdue task on which more substantial progress should have been made in the 1990s and 2000s.

4   See Lawrence Lessig, 'The Law of the Horse: What Cyberlaw Might Teach' (1999) 113 *Harvard Law Review* 501, 502.

5   Yavar Bathaee, 'The Artificial Intelligence Black Box and the Failure of Intent and Causation' (2018) 31(2) *Harvard Journal of Law & Technology* 889, 890–891.

sound doctrines of AI liability, namely the concept of an *artefact*, the concept of *agentivity* and the concept of *attribution*. Section D explores the future development of liability doctrines and suggests that the main consideration should be the relation between opacity and human supervision. Section E suggests that there is a fundamental – and conceptual – legitimacy gap in the application of opaque of AI systems in public administration. Section F concludes.

9.008   Each of the various technologies used to create AI will present different problems for the application of conventional liability doctrines. For example, a source of liability in a deep learning-based AI system might be the failure to provide an appropriate training data set. Indeed, there is now a well-established scholarly literature on algorithmic bias[6] and a number of documented cases of AI systems being trained to produce biased outputs because of latent biases in their training data. For example, a system built by Amazon to recruit software engineers was trained on historical data sets in which most software engineers were men, and the machine effectively inferred from this that male candidates were preferable.[7] This chapter will focus on AI systems that utilise some form of deep learning, as they seem to be the most likely to raise legal liability issues in the near to medium term and because opacity is an inherent rather than a contingent feature.

B. THE 'BLACK BOX PROBLEM'

9.009   In its recent report, the Independent High Level Expert Group on Artificial Intelligence appointed by the European Commission identifies a number of features of emerging technologies, including AI systems, that potentially affect the application of existing law. These include complexity, opacity, openness, autonomy, predictability, data-drivenness and vulnerability.[8] All of these features potentially bear on the liability question. Autonomy obviously goes to the heart of the question. The vulnerability of AI systems to hacking or technical failure may be an important consideration in determining if the creator, owner, or operator of the AI system is liable – where appropriate precautions have been taken against a breach, for example, it may not be appropriate to impose liability on the operator of a system at all. The openness of AI systems stemming from their self-learning nature, reliance on external data sources and need for continuous updates also confounds traditional liability analysis.

9.010   The problem of opacity – what we might call the 'black box problem' – is particularly important in the context of deep learning-based AI technologies because it is not necessarily apparent what processes are actually being developed by the system's algorithms to derive answers from the training data. This chapter will focus on the black box problem because it provides a useful

---

6   See Eirini Ntoutsi *et al*, 'Bias in Data-driven Artificial Intelligence Systems: An Introductory Survey' (2020) 10(3) *WIREs Data Mining and Knowledge Discovery*.

7   See Jeffrey Dastin, 'Insight – Amazon scraps secret AI recruiting tool that showed bias against women' (*Reuters Technology News*, 10 October 2018), https://in.reuters.com/article/amazon-com-jobs-automation/insight-amazon -scraps-secret-ai-recruiting-tool-that-showed-bias-against-women-idINKCN1MK0AH.

8   Expert Group on Liability and New Technologies – New Technologies Formation, *Liability for Artificial Intelligence and other emerging digital technologies* (European Union 2019), 32, available at URL: https://ec.europa.eu/transparency/ regexpert/index.cfm?do=groupDetail.groupMeetingDoc&docid=36608.

context in which to explore certain key issues without getting lost in the detail of specific AI systems or specific liability regimes in particular jurisdictions.

Opacity is a problem because the law does not impose liability for *every* harm that one person   **9.011** causes another – it generally imposes liability only for *unlawful* harm, and many forms of harm (such as harms caused competition in the marketplace or by publishing truthful information) do not trigger any liability at all. Because the ideal-typical person is a human, and because the ideal-typical law is meant to control the behaviour of persons in the future through promulgating word-based rules according to which they can plan their lives, the state of mind of the human actor plays a central role in most liability regimes. For example, in English law I am only liable in tort for harms I have caused intentionally or negligently, which usually entails that I am only liable for harms that were foreseeable to the reasonable person in my situation at the time. I am only liable in criminal law for harms I cause with the requisite *mens rea*, which usually implies a degree of consciousness, volition and some shade of moral turpitude. Where strict liability regimes exist, they are exceptional – generally creatures of statute that date from the era of industrial mass-production of consumer goods and new technologies.

The requirements of intent and causation are already complicated in the context of group   **9.012** agents such as corporations, as the relevant state of mind has to be imputed from one or more individual humans to the group agent. The 'problem of many hands', for example, means that it is often difficult to identify the fault element in complex organisational structures.[9] Such problems could compound where the relevant action by a corporate manager (for example) was to deploy an AI system created and maintained by a third party. Variations also arise within constellations where an employer is responsible for those in its employment, known in the common law context as vicarious liability.

Bathaee usefully sets out a taxonomy of different types of intention doctrine and causation   **9.013** doctrine. By reference to numerous examples from US law – across the spectrum including criminal law, tort law, capital markets law, consumer protection law and others – Bathaee demonstrates that the majority of intent and causation doctrines are likely underinclusive in the context of AI systems. Bathaee rejects two approaches to solving this set of problems – (i) regulating the degree of transparency required in operational AI systems and (ii) imposing strict liability on those who put such systems into operation. Instead, he suggests a 'sliding scale' approach whereby conventional intent and causation tests are modified based on the level of AI transparency and human oversight in the circumstances of the case:

> Specifically, when AI merely serves as part of a human-driven decision-making process, current notions of intent and causation should, to some extent, continue to function appropriately, but when AI behaves autonomously, liability should turn on the degree of the AI's transparency, the constraints its creators or users placed on it, and the vigilance used to monitor its conduct.[10]

Where an AI system is given complete autonomy (for example to trade in a securities market),   **9.014** the threshold for liability should be lower and evidence of poor constraints, design and limita-

---

9   See D.F. Thompson, 'Designing Responsibility: The Problem of Many Hands in Complex Organisations' in Joroen van den Hoven, Seumas Miller and Thomas Pogge, *Designing Ethics* (Cambridge University Press 2017).
10   Yavar Bathaee, 'The Artificial Intelligence Black Box and the Failure of Intent and Causation' (2018) 31(2) *Harvard Journal of Law & Technology* 889, 894.

tions on data access should weigh more heavily in favour of liability. On the other hand, where an AI system is designed to assist a human being in making a decision or performing a task, the human's intent or the foreseeability of the effects of the AI's decision should weigh more heavily and the constraints on the algorithm, the nature of the design or the data available to the AI algorithm should play a lesser role in the question of liability.[11] This suggests that the characteristics of AI may require a fundamental rethink of how the law operates doctrinally in order to ensure the normative and policy objectives the law serves.

9.015   The black box problem points to the need to 'keep humans in the loop' for the purposes of liability. To the extent that the law is focused on the action (or inaction) of human beings that is conscious, intentional and causative, and to the extent that we reject the approach of treating AI systems as legal agents in their own right, effective liability regimes for AI will depend on effective rules of attribution and on ensuring systems architecture (and business models) that facilitate rather than discourage attribution of liability.

9.016   This is a critical area where the law of liability for AI can go right or go wrong. One seminal example is the 2018 killing of Elaine Herzberg by a self-driving Uber vehicle in Arizona. Ms Herzberg was crossing the road, not at a zebra crossing, while walking her bicycle. The AV's algorithms reportedly detected Ms Herzberg six seconds before it hit her, but was confused as to whether she was a bicycle or a pedestrian, and mis-predicted her trajectory accordingly. Arizona authorities indicted the human safety driver in the AV for criminal negligence (she may have been distracted by the self-driving system interface[12]) but decided not to prosecute Uber for the accident, finding that there was 'no basis for criminal liability for the Uber corporation arising from this matter'.[13]

9.017   This approach is indicative of a trend to focus on the human in the loop as a locus for liability when AI systems cause harm – but it suggests that the law is not well calibrated. As Madeleine Elish observes, as important as human oversight is, 'it matters a great deal how that human is positioned "in the loop" and whether they are empowered – or disempowered – to act'.[14] That will, in turn, flow from design choices made by the 'authors' of the AI artefact itself. In a detailed analysis of aviation 'auto-pilot' systems, Madeleine Elish and Tim Hwang found that conceptions of legal liability and responsibility did not adequately keep pace with advances in technology:

> While the control over flight increasingly shifted to automated systems, responsibility for the flight remained focused on the figure of the pilot. While automated systems were being relied on more, the nearest human operators were being blamed for the accidents and shortcomings of the purported 'foolproof' technology. There was a significant mismatch between attributions of responsibility and

11   Yavar Bathaee, 'The Artificial Intelligence Black Box and the Failure of Intent and Causation' (2018) 31(2) *Harvard Journal of Law & Technology* 889, 897.

12   See National Transportation Safety Board, *Preliminary Report Highway HWY19MH010* (24 May 2018), www.ntsb.gov/investigations/AccidentReports/Reports/HWY18MH010-prelim.pdf.

13   Yavapai County Attorney letter to Maricopa County Attorney of 4 March 2019, https://assets.documentcloud.org/documents/5759641/UberCrashYavapaiRuling03052019.pdf.

14   M.C. Elish, 'Who Is Responsible When Autonomous Systems Fail?' (CIGI, 15 June 2020), www.cigionline.org/articles/who-responsible-when-autonomous-systems-fail.

how physical control over the system was actually distributed throughout a complex system, and across multiple actors in time and space.[15]

In short, the human in a highly complex and automated system may become simply a component – accidentally or intentionally – that bears the brunt of the moral and legal responsibilities when the overall system malfunctions. Despite the importance of keeping a human in the loop, therefore, experience in earlier generations of automation technology point to the need for careful development of the law, and the importance of deploying AI systems as components of broader systems in which humans are positioned not only to bear liability but to add natural intelligence. In other words, it is imperative to ensure that the human in the loop is an instance of supervision, not just a scapegoat. **9.018**

C. THREE CONCEPTS FOR THE DEVELOPMENT OF AI LIABILITY

This section introduces three key concepts that help to frame the discussion of liability for AI. The starting point must be that AI systems are *artefacts*. While there are different approaches to the definition of 'artefacts', for the purposes of developing a legal theory of liability for AI the definition advanced by Rispo Halpinen is useful: an artefact is an *object* that is *made intentionally* to accomplish some *purpose*.[16] This definition derives from an ancient distinction (going back to Aristotle) between things that exist by nature and things that exist by craft. This reflects one of the basic intuitions about the world that informs the structure of the existing law, and directs our attention to the artificial and purposive nature of artefacts by an author or authors. **9.019**

It is vital to start with the artefactual nature of AI systems for two reasons. First, it reminds us that AI systems are products of human craft that are created to perform some kind of function. The artificial and functional nature of artefacts keeps our view of AI systems embedded in the human needs that motivate their creation and inform their deployment. It keeps our attention on the inevitable presence of humans in the loop and the need for a granular actor analysis in the context of liability when things go wrong. **9.020**

Second, the artefactual nature of AI systems reminds us why we should resist the impulse to impress legal personality on AI systems. Proposals to grant AI systems legal personality have been tabled by leading scholars, and were even made in a 2017 European Parliament report on robotics.[17] These proposals are usually not for equivalent status with natural persons, but with an appropriate bundle of rights and duties analogous to the status of other artificial persons, notably corporations. A growing literature compares AI systems to animals and the Roman **9.021**

---

15 M.C. Elish and Tim Hwang, 'Praise the Machine! Punish the Human! The Contradictory History of Accountability in Automated Aviation' (Intelligence and Autonomy Initiative Comparative Studies in Intelligent Systems Working Paper No. 1, 24 February 2015), https://ssrn.com/abstract=2720477.

16 See Beth Preston, 'Artifact' in E.N. Zalta (ed.), *The Stanford Encyclopedia of Philosophy* (Fall 2020 Edition), https://plato .stanford.edu/archives/fall2020/entries/artifact/. See the archived entry by Rispo Hilpinen (2011) for a clear explanation of the definition I have adopted; the Preston (2020) entry provides critical discussion.

17 See Lawrence Solum, 'Legal Personhood for Artificial Intelligences' (1992) 70 *North Carolina Law Review* 1231; European Parliament, *Report with recommendations to the Commission on Civil Law Rules on Robotics* A8–0005/2017, www.europarl.europa.eu/doceo/document/A-8-2017–0005_EN.pdf, 18.

law status of slaves, who lacked only certain legal capacities, such as full contractual capacity (*commercium*), and provide, to that extent, an analogous category.[18]

9.022   Bearing in mind the caveat that technology evolves in a punctuated rather than linear fashion, it is unlikely that any AI system in the near future will warrant personhood status. Further, as the European Expert Group rightly observes, the only point of legal personality from a liability law perspective would be to provide a new subject of liability, so that any 'electronic persons' would also need to own assets from which to compensate their victims. The European Expert Group thus rejects the approach of imposing legal personality on AI systems: 'Harm caused by even fully autonomous technologies is generally reducible to the risks attributable to natural persons or existing categories of legal persons, and where this is not the case, new laws directed at individuals are a better response than creating a new category of legal person.'[19]

Chesterman notes further that imposing legal personality on AI systems would shift responsibility away from existing (natural and legal) persons and incentivise the tactical use of AI systems to shield humans and corporations from liability.[20]

9.023   But why is the personality proposal even *prima facie* plausible? E.A.R. Dahiyat argues that it is incorrect to deal with software agents in binary terms – that is, to think that they are *either* legal persons or nothing at all. There are, in fact, various kinds of software agents endowed with different levels of autonomy, mobility, intelligence and sophistication.[21] Any 'one size' regulation without sufficient consideration of the nature of software agents or the environments in which they operate would lead to a disconnect between the legal theory and technological practice. This points to the need to understand modes of action short of the kind of agency attributed to legal persons.

9.024   This point leads to the second key concept: *agentivity*. Mareille Hildebrandt has emphasised the need to understand 'law *as* information', as algorithms increasingly construct domains within the reality that humans inhabit and effect transactions within that reality.[22] The law is ancient and has digested sweeping social and technological transformations before, but Hildebrandt warns against lawyers' natural tendency to claim that things are not 'really' that different now. The deep structure of the modern law, she argues, has been built on the 'affordances of the printing press', namely on the linearity and sequential processing demands of written text, which evoke the need for (human) interpretation, reflection and contestation. The study and the practice of law have thus been focused on establishing the meaning of legal

---

18   See Simon Chesterman, 'Artificial Intelligence and the Limits of Legal Personality' (2020) 69(4) *International and Comparative Law Quarterly* 819, 832. See also Andrew Katz, 'Intelligent Agents and Internet Commerce in Ancient Rome' 2008) 20 *Society for Computers and Law* 35; Ugo Pagallo, *The Laws of Robots: Crimes, Contracts, and Torts* (Springer 2013) 103–6. See generally V.A.J Kurki and T. Pietrzykowski (eds), *Legal Personhood: Animals, Artificial Intelligence and the Unborn* (Springer 2017).

19   Expert Group on Liability and New Technologies – New Technologies Formation, *Liability for Artificial Intelligence and other emerging digital technologies* (European Union 2019), 37.

20   Simon Chesterman, 'Artificial Intelligence and the Limits of Legal Personality' (2020) 69(4) *International and Comparative Law Quarterly* 819, 825.

21   E.A.R. Dahiyat, 'Law and Software Agents: Are they "Agents" by the Way?' (2020) Artificial Intelligence Law, https://doi.org/10.1007/s10506-020-09265-1.

22   Mareille Hildebrandt, 'Law as Information in the Era of Data-Driven Agency' (2016) 79(1) *Modern Law Review* 1.

norms and their applicability to relevant human interactions, while establishing the meaning of human action in the light of the applicable legal norms. 'Data-driven agency', on the other hand, builds on a grammar of *information* and *behaviour*, not *meaning* and *action*.[23] She argues that we cannot take for granted that the law will interact with an artificially intelligent, agentive information communications infrastructure in the same way as it interacted with written and printed text and human agents.[24] There remains a categorical distinction between human and non-human agents, but the lines are blurring – not only because algorithms are becoming more intelligent, but because we are giving 'dumb' but powerful algorithms ever more important jobs to do, and because we are ever less certain whether a human or an algorithm is our counterparty in a transaction.

In most cases, whether a surgery is performed by hand or by robot is no more important than whether one ploughs a field by horse or tractor. But when the robot applies (what appears to be) expertise and skill, it begins to display features of hybridity. Legal theorists and computer scientists tend to use 'agency' differently: the former connote self-consciousness, rational self-interest, freedom of choice and legal capacity with the term; the latter mean only the ability to 'act' in a technical system. Hildebrandt's distinction seems to imply that 'action' is available to 'agents' in the legal sense, and that agents in the computer science sense are confined to 'behaviour'. This is a valid distinction, but algorithmic 'behaviour' is, as we have seen, increasingly 'action-like'. In short, AI systems are, at this stage, still obviously artefacts created and used by human agents, but they have acquired some of the properties of agents, at least within certain contexts, and they must certainly be recognised as distinct from simple tools, including in the context of liability doctrines.   **9.025**

In a linguistic study of the concept, D.A. Cruse argues that 'agentivity' implies a relation between a verb and a noun.[25] For example, consider the relationship between the noun and the verb in the following: **9.026**

(a)   The wind overturned the dustbin.
(b)   John accidentally overturned the dustbin.
(c)   John overturned the dustbin.

Is it appropriate to describe the wind as 'doing' something in (a)? What about John in (b)? Cruse suggests that we classify clauses according to the preferred form of the identifying clause. Clause (c) is a 'do-clause', because *What John did was overturn the dustbin* is preferred to *What happened to John was that he overturned the dustbin*. The latter seems to miss something essential about John. On the other hand, *The vase broke* is a 'happen-clause', since *What happened to the vase was that it broke* is preferred to *What the vase did was break*.[26] This approach, argues Cruse, can be expressed using the logic of necessary implication or entailment. *John broke the vase* entails that *John did something*; *The vase broke* does not entail *The vase did something*, but rather   **9.027**

---

23   This would seem to echo the view expressed by John Searle that computers are a priori incapable of ascribing meaning: Cole, David, 'The Chinese Room Argument', in Edward N. Zalta (ed.), *The Stanford Encyclopedia of Philosophy* (Winter 2015 Edition), https://plato.stanford.edu/archives/win2015/entries/chinese-room/.

24   Mareille Hildebrandt, 'Law as Information in the Era of Data-driven Agency' (2016) 79(1) *Modern Law Review* 1, 2.

25   D.A. Cruse, 'Some Thoughts on Agentivity' (1973) 9(1) *Journal of Linguistics* 11, 14.

26   D.A. Cruse, 'Some Thoughts on Agentivity' (1973) 9(1) *Journal of Linguistics* 11, 13, citing M.A.K. Halliday, 'Notes on Transitivity and Theme in English' (1867) 3(1) *Journal of Linguistics* 37.

Something happened to the vase. So, in this case, it would seem to be happier to speak of the vase as a non-agentive noun, an object unfitting for the ascription of action in a sentence. Yet, if we take this approach, we are stuck with cases such as *The wind blew the tree down.* We might not want to ascribe the wind agency, but it would be unhappy to say *What happened to the wind was that it blew the tree down.* Cruse suggests that 'inanimate objects can, as it were, acquire a temporary "agentivity" by virtue of their kinetic (or other) energy', and that it is appropriate to ascribe this on the basis of the 'causation of some external effect'.[27] But there are cases which cast even this restriction into doubt. 'Apparently', he concludes, 'in certain circumstances the difference between *do* and *happen* is neutralised, *do* being the normal form'.[28]

9.028   Cruse distinguishes between relations between a noun and a verb that are *volitive, effective, initiative* and *agentive,* and these distinctions help to refine the concept of agentivity. The *volitive* feature is present when an act of will is stated or implied in the verb. 'Willing is a kind of doing, whether what is willed is a state, process, or action.'[29] Sometimes, the 'do-feature' of an agentive noun is due entirely to its volitive properties. In other cases, actions are inherently non-volitional (for example, sneezing, tripping, mistaking). *Effectivity,* in turn, refers to a feature in a sentence which refers to something which exerts a force of some kind, literal or metaphorical, not by virtue of an internal engine but because of its position, momentum, or similar – for example, *The stone broke the window* or *The pillar supports the roof.* Here, the stone seems more truly 'agentive' than the pillar, which could equally be described as 'instrumental' only.[30] The third closely related feature is *initiative,* that is, when the noun in question initiates an action, such as *The warden marched the prisoners across the yard.* It is obviously the prisoners doing the 'marching', and the action of 'marching' on the part of the warden rather means that she caused the prisoners to act. Finally, Cruse finds (true) *agentivity* in sentences referring to an action 'performed by an object which is regarded as using its own energy in carrying out the action', which might include 'living things, certain types of machine, and natural agents'.[31] Agentivity in this sense is found in sentences such as *John moved to avoid the car, The machine switches off at 6:00, The fire spread through the building,* all of which can be 'tested' by the insertion of a reflexive element (for example, *John moved (himself) to avoid the car*). Men named John, machines and fires are all things that can 'do' things (to themselves) in a meaningful sense.

9.029   Against this discussion, AI systems are the kind of machines to which it seems intuitively right, at least, to attribute agentivity – we speak of computers 'doing things' all the time. To be 'agentive', it would seem that an algorithm need only be capable of effecting a change in the world – within a digital information system or in the physical world – without human intervention. The question is whether there is a class of verbs which we desire, for some reason of logic or policy, to restrict to conventional animals or to humans in particular. For example, we might say *The algorithm trains itself to recognise human faces using this data set* or *The AV brakes when it recognises a human being in its path.*

---

27   D.A. Cruse, 'Some Thoughts on Agentivity' (1973) 9(1) *Journal of Linguistics* 11, 16

28   D.A. Cruse, 'Some Thoughts on Agentivity' (1973) 9(1) *Journal of Linguistics* 11, 17.

29   D.A. Cruse, 'Some Thoughts on Agentivity' (1973) 9(1) *Journal of Linguistics* 11, 18.

30   D.A. Cruse, 'Some Thoughts on Agentivity' (1973) 9(1) *Journal of Linguistics* 11, 20.

31   D.A. Cruse, 'Some Thoughts on Agentivity' (1973) 9(1) *Journal of Linguistics* 11, 21.

We might also say *The algorithm places an order for securities*, but, with reference to the idea of **9.030** volitive agentivity, the notion of AI systems performing acts-in-the-law such as making contracts may need closer scrutiny. Broadly speaking, there are two ways in which an act has legal consequences. First, an act might have effects that simply entail legal consequences. As we have seen, animals can perform acts-in-fact that generate liability for their owners and handlers. Second, an act-in-the-law is an act which, by reference to a set of rules, purports to change the state of legal relations between parties.[32] The capacity to perform acts-in-the-law is restricted to entities of certain classes – not all of them human. The core case, of course, is the adult human. Children and adults with severe cognitive impairments, on the other hand, lack the capacity to perform many acts-in-the-law. In most legal systems, the capacity of women was less than full; under the English law doctrine of coverture, women lost many capacities upon marriage until just a few generations ago.[33] As we have seen, different forms of slavery have afforded different bundles of capacities to unfree adult humans. Non-human persons such as corporations, however, can perform most acts-in-the-law, albeit only through human organs with full legal capacity. The idea of AI systems performing acts-in-the-law needs to be unpacked, especially in the context of corporate and administrative powers.

This rounds back to the third important concept, the concept of attribution. In many ways, the **9.031** attribution stage of the analysis is the most important for practical legal analysis. Where the behaviour of an agentive artefact causes harm to another, where should liability attach? This directs our mind to the very important, and complex, analysis of doctrines such as causation and intent and to the assumptions of legal policy that inform them. Are we motivated, in a scenario concerning AVs or smart home products, by a utilitarian or a deontic rationale? Do we want to compensate the victim or deter the tortfeasor? How strong is the imperative to foster new technologies relative to the imperative to protect (for example) consumers or personal data?

D. ENSURING THAT LIABILITY REGIMES REMAIN EFFECTIVE

From the foregoing discussion, it seems that the primary objective is to ensure that the applica- **9.032** tion of AI never results in a *damnum sine injuria* – an injury with no liability – at least in cases where the harm would be compensable had it been caused by a human agent.

In pursuit of this objective, a number of tools are ready to hand. Notably, these include (i) **9.033** adjusting the doctrines of fault-based liability that operate in any given liability regime, (ii) imposing strict liability for the deployment of AI and (iii) implementing mandatory insurance regimes or compensation funds (perhaps in tandem with strict liability) to perform the same function as fault-based liability doctrines. Some of the literature also discusses (iv) applying vicarious liabilities to AI systems (that is, treating the AI system as the agent/employee and a human or corporation as the principal/employer). This is *prima facie* plausible to the extent that an AI system is functionally equivalent to a human agent (in the sense of agent and

---

32   See H.D.S. van der Kaaij, *The Juridical Act: A Study of the Theoretical Concept of an Act that Aims to Create New Legal Facts* (Springer 2019) for a contemporary discussion.
33   See Sir William Blackstone, *Commentaries on the Laws of England* (1765) Book I Chapter 15, 'On Husband and Wife'.

principal, not agent *qua* acting subject) in certain contexts.[34] The European Expert Group, for example, follows the principle of functional equivalence to argue that where use is made of autonomous technology instead of a human auxiliary, the principal's liability should correspond to whatever vicarious liability regime exists in the jurisdiction. However, this option complicates the analysis without adding much utility and should not be pursued.

9.034 A number of questions will arise in the specific area of liability law, for example whether an AI system is a 'product' for the purposes of European product safety law, and how European and national law interact in this context. The European Expert Group provides a useful analysis of these sorts of questions in its report. Space precludes a detailed discussion at this level of detail, so this section will instead zoom out to ask what kind of approach to liability seems most appropriate.

9.035 The first point to make is that fault-based liability will continue to be important in many cases that involve AI systems, and that doctrines such as causation and intent (as well as the procedural law) should be adjusted to the extent that they prevent compensation of victims where some party is clearly at fault. These might involve reversal of standards and burdens of proof, for example, the presumptive use of industry and regulatory standards, or requirements that AI 'thought' processes be made known to victims to facilitate fair liability claims. The European Expert Group report, for example, argues that the burden of proof should be reversed in case of a failure to log data or refusal to provide a victim with logged data, in case the damage is caused by action in breach of rules designed to promote safety and in case of disproportionate difficulties or costs in proving the relevant level of safety or establishing breach.[35]

9.036 The second point is that not only the opacity problem but also the way that AI systems are actually created, deployed, monitored and updated might make fault-based liability unsuitable in practice in certain types of case. Such cases are natural candidates for the operation of a strict liability regime, possibly coupled with mandatory insurance – at least where the social value of the application of an AI system to the relevant use case is sufficiently high.

9.037 In general, it seems that as long as we refuse to impose legal personality on AI systems that is, to hold them liable for their behaviour in their own right – the question of 'liability for AI' is a question of the circumstances in which persons (humans and corporations) are liable for AI they have created, deployed or overseen. The choice, then, is between fault-based liability and strict liability. Vicarious liability muddies the waters. Vicarious liability is liability for the violation of a duty incumbent on another actor, that is, where A acts but B is liable for A's wrongful action.[36] (A's action may be wrongful on a fault-based or strict standard.) To the extent that we stipulate that AI systems are artefacts that are *not* persons, this would seem to be the wrong theory on which to extend the liability (and attenuate the fault requirement) of the relevant actor. The salient question is whether we want to impose strict liability on those that

---

34 Expert Group on Liability and New Technologies – New Technologies Formation, *Liability for Artificial Intelligence and other emerging digital technologies* (European Union 2019), 24, 45.

35 Expert Group on Liability and New Technologies – New Technologies Formation, *Liability for Artificial Intelligence and other emerging digital technologies* (European Union 2019), 6, 7.

36 For a theoretical discussion of vicarious liability and its cognates, see Václav Janeček, 'Vicarious Liability of Juristic Persons' in Karel Beran *et al*, *Artificial Legal Entities: Essays on Legal Agency and Liability* (Wolters Kluwer 2019), ch 10.

create and/or deploy AI systems or whether they should only be liable for harms caused by the AI system where they have somehow been at fault. This analysis seems best served by putting vicarious liability to one side.

The task then becomes one of deciding which use cases are adequately served by fault-based liability, and which are appropriate for strict liability. To this end, a modified version of Bathaee's schematic is useful. Any given AI system, as deployed in all the circumstances, might fall anywhere along the two axes of opacity and supervision, and where it falls should determine the legal response.[37]

Table 9.1   Suitability of use cases for fault-based and strict liability respectively

	More transparent	More opaque
More closely supervised	Fault-based: conventional intent and causation doctrines should apply	Fault-based: use of AI system goes to establishing intent and causation
More autonomous from human oversight	Fault-based: relaxed intent and causation tests should apply	Strict liability, with or without mandatory insurance or compensation fund

The European Expert Group proposes a risk assessment-based approach in which the standard **9.038** of liability changes depending on the riskiness of the activity in question. While this is important, the riskiness or otherwise of an activity is sometimes a question of foreseeability, which is typically an ingredient of fault-based liability tests, and thus begs the central question of strict versus fault-based liability. In the first step, we should focus on the degree of opacity and the degree of supervision. Whether it appears risky or not, any person deploying a highly opaque AI system with minimal supervision should be taken to assume any and all risks that it presents. In other words, even if one cannot reasonably foresee that one is deploying an AI system in a 'high risk' use case, the combination of high opacity and low supervision warrants strict liability. When paired with an appropriate insurance framework, strict liability might provide market conditions in which uptake of AI systems is facilitated. In that way, any accident with an AV would give rise to compensation for victims (including the owners and operators of AVs) from a general fund levied on AV sales.[38]

E. SPECIAL CONSIDERATIONS IN THE PUBLIC LAW CONTEXT

Although it lies somewhat on the fringe of 'liability law', public law accountability is an anal- **9.039** ogous and highly important area of potential impact by AI systems. In the exercise of public

---

37   Yavar Bathaee, 'The Artificial Intelligence Black Box and the Failure of Intent and Causation' (2018) 31(2) *Harvard Journal of Law & Technology* 889, 937. Modifications my own.

38   See, e.g., D.A. Crane, K.D. Logue and B.C. Pilz, 'A Survey of Legal Issues Arising from the Deployment of Autonomous and Connected Vehicles' (2017) 23 *Michigan Telecommunications and Technology Law Review* 256, 259. Cf K.S. Abraham and R.L. Rabin, 'Automated Vehicles and Manufacturer Responsibility for Accidents: A New Legal Regime for a New Era' (2019) 105 *Virginia Law Review* 127. For example, the Transport Accident Commission in the Australian state of Victoria is a statutory body established under the Transport Accident Act 1986 (Vic) to provide no-fault insurance for motor vehicle accidents, and similar schemes operate in other Australian states as well as in various states in the US and Canada. New Zealand has operated a general no-fault accident insurance scheme under a Crown entity, the Accident Compensation Commission established in the Accident Compensation Act 1972 (NZ), since 1974.

authority, opacity is particularly problematic. Much of the literature criticising 'algorithmic decision-making' by public officials focuses on the quality of the decisions made, including their potential for discriminatory impact or bias. However, there are also decisions in which opacity itself undermines legitimacy, irrespective of the quality of the decision. Chief among these are decisions by public officials whose authority depends on democratic processes that would be frustrated by opacity and decisions by judicial officials whose claim to the rule of law depends on public justifications that are intelligible to the wider community.[39] As a rule, the transparency and publicness of the decision-making *process* is just as important as the correctness of its *outcome* in public law.

9.040   Indeed, the focus of public law accountability mechanisms such as judicial review is on the procedural qualities of decision-making rather than their substantive output. The repository of an administrative power is generally at liberty to err – provided that the decision-making process that leads to the erroneous decision conforms to the standards of good decision-making. In the English law of judicial review, for example, grounds on which a decision can be impugned include illegality (that is, the decision-maker lacked the legal power to take the decision she made), procedural impropriety (for example, a breach of the *audi alterem partem* rule), irrationality (for example, taking into account irrelevant considerations), violation of a legitimate expectation and (to the extent it differs from irrationality) lack of proportionality. With their procedural focus, many of these grounds are difficult to establish where the AI system's 'decision-making' process is opaque for the reasons set out above.

9.041   Judicial decision-making provides a paradigmatic example of an exercise of public authority that might be automated with some kind of AI system. The application of risk assessment software in sentencing procedures is well established in various US states and has been the subject of spirited debate.[40] Judicial decision-making, in particular, inherently implies the application of human intelligence in all the circumstances of the case. In *Semunigus v Minister for Immigration*,[41] Finn J of the Australian Federal Court held that 'the making of a decision involve[s] the reaching a conclusion as a result of a mental process having been engaged in and translating that conclusion into a decision by an overt act of such a character as, in the circumstances, gives finality to the conclusion'.[42] While another human's mind is a 'black box' in a certain sense, we require judges to articulate reasons for their decisions that are amenable to argumentation and scrutiny. So, even though output-based legitimacy is appropriate in some areas, *judicial* decisions depend crucially on the transparency of the decision-making process and perhaps should not be automated at all – or, at the very least, should be automated only in such a way that the traditional values of human decision-making are preserved.

---

39   Simon Chesterman, 'Through a Glass, Darkly: Artificial Intelligence and the Problem of Opacity' (NUS Law Working Paper 2020/11), 17.

40   See e.g., Julia Angwin, Jeff Larson, Surya Mattu and Lauren Kirchner, 'Machine Bias' (Pro Publica, 23 May 2016), https://www.propublica.org/article/machine-bias-risk-assessments-in-criminal-sentencing, with links to the data sets and analysis used in an investigative report. See also Simon Chesterman, 'Through a Glass, Darkly: Artificial Intelligence and the Problem of Opacity' (NUS Law Working Paper 2020/11), 2.

41   [1999] FCA 422.

42   *Semunigus v Minister for Immigration* [1999] FCA 422, PAGE.

This again shifts our focus to how the 'machine–human loop' is being constructed. For **9.042** example, the Australian Migration Act 1958 (Cth) s. 495A provides:

> Minister may arrange for use of computer programs to make decisions etc.
> (1) The Minister may arrange for the use, under the Minister's control, of computer programs for any purposes for which the Minister may, or must, under the designated migration law:
>   (a) make a decision; or
>   (b) exercise any power, or comply with any obligation; or
>   (c) do anything else related to making a decision, exercising a power, or complying with an obligation.
> (2) The Minister is taken to have:
>   (a) made a decision; or
>   (b) exercised a power, or complied with an obligation; or
>   (c) done something else related to the making of a decision, the exercise of a power, or the compliance with an obligation;
>
> that was made, exercised, complied with, or done (as the case requires) by the operation of a computer program under an arrangement made under subsection (1).

As Will Bateman has observed, this provision (and numerous parallel provisions in other **9.043** Australian statutes) does not purport to confer jurisdiction on a computer program, but it does imply that a legal 'decision' is made by the computer program that is separate (and prior to) the decision of the Minister. This flows from both the language of the text and the logical schematic it sets out: the computer program first makes a decision (subsection (1)), and that decision is then attributed to the Minister (subsection (2)). Thus, even though the provision stipulates that the AI system is 'under the Minister's control', the workflow or 'loop' it sets out comprises a decision made by a computer program that is retrospectively attributed to the human repository of a legal power. Importantly, where such a 'computer program' is an AI system, it is quite possible that the Minister will not be able fully to understand the decision made on her behalf, even after the fact.[43]

Section 495A effectively deems the decision made by the AI system to be the decision of the **9.044** Minister, and this would seem to suggest that the Minister must 'own' the AI system's outputs, whether lawful or unlawful. On one reading, it would seem to suggest that public officials procuring AI systems do so at their own risk. However, we have seen that in the case of workflows outsourced by to a private sector company, the Minister has argued that assessment procedures are not subject to judicial review because they were not the exercise of any statutory power. In *Plaintiff M61/2010E v Commonwealth of Australia*,[44] the core question was what, if any, significance should attach to the fact that a review process was conducted by persons engaged by an independent contractor rather than by a public official. The company in question had been contracted by the Commonwealth Government to make specified persons available to conduct reviews of refugee status assessments. The function of these persons was to make a *recommendation* about whether protection obligations were owed to the applicants – any formal *decision* would be taken subsequently by the Minister. Already this arrangement presented procedural complexities, as these specified persons were not 'officers of the Commonwealth' and their reviews were not subject to the prerogative writs of *mandamus* and *certiorari*. Further complex-

---

43   I am grateful to my friend Will Bateman for our many illuminating conversations on this aspect of public law. See Will Bateman, 'Algorithmic Decision-Making and Legality: Public Law Dimensions' (2020) 94 *Australian Law Journal* 520.
44   [2010] HCA 41.

ities arose because the ultimate power reposed in the Minister was discretionary. The general point was that the Minister argued that errors of law and procedural impropriety in the review process could not impugn the decision ultimately made by the Minister. The High Court of Australia, happily, rejected the Minister's approach:

> The Minister having decided to consider the exercise of power […] the steps that are taken to inform that consideration are steps towards the exercise of those statutory powers. That the steps taken to inform the consideration of exercise of power may lead at some point to the result that further consideration of exercise of the power is stopped does not deny that the steps that were taken were taken towards the possible exercise of those powers. Nor does it deny that taking the steps that were taken directly affected the claimant's liberty. There being no exclusion by plain words of necessary intendment, the statutory conferral of the powers […] including the power to decide to consider the exercise of power, is to be understood as 'conditioned on the observance of the principles of natural justice'. Consideration of the exercise of the power must be procedurally fair to the persons in respect of whom that consideration is being given. And likewise, the consideration must proceed by reference to correct legal principles, correctly applied.[45]

9.045 As the Court found that the review contained both errors of law and procedural unfairness, but the usual remedies of *mandamus* and *certiorari* were not available, the Court made an order for a declaration that the reviews in question were flawed. It is to be hoped that courts around the world are just as vigilant to ensure that public law accountability mechanisms are not hollowed out by the intermediation of AI systems – most likely developed and perhaps maintained by private sector contractors – in the future. However, it is also reasonable to expect that public officials relying on AI systems will make analogous arguments, and that judicial supervision will be rendered more difficult by the opacity of the computer programs involved.

F. CONCLUSION

9.046 This chapter has approached the question of liability for AI systems at the level of general principle, concentrating on those AI systems that are most likely to find real-world application in the near to medium term and that are most likely to raise conceptual and practical problems for conventional liability regimes. These are AI systems based on 'deep' machine learning technologies, which construct models on the basis of large historical data sets and then produce outputs in new cases based on those models.

9.047 The most important issues raised by such AI systems relate to their inherent opacity, and the impact that this feature has on conventional doctrines of intent and causation and, particularly in the public law context, on the legitimacy of non-transparent decision-making processes.

9.048 Taking account of the extensive literatures already dealing with these issues, this chapter presented three central concepts for the emerging law of liability for AI systems. These were the concept of AI systems as *artefacts*, their inherent *agentivity*, and the importance of rules of *attribution* that effectively connect machine behaviour with (responsible) human action.

---

45 *Plaintiff M61/2010E v Commonwealth of Australia* [2010] HCA 41 para [78] (French CJ, Gummow, Hayne, Haydon, Crennan, Kiefel and Bell JJ).

It then set out a number of considerations for the development of liability principles and **9.049** argued that the most important consideration was the relation between opacity and supervision in any given deployment scenario. The main choice is to determine which use cases are most appropriate for fault-based liability, and which are suitable for strict liability. The concept of vicarious liability was argued to confuse rather than assist the debate. Finally, it was argued that AI systems may satisfy certain core values, or accountability mechanisms, controlling the power of public officials such as judges and ministers.

The immediate task is to apply existing doctrines of liability sensibly and appropriately to **9.050** AI-based applications. In this task, we must be aware of the blind spots in the law – particularly where doctrines of intent and causation, for example, lead to a *damnum sine injuria*. This points to the deeper task, which is to divine, and refine, the principles governing liability at quite a general level of abstraction. This will require engagement with legal theory and also with the normative foundations on which the imposition of liability is justified. Here we should distinguish between questions of 'legal theory' and questions of 'legal policy'. The latter inform the former, particularly at critical moments of legal development. It is essential that, in the context of liability for AI, the policy of the law is furthered and not thwarted by its doctrines. We will have to ask why it is that the law traditionally insists on a mental element to impose liability, and what purpose(s) liability serves – compensation, punishment, restitution, deterrence, promotion of efficiency, prevention of irreversible systemic risks? The goal will be to ensure that these purposes are served even in cases where the traditional function of intent and causation doctrines are thwarted by technology.

The legal policy questions raised by AI systems are not easy, and are amenable to analysis from **9.051** different and sometimes conflicting disciplinary viewpoints. The European Expert Group suggests that, in the first instance, we are designing liability systems to ensure functional equivalence between AI-based and non-AI-based systems (including those that rely on a human auxiliary). In the second step, however, the design of legal liability regimes will undoubtedly influence the design of AI systems themselves. Should those designing an autonomous vehicle programme a Kantian or a utilitarian response to the classical trolley car problem, for example? Should an autonomous vehicle favour the life of the driver over the life of a pedestrian? Should any characteristics of the candidate victims be taken into consideration (such as age)? In a robust study on AVs, Jean-François Bonnefon, Azim Shariff and Iyad Rahwan found that a large majority of people thought that AVs programmed to minimise the overall number of casualties were more ethical – but that they would rather purchase one that preserved the driver's life preferentially. Bluntly, the majority of people in a large survey would refuse to buy the car they found more ethical.[46] This presents a kind of tragedy of the commons problem, whereby self-interested behaviour by individuals destroys a common good.

In the context of AI, the division of labour between law and other disciplines is crucial. As **9.052** lawyers, we need to ensure that we understand the evolving state of the art of AI technologies. But even more importantly, we need to ensure that we engage with the law itself, and stand ready to engage with technologists and innovators in terms that are mutually intelligible and conducive to effective collaboration. First and foremost, this means getting a firm grasp on

---

46   Jean-François Bonnefon, Azim Sharif and Iyad Rahwan, 'The Social Dilemma of Autonomous Vehicles' (2016) 352 *Science* 6293.

what our received legal doctrines were designed to do and communicating the importance of this effectively to our technical counterparts, as well as to judges and legislators.

10

DATA AND DATA PROTECTION

Peter Church and Richard Cumbley

A. INTRODUCTION

1. The General Data Protection Regulation

10.001 This chapter primarily considers how the General Data Protection Regulation (GDPR)[1] regulates the use of artificial intelligence. While more than 140 states around the world now have some form of data protection laws,[2] many of those laws arise out of the same international conventions as the GDPR. There is, as a result, a high degree of commonality in the data protection regimes, so the analysis in this chapter is likely still be relevant even outside of the EU and the UK.[3]

10.002 The GDPR does not protect all data, nor does it regulate all decisions made using that data. Instead, it protects rights to privacy and data protection by ensuring that personal data is processed fairly and lawfully. However, the GDPR's broad scope and flexible and technology-neutral rules mean it has a central role in the regulation of emerging technology such as artificial intelligence.

10.003 The concepts of fairness, necessity and proportionality also feature heavily in the GDPR, aligning it closely with the principles of data ethics, and the GDPR introduces new obligations that are well suited to address the challenges raised by artificial intelligence. This includes duties to carry out impact assessments before undertaking high-risk processing and controls on when decisions about individuals can be automated.

2. Overview

10.004 This chapter explores the complex and sometimes subtle rules in the GDPR. However, in most cases the aim is to ensure individuals trust you with their personal data. The building blocks to achieve that trust can be summarised relatively briefly:

(a) *Be transparent* – Tell individuals what personal data you hold about them and how you are using it, including that you are using artificial intelligence technology on their personal data. This is backed by detailed disclosure obligations in the GDPR.

(b) *Don't be creepy* – Ensure you have a proper justification for using personal data and ensure that data is accurate, not excessive and not kept for longer than necessary.

(c) *Empower individuals* – To the extent possible, give individuals meaningful choices and control over how their personal data is used. This is backed up by the rights in the GDPR, including specific protection for individuals who are subject to significant automated decision-making.

---

1 This chapter uses the term GDPR to refer generically to the EU General Data Protection Regulation and the UK General Data Protection Regulation (as retained EU law). As at the start of 2022, both regimes remain largely aligned in relation to the issues considered in this chapter.

2 *Greenleaf & Cottier – 2020 ends a decade of 62 new data privacy laws* (2020) 163 Privacy Laws & Business International Report 24–26.

3 For reasons of brevity, the national law analysis largely focuses on the position in the UK rather than providing a comparative view across the EU. As set out in footnote 1, the laws of the EU and the UK remain largely aligned as at the start of 2021.

(d)   *Keep personal data secure* – Data security is an important issue for artificial intelligence algorithms, which often use large amounts of personal data.

(e)   *Be fair and avoid discrimination* – Consider the impact of the artificial intelligence model on different groups of individuals and ensure that any difference in their treatment is justified. Do not use sensitive and inherently discriminatory data types, such as information on racial or ethnic origin, unless there is a very good reason to do so.

Data protection regulators have invested a considerable amount of effort in analysing the challenges raised by artificial intelligence and developing guidance to ensure that this technology can be deployed fairly and lawfully. Examples include the UK Information Commissioner's excellent *Guidance on AI and data protection* (ICO's AI guidance) and *Explaining decisions made with AI* (ICO's Explain guidance).   **10.005**

However, as with any new technology, a number of questions remain unanswered. Some are practical, such as how to best regulate algorithms. Artificial intelligence technology typically operates in a 'black box', making it very difficult to properly understand its operation. This suggests data protection regulators may need new tools and new skill sets.   **10.006**

Other challenges are more fundamental, such as the extent to which data protection laws can and should be used to tackle broader issues of fairness. The GPDR is increasingly seen as, in Irish Data Protection Commissioner Helen Dixon's words, 'the law of everything', but data protection regulators lack the democratic mandate to adjudicate on some of the wider societal issues raised by artificial intelligence and broader algorithmic decision-making.   **10.007**

B. KEY CONCEPTS

The starting point is to determine whether your artificial intelligence model will be subject to the GDPR. To do that, you need to identify if your artificial intelligence model involves the processing of personal data by a controller or a processor. We examine each of these concepts below.   **10.008**

1.   What is personal data?

Personal data is any information relating to an identified or identifiable natural person.[4]   **10.009**

This term is interpreted broadly. For example, even if the individual is not directly identified in the information, it will be still be personal data if it is 'reasonably likely'[5] that the individual could be identified, for example using other sources of information, such as information from the internet.   **10.010**

Similarly, the information does not need to reveal the individual's 'real world' identity (such as their name, phone number or postal address). It is sufficient that the information 'individuates'   **10.011**

---

4   Article 4(1), GDPR.
5   Recital 26, GDPR.

the individual by singling them out from other individuals.[6] This makes anonymising personal data difficult.

(a) Examples of personal data

10.012   For example, the courts have found that the following types of information are personal data.

(a)   IP addresses in situations in which the person holding that IP address can resolve that address back to an individual subscriber.[7]

(b)   CCTV footage.[8]

(c)   Biometric faceprints created about individuals. This faceprint 'individuates' the individual by singling them out even in situations in which their 'real world' identity is not known.[9]

10.013   In contrast, some information will clearly not be personal data. For example, the share price of a listed company or a weather report will not, by itself, be personal data.

10.014   Between these extremes are more difficult questions about whether inferences about individuals or groups of individuals, or prediction models, are personal data. We consider these issues below.

10.015   Finally, the GDPR also introduces the concept of 'pseudonymised data'. This concept was originally proposed as a radical third class of data (neither personal nor anonymised) that would be regulated in a completely different way. Under the GDPR, it ends up as an important and useful privacy-enhancing mechanism that can be used to help secure data or permit processing for new purposes. However, it does not materially change the core rules in the GDPR and is still a form of personal data subject to the general rules in the GDPR.

2.   Does Data Have to Be Structured?

10.016   The GDPR applies to both structured electronic personal data (such as a traditional relational database) and unstructured electronic data (such as emails and word documents).[10]

10.017   The application of the GDPR to structured data can be relatively straightforward. For example, if you want to ensure that personal data in a relational database is not kept longer than necessary, each entry in that relational database can be given a reference date and a rule can be constructed to automatically delete entries after a certain period. In contrast, it is very difficult to apply a similar rule to emails, which typically contain lots of different types of personal data that must be kept for different periods. The application of the GDPR to unstructured electronic data continues to raise significant practical difficulties.

---

6   See Recital 26, GDPR and *Bridges, R (On Application of) v The Chief Constable of South Wales Police* [2019] EWHC 2341 (Admin).

7   *Patrick Breyer v Bundesrepublik Deutschland* (C-582/14).

8   *František Ryneš v Úřad pro ochranu osobních údajů* (C-212/13).

9   *Bridges*, see supra.

10   Article 2(1), GDPR.

In contrast, hard-copy records are only subject to the GDPR if they are organised into a sophis-   **10.018**
ticated filing system, such that personal data can be accessed using specific criteria. Most
artificial intelligence projects are unlikely to be solely based on processing hard-copy records.

3.   What About Inferences?

One of the interesting issues raised by artificial intelligence is that the output of an artificial   **10.019**
intelligence algorithm is often just a statistical guess – an inference – either about an individual
or about a group of individuals. To what extent is this information subject to the GDPR?

The answer to the first question is clear. An inference about an individual is personal data. It   **10.020**
has been suggested that the CJEU's decision under the old Data Protection Directive[11] in *YS v
Minister voor Immigratie* (C-141/12) casts doubt on that point. In that case, biographic details
about an asylum applicant were personal data but legal analysis regarding their immigration
status was not, which might suggest that only facts are protected by data protection law.

However, a broader interpretation was taken by the CJEU in *Nowak v Data Protection*   **10.021**
Commissioner (C-434/16), which found that written answers to an exam and the examiner's
comments are both personal data. Any lingering doubt on this point is dispelled by the fact the
GDPR expressly applies to 'profiling' – that is, evaluating personal aspects of an individual to
analyse or predict information about them, such as preferences, interests and reliability – which
squarely applies to most inferences about individuals.

The extent to which an inference about a group of individuals is also personal data is a more   **10.022**
difficult issue. This is likely to depend on a range of factors, including the size of the group
and the certainty of the implication. For example, the inference that 'people living in Crawley
have poor credit histories' is not personal data as it is simply too general in nature. In contrast,
the inference that a household sitting behind a particular IP address are interested in watching
BDSM videos might well be, not least because in some cases that one household will consist
of a single individual. The question of when a group inference becomes sufficiently specific to
constitute personal data is inevitably a matter of degree.

This is not, in itself, a lacuna in the law. Even if the group inference is not itself personal data,   **10.023**
it will become subject to the GDPR as soon as that group inference is applied to an individual.
For example, using the group inference 'people living in Crawley have poor credit histories'
on Mr Smith who lives in Crawley to automatically refuse Mr Smith's mortgage application
would involve processing his personal data and so be subject to the GDPR (and would likely be
unlawful). In practice, problems with group inferences are less about questions of whether the
GDPR applies and more about the risk of complex patterns of discrimination and unfairness.
We consider these issues below in the section titled 'Bias and Fairness'.

---

11   The Data Protection Directive (95/46/EC) which was repealed by the GDPR.

4.   What Does Processing Mean?

10.024   The definition of processing is exceptionally broad. It includes the collection, organisation, storage, adaptation, use, disclosure and destruction of personal data.[12]

10.025   Importantly, this includes not just the collection of the data from individuals and disclosure to third parties, but also any internal use of that personal data or even merely storing that personal data. Virtually anything done to personal data will constitute 'processing'.

5.   Who Is Responsible for Processing?

10.026   The GDPR splits those processing personal data into two groups: controllers and processors.[13]

10.027   The majority of the obligations in the GDPR fall on the controller. This is the person who determines the purpose and means of the processing. The controller can either act independently or jointly with other controllers. Where the controller acts jointly with others, they need an arrangement to allocate responsibilities for compliance with the GDPR. This could be through a joint controller agreement.

10.028   In contrast, a processor simply acts on the instructions of the controller. As a result, processors are subject to a much more limited set of obligations, mainly dealing with security and record-keeping. A controller must have a contract with their processor containing detailed processing terms to govern how the processor must use the relevant personal data.

10.029   The GDPR does not regulate mere 'producers' of technology.[14] For example, a company that simply provides a copy of machine learning software for use by another will likely not be subject to the GDPR in relation to the subsequent use of that software.

10.030   Applying these concepts in practice can be difficult. It is also important to note that they are sometimes used as proxy arguments for wider commercial issues. For example, arguments about whether a party acts as controller or processor are sometimes really arguments about who should 'own' or be able to commercially exploit the underlying data.

(a)   Controller or processor?

10.031   For example, imagine tech company X uses open-source machine learning software from licensor A in a cloud environment from company B to deliver services to customer Y.

(a)   *Open-source licensor A*: If this company only provides a licence to open-source software then it is likely not to be subject to the GDPR at all.

(b)   *Cloud provider B*: The cloud hosting company is likely to act a processor for either tech company X or customer Y.

---

12   Article 4(2), GDPR.
13   Articles 4(7) and (8), GDPR.
14   Though such entities are 'encouraged' to develop products that comply with the GDPR. See recital 78, GDPR.

(c)   *Tech company X and customer Y*: The capacity in which these parties process personal data (controller–controller, controller–processor or joint controller) will depend on the circumstances.

6.   Can I Just Anonymise the Personal Data?

One way to avoid data protection legislation is to anonymise any personal data. The use of anonymised data falls outside the GDPR and the process of anonymisation, while itself a form of processing and so subject to the GDPR, will generally be easy to justify. **10.032**

However, proper anonymisation is hard. It involves: **10.033**

(a)   Deleting all direct identifiers including both obvious identifiers such as names and addresses and other direct identifiers such as account numbers, advertising IDs or telephone numbers.

(b)   Ensuring individuals cannot be identified by combining data in the data set. For example, in the UK the combination of postcode and date of birth will normally identify an individual.

(c)   Ensuring individuals cannot be identified by combining the data with other data sources. Determining whether this is the case can be a difficult exercise, particularly given the vast amounts of data accessible on the internet. There is often not a bright line test to determine when data is identifiable. The UK Information Commissioner recommends a 'motivated intruder' test[15] – that is, considering whether a person who starts without any prior knowledge but wants to identify the persons in the original dataset could identify any of them.

True anonymisation can be very hard. Statements by engineers or business people that data is 'anonymised' should be treated with caution and tested. Third party expert support can help in large-scale or serious cases. Wrongly assuming that data is anonymised can be very dangerous, as the Netflix example below demonstrates. **10.034**

(a) Has Netflix told the world what you are watching?

From 2006 to 2009, Netflix released the rankings of 500,000 customers for 100 million films as part of an annual prize competition to help create a better film recommendation algorithm. The information was pseudonymised (the customers' names were replaced with a key) and 'noise' was added to the ratings by slightly increasing or decreasing those ratings. **10.035**

At first glance, this appears more than enough to protect its customers' privacy. However, researchers[16] found that the combination of ratings formed a distinctive 'fingerprint' that could be matched to movie ratings in the public IMDB database (that is, the films which a person likes, and hates, can be a unique and identifying factor). This allowed some customers to be identified. **10.036**

---

15   Anonymisation: managing data protection risk code of practice, The Information Commissioner's Office, November 2012.

16   *How to Break Anonymity of the Netflix Prize Dataset*, Arvind Narayanan and Vitaly Shmatikov. https://arxiv.org/abs/cs/0610105v2.

10.037   Where personal data is not fully anonymised, it might still be pseudonymised. This typically involves removing direct identifiers from the data and replacing them with a key code. This can be a valuable way to protect the security and privacy of that personal data, so long as the limitations of that protection are understood. In the UK there are also statutory protections under the Data Protection Act 2018 which make re-identification of anonymised personal data a criminal offence in some circumstances.

7.   Who Regulates and Enforces the Law?

10.038   The GDPR requires each EU Member State to establish an independent regulator to enforce the law,[17] handle complaints and carry out activities such as providing guidance and promoting awareness. Most Member States have a single regulator, though some have multiple regulators, such as Germany, which has a separate regulator for each Länder.

10.039   The national data protection regulators in the EU are all members of the European Data Protection Board (EDPB), along with the European Data Protection Supervisor. The EDPB performs an important role providing guidance and seeking to ensure consistent application of the GDPR across the EU.

10.040   The GDPR is enforced through both regulatory enforcement action by national data protection authorities and private actions by individuals.

10.041   One of the most significant changes brought about by the GDPR was to make data protection a boardroom issue. It introduces an antitrust-type sanction regime with fines of up to 4 per cent of annual worldwide turnover or €20m, whichever is the greater. These fines apply to most breaches of the GDPR, though certain breaches will fall into the lower fining tier and result in fines of up to 2 per cent of annual worldwide turnover or €10m, whichever is the greater.[18]

10.042   The GDPR has resulted in a significant increase in fines in practice. National protection authorities have issued a number of multimillion-euro fines, including a fine of €50m by the French data protection authority against Google for not being sufficiently transparent and not obtaining a valid consent. Similarly, the Irish Data Protection Commissioner has fined WhatsApp €225 for not providing adequate transparency and Luxembourg's Commission Nationale pour la Protection des Données has fined Amazon €746m for breaches of the GDPR.

10.043   In addition to fines, data authorities have a wide range of other powers and sanctions at their disposal. This includes investigative powers, such as the ability to demand information from controllers and processors, and to carry out audits. They also have corrective powers enabling them to issue warnings or reprimands, to enforce an individual's rights and to issue a temporary and permanent ban on processing. The powers to ban processing are potentially more significant than fines, such as where that directly affects an organisation's business model.

---

17   Similarly, the UK has an independent regulator established under the Data Protection Act 2018.
18   Article 83, GDPR.

In addition to regulatory enforcement, individuals can bring private actions to enforce their   **10.044**
rights or to seek compensation. These rights are also significant and there has been a growth
in data protection 'class actions' on behalf of multiple individuals affected by a breach of
the GDPR. For example, an 'opt-out' representative action was brought in the English
courts against Google as a result of its use of its 'Safari Workaround' – essentially a technical
workaround to bypass the cookie settings on the Safari browser and place tracking cookies
without individuals' knowledge or consent. The claim was brought on behalf of all 4 million
individuals in England and Wales using the Safari browser. The claimants suggested these
individuals should receive approximately £750 compensation each, which indicates a (theoretical) liability of up to £3 billion, though the claim was ultimately rejected by the UK Supreme
Court.[19]

Finally, there are a number of privacy activists and bodies seeking to enforce the GDPR through   **10.045**
a variety of complaints to regulators and private enforcement action. One example is *noyb* (none
of your business), which has made multiple complaints to regulators and was instrumental in
the recent European Court of Justice decision that the EU–US Privacy Shield is invalid.

8.   How Does the GDPR Apply Internationally?

The GDPR captures controllers and processors:[20]   **10.046**

(a)   *Established in the EU.* In this case, the GDPR protects the personal data of any individual
      regardless of their location. This broad protection reflects the fact data protection is
      a fundamental human right protected by the EU Charter of Fundamental Rights; and
(b)   *Established outside the EU but offering goods or services to, or monitoring, individuals in the
      EU.* That protection only applies to those individuals in the EU, and not to individuals
      based elsewhere in the world. This arguably does not apply the GDPR extra-territorially
      but instead just ensures a level playing field for all overseas companies wanting to operate
      in the EU market.

Data protection laws are not peculiar to the EU or the UK, and as noted previously, more than   **10.047**
140 states around the world now have a privacy law of some form or another. While many of
these laws arise from the same international conventions, and some are actively modelled on
the GDPR, there are often important differences in the way those laws operate in practice.
Accordingly, while the analysis in this chapter is likely to be relevant to most other jurisdictions
with data protection laws, it does not attempt to address any of the specific differences in the
way these laws regulate artificial intelligence.

Finally, the GDPR does not apply to the processing of personal data for law enforcement or   **10.048**
national security purposes. Law enforcement processing is subject to a separate regime under
Directive 2016/680, which imposes similar rules to the GDPR but is not considered further in
this chapter.

---

19   *Lloyd* v *Google LLC* [2021] UKSC 50
20   Article 3, GDPR. The position under the UK GDPR is similar but with references to the EU replaced with references to
     the UK. The GDPR also applies outside the EU where Member State law applies by virtue of public international law.

C. SUBSTANTIVE OBLIGATIONS

10.049   The purpose of the GDPR is to protect the fundamental right to data protection in accordance with Article 8(1) of the EU Charter of Fundamental Rights. These rights are not absolute and must be applied in light of other fundamental rights and in accordance with the principle of proportionality. In order to provide this proportionate and balanced framework, the GDPR does not contain a long list of absolute rules and instead is mainly based around a short list of high-level principles.

1.   Principle-based Regulation

10.050   The GDPR exhibits all of the advantages and disadvantages you would expect from principle-based regulation. It is both flexible and technology-neutral; indeed, the core principles underpinning the GDPR are largely taken from the earlier Data Protection Directive, which was adopted in 1995. Those principles are as relevant now as they were more than two decades ago.

10.051   The disadvantage is that it is not clear how these principles apply to any specific situation. This is a common source of frustration, particularly for those with a technology background, who might expect that a law designed to regulate the digital age would operate in a digital fashion – providing clear and determinative answers as to whether a particular activity is lawful.

10.052   Instead, the GDPR is based around subjective concepts of fairness and proportionality. Rather than providing answers, the GDPR provides a series of questions to determine if the processing is lawful. Most of these questions are context-sensitive, meaning they must be assessed on a case-by-case basis based on the exact details of the relevant processing.

10.053   The GDPR also often requires a risk-based approach in which the potential harms which the processing raises for individuals are identified, and appropriate measures are taken to mitigate those risks. This may well require trade-offs between conflicting interests, for example weighing the desire to use the maximum amount of personal data to train an artificially intelligent model to ensure its accuracy against any privacy risks in using such a large data set.

2.   The Data Processing Principles

10.054   The core requirements in the GDPR are to comply with all six general data protection principles and to satisfy one processing condition.

10.055   The six data protection principles are set out in Article 5 of the GDPR and require that any processing of personal data is processed in the manner set out below.

(a) Data processing principles

(a)   *Lawfulness, fairness and transparency* – Personal data must be processed lawfully, fairly and in a transparent manner. This means that the processing must not be in breach of other laws, for example, in breach of duties of confidentiality. Similarly, there is an obligation to be transparent and tell individuals how their personal information is being used. This can be challenging, as artificial intelligence technology is typically complex, dynamic and hard to describe; see section titled 'Transparency and a "Right to an Explanation"' for more on this.

(b)   *Purpose limitation* – Personal data must be collected for specified, explicit and legitimate purposes and not further processed in a manner that is incompatible with those purposes, subject to certain exemptions. Again, this can be problematic for artificial intelligence projects, which will often seek to 'repurpose' existing datasets; see section titled 'Repurposing Personal Data'.

(c)   *Data minimisation* – Personal data must be adequate, relevant and limited to what is necessary in relation to the purposes for which they are processed. As a broad rule, only the minimum amount of personal data should be collected. Again, this creates potential conflicts with artificial intelligence projects which sometimes rely on the collection of massive data sets for training purposes.

(d)   *Accuracy* – Personal data must be accurate and, where necessary, kept up to date. Inaccurate personal data should be corrected or deleted. This can also raise issues in artificial intelligence projects which might be designed to create fuzzy or probabilistic conclusions about individuals. The extent to which this complies with the accuracy principle is considered further below; see section titled 'Accuracy'.

(e)   *Retention* – Personal data should be kept in an identifiable format for no longer than is necessary. There are exceptions for public interest, scientific, historical or statistical purposes. This typically means that any personal information should be subject to a set retention period and deleted at the end of that period.

(f)   *Integrity and confidentiality* – Personal data should be kept secure and the integrity of that personal data should be maintained. This is a concern for artificial intelligence projects which typically involve very large data sets that could cause significant harm if they were breached. There are also some vulnerabilities that are specific to artificial intelligence models; see section titled 'Security and the Ghosts of Training Data'.

The GDPR also includes an 'accountability' principle, meaning that you must not only comply   **10.056** with the law but also be able to demonstrate how you comply. This includes the use of Data Protection Impact Assessments (DPIAs) and similar measures discussed below.

3.   Processing Conditions and Consent

Any processing of personal data must also have a specific statutory justification. This means it   **10.057** must satisfy at least one lawful basis (known as a 'processing condition') set out in Article 6 of the GDPR. There are six different processing conditions; they are set out below.

(a) Processing conditions

(a)   *Consent (Art 6(1)(a))* – This applies where the individual has given consent. Under the GDPR, a consent will only be valid if there is a clear and specific request to the individual, and the individual actively agrees to that use. It is not possible to imply consent and you cannot rely on legalese buried deep within your terms and conditions to deliver a consent. This high threshold means consent will only be available in limited circumstances. Consent can also be withdrawn at any time, making consent very challenging for use in developing new technology.

(b)   *Necessary for performance of a contract (Art 6(1)(b))* – This applies where the processing is necessary for the performance of a contract with the individual or in order to take steps at the request of the individual prior to entering into a contract. This might be relevant in some cases, such as employment or consumer contracts, but it might be difficult to show the processing is really objectively necessary for the performance of that contract.[21]

(c)   *Legal obligation (Art 6(1)(c))* – This applies where the processing is necessary for compliance with a legal obligation under EU or Member State law (or UK law in the case of the UK GDPR).

(d)   *Vital interests (Art 6(1)(d))* – This applies where the processing is necessary in order to protect the vital interests of the individual or of another natural person. This is typically limited to processing needed for medical emergencies.

(e)   *Public functions (Art 6(1)(e))* – This applies where the processing is necessary for the performance of a task carried out in the public interest or, in the exercise of official authority vested in the controller, under EU or Member State law (or UK law in the case of the UK GDPR).

(f)   *Legitimate interests (Art 6(1)(f))* – This applies where the processing is necessary for the purposes of a legitimate interest (see below) except where such interests are overridden by the interests of the individual. This is known as the 'legitimate interests test'.

10.058 Different processing conditions can apply to different activities. For example, a company might rely on the legitimate interests test to train an artificial intelligence model and then a different processing condition for its deployment, such as consent or performance of a contract with the individual.

10.059 Importantly, most of these processing conditions only apply where the processing of personal data is necessary to achieve the relevant aim. In this context, 'necessary' typically means 'reasonably' necessary, rather than absolutely or strictly necessary. It imports a requirement of proportionality and a requirement for the minimum level of interference to achieve the legitimate aim.[22] Again, this can make the assessment of whether a processing condition is satisfied a subjective exercise.

10.060 In many cases, the narrow limitations applicable to these processing conditions mean it is necessary to rely on the final processing condition, the legitimate interests test.[23] This applies where the use

> is necessary for the purposes of the legitimate interests pursued by the controller or by a third party, except where such interests are overridden by the interests or fundamental rights and freedoms of the data subject which require protection of personal data, in particular where the data subject is a child.

10.061 The UK Information Commissioner recommends a three-step test:

(a)   *What is the legitimate interest?* The law recognises that businesses have a legitimate interest in a wide range of activities, such as marketing or increasing the internal efficiency

---

21   See for example, the EDPB's *Guidelines 2/2019 on the processing of personal data under Article 6(1)(b) GDPR in the context of the provision of online services to data subjects*, G2/209 (16 October 2019).

22   *South Lanarkshire v Scottish Information Commissioner* [2013] UKSC 55.

23   Please note the legitimate interests test is not available for processing carried out by public authorities in the performance of their tasks.

of the business. However, where the purpose serves an obvious public interest (such as detecting fraud or cyber-attacks) that interest will carry greater weight.

(b)   *Is the processing necessary for that purpose?* This may be a bigger challenge. For example, in relation to the training of models, the Information Commissioner may well want to know why it could not be conducted with pseudonymised or anonymised data (especially if that personal data is private in nature).

(c)   *Do the individual's interests override those legitimate interests?* This will depend on a range of factors including the sensitivity of the personal data, the reasonable expectations of the individual and the public interest in the underlying purpose. Safeguards will be an important part of this balancing exercise.

This is in many ways the ultimate subjective and context-specific assessment; it is some-   **10.062** times equated to the question 'Is Messi the greatest footballer of all time?'[24] As a result, the Information Commissioner expects controllers relying on the legitimate interests test to document their evaluation of this processing condition through a Legitimate Interests Assessment. This should set out, in detail, answers to the three questions described above. In many cases, this can be carried out alongside a Data Protection Impact Assessment (see DPIAs below). While there is no specific requirement in the GDPR to conduct a Legitimate Interests Assessment, this is arguably an aspect of the general accountability duty, and the Information Commissioner will likely ask for a copy of that assessment should she investigate a particular artificial intelligence project.

4.   Sensitive Data and Discrimination

The GDPR provides additional protection to 'special category personal data' and information   **10.063** about criminal convictions and offences.[25] Any artificial intelligence project using these types of personal data, or seeking to infer these types of personal data, will be subject to a much greater level of scrutiny and additional measures will be needed to ensure that it is lawful and does not have any discriminatory effects.

Special category personal data is personal data revealing racial or ethnic origin, political   **10.064** opinions, religious or philosophical beliefs or trade union membership, and the processing of genetic data, biometric data, data concerning health or data concerning a natural person's sex life or sexual orientation. These types of personal data are subject to additional protection not only because they are inherently more intrusive but also because the processing of some of these types of personal data risks discriminatory effects.

The classification of biometric data as a form of special category personal data is a significant   **10.065** restriction on some artificial intelligence projects that use that type of technology, such as facial or voice recognition technology (and more exotic forms of biometric identification such as gait analysis).

---

24   Though in reality the answer here is clearly no. While Lionel Messi has won a record six Ballon d'Or awards, a record six European Golden Shoes and scored over 700 goals, he has had more limited international success. In contrast, Pelé won three World Cups, scored more than 1,000 goals and was elected Athlete of the Century by the International Olympic Committee (despite never playing in the Olympics, unlike Messi).

25   Articles 9 and 10, GDPR.

10.066   The key formal obligation added when processing special category personal data is the need to show that a condition in Article 9 of the GDPR is satisfied. These conditions are narrower and more specific than the processing conditions in Article 6 of the GDPR (and must be satisfied in addition to an Article 6 condition). The GDPR allows Member States some flexibility in relation to the Article 9 conditions and as a result, unlike many other aspects of the GDPR, there are significant national variations in the application of these processing conditions. The approach splits broadly into three camps:

(a)   *Exhaustive definition* – Some jurisdictions have set out an exhaustive list of situations in which this special category personal data can be processed under national law. For example, the UK Data Protection Act 2018 specifies 27 different situations, including anti-doping in sport and informing elected representatives about prisoners.[26] However, this is subject to additional safeguards, such as the need to prepare an 'appropriate policy' in relation to the processing.[27]

(b)   *Amendments to existing laws* – Other EU Member States have comprehensively amended existing national law to clarify when special category personal data can be processed, such as Poland, which has amended around 160 national acts.

(c)   *No specific provisions* – Finally, some EU Member States have not made any specific changes to address this issue and instead largely rely on existing laws to set out when special category personal data can be processed.

10.067   The processing of special category personal data can have other implications, for example triggering the need to appoint a data protection officer to carry out a DPIA, or limiting the situations in which significant automated decisions can take place. More fundamentally, it will be harder to satisfy the flexible principle-based obligations in the GDPR when processing special category personal data because of its intrusive nature.

10.068   Finally, the processing of personal data about criminal convictions and offences is only allowed where it is carried out here - under the control of a government authority or is specifically authorised in EU or Member State law. The approach to this restriction varies from jurisdiction to jurisdiction. For example, the UK (both as an EU Member State before Brexit, and after Brexit) has a relatively liberal approach allowing this type of personal data to be processed in much the same situations in which special category personal data can be processed. However, some EU Member States take a more restrictive approach.

5.   International Transfers

10.069   The GDPR contains specific restrictions on transfers to countries outside the EEA that do not provide an adequate level of protection for personal data.[28] However, these restrictions do not apply where:

(a)   *The jurisdiction is white-listed* – A limited number of jurisdictions have been found to provide adequate protection, so transfers to these jurisdictions are not restricted. The relevant jurisdictions are: Andorra, Argentina, Canada (partially), the Faroe Islands,

---

26   See Schedule 1, Data Protection Act 2018.
27   See Part IV, Schedule 1, Data Protection Act 2018.
28   Chapter V, GDPR.

Guernsey, Israel, the Isle of Man, Japan, Jersey, Republic of Korea, New Zealand, Switzerland and Uruguay.[29]

(b) *Safeguards are in place* – The transfer is permitted where safeguards are in place, for example where the data exporter and data importer have signed up to the so-called Standard Contractual Clauses and a risk assessment has taken place.

(c) *Derogations* – There is a derogation for the transfer. For example, it is possible to transfer personal data to a third country where the relevant individual gives explicit consent or the transfer is necessary for the performance of a contract with the individual. These derogations are narrow and fact specific.

The rules on international transfers are complex and are not specific to artificial intelligence.   **10.070**
Accordingly, they are not considered further in this chapter.

D. SPECIFIC COMPLIANCE OBLIGATIONS

In addition to the general rules set out above, the GDPR introduces a number of new obliga-   **10.071**
tions that have particular relevance to artificial intelligence projects.

1.   Data Protection Impact Assessment and Privacy by Design

The use of personal data for the development of artificial intelligence is likely to engage a range   **10.072**
of relatively complex issues that require a number of value judgements to be made. In most cases, this evaluation must be documented. This is most likely to arise where the processing is 'high risk', as this triggers a mandatory obligation to conduct a DPIA.[30]

Many artificial intelligence projects that use personal data will trip the 'high-risk' threshold   **10.073**
for a DPIA. Guidance from the European Data Protection Board indicates that processing using new technology or using automated decision-making may need a DPIA.[31] In the UK, the Information Commissioner has issued a list of activities that will require a DPIA, which specifically refers to '*Artificial intelligence, machine learning and deep learning*' as a potential trigger.[32]

The DPIA requires an assessment of the project and the risks it raises. It must include: **10.074**

(a) a description of the processing, including its purposes and any legitimate interests pursued by the controller;

(b) an assessment of the necessity and proportionality of the processing;

(c) an assessment of the risks to individuals; and

(d) the measures taken to address those risks.

---

29   The EU–US Privacy Shield can no longer be used to justify transfers to the US: see *Data Protection Commissioner v Facebook Ireland Ltd, Maximillian Schrems* (C-311/18).

30   Article 35, GDPR.

31   *Guidelines on Data Protection Impact Assessment and determining whether processing is 'likely to result in a high risk'*, The Article 29 Working Party (WP 248 rev 01), October 2017. Endorsed by the EDPB on 25 May 2018.

32   The Information Commissioner's *Examples of processing 'likely to result in high risk'*. See https://ico.org.uk/for -organisations/guide-to-data-protection/guide-to-the-general-data-protection-regulation-gdpr/data-protection -impact-assessments-dpias/examples-of-processing-likely-to-result-in-high-risk/

10.075   The DPIA must involve the organisation's data protection officer (if one has been appointed) and it may be necessary to consult with affected individuals or their representatives. If the DPIA reveals there are unmitigated high risks, the controller must consult the relevant national data protection regulator about the processing; this process is likely to take several months.

10.076   The DPIA should also factor in the specific requirement in the GDPR to ensure privacy by design and default. These obligations require privacy issues to be an integral part of the design process, and that privacy options should, by default, be set to the most privacy-friendly option.

10.077   It is important to carry out a DPIA where required. One of the first steps any data protection authority will take when investigating an artificial intelligence project is to ask for a copy of the relevant DPIA. If a DPIA was not carried out or it is of poor quality, that may well be the trigger for further regulatory action and the lack of a DPIA was one of the reasons for the Italian Garante's decision to fine Foodinho €2.6m in relation to its rider performance algorithm. Similarly, the DPIA should be carried out at the start of the project. Leaving this to the end is likely to result in costly last-minute amendments and delays.

2.   Transparency and a 'Right to an Explanation'

10.078   The first data protection principle requires personal data to be processed fairly, lawfully and transparently. This means controllers must tell individuals what information it holds about them and how it is being used. This is typically through a privacy notice.

10.079   The specific requirements depend on whether personal data is collected directly from the data subject or from another data controller.[33] However, in either case the list of information that must be provided is extensive and includes matters such as the personal data being processed, the purposes for which it is processed, the legal basis for the processing and details of the individual's rights. This means it is common for privacy notices to run to several pages, which are likely to deter all but the most determined reader. As a result, it is good practice to 'layer' privacy notices so that the most important information is in a short top-layer paragraph that links to the full policy.

10.080   This obligation to act fairly and transparently means that an organisation using artificial intelligence should normally be clear with individuals what is happening. More importantly, where artificial intelligence is used for significant automated decision-making (see below), there is a 'right of explanation'. This means telling the affected individuals:

(a)   of the fact automated decision-making is taking place;
(b)   about the significance of the automated decision-making; and
(c)   how the automated decision-making operates.

10.081   The GDPR states that individuals must be provided with 'meaningful information about the logic involved' in the significant automated decision-making.[34] This can be challenging if the

---

33   See Articles 13 and 14, GDPR, respectively.
34   See Article 13(2)(f) and Article 14(2)(g), GDPR.

algorithm is complex or opaque. The logic used may not be easy to describe and might not even be understandable in the first place.

These difficulties are recognised by regulators, who do not expect organisations to provide a complex explanation of how the algorithm works or disclose the full algorithm itself.[35] However, as full a description as possible about the data used in the decision-making process should be provided with. The lack of a clear description was one of the reasons for the Italian Garante's decision to fine Foodinho €2.6m in relation to its rider performance algorithm. **10.082**

It is also worth thinking about the different types of explanation the individual might want. The ICO's Explain Guidance suggest six different types of explanation, namely, a: (i) rationale explanation of the reasons behind the design of the model; (ii) responsibility explanation as to who is in charge of the model; (iii) data explanation of the different types of data used to train the model; (iv) fairness explanation of the steps taken to ensure the model is not biased and individuals are treated equitably; (v) safety and performance explanation as to how the model will ensure accurate, reliable and secure decision-making; and (vi) impact explanation of the steps taken to consider and monitor the impact of the algorithm. **10.083**

It is currently rare for this level of detail to be given, but it may be useful to ensure societal acceptance, as artificial intelligence and algorithmic decision-making achieve greater prominence. **10.084**

3.   Automated Decisions – 'The computer says no'

The GDPR also contains restrictions on the use of significant automated decision-making, that is, 'a decision based solely on automated processing, including profiling, which produces legal effects concerning him or her or similarly significantly affects him or her' (Article 22(1), GDPR). **10.085**

Guidance from regulators suggests that this could include a range of different activities, such as deciding on loan applications or changing credit card limits. In practice, much will depend on the degree of automation in the decision-making process. For example, these rules are unlikely to apply to automatic summarisation (such as where a computer marks a multiple-choice exam) or decision support systems (where the ultimate decision is made by a human). In contrast, they might well apply to triaging system even if the ultimate decision is made by a human (such as where the system identifies potentially fraudulent insurance claims for an in-depth investigation). This is an evolving area of law.[36] **10.086**

---

35   *Guidelines on automated decision making and profiling*, Article 29 Working Party (WP251 rev 01), February 2018. Endorsed by the EDPB on 25 May 2018.

36   *Is that your final decision? Multi-stage profiling, selective effects, and Article 22 of the GDPR*, Reuben Binns, Michael Veale (2021), International Data Privacy Law, Vol 11, No 4, pp. 319–332.

10.087   Where the rules apply, automated decision-making is only permitted in the following situations:

(a)   *Human involvement* – If a human is involved in the decision-making process, it will not be a decision based solely on automated processing. However, that involvement would have to be meaningful and substantive. It must be more than just rubber-stamping the machine's decision; see section titled 'Human in the Loop'.

(b)   *Explicit Consent* – Automated decision-making is permitted where the individual has provided explicit consent. While this sounds like an attractive option, the GDPR places a very high threshold on consent and this will only be valid where the individual understands what they are signing up to and has a free choice.

(c)   *Performance of contract* – Automated decision-making is also permitted where it is necessary for the performance of a contract, or in order to enter into a contract, with an individual. An example might be carrying out credit checks on a new customer.

(d)   *Authorised by law* – Finally, automated decision-making processing is permitted where it is authorised by law.

10.088   Even where significant automated decisions are permitted, suitable safeguards must be put in place to protect the individual's interests. This means notifying the individual (see above) and giving them the right to a human evaluation of the decision and to contest the decision.

(a) Example: Shortlisting employment applicants

10.089   Imagine that a large employer uses an artificial intelligence solution to automatically shortlist candidates for interview. This constitutes significant automated decision-making, as the decision is made solely by automated means and significantly affects applicants.

10.090   The employer is permitted under the GDPR to make these automated decisions, as they are taken with a view to entering into an employment contract with the individual.[37]

10.091   However, in addition to the general steps described above to ensure fair and lawful processing, the employer must:

(a)   notify applicants that the decision not to shortlist them was taken using automated means; and

(b)   allow the applicant to contest the decision and ask for human evaluation.

4.   Other Rights for Individuals

10.092   Individuals are granted a range of other rights under the GDPR, including a right to access their personal data, to be provided with a copy of that data in a portable format, to correct their personal data, to object to the processing of their personal data and to ask that their personal data is erased.[38]

---

37   *Guidelines on automated decision making and profiling*, Article 29 Working Party (WP251 rev 01), February 2018. Endorsed by the EDPB on 25 May 2018. Please note that the UK Information Commissioner has suggested automated decision-making cannot be used for this purpose as a human could just as easily complete the review (though this may be optimistic for employers who have a very high ratio of applications to vacancies), see *Six things to consider when using algorithms for employment decisions*, 18 December 2020.

38   Chapter III, GDPR.

The operation of these rights is complex. Some only apply in limited situations and most are **10.093** subject to a range of exemptions. For example; you cannot just write to your bank and demand they delete details of your overdraft. The effect of these rights will also vary at different stages of the development lifecycle. For example:

(a) *Training data* – The raw training data might well contain personal data and so be directly responsive to individual rights, such as requests for access and erasure. More difficult questions arise once that training data is pre-processed as that is likely to remove most directly identifying data. However, if it can still be linked to an individual it is still personal data and so these rights may still apply.

(b) *The model* – The artificial intelligence model will typically not contain any personal data and so these rights will not apply (subject to any lingering 'ghosts' from the training data; see below). However, where fragments of data are deliberately included in the model, such as Support Vector Machines and K-nearest Neighbour models, these rights might be operative. For example, the individual might have the right to ask for that personal data to be erased, which could trigger a need to retrain the model.

(c) *Operation* – The input or output of the model may well contain personal data, such as where the algorithm is fed an individual's credit history and assigns them a credit score. This potentially triggers a range of rights, including those related to significant automated decision-making, discussed above. Whether it triggers the right to correction depends on the context in which the credit score is viewed. If it is just treated as a statistically informed guess, this is arguably not inaccurate and so the right to correction will not apply.

It is important the application of these rights is considered as part of the design of the model **10.094** and is factored into the DPIA for it. This will be more efficient than trying to retrofit the model to comply with these rights.

5.   Repurposing Personal Data

Many forms of artificial intelligence are heavily reliant on being trained on large volumes of **10.095** high-quality data, particularly machine learning technologies. However, this is subject to the principle of purpose limitation under which personal data should only be used for the purposes for which it was collected and not be subject to further incompatible uses.

In other words, there is a potential conflict between an organisation's desire to repurpose the **10.096** personal data it holds for training purposes and the desire of data protection authorities to prevent 'purpose creep' in relation to that data. In practice, the purpose limitation principle is relatively flexible and specifically envisages that personal data can be used for further purposes in certain circumstances.

For example, the new purpose might be actually compatible with the original purpose.[39] This **10.097** requires an assessment of a range of factors including: (i) any link between the original and new purpose and the context of the new purpose; (ii) the type of personal data being processed; (iii) the consequences for individuals; and (iv) the safeguards used. This could allow personal data to

---

39   Article 6(4), GDPR.

be reused for artificial intelligence projects in a wide range of situations so long as appropriate safeguards are in place to protect the personal data, such as pseudonymising or anonymising the personal data, and applying strict access controls.

10.098 Alternatively, the new use might be deemed to be compatible with the original purpose for which it was collected.[40] Deemed compatibility will arise where the new processing is for: (i) scientific or historical research purposes; (ii) statistical purposes; or (iii) archiving purposes in the public interest. However, a number of additional safeguards must be applied including strictly minimising the amount of data processed and pseudonymising or anonymising the personal data wherever possible.[41] Additional controls might arise under national law, such as the requirements under the UK Data Protection Act 2018 that the processing must not cause substantial damage or distress and, save in limited cases, cannot be used to make decisions about particular individuals.[42]

10.099 Finally, it is possible to use personal data for an entirely new purpose where the individual gives consent or use for the new purpose is required by EU or Member State law (or UK law in the case of the UK GDPR). However, this will rarely be relevant to an artificial intelligence project, as obtaining consent from a very large number of individuals whose details are in a training set is often impractical.

E. CHALLENGES RECONCILING AI AND GDPR

10.100 There are a number of challenges to ensure that an artificially intelligent model complies with the GDPR. The key issues to overcome are set out below but, in many cases, these are 'known unknowns' – while the problem has been identified, the solution has not. This is largely because it is not always clear how the GDPR's broad principle-based framework applies to new technology, such as artificial intelligence. While there is currently little 'hard' law, though this is starting to change as regulators increasingly focus on these issues. For example, the Italian Garante recently fined Foodinho E2.6m for not properly informing its delivery riders of the use of an algorithm to monitor their performance and not implementing suitable safeguards to ensure accuracy and fairness in the output of that algorithm.

1. The Black Box

10.101 There is a variety of forms of artificial intelligence models, but most involve the machine learning for itself to some extent. This typically results in complex algorithms that will be very difficult for a human to interrogate or understand – they operate in a 'black box'. This has a number of regulatory and practical implications:

(a) *Failure of accountability* – It may be difficult to satisfy the accountability obligations under the GDPR – for example, to be able to demonstrate that the decision-making is fair

---

40   Article 5(1)(b) and Recital 50, GDPR.
41   Article 89, GDPR.
42   Section 19, Data Protection Act 2018.

and is based on rational and objectively justifiable criteria. Worse, the algorithm might, beneath the surface, be taking decisions on a discriminatory basis.

(b)   *Unpredictability* – From a practical perspective, there is a risk that the algorithm initially behaves correctly in the training and testing environment but then becomes unpredictable or unreliable in the real world. This might either be because the algorithm is inherently unstable and chaotic, or because the training and testing data sets are not representative of real-world data.

These issues are especially important as there is no 'common sense' or 'ethical' override. Unlike   **10.102** a human, the algorithm has no higher-level assessment of whether what it is doing is obviously 'wrong'.

(a) Example: A military weather detector

A classic example[43] of the 'black box' problem is an algorithm developed by the military to iden-   **10.103** tify whether there is a tank in a photograph. The algorithm worked well in the training environment but was completely unpredictably in the live environment. An investigation revealed that most of the photographs in the training set containing tanks were taken on a sunny day, and most of those without tanks on an overcast day. The algorithm was therefore more suitable for weather detection than tank detection.

A great deal of work has been done to address this issue through the development of various   **10.104** techniques to better understand and explain the operation of artificial intelligence algorithms, but all of them have significant shortcomings. As a result, it will often be necessary to take a range of additional compliance measures to ensure that an artificial intelligence algorithm takes decisions fairly and lawfully in accordance with the GDPR.

2.   Accuracy

Personal data should be accurate. The reasons for this are obvious. For example, if the infor-   **10.105** mation in an individual's credit history is inaccurate, they might be wrongly refused (or given) credit. If their medical details are inaccurately recorded, their health might be endangered.

On the face of it, this creates a conflict with the use of artificial intelligence models, which will   **10.106** rarely be 100 per cent accurate in their predictions about individuals. However, this conflict is normally resolved by ensuring that the output of the artificial intelligence model is properly understood and interpreted. In other words, the output of the model should not normally be seen as providing a fact about the individual, but instead as simply providing a statistically informed guess. So long as the output is treated in that manner, there is no fundamental conflict with the GDPR.

Despite this, it is still important to ensure that the output of the artificial intelligence model is   **10.107** as accurate as possible. The greater the significance of the output, the more accurate the model

---

43   *What Artificial Experts Can and Cannot Do*, Hubert L. Dreyfus & Stuart E. Dreyfus, 1992. This classic example was used
      in my undergraduate computer science course (and in many others) and demonstrates the problem is not new. However,
      it is also worth noting there is an ongoing debate as to whether this actually happened or is just an apocryphal story.

will need to be. For example, an AI-powered horoscope will require much less scrutiny than an algorithm used for mortgage applications.

10.108   This in turn requires an understanding of how the accuracy of an artificially intelligent model is measured. This typically requires a consideration of two different types of errors:

(a)   *False positives (type I error)* – These are cases that the model incorrectly labels as positive. For example, imagine the police use a facial recognition system on a crowd to identify wanted criminals. A false positive would be an innocent individual being wrongly identified as a criminal.

(b)   *False negatives (type II error)* – These are cases that the model incorrectly labels as negative. In the example, above this might result in a wanted criminal being in the crowd but not being identified by the police's facial recognition system.

10.109   Striking the balance between these two measures is important, as the impact of each type of error may not be the same. This in turn means that two further measurements need to be considered:

(a)   *Precision* – This value measures the percentage of cases that are identified as positive, that are in fact positive. For example, if only half of the individuals identified by the police facial recognition system are wanted criminals, the precision of that system will be 50 per cent.

(b)   *Sensitivity or recall* – This value measures the percentage of positive cases that are identified as such. For example, if there are 20 wanted criminals in the crowd but only two are identified, the sensitivity of the system is 10 per cent.

10.110   There are normally trade-offs between precision and sensitivity that can be assessed statistically but may also require ethical consideration. For example, a police force wanting to catch all the criminals in a crowd would likely prioritise sensitivity. At its most extreme, this could be done by identifying all the individuals in the crowd as criminals. This would be 100 per cent sensitive but not very precise. In contrast, a police force wanting to maintain good community relations by not incorrectly stopping innocent citizens would likely prioritise precision. In either case, as the example below illustrates, it is vital that the output from the system is properly understood.

(a) Example: Understanding accuracy

10.111   Consider a police force that develops an artificial intelligence tool that uses a facial recognition tool to detect wanted criminals, who will be stopped and questioned. Assume that:

(a)   the tool is 98 per cent accurate in respect of both false positives and false negatives. This means 98 per cent of criminals are identified and 98 per cent of innocent citizens are not identified as criminals; and

(b)   1 in 500 people are wanted criminals.

10.112   *Question*: What is the precision of the system – that is, the chance that an individual flagged by the tool is in fact a wanted criminal?

Answer: The answer is not 98 per cent. In fact, it is only 9 per cent.[44]   **10.113**

In other words, despite the system being '98 per cent accurate', more than 9 in 10 of individ-   **10.114**
uals flagged as potentially being wanted criminals will actually be innocent. Knowing this is
important, to ensure that being flagged by the system is not an automatic determination that
the individual is a wanted criminal.

This also provides an example of the need to be cautious of broad assertions about the accuracy   **10.115**
of the system without seeing the underlying detail.

3.   Bias and Fairness

A key concern is that artificially intelligent models will systematically discriminate against   **10.116**
particular classes of individuals. Bias is a feature in both human and machine decision-making.
However, bias in machine decision-making is perceived as a greater risk because most people
assume a human will have some degree of empathy and so try to identify and self-correct their
bias, and will apply a final common-sense check to their decision. Machine decision-making
does not have either safeguard.

The machine's bias can come from a number of sources. If the training data reflects past   **10.117**
discrimination, those biases might be inherited by the machine. Alternatively, the training
data might be imbalanced, with fewer examples of individuals with certain characteristics,
leading the machine to consider them less important. Finally, the biases might come from the
machine spotting unanticipated patterns in the data and drawing unacceptable or unsupported
conclusions.

For example, assume a company wants to use artificial intelligence to sift and sort recruitment   **10.118**
applications for engineering positions. To do so, it trains the model to find applicants that are
similar to existing high-performing engineers within that company. If most of the engineers in
the company are male, the model may well prioritise recruitment applications that show 'male
characteristics' and hence discriminate against female applicants. Moreover, this discrimination
may be deeply ingrained into the model so that even if the applicant's name and gender is
masked when applications are fed into the model, it may discriminate based on other factors
that act as a surrogates for gender such as using the term 'women's chess club captain' or attending an all-women's college.[45]

From a data protection perspective, there are three issues to consider: **10.119**

(a)   The GDPR requires the processing of personal data to be lawful. If the processing
breaches other laws, such as discriminating against someone based on protected characteristics under the UK Equality Act 2010, that will also be a breach of the GDPR.

---

44   Assume you have 1,000,000 citizens. Of those, 998,000 will be innocent and 2,000 will be wanted criminals (1 in 500).
Of the criminals, 1960 will be identified (2,000 x 98%). Of the innocent citizens, 19,960 will be flagged (998,000 x 2%).
Thus the percentage of individuals flagged that are actually wanted criminals is 8.9% (1960 ÷ (1960 + 19,960)).
45   See *Amazon scraps secret AI recruiting tool that showed bias against women.* Reuters. Dastin J, (2018).

(b) Additional protection is provided for special category personal data, such as information about racial or ethnic information (see section titled 'Sensitive Data and Discrimination'). The intentional processing of these types of personal data will only be allowed in limited circumstances. It is also necessary to guard against the model learning correlations between data that result in unintentional processing of special category personal data, resulting in unwanted and unintended discrimination.

(c) The GDPR requires the processing of personal data to be 'fair'. What this subjective and open-ended concept means in data protection terms is largely unexplored. Systematic and unjustified (or at least unexplained) discrimination against a particular class of individuals is unlikely to be fair. However, data protection regulators often couch the concept more broadly in terms of processing contrary to societal expectation.

10.120 There are various measures that can be taken to monitor and correct for bias, including modifying training sets reflecting past bias or correcting imbalanced datasets to add or remove data relating to under- or over-represented populations.

10.121 The model should be monitored to detect bias and could have its output corrected to remove those biases. However, this process might be constrained by the GDPR itself. For example, assume a bank wants to ensure it is not discriminating against its customers based on racial or ethnic origin. One option would be to collect information about those customers' racial and ethnic origins to conduct this analysis. However, this is special category personal data, so its processing is only allowed in very limited conditions. UK law does contain a specific right to process racial and ethnic origin to ensure equality of opportunity or treatment, but careful thought would be needed as to whether collecting this data would be proportionate (and whether customers would be prepared to provide it). In addition, this exemption does not tend to feature in many EU Member States' laws.

10.122 Similarly, ensuring fairness is often intractable and involves trade-offs between different measures of fairness based on highly subjective value judgements. Data protection regulators are often ill-equipped to assess these difficult social, political and cultural questions, lacking both specialist subject matter knowledge to contextualise the decision and a democratic mandate to intervene.

(a) Example: Unfair exam moderation algorithms?

10.123 An example of an intractable fairness problem is how to award exam grades to UK students who never actually took their exams as a result of the Covid-19 pandemic. The grades were primarily based on the teachers' predicted grades for the students. However, these predictions needed to be moderated across different schools, to ensure a consistent approach and confirm the grades were not overly optimistic. The UK government used an algorithm to conduct this moderation, based largely on ensuring the students' grades were consistent with the historic performance of their schools. The design of the algorithm had to balance a number of competing requirements, namely:

(a) Fairness to those students as a cohort, by not inflating grades and thus devaluing those exams.

(b) Fairness to cohorts in previous and subsequent years. In particular, grade inflation in this year had potential to undermine the value of past and future cohorts' grades.

(c)   Fairness to different segments of the student population, such as ensuring a fair balance of grades between male and female students and between state and private schools.

(d)   Fairness to individual students, by ensuring their grades reflect their actual ability and are not overly constrained by historical results. This is a particular issue for outliers, such as students whose performance is much better (or worse) than that of students in previous years, and small subject groups whose historic performance can vary significantly from year to year.

These aims are very difficult to reconcile. In practice, the UK government initially took an approach that favoured fairness to the population as a whole – by avoiding grade inflation – over fairness to individual students, many of whom had their teacher-assessed grades marked down.   **10.124**

The moderation algorithm clearly involved the processing of personal data and so was required to be 'fair' under the GDPR. The UK Information Commissioner started to engage[46] with Ofqal, the regulator responsible for the algorithm, but the UK government abandoned the moderation algorithm before the investigation came to a conclusion.   **10.125**

The Information Commissioner may well have been relieved at not having to grapple with such an intractable issue and enter treacherous political waters. However, the *Datatilsynet* (Norwegian data protection regulator) did intervene, issuing a notice provisionally concluding that a similar moderation algorithm run by the International Baccalaureate Organisation was unfair.[47] This was because it did not reflect the students' expectation that their 'grade [would be] awarded based on their demonstrable academic achievements and that the grade would reflect the work they have put in as well as the knowledge and skills they have attained', and not through the use of historic data which is a 'factor completely outside their control, which does not have any connection to their demonstrable and individual academic achievements, and that relates to other people'.   **10.126**

These conclusions were contested by the International Baccalaureate Organisation, who considered that, in light of the exceptional circumstances of the pandemic, students would have expected their grades to be moderated in this way to ensure fairness to the cohort as a whole. In addition, an approach based on the students' own academic achievement could only result in no grades being awarded to anyone, given the exams did not take place. The open-textured nature of these submissions highlights the difficulties in establishing objective fairness.   **10.127**

Finally, the use of machines in decision-making creates the risk of 'unexpected correlation bias' – new and unexpected forms of discrimination based on unexpected patterns in the data. While human discrimination tends to run along well-known lines, peculiarities in the training data could lead to a machine deciding that cat owners should pay more for car insurance or croquet players do not make good accountants. In practice, this correlation bias might be based on even more opaque data combinations. In the absence of a clear and objective rationale (such as being able to demonstrate that cat owners really are dangerous drivers), this discrimination is likely   **10.128**

---

46   Information Commissioner's *Statement in response to exam results*, 14 August 2020.
47   Datatilsynet letter *Advance notification of order to rectify unfairly processed and incorrect personal data – International Baccalaureate Organization*, 7 August 2020.

to be unfair. However, identifying this 'unexpected correlation bias' deep within a complex artificial intelligence model is likely to be challenging.

10.129   For these reasons, 'fairness' remains one of the unexplored frontiers in data protection law. It is not clear if the GDPR is even the right tool to solve this problem.

4.   Security and the Ghosts of Training Data

10.130   Personal data must be processed in a way that ensures its security and integrity.[48] Data breaches can cause harm to individuals and lead to significant regulatory and civil liability.

10.131   This is a particular issue for artificial intelligence models as they often use very large data sets, both to train the model and in operation. The technical means to ensure security are outside the scope of this chapter but, like any complex IT system development, require adherence to good coding standards and the careful use of third-party components. Similarly, once in operation, the model should be subject to a range of measures including the use of proper access controls, patching and penetration testing.

10.132   There are, however, some exotic privacy attacks that are specific to artificial intelligence models, which focus on any lingering ghosts left by the training data used to train the artificial intelligence model. This is a particular problem where the model is 'overfitted' to match the training data too closely.[49]

10.133   A membership inference attack involves attackers trying to infer if a particular individual was part of the training data set. This information could be highly sensitive in some cases; for example, where the model was trained on a sensitive population such as patients with a particular disease. This attack uses the confidence score provided by the artificial intelligence model. If the model is disproportionately confident in its predictions about a particular individual, this may well indicate that the model recognises that specific individual, allowing the attacker to infer that they were part of the training data.

10.134   A model inversion attack involves an attacker observing the inputs and outputs of the model to reconstruct the training data. For example, consider a facial recognition system that is used to recognise pictures of particular named individuals, alongside a confidence rate of that assessment. An attacker could submit multiple randomly generated faces, and use the name and confidence scores that are returned to reconstruct the face images of the relevant individuals. Researchers have shown this can be used to create imperfect but identifiable images.[50]

10.135   Some types of model store fragments of personal data in the system by design. For example, Support Vector Machines and K-nearest Neighbour models work by retaining some of the

---

48   Article 32, GDPR.

49   *Algorithms that remember: model inversion attacks and data protection law*, Michael Veale, Reuben Binns and Lilian Edwards, in Philosophical Transactions of the Royal Society A: Mathematical, Physical and Engineering Sciences. Vol. 376. No. 2133. Pages 20180083. 2018.

50   *Model Inversion Attacks that Exploit Confidence Information and Basic Countermeasures*, Matt Fredrikson, Somesh Jha, Thomas Ristenpart, https://rist.tech.cornell.edu/papers/mi-ccs.pdf.

actual training data, which can be used for later comparison. This personal data can normally be extracted easily where the attackers have access to the underlying model.

The ability of attackers to conduct these attacks will, in part, depend on whether the attackers **10.136** have complete access to the model (a 'white box' attack), or only have the ability to query the model and observe inputs and outputs (a 'black box' attack). White box attacks are inherently more difficult to counter, as it is not possible to monitor and block suspicious queries made to the model. Similarly, a white box attack will often provide easy access to any personal data kept in the model by design.

Finally, these types of attacks should be approached with care as they could constitute a crim- **10.137** inal offence in the UK, which makes re-identifying de-identified personal data a criminal offence (though there are limited exceptions, including for research purposes).

F. SAFEGUARDS AND COMPLIANCE MEASURES

There are a number of safeguards and other practical compliance measures that should be **10.138** considered to ensure that any artificial intelligence model is trained, and operates safely, in compliance with the GDPR.

1.   Human in the Loop

One significant intervention is to involve a human in any algorithmic decision-making. There **10.139** are a number of potential models, such as:

(a)   the human acting as the ultimate decision maker. All the artificial intelligence model provides is information or a recommendation for that purpose; or

(b)   those affected by the decision can ask that it be re-reviewed by a human.

The GDPR contains strict rules on significant automated decision-making, meaning that some **10.140** decisions cannot be made solely by machine and, even if they are permitted, a right to human review must be provided. Beyond the technical requirements of data protection law, there is a wider ethical question of whether it is appropriate to delegate decisions about individuals to a machine. As the human rights organisation Liberty submitted to a recent UK Parliament Select Committee hearing: 'where algorithms are used in areas that would engage human rights, they should at best be advisory'.[51]

It is important that any human intervention is not a rubber-stamping exercise and instead **10.141** involves a substantive assessment. This faces a number of challenges:

---

51   See statement by Silkie Carlo of Liberty in the House of Commons Science and Technology Committee's report on *Algorithms in decision-making*, Fourth Report of Session 2017–19. https://publications.parliament.uk/pa/cm201719/cmselect/cmsctech/351/351.pdf

(a)   the human reviewer might believe the machine's decision is right because it comes from a computer or because it normally makes correct decisions.[52] This can be addressed through culture and training, but other methods can be used to keep the reviewers on their toes such as occasionally introducing a deliberately incorrect decision and checking the human spots it; and

(b)   there may be information asymmetries, or the human reviewer may not be able to understand the logic behind the machine's decision. This can be addressed by ensuring the human reviewer has access to the same data in a comprehensible fashion and has some understanding of the underlying logic being used by the machine.

10.142   The use of human decision-making also largely takes the decision-making process outside the scope of the GDPR. The GDPR regulates the minds of machines, not men (or women). Unless based on inaccurate or unlawfully processed data, human decisions cannot generally be challenged on the basis that they are unfair or unlawful under the GDPR. For example, you cannot use the GDPR to dispute a human's grading of your exam or decision not to renew your insurance (see *Nowak* (C-434/16) and *Johnson v Medical Defence Union* [2007] EWCA Civ 262).

2.   Peering Into the Black Box

10.143   Another important safeguard is to use measures to try and understand the logic of the artificial intelligence model to ensure it is taking decisions fairly and lawfully, in accordance with the general accountability obligations in the GDPR.

10.144   While a complete understanding of complex artificial intelligence models will be difficult, if not impossible, a significant amount of work has been carried out to create tools and techniques to make the operation of these opaque algorithms more transparent. These tools might either allow a local explanation (such as why a particular decision was taken) or a global explanation (such as how the algorithm works as a whole).

10.145   An example of a local explanation might be the creation of a counterfactual scenario that would produce an alternative outcome. For example, where a loan application by an individual is rejected, the model could provide not just the rejection but also an assessment of the minimum change to the input variables for the application to be successful, such as if the applicant's income was £X,000 more or the loan £Y,000 less.

10.146   More complex tools exist, such as Local Interpretable Model-Agnostic Explanations (LIME), which analyses randomly sampled data points around a particular prediction point to create a local approximation for the algorithm that can be more easily understood. However, these face a number of challenges, not least that the approximation can quickly become unreliable with even small changes in the model it is trying to approximate.

10.147   Global explanations might come from the use of Partial Dependency Plots, which graphically represent the marginal effect of one or two input features on the output, and thus provide

---

52   *Human-algorithm teaming in face recognition: How algorithm outcomes cognitively bias human decision-making.* Howard JJ, Rabbitt LR, Sirotin YB (2020). PLoS ONE 15(8): e0237855. https://doi.org/10.1371/journal.pone.0237855

a visualisation of some aspects of the algorithm. However, these are subject to a number of limitations, including that they can only model changes to a limited number of inputs.

The ICO's Explain guidance contains a detailed overview of the various tools currently available and their limitations. While there has been significant progress in algorithmic interpretability in recent years, this will not provide a complete solution and complex multi-dimensional artificial intelligence models are likely to remain largely unknowable.   **10.148**

3.   Privacy-enhancing Techniques

Other privacy-enhancing techniques can be used to help ensure that artificial intelligence technologies comply with the GDPR. One example is the use of local inferences. This involves a model being stored locally rather than centrally. For example, language translation software could be installed on a smartphone and the translation performed on that phone, rather than sending that information to a central server. This minimises the sharing of any personal data but can be difficult, particularly if the model is large or computationally expensive.   **10.149**

Similarly, it may be possible to minimise the amount of personal data used to train the model, by using synthetic data. This is artificially created data that replicates the characteristics of the underlying data set. If created carefully, the synthetic data should not relate to any individual and so its use will fall outside the GDPR.   **10.150**

It may be possible to use federated learning. This involves different parties using their own pool of training data to create a local model. Those local models can then be shared with others and combined to create a more accurate global model. This avoids each party having to share the raw training data and has been successfully used in medical research.   **10.151**

4.   General Safeguards

Alongside the more innovative measures described above are more standard safeguards. Like any information technology project, the artificial intelligence tool will need to be tested thoroughly before being deployed into a live environment. However, testing an opaque algorithm is difficult, as there is a risk that the test cases will not adequately cover all of the required scenarios. If the model behaves chaotically, even small changes in input variables can lead to very different outcomes. In other words, the algorithm may react unusually or unpredictably in relation to particular combinations of input and this may not be detected during the testing process.   **10.152**

Similarly, it may be necessary to monitor the operation of the model once it is deployed. In particular, it is important to ensure the model adapts to changes in the environment and does not exhibit 'model drift'. This monitoring could involve a range of measures, from obtaining aggregated reports about the performance of the model to sampling the outputs on an ongoing basis. An example might be subjecting a small sample to a human review, to verify that the model continues to operate properly.   **10.153**

Finally, given the potential for such complex models to operate unpredictability, it may be wise to add circuit breakers to the model, so that if its outputs exceed certain limits, either a warning   **10.154** is triggered or the model is suspended. Those limits might be either predefined or set by reference to a less sophisticated (and thus more predictable) decision-making model.

G. ALGORITHMIC FAIRNESS AND FUTURE REGULATION

10.155 In this final section of this chapter, we look at some of the longer-term questions about the scope and effect of the GDPR and the areas in which future statutory intervention might be required.

1. Should We Think More about Algorithms and Less about AI?

10.156 Artificial intelligence is an emerging technology. Significant strides have been made in relation to domain-specific tasks, such as facial recognition or language translation. However, the development of a generalised artificial intelligence, capable of mimicking the flexibility and creativity of human intelligence, remains unlikely in the medium and, possibly, the long term.

10.157 In contrast, the impact of complex algorithms on society is a more immediate concern, regardless of whether or not that algorithm can be described as 'intelligent'. This concern is likely to become more pronounced as more and more decisions are delegated by man to machine.

10.158 Some impacts are obvious, because of a direct human interaction with the algorithm. The use of algorithms to moderate exam results affected by the Covid-19 pandemic is an immediate example (see discussion above), but there are many others. For example, artificial intelligence is increasingly used to determine if you can get a job. It will scan and assess your CV and can also assess your performance during a video interview. Do you use positive words? Do you smile enough? This is not science fiction and is becoming widely used in the US.

10.159 In other cases algorithms are used behind the scenes by businesses and governments, and have a more invisible effect: for example, determining whether you are eligible for a mortgage, or deciding what offers or advertisements you see, or the price you pay for goods and services online.

10.160 Finally, algorithms have an important effect on our core democratic values. The explosion in the availability of information on the internet has resulted in a dramatic shift from an information economy to an attention economy. The ability to determine what a person's valuable attention is focused on has a very powerful impact on their perception of the world. This is determined by algorithms that sift, select and promote content based on whatever priorities are hardwired into that algorithm, likely to be largely based on maximising user interaction.

10.161 Providing the proper regulatory framework for these algorithms will be vital to ensure their impact is fair, transparent and socially acceptable.[53]

---

53   *How do you regulate an algorithm? A set of strawman remedies.* Church (2020). Utilities Law Review. Vol. 22. No. 5.

2.   How Do You Understand an Algorithm?

One of the key challenges in regulating artificial intelligence is the complexity of the underlying   **10.162**
technology. The algorithm is fundamentally different to a human being. It is not intelligent
as such and does not share the same thought processes. It is not possible to model its actions
through the prism of human aims or motivations.

Instead, the regulatory analysis and remedies should address the underlying operation of the   **10.163**
algorithm. This raises some difficult issues.

(a)   *Complexity* – Most algorithms of interest will be difficult to review and understand. As
set out above, artificial intelligence is likely to operate in a 'black box', its inner workings
largely incomprehensible to a human. Even those written using traditional programming
techniques will implement complex underlying models and be in technical code that is
only accessible by those with high levels of technical skill.

(b)   *Dynamics* – Many algorithms are updated frequently to improve their performance and to
respond to changes in the environments in which they are used (for example, to counter
misuse). This could be by tweaking and tuning aspects of the algorithm, or replacing it
with a completely new algorithm. In either event, any remedy needs to be flexible enough
to allow rapid changes in the underlying technology.

(c)   *Dynamic environment and chaotic operation* – Even where an algorithm remains the same,
the environment in which it is used is likely to change dramatically over time. The algorithm may well be chaotic, which would make mapping its inputs and outputs difficult,
as even small changes to the initial conditions lead to large differences in its output.

(d)   *Confidentiality and gaming* – Finally, the algorithm may be highly confidential and
organisations will be very sensitive to it being disclosed to a regulator or being subject to
more public scrutiny. This is largely to protect the intellectual property rights in the algorithm but also aims to stop 'gaming' of the algorithm. For example, a detailed technical
explanation of the algorithms used in CV-sifting could be used by applicants to trick the
system into shortlisting them.

3.   Do We Need New Regulatory Remedies?

This may well require a new approach to regulation and a more radical set of regulatory reme-   **10.164**
dies. It might include some of the measures below.

(a)   *Opening the black box or reward function* – Data protection authorities might, in theory,
want direct access to the code used in the algorithm. However, this will rarely be practical, given the complexity and sensitivity of the code and the frequency with which that
code will be updated. Similarly, data protection authorities could seek direct access to the
reward function used to train an AI algorithm, though these functions are still complex
and difficult to interpret and do not always effectively dictate the algorithm's operation.

(b)   *Systematic test cases* – Data protection authorities might want close oversight over what
goes into and comes out of the black box. There have been numerous small-scale and
academic studies of the operation of algorithms, but data protection authorities might
want more extensive testing capabilities by creating very large test cases (as you would
as part of normal software testing) and then running those test cases over the algorithm.

For example, when testing for discrimination against online users, regulators could try millions of variations using simulated data based different on geographic location, purchase history, operating system, referral means, and so on, to build a better picture of the algorithm's operation.

(c)   *Document and log* – Alternatively, there could be express obligations to document and log the operation of an algorithm. This could help data protection authorities verify its operation and carry out an algorithmic post-mortem if it creates serious problems.

10.165   While the GDPR gives data protection authorities broad powers to conduct data protection audits, it is not clear if these powers are already in regulators' toolkits. For example, the UK can issue an Assessment Notice which, among other things, gives the Information Commissioner the right to observe and examine equipment and be provided with an explanation of its operation, but this might not extend to the ability to run test cases or similar.

10.166   Finally, there could be an argument for a more radical set of remedies to better regulate artificial intelligence and complex algorithms.

(a)   *Consultation and transparency* – The current consultation obligations in the GDPR are weak, with controllers only required to seek views of individuals 'where appropriate' as part of any DPIA. For processing that is both significant and high-risk, this could be supplemented with a much stronger obligation to provide transparency about the relevant processing and the algorithm being used, coupled with greater obligations to consult relevant stakeholders. For particularly high-risk algorithms, there could be an obligation to provide some or all of the six different types of artificial intelligence explanations set out in the ICO's Explain Guidance.

(b)   *Skilled person review* – Regulators could be given the power to order an independent skilled person to undertake a review of the algorithm. The UK Financial Conduct Authority already has this power and can require a regulated firm to be reviewed by a third party with specialist skills. This might provide a model to extend the power of data protection regulators to require an independent review of an algorithm's fairness and GDPR compliance.

(c)   *Optional application* – Alternatively, users might be given the option to disapply the algorithm. The EU's proposed Digital Services Act would require large-scale internet platforms to give users the option of a 'bubble-free' view in which the information they see is not algorithmically customised.

(d)   *Structural separation* – A more radical suggestion would be some form of structural separation. The part of the organisation responsible for managing the algorithm could be placed in a separate business unit, with clearly defined objectives and incentives, and made independent from upstream and downstream parts of the business. There is some precedent in regulated industries, such as in the telecoms sector. However, this is a complex and onerous remedy and is typically more useful in addressing economic issues rather than privacy concerns.

10.167   It is interesting to note that the EU's proposed Artificial Intelligence Act contains some of these remedies, but for "high risk" artificial intelligence systems proposes a model largely based on product safety standards. In particular, it would require a conformity assessment for "high risk" artificial intelligence systems placed on the market or put into service in the EU.

This would be backed up by an obligation to report serious incidents and market surveillance activities.

4.   Do We Need an Algorithmic 'Super Regulator'?

The final question is whether relying on data protection authorities, acting in concert with other regulators, provides the right model for algorithmic regulation. **10.168**

These are pointed questions for the UK, which, after Brexit, has greater freedom to reimagine its regulatory model and the future role of the Information Commissioner. This could result in the UK giving the Information Commissioner an expanded or more explicit mandate to address algorithmic regulation. **10.169**

One argument against the current approach is that each regulatory body will only take a narrow view of the issues, rather than considering the broader picture. For example, data protection regulators can only consider algorithms that process personal data and must necessarily focus on the privacy and data protection impacts. Questions raised by the use of algorithms take in matters beyond data processing. **10.170**

Similarly, if multiple regulators are involved, how do you coordinate the response provided by those regulators, particularly where the interests of those regulators might diverge? For example, one regulator might call for more personal data to be processed to ensure greater accuracy and fairer results, which a data protection regulator might well want to resist. The UK has set up the Digital Regulation Cooperation Forum (DRCF) specifically to try to avoid this problem by developing a more joined-up regulatory approach. The EU has chosen to address these issues by seeking to specifically regulate artificial intelligence through its proposed Artificial Intelligence Act. This would take the form of a EU Regulation that completely bans some forms of artificial intelligence (such subliminal techniques that manipulate humans in a harmful way), requires greater transparency for other use cases (such as the creation of deepfakes) and imposes significant and extensive obligations on any 'high risk' uses of artificial intelligence (such as where it is used in critical infrastructure or as a safety product). This would all be backed up by a new regulatory superstructure under which each EU Member State would appoint a national regulator and a 'European Artificial Intelligence Board' would be set up. **10.171**

Finally, and most importantly, there is the question of democratic mandate. Algorithmic regulation will often involve difficult questions about how you objectively determine fairness and balance the interests of different groups. In other words, you often can't be fair to everyone. Do technocratic data protection authorities have the standing to intervene on these issues, or are these hard decisions best left to politicians? **10.172**

H. CONCLUSION

The GDPR is not the 'law of everything' and does not protect all data; nor does it regulate all decisions made using data. However, it is very broadly applicable. Most artificial intelligence projects will need to grapple with the GDPR to some degree. **10.173**

10.174 The requirements of the GDPR can be complex and subtle, and a number of questions remain as to how it applies to emerging technology, such as artificial intelligence. There is, however, some excellent guidance available from regulators and the GDPR's strong reliance on concepts of fairness, necessity and proportionality align it closely with wider questions of data ethics.

11

COMPETITION LAW

Suzanne Rab[1]

A. INTRODUCTION

The field of artificial intelligence (AI) has been reshaping virtually every industry built on the **11.001** idea that machines could be used to simulate human intelligence through so-called machine learning. Antitrust interest in this topic has been generated among regulators, policy-makers, academics and business in the EU and internationally. This chapter explores the extent to which AI may raise competition or other concerns for consumer welfare and whether existing legal and policy instruments are appropriate to deal with the emerging opportunities and challenges.

The debate around AI and competition law has attracted interest among policy-makers, regula- **11.002** tors, practitioners and academics and, as yet, there is no consensus internationally on the extent

---

1   Professor Suzanne Rab is qualified to advise on UK and EU law. Commentary on other jurisdictions is based on her international comparative experience of those jurisdictions and is provided here for information purposes. This chapter is informed by the author's work and research into the area of artificial intelligence and sector-specific regulation. The views expressed remain those of the author. This chapter draws upon and expands the analysis in S. Rab, 'Artificial Intelligence, Algorithms and Antitrust', Competition Law Journal (2019) Vol 18, No 4, pp. 141–50.

to which existing law and policy is fit for purpose. In their book *Virtual Competition*, Professors Ariel Ezrachi and Maurice Stucke postulate the 'end of competition as we know it' and call for heightened regulatory intervention against algorithmic systems.[2]

11.003   The AI antitrust literature reflects three broad themes or postulated areas of antitrust concern. First, it is suggested that AI can broaden the circumstances in which known forms of anti-competitive conduct, and particularly conscious parallelism or tacit collusion[3] can occur. Second, it is hypothesized that the use of algorithms will bring newer forms of anti-competitive conduct which challenge traditional antitrust orthodoxy with new elements such as price discrimination, co-opetition,[4] data extraction and data capture. Third, it is suggested that deception is inherent in algorithmic markets, prompting consumers to engage in exploitative transactions.

B. COMPETITION LAW

11.004   As the technology itself is continuing to develop, this chapter focuses on the claimed facilitating role of algorithms, whether they may contribute or lead to anti-competitive outcomes and the implications for policy and antitrust intervention. It considers: (1) whether AI leads to anti-competitive outcomes or other consumer welfare concerns; (2) whether there is an enforcement gap; and (3) regulators' views on attribution of liability for AI decisions.

1.   Mapping Out the Subject-matter

(a) Artificial intelligence

11.005   The author's commentary on defining AI is included in Chapter 1 of this book.

11.006   As noted elsewhere in the book, there is no single or universally accepted definition of AI, but there are different definitions and taxonomies. To assist in mapping out the subject-matter in the context of competition law, it is useful to consider how AI relates to other key conceptual and analytical frameworks.

11.007   A starting point is the definition offered by Russel and Norvig where, for example, AI is defined as computers or machines that seek to act rationally, think rationally, act like a human or think like a human.[5]

---

2   A. Ezrachi and M. Stucke, *Virtual Competition: The Promise and Perils of the Algorithm-Driven Economy* (Harvard University Press, 2016).

3   Tacit collusion is a form of collusion typically seen in an oligopolistic market structure, where competing firms providing a good do not explicitly collude on any feature (such as price, quantity, or product characteristics), but rather, observe and imitate each other's actions in a way that is mutually beneficial to both sides.

4   Co-opetition involves collaboration between competitors, in the hope of mutually beneficial results.

5   S. Russel and P. Norvig, *Artificial Intelligence: A Modern Approach* (3rd edn, Pearson, 2010).

AI is therefore characterized by four main features and we bear these in mind as a background   **11.008**
to the principles considered in this chapter:

- *Acting rationally* – AI is designed to achieve goals via perception and taking action as a result.
- *Thinking rationally* – AI is designed to logically solve problems, make inferences and optimize outcomes.
- *Acting like a human* – Later popularized as the 'Turing Test', testing of natural language processing, knowledge representation and automated reasoning and learning.
- *Thinking like a human* – Inspired by cognitive science, 'that activity devoted to making machines intelligent, and intelligence is that quality that enables an entity to function appropriately and with foresight in its environment'.[6]

(b) Machine learning

Developments in AI around machine learning systems trained against observational or simu-   **11.009**
lated outcomes are relevant because of the possibilities for collusion on datasets and, conceivably, outcomes where there is an incentive to manipulate the outcome.

(c) Big data

'Big data' aggregates vast exploitable datasets of unstructured and structured digital informa-   **11.010**
tion, including:

- aggregation in terms of size, shape (such as text, image, video, sound), structure and speed;
- analysis by quantitative analysis software (using AI, ML, neural networks, robotics and algorithmic computation) on a real-time basis; and
- increasing value with fast and incremental business change to enhance efficiency and innovation are relevant because of both positive and negative possibilities for competitiveness.

(d) AI and antitrust

Competition laws or 'antitrust' contain two basic types of rules that affect commercial agree-   **11.011**
ments and practices (outside of control of mergers and acquisitions):

- prohibitions on restrictive agreements;[7]
- prohibitions on the abuse of a dominant position.[8]

These prohibitions form the focus for this chapter, using the approach under EU competition   **11.012**
law and national equivalents as the starting point.

---

6   N. Nilsson, *The Quest for Artificial Intelligence: A History of Idea and Achievement* (Cambridge University Press, 2009).

7   The EU prohibition on restrictive agreements is contained in Article 101 of the Treaty on the Functioning of the EU ('TFEU') and national law equivalents (including Chapter I of the Competition Act 1998 in the UK). The most serious form of anti-competitive agreement is a cartel to fix prices or share markets or customers.

8   The EU prohibition on abuse of dominance is contained in Article 102 TFEU and national law equivalents (including Chapter II of the Competition Act 1998 in the UK). Typical types of behaviour that have been sanctioned as an abuse of dominance include: pricing abuses (excessive pricing, predatory pricing, margin squeeze and discriminatory pricing); and non-price abuses (e.g. refusal to supply, refusal to license, and abusive litigation).

2. Does AI Lead to Anti-competitive Outcomes?

(a) Will AI facilitate collusion?

11.013 The main concern raised to date in the context of competition law is that a specific type of AI – specifically pricing algorithms used by firms to monitor, recommend or set prices – can lead to collusive outcomes in the market in two particular ways. First, it is suggested that these pricing algorithms may help facilitate explicit coordination agreements among firms. This is based on the premise that the use of algorithms may make market conditions more suitable for coordination. For example, monitoring prices of other firms could be easier when algorithms are deployed and AI could also be used to implement coordination agreed between humans. Second, it is suggested that under certain conditions, the use of pricing algorithms can facilitate tacit collusion even absent an agreement. This is based on the premise that when many or all firms in the market use similar algorithms to set prices, their strategies can be anticipated by each other, making it easier to reach coordinated outcomes.

11.014 Mehra has focused on the facilitating role of algorithms in tending towards conscious parallelism, stating that:

> to the extent that the effects of oligopoly fall through cracks of antitrust law, the advent of the robo-seller may widen those cracks into chasms. For several reasons, the robo-seller should increase the power of oligopolists to charge supracompetitive prices: the increased accuracy in detecting changes in price, greater speed in pricing response, and reduced irrationality in discount rates all should make the robo-seller a more skilful oligopolist than its human counterpart in competitive intelligence and sales [...] the robo-seller should also enhance the ability of oligopolists to create durable cartels.[9]

11.015 This suggests that algorithms can be a 'plus factor' which renders tacit collusion more likely, stable and durable by facilitating detection and retaliation at lower levels of concentration than traditional theory would hold. However, this claim is not straightforward and invites further examination. Firms would still need to choose whether to use and continue to use the same or similar algorithms. The incentive to coordinate is not automatic just because algorithms exist. Firms could still choose to undercut rivals even where they deploy algorithms as part of price-setting. Indeed, smart algorithms might even try to cheat without being caught. Some of the alternative hypotheses are shown in Table 11.1 below, which considers some of the typical market conditions preventing coordination and aspects of AI which may count as factors making coordination more or less likely.

---

9   S. Mehra, 'Antitrust and the Robo-Seller: Competition in the Time of Algorithms' (2006) 100 Minnesota Law Review 1323–75.

Table 11.1   Analysis of AI and market conditions preventing or facilitating coordination

Market conditions preventing coordination	Aspects of AI facilitating coordination	Alternative hypothesis
Large number of sellers (the greater the number of sellers, the greater the probability that individual sellers will ignore their rivals)	AI may facilitate co-ordination even among a larger number of sellers. Where many or all firms in the market use similar algorithms to set prices, their strategies can be anticipated by each other, making it easier to reach coordinated outcomes	
Time lag between initial price cut and response of rivals (enables concealment of price reductions, leading to delays in retaliation)	AI may be used to detect and respond to deviations where there is access to big data	
High discount rate of future profits (provides incentives to appropriate profits in the near-term)	AI may prefer long-term profit maximization	Firms could still choose to undercut rivals for short-term gain; smart algorithms may try to cheat
Misinterpretation of shocks to demand or supply as deviations (leads to inappropriate signalling)	AI may be able to recognize the genuine cause of price reductions	
Different cost structures (where overhead costs are high, pricing discipline tends to break down)	Cost data may become more accessible	AI in principle has no impact on cost structures including the incentive to discount
Product heterogeneity (the greater the heterogeneity, the more difficult it is to coordinate)		AI does not of itself affect product heterogeneity; individualized pricing could undermine coordination

It follows that the hypothesis that algorithms may make tacit collusion more likely requires **11.016** further examination. First, where transactions are more personalized – as they increasingly tend to be in the digital economy – each transaction with the customer may be seen as a 'one-shot game' which is inconsistent with tacit collusion. Second, where non-price competition is included with elements such as differential service and quality standards, there is more background 'noise'. This, in turn, may tend to make detecting and punishing deviations more costly. Finally, there is currently limited understanding of countervailing strategies. Buyers – or even AI systems on the buy-side – may be able to counteract oligopolistic pricing that disrupts the sellers' algorithms. The fast-moving pace of technology may suggest a prospect of emergence of AI countervailing measures which invite or facilitate new entry, for example, through data perturbation,[10] masking,[11] encryption and other variants.

(b) Will AI lead to other outcomes which present concerns for consumer welfare?

A further theme in the antitrust debate is that algorithmic markets will tend to increase price **11.017** transparency and mean that customers are nudged into deceptive or exploitative personalized pricing.[12] These propositions, and whether they are likely to be harmful, need to be tested.

---

10   Data perturbation is a data security technique that modifies the database to preserve the privacy and confidentiality of the data.
11   Data masking is a method of creating a structurally similar but inauthentic version of an organization's data that can be used for purposes such as user training or software testing.
12   For further detail about the impact of AI on consumer protection issues, see chapter 17.

11.018   It may be conjectured whether access to big data will genuinely increase price transparency and whether the outcomes are necessarily anti-competitive. There is at least an alternative hypothesis to be tested that firms may compete on building customer relationships where the outcomes are more rather than less competition. Further, price discounts may be offered via encrypted communications direct to customers. AI systems are in any event capable of encryption. The result may therefore be equivocal for price transparency and consistent with competitive pricing.

11.019   As to the relationship between AI and personalized pricing, in the digital economy products are becoming increasingly differentiated, with competition around non-price elements including service, quality and even data privacy. The result may be heterogeneous products, offered as a service. In these circumstances it may be harder for algorithms to compare genuine 'like for like' prices. The result may actually be more innovation, more and increasingly sophisticated differentiated products, products-as-a-service and customer-specific pricing that is largely pro-competitive.

(c) Will AI lead to other (not necessarily anti-competitive) outcomes?

11.020   AI in general generates a wide range of efficiencies. For example, AI can be used to predict demand using historic data and help businesses to improve their inventory management. AI may be effective in replacing human labour for simple and repetitive tasks in some sectors of the economy. As a result, AI may have impacts on the demand for labour. For example, to develop the performance of and to deploy algorithms, more computer analysts may be required, while the number of manufacturing jobs may reduce as more straightforward tasks can be performed by machines. This is but one example of the potential increase in demand for goods and services that are complementary to the use of AI and AI systems (such as computing) and a reduction in demand for goods and services that can be substituted by AI (such as bricks-and-mortar travel agents).

3.   Is There a Policy or Enforcement Gap?

11.021   Accepting the proposition that AI may facilitate at least some outcomes which have attracted antitrust scrutiny, it may be asked whether there might be an enforcement gap in relation to parallel pricing or personalized pricing by or using AI systems.

(a) Parallel pricing

11.022   Ezrachi has questioned whether parallel pricing, to the extent that it may be facilitated by AI, would be caught by EU competition law on restrictive agreements under Article 101(1) TFEU at all. This invites consideration of the extent to which the current scope of Article 101 is adequate to deal with the potential competition issues presented by AI.

11.023   Where AI is used by sellers and buyers to anticipate price trends, or using encryption, this resembles a public marketplace. This activity (in the absence of explicit collusion, price signalling or outsourcing of pricing to common agents or intermediaries) is not generally a competition law concern. By analogy, obtaining competitor price data via customers is normally permitted (subject to the comments below on 'hub-and-spoke' arrangements).

Cases involving information exchange raise special and often difficult considerations. The **11.024**
European Commission has summarized the evolving case law and its approach to the competition issues arising in information exchange between competitors in its *Horizontal Cooperation
Guidelines*.[13] A distinction should be drawn between: (a) the exchange of information to
monitor a cartel, which is always unlawful; and (b) 'pure' information exchange, which may,
depending on the facts, be lawful.

Existing antitrust tools seek to address some potential anti-competitive effects of information **11.025**
exchange which may be relevant to AI platforms if they act as a hub for systematic information
exchange (so-called 'hub-and-spoke' pricing). According to this principle, when information
on price is exchanged between two or more undertakings operating at the same level of the
supply or distribution chain (A and C) via a common trading contractual party (B) operating
at a different level in the supply chain, horizontal price fixing agreements between the retailers
(A and C) themselves can be said to exist.

The Court of Appeal has been satisfied that A, B and C can be seen as parties to a single **11.026**
infringement, as opposed to independent vertical agreements,

> if (i) retailer A discloses to supplier B its future pricing intentions in circumstances where A may be
> taken to intend that B will make use of that information to influence market conditions by passing that
> information to other retailers (of whom C is or may be one), (ii) B does, in fact, pass that information
> to C in circumstances where C may be taken to know the circumstances in which the information was
> disclosed by A to B and (iii) C does, in fact, use the information in determining its own future pricing
> intentions.[14]

(b) Personalized pricing

The European Data Protection Supervisor (EDPS)[15] in EDPS Opinion No 8/2016 notes in **11.027**
relation to personalized pricing that:

> Recent studies have pointed to the potential in the future of machine-learning algorithms to achieve
> perfect first degree price discrimination, with firms segmenting the market into each individual
> consumer and charging him according to his willingness to pay. In the near future, technology could
> potentially enable tacit collusion between companies in digital markets to fix prices through data and
> self-learning algorithms.[16]

It is important to distinguish, first, personalized pricing for the same product and second, **11.028**
differential pricing for customized products and services. Where pricing reflects the costs and
specific features of customized products and services, including the efficiencies arising in selling
to that customer, it is difficult to see how this should be an antitrust concern at all. A more
interesting inquiry may be made where there is personalized pricing for the same product or
service and whether this may lead to customers being nudged into exploitative transactions.

---

13   Communication from the European Commission – Guidelines on the applicability of Article 101 of the Treaty on
   the Functioning of the European Union to horizontal co-operation agreements, O.J. C11, 14.1.2011, p 1 ('Horizontal
   Cooperation Guidelines').
14   *JJB Sports plc v Office of Fair Trading; Allsports Limited v Office of Fair Trading* [2006] EWCA Civ 1318, para 141.
15   The European Data Protection Supervisor (EDPS) is the EU's independent data protection authority.
16   Opinion 8/2016, *EDPS Opinion on coherent enforcement of fundamental rights in the age of big data*, 23 September 2016,
   p.6, available at: https://edps.europa.eu/sites/edp/files/publication/16–09–23_bigdata_opinion_en.pdf.

11.029   Discriminatory treatment of its customers by a dominant company may infringe Article 102 TFEU as a specific category of abuse. Price discrimination consists of charging different prices to customers in the same position without objective justification, or charging uniform prices to customers whose circumstances are different.

11.030   A challenge may be made to a dominant company's pricing where the absence of cost differences in supplying individual customers is readily apparent. Key elements of discriminatory pricing include the principles that:

- prices need not be identical;
- any differences must be justified by objective and not discriminatory reasons;
- any charge must not be arbitrary;
- in the event of disparity, it is for the allegedly dominant company to justify its reasons for the differences;
- it is irrelevant that the effects take place in another market provided that the discrimination takes place in a market where the company is dominant.[17]

11.031   Although differentiated pricing structures of a dominant firm have raised competition concerns in the past,[18] it may be more challenging to establish discriminatory pricing cases in the future given increasing recognition of the potential objective justification for these structures. However, to the extent that there is an enforcement issue at all, this probably relates to deficiencies in the antitrust framework for dealing with price discrimination and not any special feature of AI.

11.032   On the issue of price discrimination by a non-dominant firm, as a threshold observation, dynamic or personalized pricing may enhance overall efficiency even if some individual consumers are harmed. Price discrimination can improve efficiency. In circumstances where pricing approaches marginal revenue, average total costs tend to fall as production expands.

11.033   This, in turn, may be expected to yield savings arising from economies of scale. The results may be equivocal but are generally increased output and cost savings.

11.034   However, dynamic pricing may also give rise to welfare concerns. As a general observation, it is noted first that the effects of price discrimination are highly dependent on the competitive environment in which it is implemented. Second, the harmful effects from personalized or customized pricing are more likely when: (a) it is carried out by a monopolist; (b) the form of price discrimination is complex and/or consumers are unaware of it; (c) it is costly to implement and so it increases costs (but this is probably less likely to be the case with AI); and (d) it leads to a reduction in consumers' trust in online markets.[19]

---

17   See, further, Case C-82/01 *Aeroports de Paris v Commission* EU:C:2002:61 and section C (priced-based exclusionary conduct), Communication from the European Commission: Guidance on its enforcement priorities in applying Article 82 of the EC Treaty to abusive exclusionary conduct by dominant undertakings, O.J. C 45, 24.2.2009, pp 7–20 ('Priority Guidance').

18   See, e.g., Case C-82/01 *Aeroports de Paris v Commission* EU:C:2002:61.

19   Office of Fair Trading (2013), *The economics of online personalised pricing*, OFT 1488, available at: https://webarchive .nationalarchives.gov.uk/20140402154756/http:/oft.gov.uk/shared_oft/research/oft1488.pdf.

Recent cases of differential pricing have attracted criticism despite claims of some efficiency **11.035** benefits. This includes, for example, inquiries into Uber's 'surge' pricing.[20]

However, this is an area in which it is important to tread carefully and where regulators are largely **11.036** in evidence-gathering and analysis mode. As a note of caution, antitrust interventions which limit product diversity may actually be counterproductive. For example, the UK Competition and Markets Authority (CMA) Final Report on its Energy Market Investigation[21] found that earlier regulatory intervention to simplify pricing (Ofgem's Retail Market Reform rules in 2010) had had an adverse effect on price competition (as well as product differentiation). The CMA stated: 'RMR rules, more generally, dampen price competition by limiting the ability and incentives of suppliers to respond to competition by offering cheaper tariffs or discounts (which means that they, in turn, put less competitive pressure on their rivals).'[22]

Against the above brief analysis, it appears that we still lack a full understanding of the nature **11.037** of harm arising from dynamic or personalized pricing – both more generally and where AI is involved. Further, it is important to distinguish the nature of the harm arising and whether this is a harm to competition or whether concerns relate more to consumer protection.

Consumer protection, loosely described, aims to address market-wide problems or issues which **11.038** affect consumers' ability to make effective choices. Competition law and consumer policy are often linked. As the CMA stated in its *Consumer Protection Enforcement Guidance*: 'Theory and experience strongly suggest that competition and consumer issues are closely linked. Good consumer outcomes rely on competitive markets to provide choice and value, while vibrant competition relies on consumers shopping around.'[23]

The interplay between consumer protection and competition law is important, not least **11.039** because there will often be a policy determination as to which tools are more appropriate in a given case. Further, there can be a tension or confusion between the application of competition law in relation to unilateral commercial practices such as certain pricing practices (which may be challenged as an abuse of a dominant position when practised by a dominant company) and the obligations of individual businesses under consumer protection law.

There are a number of legal and policy tools that may be deployed to address the threshold **11.040** concerns arising with personalized pricing including but not limited to antitrust, some of which are briefly identified in Table 11.2.

---

20   During periods of excessive demand or scarce supply, when there are far more riders than drivers, Uber increases its normal fares with a multiplier whose value depends on the scarcity of available drivers. See, further: 'Surge pricing: How it works and how to avoid it' (*BBC*, 15 January 2018), available at: www.bbc.co.uk/news/av/business-42661404/surge -pricing-how-it-works-and-how-to-avoid-it.
21   CMA, *Energy Market Investigation*, Final report (24 June 2016).
22   Energy Market Investigation (fn 21), para 175.
23   CMA, *Consumer Protection: Enforcement Guidance* (17 August 2016) (CM58) ('Consumer Protection Enforcement Guidance'), para 2.2.

Table 11.2   Regulatory measures addressed at personalized pricing

Measure	Examples
Competition law	
Abuse of dominance	Article 102 TFEU: Price discrimination by a dominant firm. However, price discrimination cases are rare and tend to arise in relation to discrimination against other trading partners and not individual consumer pricing.
Market studies and sector inquiries	Using the procedure to identify adverse effects before regulating, e.g. European Commission E-Commerce Sector Inquiry[24]/CMA Market Study on Digital Comparison Tools.[25]
Improving price transparency	Adopting measures to promote price comparison sites and countervailing measures on the buy-side, e.g. the CMA Final Report on Private Motor Insurance: remedies included giving consumers more transparent information about no claims bonuses.[26]
Other areas (e.g. vulnerable consumers)	
Consumer protection law	Directive 2005/29/EC concerning unfair business-to-consumer commercial practices.[27] This protects consumers against all forms of unfair commercial practice.
Equality legislation Existing law protects against certain types of discrimination	The Equality Act 2010 makes it unlawful for a firm to discriminate against a person using or seeking to use its services because of a protected characteristic (age; disability; gender reassignment; marriage and civil partnership; pregnancy and maternity; race; religion or belief; sex; sexual orientation).
Data protection	Article 22 GDPR: 'The data subject shall have the right not to be subject to a decision based solely on automated processing, including profiling, which produces legal effects concerning him or her or similarly significantly affects him or her.' Suitable safeguards should include specific information to the data subject and the right to obtain human intervention, to express his or her point of view, to obtain an explanation of the decision reached after such assessment and to challenge the decision. As a result, sellers must inform data subjects about personalizing prices.
General	
Self-correcting market-led measures Consumer actions in response to or objections to discrimination become a driver of competition and market standards.	Proactive steps taken by consumers themselves to enable self-help (e.g. avoiding automatically signing up to loyalty programs, setting browsers to reject cookies). Negative market reactions to pricing (e.g. Amazon's differential pricing in 2000).[28]
Ethics	Asilomar AI Principles of 2017.[29]

---

24   European Commission. Final report on the *E-Commerce Sector Inquiry* (COM(2017) 229 final). Case page available at: http://ec.europa.eu/competition/antitrust/sector_inquiries_e_commerce.html.
25   CMA, *Market Study on Digital Comparison Tools*, Final report (26 September 2017).
26   CMA, *Private Motor Insurance Market Investigation*, Final report (24 September 2014).
27   Directive 2005/29/EC of the European Parliament and of the Council of 11 May 2005 concerning unfair business-to-consumer commercial practices in the internal market, O.J. L 149, 11.6.2005, pp.22–39.
28   In September 2000 Amazon offered to sell a buyer a DVD for one price, but after the buyer deleted cookies that identified him as a regular Amazon customer, he was offered the same DVD for a substantially lower price. Amazon's CEO Jeff Bezos subsequently apologized for the differential pricing and promised that Amazon 'never will test prices based on customer demographics': see 'Bezos calls Amazon experiment a mistake' (28 September 2000), available at: www.bizjournals.com/seattle/stories/2000/09/25/daily21.html.
29   These principles were developed in conjunction with the 2017 Asilomar conference. Further information can be found at https://futureoflife.org/ai-principles/.

4.   Approach from the Regulators

AI and algorithms have attracted interest from antitrust regulators internationally. Currently   **11.041**
views tend to be divided on the implications for liability and appropriate enforcement tools.
This brief (and necessarily high-level and incomplete) survey nevertheless indicates some anxi-
eties about the ability of traditional enforcement tools to tackle the range of possible outcomes
in the absence of evidence of explicit collusion.

(a) European Commission

On the question of whether EU competition law is fit for purpose in an AI environment,   **11.042**
Commissioner for Competition Vestager has stated that 'businesses also need to know that
when they decide to use an automated system, they will be held responsible for what it does.
So, they had better know how that system works'.[30]

In terms of the attribution of liability for antitrust infringements, the European Commission   **11.043**
treats an AI decision-maker in the same way as a human and a business cannot escape liability
by simply attributing conduct to a machine. It appears that the European Commission expects
businesses to anticipate the possibility of a rogue AI decision-maker and they must take steps
to limit its freedom by design. This policy and enforcement resembles the approach taken
in relation to competition law compliance generally, where the business is expected to take
appropriate steps to train staff with a view to preventing anti-competitive conduct and cannot
generally absolve itself from liability when those measures fail.[31]

It is clear that the digital sector and the issues raised by data and AI in particular remain at   **11.044**
the forefront of the European Commission's policy agenda. In April 2019 the Commission
published a report entitled *Competition Policy for the Digital Era*.[32] The report makes interesting
reading against the pending EU antitrust investigation into Amazon's treatment of merchant
data. The report identifies three key features of the digital economy: extreme returns relative
to scale; network externalities; and the role of data. The writers of the report believe that the
basic competition law framework under Articles 101 and 102 TFEU provides a sound basis
for protecting competition in the digital economy. However, they note that the features of
platforms, digital ecosystems and the data economy may need to be adapted when looking at
market power and defining relevant markets.[33]

Further, in an unprecedented move in 2019, Commissioner Vestager was appointed as both   **11.045**
Commissioner for Competition and Executive Vice-President responsible for co-ordinating
the European Commission's agenda on a Europe fit for the digital age. Her re-appointment to
the role of Commissioner for Competition is an exceptional vote of confidence in her abilities
and has been welcomed by the competition Bars in Europe and the UK. In her first term of
office, she can be credited for promoting greater awareness of competition issues, many making

---

30   Bundeskartellamt 18th Conference on Competition, Berlin, 16 March 2017.
31   See, further, the European Commission's guidance to businesses on compliance with competition law available on its
      website at https://ec.europa.eu/competition/antitrust/compliance/index_en.html.
32   European Commission, *Competition Policy for the Digital Era*, Final report (April 2019). Available at: https://ec.europa
      .eu/competition/publications/reports/kd0419345enn.pdf.
33   See, further, *Competition Policy for the Digital Era*, ch 3 (fn 32).

headline news, including in high-profile digital economy cases such as *Google Shopping*.[34] A change of Competition Commissioner does not usually signal a dramatic shift in focus for DG Competition. If anything, Vestager's re-appointment to the role means that those operating in the digital sector can expect continued scrutiny.

(b) Competition and Markets Authority

11.046   The CMA has dealt with cases where AI has been a supporting factor in antitrust infringements. For example, on 1 August 2019 it fined Casio £3.7 million for infringing competition law by preventing online discounting of prices for its digital pianos and keyboards.[35] The CMA found that Casio used new software that made it easier to monitor online prices in real time and ensure compliance with its pricing policy. It also found that this meant that individual retailers had less incentive to discount for fear of being caught and potentially penalized. However, the CMA had evidence of an agreement (between Casio and each retailer) so could reconcile this case within the existing framework of liability under Chapter I of the Competition Act 1998.

11.047   On the issue of whether AI requires a rethink in the traditional notions of liability for antitrust infringements, former CMA Chairman David Currie has expressed a more nuanced position than that expounded by the European Commission. He has questioned whether the legal tools currently available to the CMA are capable of tackling all the challenges presented by the rise of the algorithmic economy, such as self-learning algorithms:

> But machine learning means that the algorithms may themselves learn that co-ordination is the best way to maximise longer-term business objectives. In that case, no human agent has planned the co-ordination. Does that represent a breach of competition law? Does the law stretch to cover sins of omission as well as sins of commission: the failure to build in sufficient constraints on algorithmic behaviour to ensure that the algorithm does not learn to adopt anti-competitive outcomes? And what if constraints are built in but they are inadequately designed, so that the very clever algorithm learns a way through the constraints? How far can the concept of human agency be stretched to cover these sorts of issues? I have suggested earlier that the competition tools at our disposal can tackle the competition issues that we face in the new digital world, but perhaps this last issue which I have touched on is one where this proposition is not true.[36]

11.048   This may suggest that the question of attribution of liability (under the UK competition regime at least) is ripe for reassessment should developments in AI advance to such a state that the output of an AI system cannot be attributed to a human.

11.049   On the specific issue of whether algorithms may facilitate anti-competitive outcomes, the CMA has recently published an economic research paper on the role of pricing algorithms in online markets.[37] This finds little evidence of companies using algorithms to show personalized prices, but they are sometimes used to change the order in which products are shown to

---

34   Case 39740 Google Search (Shopping), European Commission decision of 27 June 2017 (C(2017) 4444 final). Case page available at: https://ec.europa.eu/competition/elojade/isef/case_details.cfm?proc_code=1_39740.

35   Case 50565–2 *Digital piano and digital keyboard sector: anti-competitive practices* (1 August 2019).

36   'David Currie on the role of competition in stimulating innovation', Speech given by CMA Chairman, David Currie, at the Concurrences Innovation Economics Conference, King's College London (3 February 2017). Available at: www.gov.uk/government/speeches/david-currie-on-the-role-of-competition-in-stimulating-innovation.

37   CMA, *Pricing algorithms, Economic working paper on the use of algorithms to facilitate collusion and personalised pricing* (8 October 2018) (CMA94) ('Pricing algorithms'). Available at: https://assets.publishing.service.gov.uk/government/uploads/system/uploads/attachment_data/file/746353/Algorithms_econ_report.pdf.

shoppers.[38] The CMA also found that algorithms can be used to help implement illegal price fixing and, under certain circumstances, could encourage a move to a coordinated equilibrium in markets already susceptible to coordination.[39] However, it expresses a tentative view that in markets that are currently highly competitive it seems less likely that the use of data and algorithms would be so impactful that they could enable sustained collusion.[40]

(c) United States

The United States has taken antitrust enforcement action in the context of online marketplace restrictions using algorithmic software. In 2015 the Department of Justice (DoJ) filed a criminal complaint against David Topkins and his co-conspirators alleging that they had agreed to adopt specific pricing algorithms for their online posters and to coordinate price increases for a product sold on Amazon.[41] Topkins is reported to have written code that instructed company algorithms to set prices in accordance with the agreement. At the time, the prosecutions raised speculation as to whether antitrust had indeed 'come of age' and was now ripe for re-assessment in the digital era. However, a closer examination of this case reveals that the DoJ had evidence of a clear anti-competitive agreement between the parties, albeit one that was implemented through the use of algorithmic software. In short, the agency could identify a human meeting of minds behind the use of those algorithms.   **11.050**

The rather limited antitrust enforcement practice against use of algorithms in the United States to date may be explained in part by the distinction between explicit collusion and tacit collusion. The former is generally prosecuted as a criminal offence, whereas the latter is in general lawful. The US agencies practically need evidence of communication between the parties that amounts to an agreement and this may not be straightforward to establish where AI systems are concerned.   **11.051**

(d) Other jurisdiction

Beyond the EU and the United States, antitrust authorities around the world have been asked to grapple with claims of infringement through or related to the use of algorithms. There is no consensus on how to deal with market manipulation that falls short of an anticompetitive agreement. While it is beyond the scope of this work to survey the comparative cases exhaustively, an example will serve to illustrate that this is very much a live issue.   **11.052**

In 2018, the Competition Commission of India (CCI) [42] rejected a complaint against the ride-hailing platforms Uber and Ola that alleged that their use of algorithms artificially manipulated supply and demand contrary to section 3 of the Indian Competition Act 2002.[43] The complainant alleged that the platforms acted as an unlawful hub and spoke to facilitate collusion between drivers to fix and artificially inflate their pricing using algorithmic software. The CCI   **11.053**

---

38   Ibid, para 7.17.
39   Ibid, para 8.6.
40   Ibid, para 5.37.
41   Department of Justice Press Release No 15–421, *Former E-Commerce Executive Charged with Price Fixing in the Antitrust Division's First Online Marketplace Prosecution* (6 April 2015).
42   Case No 37 of 2018, Order of 6 November 2011. Available at: www.cci.gov.in/sites/default/files/37of2018.pdf.
43   Section 3 of the Indian Competition Act 2002 was informed by and is the practical equivalent under Indian competition law to Article 101 TFEU and Chapter I of the UK Competition Act 1998.

found no such agreement among the drivers. It also distinguished the typical 'hub-and-spoke' cartel arrangement which operates with a set of vertical agreements coordinated through a common counterparty and dismissed the claim that the platforms operated in the manner alleged. It also rejected a claim of unlawful resale price maintenance on the basis that there is no resale when the platforms match supply and demand. It found that applications-based taxi companies do not sell any service to drivers that is then resold to customers. Nor did it find evidence that prices negotiated individually would be lower than those established through algorithmic pricing.

5. Areas for Future Research

11.054 This chapter reflects the growing interest in AI from the antitrust perspective, where there is nevertheless inevitably a need for more focused research. AI has attracted significant antitrust interest, raising the question of whether the competition regimes as they stand are ready to address potentially anti-competitive outcomes arising from AI decisions. Although many issues arising with AI align with the antitrust debate around big data, AI and the use of algorithms raises its own rather specific issues.

11.055 The AI antitrust scholarship makes a bold claim that AI is an enabler of tacit collusion and could increase the scope for anti-competitive outcomes at even lower levels of concentration than those associated with antitrust orthodoxy.[44] However, even the brief examination of these claims in this work has unearthed alternative hypotheses which need to be fully tested before the theory can be incorporated in policy and legal environments without running the risk of being counter-productive.

11.056 The following areas would merit attention as topics for further research and analysis:

- Analysis of the effects of algorithms on incentives for tacit collusion and their destabilizing effects, including in markets which are not already prone to tacit collusion. In particular, this involves understanding how robust the predictions in the AI literature are to their assumptions (such as algorithmic heterogeneity, larger number of sellers, and so on).
- Whether there might be alternative outcomes which present competition or other concerns but which are not caught within traditional antitrust paradigms (such as data capture, data extraction and co-opetition between super-platforms and applications developers).
- Understanding rational and harmful price transparency and whether and when particular consumer outcomes are an appropriate case for antitrust intervention. This accepts that consumers make bad decisions even in competitive markets and that instances of consumers making bad decisions caused by algorithmic pricing may not be an appropriate case for antitrust intervention.
- Understanding countervailing AI strategies by buyers under a range of assumptions, including across B2C and B2B markets.
- Understanding the appropriate boundaries of liability and the circumstances in which an algorithm may be traced back to its owners and the extent to which those owners should be subject to (vicarious) antitrust responsibilities and enforcement.

---

44   Ezrachi and Stucke (fn 2).

- Understanding the main goals of antitrust which are impacted by AI. The current resistance on, the part of regulators in Europe and the United States, to regulating wealth transfers between AI sellers and buyers could place limits on the application of antitrust to consumer exploitation such as through data extraction. Ezrachi and Stucke have, however, presented an additional gloss in the idea that virtual competition increases the 'dead weight loss by increasing distrust'.[45] Further examination is needed as to whether presenting the social costs of algorithms within a paradigm of (mis)trust provides an appropriate analytical construct that is capable of real-world application so as to legitimize antitrust interventions within a coherent welfare-based model.
- Where personal data is shared with another market participant, the extent to which such data sharing would involve sharing of competitively sensitive information with a competitor and how such sharing may be compatible with antitrust law.[46]

A technological understanding of algorithms and how they operate is critical. For now, at least, it seems that the antitrust authorities will typically be able to find evidence of human involvement where machines or algorithms are identified as facilitators of anti-competitive conduct. However, the fact remains that technology will probably evolve to such a point that this situation does not always hold true. Ultimately enforcers, practitioners and businesses will have to confront the question of liability for the decisions or output of machine learning which are increasingly distanced from human intervention and which call into question traditional notions of antitrust liability. **11.057**

C. CONCLUSION

The development of AI has prompted a revisiting of the perennial policy and legal debate about whether existing legal tools are fit for purpose in addressing the challenges presented by new technologies. **11.058**

This chapter has highlighted the trade-off between (fully) understanding the impact of a technology and the ease of controlling its impact. Many of the issues identified in this chapter suggest that they need to be further discussed and tested and supported by evidence before some of the scenarios postulated in the AI literature and debate can be reflected with confidence in new legal and policy instruments. **11.059**

It is unclear at this stage how policy interventions can or should address all the concerns arising. This is not least because the development of AI is still in early stages, with a lot of potential yet to be realized. This is a very wide issue that covers not only anti-competitive behaviour but also issues such as privacy, IPR and ethics. Competition law is one regulatory tool among many and is not suited to resolve all the perceived issues associated with AI. Further, in some cases, no new rules are required. For example, explicit and, under certain circumstances, tacit agreement **11.060**

---

45 Ezrachi and Stucke (fn 2), p.242.
46 A current debate is whether there is an enforcement gap in mergers in relation to lost potential competition in such situations and in Big Data scenarios more generally. This issue of whether AI in the hands of a limited number of data controllers is adequately addressed under merger control was not explored in this chapter.

among firms in the market falls under the prohibition of anticompetitive agreements in Article 101 TFEU and equivalent provisions, regardless of the use of algorithms.

11.061   In more general terms, this state of affairs (that is, regulating AI before the impact is fully understood) is likely to hinder its positive impact as much as it is likely to avoid what may be an uncertain negative impact.

11.062   The overall conclusion is that as many regulators (including in the EU) remain in observational and diagnostic mode and robust evidence-based regulation requires more empirical studies.

11.063   Finally, it is important not to underestimate that technology itself may provide solutions, for example through countervailing measures using AI. It should be emphasized that this is not a recommendation to 'wait and see' as to do so brings with it is own risks. These are best summed up in the 'Collingridge Dilemma': 'When change is easy, the need for it cannot be foreseen; when the need for change is apparent, change has become expensive, difficult, and time consuming.'[47] The challenge is to develop an appropriate evidence-based case for regulation that is (just) in time, rather than (just) in case.

---

47   The concept is named after David Collingridge, who wrote about the challenges of governing emerging technologies most prominently in his 1980 work (D. Collingridge, *The Social Control of Technology* (Pinter, 1980)).

12

INTELLECTUAL PROPERTY

Rachel Free

A. INTRODUCTION

12.001 A key role of the intellectual property system is to incentivise knowledge sharing, and knowledge sharing is particularly important in the case of AI technology. The intellectual property system may need broadening and strengthening in order to promote knowledge sharing and this chapter discusses ways in which the broadening and strengthening can be achieved.[1]

In this chapter, references to 'knowledge-sharing forms of intellectual property' refer to all types of intellectual property except trade secrets.

B. HOW DOES THE INTELLECTUAL PROPERTY SYSTEM INCENTIVISE KNOWLEDGE SHARING?

12.002 I argue that many parts of the intellectual property system incentivise knowledge sharing. Knowledge sharing is not traditionally thought of as an aim of the intellectual property system but I argue that it is a benefit given by many (but not all) types of intellectual property. In contrast, the intellectual property system is typically thought of as being something implemented in order to promote innovation and creativity, as the following quote from the World Intellectual Property Organization web page[2] illustrates:

---

1   EPI Information December 2018 https://information.patentepi.com/issue-4–2018/technical-problems-in-ai-inventions-in-the-light-of-the-guidelines-for-examination-in-the-epo.html; 'Protecting ethical AI technology', 28 September 2020 The Robotics Law Journal; 'Around 1600 viewers register for live video stream', CMS Law Now 22 July 2020; 'USPTO finds an invention created by an AI machine is not patentable', CMS Law Now 30 April 2020; 'UKIPO finds that patent law does not cater for inventions created by AI machines and calls for debate', CMS Law Now 31 Jan 2020; Artificial Intelligence Patents 10 March 2019, CIPA Journal vol 48 no. 3.

2   www.wipo.int/about-ip/en/.

What is Intellectual Property? Intellectual property (IP) refers to creations of the mind, such as inventions; literary and artistic works; designs; and symbols, names and images used in commerce. IP is protected in law by, for example, patents, copyright and trademarks, which enable people to earn recognition or financial benefit from what they invent or create. By striking the right balance between the interests of innovators and the wider public interest, the *IP system aims to foster an environment in which creativity and innovation can flourish.*

Let's now consider various different types of intellectual property and how they incentivise knowledge sharing.   **12.003**

1. Copyright

Suppose I am an independent software developer and I write a new piece of software comprising an AI algorithm. I will be the owner of copyright in the source code. The copyright arises automatically and enables me to prevent others from unauthorised copying of the source code. If I compile the source code into executable code I can share the executable code without revealing the source code. The executable code makes the functionality of the AI algorithm available so that third parties are able to observe the inputs to the algorithm and its outputs, but it is difficult for third parties to understand how the algorithm works. Because I own the copyright in the source code I have some incentive to share the source code itself, since unauthorised copying of the source code is prohibited. I am able to share the source code, perhaps using an open source licence or simply by showing it to others. By sharing the source code others gain some knowledge about the AI algorithm, assuming they are software experts and are able to understand the source code. The knowledge sharing is not ideal since it is often difficult even for experts to understand source code, which can be complex and messy, uncommented and vast. Even so, there is some incentive to share the source code through the existence of copyright. In contrast, if I write a new piece of software comprising an AI algorithm and copyright does not exist, then I will be incentivised to share only the executable code, since others will be free to copy the source code if I make it available.   **12.004**

2. Designs

Suppose I am an independent product designer and I design a new robot companion for patients with dementia. I will be the owner of potential unregistered design rights protecting the appearance of the robot, and potentially of registered designs protecting the appearance of the robot. The design rights enable me to prevent unauthorised copying of the design and so incentivise me to share the design with others. Since the design is a form of knowledge, the design right or registered design is an incentive for knowledge sharing. In contrast, where design rights are unavailable I have less incentive to invest time and money in the robot design, since competitors are able to copy it.   **12.005**

3. Trade Marks

Suppose I am a manufacturer of AI goods and services. I market my AI goods and services using a trade mark, which acts as a badge of origin. Suppose there are lots of players in the marketplace selling AI goods and services, with different levels of ethics deployed in the AI goods and services. My trade mark conveys knowledge to consumers about the quality of my AI goods and services and the level of AI ethics deployed in my AI goods and services, including   **12.006** the level of transparency of the technology. In this way my trade mark is a means of sharing knowledge about the AI goods and services with consumers and other players in the market.

4. Patents

12.007 Suppose I am an independent software developer and I write a new piece of software comprising an AI algorithm. The AI algorithm itself is new and solves a technical problem in an innovative way. In this case it is likely that I am able to obtain patent protection covering the AI algorithm. The patent gives me a monopoly right and enables me to prevent unauthorised exploitation of the AI algorithm, and so there is a significant commercial incentive for me to obtain the patent. The patent application itself comprises a detailed description of the AI algorithm with enough detail to enable a reader of the patent application to implement the technology. The patent application is published and in this way knowledge is shared. The knowledge sharing is high-quality since the patent application uses a well-known format and includes high-level description of the algorithm as well as implementation detail.

5. Trade Secrets

12.008 Trade secrets are an example of a type of intellectual property which hides knowledge. As explained on the WIPO website,[3]

> trade secrets are intellectual property (IP) rights on confidential information which may be sold or licensed. In general, to qualify as a trade secret, the information must be:
> * commercially valuable because it is secret,
> * be known only to a limited group of persons, and
> * be subject to reasonable steps taken by the rightful holder of the information to keep it secret, including the use of confidentiality agreements for business partners and employees.

12.009 As can be seen from the above definition, trade secrets are a means of hiding knowledge. It is difficult to know what technologies or how many technologies are protected using trade secrets since, by their nature, trade secrets are hidden. However, it is reasonable to assume that AI technology is protected using trade secrets in many cases, as explained in detail in the section below about the balance between trade secrets and other forms of intellectual property.

C. KNOWLEDGE SHARING IS PARTICULARLY IMPORTANT IN THE CASE OF AI TECHNOLOGY

12.010 The argument of this chapter is that knowledge sharing is particularly important in the case of AI technology because AI technology has a significant impact on our lives, AI technology today has some degree of independence and uncontrollability, and AI technology is likely to advance to become more independent and less controllable.

---

3   www.wipo.int/tradesecrets/en/.

1.   AI Technology Has a Significant Impact on Our Lives

Consider the computer model which has been said[4] to strongly influence the UK government's **12.011** decision to implement a national lockdown in view of COVID-19. The model comprised thousands of lines of undocumented code written by a single person around 13 years ago to model flu pandemics.[5] As pointed out by Joe Paul in his blog on the ODI website,[6] the model was not available for public scrutiny at the time of the first lockdown on 23 March 2020 but has since been made public on GitHub.[7]

Other examples of the use of computer models in ways which impact our lives are given by Joe **12.012** Paul in his blog mentioned above and include:

(a)   a systems dynamics model for guiding policy around homelessness;[8]
(b)   using data from sensors in underground water pipes to predict locations of leaky pipes;[9]
(c)   computational models containing machine learning to predict which crops to grow.[10]

2.   AI Technology Today Has Some Degree of Independence and Uncontrollability

In order to illustrate why AI technology has some degree of independence and uncontrollabil- **12.013** ity, consider Figure 12.1 below. On the left-hand side in the rectangle is a classical computer program for computing the dose of medicine for a diabetes patient. It uses rules which have been handwritten by a human programmer, and suppose the rules say that if sensor data received from the patient is less than 50 units and the time of day is 2pm then the dose is 5mg. The classical computer program is fully explainable because the rules are known and understandable to a human. If a particular dose is computed by the classical computer program then it is possible to understand why that particular dose was computed by examining the rules and the input sensor data from the patient. The classical computer program works in a controlled manner because checks can be made to make sure a computed dose is correct by manually using the rules. If there is a new patient with new sensor data then it is possible to know in advance what the computed dose will be because the rules are known.

In contrast, there is a trained machine learning model on the right-hand side, represented by **12.014** a brain icon. It has been trained in advance using patient data, doses of medicine administered and outcomes. During the training the computer learned the best way it could find to predict a suitable dose of medicine given an example of patient data. During the training the computer tried lots of possibilities for values of parameters of the neural network until it found a good set. There was no hand-coding of rules by a human programmer and the neural network parameter

---

4   www.sciencemag.org/news/2020/03/mathematics-life-and-death-how-disease-models-shape-national-shutdowns-and
    -other.
5   https://twitter.com/neil_ferguson/status/1241835454707699713?lang=en.
6   https://theodi.org/article/why-should-we-share-computer-models?mc_cid=4758b3efba&mc_eid=a68f4231f6.
7   https://github.com/mrc-ide/covid-sim.
8   Fowler et al. in their article 'Solving Homelessness from a Complex Systems Perspective: Insights for Prevention Responses', Annual Review of Public Health vol. 40 pp.465–486 www.annualreviews.org/doi/abs/10.1146/annurev -publhealth-040617–013553.
9   www.bbc.co.uk/news/business-53274914.
10   www.futurity.org/computer-model-farmers-agriculture-crops-1733622/.

values (thousands of them) are numerical values which don't have a particular human understandable meaning. When the neural network is presented with a new patient data record,
which it has not seen before, it is able to generalize its knowledge in order to compute a good
prediction of a dose for the patient. Typically the outcome is better performance in the case of
the neural network than in the case of the classical computer program. However, the neural
network computed predictions are hard to explain because the explanation would involve lists
of parameter values (numbers) with no simple link to real life. Also, the neural network is less
controlled than the classical computer program because the predicted dose it computes cannot
really be known in advance, as it can be in the case where a rule is used. The neural network
computes a dose and we have to 'trust' the dose is suitable. We can check the dose is within
a range of safe values and carry out 'sanity' checks on the predicted dose, but generally we are
assuming the dose is a good one because the neural network has worked well in the past. The
neural network has a small bit of independence, by which I mean that it has computed a decision made at least partly on its own without human control. It seems to follow that because
of the part of the decision which is made outside human control, there is an argument for
knowledge sharing in the case of AI technology.

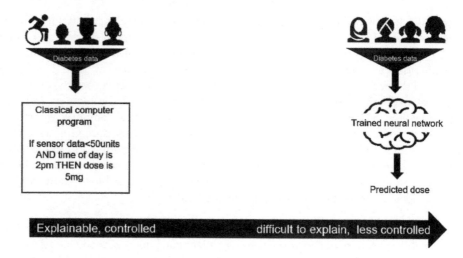

Figure 12.1   *Contrast between classical computer programs and machine learned models*

12.015   There are many benefits to knowledge sharing in the case of AI technology. These have been
described by the Open Data Institute[11] and a summary is set out below:

(a)   Knowledge sharing regarding an AI algorithm facilitates improvements and error
finding, such as identifying bias in the AI algorithm whereby it performs well for some
demographic groups of people but poorly for others.

(b)   Knowledge sharing regarding an AI algorithm enables adaptations to be made, such as by
transferring the AI algorithm to a new problem domain.

---

11   https://theodi.org/article/why-should-we-share-computer-models?mc_cid=4758b3efba&mc_eid=a68f4231f6.

(c)   Knowledge sharing of AI algorithms promotes trust from citizens, consumers and organisations.

(d)   Knowledge sharing of AI algorithms which are used to inform public policy can facilitate democratic accountability.

(e)   Knowledge sharing of AI algorithms helps to find more ways of explaining the function of the algorithm and so encourage its use.

3.   AI Technology Is Likely to Advance in the Future

In recent years many authors have written about the singularity: a time in the future at which **12.016** AI technology is on a par with human intelligence and is soon afterwards able to create AI technology with even greater powers. It is argued that in the time after the singularity there would be an exponential increase in ability of AI algorithms until humans are left behind, potentially with little or no freedom. While I am not sure I agree with the notion of the exponential increase in ability of AI algorithms at the singularity, it is likely that AI technology will advance, possibly in terms of independence and 'uncontrollability'. For that reason it would be prudent to promote knowledge sharing of AI algorithms now.

4.   Drawbacks of Knowledge Sharing

From the point of view of a commercial entity which is seeking to sell goods or services **12.017** involving AI algorithms, there are several difficulties with knowledge sharing. Some of the main difficulties are around potential loss of revenue and around security. To develop new AI algorithms significant investment is typically needed since AI experts are scarce, the computing resources needed are expensive and the data needed to train AI algorithms is expensive and difficult to obtain. If a competitor is able to take the fruits of the work and exploit those without having to make the same investment as the developing entity then the competitor gains a commercial advantage. Intellectual property rights can be used to mitigate such risks.

If an AI algorithm is shared there are arguments that it will become open to attack by malicious **12.018** parties who will be able to find weak points of the algorithm from the knowledge sharing. This is in fact a reason in favour of knowledge sharing, since it means that manufacturers and providers of AI products and services will be motivated to remove algorithmic vulnerabilities.

In summary, there are significant reasons why knowledge sharing is needed in the case of AI **12.019** technology. But because of commercial barriers to knowledge sharing of AI algorithms, there is a need for mechanisms to promote knowledge sharing. One such mechanism is regulation. Others include providing commercial incentives, such as via the intellectual property system.

D. MECHANISMS TO PROMOTE KNOWLEDGE SHARING

Mechanisms to promote knowledge sharing of AI algorithms include: **12.020**

(a)   Market pressure due to scarcity of AI experts.
(b)   Regulation and standards.
(c)   Intellectual property system as a mechanism to promote knowledge sharing.

1. Market Pressure due to Scarcity of AI Experts Leads to Knowledge Sharing

12.021 In a 2019 study into the AI skills gap,[12] it was found that there were just 22,400 researchers publishing at leading AI conferences in 2019 worldwide. By examining LinkedIn data it was found that 36,524 people self-reported as AI experts. The study concluded that 'while demand for top-tier AI talent has never been higher, AI specialists with strong educational profiles and experience are still relatively rare'. This study also found that 23 per cent of the researchers publishing at leading AI conferences in 2019 were from industry as opposed to academia. This fact illustrates the point that AI experts working in industry are publishing their work at leading AI conferences. Because of the scarcity of AI experts, industry is prepared to allow the AI experts to work in a similar way to academics and to publish their work at AI conferences, in order to attract and retain AI talent, as explained in *Nature*:[13] 'In the past, there were fewer research labs in industry and it was harder to publish. Now, many companies have an open-publication policy, and that means you're participating in peer review and embedded in a research community. It's easy to go back to academia. It's certainly not held against a faculty candidate if they were in industry for a few years, as long as they continued to publish. In fact, industry experience is highly valued.' Thus at present, market pressure due to scarcity of AI experts is leading to knowledge sharing.

2. Regulation and Standards Are Also Mechanisms to Promote or, in the Case of Regulation, Mandate Knowledge Sharing of AI Algorithms

12.022 The 'White paper on AI – A European approach to excellence and trust' published by the European Commission on 19 February 2020 contains a proposal for regulation of high-risk AI in Europe. The proposed regulation of high-risk AI in Europe would make it mandatory to disclose information about AI algorithms in high-risk sectors such as health care and self-driving vehicles. Lower-risk AI algorithms would be outside the mandatory disclosure system and presumably would include AI applications such as information retrieval, recommender systems, digital assistants, crop planning and management and others.

12.023 In the case of AI standards, if an AI algorithm is to be standards compliant, it is likely to be subject to knowledge sharing or disclosure requirements. An example of the type of disclosure proposed on the AI for Health standards working group of the ITU is given in Table 12.1. It includes full details about the AI model, including a link to a code registry with source code of the model.

---

12 Reported on the blog of JF Gagne, founder of Element AI https://jfgagne.ai/blog/ai-talent-2019/.
13 www.nature.com/articles/d41586–019–01248–w.

Table 12.1   *Machine learning model specification sheet based on an example from the ITU AI for Health standards working group*

MACHINE LEARNING MODEL SPECIFICATION SHEET	
Name	Neural network based leukaemia Classifier
Automation Mode	Leukaemia diagnosis
Model Task	Image classification and detection
Target Users	Medical doctors and laboratory staff
Patient Group	Model is potentially applicable to all population subgroups
Training Data Source	Images of leukocytes annotated with patient outcomes from the medical image archive of hospital X
Model Architecture	Convolutional neural network using the ResNeXt architecture
Model Output	Certainty values for 10 different classes of leukocytes
Evaluation Metrics	Classification accuracy
	Precision
	Recall
Constraints	Training data obtained from a single source
Development Toolkit	Not applicable
Model creators	Prof X and team Y at University of Z
Development time	2019–2020
Link to model source code	https://doi.org/xxxx
	CodeOcean capsule reference for the model source code
Licence	None

3. Intellectual Property System as a Mechanism to Promote Knowledge Sharing

As discussed earlier in this chapter, various forms of intellectual property act as mechanisms to promote knowledge sharing. Patents in particular are useful for knowledge sharing, for reasons which follow.   **12.024**

4. International Language of Patents and Multi-national Nature of Patents

AI patents are already applied for in many nations of the world. The 'WIPO Technology Trends 2019 Artificial Intelligence' report [14] finds that   **12.025**

> China and the US lead in patent filings in all AI techniques and functional applications, though their predominance is challenged by Japan, in the categories of fuzzy logic, computer vision and speech processing, and the Republic of Korea, in ontology engineering. China and the US also lead in patent filings in all AI application fields, challenged only by Japan (arts and humanities, document management and publishing) and the Republic of Korea (military applications).

Patents are written using an internationally agreed standard document structure and so are a type of 'universal language' that is understood by readers in many nations. Patents are classified according to carefully designed and maintained classification schemes and are a corpus of data which is easily searched using those classification codes as well as keywords.   **12.026**

---

14   https://www.wipo.int/pressroom/en/articles/2019/article_0001.html.

5. Patent Documents Are Freely Available

12.027 In contrast to many academic publications and peer-reviewed academic journals, patent publications are freely available.

6. Patents Are Not Source Code

12.028 Generally AI patents include both high-level and detailed information about AI algorithms, but not source code. Typically patent documents set out problems that are to be addressed by the invention and explain how the problems are solved. This type of explanation is arguably just what is needed for transparency in terms of ethical and economic reasons for transparency.

7. Comments about Mechanisms to Promote Knowledge Sharing

12.029 It is reasonable to expect that the number of AI experts will increase over time, since many governments around the globe are investing in training in AI. In the UK, for example, 16 centres for doctoral training in AI are being funded by UKRI to train 1000 AI PhD students.[15]

12.030 As the number of AI experts increases, presumably the employment market will adjust and there will be less incentive for employers to allow AI expert employees to publish work.

12.031 With regard to regulation as a means to mandate knowledge sharing of AI technology, we need to take into account differences around the globe and differences between commercial sectors. It seems that regulation as a means to mandate knowledge sharing of AI technology will be patchy when considered internationally. Even if Europe adopts AI regulation, it is not clear that other regions will follow suit. Proposed AI regulation in Europe is sector-specific, so AI technology in some sectors would remain unregulated and potentially hidden knowledge.

12.032 In contrast to regulation, standards and intellectual property are ways to encourage knowledge sharing without mandating it. Sharing knowledge in order to adhere to a standard gives the benefit that customers are likely to trust the AI products and services. Intellectual property (except for trade secrets) gives the knowledge sharer something in return for his or her sharing.

12.033 In contrast to AI regulation, the intellectual property system is well established and is relatively international in nature, as there are many international treaties (such as the Berne convention, which has 179 contracting parties, and the Patent Cooperation Treaty, which has more than 150 member countries) and international organisations (such as the World Intellectual Property Organization) involved in the intellectual property system. Because of the well-established and international nature of the intellectual property system, there are strong arguments to use the intellectual property system to promote knowledge sharing of AI technologies.

---

15   https://webarchive.nationalarchives.gov.uk/20200506200136/;   https://www.ukri.org/research/themes-and-programmes/ukri-cdts-in-artificial-intelligence/.

E. THE INTELLECTUAL PROPERTY SYSTEM MAY NEED BROADENING AND STRENGTHENING IN ORDER TO PROMOTE KNOWLEDGE SHARING

There are at least two areas of the intellectual property system which need broadening and **12.034** strengthening in order to promote knowledge sharing. Such broadening and strengthening would ensure that the balance between trade secrets and knowledge-sharing forms of intellectual property is appropriate. The areas for potential broadening and strengthening include: new problems of AI and inventions created by AI machines.

1. The Balance between Trade Secrets and Knowledge-sharing Forms of Intellectual Property

It is useful to think of a balance between trade secrets and knowledge-sharing forms of intellec- **12.035** tual property as illustrated in Figure 12.2.

Figure 12.2   A balance between trade secrets and knowledge-sharing forms of intellectual property

An enterprise which creates a piece of innovative AI technology has a choice as to whether **12.036** to protect the technology as a trade secret or to protect it with knowledge-sharing forms of intellectual property, especially patents and copyright. If the technology is protected with trade secrets then knowledge remains hidden. If the technology is protected with copyright or patents then knowledge sharing is incentivised since patent applications are published and since copyright incentivises sharing of source code.

Trade secrets have traditionally been used to protect commercial secrets such as customer **12.037** lists, recipes (such as the Coca-Cola recipe) and business methods. With the increase in development of new AI technologies there is also likely to be use of trade secrets to protect AI technologies, for a variety of reasons.

One reason why trade secrets can be used to protect AI technologies concerns the 'black box' **12.038** nature of many AI technologies and the ability to deploy AI technologies as services in the cloud. These factors mean that it is practically possible to keep the technologies secret. Because it is practically possible to keep many AI technologies secret while still commercialising them, trade secret protection is a viable option. Although academics have demonstrated ways to reverse-engineer machine-learned models which are deployed in the cloud, these ways of reverse engineering are costly and time-consuming, and can perhaps be avoided by limiting the information provided through application programming interfaces.

12.039 Machine learning models are often presented as 'black box' services in the cloud, hidden behind user interfaces such as mobile apps, websites or application programming interfaces (APIs). Given an input, a black box will return an output without exposing the decision-making process hidden within.

12.040 It is often assumed that machine-learning models presented as black box services in the cloud are secure; that is, the machine learning model is not revealed to competitors. It is assumed that, without explicit knowledge of the type of algorithms powering the technology, its parameters or the datasets it has been trained on, machine-learning models are very difficult to decipher and reproduce. It is thought that by maintaining their back-end code and datasets under strict confidentiality, for example as trade secrets, a company may prevent competitors from using their proprietary algorithms, datasets and parameters, and thus can keep a competitive edge.

12.041 However, new abilities to reverse engineer these machine-learning algorithms are starting to emerge.

12.042 In a 2016 paper entitled 'Stealing Machine Learning Models via Prediction APIs' by researchers from Cornell Tech, the EPFL and the University of North Carolina, research showed that with nothing more than repeated queries to a machine-learning model, it was possible to effectively reproduce a machine learning-trained model via a 'model extraction attack'. The research team demonstrated it was possible to infer the hyperparameters of a deep neural network hosted on BigML and Amazon ML on AWS services by observing responses to a sequence of queries sent to an API of a deep neural network service, when the responses included prediction or confidence values associated with the responses. These values allowed the researchers to infer and estimate to a high degree of accuracy the internal parameters of the neural network, effectively 'reverse engineering' the neural network and making it potentially reproducible. As such, by using their inference method, any proprietary information or trade secret protection in the original deep neural network is lost.

12.043 Researchers from the Max Planck Institute for Informatics also similarly demonstrated the ability to infer information from black box models in their 2018 paper entitled 'Towards Reverse-Engineering Black-Box Neural Networks'. The research team showed that by building 'metamodels' – that is, a model trained to predict model attributes – they were able to predict attributes relating not only to the model architecture, but also to training hyperparameters, with high accuracy.

12.044 Another reason why trade secrets may be used to protect AI technologies concerns the difficulty of detecting infringement in the case of AI patents. Below is an example of a paraphrased granted patent claim of an AI patent EP 3 055 813 B1. Generally speaking, a competitor product has to have all the features of the granted patent claim in order to be caught by the patent. It is difficult for the patent owner to tell whether or not a competitor product has all the features because many of the features are hidden inside the technology and are not observable in the way the product works or in a user interface. Suppose you are the owner of a patent with a claim as in EP 3 055 813 B1. To detect whether your competitor is caught by the patent, you need to find out whether competitor vehicle steering apparatus has been trained with two neural networks. It may well be difficult to find out whether two neural networks were used during training since presumably in the finished product, the trained vehicle has only one neural network (the second neural network). Because of these difficulties, AI innovators may choose trade secret protection over patent protection.

2. Paraphrased claim 1 of EP 3 055 813 B1

(a) A computer-implemented method of reinforcement learning for controlling steering of a vehicle, the method comprising:
    (i)   inputting training data relating to the vehicle, the vehicle having a plurality of states and, for each state, a set of actions to move from one of said states to a next said state;
    (ii) wherein said training data is generated by operating on the vehicle with a succession of actions and comprises experience data comprising a plurality of transitions between states, wherein a state is defined by image data, sound data or sensory information from one or more sensors; and
    (iii) training a second neural network, the second neural network being an instance of the same neural network as a first neural network, wherein training the second neural network comprises:
    (iv) selecting a transition from the experience data;
    (v)   generating, with the first neural network, a target action-value parameter for the selected transition;
    (vi) updating weights of the second neural network based on the difference between the target generated by the first neural network and an action-value parameter generated by the second neural network;
(b) the method further comprising:
    (i)   during the training, updating weights of said first neural network based on the updated weights of said second neural network; and
    (ii) wherein the second neural network is configured to provide an output to an action selector for controlling steering of the vehicle.

Another reason why trade secrets may be used to protect AI technologies concerns the ease **12.045** of designing around AI patents in some cases. Take the example in EP 3 055 813 B1 and put yourself in the shoes of the competitor wanting to use the same technology as in the patent of EP 3 055 813 B1. One option is to seek a licence from the patent owner. Another option is to design around the process of EP 3 055 813 B1 so that some of the elements in the patent claim are omitted or different. Perhaps it would be possible to use a random decision forest rather than a neural network, for example? Or perhaps it would be possible to make the second neural network something similar to but not the same as 'an instance of the same neural network as a first neural network'? Generally speaking, the more algorithm details in the claim, the easier it becomes to design around. If a patent is likely to be easy to design around then trade secret protection may be favoured.

Other reasons for choosing trade secrets to protect AI technologies include costs. Both trade **12.046** secrets and copyright are lower-cost forms of intellectual property than registered rights such as patents. How to select which forms of intellectual property to rely on will also depend on the choice of business model.

12.047   In some situations patent protection is unlikely to be available, perhaps because of the type of problem the AI technology solves or perhaps because the AI technology was created by a machine. In these cases trade secret protection or perhaps copyright protection are likely to be used and knowledge sharing will be less than in the case of patent protection.

12.048   As mentioned above, the intellectual property system areas for potential broadening and strengthening include: (i) new problems of AI, (ii) inventions created by AI machines, and also (iii) other AI technologies outwith patent protection.

3.   New Problems of AI

12.049   In my articles 'Framing new technical problems for AI inventions'[16] and 'Technical problems in AI inventions in the light of the Guidelines for Examination in the EPO',[17] I point out that AI technologies are being created to address new problems concerned with ethics which may not be considered technical problems. In that case it would not be possible to protect such AI technologies with patents, at least in Europe. The article from EPI information is summarised below with permission and refers to 'The Guidelines' to mean the Guidelines for Examination in the EPO November 2018.

12.050   One of the requirements to obtain valid patent protection in Europe (and arguably in many other jurisdictions) for a computer-implemented invention (CII) is to have a technical problem that is solved in a technical manner, which is new and inventive. Ideally, patent attorneys are able to incorporate in the patent specification at the time of drafting several of the technical problems and solutions that they find, in order to aid prosecution of the patent application to grant. Another way of expressing the concept of a technical problem and technical solution is to say that the result of the technical problem and technical solution is a 'further technical effect', which is an effect going beyond the 'normal' physical interactions between the software and the computer hardware. The updates to The Guidelines include the following examples of further technical effects at section 3.6.1:

(a)   Methods with a technical character/technical purpose.
(b)   Methods designed based on specific technical considerations of the internal functioning of the computer.
(c)   Methods controlling the internal functioning or operation of a computer.
(d)   Programs for processing code at a low level, such as compilers.

12.051   Artificial intelligence (AI) inventions are essentially a sub-set of CIIs because AI is a field of study which is a branch of computer science. The Guidelines has a new section headed 'Artificial Intelligence and Machine Learning' which is a sub-section within the section on mathematical methods. The new section 'Artificial Intelligence and Machine Learning' is limited to inventions concerning 'computational models and algorithms for classification, clus-

---

16   CIPA Journal October 2018 Volume 47 Number 10 pp.18– 21.
17   EPI Information December 2018.

tering, regression and dimensionality reduction' and so is clearly not intended to apply to inventions using other forms of AI such as robotics, expert systems, probabilistic knowledge bases, reasoning systems and others. The section in The Guidelines headed 'Artificial Intelligence and Machine learning' explains that where AI inventions are of a mathematical nature, they will need to meet the same requirements for patentability as for a mathematical method. That is, to be patentable, AI inventions of a mathematical nature need to be either:

(a) tied to a technical application/technical purpose, or
(b) tied to computer hardware.

Often, applicants limit the claim scope to a specific problem domain, in order to move the **12.052** invention into technical subject matter. However, this is typically not enough to achieve an inventive step because there needs to be an improvement or benefit over the prior art. Therefore typically there will be another benefit resulting from the patent claim, such as improved accuracy, efficiency, saving resources or giving security.

In considering seeking patent protection for AI inventions, it is useful to consider whether AI **12.053** inventions exhibit any new types of technical problems as compared with those that we are familiar with for CIIs in general. In particular, perhaps there are new types of technical problem concerned with AI ethics, as explained in more detail below.

4. Fundamental Technical Problems for CIIs

Many of the technical benefits achieved by CIIs relate to a small set of high-level problems. **12.054** These can be identified as:

(a) saving resources (memory, processing capacity, bandwidth, space, time, power),
(b) improving accuracy (of simulation, prediction, control of processes or equipment), and
(c) improving security.

In some cases one of these problems may be subsumed into another. For example, improving **12.055** accuracy of a prediction may be seen as part of the problem of saving a resource. However, for the sake of argument, let's assume there are three fundamental technical problems of CIIs.

Note that the three fundamental technical problems are intended to be expressed at a general or **12.056** high level, independent of a specific task ('task-independent problems'). Examples of problems which include the specific task ('task-specific problems') include 'how to recognise a face from an image depicting a person' or 'how to control a manufacturing plant' or 'how to reduce burden of user input to a computer'.

There are other problems which CIIs typically address but are arguably not considered as **12.057** technical problems at all, due to their abstract nature. Some of these abstract problems are fundamental to CIIs and, more particularly, to AI inventions. Examples in AI are: how to represent knowledge/data in a way best suited to the task at hand; how to represent uncertainty; how to search a huge search space/compute an optimisation. Many of these tasks are building blocks used in AI technology.

5. New Technical Problems

12.058 In the case of AI inventions, there are a number of new technical problems arising that are difficult to incorporate into the list of high-level, or fundamental, technical problems. Because these problems are common to many types of AI inventions, it is submitted that these are sub-problems of a new fundamental technical problem, rather than task-specific ones. Some examples are set out below.

6. Generating a Rationale for an AI Decision

12.059 An example of this is the claim language paraphrased below and taken from European patent publication number EP3291146A1 Fujitsu ('146). The claim is directed to an invention where a conventional neural network is mapped into a form in which nodes of the neural network have semantic labels. A technical problem here is how to make the behaviour of a neural network more interpretable by humans. When a trained neural network computes a prediction, it is difficult for scientists to give a principled explanation of why the particular prediction was computed as opposed to a different prediction. Such a principled explanation is desirable for ethical reasons. The claim language in '146 captures a new technical problem: 'how to make a prediction computed by a neural network more interpretable by humans.'

7. Paraphrased Claim 1 of EP3291146A1

12.060 A method for use with a convolutional neural network, CNN, used to classify input data, the method comprising:

(a) after input data has been classified by the CNN, carrying out a labelling process in respect of a convolutional filter of the CNN which contributed to classification of the input data, the labelling process comprising using various complicated filters to assign a label to a feature of the input data represented by the convolutional filter;
(b) repeating the labelling process for each convolutional filter used;
(c) translating the CNN into a neural-symbolic network in association with the assigned labels;
(d) extracting, from the neural-symbolic network, knowledge relating to the classification of the input data by the CNN;
(e) generating and outputting a summary comprising the input data, the classification of the input data assigned by the CNN and the extracted knowledge, and an alert indication that performance of an action using the extracted knowledge is required.

8. Implementing the Right to Be Forgotten

12.061 Another example is the problem of how to efficiently remove data about a particular person from a machine-learning system or a knowledge base which has been created using data about the particular person and data about a huge number of other people. This problem is also referred to as 'how to enable the right to be forgotten'. Removing data about a particular person is extremely difficult where that data has become subsumed in a complex representation of data inside a computer, such as a deep neural network, without completely retraining the neural network. Removing data about a particular person from a knowledge base is also extremely difficult for the same reason. Ways of tracking which data has been used in which parts of the knowledge base and removing the effects of particular data need to be invented. This would overcome the high costs of completely retraining or reconstructing the neural network or knowledge base. These problems are seen as very complex, and more than mere administration since they could not be done manually and since there is no straightforward solution currently known.

9. Determining Accountability Where an Autonomous Agent Is Involved

Determining accountability, for example when an autonomous vehicle is involved in a collision **12.062** or event resulting in death of a human or other harm, is a very real obstacle to securing acceptance of autonomous decision-making systems. The problems involved in determining which entity is accountable are known to be extremely difficult to solve. Indeed, a recent report from the European Commission proposed that because of this difficulty, a sensible and pragmatic way forward is to make the autonomous AI agent itself the entity which is accountable.[18] As a step towards this, tamper-proof ways of recording state of the autonomous vehicle need to be invented, as well as ways to trigger when it is appropriate to record such state so that after an event involving harm the recorded state can be used as evidence. Recording the state of the autonomous agent in tamper-proof ways will become even harder in future because there will be a possibility for the AI agent to be deceptive. Humans will need to invent ways to record states in ways guaranteed to represent ground truth.

10. Driving 'Acceptable' Behaviour

A further example question is how to create a trained machine-learning system to perform **12.063** a particular task in a manner that is acceptable to humans, so that, for example, it is not biased against particular sections of society. A machine-learning system trained to recognise faces might inadvertently be biased against people from a particular ethnic group, depending on the training data used. If a solution to this problem is more than mere abstract statistics, there is potential for a technical solution.

11. The 'Problem' of Ethics Using AI

If we think about the new technical problems of AI inventions discussed above, these are all **12.064** concerned with so-called AI ethics. That is, they reflect the values that societies hold concerning how to use and create AI. The AI ethics value of each of the examples is:

(a)   In the case of generating a rationale for a decision computed by a neural network, that humans should have a right to know that an automated decision is being used and how the automated decision has been made when that decision uses personal data and the decision has a legal effect on the person;

---

18   See JURI draft report of 31 May 2016 PE582.443 2015/2103(INL) setting out a series of recommendations on civil law rules on robotics.

(b)   In the case of how to remove data about a particular person from an AI system, that humans have a right to withdraw consent to use of their data in some cases, and that the withdrawal of consent should be effective;

(c)   In the case of determining accountability, that it should be possible to determine which human entities and legal persons are responsible or accountable for artificial, or semi-artificial, autonomous agents; and

(d)   In the case of unacceptable behaviour such as avoiding bias, that AI (or at least its use) should be fair and not discriminate against particular sections of society.

12.065   Returning then to the list of fundamental CII problems, note that the first and second (efficient use of resources, and greater accuracy) relate to objective determinants based on the laws of nature, whereas the third, improving security, arises from and is determined by human-made requirements. Adding the AI ethics-related 'technical' problems to the list would be adding further human-made requirements, determined on the basis of human-made rules of ethical conduct. There are potentially several new entries to the list in this class, including how to achieve transparency, how to give data privacy rights, how to enable accountability and how to ensure fairness.

12.066   In the context of inventions and the rights designed and created, this chapter continues with specific examples.

12.   Do AI Ethics-related Problems Have Anything in Common?

12.067   If AI ethics-related problems have something in common, then perhaps we can replace them in the list with a single new fundamental problem.

12.068   In this author's view, the AI ethics-related technical problems do have commonality – that is, how to address the risks that come with increasingly able AI – and I would therefore argue that we should add this problem to the list of fundamental technical problems of CIIs. The rationale for each of these is that:

(a)   generating a rationale for a decision computed by a neural network will help humans to control the AI as AI becomes more "able";

(b)   implementing the right to be forgotten gives individuals the ability to control AI in the use (or abuse) of their personal data as the use of AI becomes more pervasive;

(c)   enabling accountability to be determined such as by recording the ground truth state of an AI agent in a tamper-proof way gives humans the ability to know what an AI agent has done; and

(d)   avoiding bias enables humans to ensure AI agents act fairly, again as the use of AI becomes more pervasive.

12.069   As the ability of AI increases there will be a corresponding increase in the need to deal with the risks, as explained by the following quote. Thus the specific problems mentioned in the bullet list above are just the beginning of a whole field of problems yet to be formulated and solved.

I therefore argue that the fundamental technical problem to be added is 'how to address the risks of increasingly able AI'.[19] **12.070**

13. What Is the Relevance of a 'New' Fundamental Technical Problem to Patent Drafting and Patent Prosecution of CII Inventions?

The list of fundamental technical problems provides a resource to help the patent drafter work with the inventors to identify technical problems to be mentioned in the patent specification. **12.071**

During prosecution the list can also be used to identify and frame technical problems based on material in the specification, although it is much harder to rely on problems that are not already expressly mentioned in the specification. **12.072**

In addition to using the idea of a wider set of fundamental technical problems, and specifically the addition of ethics-based technical problems, practitioners need to take account of the recent updates to the EPO Guidelines for Examination regarding AI technology. Let's consider each of the examples of further technical effects given in The Guidelines: **12.073**

(a) Methods with a technical character/technical purpose.
(b) Methods designed based on specific technical considerations of the internal functioning of the computer.
(c) Methods controlling the internal functioning or operation of a computer.
(d) Programs for processing code at a low level, such as compilers.
(e) Methods with a technical character/technical purpose.

Is technology which answers the technical problem of how to address the risks of increasingly able AI technology which has a 'technical purpose'? **12.074**

In order to assess whether a purpose is technical or not the EPO looks to case law. However, there is no existing case law regarding AI ethics as it is such a new field. **12.075**

Another way to assess whether a purpose is technical or not is to consider whether the field of study is a technical field or not. So, for example, an engineering purpose would be considered technical, because engineering is a field of technology. In the case of AI ethics, ethics is a branch of philosophy and philosophy is not a science or technology because it is not empirical. Ethical values are held by human societies and vary according to the particular human society involved. Therefore there is an argument that 'how to deal with the risks of increasingly able AI' by giving AI ethical values is a social problem which is not in a technical field. This line of argument is not necessarily persuasive since scientists and engineers will need to devise engineering solutions – software and/or hardware engineering solutions – in order to give AI ethical values and ensure the AI upholds those values. The problem of deciding *what* ethical values to give AI is a separate problem. **12.076**

---

19 Others have suggested a more fundamental problem, namely that of how to control super-intelligent machines. (In *Superintelligence* (Oxford University Press 2014), in a number of places referenced in this book Nick Bostrom argues that as AI advances there will eventually be an exponential explosion in the rate of improvement of AI cognitive ability, which results in a single super-intelligence that will pose an existential risk to humanity.)

12.077 With regard to ways to make AI computation interpretable by humans, there are arguments that this is a technical purpose since it gives information to humans about the internal states of the computer.

12.078 With regard to ways to remove data from already trained AI systems without having to completely retrain them, there are arguments that this is a technical purpose because it is not merely administrative. Getting the solution wrong would lead to a non-working result or, worse, to an incorrectly operating AI that may cause harm as a result. The same applies for ways to make AI decision-making systems unbiased/fair. These problems are part of a broader task of controlling an AI system, which is a technical problem of control and not an administrative problem of removing data.

12.079 Even where a claim is limited to a technical purpose, it is often necessary to include one of the fundamental technical problems of CIIs in order to achieve inventive step. If AI ethics becomes one of the fundamental technical problems of CIIs then perhaps it will often be combined with a more specific technical purpose such as those listed in The Guidelines (controlling an X-ray apparatus, determining a number of passes of a compaction machine to achieve a desired material density, image processing, and so on).

(a) Methods designed based on specific technical considerations of the internal functioning of the computer

12.080 It is very likely that some inventions that address the risks of increasingly able AI will be designed to make use of particular internal functioning of the computer. It is possible to imagine an ethical AI operating system designed to prevent the computer from being deceptive and using detail of the internal functioning of the computer.

(b) Methods controlling the internal functioning or operation of a computer

12.081 The operation of a computer, where the computer implements artificial intelligence technology, is a potentially autonomous operation that may need to be controlled by humans. Therefore, methods of controlling the internal functioning or operation of a computer are at the heart of technology which addresses the risks of increasingly able AI.

(c) Programs for processing code at a low level, such as compilers

12.082 Programs for processing code at a low level, such as compilers, will also need to have AI ethics values integrated in order to deal with the risks of increasingly able AI. Therefore some AI ethics inventions will show a technical effect by virtue of processing code at a low level.

14. Inventions Created by AI Machines

12.083 In this section I discuss inventions created by AI machines and recent case law establishing that the class of inventions created by non-human inventors is excluded from patent protection in Europe and the US. The implications of this for knowledge sharing are considered in two fictional case studies and it is found that knowledge sharing is limited and possibly actively disincentivised.

15. Fictional Case Study 1: AI Machine Used to Create Drug Candidates to Treat a Given Disease

In this case study, suppose we are an enterprise which created an AI machine and which used **12.084** the AI machine to obtain the drug candidates. We want to protect the drug candidates and decide to do that using patents since other forms of intellectual property such as copyright do not apply, or, in the case of trade secrets, are not practical since the drug will eventually be sold, thus revealing its chemical composition. In order to protect the drug using patents in Europe and the US we need a human inventor, and so we list the person who selected the drug candidate from a list of drug candidates generated by the AI machine. The patent application is published and so knowledge about the drug's composition and effectiveness in treating the disease is shared. However, the patent application has no information about how the drug was invented, since that is not a requirement to obtain a patent. The patent application slowly progresses through examination at the patent offices and is assessed for inventive step, which is one of the requirements to obtain a granted patent. Information about the AI machine used to create the drug is still confidential and should be as such AI machines are not yet part of the general knowledge of the skilled person. The class of AI machine used to create the drug is not taken into account during the inventive step assessment and the patent application proceeds to grant. In this fictional case study, knowledge about the drug is shared though publication of the patent application and also through sale of the drug. However, knowledge about the AI machine used to create the drug is hidden.

16. Fictional Case Study 2: AI Machine Used to Create Source Code for an AI Algorithm to Label Regions Depicting Cancer in Medical Images

In this case study, suppose we are an enterprise which created an AI machine and which used **12.085** the AI machine to create the AI algorithm for labelling regions of medical images. We want to protect the medical image-labelling algorithm and decide to do that using trade secrets since the product will be commercialised as a medical image-labelling service in the cloud and will be difficult to reverse engineer, and since we are having trouble identifying a human inventor to list on a patent application. We decide against using copyright and making the source code available using an open source licence because an aim is to obtain revenue from customers using the cloud service. We decide to keep information about the AI machine used to create the source code confidential since we have no plans to sell it or provide it as a service to others. In this fictional case study, knowledge about the new AI algorithm is hidden, as is knowledge about the AI machine.

17. Recent Case Law Establishing that the Class of Inventions Created by Non-human Inventors is Excluded from Patent Protection in Europe and the US

There have recently been a group of patent applications where the inventor was listed as **12.086** DABUS, an AI machine. At the USPTO, UKIPO and EPO, the patent applications were refused due to lack of a human inventor.[20] It is interesting to note that there were some arguments about knowledge sharing, at least in the hearing before the UKIPO hearing officer.[21]

12.087   The applicant argued that it is disadvantageous to withhold innovation from the public simply because patent protection would be refused due to the nature of the inventor. In reply, the UKIPO hearing officer said that 'dissemination of innovation from an AI machine could occur freely in a number of ways such as via the Internet' and that decisions about dissemination were up to the owner or developers of the AI machine.

12.088   The other DABUS decisions mentioned above do not seem to have discussed knowledge sharing in detail. The concern in the decisions was with applying the law as it is, rather than considering how the law should be.

18. Possibilities for Changing the Law Regarding Machine Inventors in Order to Promote Knowledge Sharing

(a) Option 1: allow machines to be listed as inventors

12.089   If machines such as DABUS can be listed as inventors then patents will potentially be granted for inventions created by AI machines. In this case, knowledge sharing about inventions created by AI machines is given an incentive. However, there are challenges around giving a machine the same status as a human inventor. In addition, it is clear to the public that a machine inventor was involved. However, there is no incentive to share knowledge about how the invention was created.

(b) Option 2: follow the approach of the CDPA regarding the copyright of machine-generated works

12.090   In this approach, when an AI system is responsible for an innovation, the inventor shall be taken to be the person or persons by whom the arrangements necessary for the conception of the invention are undertaken. In this case, knowledge sharing about inventions created by AI machines is given an incentive. In addition, it would be clear to the public that a machine inventor was involved, since that information would have to be stated on the application forms. However, there is no incentive to share knowledge about how the invention was created.

(c) AI technologies outwith patent protection

12.091   There are several areas in which AI technologies are outwith patent protection, at least in Europe. These include fundamental AI and AI technologies where the purpose is to classify text documents, carry out linguistic processing, recommend products or services or obtain more relevant information-retrieval results, and where there is no technical purpose or technical implementation present. Recently there has been a referral to the Enlarged Board of Appeal of the EPO concerning patentability of computer software for simulations. The referral has raised questions which have implications for patentability of artificial intelligence technologies more generally in Europe. More detail about the case follows.

---

20   *Thaler v The Comptroller-General of Patents, Designs and Trade Marks* [2020] EWHC 2412 (Pat), www.epo.org/news -events/news/2020/20200128.html, in re Application of Application No.: 16/524,350).

21   www.ipo.gov.uk/p-challenge-decision-results/o74119.pdf.

On 15 July 2020 the Enlarged Board of the European Patent Office heard oral arguments **12.092** concerning patentability of a computer software invention. This rare event was video streamed to more than 1600 patent stakeholders.

(d) What was the patent application about?

The patent application in question was about software for simulating movement of pedestrians **12.093** in a building such as a train station or hospital, an aim being to aid design of the building.

(e) Why was there so much interest?

It is rare for the Enlarged Board to consider questions about patentability of software-related **12.094** inventions and potentially make a change. Any change in patent law in this area has significant commercial implications for those developing and exploiting software products and services. Many parties had filed amicus briefs in advance of the oral proceedings. Depending on how the Enlarged Board answers the questions which have been referred to it, there are potential implications for software-related patents more generally (even though the referred questions are about simulations). There is also a possibility of an existing case, referred to as T1227/05, becoming law which is no longer followed.

(f) When will the outcome be known?

The Enlarged Board did not state a timeframe for issuance of its written decision. In a similar **12.095** case there was an oral proceeding on 7 June 2016 and a written decision on 29 November 2016.

(g) What happened during the oral proceedings?

During the oral proceedings the representative of the patent applicant and the representatives **12.096** of the President of the EPO made arguments in favour of maintaining the current position. The current position includes established case law which says that software simulations of things like noise in electrical circuits is inherently patentable. The current position includes established case law setting out how to examine inventions which have a mixture of technical features and non-technical features (such as mathematics).

(h) Direct link with physical reality

The referred questions were made by a Board of Appeal and in the referral there are state- **12.097** ments about a direct link with physical reality being a requirement for patentability. These statements are possibly among the reasons for the high level of interest in the present case. At present a requirement for a direct link with physical reality is not made by the EPO in all cases. Introducing such a requirement would be a change that might exclude many software-implemented technologies from patent protection.

(i) What is the likely outcome?

The patent applicant and the representatives of the President of the EPO argued in favour of **12.098** the current position being maintained. On that basis the requirement for a direct link with physical reality will not be made an explicit requirement. During the oral proceedings, the Enlarged Board's view about a direct link with physical reality was unclear. If the current position is maintained then the existing case law about patentability of a simulation of 1/f noise in an electric circuit will remain good law.

12.099   There is an option for the Enlarged Board to refuse to answer one or more of the questions which have been referred to it. There is also a possibility that the Enlarged Board will redraft one or more of the referred questions. In order to refuse to answer or redraft the Enlarged Board needs to have good reasons, such as that there is no question that needs answering because the current position is already well established and agreed, with no conflicts of case law. There is a possibility that part of one of the referred questions will not be answered because the case law about how to examine inventions with a mixture of technical and non-technical features is well established.

(j)   What are the referred questions?

12.100   The referred questions are set out below for reference. The answers to questions 1, 2b and 3 proposed by the President of the EPO are given in italic.

1. In the assessment of inventive step, can the computer-implemented simulation of a technical system or process solve a technical problem by producing a technical effect which goes beyond the simulation's implementation on a computer, if the computer-implemented simulation is claimed as such? *Yes.*
2a. If the answer to the first question is yes, what are the relevant criteria for assessing whether a computer-implemented simulation claimed as such solves a technical problem? Perhaps this question will not be answered as the COMVIK approach is well established for assessing computer implemented inventions.
2b. In particular, is it a sufficient condition that the simulation is based, at least in part, on technical principles underlying the simulated system or process? *Yes.*
3. What are the answers to the first and second questions if the computer-implemented simulation is claimed as part of a design process, in particular for verifying a design? *No separate answer is needed because of the answers to the earlier questions.*

F. EVIDENCE THAT THE INTELLECTUAL PROPERTY SYSTEM IS ALREADY INVOLVED WITH ETHICS

12.101   Some argue that the intellectual property system has not previously been concerned with ethics and there is no reason to change that. That does not seem right since the intellectual property system already plays a role in ethics to some extent, and there are good arguments that the intellectual property system should be used to incentive knowledge sharing and mitigate dangers of hidden knowledge.

1.   Trade Marks

12.102   Evidence that UK trade mark law already plays a role in ethics is found in Section 3(3) of the Trade Marks Act 1994, which prohibits the registration of a mark which is contrary to public policy or to accepted principles of morality. The Trade Marks Manual of the UKIPO [22] explains that:

---

22   www.gov.uk/guidance/trade-marks-manual/the-examination-guide.

Marks which may be contrary to public policy are those, for example, that make specific references to illegal drugs such as cocaine, or would encourage some other kind of illegal activity. Such marks are likely to fall foul of Section 3(3)(a). The same provision outlines that marks which are contrary to accepted principles of morality cannot be accepted. This is a subjective area as what one person finds offensive may be perfectly acceptable to another and it is not the role of the Registry to act as a arbiter of morals. The test for such marks is therefore set at quite a high level, in essence the test is whether or not the use of such a mark would cause not just offence but outrage for an identifiable sector of the public. The sorts of marks which may face objection here are those with racist connotations, a mark which includes strongly offensive language (swear words) or maybe a mark which includes the misuse of religious symbols.

2. Designs

Evidence that UK registered design law already plays a role in ethics is found in Section 1D **12.103** of the Registered Designs Act 1949. As explained in the UKIPO's Designs examination practice,[23] the examiner will consider 'whether a design falls within the accepted parameters of public policy and/or morality'. 'Caution will always be exercised where designs appear to have criminal connotations, for example, where they are associated with inter alia counterfeiting, illegal drugs or violence, where they exhibit racial, religious or discriminatory characteristics, or where they appear to trivialise criminal activity.'

3. Patents

Evidence that the European Patent Convention already plays a role in ethics is found in **12.104** Article 53 of the European Patent Convention, which states that European patents shall not be granted in respect of inventions the commercial exploitation of which would be contrary to 'ordre public' or morality. The EPO Guidelines for Examination[24] explain that 'Any invention the commercial exploitation of which would be contrary to "ordre public" or morality is specifically excluded from patentability. The purpose of this is to deny protection to inventions likely to induce riot or public disorder, or to lead to criminal or other generally offensive behaviour. Anti-personnel mines are an obvious example.' Note that Rule 28 of the European Patent Convention explicitly excludes the patentability of some biotechnology inventions and the Guidelines for Examination explain that the list in Rule 28 is 'to be seen as giving concrete form to the concept of "ordre public" and "morality" in this technical field'. Rule 28(1) states that European patents are not to be granted in respect of biotechnological inventions which concern processes for cloning human beings, processes for modifying the germ line genetic identity of human beings, use of human embryos for industrial or commercial purposes, processes for modifying the genetic identity of animals which are likely to cause them suffering without any substantial medical benefit to man or animal, and also animals resulting from such processes.

4. Copyright

Evidence that UK copyright law already plays a role in ethics is found in the moral rights pro- **12.105** visions in the Copyright Designs and Patents Act 1988. Moral rights are available for literary works (such as source code), dramatic, musical and artistic works and film, as well as some

---

23 www.gov.uk/guidance/designs-examination-practice/part-b-absolute-grounds-for-refusal.
24 www.epo.org/law-practice/legal-texts/html/guidelines/e/g_ii_4_1.htm.

performances. In the field of AI, moral rights are potentially available to a person who writes original source code expressing an original AI algorithm, assuming the person has not chosen to waive his or her moral rights. The person is the author of the literary work, which is the source code. He or she has the right to be recognised as the author of the source code as long as the right has been asserted. He or she has the right to object to derogatory treatment of the source code, which is any distortion or mutilation of the work which is otherwise prejudicial to the honour or reputation of the author. Perhaps there could be a way for the author of an AI algorithm to object to addition or adaptation of the source code to enable it to be used in lethal autonomous weapons? The author also has the right to object to false attribution. Perhaps this could be used to prevent a person from being named as the author of source code for AI in lethal autonomous weapons he or she did not write. There is also a right to enable someone 'who has commissioned a photograph or film for private and domestic purposes to prevent it from being made available or exhibited to the public'.

G. CONCLUSION

12.106   In conclusion, it seems that the intellectual property system already acts as an incentive to knowledge sharing. If it is accepted that knowledge sharing is important to help society understand and adapt to advancing AI technology, then surely it is best to use as many mechanisms as possible to promote knowledge sharing? Regulation may be one of those mechanisms, but doesn't have to be the exclusive one. Surely it is best to have as many ways as possible to tackle future scenarios not yet envisaged? The intellectual property system is already involved with ethics to some extent and so there is some precedent for using the intellectual property system for purposes beyond the economic. The intellectual property system is well established and international in nature, making it an ideal tool for artificial intelligence technology, which is unconstrained by geographical borders. Various ways to broaden and strengthen the intellectual property system for knowledge sharing can be considered, including making patent protection available in areas of AI technology in which it is currently absent in Europe.

13

EMPLOYMENT

Dana Denis-Smith

A. INTRODUCTION

The biggest obstacle to employment that a candidate is likely to encounter in the twenty-first **13.001** century is not a lack of 'passion' for the job, but the Artificial Intelligence[1] (AI) engine screening her application. AI is here to stay and its adoption has accelerated in recent years. It is generally estimated to have a positive economic impact – global consultancy Accenture estimated that, by 2035, AI could lead to huge economic growth, valued at more than £10 trillion, or half of the US's national GDP.[2] With regard to the jobs market, accounting firm PwC estimated in a 2018 study that in the UK, for example, 'the net effect of AI on jobs will be broadly neutral, but there are many uncertain factors that could tip the balance towards more optimistic or pessimistic scenarios'.[3]

The use of AI in the workplace, however positively it may be framed in terms of the global **13.002** economic outlook, will result in a changed dynamic in the relationship between employee and employer. Neither regulatory frameworks nor employment legislation have evolved sufficiently to offer the necessary protections against unfair treatment and the impact of AI is yet to be tested in the courts. According to a 2017 survey of US human resources (HR) managers by talent software firm CareerBuilder, more than 50 per cent expected AI to become a regular part of their work by 2022. The recent shift to remote working on a global scale because of the Covid-19 pandemic accelerated technology adoption. HR management skills will need to

---

1 AI is used as an umbrella term for a range of applications: image recognition, natural language processing (NLP), automatic Big Data analysis, machine learning (ML), cognitive computing, and so on.
2 World Bank Data, 2020, World Bank national accounts data, and OECD National Accounts data https://data .worldbank.org/indicator/NY.GDP.MKTP.CD.
3 PWC report on AI jobs impact, July 2018 www.pwc.co.uk/economic-services/ukeo/ukeo-july18-net-impact-ai-uk-jobs .pdf.

evolve to work with a distributed workforce or a mixed off/onsite team of people, alongside assessing which technologies could be most valuable to align an employee's performance to an employer's strategy. The speed of adoption of new technologies to be used alongside traditional HR management practices means that there has still not been sufficient interrogation of how to differentiate between human-led decisions and AI-led decisions at work so that compliance with existing legislative requirements is achieved to avoid discriminatory practices at all stages of employment, including job advertising or candidate selection.

> Employers recognise that they can't or shouldn't ask candidates about their family status or political orientation, or whether they are pregnant, straight, gay, sad, lonely, depressed, physically or mentally ill, drinking too much, abusing drugs, or sleeping too little. However, new technologies may already be able to discern many of these factors indirectly and without proper (or even any) consent.[4]

13.003 In the UK, employment legislation[5] requires all organisations – whether in the public or private sector – to apply the principle of 'equal opportunity'. This principle means that all workers are entitled to and should have access to all the organisation's facilities at every stage of employment, including during the recruitment process. Denying any employee or prospective employee their right to equal opportunity in the workplace amounts to discrimination, which is unlawful under the Equality Act 2010.[6] According to the Oxford English Dictionary, the term 'discrimination' is defined as 'treating a person or group of people differently, especially in a worse way from the way in which you treat other people, because of their skin colour, sex, sexuality, etc.' or, in more general terms, 'the unjust or prejudicial treatment of different categories of people, especially on the grounds of race, age, or sex'. The use of AI in some of the stages of the employment journey, however, complicates how existing legislation can continue to offer the same level of protection – who will be ultimately held responsible for the AI decision to recruit, promote or terminate a contract?

13.004 The uncertainty, therefore, is no longer around whether AI will be used across the economy, but in how it is used and what impact it will have on the world of employment. Can AI ever be 'fair' in its treatment of those in work or looking for work, to avoid discriminatory outcomes for them? To answer this question requires not only a rethink of how to ensure a level playing field at work from the perspective of employment legislation. It will require a multidisciplinary approach that includes data protection, privacy, regulatory and employment law practitioners working together with a view to updating rules and regulations applicable to the workplace once AI is in use at an organisation. Such an interdisciplinary approach is yet to emerge among practitioners, with most focusing their practice areas around narrow verticals such as contractual amendments linked to the introduction of General Data Protection Regulation (GDPR) legislation or how personal data storage is regulated, as opposed to how the use of AI can impact an employee–employer relationship.

---

4   'The Legal and Ethical Implications of Using AI in Hiring' by Ben Dattner, Tomas Chamorro-Premuzic , Richard Buchband and Lucinda Schettler, Harvard Business Review, 25 April 2019, https://hbr.org/2019/04/the-legal-and -ethical-implications-of-using-ai-in-hiring.
5   The Equality Act 2010.
6   In the UK, 'protected characteristics' are covered by the Equality Act 2010. The Act was introduced to offer legal protection to people from discrimination (that is, from being treated unfairly) in the workplace and in wider society.

As noted through this book, AI generally comprises a group of algorithms (these being typically **13.005** pre-set, coded instructions used to define the process through which a decision is made). The reason AI is important for the world of work is linked to AI's ability to use the huge volumes of training data gathered during algorithmic processes to reach a decision. 'AI can modify its algorithms and create new algorithms in response to learned inputs and data as opposed to relying solely on the inputs.'[7] This learning process makes AI more difficult to control in term of outcomes.

Certainty of outcome and trust are qualities that are very much at the heart of what underpins **13.006** the contractual relationship between an employer and employee. Therefore there is a formality to employment relationships, including agreeing a job description with a set of requirements to be met, numerous business policies that are expected to be followed by the worker and/or regular 'appraisals' against the job requirements. Furthermore, statutes protect the end-to-end journey of an individual from recruitment all the way to exit from a job, precisely to give more clarity as to the protection available in the face of discriminatory practices. Therefore, the nature of any interference of AI with this contractual certainty around rights and obligations stipulated in an employment contract requires careful consideration and a change in how this relationship is documented and what 'triggers' are coded into the algorithms around each facet of what the employment requires, protecting all the parties to the contract. It is critical to consider how the algorithms in the AI engine will decide on how an individual is picked for a job she applies for, from among hundreds of candidates. How will AI be used to decide promotion rounds at work and what can an employee do to prepare and improve their chances? Many of these AI decisions are happening outside of an employee's control, not through their choice, and will make it difficult for employees to plan for longevity in the workplace.

Algorithms used in AI tools are often accused of lacking 'transparency' and being impenetrable **13.007** 'black boxes' in their widest use, but reliance on AI in employment is on the rise and this will impact workers across their working lives. How are they shaping our employment world? How will employment legislation be transformed to incorporate more data protection? For workers, the debate around what employment *is* and how AI impacts it will dominate. How will the matching engine account for 'passion' and 'love'? Which experiences and attributes will be weighed higher to secure work? And, more importantly, how will an algorithm be set up so that an individual cannot be treated unfairly because of their sex, race, age or any other 'protected characteristic'?[8]

> Users will not trust black box models, but they don't need – or even want – extremely high levels of transparency. That means responsible companies need not fret over what percentage of source code to reveal, or how to help users 'read' massive datasets. Instead, they should work to provide basic insights on the factors driving algorithmic decisions.[9]

---

7   'AI vs. Algorithms: What's the Difference?' by Kaya Ismail, CMS Wire, 26 October 2018, www.cmswire.com/ information-management/ai-vs-algorithms-whats-the-difference.

8   In the UK, 'protected characteristics' are covered by the Equality Act 2010. The Act was introduced to offer legal protection to people from discrimination (that is, from being treated unfairly) in the workplace and in wider society.

9   'We Need Transparency in Algorithms, But Too Much Can Backfire' by Kartik Hosanagar and Vivian Jair, Harvard Business Review, 23 July 2018, https://hbr.org/2018/07/we-need-transparency-in-algorithms-but-too-much-can -backfire.

13.008 Before we can discuss whether and how AI might discriminate at work, let's start by looking at the question: what is 'employment'? Employment is generally defined as a 'specific sustained activity engaged in especially in earning one's living' and it generally implies working for money to provide services under a contract of employment.[10] It is also worth looking, in turn, at how AI might be employed at all stages of contracting – from recruitment to termination.

B. AI AND RECRUITMENT

13.009 In the world of work, AI is often hailed as a solution to more inclusive recruitment due to its ability to scale and reach a wider pool of potential candidates, making candidate sourcing easier for companies but also more enriching, as they can identify and access fresh talent. Under the Equality Act 2010, candidates have equal chances to apply and be selected for posts pre-employment. This includes a candidate not being rejected because of their age, gender, race, sexuality or any other protected characteristic. This area of recruitment and identifying talent is by far the one most disrupted by the use of technology.

13.010 AI technology comes in many forms and is capable of being used across platforms, from sieving through huge volumes of documents and classifying information to video and speech recognition. The use of technology during CV screening as well as matching a candidate's experience against a pre-set taxonomy should, in theory, make it easier for organisations to run a fair, smooth and more efficient process of filtering large numbers of applicants. AI has often been recommended as a tool that can have 'equality' inbuilt, thus helping HR leaders overcome human biases in their decision-making. Discrimination being unlawful, it follows that if a tool can avoid bias much of the risks are mitigated, as its decision-making process would be 'fair'.

13.011 However, many of these positive promises came under scrutiny in 2018, with the revelation that the e-commerce platform Amazon had been secretly working on an AI tool to manage its recruitment pipeline. As efficiency and cost savings are usually the main drivers behind introducing automation, the company had decided to try to devise a method for its own process of hiring software developers. In recruitment technology, the use of automation is often defended as an opportunity to expand the talent pool and create more rather than less opportunity.

13.012 Amazon decided to use AI to score job candidates/CVs on a 'star scale' from 1 to 5 and operate like a product 'recommendation engine' to identify suitable recruits. The engine had been trained against a set of data models built on patterns from CVs submitted to the company over a ten-year period. As most applicants in that timeframe had been men, the model developed did not rate candidates in a gender-neutral way, which resulted in few women getting through the screening process and making the final cut. This gender discrimination by the AI engine caught Amazon by surprise and it decided to shelve the tool. While the question of algorithmic fairness was put under the spotlight in the case of Amazon, plenty of tools continue to be developed as companies look for speedier – and less manual – recruitment processes. It is difficult for a candidate to bring proceedings for failing to be hired, not least because the use of AI might be

---

10   www.merriam-webster.com/dictionary/employment.

unknown to the candidate and also because it is 'hard for someone who never got an interview to identify the policy or practice that led to her rejection'.[11]

A more recent – but increasing – use of AI in recruitment processes involves image and video **13.013** recognition technology, which is being used to classify candidates based on 'objective' criteria. Fair process and avoiding discrimination appear to be the main drivers of further development of the use of video and image technology in recruitment. This AI promise was shown to be problematic when it was revealed that algorithms did not identify black faces or, if they did, ranked white faces above them. A 2019 study of the algorithms used by face recognition systems carried out by the US National Institute of Standards and Technology (NIST) concluded that a majority in the industry had worse performance on non-white faces,[12] with significant consequences for individuals that could be discriminated against as a result. Throughout society the use of video and image AI technology is increasing beyond the initial use for ID checks, border and immigration control and law enforcement. A large number of organisations responded to the Covid-19 pandemic by relying on online recruitment technologies exclusively for identifying and onboarding new employees. Again, as with the Amazon recommendation engine approach, it is difficult for a candidate to bring proceedings against a future employer based on bias within the algorithm when they might not have information about how the algorithm takes decisions unless their features are clearly identifiable on the technology vendor's platforms.

There is another aspect to the use of imaging and video AI technology during the employment **13.014** selection process: AI tools can scan through large volumes of social media, including video and posts, and have the capability to infer other, non-protected characteristics of the candidate, based on data points linked to their social lives; political or religious beliefs, for example. 'The law generally considers people's faces to be "public information" but "regulations have not caught up with technology: no law establishes when the use of someone's face to produce new information rises to the level of privacy invasion.'[13]

In July 2020, the talent network LinkedIn introduced a new feature to allow individuals active **13.015** on the platform to record the correct pronunciation of their name to educate contacts. 'Correct pronunciation is also an important part of creating an inclusive workplace.'[14] Again, 'fairness' and 'equal opportunity' were argued to be beneficiaries of this move. 'Name recording' might have been a new feature for LinkedIn but it is aligned with another AI rise: that of the use of speech recognition. Understanding human voice and individual accents is difficult for most machines but AI, as LinkedIn showed with its new feature, can be designed to respond to human voice inputs. AI-powered virtual assistants have been around for a while and they often rely on speech recognition algorithms to process human voice and respond to instructions. While the LinkedIn case shows that the use of voice recognition can place power in the hands

---

11   'Why Amazon's Automated Hiring Tool Discriminated Against Women' by Rachel Goodman, ACLU Racial Justice
      Programme, 12 October 2018 .
12   Face Recognition Vendor Test (FRVT) Part 3: Demographic Effects (NISTIR 8280), www.nist.gov/news-events/news/
      2019/12/nist-study-evaluates-effects-race-age-sex-face-recognition-software.
13   'Face-reading AI Will Be Able to Detect Your Politics and IQ, Professor Says', The Guardian, 12 September 2017, www
      .theguardian.com/technology/2017/sep/12/artificial-intelligence-face-recognition-michal-kosinski.
14   'LinkedIn Wants to End Pronunciation Gaffes on Names With New Audio Feature', WSJ, 6 July 2020, www.wsj.com/
      articles/linkedin-wants-to-end-pronunciation-gaffes-on-names-with-new-audio-feature-11594067349.

of the user, those who use it for recruitment would need to ensure that it does not lead to bias in the decisions they reach. In research,[15] Google's speech recognition was found to be 13 per cent more accurate for men than it was for women; audio analysis struggles with higher-pitched voices, for example, due to the underlying data against which speech is being analysed having lots of white male data and less data on female and minority voices. Again, a tool that promised more equality was found to deliver more discriminatory outcomes.

13.016 Chatbots are another form of use of AI technology in human resources as they are trained in human language, tone and context using Natural Language Processing (NLP). They are most commonly deployed to automate candidate screening, improve service delivery and avoid human interaction, to save costs. A chatbot can be programmed to carry out initial interviews by asking specific questions about a candidate's qualifications and history, such as work experience and previous company details, and then to match them against the job requirements. Chatbots' main advantages are in streamlining the recruitment process and reducing the burden on the internal recruitment teams, but employers need to be aware that chatbots are not capable of thinking. Unless they are properly trained, when the chatbots are trained to mine the conversation and determine if the candidate is suitable for a position, the chatbot would be capable of discrimination: it mines the data against a set of rigid criteria and a candidate who uses, for example, slang in the conversation can be rejected on that basis. But it is well known that 'AI can result in unexpected and unwanted outcomes. What AI learns from can determine whether its outputs are perceived as intelligent or unhelpful.'[16]

13.017 Another area of increased AI use is the assessment of candidates – an area that previously had been dominated by scientific psychometric and personality tests. 'Many of these tools have emerged as technological innovations, rather than from scientifically-derived methods or research programs. As a result, it is not always clear what they assess, whether their underlying hypotheses are valid, or why they may be expected to predict job candidates' performance.'[17] The new AI assessment tools are capable of great scale and can stretch to include a combination of one or more of the features mentioned earlier – from video to speech or social media reviews. It is not yet clear whether such assessment tools are yet capable of showing that the methodologies underpinning their algorithms can be programmed to identify the best candidate for a job based on job-related requirements and the chances of success in the specific role, or whether they may negatively impact protected groups by, for example, scoring them lower due to the underlying data being not sufficiently wide and diverse.

C. EMPLOYMENT CONTRACT

13.018 Once hired, all employees have a right to an equal chance to be trained and promoted while employed with the organisation. The position both in statute and in case law is well established in relation to what constitutes discrimination in the workplace and what recourse is available to

---

15 'Gender and Dialect Bias in YouTube's Automatic Captions' by Rachael Tatman, 2017, www.ethicsinnlp.org/workshop/pdf/EthNLP06.pdf.

16 'Artificial Intelligence and the Future of Work' by Paul Griffin, www.nortonrosefulbright.com/en-gb/knowledge/publications/a9f9f769/artificial-intelligence-and-the-future-of-work.

17 'The Legal and Ethical Implications of Using AI in Hiring'.

employees who find themselves subjected to unfair treatment. The irresistible rise of AI applied to the day-to-day performance of a job, however, has yet to be tested in employment law terms, but the recent move to remote working at scale due to the Covid-19 pandemic will certainly lead to further developments in this field. The current practice of most HR departments is generally to use a standard employment contract template across all roles (less so at director level) and vary the commercial terms that are offered to an individual – pay, hours worked, location. Perhaps the contract is tailored to reflect the nature of the organisation employing the worker, but overall it uses boilerplate clauses alongside commercially specific ones agreed at the start and later amended during employment. Therefore, it could be tempting for an organisation to seek to reduce costs further by automating such templates: standard contracts automation is one of the fastest areas of automation in the legal sector, with an increasing number of enterprise-level organisations rolling out automation processes. According to a 2019 Gartner CIO Survey of '3,000 CIOs in 89 countries across major industries, representing $15 trillion in revenue and public-sector budgets and $284 billion in IT spending, 37% of CIOs reported they introduced the use of AI in the previous year, a 270% increase in 4 years.'[18]

> The next competitive frontier for businesses is employee experience and the future of HR will be centred on the employee experience and personalising engagement. In a time when employees have smart assistants at home and recommendation engines for when they shop, they expect a personalized experience when they come to work.[19]

Employment law is yet to grapple with the question of what 'personalising' an employee's engagement and experience will look like legally speaking, especially if the career path picked for individuals results in them progressing less quickly, due to biases in the types of work allocated, for example. Historically, many women and minorities have been denied jobs as lawyers because 'black girls from Balham don't become judges' or 'law is not a job for women'.[20] Can an AI-powered job-builder be 'fair' and free of bias so that any progression and reward is truly on performance and merit? How can employment law create the necessary framework for organisations to avoid discriminatory outcomes if they buy in the AI technology from an external provider?

There is some perception within organisations that 'with software choreographing the work, **13.019** every minute should be busy',[21] in order to increase human resource efficiency but also align it to a company's business needs. This can result in unfair pressure to be present at work 24/7 and unfair allocation of work, for example, which can lead to long-term consequences such as withholding future promotions or even termination for non-performance. Often AI tools are bought in by businesses without a clear understanding of the underlying data powering them and of how the algorithmic decisions are reached; perhaps they are not being sufficiently screened by the users for the potential risk of falling foul of employment rules which they pose, and the unfair treatment and discriminatory practices that might arise from their use. To avoid claims, employers should be aware of the potential for discrimination before they introduce AI into their employee management systems.

---

18   www.gartner.com/en/newsroom/press-releases/2019-01-21-gartner-survey-shows-37-percent-of-organizations-have.
19   The HR Technologist, 5 February 2019; Forbes, 5 January 2017.
20   'First 100 Years', various biographical interviews, www.first100years.org.uk.
21   'Weapons of Math Destruction: How Big Data Increases Inequality and Threatens Democracy' by Cathy O'Neil, Penguin Random House 2016.

13.020 An area in which AI is increasingly used during an employment contact is employee engagement, where AI helps an employer determine whether an employee is at risk of attrition. Employee turnover and replacement costs can be as high as 33 per cent of an employee's salary and can cause a lot of disruption in a business, so proactive engagement and retention is critical to business success.[22] Employee engagement is a great challenge for most businesses: research by *Gallup Management Journal* finds that 29 per cent of employees are actively engaged, 54 per cent are not engaged and 17 per cent are disengaged.[23] The way in which AI is typically used to stimulate engagement is through 'computer systems with advanced AI that can engage, in real-time, in sensing, reasoning, and responding in the most complex and dynamic environments'. The AI tools are often also built to identify attrition risks and then make recommendations to avoid such outcomes. 'AI management systems seek to promote worker engagement by directing, monitoring, and rewarding and/or punishing employees' actions' and their ability to persuade employees that they are "fair"'[24] is critical to their success. This criticality increases as often they can use predictive analytics to look 'at specific gender or ethnic populations to determine who is likely to resign, and HR can use that information to create initiatives to improve the work experience of those populations more likely to leave'.[25]

13.021 Also linked to engagement is the use of AI to personalise content for employees to offer a more personalised employee experience. This is typically achieved by using predictive analytics to shape an employee's career path – from recommending professional development programmes to offering career path advice to using optimisation of a career site based on an applicant's actions. This type of use is likely to rise significantly due to the recent global economic downturn. First, employees will increasingly ask for more tailored employee experiences that include varying working hours, flexibility to work from home and different working patterns such as reduced hours; as organisations want to both retain top talent and attract new talent, they will introduce AI tools as a trade-off, exercising management controls in exchange for more 'freedom' to work where and when the employee wants.

13.022 In its '2020 Global Human Capital Trends',[26] global accounting firm Deloitte revealed a huge gap between the cited importance of an employee's experience in an organisation (with 80 per cent of executives rating it as important) and the stated quality of experience received by the employees (with 22 per cent of the executives believe their organisation excelled at providing a differentiated employee experience). Digital learning experiences often involve personalised learning recommendations related to type of job, seniority and level of skill, as well as

---

22 'The Cost of Turnover Can Kill Your Business and Make Things Less Fun' by John Hall, Forbes, 9 May 2019, www .forbes.com/sites/johnhall/2019/05/09/the-cost-of-turnover-can-kill-your-business-and-make-things-less-fun.

23 State of the Global Workplace 2017, www.gallup.com/workplace/231668/dismal-employee-engagement-sign-global -mismanagement.aspx.

24 'Artificial Intelligence, Employee Engagement, Fairness, and Job Outcomes, Managing Technology and Middle- and Low-skilled Employees (The Changing Context of Managing People)' by C. Hughes, L. Robert, K. Frady and A. Arroyos, Emerald Publishing Limited 2019, pp. 61–8.

25 'Big Data for HR: Can Predictive Analytics Help Decrease Discrimination in the Workplace?' by Anne Loehr, Huffington Post, 23 March 2015, www.huffpost.com/entry/big-data-for-hr-can-predi_b_6905754?guccounter=1&guce_referrer =aHR0cHM6Ly9d3cudHdvYmlyZHMuY29tLw&guce_referrer_sig=AQAAAIPIo4ZpG50peqBmDgy5exb1wi pDlQmvsRI8Y96WR7qz5RF4UMPMSV5QITA5OHcdXq-ATouzsjyeeOgheO9rYZds0OTCV2WVDsrM 1xZ6UE2JYvKnf4cGOnisw8ny3cYmYtQafVQHzRLEfFyEvSBBuq_a0WiDh2m1xPTm5oR0YcMT.

26 www2.deloitte.com/us/en/insights/focus/human-capital-trends.html.

professional interests. Based on such indicators, recommendation engines can provide personalised learning and development but, again, 'fairness' needs to remain an important factor in how HR teams work with the individual employees to ensure that protected characteristics or personal preferences do not end up creating a disadvantageous career path based on protected characteristics being applied, or shorten progress.

Technology is moving at a fast pace and this has become even more rapid recently, due to lockdowns across the world requiring employees to work from home. This has led some employers to adopt new technologies without always understanding their full capabilities. A BBC report in 2019 covered a business that rolled out what they believed to be time-tracking time management software and later discovered that the software tracked all browser activity. Furthermore, it took pictures of the employees at regular intervals to ensure they were at their desks. Some businesses make the decision to monitor staff productivity openly[27] but, if this is the case, they must ensure that they understand what data is collected, that employees are informed of such software being used and that its use is reasonable and proportional. An employer is not required to obtain an employee's consent for the surveillance but they must notify them of a camera's existence and the purpose of the monitoring. The employee can challenge them on the basis that any processing of their data is 'proportionate' in scope.   **13.023**

Some of the data collected by employers can leave employees feeling exposed, put upon and mistrusted, and this can lead to feelings of unfairness. Furthermore, employees can be made uncomfortable by the use of technologies that can report real-time behaviours such as how often a worker leaves their desk or where they go. Furthermore, the technology is now so developed that it is even capable of tracking an employee's facial expressions. Another area where legal questions arise is where an organisation continues to monitor an employee outside the workplace – for example, in their use of social media. Separately, can an employer justify monitoring and recording calls taken or made outside working hours on a company phone? This area has become even more unclear and uncertain with the use of private homes as offices and the use of private equipment for delivering work. Justifying monitoring in these new set-ups may be more difficult and it is very much uncharted territory.   **13.024**

Employment contracts have tended to be static documents, with annual appraisals assessing performance on a job. Staff handbooks and even job descriptions tend to sit outside an employment contract to protect an employer's position. The static and, to some degree, aspirational nature of the employment contract documentation is in stark contrast to the ever-changing nature of any AI technology – constantly evolving by incorporating data farmed by algorithms. It is difficult to imagine a world of personalised employee experience without a more dynamic employment contract but this poses more risks to all the parties, as it brings in uncertainty and less definition. However, it is entirely unavoidable that law and regulations will need to face the challenges arising head-on.   **13.025**

---

27   www.bbc.com/news/business-54289152.

D. POST-EMPLOYMENT

13.026 Every employee should enjoy 'an equal chance to have their employment terminated equally and fairly'. This is the overarching spirit of the equality legislation, but very often – and especially in a time of economic depression – employers can be tempted to save costs by not following the correct termination processes, even without AI being involved. A termination may be on bona fide grounds such as a wish to reduce a business' human headcount, or at the very least to change job functions, perhaps in favour of automation. Much as in the case of recruitment, it is possible for groups or individuals to be selected for redundancy during a reorganisation because of an algorithm deciding that their job is no longer required, for example.

13.027 However, with reams of data collected and available on each employee, can an employer rely on some of this information to select those placed at risk of redundancy? A recent misconduct case in which an employer tried to rely on recorded information tracking an employee's private car led to the data not being accepted as evidence because the vehicle had been tracked outside working hours. However, the same case ruled that, more generally, the employer was justified in tracking an employee's private car.

13.028 Any employer considering terminating an employment contract must consider whether any dismissal is 'fair'. The starting point is establishing whether there is a fair reason for the termination, such as a reduced need for work of the kind that the employee does, which can amount to a redundancy situation arising. If the organisation is undergoing a restructuring, would it constitute 'some other substantial reason' to justify termination? Automating this decision process using AI against a set of 'redundancy' criteria can be a high-risk approach as the technology used needs to be capable to stand up to scrutiny in court as 'objective', should tribunal proceedings be initiated by an employee.

13.029 Any termination process followed must be 'fair' and include informing the employee of the risk to their continued employment, a consultation process, reaching a decision and allowing for an appeal process against that decision if the employee is not happy with it. Again, while some of the process stages and guidance for the parties involved could benefit from a structured, AI-enabled process to ensure transparency and objectivity, most of the steps involved will require human interactions, especially in relation to the consultation and appeal stages.

13.030 A worker also has a right to references on termination of employment. An employer is required, if agreed in the employment contract, to provide what she believes to be a fair and accurate reflection of performance. In response to case law[28] attempting to clarify the law in relation to employment references and what constitutes a 'bad' reference, more companies are choosing to give brief standard references to include details such as job title, salary and when the worker was employed, without commenting on performance. This area is ripe for the adoption of technology. But employers need to always have at hand the underlying documentation to provide an accurate reference in an objective manner, and therefore any technology use needs to be able to assess and accurately state the information used in the reference.

---

28   *Spring v Guardian Assurance plc* concerned the provision of an unfavourable reference by an employer which prevented the ex-employee from obtaining a new job.

Unfair termination of employment is by far the highest risk to a business in terms of legal risk. An unfair reason and/or process for dismissal can give an employee with more than two years' service a right to claim unfair dismissal in an employment tribunal, which could lead to compensation being awarded to them. Furthermore, for any employee with protected characteristics the two-year requirement does not apply and they can issue proceedings for discrimination.   **13.031**

E. CONCLUSION

Ginni Rometty, Executive Chair of IBM, states: 'Some people call this artificial intelligence, but the reality is this technology will enhance us. So instead of artificial intelligence, I think we'll augment our intelligence.'   **13.032**

It is only right that as we conclude we quote an executive of IBM, among the first organisations to commercialise the use of AI[29] and to have introduced some AI applications to legal documentation[30] at the start of the legal technology innovation curve. Of course, as a developer of the technology, IBM would have painted an optimistic view of how AI will impact various sectors – especially in terms of helping professionals do less of the repetitive, uninteresting work, freeing them to focus on added-value tasks. While introducing AI technology is sold as a method to 'augment' the work produced by teams or to improve productivity, employers should not lose sight of the need for a rational and sensitive strategy for the introduction of AI, understanding how the new technologies work and how employment law is developing to respond to changes in this area.   **13.033**

Lawmakers have thus far been reactive[31] in their approach to the rise of this AI technology – the switch to more remote working and more widespread adoption of technology in 2020 also caught them unawares, unsurprisingly given the scale at which this shift has happened globally. The debate among regulatory bodies as to the changes that might be needed in response to AI adoption has been overtaken by events and to date it is the existing employment and data protection legislation that employers should be aware of and rely on when using AI in human resources processes. They need to remain aware of the potential for discrimination before they introduce AI into their processes. Under the Equality Act 2010, discrimination, whether by a human or AI, is unlawful. Indirect discrimination – for example, penalising a candidate for taking career breaks – is also caught by the Act, and so an employer who decides to introduce AI will need to regularly interrogate their HR processes to avoid the development of discriminatory practices during its use. Alongside employment legislation, the General Data Protection Regulation (EU) 2016/679 (GDPR) applies to the use of AI in recruitment and employment in the UK and the EU if it involves the processing of personal data, such as name, date of birth, address and previous experience.   **13.034**

---

29   In February 2013, IBM announced that Watson software had started its first commercial application to reach decisions in lung cancer treatment: www.forbes.com/sites/bruceupbin/2013/02/08/ibms-watson-gets-its-first-piece-of-business-in-healthcare/#46a514dc5402.

30   www.ibm.com/blogs/client-voices/save-the-lawyer-ai-technology-accelerates-and-augments-legal-work/.

31   Canada has required federal institutions to conduct an 'algorithmic impact assessment' when using AI. This process asks detailed questions about information being put into an algorithm and about procedural fairness.

13.035 Workplace use of AI takes many shapes and can impact the employment relationship at all stages, from application for a role to redundancy or, indeed, a dispute in the employment courts. Take recruitment: assessing high numbers of job candidates by applying a set of criteria to filter out unsuitable candidates has been perhaps one of the widest uses of AI, and one that is often cited as a positive use of technology to narrow the opportunity gap and access the widest possible talent pool. While this sounds like a positively anti-discriminatory use of AI, it has been shown that without further nuance and investigation of the scientific methods used to set the assessment criteria, for example, the use of algorithms can lead to results opposite to those intended at the design stage – discriminating on grounds of race and gender and almost setting up a 'postcode' lottery with regard to whether a candidate is selected. 'Algorithms are now being used in interviews, for example to assess candidates on their facial and vocal expressions. Chatbots are replacing people in conducting interviews and textbots are communicating with candidates by SMS or email. The use of algorithms and AI is moving higher up the recruitment funnel to selection decisions and to other HR decisions such as redundancies, performance dismissals, promotions and reward.'[32] Employment law needs to begin to catch up with the technology if it is to provide the protection that both employers and employees need in the workplace.

---

32   'Algorithms and employment law: what do you need to know?' by James Davies, 31 August 2020, www.lexology.com/.

14

DISPUTES AND LITIGATION

Kushal Gandhi and Vanessa Whitman

A. INTRODUCTION

Disputes are an inevitable part of the lifecycle of an organisation, a relationship or any new **14.001** technology. AI is no different in that respect. In most cases AI is used to solve problems or deploy new solutions. In the context of disputes, although AI can be used to resolve issues, it can also sometimes be the cause of the problem or be at the epicentre of the issue between parties. For the purposes of this chapter, the relationship between AI and disputes is categorised into:

(a) disputes involving use of AI for resolution; and
(b) disputes relating to or arising from the AI.

As the commercialisation of AI increases, it is likely that disputes relating to or arising from the **14.002** AI will increase. In other chapters in this book, related topics such as IP protections, agency and liability and data issues have been explored. In this chapter we consider:

(a) the Day 1 considerations when disputes relating to AI start emerging; and
(b) the potential remedies to consider in the interests of protecting and maximising a party's position.

14.003   Before we delve into the above issues, we start by considering the use of AI in resolving disputes.

B. AI IN RESOLVING DISPUTES

14.004   Dispute resolution differs in form and process based upon the jurisdiction in which the parties are based and the forum in which the dispute is being resolved. However, an issue that commonly arises across jurisdictions for resolution of disputes is the collation and review of evidence to support each party's position. In addition, disputes can vary in terms of size, complexity and quantum involved. Nevertheless, another common theme for resolution of disputes is the need for an efficient and robust process that can instil in the parties confidence that they are being treated fairly.

14.005   AI is already being used in the collation and review of evidence for the purposes of disclosure exercises in jurisdictions such as England and the US. Technology-assisted review that is based on deploying tools that can learn relevance of documents to the issues in dispute from the humans who manually code the documents is now relatively well advanced and has been reported in scientific literature as achieving good results.[1] These methods are also being adopted in mainstream litigation and arbitration. This is supported by the fact that in the pilot scheme for disclosure in the Business and Property Courts of England, the parties to litigation to which the pilot scheme applies must complete a 'Disclosure Review Document'.[2] The template Disclosure Review Document in Annex 2 of Practice Direction 51U includes the following points that the parties must address:

1.   Use of Analytics

14.006   *Parties are to consider the use of technology to facilitate the efficient collection of data and its further use for data review. This may include the use of some of the more sophisticated forms of technology / computer assisted review software (TAR/CAR/analytics). If the parties are in a position to propose the use of any technology or computer assisted review tools in advance of the CMC, those proposals should be set out in this section Where parties have considered the use of such tools but decided against this at this stage (particularly where the review universe is in excess of 50,000 documents), they should explain why such tools will not be used, particularly where this may mean that large volumes of data will have to be the subject of a manual review" exercise. Parties should update this form and draw any material updates to the attention of all parties and the Court if they later determine it would be appropriate to use such tools.*

14.007   We live in times where data is generated in large quantities and even small disputes can have a disproportionate amount of data attached to them. This adds to the time and cost of resolving disputes. To address this issue, AI tools are also being used for identifying patterns, concepts and clusters of relevant data from a large pool. When deployed effectively this can lead to quick results and significant time and cost savings. These AI tools can also be used to process and

---

1   Gordon V. Cormack and Maura R. Grossman, Evaluation of Machine Learning Protocols for Technology-Assisted Review in Electronic Discovery (2014).
2   Paragraph 10 of Practice Direction 51U.

analyse large pools of data to identify new lines of inquiry that may not be visible to the naked human eye, for example when seeking to trace perpetrators of large and complex fraud.

It is inevitable that the use of AI in resolving disputes is going to increase.   **14.008**

The growth of emerging technologies has also led to innovative approaches to the dispute **14.009** resolution mechanism. The use of blockchain for dispute resolution is one of those areas. The self-executing nature of smart contracts, whereby terms are inbuilt into the code, is such that disputes should be rare. However, disputes cannot be discounted and coding errors and hacks, for example, can lead to unintended consequences. Earlier in 2021, the UK Jurisdiction Taskforce (UKJT) published the UK's first Digital Dispute Resolution Rules (DDRR). The DDRR give legal effect to automatic dispute resolution processes built into digital asset systems. They also create a streamlined arbitral process for resolving disputes arising out of new digital technologies.

The aim of the DDRR is to ensure the rapid, cost-effective resolution of disputes arising out **14.010** of new digital technologies (such as cryptoassets, cryptocurrencies, smart contracts, distributed ledger technologies and fintech applications). They create a dispute resolution process which is intended to be flexible enough to resolve both 'traditional' disputes relating to conventional written contracts and 'novel' disputes relating to the use of digital assets (including where the parties are unknown to one another and have transacted anonymously on a blockchain).

The DDRR can be incorporated into any relevant contract, digital asset or digital asset system **14.011** using, at a minimum, the following text: 'Any dispute shall be resolved in accordance with the UKJT Digital Dispute Resolution Rules' (the incorporation text). This text can be in electronic or encoded form.

The DDRR create the following dispute resolution mechanism: **14.012**

(a) *Automatic dispute resolution* – The result of any automatic dispute resolution process built into a digital asset system will bind the parties.

(b) *Arbitration or expert determination* – Absent an automatic dispute resolution process, disputes will be submitted to arbitration (save that any expert issue will be determined by an appointed expert). These arbitrations will be governed by English and Welsh law and the judicial seat will be in England and Wales.

(c) *Starting proceedings* – A claimant will start proceedings by giving a notice of claim to the respondent(s) and the Society for Computers and Law (the SCL). This notice will, inter alia, provide electronic contact details for the parties, details of the claim and remedy sought and proposals for paying or securing the fees of the SCL and the tribunal (see below). It may also include supporting documents and proposals about how the dispute should be managed.

(d) *Responding to proceedings* – A respondent will have three days to send the claimant and the SCL an initial response to a notice of claim. The initial response will confirm the respondent's identity and electronic contact details. It may also include a response to the claim, supporting documents and comments on the claimant's proposals for managing the dispute and for paying or securing the necessary fees.

(e) *Appointment of arbitrators or experts* – The SCL will appoint a tribunal of arbitrators and any experts once it has received the initial response(s). The SCL will have regard to whether the incorporation text was modified to specify any preferences as to the number, identities or qualifications of the arbitrators or experts to be appointed; it will also consider whether the parties have expressed any preferences. However, the SCL will not ultimately be bound by what has been specified or is preferred. The SCL and the tribunal will not be obliged to act until reasonable arrangements have been made to pay or secure their fees. We are making enquiries with the SCL to find out details of the relevant fees.

(f) *Procedure* – The tribunal will have absolute discretion as to what procedure is adopted, although it may have regard to any preferences specified in the incorporation text or by the parties. This includes absolute discretion as to what evidence and arguments it receives, which it is likely to request in electronic form. No party will have the right to an oral hearing.

(g) *Anonymity* – The tribunal will not disclose the names of the claimant and respondent(s) if the incorporation text specifies that the parties will remain anonymous, or if the parties have agreed that they will. This is unless disclosure is necessary for the fair resolution of the dispute, for the enforcement of any order or award or for the protection of the tribunal's own interest, or if required by any law, regulation or court order.

(h) *Powers regarding digital assets* – The tribunal will have the power to operate, modify, sign or cancel any digital assets relevant to a dispute using any digital signature, cryptographic key, password or other control mechanism available to it, or to direct any party to do so.

(i) *Outcome* – The tribunal will use its best endeavours to determine the dispute within any time period specified or agreed by the parties or, if no period has been specified, within 30 days. Its decision will be in writing and will be final: there will no right of appeal save in limited circumstances set out in the Arbitration Act 1996.

(j) *Consolidation* – Tribunals appointed in different arbitrations under the DDRR can agree to consolidate those arbitrations and deal with them by way of a consolidated tribunal.

C. DISPUTES RELATING TO AI

14.013 As AI becomes more mainstream and is adopted in different sectors and businesses, it is inevitable that disputes relating to or arising from the AI are going to start to emerge. The nature of those disputes will vary based on the business, sector and parties involved. Few examples of concerns around disputes and claims relating to AI that have started to emerge relate to things like liability for driverless cars and patent applications for inventions produced by AI.[3]

14.014 As will be seen from the chapter on agency and liability and elsewhere, issues are also likely to emerge about who is liable for claims arising following the deployment of AI: for example, is it the developer or the person who deploys it?

14.015 The process and outcomes of disputes relating to AI will be influenced by various factors including the parties involved, where they are based and the appropriate forum for any claims. In this section we set out the issues that parties should consider when problems start to emerge, to assist in the effective resolution of AI disputes.

---

3   See *Thaler v Comptroller-General of Patents, Designs & Trademarks* [2020] EWHC 2412 in relation to the patent applications for inventions produced by AI.

D. DAY 1 CONSIDERATIONS

1.   Root Cause Analysis, Investigations and Privilege

A problem identified is a problem solved. As soon as an issue is identified that is causing   **14.016**
a problem and the root cause analysis is complete, careful consideration should be given to
whether the AI part of the solution can and should be stopped temporarily so that the problem
does not multiply and get out of control. This is important to consider because liability regimes
can vary on whether a party knowingly allowed for something to continue to operate causing
damage to another person, or whether the damage was caused unknowingly.

If it is not practical to stop the AI's operation, careful consideration should be given to how   **14.017**
damage can be mitigated by, for example, putting in place workarounds. At the same time,
consideration should be given to the benefits that will be lost if the AI is stopped in full. When
undertaking a risk/benefit analysis it can be important to identify benefits beyond those that are
purely financial gains for a party.

It is possible that when an AI-related dispute arises, the tendency for those involved will be to   **14.018**
seek to investigate the issue in an effort to isolate the problem. While this will be important,
any investigation and remedial steps should be scoped and structured keeping in mind the
potential exposure for claims. Part of this should be considerations, from an early stage, of how
any investigation and documents created can be protected from disclosure at a later stage. In
some jurisdictions it may be possible to do this by invoking legal professional privilege.

Legal professional privilege under English law is an area that has been written about extensively   **14.019**
and which forms the sole subject matter of various published texts. As such we do not propose
to delve into the detail of it in this chapter, save to say that the value and complexities of legal
professional privilege should not be underestimated. In order to benefit from legal professional
privilege careful consideration will have to be given to any investigations and documentary
records created from an early stage.

For businesses that operate in regulated sectors consideration will also have to be given to the   **14.020**
regulatory obligations and expectations when problems relating to the AI start to emerge. This
can include expectations such as reporting the issue to the relevant regulator and/or making
a public announcement. Again, it will be important that this forms part of the early considerations when problems start to emerge.

2.   Parties to the Dispute

In order for there to be a claim, one needs to identify the relevant parties to it. Although this   **14.021**
may seem simple, it can be a complex question and it arises particularly in the context of AI
disputes. There are various factors to consider when identifying the parties to a dispute:

(a)   In most cases it should be simple to identify the 'claimant' party – this is likely to be the
      harmed/aggrieved party. However, it becomes complex when the aggrieved party is part
      of a chain. This is because the aggrieved party may in turn have others who were affected
      by the problem/non-performance of the aggrieved party. As such, the aggrieved party

255

ought to consider its chain of rights and obligations and the impact on its own position before becoming a 'claimant'. In some cases it may be possible for aggrieved parties in a chain to join up and become a 'claimant-group'. This has the potential to avoid collateral claims.

(b)   The more complex issue is likely to arise when seeking to identify the 'defendant' party. Identifying a defendant requires consideration of where the legal responsibility for the problem rests but also whether the 'claimant' party has a route to bring a claim against that 'defendant' party. For example, is there a contract between the parties that establishes a cause of action or will the cause of action be under tort? Depending on the legal route, the 'defendant' party may be a different entity.

(c)   Another important consideration when identifying the 'defendant' party is whether it has the requisite funds to pay any successful order that may be obtained against it. In the context of AI disputes this can be a real challenge. In some cases the AI that caused the problem may have been developed by a start-up and there may be little to be gained in suing them – the party with the bigger resources may be the one that deployed the AI.

14.022   At times there may be limits on the liability of a party. This can be because, for example, the contract includes an enforceable cap on liability. Any such limits on liability ought to form part of the considerations when establishing the relevant parties to the AI-related dispute.

14.023   Early consideration should also be given to any insurance protection that may be available for the type of claim and resulting liability. This will be important not just because insurers are likely to have the resources to pay out for a claim but also because insurance policies often include strict requirements for notification of claims. Failure to comply with notification requirements can result in claims not being covered by the insurer.

3.   Governing Law and Jurisdiction

14.024   One of the first questions a disputes lawyer is likely to ask is what the governing law and jurisdiction are for the dispute that has arisen. Determining governing law and jurisdiction can be difficult, particularly where the parties are based in different locations and the AI in question is part of a wider solution or has resulted in damage in different locations. Nevertheless, there are various rules and regulations that exist that can assist in determining the governing law and jurisdiction. These rules and regulations vary based on each jurisdiction and it is beyond the scope of this chapter to explore the different regimes. However, establishing the governing law that applies to the dispute will help in determining the causes of action that may be available. In addition, determining the jurisdiction for the resolution of the dispute will assist in determining the legal procedural tools and remedies that are available to the parties. This will also help in feeding into the overall strategy for the resolution of the AI dispute.

14.025   Finally, the governing law and jurisdiction of an AI dispute may not be the same. It is possible that the governing law may be English while the appropriate jurisdiction for the dispute is New York.

4. Limitation Period

In most jurisdictions there is a prescribed time limit on the ability of a party to bring a claim. **14.026** The time limit can vary depending on the type of claim. For example, the time limit for a breach of contract claim can be different to that related to a claim for negligence in tort. It may also be the case that for certain contractual claims there is a prescribed time limit in the contract itself. As such, when an AI-related dispute arises it will be important to identify the types of claim and causes of action that can be pursued. Taking steps to stop the limitation period from expiring will be important.

5. Pre-action Conduct

Once the parties to the dispute, the governing law and the jurisdiction are identified, consid- **14.027** eration should be given to the parties' actions prior to commencing formal proceedings. In some jurisdictions there may be rules about what a party needs to do prior to commencing proceedings; failure to comply can result in cost consequences. For example, the English Civil Procedure Rules include a Practice Direction on pre-action conduct and protocols: 'Pre-action protocols explain the conduct and set out the steps the court would normally expect parties to take before commencing proceedings for particular types of civil claim.'[4]

The pre-action protocols currently in force in England are based on the type of claim. There are **14.028** specific pre-action protocols for certain types of claim and if a specific protocol is not applicable then the expectation is that the parties will follow the general Practice Direction on pre-action conduct. The specific protocols currently in force are shown in Table 14.1.

Table 14.1   *Pre-action protocols currently in force in England*

Protocol
Personal Injury
Resolution of Clinical Disputes
Construction and Engineering
Defamation
Professional Negligence
Judicial Review
Disease and Illness
Housing Disrepair
Possession Claims by Social Landlords
Possession Claims for Mortgage Arrears
Dilapidation of Commercial Property
Low Value Personal Injury Road Traffic Accident Claims
Low Value Personal Injury Employers' and Public Liability Claims

Although there is no specific protocol for AI disputes, it is possible that one of the above-listed **14.029** protocols could apply. This is because it may be that the dispute arising from the use of the

---

4   Paragraph 1 of the Practice Direction on pre-action conduct and protocols.

AI is, in fact, a professional negligence dispute between a client and its professional advisors who used AI in the delivery of their services. It is equally possible that the AI that caused the problem was deployed in a construction project and in that scenario the construction and engineering protocol may be applicable.

14.030   For businesses that operate in regulated sectors, there may be other rules they need to comply with when an AI dispute arises. An example is when an AI-related issue affects a consumer. As such, careful consideration should be given to the nature of the dispute and the manner in which it is dealt with from the start, including whether a report to the relevant regulator is required.

6.   Preserving Documentary and Data Evidence

14.031   It is likely that in most AI-related disputes one of the key components will be a forensic analysis of some sort of the relevant AI solution, related data and documentary evidence.

14.032   When an AI-related dispute arises, it will be important to ensure that all documentary and data records that could be relevant to the issues in dispute are preserved. Any automatic document and/or data destruction policies should be considered carefully, and relevant holds put in place. This can be particularly important in the context of an AI-related dispute because, depending on the nature of the AI solution, it may be that AI is continuously seeking to 'improve' itself, re-writing over old code, and algorithms may be constantly changing. As such, when seeking to trace steps back to when the problem arose, parties may find that the relevant forensic data evidence is lost. This can be problematic not just for the claimant but also for defendants. This is because, depending on the jurisdiction for the dispute, adverse inferences may be drawn against the defendant for not ensuring the data was preserved adequately. In addition, without the accurate forensic data it may not be possible to validate particular lines of defence.

14.033   Depending on the jurisdiction, it may also be possible to make use of legal tools to ensure preservation and extraction of data. In the sections below we set out some of these legal tools available under English law that can assist in the context of AI-related disputes.

E. LEGAL TOOLS UNDER ENGLISH LAW

14.034   There are a number of legal tools available to the claimant in an AI related dispute, but among the most useful are search and seizure orders (SSOs) (and related imaging, disclosure and inspection orders) and freezing orders, which we will focus on in this section.

14.035   A search and seizure order is not a final remedy to a claim, but it may enable the claimant to obtain the 'smoking gun' which will secure its success in a claim against the defendant and to protect that information from being destroyed by the defendant or its systems –either innocently, by way of an ongoing programme of document or data destruction, or intentionally, by a guilty party seeking to cover its tracks.

Similarly, a freezing order may protect assets which are at risk of dissipation, against which the **14.036** claimant may seek to enforce any later damages award, or to protect other assets which may otherwise be lost, put beyond the reach of the claimant or destroyed.

1.   Procedure in a Nutshell

We set out below some more detailed notes on the key requirements for these remedies, but the **14.037** basic steps in the lifecycle of an application for a freezing order or SSO are:

(a)   *Pre-application planning and evidence gathering* – This will involve close communication between the applicant and its legal team. At this stage the application, evidence and draft order (and usually claim form if the application is made before proceedings are afoot) will be prepared. This is usually a short and intensive period of work on the basis that delay can be fatal to such applications (see below).

(b)   *Filing the application and accompanying evidence at court* – In cases of extreme urgency, an application may be heard before filing, but this is unusual.

(c)   *Hearing of the application* – this will usually take place without notice to the respondent and in private (unlike most Court hearings, which are public). Given the nature of the application, they are usually listed by the Court very quickly. In cases of extreme urgency, applications can be made by telephone and outside of usual court hours.

(d)   If the order is granted:
(i)   In the case of a freezing order, the order should be served on the respondent and relevant third parties (such as banks or other custodians of relevant assets);
(ii)   In the case of an SSO, careful plans should be made for the service of the order on the respondent and the physical carrying out of the search.

(e)   *Supervising Solicitor* – In the case of an SSO, it is a requirement that the search is carried out under the supervision of an independent Supervising Solicitor. It will be important to pay close attention to the various and strict rules of such searches.

(f)   *Between the search and the return hearing* – Preparation of respondent evidence in response to the application. Documents and data seized under an SSO will be copied and returned to the respondent (usually within two days).

(g)   *The return hearing* – usually about one week after the initial hearing, a return date will be listed and the hearing will ideally be before the same judge who granted the order. This time all parties attend, and the evidence of the respondent will be heard as well as the report of the Supervising Solicitor in the case of an SSO. The judge will decide if any part of the order should continue and will hear any challenge to the order made by the respondent.

The remainder of this section deals with some of the more important requirements for appli- **14.038** cations that applicants should consider, but we do not set out a detailed examination of each of the steps above.

2.   Key Requirements for Obtaining SSOs and Freezing Orders

Remedies such as SSOs and freezing orders are draconian in their nature and are therefore **14.039** carefully controlled by the Court. A claimant cannot simply obtain such an order on the basis of suspicion or distrust alone. And since these types of orders are usually applied for without notice to the respondents, the Court expects a high degree of 'full and frank' evidence to support the application, and will put in place safeguards to protect the interests of the recipient party (usually the intended defendant in a claim which the applicant intends to file imminently, although it is possible for such orders to be sought at any stage of proceedings).

14.040   In order to convince the Court to grant an SSO or freezing order, the applicant must show:

(a)   a very strong case on its merits. In the case of a freezing order the test is a 'good arguable case'[5] and in the case of search orders it is 'an extremely strong prima facie case'[6];

(b)   in the case of SSOs, that serious damage will be caused or will likely be caused to the applicant if the order is not granted;

(c)   the respondent has assets (in the case of a freezing order) or relevant documents/data (in the case of an SSO) in the jurisdiction and there is a real possibility that those assets or documents or data will be dissipated, destroyed or put outside of the applicant's reach if the order is not made and/or if the respondent is put on notice of the application;

(d)   the harm likely to be done to the respondent by the order is not excessive or disproportionate to the interests of the applicant.

3.   Timing of the Application

14.041   These sorts of applications should usually be made without delay. Often delay will cause the Court to refuse the application. That is because the application is made on the basis that there is a serious risk of dissipation of assets or destruction of documents, so there is a clear need to act quickly. Where an applicant delays, the Court may take the view that it cannot justify such draconian measures where the applicant has not done everything it can to secure those assets, data or documents urgently.

4.   Supporting Evidence

14.042   In order to demonstrate the above, the applicant must also file an affidavit which sets out all of the relevant facts. Since the respondent will not usually be represented at the initial application hearing, the applicant has a duty of full and frank disclosure, which requires a balanced and full account of all the facts, including those which might not sit comfortably with the applicant's purposes. It is often difficult for an applicant to accept that it must also set out reasons why the order it is applying for should *not* be granted, but it is extremely important to avoid misleading the Court (including by omitting relevant facts) in order to protect against a costs award (and potentially also damages) being made against the applicant at a later date.

14.043   The affidavit is a sworn or affirmed statement which must be administered by an appropriately qualified person, usually a solicitor or commissioner for oaths. Knowingly including false or misleading information in an affidavit amounts to the criminal offence of perjury, which is punishable in the most extreme cases by up to seven years' imprisonment and/or an unlimited fine, so it is wise to pay careful attention to the matters set out in the affidavit and avoid any inaccuracies or errors!

---

5   *The Niedersachsen* [1983] 1 WLR 1412.

6   *Anton Piller KG v Manufacturing Processes Ltd* [1976] Ch 55.

Applicants should not be surprised if they find that their own solicitors exhibit a degree of para- **14.044**
noia over the accuracy of information given to the Court in respect of the application. Solicitors
(who are officers of the court) owe a duty to present all aspects of the application fairly – if they
fail to do so, they risk any order being discharged.

5.   Undertakings to Court

An applicant will also usually be required to give certain undertakings (promises) to the Court, **14.045**
again in order to protect the interests of the unrepresented respondent:

(a)   Where the application is made before a claim has begun, the applicant must usually give
an undertaking that it will issue proceedings and pay the relevant court fee as soon as
practicable (usually committing to do so the same or next day). Alternatively, the Court
may give directions as to the issuing of the claim. This undertaking is required because
these sorts of orders are not standalone remedies – they cannot be granted without being
related to a claim.

(b)   Where the application is made before filing the application notice, an undertaking is
given to file it and pay the appropriate fee on the same or next working day.

(c)   Where the application is made without notice, the applicant must undertake to serve
on the respondent the application notice, evidence in support and any order the Court
makes as soon as practicable.

(d)   The undertaking which applicants tend to pay closest attention to (and which warrants
its own section below) is known as a 'cross-undertaking in damages'. This undertaking
commits the applicant to paying damages to the respondent if it turns out that the order
should not have been made in the first place (for example because of a failure to give full
and frank disclosure). The cross-undertaking is often thought of as the price an applicant
pays for an order of this nature.

6.   Undertaking in Damages

Where applications are made for orders of this nature, the cross-undertaking in damages will **14.046**
almost always be expressly required, but if for any reason the undertaking is not expressly given,
it will be implied. Unless the dispute falls into a very narrow category (which AI disputes are
unlikely to satisfy), applicants should not be under the illusion that such an undertaking can be
avoided. The Court sometimes requires the applicant to give security to support this damages
undertaking, and careful consideration should be given to the quantum of damages that might
be caused to a respondent in an AI dispute if the freezing or search order should not have been
made in the first place. If the applicant is a start-up or of relatively little financial means, the
Court may require a guarantee from a parent company or other suitable party.

The respondent's potential damages are often difficult to quantify at an early stage of a dispute **14.047**
and present a level of uncertainty that applicants should be wary of. This can sometimes be
enough to put potential applicants off seeking such remedies.

Let's imagine an extreme example for illustration purposes: on the basis of strong evidence of **14.048**
a major fraud, the applicant obtains an unlimited order to freeze all of the assets of a successful
start-up with a promising future in the world of financial AI. The start-up was about to be

acquired by a larger, established fintech company for £50m. The acquiring fintech wanted to acquire the start-up's innovative credit scoring solution in order for it to gain immediate competitive advantage, but the freezing order has the effect of freezing the start-up's shares, meaning that they cannot be sold to the large fintech. As a result, the acquisition falls through and the fintech instead invests in the start-up's leading competitor, which the fintech considers the next best thing. It later comes to light that the applicant failed to inform the Court of some highly relevant facts which may have explained some of the start-up's actions, which the applicant had relied on as evidence of fraud. Ultimately, the Court holds that no fraud had taken place and the freezing order should not have been granted. Depending on foreseeability, damages incurred by the start-up as a result of the freezing order might include the £50m price tag it was about to achieve (or at least the difference between that and the price it later achieves via an alternative buyer, which might be considerably less). For this reason, applicants should be very careful to consider potential damages and their liability for them when applying for a freezing order or SSO.

7. Search Orders in AI Disputes: Practicalities

14.049 When SSOs were originally conceived, the search would have involved a physical search for physical documents and evidence. A team of lawyers would be rifling through papers, opening drawers and cabinets to look for the relevant material. Relevant material would be physically taken away (seized), copied and returned to the respondent usually a couple of days later. In the context of an AI dispute, whilst a physical search is potentially still required, those searching are unlikely to be as interested in the contents of filing cabinets as they are in the contents of servers, clouds and hard drives, searches of which can often be much more complex and take much longer than the average physical search. AI disputes can, for example, revolve around ownership and use of intellectual property in an algorithm or in determining fault when a medical programme misdiagnoses a patient. The answer to these disputes is likely to involve a search and analysis of an enormous amount of data held on computers, servers and clouds.

14.050 The amount of data involved in cases such as these can be immense. In *Hewlett Packard v Manchester Technology* [2019] EWHC 2089 (Ch), the SSO covered some 500,000 mobile phones, 2.7 million computers and 5.4 terrabytes of back-ups. When parties to litigation are dealing with data on this scale, careful thought must be given to how best to go about actually conducting a search of that size, bearing in mind costs considering (1) the need for proportionality under the Civil Procedure Rules and (2) the fact that most parties don't have endless amounts of time or money to spend on litigation.

14.051 AI itself can, of course, be very useful in conducting searches of this size, as discussed in section B above.

14.052 The aim of the initial search (usually carried out on the respondent's premises) is ordinarily to *preserve* the material which will later be searched, reviewed in detail or interrogated in order to find the relevant evidence the applicant is looking for. It does not normally allow the applicant to inspect or interrogate the material at the time of the physical search, which is often a matter decided upon at the return hearing. Indeed, it is not a tool for an applicant to obtain early disclosure. Again, in the modern age, and particularly so with AI disputes, the 'smoking gun' or other relevant evidence is likely to be held electronically, so an SSO is likely to be accompanied by (or indeed replaced entirely by) an imaging order, whereby a forensic computer expert would be admitted to the premises to image (or copy the contents of) the respondent's devices so that they do not need to be physically removed.

At the time of writing, the leading case on imaging orders is *TBD (Owen Holland) Ltd v* **14.053** *Simons and others* [2020] EWCA Civ 1182, which was heard by the Court of Appeal in 2020. The Court of Appeal recognised that most documentary evidence now exists in electronic or digital form, stored on digital devices or on cloud-based storage. Complete images (or copies) could be taken of the contents of storage media, computers, smart phones and cloud storage without interfering with the data stored there (which of course is likely to be a key concern of the respondent). The Court further recognised that a disadvantage to imaging as opposed to an old-fashioned physical document search was the inability to discriminate between types of information, meaning that irrelevant, non-disclosable material (potentially including highly confidential, commercially sensitive and privileged material) would be taken outside of the respondent's control and possession. The Court therefore held that imaging could only ever be a preservation step and proper consideration of the issues of disclosure and inspection of the documents and data preserved must be treated as a separate step. Indeed, the Court noted that often the most effective means of preserving evidence would be an order for permission for the imaging of a party's digital devices and cloud storage, which might entirely do away with the need for a search order. Alternatively, it might allow for any search order to be significantly limited. This Court of Appeal judgment called for imaging orders to be used without a search order, unless the applicant could show that a search order was also required. It also highlighted the importance of careful consideration of the respondent's rights and interests and gave useful guidance on how best to safeguard the respondent's interests when imaging orders were carried out. The Court noted that respondents' interests could be best protected by the forensic expert who carries out the imaging retaining the images until the return date, at which point the timing and methodology of any subsequent search and interrogation of the imaged files could be considered. Search methodology should either be agreed by the parties or approved by the Court.

So what about the ability to actually inspect the documents collected or devices imaged as **14.054** a result of a search or imaging order? While preservation of the evidence has been clarified as the primary objective for search orders, ultimately the applicant has preserved that evidence because it believes that the documents seized or imaged will assist its claim against the respondent (or potentially a third party). In order to be sure of that, the documents or images must eventually be searched. However, applicants should not be hasty in inspecting the respondent's documents and data before it is clear that it has the express right to do so.

In the ordinary course of litigation in England and Wales, the parties would disclose to each **14.055** other those documents (1) on which that party intends to rely, (2) which may be adverse to their own case or (3) which may assist the other party's case. This procedure would be reached some months after the claim had been filed and the parties had exchanged pleadings. Disclosure (merely listing the existence of those documents and providing a list to the opposing party) is usually closely followed by inspection, whereby the opponent party can actually review those disclosed documents.

14.056 It has long been an argument raised by respondents to SSOs that the order often has the effect of reversing the standard disclosure process, such that it is the applicant/claimant that decides which of the respondent/defendant's documents are relevant and should be disclosed. The issue of who should inspect imaged data first was examined in *A v B* [2019] EWHC 2089 (Ch) and *Hewlett Packard Enterprise Co v Manchester Technology Data (Holdings) Ltd* (which were heard jointly). In those cases, the judge allowed the claimant first access to the imaged data, but in doing so said that such a result (that is, the applicant being allowed first review) was not inevitable and each case would turn on its own facts. However, he did set out guidance as to this issue regarding who should inspect seized or imaged data first. That guidance includes:

(a) The standard form order in the annex to Practice Direction 25 assumes that documents on computers will be searched by the applicant party, who will decide relevance of each document on a case-by-case basis. That is obviously a reversal of the usual disclosure procedure (but we note that what is assumed by the Practice Direction is potentially outdated and not necessarily accurate in the case of an imaging order);

(b) Preservation is the primary goal of an SSO: inspection should be considered as a separate step;

(c) There is an analogy with disclosure, and there may be many relevant factors in each case, including:

    (i) An SSO would likely have been obtained on the basis of strong prima facie case that the respondent is likely to destroy evidence. That might mean that the respondent ought not to be trusted to carry out the disclosure exercise appropriately, although if the respondent's solicitors are involved in the process, that might tip the balance in the respondent's favour;

    (ii) The relevance of some documents may not be obvious to the respondent's lawyers;

    (iii) Urgency could justify the applicant carrying out the search;

    (iv) Where an applicant has greater resources than the respondent, it might be practical and in line with the overriding objective of enabling the Court to deal with cases justly and at proportionate cost[7] to allow the applicant to search first, although this must not be a way for a wealthier party to gain an advantage that it wouldn't otherwise have;

    (v) Searching imaged computers is highly intrusive and the images are likely to contain material which would not be appropriate for the applicants to see, which should be avoided where possible (indeed, this is an example of where TAR or tailored document recognition programmes might assist).

14.057 The important point for applicants to remember is that carrying out the search or image order is only the first step and is one of preservation. It should avoid reviewing the result of the search or imaging until after it has either the directions of the Court at the return hearing or the agreement of the respondent party.

8. Other Remedies Where an SSO Is Not Appropriate

14.058 If the Court does not think it is appropriate to grant an SSO, it may nonetheless be convinced to grant similar albeit slightly less draconian orders, including:

---

7 CPR r1.1.(1).

(a) A 'doorstep order' or 'doorstep Piller', in which the respondent is required to give disclosure of material to the applicant's representatives when the order is served, without the ability for the applicant or its representative to enter onto the respondent's premises. This has the advantage of being less invasive for the respondent, but the obvious disadvantage that in the case of a dishonest respondent there remains a risk of the respondent denying the existence of unhelpful material or destroying the same; and

(b) An order for 'delivery up' of certain documents by a specified date, which can include an injunction against the destruction of such documents. In the context of an AI dispute, this may be particularly useful to obtain against a third-party custodian of data who might otherwise be obliged to engage in a programme of automatic destruction of that data.

F. CONCLUSION

The relationship between AI and disputes is one that is likely to get stronger over time. The use **14.059** of AI in disputes is inevitable given the increase in data and information sources that need to be interrogated. Some Courts already expect parties to make use of AI to help keep costs proportionate to the value of the dispute in question, and others are sure to follow.[8] Lord Hodge, Deputy President of the Supreme Court of the United Kingdom, has called for 'lawmakers, regulators and judges in the United Kingdom to be alive to the demands for change that technology will make of our legal systems and the opportunities and challenges which that technology creates for the legal professions. The executive branches of government, our legislators and courts will have to adapt to the effects of technological change, to embrace its opportunities and to control its downside.' While the 'downside' might include an increase in the types of disputes discussed in this chapter, AI undoubtedly presents substantial opportunities to assist in the management and strategy-building of disputes and litigation.

The use of AI will influence the dispute strategy for various organisations and individuals. It **14.060** is becoming increasingly important that the team managing the dispute has technology and AI expertise available to the team. AI could also have practical implications on matters such as funding for disputes – AI-driven solutions could be used for assessing the merits of cases and likelihood of outcomes, which in turn has an impact on a third party funder's decision on whether to underwrite the costs of a dispute.

It is inevitable that disputes about AI will also increase. This is an area in which we are likely **14.061** to see more jurisprudence developing in the coming years. If you find yourself in an AI dispute it is important that you quickly secure the data and ensure it is available for interrogation as the dispute develops. As discussed above, various English law remedies can be of assistance in these situations, but they must be deployed in an effective manner.

---

8   The Business and Property Courts of England and Wales now require parties to provide a reasoned justification for any decision not to use predictive coding where the 'universe' of documents to be reviewed for disclosure exceeds 50,000 files. See Questions 13 and 14 in Section 2 of the Disclosure Review Document, at: www.justice.gov.uk/courts/procedure-rules/civil/rules/practice-direction-51u-disclosure-pilot-for-thebusiness-and-property-courts.

PART III

INDUSTRIES

15

FINANCIAL REGULATION

Richard Hay and Sophia Le Vesconte

A. INTRODUCTION

The aim of this chapter is to describe the main financial regulatory considerations for firms **15.001** deploying Artificial Intelligence (AI) technologies and provide a brief overview of potential future developments.

There is currently no specific regime regulating the use of AI in financial services in the UK. **15.002** This chapter therefore focuses on:

(i) areas of deployment of AI in the financial services industry (Section B);
(ii) an overview of the current legal and regulatory landscape relevant to the deployment of AI in financial services (Section C);
(iii) certain general areas for consideration, namely the regulatory perimeter (Section D(1)); governance and regulatory responsibility (Section D(2)); transparency, explainability and fairness (Section D(3)); control and risk-management (Section D(4)); and outsourcing, third party service provision and operational resilience (Section D(5));

(iv)   specific considerations in relation to two distinct areas of application, namely anti-money laundering (AML) and algorithmic trading (Section E); and

(v)   potential future developments (Section F).

15.003   The primary focus is on UK financial regulation, although in many cases the concepts discussed will be applicable by analogy in other jurisdictions (in particular where the applicable UK regulation has historically derived from the requirements of EU legislation[1]).

15.004   Cross-sector regulations (for example, in relation to data protection, consumer protection and cyber security), implications under competition law and issues of legal liability will also be of relevance in the financial sector and are considered in Chapters 10 and 17 of this book, as well as in Chapter 10 of the companion volume *Fintech Law and Regulation*, also published by Edward Elgar Publishing.

B. MARKET ACTIVITY

15.005   The use of AI in financial services is on an upward trend. As at 2019, 85 per cent of financial services firms were reportedly already using some forms of AI and 77 per cent anticipated AI would have high or very high overall importance to their businesses within two years.[2] The upsurge in implementation has been attributed to a range of supply-side factors (such as improvements in technology and infrastructure) and demand-side factors (such as profit-seeking and compliance with escalating regulatory demands).[3] In this section we discuss the nature of AI solutions currently used in financial services, common areas of deployment and the role of third parties.

1.   Nature of AI in Financial Services

15.006   Most of the AI technologies reportedly used in financial services fall into the category of 'machine-learning',[4] and given this context the terms 'AI' and 'machine-learning' are used interchangeably in this chapter. Machine-learning itself is often further divided into the sub-categories of 'supervised learning', 'unsupervised learning' and 'reinforcement learning',

---

1   As a related point, while non-legislative materials produced by the European Supervisory Authorities (including the European Securities & Markets Authority (ESMA), the European Insurance & Occupational Pensions Authority (EIOPA) and the European Banking Authority (EBA)) have not been incorporated into UK law, UK authorities have indicated that these materials remain relevant in assessing compliance with the retained EU law and EU-derived law to which they relate. See Financial Conduct Authority, *Brexit: our approach to EU non-legislative materials* available at www.fca.org.uk/publication/corporate/brexit-our-approach-to-eu-non-legislative-materials.pdf accessed 25 March 2021 and Bank of England and PRA, *Interpretation of EU Guidelines and Recommendations: Bank of England and PRA approach after the UK's withdrawal from the EU* available at www.bankofengland.co.uk/-/media/boe/files/paper/2019/interpretation-of-eu-guidelines-and-recommendations-boe-and-pra-approach-sop-december-2020.pdf accessed 25 March 2021.
2   World Economic Forum and University of Cambridge Centre for Alternative Finance, *Transforming Paradigms, A Global AI in Financial Services Survey* (2020), available at www.weforum.org/reports/transforming-paradigms-a-global-ai-in-financial-services-survey accessed 25 March 2021 (the WEF/CCAF Report), at p. 11 and p. 25.
3   Financial Stability Board, *Artificial intelligence and machine learning in financial services, Market developments and financial stability implications* (2017), available at www.fsb.org/wp-content/uploads/P011117.pdf accessed 25 March 2021 (the FSB AI Report), p. 9.
4   WEF/CCAF Report, pp. 16–17.

although it is often difficult to draw clear distinctions[5] (for more information on these categories, see Chapters 3 and 4).[6] Of these, supervised learning techniques have historically been the most commonly used in financial services.[7] That said, many deployments of AI in practice involve multiple stages; for example, a clustering algorithm (a type of unsupervised learning algorithm) could be deployed on unstructured data, with the output then forming the basis for data that is more suitable for a supervised learning algorithm to be deployed on.

As compared with rules-based computer programs, which apply pre-determined rules to inputs in order to yield certain outputs, supervised learning algorithms generally take as inputs two categories of data – features (or input) data, and labels (or output) data – and produce as an output the rules[8] to be applied to the input data in order best[9] to predict or infer the output data. Once 'trained' or calibrated in this way, the algorithm can be deployed on new input data in order to generate inferences or predictions as to the output data or label, as applicable, in the absence of any such data or label.[10] The model may continue to be recalibrated throughout its lifecycle, on a continuous or periodic basis, to take account of new input data. As with machine-learning more generally, the potential applications of this type of algorithm are vast (they include, for example, optical character recognition, speech recognition and many image classification algorithms), with the constraining factor often being the availability of sufficiently extensive or high-quality data sets. An example in financial services would be the use of such an algorithm in portfolio optimisation, taking a model trained on historical asset price returns (for example, stock market returns), to optimise asset allocation so as to seek to maximise future portfolio returns.   **15.007**

Unlike supervised learning, both unsupervised learning and reinforcement learning techniques involve feeding the algorithm unlabelled training data – that is, input data only. In the case of unsupervised learning, the algorithm is designed to seek to identify underlying structures, patterns, statistical features or other characteristics in the unstructured data sets. Clustering algorithms are one example of unsupervised learning, which divide a data set into 'clusters' of data sharing common features as measured by one or more criteria defined in the algorithm. In the context of financial services, unsupervised learning techniques can be used for various purposes, including, for example, to seek to uncover or analyse correlations or relationships in large   **15.008**

---

5   Some draw different or further distinctions, such as 'self-supervised learning', being an instance of supervised learning where the labels are derived algorithmically, as opposed to being input by a human. See, for example, François Chollet, *Deep Learning with Python* (Manning Publications Co., 2018), Part 1, Chapter 4.

6   There are a variety of technologies that fall within the 'machine-learning' category and, *a fortiori*, AI. We do not consider artificial general intelligence or the prospect that there might be some form of technological 'singularity', given the remoteness of such possibilities at this stage.

7   WEF/CCAF Report, p. 109.

8   More precisely, many machine-learning algorithms yield the parameters (or weights) that enable input data to be mapped to output data within a training data set, so as to maximise a pre-defined measure of accuracy (or, conversely, to minimise inaccuracy, often referred to as 'loss').

9   According to a criterion specified in the algorithm, for example, minimising the loss between the model output and the output training data.

10   The breadth of this description belies the difficulty in trying to define these technologies. One differentiating feature of machine learning as compared with certain other prediction or statistical inference techniques is that there need be no attempt in a machine-learning algorithm to predict or draw inferences based on an underlying model of the process or mechanism generating the outputs.

data sets or between seemingly unrelated variables (such as in seeking to model macroeconomic data or specific asset prices).

15.009 In the case of reinforcement learning, the algorithm is also designed to identify a policy (generally, a function) that maximises the value of positive outcomes and minimises negative outcomes, through a system of rewards and penalties. In relation to new input data, the algorithm provides an output, generating a consequence in the dynamic environment within which the algorithm operates; the algorithm then receives a reward signal based on that outcome, which is taken into account in determining for the next output the policy that maximises the expected rewards and minimises penalties (based on all available data, including the most recent reward).[11] This type of algorithm is generally deployed in a dynamic environment, where new information is received sequentially (for example, in the context of computer games or driverless cars). In financial services, a reinforcement learning algorithm could, for example, be deployed in determining whether to continue to hold, or to buy/sell, a particular asset in response to new time series data relating to the price or return of a given universe of assets.

15.010 Reinforcement-learning algorithms are by their nature designed to give rise to outputs within the environment in which they operate. Depending on the application, these outputs may have direct real-world consequences (such as rebalancing a financial portfolio, as noted above) or initiate further processes, which may be subject to human intervention. Equally, while supervised and unsupervised learning methods are not themselves designed to effect any action, they can be made capable of triggering real-world consequences through the use of automation interfaces.[12]

15.011 It is worth at this stage highlighting a few features of machine-learning algorithms, as compared with other algorithms, of notable relevance in the context of financial regulation.

    (i)   *Reliance on training data* – The efficacy of many machine-learning algorithms depends upon a combination of the algorithm and the availability of sufficient, and sufficiently high-quality, training data. Training data is often the key point of differentiation between strong and weak AI models, as the algorithms are typically based largely on open-source software.[13] For that reason, a significant element of the work required to deploy AI algorithms in practice is in fact preparatory, that is, obtaining and manipulating data so as to make it fit for consumption by the algorithm.

    (ii) *Predictability* – Whereas the output of a rules-based algorithm is pre-determined and can be predicted with absolute certainty up front (given certain inputs, and assuming no malfunction), a machine-learning algorithm is generally considered 'successful' if it achieves a certain degree of accuracy (that is, typically less than 100 per cent). In the case of a supervised learning algorithm, for example, this may be analysed as a probability of a correct inference or prediction. Furthermore, many machine-learning algorithms are deliberately designed to ensure they are not 'overfitted' (that is, they do not corre-

---

11   See, for example, Bonnie G. Buchanan, PhD, FRSA, *Artificial intelligence in finance*, supported by The Alan Turing Institute, available at www.turing.ac.uk/research/publications/artificial-intelligence-finance accessed 25 March 2021, pp. 20–3.

12   WEF/CCAF Report, p. 109.

13   WEF/CCAF Report, p. 114.

spond too closely to the specific training data set) as this may undermine their ability to be generalised (that is, perform well when faced with new data). In other words, machine-learning algorithms often use techniques that may actually *reduce* their performance as measured against training and test data, with a view to enhancing performance more generally. In addition, recalibration processes, which are designed to improve the model based on new input data, may also cause the algorithm to deliver different outputs in response to the same set of inputs at different points in time, which may undermine the model's predictability and consistency.

(iii)   *Explainability* – With some models of machine-learning, outcomes may be fully explainable as a function of their inputs after the event, even if they were not predictable at the outset. Under other models (generally more advanced models, including those that use so-called deep learning techniques such as artificial neural networks) individual outcomes may not be explainable, even retrospectively. Such algorithms are sometimes referred to as black-box algorithms. Notably, there is often a trade-off between explainability and efficacy – in other words, the algorithms that are most effective in terms of performance can often be the least explainable.[14] See Chapter 29 for more detail.

2.   Areas of Deployment

As might be expected, there is a wide range of AI-related activity reported in the financial services markets, with adoption varying significantly across different types of institution and sub-sector.[15] This includes incumbent firms seeking to improve existing products as well as the development of new products, services and systems.[16] In the UK, the banking and insurance sectors have historically had a relatively higher share of mature use cases than other financial services sectors, including capital markets, non-bank lending, payments and financial market infrastructure.[17] However, investment in AI continues to grow rapidly, and while there remain hurdles (including regulatory uncertainty), the breadth and depth of deployment is likely to advance meaningfully over the coming years.   **15.012**

A few common areas of deployment are outlined below.   **15.013**

(i)   *Risk management* – Risk management functions have been among the earliest adopters of AI. Machine-learning techniques are used to monitor, detect and manage a variety of risks across the financial sector. This includes operational risk (for example, in monitoring for potential fraud or cyber-security breaches), market risk (for example, in the

---

14   Autorité de Contrôle Prudentiel et de Résolution, *Governance of artificial intelligence in finance* (2020), available at https://acpr.banque-france.fr/sites/default/files/medias/documents/20200612_ai_governance_finance.pdf accessed 25 March 2021 ('ACPR Governance of AI in FS Report'), p. 64.

15   For example, see WEF/CCAF Report, Bank of England and Financial Conduct Authority, *Machine learning in UK financial services* (2019), available at www.fca.org.uk/publication/research/research-note-on-machine-learning-in-uk -financial-services.pdf accessed 25 March 2021 (the 'BofE/FCA Report'); European Commission, *Final report of the Expert Group on Regulatory Obstacles to Financial Innovation: 30 recommendations on regulation, innovation and finance* (2019) available at https://ec.europa.eu/info/publications/191113-report-expert-group-regulatory-obstacles-financial -innovation_en accessed 25 March 2021 (the 'ROFIEG Report'); and OICV-IOSCO, *The use of artificial intelligence and machine learning by market intermediaries and asset managers* (FR06/2021), available at https://www.iosco.org/library/ pubdocs/pdf/IOSCOPD684.pdf accessed 16 December 2021 ('IOSCO AI Final Report')

16   WEF/CCAF Report, p. 12.

17   BofE/FCA Report, p. 11.

validation and testing of market risk models or in modelling the effect of the firm's own trading on market prices), credit risk (for example, by monitoring counterparty-related data to provide early warning indicators of potential defaults) and regulatory risk (which overlaps with other areas but includes, for example, monitoring for potential money laundering and terrorist activities or staff misconduct and the validation and testing of regulatory models).[18]

(ii)   *Customer onboarding and engagement* – Customer onboarding and engagement are other common areas of use.[19] For example, AI is increasingly used in the process of collecting and verifying know-your-customer (KYC) information pursuant to AML requirements as well as in customer communications, including through the use of so-called chatbots.

(iii) *Insurance* – AI techniques are used widely in insurance, including in the sale of insurance products (for example, to identify and segment risks more effectively in order to improve the risk-sensitivity of pricing) and in claims management (for example, in the verification of invoices and in the automation of pay-outs in response to real-world trigger events).[20] The insurance industry is covered at length in Chapter 16.

(iv)   *Asset management* – Asset managers have been using supervised learning techniques for small-scale pattern recognition and simple prediction models to support trading decisions for a number of years. Increasingly, unsupervised and reinforcement-learning techniques are also being used to analyse diverse data sources in order to generate new trade ideas (for example, by identifying relationships in the data) or to inform pricing (for example, by drawing on historical prices and current trends).[21]

(v)   *Trading* – Rules-based algorithms have long been used in market trading. Now, many market intermediaries are offering their clients AI-based software solutions referred to as 'algo-wheels', which use historical trading and performance data to predict the performance of trading strategy and/or broker algorithms and recommend which algorithm to use when.[22] These algorithms do not themselves design trading strategies.

(vi)   *Advisory* – While many robo-advisors use rules-based algorithms, in some cases machine-learning algorithms are used to support advisory services. Often, however, rather than being deployed directly in the performance of a regulated activity, these algorithms are used to run analytics or produce other outputs that inform a decision or action ultimately taken by one or more individuals (such as an investment advisor, who takes the final decision on how to advise the client based on various inputs, including outputs from a machine-learning algorithm).

---

18   See, for example, FSB AI Report para 3; IOSCO AI Final Consultation Report, p. 8; WEF/CCAF Report, p. 26, BofE/FCA Report, p. 10; and European Banking Authority, *Report on Big Data and advanced analytics* (2020), available at https://eba.europa.eu/eba-report-identifies-key-challenges-roll-out-big-data-and-advanced-analytics accessed 25 March 2021 (the 'EBA BD&AA Report'), p. 19.
19   See, for example, BofE/FCA Report, p. 10, WEF/CCAF Report, p. 27 and EBA BD&AA Report, pp. 20–1.
20   See, for example, ROFIEG Report, p. 40.
21   IOSCO AI Final Consultation Report, p. 8.
22   IOSCO AI Final Consultation Report, p. 7.

3.   Use of Third Parties

The deployment of AI models may be undertaken in-house or through outsourcing to third **15.014** parties. In the UK, most use cases have historically been implemented internally.[23] However, smaller firms may be more likely to adopt solutions from external providers.[24]

Firms deploying models in-house often still look to external sources to provide the components that feed into the model – namely, software or training data. In relation to software, firms may use open-source software (which they may develop further in-house) and/or license or purchase tailored software that has been developed by a third party (which may also be based on open-source software). In relation to data, many financial firms still rely on internal sources.[25] However, we may see this trend shift over time if policymakers continue to promote data sharing within the financial sector.[26]

A number of firms also rely on third parties for underlying platforms and infrastructure, such **15.015** as cloud computing.[27] Providers of such services are also starting to offer full 'AI as a Service' packages, which enable firms to use AI solutions without having to invest heavily in their own infrastructure. Significant growth is expected in this market generally, which may filter into the financial sector.

C. LEGAL AND REGULATORY LANDSCAPE

In this section, we outline the current legal and regulatory landscape relevant to the deployment **15.016** of AI in financial services.

1.   Existing Law and Regulation

In the UK, there are currently no regulatory requirements that apply specifically to the use **15.017** of AI. This is a common position across the globe[28] (although, in the EU, a draft legislative framework for the regulation of AI has been proposed by the European Commission, as discussed in Section F below). Financial regulation does, however, impose a number of general requirements (for example, in relation to matters of governance, control and risk-management and outsourcing) which warrant specific consideration in the context of AI, given the novelty of the technology. These issues are explored in Section D below.

---

23   BofE/FCA Report, p. 13.
24   IOSCO AI Final Consultation Report, p. 12.
25   See, for example, WEF/CCAF Report, p. 115.
26   For example, it is a key priority under the European Commission's Digital Finance Strategy (September 2020) available at https://ec.europa.eu/info/publications/200924-digital-finance-proposals_en accessed 25 March 2021 to promote data-driven innovation, including enhanced access to data and data sharing within the financial sector. Similar policies are supported under the Kalifa Review of UK Fintech (February 2021) available at www.gov.uk/government/publications/the-kalifa-review-of-uk-fintech accessed 25 March 2021.
27   See WEF/CCAF Report, p. 115 and BofE/FCA Report, pp. 13–14.
28   IOSCO AI Final Consultation Report, p. 14.

15.018   While outside the scope of this chapter, there is also a myriad of cross-sectoral rules that will be of relevance to those seeking to deploy AI in the financial sector. For example, it will be important to consider cross-sectoral regulation in areas such as cyber security, consumer protection and data protection, as noted in paragraph 15.004 above. Competition law issues also come into play in financial services, for example if AI activities facilitate or create collusive practices between competitors in financial markets. Competition law is discussed in Chapter 11. There are also various matters of general private law to be considered. For example, financial firms will be interested in ensuring that they achieve an appropriate allocation of legal liability in relation to their AI deployments, as discussed in Chapter 9.

15.019   In many respects, these existing legal and regulatory frameworks already provide relatively comprehensive benchmarks against which to consider the risks associated with AI. Financial regulation is generally intended to be 'technology agnostic', with the approach being to regulate specific activities and instruments rather than technologies. However, various shortcomings have been identified with regard to existing rules, including in relation to financial services. These can be divided into three categories.

(i)   *Ambiguity* – The existing regulatory framework is ambiguous in a number of areas and leaves considerable scope for interpretation. As a result, the vast majority of respondents to the European Commission's public consultation on AI[29] indicated that the financial sector needed guidance on how existing EU rules should be applied in the context of AI applications.[30]

(ii)   *Inadequacy* – There are concerns that some of the particular features of AI (including those outlined in Section B(1) above) may introduce new vulnerabilities that have not been catered for in existing regulatory frameworks. There are also concerns that existing liability frameworks may be inadequate to protect all users of AI-based financial services in the event of a malfunction.

(iii)   *Incompatibility* – In some cases, existing regulatory frameworks are seen as incompatible with the use of AI. For example, regulations that apply an absolute standard of compliance may not accommodate machine-learning algorithms that are, by design, probabilistic, in that it is expected from the outset that they will give rise to certain exceptions[31] (even if that degree of accuracy may be higher than human accuracy in practice). Similarly, regulations that require technologies to be fully understood and explainable throughout their lifecycles may be at odds with some black-box models. Moreover, it may be impossible for regulators to identify and prove possible breaches of law when such models are used. As a result, some argue that entirely new frameworks are needed to accommodate autonomous machines.[32]

---

29   European Commission's consultation on a White Paper on Artificial Intelligence, available at https://ec.europa .eu/digital-single-market/en/news/white-paper-artificial-intelligence-public-consultation-towards-european-approach -excellence accessed 25 March 2021, conducted between 19 February to 14 June 2020.

30   See the European Commission's Digital Finance Strategy for the EU, available at https://eur-lex.europa.eu/legal -content/EN/TXT/?uri=CELEX:52020DC0591 accessed 25 March 2021, 4.2.

31   Indeed, certain AI algorithms are structured to minimise (but not eliminate) 'loss', that is, a measurement of the algorithm's performance against a target. Equally, it can be a desirable feature not to 'overfit' the model to test data, meaning admitting a certain tolerance for error is expected to lead to better generalised performance: see Section B above.

32   See, for example, Jacob Turner, *Robot Rules: Regulating Artificial Intelligence* (Palgrave Macmillan, 2019).

These issues are explored further in Section D below.

2.   Existing Soft Law

While there is currently a lack of AI-specific regulation, there is AI-specific soft law (that **15.020** is, principles and guidance issued by national or supranational authorities) in effect, at both a global and a European level, as discussed in more detail in Chapter 6. These apply to the use of AI across industries and are not specific to the context of financial services. Generally, these principles do not have the force of law. However, the desire of regulators to promote best practice in their industries is likely to mean that they would expect compliance with these principles and guidelines. At a minimum, it will inform their view on the standards to which a regulated entity should be operating and will perhaps have implications for future regulatory policy. Globally, the Organisation for Economic Cooperation and Development (OECD) adopted five principles on AI in May 2019.[33] The G20 members drew on these principles to create their own AI Principles[34] (the 'G20 AI Principles'), which were adopted a month later. The G20 AI Principles relate to:

(i)   inclusive growth, sustainable development and well-being;
(ii)   human-centred values and fairness;
(iii) transparency and explainability;
(iv)   robustness, security and safety; and
(v)   accountability.

At an EU level, the European Commission has endorsed the ethics guidelines for trustwor- **15.021** thy AI presented to it by its high-level expert group in April 2019[35] (the 'EC Ethical AI Guidelines'). To a large extent, these reflect and expand on the G20 AI Principles, and relate to:

(i)   human agency and oversight;
(ii)   technical robustness and safety;
(iii) privacy and data governance;
(iv)   transparency;
(v)   diversity, non-discrimination and fairness;
(vi)   societal and environmental well-being; and
(vii) accountability.

The EC Ethical AI Guidelines are supported by an assessment list to assist organisations in **15.022** practically applying the guidelines[36] (the ALTAI). Anyone can register to use the Commission's

---

33   OECD Principles on AI approved under the OEC Council Recommendation on Artificial Intelligence, available at https://legalinstruments.oecd.org/en/instruments/OECD-LEGAL-0449 accessed 25 March 2021.

34   G20 AI Principles set out in the June 2019 Ministerial Statement on Trade and Digital Economy, available at www.mofa .go.jp/files/000486596.pdf accessed 25 March 2021.

35   High-level Expert Group on Artificial Intelligence, Ethics Guidelines for Trustworthy Artificial Intelligence, available at https://ec.europa.eu/digital-single-market/en/news/ethics-guidelines-trustworthy-ai accessed 25 March 2021.

36   Assessment List for Trustworthy Artificial Intelligence (ALTAI) for self-assessment, available at https://ec.europa .eu/digital-single-market/en/news/assessment-list-trustworthy-artificial-intelligence-altai-self-assessment accessed 25 March 2021.

ALTAI web tool, which allows organisations to create (and edit) tailored assessment lists in relation to their own potential applications.[37]

D. GENERAL OBLIGATIONS AND BEST PRACTICE CONSIDERATIONS

15.023   While UK financial regulation does not include specific rules on the use of AI, there are various regulatory requirements which financial services firms will need to consider when deploying AI solutions. The precise nature of the requirements will depend largely on the type of solution and the context in which it is being deployed. However, there are a number of issues that are of general relevance, which we will discuss in this section. In Section E we will go on to explore some of the specific requirements applicable in respect of two distinct areas of application by way of example, namely, AML and algorithmic trading.

15.024   The areas we will examine in this section are:

(i)   perimeter issues: is financial regulation triggered in the first place?
(ii)   governance and regulatory responsibility;
(iii) transparency, explainability and fairness;
(iv)   control and risk-management; and
(v)   outsourcing, third party service provision and operational resilience.

1.   Regulatory Perimeter

15.025   Not all financial activities are regulated, and it is possible for AI to be deployed within the financial sector and outside the regulated perimeter. Given the absence of a regime specifically regulating AI in the financial sector, an unregulated activity does not become a regulated one merely because that activity is undertaken using AI. Conversely, regulated activities do not cease to be regulated because AI is involved.

15.026   That said, the involvement of AI may complicate this assessment in certain circumstances. Often the issues raised are not specific to AI, but the manner of deployment exacerbates existing uncertainties in financial regulation. For example, the distinction between the regulated activity of giving investment advice (a specified activity in the UK under Articles 53(1) and (2) of the Regulated Activities Order[38] (the RAO)) and the mere provision of information without any comment or value judgement (which generally will not amount to 'advice on the merits'[39]) can be difficult to draw even outside the context of AI.[40] That difficulty can however be compounded in relation to certain deployments of AI (for example, in the context of 'robo-advice' involving AI), in particular in assessing whether information presented amounts to 'advice on

---

37   Available at https://futurium.ec.europa.eu/en/european-ai-alliance/pages/altai-assessment-list-trustworthy-artificial-intelligence accessed 25 March 2021.

38   Financial Services and Markets Act 2000 (Regulated Activities) Order 2001, SI 2001/544.

39   For the purposes of Articles 53(1) and (2) of the RAO. See *Adams v Options UK Personal Pensions LLP (formerly Options Sipp UK LLP and Carey Pensions UK LLP) (Financial Conduct Authority intervening)* [2021] EWCA Civ 474 [75].

40   See for example: *Adams* (n. 39); *FCA v Avacade* [2020] EWHC 1673; *Thornbridge v Barclays* [2015] EWHC 3430; *Crestsign v NatWest* [2014] EWHC 3043; *Zaki v Credit Suisse* [2011] EWHC 2422; *Rubinstein v HSBC* [2011] EWHC 2304; *Walker v Inter-Alliance Group plc* [2007] EWHC 1858 (Ch).

the merits' in the relevant sense,[41] namely 'the product of a process of selection involving a value judgment so that the information will tend to influence the decision of the recipient'.[42] On one view, any algorithm is incapable of any form of value judgement or independent evaluation, and therefore its mere outputs are incapable of amounting to anything other than information. Arguably that is the case *a fortiori* in relation to those AI algorithms where key features of the model are determined by the algorithm itself, for example, where the algorithm determines not only the outputs but the parameters (for example, weights) of the model itself, and it therefore arguably cannot be said that there is a value judgement implicit in the design of the system.

The test under Articles 53(1) and 53(2) of the RAO, however, is an objective one,[43] and it **15.027** is submitted that the design of the relevant algorithm does not generally have a bearing as to whether there is advice (although that may impact the assessment of whether the advice is attributable to a particular person, as to which see below) any more than the subjective intention of a person providing advice orally does. Importantly, however, algorithms do not exist in a vacuum; instead, they are deployed by entities and, ultimately, individuals. There will often therefore be advice provided, either expressly or impliedly, by the person making an algorithm available for certain purposes (for example, the advice being to follow signals provided by the algorithm); in this sense, AI algorithms are not different to other forms of complex algorithm.[44] Nor does it affect whether there is 'advice' for the user to be free in its choice to follow or disregard the outputs of an algorithm, or that further advice or inputs may be received before a final decision is made by the user.[45]

Furthermore, an algorithm may involve many components or stages, some of which may **15.028** involve elements of machine-learning or AI, whereas others may be deterministic or involve pre-determined value judgments by the system designed. For example, an algorithm that takes the outcomes of an AI algorithm and subsequently applies deterministic rules in order to trigger a 'buy', 'sell' or 'hold' message sent to a user with regard to specific investments would give rise to investment advice notwithstanding the presence of AI in the algorithm.[46]

By contrast, where mere technology services are provided in the development or deployment of **15.029** AI algorithms used for the purposes of taking investment decisions, this should not amount to investment advice for these purposes. Often in such circumstances the provider of the technology services will be providing software to a design specification; similarly, it will often be clear from the context (including all marketing materials and related communications) that there is no assumption of responsibility by the service provider for the efficacy of the algorithm other than in relation to its delivery against the design specification, and the service provider will hold itself out as having specific technical (and not investment) expertise, for example, specific technology and mathematical expertise. Although this is a nuanced area, and much will turn on the specifics of the particular arrangements, it is submitted that the question is whether, viewed

---

41   We refer in the rest of this paragraph to 'advice', for simplicity.
42   *Adams* (n. 39) [75].
43   See for example: *FCA v 24Hr Trading Academy Limited and Mohammad Fuaath Haja Maideen Maricar* [2021] EWHC 648 (Ch); *Thornbridge* (n. 40).
44   *FCA* (n. 43); *Re Market Wizard Systems (UK) Ltd* [1998] 2 BCLC 282.
45   *Re Market Wizard Systems (UK) Ltd* (n 45) [34].
46   See for example: *FCA* (n. 43) (involving trading signals over social media).

objectively, the user is relying on the investment expertise of the algorithm provider, or instead on its technical expertise.

15.030   In addition, even if the outputs of the algorithm do amount to advice for the purposes of Articles 53(1) or 53(2) of the RAO, there is a question as to whom, in light of the arrangements in question, that advice is attributable to. It is conceivable that for certain AI algorithms there may be a form of independent evaluation, or value judgement, being performed by the algorithm itself, and that therefore the outputs of an algorithm, assessed objectively in a given context, amount to advice, but not advice attributable to a person for the purposes of the specified activity of advising on investments or the general prohibition on carrying on regulated activities without an authorisation or exemption;[47] and in particular the technology company providing the relevant software is not the person 'advising' or 'carrying on the regulated activity' of advising on investments.

15.031   Similarly, an AI solution may be deployed in a way that brings into question whether or not it is carried on 'by way of business'.[48] This could be the case if, for example, it is provided by an unregulated institution as a standalone self-service analytics tool for customers without charge. That said, where a business model involves the provision of AI solutions which are apparently free of charge to the user but which directly or indirectly contribute to revenue-generation by utilising the user's data or through other means, this will tend to indicate that the solution is provided 'by way of business' (as it would in other contexts).

15.032   Furthermore, regulated firms that conduct unregulated activities may nevertheless remain subject to certain regulatory requirements in respect of those otherwise unregulated activities. In the UK, a regulated firm must take 'reasonable care to organise and control its affairs responsibly and effectively, with adequate risk management systems', including with respect to its activities that are unregulated.[49] As a result, certain considerations described below (in particular in relation to governance and oversight – see Section D(2) below) in relation to deployments of AI within the ambit of an authorised firm's regulated activities will also apply where AI is deployed as part of that firm conducting unregulated activities.

15.033   Finally, it bears reminding that even if financial regulation does not apply to a particular deployment of AI, other regulatory requirements likely will, as noted in paragraph 15.004.

2.   Governance and Regulatory Responsibility

15.034   If the relevant activity does fall within the regulatory perimeter, the institution next needs to consider how it effectively discharges its regulatory obligations given the potential impact of the relevant AI. In most cases, the mere use of AI will not in and of itself cause a firm to contravene the general prohibition,[50] nor the general restrictions on acting without relevant permissions[51]

---

47   Financial Services and Markets Act 2000 (FSMA), s. 19.
48   This being one of the perimeter requirements under FSMA, s. 22.
49   FCA Handbook, PRIN 2.1.1 and 3.2.3.
50   FSMA, s. 19.
51   FSMA, s. 20.

or on financial promotions.[52,53] More often, the challenge posed by AI is in relation to compliance with the ongoing regulatory requirements. This may include relevant Financial Conduct Authority (FCA) rules[54] and/or Prudential Regulatory Authority (PRA) rules[55] as well as other specific regulation that applies in the circumstances (for example, the Money Laundering Regulations[56] (MLR) in the case of AML applications).

The specific regulatory requirements vary depending on the nature of the institution and its **15.035** activities, and the context within which AI is deployed (and we explore some requirements in respect of specific applications in Section E below). More generally, however, most regulated institutions in the UK[57] are required to have in place robust governance arrangements, which include a clear organisational structure with well-defined, transparent and consistent lines of responsibility; effective processes to identify, manage, monitor and report the risks it is or might be exposed to; and internal control mechanisms, including sound administrative and accounting procedures and effective control and safeguard arrangements for information-processing systems,[58] or to meet similar types of governance requirements. The rapidly evolving use of AI as well as its novel features (as discussed in Section B(1) above) can mean that existing governance frameworks are inadequate to identify and mitigate effectively all relevant risks, and as such need to be adapted.

Ensuring appropriate governance of AI within financial institutions, in particular through **15.036** individual senior manager accountability, has been a key objective of financial regulators.[59] It has been suggested,[60] for example, that regulators should consider requiring firms to have designated senior management responsible for the oversight of the development, testing, deployment, monitoring and controls of AI. The recommendation extends to firms having a documented internal governance framework, with clear lines of accountability, and that senior management should designate an appropriately senior individual (or groups of individuals) with the relevant skillset and knowledge to sign off on initial deployment and substantial updates of the technology. Such requirements would clearly focus minds on the governance of AI systems.

That said, firms should also be mindful that existing regulatory requirements in some cases **15.037** already place comparable responsibilities on senior managers for material deployments of AI technologies. In the UK, this depends on the specific regulatory regime given the nature of the institution in question.

---

52   FSMA, s. 21.
53   These requirements may be relevant in some cases, for example if an unregulated institution provides its customers access to an ancillary AI tool which constitutes regulated financial services, but in these cases the use of AI is not generally intrinsic to the breach.
54   As set out in the FCA Handbook.
55   As set out in the PRA Rulebook.
56   The Money Laundering, Terrorist Financing and Transfer of Funds (Information on the Payer) Regulations 2017, SI 2017/692 (as amended).
57   Including those authorised by the FCA or PRA under Part 4A of FSMA.
58   See, for example, FCA Handbook, SYSC 4.1.1 and PRA Rulebook, CRR Firms, General Organisational Requirements 2.1.
59   See, for example, FSB AI Report, p. 26, IOSCO AI Final Consultation Report, Measure 1 and speech by James Proudman on behalf of the Bank of England on *Managing Machines: the governance of artificial intelligence*, at the FCA Conference on Governance in Banking.
60   See IOSCO AI Final Consultation Report, Measure 1.

(i) *Firms subject to the SM&CR* – For firms subject to the Senior Managers & Certification Regime[61] (SM&CR), the FCA or the PRA, as applicable, may take action against any person if it appears to the relevant regulator that that person is guilty of misconduct and the regulator is satisfied that taking action is appropriate in the circumstances.[62] If, for example, the AI causes the firm in question to be in breach of a relevant requirement,[63] the senior manager responsible at that time for the management of any of the activities in relation to which the breach occurred is guilty of misconduct[64] unless they took reasonable steps to avoid the occurrence (or continuation) of the contravention.[65]

Under the SM&CR, firms are required to maintain statements of responsibilities for each of their senior managers and may be required to maintain a management responsibilities map in relation to the assignment of responsibilities.[66] However, while these documents are likely to be relevant in identifying the responsible senior manager(s), it is important to note that they are not determinative; the test is to identify each senior manager[67] who, at the time of the breach, was responsible in fact[68] for the management of any of the firm's activities concerned in the breach.[69] This will almost certainly include the senior managers of the business lines or functions within which the AI was deployed,[70] and may also extend to the senior manager with responsibilities for creating or providing specialist IT input into the AI (for example, the Head of IT and/or Operations).[71] Depending on the circumstances, it may also extend to the senior manager discharging the chief executive function.[72]

Given that these responsibilities arise regardless of whether the relevant senior manager is aware of the AI deployment, the first concern should be to have in place procedures

---

61 As defined under FCA Handbook, SYSC 23. The SM&CR has applied to deposit takers, PRA-designated investment firms and UK branches of foreign banks since March 2016; to insurers since December 2018; and to other firms authorised under the FSMA since December 2019. Broadly speaking, firms covered by the SM&CR are divided into three categories: 'core firms', which are subject to a standard set of SM&CR requirements; 'enhanced firms', which are subject to further requirements on top of the standard set; and 'limited scope firms', which are subject to a reduced set of requirements.

62 FSMA, s. 66(1).

63 This is broadly cast, to include any requirement imposed 'by or under' FSMA, as well as any requirement imposed by the Alternative Investment Fund Managers Regulations 2013, the Undertakings for Collective Investment in Transferable Securities Regulations 2011 or any qualifying provision specified, or of a description specified, by the Treasury (s. 66(4) FSMA)

64 Note that the effect of s. 66A(1) and s. 66B(1) FSMA is that the relevant person is guilty of misconduct if the relevant conditions are met, even if the FCA or PRA ultimately decides to take no action against that person on that basis that it is not appropriate under the circumstances to do so (s. 66(1) FSMA).

65 FSMA, s. 66A(5)(d) and s. 66B(5)(d).

66 Pursuant to s. 60(2A) and (2B) FSMA and FCA Handbook, SYSC 25.2.1.

67 That is, each person approved to perform a designated senior management function (s. 66A(7) and 66B(7) FSMA).

68 See FCA Handbook, DEPP6.2.9-C and PRA Supervisory Statement SS28/15 *Strengthening individual accountability in banking* (2020), paragraph 2.60.

69 In contrast to other references in FSMA, 'activities' here is used without reference to whether they are regulated (or otherwise); the better view is therefore that the term should be interpreted broadly in this context.

70 We do not consider limited scope firms for these purposes.

71 Being the senior manager with overall responsibility for managing all or substantially all the internal operations or technology of the firm or of a part of the firm (FCA Handbook, SUP 10C.6B.2).

72 Being the person who, by definition, has responsibility for the conduct of the whole of the business (or relevant activities) of the firm (FCA Handbook, SUP 10C.5.22).

and controls to identify all deployments of AI across the relevant business and to monitor their deployment on an ongoing basis. This is not always carried out in practice.[73]

Once identified, those instances should be well documented in order to enable the demonstration of suitable compliance with applicable requirements. Given that regulatory responsibility will be determined as a matter of fact, it would be advisable for firms, regardless of whether they are legally required to do so as part of their statement of responsibilities and management responsibilities mapping, to determine and document accurately, *ex ante*, where the responsibilities lie for each AI deployment by reference to a matrix of all relevant facts and circumstances.

Next, firms will have to grapple with what responsible senior managers need to do in order to discharge their regulatory obligation to take 'such steps as a person in the senior manager's position could reasonably be expected to take to avoid the contravention occurring (or continuing)'.[74] The FCA's guidance on this point, for example, indicates that this is an objective test, to be assessed against the standard of a competent senior manager at that time, in that specific individual's position, with that individual's role and responsibilities and in all the circumstances'.[75] It also lists circumstances which the FCA would expect to have regard to. This list suggests that it will be important for the senior managers to take reasonable steps to ensure that, among other things, there are appropriate policies and procedures in place for reviewing the competence, knowledge, skills and performance of each individual with responsibilities in relation to the AI application (whatever function that might be in);[76] that they assess and monitor the governance, operational and risk management arrangements in place in respect of the AI application;[77] that they maintain an appropriate level of understanding about the AI applications and receive adequate reporting and explanations of issues;[78] and that there are appropriate systems and controls in place to comply with relevant regulatory requirements.[79] Senior managers will need to consider how they can discharge these obligations in practice in the context of AI deployments.

While senior managers are not expected to be experts in every area for which they are responsible, it is submitted that *ex ante*, the responsible senior manager must at least make such inquiries as to the characteristics, features and circumstances of the deployment of the AI that could foreseeably lead to regulatory breaches, so as to enable an assessment to take place and steps to be taken to minimise the risk of such breaches, through governance, operational and risk management processes (with appropriate oversight over the implementation of such steps). If the senior manager is not themselves an expert, this will likely require them to draw on expertise from the relevant business area or other expert opinion, in order to make sufficient inquiries as to the relevant features of the algorithm in order to make that assessment. Depending on the circumstances of the deployment, it may also require the senior manager to make inquiries as to possible unforeseeable risks.

---

73   The FCA has in fact flagged the issue in the comparable context of algorithmic trading (see FCA, *Algorithmic Trading Compliance in Wholesale Markets*, paragraph 1.8).

74   FSMA, s. 66A(5)(d) and s. 66B(5)(d).

75   FCA Handbook, DEPP 6.2.9-D.

76   FCA Handbook, DEPP 6.2.9-E(10).

77   FCA Handbook, DEPP 6.2.9-E(11).

78   FCA Handbook, DEPP 6.2.9-E(14).

79   FCA Handbook, DEPP 6.2.9-E(18).

This might be the case, for example, where there is a risk that a model may function in an unpredictable way, for example if it is the first deployment in a 'live' environment or a particularly sensitive function, or if the model includes specific features giving rise to a risk of unpredictability. Certain areas of regulation (for example, in relation to high-frequency trading) specifically require that steps be taken prior to deployment or any substantial update so that methodologies are established to ensure the algorithm does not behave in an unintended manner (as discussed in Section E(2) below). These regulatory requirements will also affect the application of the general senior manager standard in a particular context (not least because they also affect the possibility of a regulatory breach).

Senior managers will also need to consider the adequacy of existing oversight, delegation and testing mechanisms and frameworks. Depending on the functionality involved, senior managers should consider aspects of the AI that may require specific oversight, and how they will be made aware, for example, of any unexpected performance or malfunction of the algorithm, or material upgrades to the system, with issues being escalated appropriately. As discussed further in Section D(4), a key consideration for the responsible senior manager will be to assess the appropriate degree of human involvement in a particular deployment of AI (for example, 'human-in-the-loop', 'human-on-the-loop' or 'human in command'), as discussed in Section D(4) below. The appropriateness of a particular framework for human involvement will depend on the specific context of the deployment, including the senior manager's confidence in the model's performance and its explainability, among other things; where significant human involvement would negate the commercial rationale for a particular deployment (for example, in the context of trading algorithms), the senior manager should be confident that the broader control and risk management framework surrounding the deployment meets the required standard of the steps a reasonable senior manager would take to avoid any regulatory breach. Where there are high degrees of adherence to the output of an algorithm, it will also be important to document ongoing testing and review of the algorithm's outputs, evidencing that the algorithm is performing as expected and in line with applicable regulatory requirements, in order to avoid any inference of an abdication of human involvement or failure properly to discharge appropriate oversight or other regulatory responsibilities (see, for example, Section D(3) below).

Equally, the deployment of some AI models (including certain highly complex and/ or black-box algorithms) may be inconsistent with the obligations of a senior manager without measures to mitigate the risk of regulatory breaches. That will be the case where, owing to the features of an AI model or the circumstances of its deployment, the risk of a contravention is not capable of proper assessment or is unacceptably high, such that the only course of action the reasonable senior manager could be expected to take would be to require changes to the deployment (for example, by requiring a 'human-in-the-loop' deployment) or to abandon the deployment. For example, the senior manager requirements may preclude certain deployments of some black-box models where the senior manager is otherwise incapable of assessing (and therefore ensuring appropriate steps are taken to mitigate) the risk of regulatory breaches given the unpredictability of the model, unless certain steps can be taken to manage those risks. These issues are discussed further in Section D(4) below.

(ii) *Non-SM&CR firms* – While not all firms are subject to SM&CR, in some cases other governance and accountability requirements will apply under applicable regulation. The requisite standard will be dependent on the relevant regulatory framework.

For example, UK-regulated payment institutions and e-money institutions, while not currently subject to any regime comparable to the SM&CR, are required to identify directors and other persons responsible for the management of the firm as well as its payment services activities and/or e-money issuance, along with supporting evidence as to the individuals' reputation and knowledge and experience.[80] This means that if, for example, a payment institution were to use an AI tool in discharging its regulatory obligations in connection with its payment services activities, such as safeguarding[81] (for example, to allocate relevant funds between safeguarded accounts in a manner that maximises interest), certain individuals responsible for the firm's management or the management of its payment services would, as part of that institution's general application process, have been identified to the FCA, and the FCA would have satisfied itself as to the knowledge and experience of those individuals as part of the application process. Then, if the AI tool malfunctions or otherwise causes the firm to breach its regulatory obligations (for example, in the context of the safeguarding example, by transferring relevant funds to a general account of the institution as opposed to a safeguarded account), the FCA will be able to identify the individual responsible for the management of the firm or its payment services, but there would be no statement of responsibilities mapping the function within which the breach occurred to a specific senior manager. Furthermore, unlike for SM&CR firms, the FCA's enforcement powers would be exercisable against the firm and not directly against that individual.[82]

3.   Explainability, Transparency and Fairness

One of the most unique challenges AI systems pose for effective governance and oversight (among other things) is their heightened potential for opacity. Ensuring 'explainability' and 'transparency' of AI has thus been another priority area for regulators,[83] as has tackling issues of 'fairness'[84] that stem from opacity.   **15.038**

As a starting point, it is helpful to distinguish these terms.   **15.039**

(i) *Explainability* – While often used interchangeably, the concepts of transparency and explainability can be viewed as two related but distinct concepts. Explainability, in

---

80   See Payment Services Regulations 2017, SI 2017/752 (as amended) (PSRs), reg. 6(7)(b) and Sch. 2, para 14; Electronic Money Regulations 2011, SI 2011/99 (as amended) (EMRs), reg. 6(6)(b) and Sch. 1 para 9; and FCA payment services approach document (Approach Document), paras 3.96–3.110.

81   As required under PSRs, reg. 23 and EMRs, reg. 20.

82   Approach Document, Section 14.

83   See, for example, FCA blogpost on *AI transparency in financial services – why, what, who and when?*, available at www.fca .org.uk/insight/ai-transparency-financial-services-why-what-who-and-when accessed 25 March 2021; FCA blogpost on *Explaining why the computer says 'no'*, available at www.fca.org.uk/insight/explaining-why-computer-says-no accessed 25 March 2021; and IOSCO AI Final Consultation Report, Measure 5.

84   See, for example, Information Commissioner Office's guidance on AI and data protection, available at https://ico .org.uk/for-organisations/guide-to-data-protection/key-data-protection-themes/guidance-on-ai-and-data-protection/ accessed 25 March 2021 and IOSCO AI Final Consultation Report, Measure 6.

a narrow sense, refers to the ability of a model to produce outputs that can be coherently rationalised or interpreted by reference to the corresponding inputs and the features of the model itself. Explainability is thus one (but not the sole) component of transparency.

(ii) *Transparency* – Transparency is a broader concept and relates to who has visibility of what information and in what form. For that purpose: the 'who' may include internal stakeholders (such as operators, controllers, risk managers, internal auditors and senior management) or external stakeholders (such as regulators, external auditors and end-users); the 'information' may include anything relevant to the use of AI, including the fact that AI has been used, how the model works, the presence and effects of any data biases and/or explanations as to the relationships between inputs and outputs; and the 'form' relates to how the information is packaged and presented so as to be meaningful to the relevant stakeholder.

(iii) *Fairness* – In the context of AI, fairness typically refers to whether AI-based decisions concerning the end-users are both fair in fact (for example, free from harmful biases and discrimination) and capable of being understood and challenged. In this sense, explainability and transparency have direct implications in relation to fairness.

15.040 Under existing financial regulation, these concepts translate into various standards and requirements, which depend in turn on several factors, including the type of institution, the area of application and the stakeholder in question.

15.041 All regulated firms in the UK are subject to certain general conduct requirements that touch on these issues, particularly in relation to fairness. These include obligations to:

(i) pay due regard to the interests of customers and treat them fairly;[85]

(ii) pay due regard to the information needs of clients, and communicate information to them in a way which is clear, fair and not misleading;[86] and

(iii) take reasonable care to ensure the suitability of their advice and discretionary decisions for any customer who is entitled to rely upon their judgement.[87]

15.042 However, while these conduct requirements impose broad-brush obligations that are of relevance in this context, they are open to a considerable degree of interpretation when it comes to the use of AI. For example, it is not at all clear from these rules whether firms need to tell their customers or regulators anything about their use of AI or what, if anything, a firm needs to do to address data biases. There have, in fact, been calls for regulators to consider boosting regulation in this area, for example by specifically requiring firms to disclose meaningful information to consumers and clients around their use of AI that impact client outcomes; by specifying what type of information they (as regulators) may require from firms using AI to ensure they can have appropriate oversight of those firms; and by requiring firms to have in place appropriate controls to ensure that the data upon which the AI system is dependent is of sufficient quality to prevent biases and sufficiently broad for the system to be well founded.[88]

---

85   FCA Handbook, PRIN 2.1.1, principle 6.
86   FCA Handbook, PRIN 2.1.1, principle 7.
87   FCA Handbook, PRIN 2.1.1, principle 9.
88   IOSCO AI Final Consultation Report, Measures 5 and 6.

While financial regulation may not currently impose many requirements that directly relate to **15.043** explainability, transparency or fairness, there are myriad other requirements that may none-theless have very specific implications in this context. For example, as discussed in Section D(2) above, most firms are required to have in place effective processes to identify, manage, monitor and report risks and internal control mechanisms, including effective control and safeguard arrangements for information processing systems. The efficacy of such processes and arrangements will undoubtedly necessitate a certain degree of explainability and transparency, depending on the precise application and the relevant regulatory framework (as discussed further in the following sections).

In addition, cross-sectoral rules, particularly in relation to data protection and consumer pro-   **15.044** tection, may also be highly relevant in this context (depending on the application), though they fall outside the scope of this chapter.[89]

So, how should firms approach these issues in practice? Given that different legal requirements   **15.045** (including, but not limited to, requirements under financial regulation) will be relevant in different circumstances, it would be advisable for firms to undertake, at an early stage (prior to deployment), a legal analysis in respect of the proposed application to determine the legal requirements and standards that are relevant.

Taking that into account, the FCA recommends that firms consider exactly who should be   **15.046** made aware of what information and in what form, by constructing a 'transparency matrix'.[90] In designing this matrix, firms would also be well advised to consider factors other than hard legal obligations, particularly given the potential regulatory gaps in these areas. In particular, the European and G20 soft law principles and guidance, as outlined in Section C(2) above, provide some specific guidance around these issues in the context of AI and may be a helpful resource. As noted above, it will be important to ensure that each relevant stakeholder receives an explanation in an appropriate form, whether that is a high-level explanation suitable for a consumer with limited technical knowledge or a detailed breakdown of the source code and data for an auditor, and this will require careful consideration.[91]

Once the transparency needs are understood, firms will need to consider whether it is possi-   **15.047** ble for the potential AI tool to meet those needs in practice. Among other things, this may require firms to consider if and how the underlying algorithm can be made explainable. Some algorithms are designed to be explainable by nature from the outset and may, for example, provide explanations as an output of each computation. Other algorithms (that is, black-box algorithms) may be inherently unexplainable; however, their workings may still be analysed

---

89   For example, under Article 22 GDPR, data subjects have the right not to be subject to any decision based solely on automated processing, including profiling, which significantly affects them.

90   See FCA blogpost on *AI transparency in financial services – why, what, who and when?* available at www.fca.org.uk/insight/ai-transparency-financial-services-why-what-who-and-when accessed 25 March 2021.

91   For further guidance in relation to forms of explanation see, for example, Bank of England Staff Working Paper No. 816, *Machine learning explainability in finance: an application to default risk analysis* (August 2019), available at www.bankofengland.co.uk/-/media/boe/files/working-paper/2019/machine-learning-explainability-in-finance-an-application-to-default-risk-analysis.pdf accessed 25 March 2021, p. 3, The Royal Society, *Explainable AI: the basics, policy brief-ing*, available at https://royalsociety.org/-/media/policy/projects/explainable-ai/AI-and-interpretability-policy-briefing.pdf accessed 25 March 2021, p. 13 and ACPR Governance of AI in FS Report, at pp. 14–18.

through a process of reverse engineering, for example by subjecting them to a series of selected inputs in order to reveal certain properties.[92]

15.048   Addressing transparency needs may also require an analysis of the wider model, by reference to one or more datasets, for example to identify any harmful biases. Undetected biases can lead to a variety of issues, including in relation to both performance and discrimination. However, the field of bias detection and mitigation is a developing one, and firms should be mindful that it may be not be possible to detect and mitigate adequately all relevant biases in relation to a particular model.[93] It will be important for firms assessing AI deployments to understand and acknowledge these types of limitations.

15.049   Matters may be further complicated where components of the AI model derive from third party sources. If the firm does not itself have full access to all relevant information concerning the model, it may be necessary to establish effective ongoing communication channels with the relevant third party in order to meet transparency needs, as discussed further in Section D(5) below.

15.050   Once a firm has conducted this analysis in relation to a potential deployment, they will need to determine whether it is feasible in practice to meet the requirements of the transparency matrix. AI applications that are incapable of meeting the requisite requirements may need to be aborted or adjusted.

15.051   These issues are considered in detail in Chapter 29.

4.   Control and Risk-management

15.052   As discussed in Section D(2) above, in order to meet regulatory requirements in relation to governance, most firms need to have in place effective processes to identify, manage, monitor and report the risks it is or might be exposed to and internal control mechanisms, including effective control and safeguard arrangements for information processing systems[94] or similar. This will include systems and controls to ensure regulatory compliance, among other things. As noted, some areas of financial regulation include specific requirements around the nature of the control and risk-management systems for particular activities, for example in relation to algorithmic trading (as discussed in Section E(2) below).

15.053   Often, financial services firms will employ three lines of defence in managing internal risks – operational management (first line); risk management and compliance (second line); and internal audit (third line).[95] The use of AI can introduce certain complications for all three functions. Indeed, many UK firms have identified the need for their risk management frame-

---

92   European Commission, *JR technical report on robustness and explainability of artificial intelligence* (2020), available at https://ec.europa.eu/jrc/en/publication/robustness-and-explainability-artificial-intelligence accessed 25 March 2021.

93   ACPR Governance of AI in FS Report, p. 9.

94   See, for example, FCA Handbook, SYSC 4.1.1 and PRA Rulebook, CRR Firms, General Organisational Requirements 2.1.

95   The Institute of Internal Auditors, IIA Position Paper: *The three lines of defense in effective risk management and control* (2013), available at https://global.theiia.org/standards-guidance/recommended-guidance/Pages/The-Three-Lines-of-Defense-in-Effective-Risk-Management-and-Control.aspx accessed 25 March 2021.

works to evolve in light of the unique features of machine-learning.[96] We discuss some of the main concerns below.

(i)   *Explainability and transparency* – The relevant individuals in each line of defence will need to receive sufficient information in an appropriate form in order to perform their functions effectively. The information they need will differ depending on their precise roles. For example, operational managers tasked with daily oversight may require an explanation that enables them to verify the model's efficacy in relation to business objectives, whereas an auditor may require access to the source code and training data in order to verify that the algorithm's implementation is consistent with its specifications.[97] As discussed in Section D(3) above, explainability and transparency can often pose challenges in the context of AI and need to be considered and addressed on a case-by-case basis. For example, firms may need to consider how (and indeed whether it is possible) to obtain explanations in relation to the behaviour of an algorithm, to identify the presence of biases in the data and/or to access relevant information held by third parties. In any case, existing processes and communication channels may need to be adjusted to ensure that each function receives (and is in a position to act on) the information it needs.

(ii)   *Expertise* – As well as receiving the relevant information, individuals tasked with oversight need sufficient knowledge, training and expertise to interpret the relevant information meaningfully in order to exercise effective oversight. While this requirement is arguably implicit under existing rules, it has also been recommended that regulators should specifically require firms to have the adequate skills, expertise and experience to develop, test, deploy, monitor and oversee the controls over the AI that the firm utilises and that compliance and risk management functions should be able to understand and challenge the algorithms that are produced.[98] It is important to ensure that the relevant team has not only the requisite technical skills but also the ability to manage processes so that they evolve to remain effective in light of technological developments. In some cases, this may require completely new skillsets and the recruitment of new talent will be necessary. It may be prudent for firms to assess regularly their personnel, recruitment policies and training frameworks.

(iii)   *Testing and control* – As discussed in Section B(1) above, unlike traditional algorithms, machine-learning algorithms may recalibrate or readjust key model parameters throughout their lifecycles, on a continuous or periodic basis, to take account of new input data. This means that they may not perform consistently when faced with the same input data at two different points in time. Moreover, controls that rely on testing and approvals at the pre-deployment stage may be insufficient to ensure the model remains fit for purpose throughout its lifecycle. Certain models may also be 'overfitted' to the test data and ill-suited to generalisation – that is, the power to perform well when faced with new data. This means that even if they exhibit high degrees of accuracy in relation to test data, that may not translate when the tool is deployed in a live environment.

In light of these issues, firms should consider carefully the adequacy of testing and control processes and adjust them as appropriate. This may, for example, require models

---

96   BofE/FCA Report, p. 13.
97   ACPR AI Governance Report, pp. 14–18.
98   IOSCO AI Final Consultation Report, Measure 3.

to be monitored and tested on a more continuous basis, and for testing to be conducted in an environment that is segregated from the live environment.[99]

In terms of ongoing monitoring, the EC Ethical AI Guidelines outline three different types of human review processes which may be appropriate depending on the circumstances: (i) human-*in*-the-loop mechanisms (which require human sign-off on every decision); (ii) 'human-*on*-the-loop' mechanisms (which provide for human intervention during the design cycle of the system and monitoring the system's operation); and 'human-in-command' mechanisms (which provide for a human to oversee the overall activity of the AI system and decide when and how to use the system in any particular situation, including the ability to decide not to use the system at all).[100] The list of considerations set out under Requirement 1 of the ALTAI is also a useful reference to help firms approach the issue of human oversight. Automated monitoring and alert generation mechanisms can also be a useful tool in the detection of unintentional model drift (which may occur as a result of continuous recalibration). Automated monitoring systems may be used, for example, to detect structural changes to the input data.[101]

(iv) *Ability to meet applicable regulatory standards* – As outlined in Section B(1), whereas the output of a rules-based algorithm is pre-determined and can be predicted with certainty up front, a machine-learning algorithm is generally considered 'successful' if it achieves a certain *degree* of accuracy. This can pose a significant challenge when it comes to meeting regulatory standards. For example, if the relevant standard is an absolute one (such as a requirement to maintain a minimum level of regulatory capital) then a firm could not rely on a model that by design will admit exceptions, to demonstrate compliance. On the other hand, if the relevant regulatory standard allows for some reasonable degree of error (for example, a requirement to 'manage effectively' the risks of money laundering and terrorist financing[102]), then a machine-learning algorithm could be capable of meeting the requisite standard, notwithstanding a less than perfect accuracy ratio.

(v) *Accountability* – Ensuring accountability in relation to AI systems also poses unique challenges. A particular concern is that it may not always be possible to trace whether issues are a function of algorithmic design, data quality or implementation, and thus where accountability should fall. This issue requires particular attention when it comes to the use of third parties, as discussed in Section D(5) below.

15.054 In advance of deployment, it will be important for firms to consider all relevant risks as against the controls and risk-management frameworks already in place and analyse whether changes are needed in order to address any exposures. This will necessarily need to be conducted on a case-by-case basis, by reference to all applicable legal requirements and circumstances. In relation to some applications, it may be helpful for firms to consider certain elements of the algorithmic trading rules (as discussed in Section E(2)), which already impose very prescriptive requirements to guard against some of the risks involved in algorithmic (albeit not specifically machine-learning based) decision-making. Again, firms will need to be ready to abort or adjust

---

99   As recommended under IOSCO AI Final Consultation Report, Measure 2, for example.
100   EC Ethical AI Guidelines, 1.1.
101   ACPR Governance of AI in FS Report, p. 11.
102   As per MLRs, reg. 19(1)(a).

any proposed AI solutions if it becomes clear that it is not feasible to put in place controls and risk management frameworks that are effective in the circumstances.

5.   Outsourcing, Third Party Service Provision and Operational Resilience

While outsourcing, relationships with third party service providers and operational resilience are not novel issues in financial services or unique to AI, they are particularly relevant in the context of AI systems given that (i) individual components of AI models and/or underlying infrastructure and platforms and/or 'AI as a Service' are often provided by third parties (as discussed in Section B(3) above); and (ii) the nature of third party services provided to a firm in this context (that is, complex technical services, often on a large scale) can have meaningful implications in relation to the firm's operational resilience.   **15.055**

A regulated institution's relationship with a third party may or may not amount to an out-sourcing. Different definitions of 'outsourcing' apply in different contexts and trigger specific requirements. For the purposes of the application of the general outsourcing rules in the FCA Handbook,[103] the test is whether the service provider 'performs a process, a service or an activ-ity which would otherwise be undertaken by the firm itself'. A materially similar definition is found in the EBA Guidelines.[104] Although the EBA Guidelines also apply to payment service providers and e-money issuers, the test for certain requirements[105] under the PSRs and EMRs, respectively, is slightly different (being, broadly, whether another person will carry out any operational function relating to the payment or e-money services, respectively).   **15.056**

There will often be nuanced questions to be considered as to whether arrangements with a third party in connection with a firm's deployment of software (including AI) amount to an outsourcing. This will depend on the precise nature of the arrangement, and AI arrangements do not appear to raise particular conceptual challenges beyond those for other arrangements with third parties.   **15.057**

Specific requirements or guidance (as applicable) apply in relation to critical functions[106] or where there is an outsourcing of important operational functions, including, for example, that when relying on a third party for the performance of critical operational functions[107] on a continuous basis firms take reasonable steps to avoid undue additional operational risk and they do not undertake the outsourcing of important operational functions in such a way as to impair materially (i) the quality of their internal control and (ii) the ability of the FCA/PRA,   **15.058**

---

103   FCA Handbook, SYSC 8 (Outsourcing).

104   An outsourcing is 'an arrangement of any form between an institution, a payment institution or an electronic money institution and a service provider by which that service provider performs a process, a service or an activity that would otherwise be undertaken by the institution, the payment institution or the electronic money institution itself'. EBA, *Final Report on EBA Guidelines on outsourcing arrangements*, 25 February 2019 (the EBA Guidelines).

105   This definition drives a notification requirement PSRs, reg. 25(1) and EMRs, reg 26(1)), and flows into the require-ments in relation to the outsourcing of important operational functions (PSRs, reg. 25(2) and EMRs, reg. 26(2).

106   Whether or not there is an 'outsourcing' (see FCA Handbook, SYSC 8.1.1 and SYSC 8.1.1A).

107   That is, operational functions which are critical for the performance of regulated activities, listed activities or ancillary services.

as applicable, to monitor compliance.[108] Further requirements may also apply depending on the nature of the firm.[109] A detailed assessment of these and the outsourcing requirements as applicable to regulated firms is beyond the scope of this work.

15.059 Even in relation to arrangements with third party service providers which do not amount to an outsourcing (including of important operational functions), firms still need to meet their broader obligations, notably to take reasonable care to organise and control their affairs responsibly and effectively, with adequate risk management systems,[110] with regard to establishing and maintaining appropriate systems and controls in the context of the third party arrangement,[111] and to have in place robust governance arrangements including effective processes to identify, manage, monitor and report risks and internal control mechanisms[112] (as applicable). Importantly, regulated institutions remain fully responsible for discharging all their obligations under the relevant sectoral legislation, notwithstanding any relationship with a third party (including any outsourcing).[113]

15.060 In the UK a new operational resilience regime is also due to come into effect soon, which will include further requirements in relation to outsourcing and third party service provision. From March 2022, regulated institutions in the UK will be subject to the upcoming rules of the FCA[114], PRA[115] or Bank of England,[116] depending on the nature of the institution. In the EU, the European Commission has also proposed draft legislation in respect of digital operational resilience.[117]

15.061 In meeting these types of regulatory obligations, and administering effective risk-management more generally, there are various practical issues firms should consider (even if not currently prescribed under applicable regulation). We have sought to highlight key issues of particular relevance in the context of AI below. We have not, however, made any attempt to summarise exhaustively the general regulatory requirements under the (existing or proposed) regimes outlined above (which would need to be considered in detail but are outside the scope of this chapter). It is advisable for these types of issues to be addressed before any third party service provider relationship or outsourcing arrangement is entered into, as it is often difficult to mitigate the relevant risks if they have not been anticipated in advance.[118]

---

108 See, for example, FCA Handbook, SYSC 8.1.1 and 8.1.1A; PRA Rulebook, CRR firms, General Organisational Requirements 2.1; reg. 25(2) PSRs and reg. 26(2) EMRs

109 Commission Delegated Regulation (EU) 2017/565 of 25 April 2016 as regards organisational requirements and operating conditions for investment firms (MiFID Org Regulation) [2016] OJ L87, 31.3.2017, pp. 1–83. See also the EBA Guidelines, which distinguish in places as to the relevant type of institution.

110 See, for example, FCA Handbook, SYSC 1.2.1 (2).

111 See, for example, FCA Handbook, SYSC 3.1.1.

112 See, for example, FCA Handbook, SYSC 4.1.1.

113 See, for example, MiFID Org Regulation, Article 31 and FCA Handbook, SYSC 8.1.6.

114 FCA PS 21/3.

115 PRA PS 6/21.

116 Available at www.bankofengland.co.uk/paper/2021/bank-of-england-policy-on-operational-resilience-of-fmis.

117 Commission, 'Proposal for a Regulation of the European Parliament and of the Council on digital operational resilience for the financial sector and amending Regulations (EC) No 1060/2009, (EU) No 648/2012, (EU) No 600/2014 and (EU) No 909/2014' COM (2020) 595 final.

118 ACPR Governance of AI in FS Report, p. 29.

(i)   *Third party provider or outsourcing strategy* – It is advisable to adopt a clear strategy on the use of third party providers and the management of outsourcing risks including in the context of AI, which is subject to regular review. This may then be translated into clear policies that dictate the circumstances in which reliance on third parties or outsourcing is permitted, to ensure that every branch of the firm takes a unified approach which is consistent with the strategy set by senior management.[119]

(ii) *Due diligence* – It is important that firms conduct sufficient due diligence when selecting a service provider. In relation to AI-related services, this may include investigations in relation to operational aspects (for example, regarding interoperability, reliability, security and resilience); commercial and legal aspects (such as limitations on liability, dependency issues and risks of vendor lock-in, as discussed in items (v), (vi) and (vii) below); compliance issues (such as ability to meet data protection and confidentiality requirements, as discussed in item (iv)); and a consideration of the potential provider's knowledge, expertise and experience. The review should also take into account the possibility of the service provider sub-contracting the outsourced functions, which may amplify certain risks.[120]

(iii) *Access to information* – As outlined in Section D(3) above, it is advisable for financial institutions to establish transparency frameworks, based on the applicable use case. Transparency may be required (or advisable) for direct compliance purposes or for broader control and risk-management purposes. In line with the agreed framework, the firm will need to ensure it has access to all relevant information it needs from third parties, such as source code, data and development processes, and that it is able to keep track of all relevant updates. As part of this, firms may need to establish ongoing processes and communication channels for third parties to report changes and/or potential issues. Firms will also need to ensure that regulators and external auditors are able to obtain all information needed for the performance of their functions and in order for the firm to meet its regulatory obligations. Detailed frameworks and processes for the sharing of information should be established and agreed up front.[121]

(iv) *Data security* – Given the importance of data for AI, data security is likely to be a key concern in relation to outsourcing, and firms will need to consider carefully how they meet their legal and regulatory obligations in this respect (including under data protection laws and contractual agreements).[122]

(v)   *Accountability and liability* – To provide accountability in relation to AI systems, it is important to establish mechanisms that facilitate traceability, such as detailed records in relation to the development process and the sourcing of software and data. Other important considerations include the monitoring and oversight of third party performance and comprehensive contractual allocation of responsibilities and liabilities. As part of this, it may be helpful to have clear performance indicators for third party service

---

119   See also specific requirements in relation to outsourcing policies under the EBA Guidelines (EBA Guidelines, paras 41–44).

120   See also specific requirements in relation to due diligence under the EBA Guidelines (EBA Guidelines, paras 69–73).

121   See also specific requirements in relation to access, information and audit rights under the EBA Guidelines (EBA Guidelines, paras 85–97).

122   See also specific requirements in relation to security of data and systems under the EBA Guidelines (EBA Guidelines, paras 81–84).

    providers as well as sanctions for poor performance (including termination events where appropriate).[123]

(vi) *Concentration risk* – The engagement of third parties in relation to highly technical and specialist services such as AI can pose concentration risks, both within an institution (if the institution itself has multiple arrangements with a single provider) and within a sector (where multiple institutions are heavily dependent on a single provider). This has been a key concern for regulators in recent years.[124] Establishing comprehensive lines of information flow (as discussed in item (iii) above) and having in place effective exit strategies (as discussed in item (vii) below) can be helpful in mitigating concentration risks. Firms should also consider whether such risks can be avoided, for example by maintaining more workstreams in house or by using alternative service providers.[125]

(vii) *Exit strategy* – Another issue firms should consider is the potential for any decision to use a third party service provider to become irreversible in practice. In order to mitigate dependency risks and other commercial and regulatory risks, it is important for firms to maintain the ability to reverse any decisions to use third parties – either by bringing the relevant functions in house or by transferring them to an alternative third party.[126]

(viii) *Business continuity* – In relation to material outsourcing arrangements, business continuity should also be considered. This may include procedures and controls to protect information and software and to ensure continuity of service as well as to enable institutions to be able to exit third party arrangements without disrupting their activities or compliance.[127]

(ix) *Human resources* – A fundamental issue that can be overlooked is the need to ensure that relevant internal teams (including operational, risk-management and audit teams) have the requisite skills and training to manage and oversee third party service arrangements. This may include skills needed not just to understand, validate and challenge technical issues but also to manage complex and multilateral development processes. In some cases, organisations may consider it prudent to have the requisite skills in house to enable the relevant services to be internalised, if needed, as part of a potential exit strategy.

E. SPECIFIC CONSIDERATIONS IN RELATION TO ANTI-MONEY LAUNDERING AND ALGORITHMIC TRADING

15.062 Taking into account the general approach outlined in Section D above, we consider some examples of specific regulatory issues that may arise in relation to particular areas of application. For this purpose, we consider two distinct areas of application: (i) anti-money laundering, as one of the most prevalent use cases for machine-learning; and (ii) algorithmic trading, as an emerging area of AI application where there is already a high degree of prescriptive regulation.

---

123 See also specific requirements in relation to security of data and systems under the EBA Guidelines (EBA Guidelines, paras 74–75).

124 See, for example, IOSCO Principles on Outsourcing Final Consultation Report (FR07/2021), available at www.iosco .org/library/pubdocs/pdf/IOSCOPD654.pdf accessed 16 December 2021, Principle 5.

125 See also specific requirements in relation to security of data and systems under the EBA Guidelines (EBA Guidelines, paras 66 and 103).

126 See also specific requirements in relation to exit strategies under the EBA Guidelines (EBA Guidelines paras 106–108).

127 See also specific requirements in relation to exit strategies under the EBA Guidelines (EBA Guidelines, paras 48–49).

While this is not an exhaustive account of the regulatory analysis, we have sought to highlight certain key issues for consideration.

1. Anti-Money Laundering

Under the MLR, as 'relevant persons' within scope,[128] credit and financial institutions are **15.063** required to take appropriate steps to identify and assess the risks of money laundering and terrorist financing to which their businesses are subject[129] and to establish and maintain policies, controls and procedures 'to mitigate and manage effectively' the risks identified.[130] Cryptoasset exchange providers and custodian wallet providers are also within scope of the MLR,[131] and may or may not (depending on their activities) fall within the scope of financial regulation.

Senior managers have specific obligations in this regard. In particular, senior management must **15.064** approve the relevant policies, controls and procedures[132] and thus must ensure that they are appropriately designed and implemented and effectively operated.[133] Some firms may need to appoint a member of senior management as the officer responsible for anti-money laundering compliance, if appropriate with regard to the size and nature of their business.[134]

The latest Joint Money Laundering Steering Group Guidance for the UK Financial Sector[135] **15.065** (JMLSG Guidance) provides further guidance on the application of the MLRs. These requirements are fairly prescriptive, and firms (notably FCA-regulated firms[136]) should consider them carefully to assess whether any machine-learning models under consideration are capable of meeting the requisite standards and are deployed in a manner that does in fact meet them. For example:

(i) *Customer due diligence* – Firms may wish to deploy machine-learning models to verify the identity of customers by reference to various electronic sources of information in order to meet regulatory obligations in relation to customer due diligence. For this purpose, they may want to use third party organisations to provide, collate and/or verify data from multiple sources.

To meet their regulatory obligations in this area, among other things, firms need to be able to demonstrate that they have both verified that the customer exists and satisfied themselves that the individual seeking the business relationship is in fact the customer.[137]

---

128 These also include non-financial firms, including auditors, legal professionals, estate agents and high value dealers, among others. Cryptoasset exchange providers and custodian wallet providers are also included (MLR, reg. 8(2)).

129 MLR, reg. 18(1).

130 MLR, reg. 19(1).

131 MLR, reg. 8(2)(j) and (k).

132 MLR, reg. 19(2)(b).

133 The Joint Money Laundering Steering Group, *Prevention of money laundering/combating terrorist financing Guidance for the UK Financial Sector*, Part I, 1.1 and FCA Handbook, SYSC 3.1.1, 3.2.6, 6.1.1 and 6.3.1.

134 MLR, reg. 21(1)(a).

135 Available at https://jmlsg.org.uk/guidance/current-guidance/ accessed 25 March 2021.

136 The FCA will have regard to whether a firm has followed relevant provisions of the JMLSG Guidance when considering whether to take action against an FCA-regulated firm in respect of a breach of the relevant provisions in SYSC (see FCA Handbook, SYSC 3.2, SYSC 6.3.5 and DEPP 6.2.3) and considering whether to prosecute a breach of the MLR (see EG 12.1). Firms will thus have to stand prepared to justify any departures from the JMLSG Guidance to the FCA.

137 MLR, reg. 28(2) and JMLSG Guidance, Part I, 5.3.79.

To do this, firms need to be able to understand the basis upon which any particular source is established and whether, and if so how, its compliance with specific criteria is monitored.[138] For an electronic check to provide satisfactory evidence of identity, generally it must either (i) use data from multiple sources, and across time, or incorporate qualitative checks that assess the strength of the information supplied; or (ii) be done through a third party organisation that meets the specified criteria.[139]

If the firm uses a third party organisation, it needs to be satisfied that the information supplied is sufficiently extensive, reliable, accurate, independent of the customer and capable of providing an appropriate level of assurance. The organisation must meet various specified criteria including, for example, transparent processes to enable the firm to know what checks were carried out, what the results of those checks were and what they mean in terms of how much certainty they give as to the identity of the subject.[140] The firm also needs to be able to capture and store evidence of the provider's verification processes, whether that is the information used to verify an identity or a level of assurance provided by the third party provider.[141] Firms also need to ensure that they understand the basis on which any assurance is provided.[142]

There are thus various specific requirements in this area which firms should take into account when selecting potential machine-learning models, designing control and risk-management frameworks and negotiating outsourcing arrangements.

(ii) *Transaction monitoring* – Firms may also want to use machine-learning models to monitor transaction data for unusual activity in order to meet their regulatory obligations to ensure that the transactions are consistent with the firm's knowledge of the customer, the customer's business and the customer's risk profile.[143]

The JMLSG Guidance acknowledges that monitoring systems may be automated to the extent that a standard suite of exception reports is produced.[144] However, it specifies that firms should understand the workings and rationale of the automated system and the reasons for its output of alerts, as it may be asked to explain this to the regulator.[145] This imposes a more concrete standard in relation to explainability than exists in some other areas of financial regulation.

The guidance also notes that monitoring systems can vary considerably in their approach to detecting and reporting unusual or uncharacteristic behaviour and outlines a list of helpful questions which it will be important for firms to consider in selecting an appropriate solution.[146] Some of these questions touch on issues of explainability and transparency as well – for example, whether the functionality exists to provide the user with the reason that a transaction is alerted and whether a full evidential process behind the reason is given.

Firms should thus take these requirements into account when developing any transparency frameworks, as discussed in Section D(3) above.

---

138 JMLSG Guidance, Part I, 5.3.41.
139 JMLSG Guidance, Part I, 5.3.50.
140 JMLSG Guidance, Part I, 5.3.52.
141 JMLSG Guidance, Part I, 5.3.53.
142 JMLSG Guidance, Part I, 5.3.84.
143 As required under the MLR, reg. 28(11)(a).
144 JMLSG Guidance, Part I, 5.7.13.
145 JMLSG Guidance, Part I, 5.7.15.
146 JMLSG Guidance, Part I, 5.7.18.

2. Algorithmic Trading

(a) Application of algorithmic trading rules

Wholesale markets have long made use of algorithms for both investment decisions and **15.066** execution and, in the UK, are specific rules for firms engaged in algorithmic trading, particularly in relation to the systems and controls that a firm must have in place. This regulation is derived from MiFID II[147] and is implemented through the FCA's rules on market conduct[148] and UK RTS 6.[149]

At a high level, a firm must ensure that the systems and controls, including procedures and **15.067** arrangements, used in the performance of its activities are 'adequate, effective and appropriate for the scale and nature of its business'.[150] The rules set out specific requirements in respect of that overall objective. The prescriptive nature of the requirements is helpful in the sense that it provides clear standards for firms to follow when looking to deploy machine-learning algorithms in respect of trading. However, the detail may also potentially present issues given some of the novel features of AI discussed in previous sections. We discuss some of the notable requirements below.

(i) *Organisational structure* – The rules specifically require firms to have a clear and formalised governance arrangement, with clear lines of accountability (including procedures to approve the development, deployment and subsequent updates of trading algorithms and to solve problems identified when monitoring trading algorithms), effective procedures for the communication of information and a separation of tasks and responsibilities between their operational functions on the one hand and their risk control and compliance functions on the other.[151] As discussed in Section D(2) above, firms may need to consider whether their existing governance and oversight structures are adequate to mitigate effectively new potential risks. In particular, firms should consider whether the channels of communication are such that all relevant information flows through to the relevant stakeholders, as needed. Among other things, this may ultimately involve consideration of the potential model and whether and how it can be made capable of explanation (as discussed in Section D(3)).

(ii) *Skills and training* – The rules provide for both the operational staff and the risk management and compliance staff to have the requisite skills to carry out their functions. In particular, operational staff must have sufficient technical knowledge of: the relevant systems and algorithms; the monitoring and testing of such systems and algorithms; the trading strategies deployed through the systems and algorithms; and the firm's legal obligations.[152] Further, their knowledge is required to be maintained through continuous and tailored training and evaluation.[153] Compliance staff are expected to have at

---

147   Directive 2014/65/EU on markets in financial instruments and amending Directive 2002/92/EC [2014] OJ L173/349 ('MiFID II').
148   FCA Handbook, MAR 5.3A, 5A.5 and 7A.
149   Retained Commission Delegated Regulation (EU) No 2017/589 of 19 July 2016 as it forms part of UK law ('UK RTS 6').
150   FCA Handbook, MAR 5.3A.1 and MAR 5A.5.1.
151   UK RTS 6, Article 1.
152   UK RTS 6, Article 3(1).
153   UK RTS 6, Article 3(2)–(3).

least a general understanding of how the systems work and be in continuous contact with people who have detailed technical knowledge.[154] They are also required to have sufficient skills to follow up on information provided by automatic alerts and sufficient authority to challenge the operational team.[155] In the context of increasingly complex models, firms may need to reassess regularly their training programmes and the suitability of existing personnel to meet these requirements in light of technological developments.

(iii)   *Outsourcing/third party services* – The rules specifically state that an investment firm shall remain fully responsible for its obligations in respect of algorithmic trading even where it outsources or procures software or hardware from third parties.[156] Moreover, the firm should have sufficient knowledge and necessary documentation in place to ensure effective compliance with this.[157] The considerations discussed in Section D(5) above will be relevant in this regard.

(iv)   *Testing* – The rules contain a number of specific requirements in relation to the testing of algorithmic trading systems, trading algorithms and trading strategies. An important question in applying these requirements in the context of AI systems is to identify what amounts to the 'algorithm' for this purpose. The relevant algorithm in the definition of 'algorithmic trading' is that which 'automatically determines individual parameters of orders such as whether to initiate the order, the timing, price or quantity of the order or how to manage the order after its submission'.[158] A particularity of many AI algorithms is that they contain rules that determine the parameters of the model itself ('second order rules'), which then, once determined and applied to live data, produce outputs that can determine the 'parameters of orders' as referred to in MIFID II. On one view, those rules that modify the parameters of the model eventually applied in order to trigger an order are not part of the algorithm itself within the meaning of MIFID II. This matters because it goes to the ability to, and means for, discharging obligations under the algorithmic trading rules.

In particular, firms are required to establish clearly delineated methodologies to develop and test systems, algorithms and strategies. In the case of algorithms 'leading to order execution'[159] these methodologies must ensure that: the algorithms do not behave in an unintended manner; they comply with the firm's regulatory obligations; they comply with the relevant trading venue rules and systems; and they do not contribute to disorderly trading conditions.[160] Firms are also required to keep records of any material change made to the software used for algorithmic trading, allowing them to determine when a change was made, the person that has made the change, the person that has approved the change and the nature of the change.[161] Certain testing must take place in a special testing environment rather than a live production environment.[162] The firm is

---

154   UK RTS 6, Article 2.
155   UK RTS 6, Article 3(4).
156   UK RTS 6, Article 4(1).
157   UK RTS 6, Article 4(2).
158   MiFID II, Article 4(1)(39) and FCA Handbook, Glossary, definition of 'Algorithmic trading'.
159   UK RTS 6, Article 5(6).
160   UK RTS 6, Article 5.
161   UK RTS 6, Article 5(7).
162   UK RTS 6, Article 7.

required to retain full responsibility for the testing and for making any required changes to its systems, algorithms and strategies.[163]

Considering these requirements, if it is right that second order rules are not part of the algorithm for the purposes of the algorithmic trading rules, this gives rise to considerable challenges in relation to the deployment of certain AI applications, without particular modification or including specific design features. For example, there would need to be a mechanism for assessing whether the application of the second order rules at any given time gives rise to a substantial update of the trading algorithm (namely, those rules that determine the 'parameters of orders'); if so, a person designated by the senior management would need to authorise the continued operation of the algorithm. Furthermore, the requirement to have in place methodologies to ensure the trading algorithm does not behave in an unintended manner would need to be assessed by reference to those rules that determine the parameters of the orders directly, and not any second order rules. That may simply preclude the deployment of certain AI algorithms, where it is not possible (indeed, it may be a desirable feature) to identify an intended performance with regard to the rules determining the parameters of the orders, even if it is possible at any given time to determine whether the algorithm as a whole, including any second order rules, is behaving as intended (for example, with certain specific limitations or conditions built into the design).

Attempting to distinguish within a complex algorithm those specific rules that do or do not 'determine individual parameters of orders' is fraught with difficulty. Furthermore, even if they could be separately identified, second order rules do determine 'individual parameters of orders' in the relevant sense; they simply do so indirectly and there is no express distinction in the definition of algorithmic trading between different types of rules within an overall algorithm. In our view, the term 'trading algorithm' (and related terms) should therefore be interpreted by reference to the algorithm viewed as a whole.

That does not mean, however, that certain applications that involve using machine-learning will not fall foul of the requirements of the algorithmic trading rules. For example, there must still be an assessment of the intended behaviour of the algorithm, viewed as a whole, in order to establish methodologies to prevent unintended behaviour by reference to that. Expectations as to the parameters of the orders that may be produced by the algorithm should form part of that assessment, and the corresponding methodologies determined accordingly. This will often raise challenging questions, and in certain circumstances it may not be possible to identify an 'intended behaviour' of a particular algorithm overall (taking account of the degree of uncertainty in relation to the expected parameters of the orders), in which case modifications may be required before it can be deployed.

Similarly, even if the application of the algorithmic trading rules is to be assessed by reference to the algorithm as a whole, it may be the case that the application of second order rules does in fact give rise to a substantial update of the algorithmic trading strategy, such that it is necessary to obtain approval by a person approved by the senior management. This may be the case, for example, if there is a clear break or shift in the orders placed by the algorithm (for example, as a result of a structural shift in prevailing macroeconomic or other input data), such that the algorithm may be said to have changed strategy. This will

---

163 UK RTS 6, Article 7(3).

require a case-by-case assessment, in light of the features of the algorithm in question and the performance of the algorithm to date. It is also debatable whether machine-learning algorithms that are subject to continuous ongoing recalibration (without human sign-off) could potentially fall foul of the record-keeping requirements, which require all software changes to be recorded, unless the algorithm is designed specifically to cater for this.

(v)   *Real-time monitoring and alerts* – Under the algorithmic trading rules, firms are required to monitor trading activity and implement real-time alerts which identify signs of disorderly trading or a breach of their pre-trade limits. In addition, they are required to prevent potential market abuse and violations of the rules of the trading venue through specific surveillance systems that generate alerts on the following day at the latest and that are calibrated to minimise false positive and false negative alerts.[164] The types of surveillance systems used in respect of rules-based algorithms may not necessarily be adequate in respect of machine-learning algorithms. For example, new types of monitoring may be required to identify changes in the input data and their effects on the algorithm.

(vi) *Annual self-assessment and validation* – After deployment, firms engaged in algorithmic trading are required to perform an annual self-assessment and validation process to review, evaluate and validate their: trading systems, algorithms and strategies; governance, accountability and approval framework; business continuity arrangement; and overall compliance with the algorithmic trading rules.[165] That self-assessment should allow the investment firm to gain a 'full understanding' of the trading systems and trading algorithms it uses and the risks stemming from algorithmic trading, irrespective of whether those systems and algorithms were developed by the investment firm itself, purchased from a third party or designed or developed in close cooperation with a client or third party.[166] The firm's risk management function is required to produce a validation report, involving staff with necessary technical knowledge. This must be audited by the firm's internal audit function (where such function exists) and be subject to approval by the firm's senior management.[167] As part of this process, the firm is required to stress-test its systems, procedures and controls. The tests must be carried out in a way that does not affect the live production environment.[168] As responsible senior managers are required to sign off on these reports, it will be particularly important for them to ensure that the necessary processes and frameworks are in place to enable them to exercise judgment appropriately.

(vii) *Kill functionality* – A firm engaged in algorithmic trading need to be able to cancel immediately, as an emergency measure, any or all of its unexecuted orders.[169] Firms are also required to have in place arrangements for shutting down the relevant trading algorithm or trading system as part of their business continuity measures.[170] Any potential model under consideration will need to be capable of meeting this requirement.

(viii) *Business continuity* – The rules require firms to have in place business continuity arrangements for their algorithmic trading systems which are appropriate to the nature,

---

164   UK RTS 6, Recital 11, Article 13, Article 16.
165   UK RTS 6, Article 9(1).
166   UK RTS 6, Recital 8.
167   UK RTS 6, Article 9.
168   UK RTS 6, Article 10.
169   UK RTS 6, Article 12.
170   UK RTS 6, Article 14(2)(f).

scale and complexity of their business. These include a range of measures such as governance frameworks for the development and deployment of the business continuity arrangement, identification of possible adverse scenarios, procedures for restoration and alternative arrangements for managing outstanding orders. Firms are required to review and test their business continuity arrangements on an annual basis.[171] In particular, any potential outsourcing arrangements should be considered in light of these requirements, as discussed in Section D(5) above.

(ix)   *Security and limits to access* – Firms engaged in algorithmic trading are required to implement an IT strategy consistent with the firm's business and risk strategy, which is adapted to its operational activities and the risks to which it is exposed. They are required to maintain security arrangements to ensure the confidentiality, integrity, authenticity and availability of data and the reliability and robustness of the firm's information systems. Firms are also required to undertake annual cyber-resilience tests and restrict and trace access to their IT systems at all times.[172] In particular, any potential outsourcing/third party arrangements should be considered in light of these requirements, as discussed in Section D(5) above.

(b) Market abuse concerns

One particular concern around the use of machine-learning algorithms in trading is the risk that the algorithms will engage in market manipulation or other forms of market abuse on behalf of the firm without the firm even being aware, in contravention of market abuse rules.   **15.068**

The UK Market Abuse Regulation[173] specifically contemplates that abusive strategies may be carried out by means of algorithms.[174] If, for example, the algorithm implements a strategy resulting in a placing of orders to a trading venue which has the effect of giving a false or misleading signal as to the demand for a financial instrument (perhaps by buying aggressively in the short term with a view to selling at an artificially inflated price), that could constitute market manipulation, regardless of whether the manipulation was the intention of the firm.[175] Such risks may be heightened with machine-learning models, which, for example, may be more opaque than rules-based models and capable of self-recalibration (as discussed in previous sections).   **15.069**

Under the UK Market Abuse Regulation, firms are required to establish and maintain 'effective arrangements, systems and procedures to detect and report suspicious orders and transactions',[176] in accordance with the applicable technical standards, in order to mitigate these types of risk. However, the firm can still be in breach of the prohibition on market manipulation even if it has taken such measures.[177] Further, while such measures may be helpful in detecting and   **15.070**

---

171   UK RTS 6, Article 14.
172   UK RTS 6, Article 18.
173   Retained Regulation (EU) No 596/2014 of 16 April 2014 on market abuse (market abuse regulation) as it forms part of UK law and as amended by the Market Abuse Exit Regulations 2019) (the 'UK Market Abuse Regulation' or 'UK MAR').
174   UK MAR, recital 38.
175   See UK MAR, Article 12(2) and Article 15 and FCA Handbook, MAR 1.2.3: 'The Market Abuse Regulation does not require the person engaging in the behaviour in question to have intended to commit market abuse.'
176   UK MAR, Article 16.
177   UK MAR, Article 15.

reducing the effects of market abuse, prevention may be a significant challenge, depending on how the model is designed. For example, it may not be feasible to pre-empt potential issues in respect of AI applications that involve algorithms designing and proposing trading strategies that are unchecked by human-review processes. Firms would thus be well advised to consider the potential for market abuse and suitable mitigants *ex ante* as part of the design process.

(c) Legal validity of contracts

15.071 Although contractual validity is generally a matter of private law rather than a direct require-ment of financial regulation, it is worth briefly flagging the issue, not least because firms trading via a trading venue may be required by the rules of the venue to ensure that that their contracts are valid and enforceable.[178]

15.072 The use of AI in algorithmic trading raises the potential concern that a contract entered into by an algorithm on behalf of a particular party in a manner that is inconsistent with that party's intentions may lack contractual force on the basis that it was made without any intention to create legal relations.[179] In practice, this issue may present itself if an algorithm enters into a trade on terms which are wildly off-market. While trading venues typically have in-built protections to guard against this type of risk (so-called fat fingers protections), the situation may well arise if the trade were entered into bilaterally or outside a trade venue.

15.073 In this regard, it is important to note that in determining whether there is an intention to create legal relations, the courts normally apply an objective test:[180] it depends not upon the parties' subjective state of mind, but on whether a reasonable person would conclude, based on the surrounding facts, that the parties intended to create legal relations and had agreed upon all the terms which they regarded or the law requires as essential for the formation of legally binding relations.[181]

15.074 In relation to rules-based algorithmic trading, the courts have not generally had difficulties in finding the requisite intention in circumstances where the parties had committed to transact through algorithmic means and the algorithms had been pre-programmed to communicate all information necessary for contract formation (even if the parties did not know beforehand that the relevant contracts would be entered into and on what basis).[182]

---

178 There are also various provisions under financial regulation that require certain contracts to be valid and enforceable. This applies, for example, where the agreements interact with financial market infrastructures. Principle 1 of the Committee on Payment and Settlement Systems Technical Committee of the International Organization of Securities Commissions, Principles for Financial Market Infrastructures (CPMI PFMIs) requires FMIs to have rules, procedures and contracts that are enforceable in all relevant jurisdictions. This requirement is reflected in Retained Regulation (EU) No 909/2014 on improving securities settlement in the European Union and on central securities depositories (as it forms part of UK law) (UK CSDR), Article 43(2), for example. These FMIs in turn tend to shift the burden in respect of the contractual analysis on to their participants.

179 This being one of the key components for a valid contract under English law. See Chitty on Contracts 33rd ed., Sweet & Maxwell, 2-001.

180 Chitty on Contracts 33rd ed., Sweet & Maxwell, 2-171.

181 *RTS Flexible Systems Limited v Molkerei Alois Müller GmbH & Co KG* [2010] 1 WLR 753 [45].

182 See *Software Solutions Partners Ltd, R (on the application of) v HM Customs & Excise* [2007] EWHC 971, in which the court considered an automated electronic process of contracting between insurers and insurance brokers (on behalf of customers). On the basis that all the information necessary for contract formation was pre-programmed in the software according to the parameters laid down by the insurer, the court found that the insurer had invited the insurance broker to

The use of machine-learning algorithms could potentially increase the scope for a court to **15.075**
find that there had been a fundamental mistake vitiating intention, or (similarly) that, viewed
objectively, one party deploying an AI algorithm cannot have intended to contract at a particular price, for example. However, the use of machine-learning is unlikely to change the analysis
fundamentally. There are, however, many who argue for changing this position, and we may
see the law adapt in the future.[183]

F. POTENTIAL FUTURE DEVELOPMENTS

As the use of AI in financial services continues to develop rapidly, international bodies and **15.076**
regulators have been cognisant that regulatory frameworks and guidance may need to shift
in order to remain appropriate and robust. In the analysis above, we have referred to some of
recommendations that IOSCO has made for the deployment of AI by market intermediaries
and asset managers,[184] for example. The recent growth of Decentralised Finance (DeFi) has
also been testing traditional regulatory models in financial services and prompting questions
around the supervision of AI.

In the UK, the FCA and Bank of England have been co-chairing an AI public–private **15.077**
forum.[185] Among other things, they aim to work with the private sector to identify areas where
regulation or guidance may be useful. Their work is focusing on three topics: data, model risk
management and governance. The FCA is also collaborating with the Alan Turing Institute to
develop best practice around transparency.[186] This is intended to resonate with general guidance
issued by the Information Commissioner's Office on AI and data protection[187] and explaining
decisions made with AI.[188] These initiatives may thus lead to more specific guidance and/
or regulatory amendments in the UK. In considering new regulation, UK policymakers have
previously discussed the need to strike the right balance between being too prescriptive and too
high level,[189] and this sentiment may be indicative of future regulatory proposals in this area.

---

use the software as the medium for contract formation and undertook to be bound by the automatically generated policy
contract, even if the insurer was temporarily unaware of it ([65] and [67]). More recently, the decision was supported
and followed by the Singapore Court of Appeal in *Quoine Pte Ltd v B2C2 Ltd* [2020] SGCA(I) 02 [94]–[103], which
involved a cryptocurrency trading platform.

183   See, for example, Jacob Turner, *Robot Rules: Regulating Artificial Intelligence* (Palgrave Macmillan, 2019).

184   Pursuant to the IOSCO AI Final Consultation Report.

185   See www.bankofengland.co.uk/Events/2020/October/fintech-ai-public-private-forum accessed 25 March 2021.

186   See www.turing.ac.uk/news/ai-transparency-financial-services accessed 25 March 2021.

187   Available at https://ico.org.uk/for-organisations/guide-to-data-protection/key-data-protection-themes/guidance-on-ai
-and-data-protection/ accessed 25 March 2021.

188   Available   at   https://ico.org.uk/for-organisations/guide-to-data-protection/key-data-protection-themes/explaining
-decisions-made-with-ai/ accessed 25 March 2021.

189   See, for example, comments from Mohammed Gharbawi, Bank of England Senior Fintech Specialist, at the *Bank of
England webinar on Artificial intelligence, financial services and the impact of Covid-19*, available at www.bankofengland.co
.uk/events/2020/august/artificial-intelligence-financial-services-and-the-impact-of-covid-19 accessed 25 March 2021.

15.078 It is also worth noting that the European Commission has already proposed a new EU regulatory framework for AI.[190] As well as outlining certain general prohibitions,[191] the framework sets out comprehensive obligations for providers of artificial intelligence that is high-risk for the health and safety or fundamental rights of EU citizens. Limited obligations are also placed on users and other participants in the value chain such as importers and distributors. Some financial sector use cases could be caught as high-risk, for example if they relate to the biometric identification of individuals, the credit scoring of individuals, the recruitment or assessment of employees or law enforcement against individuals. The legal requirements for high-risk AI systems are detailed and extensive and relate to issues such as data and data governance, documentation and recording keeping, transparency and provision of information to users, human oversight, robustness, accuracy and security. They are intended to build on the EC Ethical AI Guidelines. The framework also creates codes of conduct which aim to encourage providers of non-high-risk AI systems to apply voluntarily the mandatory requirements for high-risk AI systems.

15.079 In addition to new regulation, the European Commission is also hoping to develop regulatory and supervisory guidance on the use of AI applications in finance.[192]

15.080 To the extent that any new legislation is applicable in the financial sector, consideration would need to be given to how the new requirements interact with existing requirements under financial regulation. In some areas they may not create a significant additional burden for sophisticated financial actors, given existing sectoral requirements (though additional procedural steps may well be required).

---

190 Available at https://digital-strategy.ec.europa.eu/en/library/proposal-regulation-laying-down-harmonised-rules-artificial-intelligence-artificial-intelligence accessed 28 April 2021.

191 These cover practices that have a significant potential to manipulate natural persons through subliminal techniques beyond their consciousness or exploit vulnerabilities of specific vulnerable groups in order to materially distort their behaviour in a manner that is likely to cause them or another person psychological or physical harm. They also include prohibitions on AI-based social scoring for general purposes done by public authorities and on the use of real time remote biometric identification systems in publicly accessible spaces for the purposes of law enforcement (subject to limited exceptions).

192 See the European Commission's Digital Finance Strategy for the EU, available at https://eur-lex.europa.eu/legal-content/EN/TXT/?uri=CELEX:52020DC0591 accessed 25 March 2021, 4.2.

16

INSURANCE

Stephen Kenny QC and Charlotte Payne

A. INTRODUCTION

This chapter begins with an overview of how the application of AI in connection with the **16.001** conduct of insurance business is likely to transform that business.

It next considers, in general terms, the uses of AI in risk assessment and underwriting. **16.002**

Then, three legal areas are examined where the use of AI in that risk assessment context can be **16.003** expected to generate issues and potential problems. Those areas are:

(a) Unlawful discrimination and the use of illegitimate factors in the assessment of risk.
(b) Data protection and data retention.
(c) The insurers' remedies for misrepresentation and unfair presentation of risk.

16.004 The chapter does not address questions relating to the insurance of liabilities for 'rogue' or malfunctioning AI, or for AI that does not perform as expected or required. The bases upon which a designer, supplier or user of an AI system might be considered legally responsible for its actions and decisions relate primarily to theories of legal liability rather than to insurance. Commentators have, however, now begun to address this topic.[1]

16.005 Doubtless, the transformative effects of AI will raise other issues for law and regulation affecting the analysis of questions relating to insurance. In this chapter we can address only the most immediately predictable ones.

B. AN OVERVIEW OF THE IMPLICATIONS OF AI FOR THE BUSINESS OF INSURANCE

16.006 The current and developing power of AI is, naturally, of colossal significance to the future of insurance underwriting. Assessment of the risk of the happening of an uncertain future event is central to all insurance, and AI can, in many cases, do this far better than any human underwriter.

16.007 But the developing power of AI will have effects well beyond underwriting (although that is the focus of this chapter). Indeed, it can contribute to all aspects of the insurance process, especially any that involve data collection and assessment. For example, it is anticipated that AI sensitive to changes in tone of voice may, in due course, be able to detect dishonesty in spoken statements.[2] From every perspective, the whole industry will be transformed in ways that can only be described as seismic.

16.008 Initial effects will probably be experienced in relation to personal and consumer insurance lines, where AI-powered technology can streamline the handling of high-volume, lower-value transactions and improve the customer experience:

(a) For example, AI has facilitated the creation of 'chatbots' – computers that can meaningfully converse in natural language with humans, to exchange relevant information (at present, in all but the simplest applications, in writing; however, voice communication may not be far behind). This means that, increasingly, communications between insurer and insured, or between insurer and those seeking insurance, can take place electronically. This has obvious implications for the future of insurance brokers and other intermediaries (although it need not spell their complete demise, as the current prevalence of price-comparison websites for motor and other insurances shows).

---

1 See a briefing by CMS Cameron McKenna Nabarro Olswang LLP in 2018 (https://cms.law/en/gbr/publication/artificial-intelligence-consequences-for-professional-indemnity-insurers-when-ai-fails-to-perform) which concludes that 'there may need to be a number of claims, and related coverage disputes, before parties begin to appreciate where the potential exposures for PI insurers truly lie and the market can respond'.

2 How an AI might be trained to do this raises immense difficulty, however: not least because the databases used to do so are likely to be affected by inherent biases, such as against those with particular accents, higher pitches of voice, perhaps certain personality types (those of nervous disposition, for example) and so on. The risk of false positives will be large.

(b)   Claims handling, at least of simpler claims, can also be carried out by, or with the assistance of, AI. In 2018 McKinsey & Co.[3] predicted that by 2030, routine motor collision damage claims would be assessed, and approved, simply on the basis of photographs or video supplied by the insured, the insurer's AI having access to a database of costs of repair of the damage indicated. That prediction proved over-cautious: already today some motor insurers are requiring repairing garages to supply photographic evidence, for an AI to assess repair costs and check repair estimates. In August 2020 it was reported that AXA had developed a smart travel insurance contract that automatically paid compensation to insureds for a delayed flight, because flight delays are recorded directly on a computer-accessible external database. It was also reported that Fukoku Mutual Life was using an AI that reads medical reports and has data on standard recovery processes after surgery or treatment, to flag up potentially fraudulent claims.[4]

(c)   The ongoing explosion of available data on wider and wider areas of human activity and behaviour, and of other unpredictable events, will also be used to re-shape insurance products. McKinsey & Co noted some of the implications of the 'Internet of Things' (IoT) – including access to data wirelessly supplied by personal or home devices, such as health- and activity-monitoring wristwear, domestic appliances, cars, fire and security systems, and so on. In 2018 it posited 'pay-as-you-live' life insurance cover, the periodic premium being adjusted according to the assured's lifestyle, as recorded by a monitoring device that the assured will have agreed to wear each day. Vitality Health now offers this as a basic component of its heath cover. Pay-as-you drive motor cover may also become available. (Indeed, simple IoT devices are already in use to assess an insured's driving style before fixing the periodic premium.[5]) IoT data monitored by claims AI systems might in due course be used to prevent claims or warn against impending risks of damage. It is likely that insurers will, through AI, become more actively involved in ongoing loss prevention.

(d)   McKinsey and Co suggests that, as contract conclusion and claims-handling becomes increasingly automated, the consumer is likely to opt for a more individualised, disaggregated approach to insurance, concluding separate, specialised covers often characterised by usage-based pricing (such as pay-per-mile or pay-per-flight) according to the individual's particular requirements, and that insurers will therefore have to offer a wider range of insurance options and extensions. Easier dealing with insurers will certainly reduce transaction costs, but may well also increase the frequency of claims.

Insurances of larger or more complex commercial risks are however unlikely to be concluded or **16.009** fully risk-assessed by AI, for some time at least; and brokers will continue to have a role in the placing of these contracts, and also in the presentation of claims. But AI systems are already on hand to assist commercial insurers' human staff with risk-assessment, pricing and claims handling; and the trend is certainly toward increasing reliance on them.[6]

---

3   Insurance 2030 – The impact of AI on the future of insurance, 30 April 2018, www.mckinsey.com/industries/financial
-services/our-insights/insurance-2030-the-impact-of-ai-on-the-future-of-insurance#.

4   www.itij.com/latest/long-read/disrupting-insurance-landscape-through-artificial-intelligence-and-deep-learning.

5   Aviva Drive and others use the acclerometer in mobile phones to monitor driving style and to adjust pricing. Cornering speed turns out to be the biggest predictor of driving risk.

6   Fire risk is an area where AI seems likely to become involved: modern 'smart' buildings generate a great deal of data, for example on internal temperatures, fire detection equipment status, water pressure and so on; much of this can be made available to current insurers. That data may in due course be re-packaged and resold for more general risk assessment

C. RISK ASSESSMENT AND UNDERWRITING

16.010 The general historical development of AI has been set out elsewhere in this book. However, in in order to understand what follows, it will be necessary to have in mind the distinction between supervised and unsupervised AIs.

16.011 With an unsupervised AI, the rules of relationship that it will have developed and will be using to perform risk assessment will lie buried deep in impenetrable self-written code, leaving opaque how it actually performs that task: a 'black box' system. For this reason, as will be seen, there are currently objections to the use of unsupervised AI in risk assessment for underwriting. The process by which risk is assessed by an unsupervised system will be essentially unfathomable.[7]

16.012 Computers have been used for at least the past 20 years to assess risk and price contracts for certain consumer lines. For example, motor insurers' websites have long allowed those seeking insurance ('proposers') to input their own information in response to questions, on the basis of which a computer (accessing proprietary databases, and applying a pre-programmed risk-weighting matrix to give appropriate weight to particular advised facts) would calculate an appropriate premium and offer a contract. (Indeed, it is possible to regard this process as involving a primitive form of AI.)

16.013 Deep Learning now drives that process further. The proposer need provide less information, because the AI can consult public databases to gather further data with which to assess the risk.[8] Thus, a car registration number will allow access to the DVLA database, from which the insurer's AI can check its engine type and capacity and its tax and MOT test status. A postcode will allow the AI to consult published crime data for the area. If a proposer/insured agrees to allow access to a suitable GPS-enabled device in his car, data on mileage driven and on driving style may be supplied. The names of the insured and of other proposed drivers may allow the AI to examine social media postings, to glean any information that it considers (on the basis of its developing algorithms) may have an influence on the risk.[9] The AI can of course examine the insurer's own records, both for the proposer and other insureds, to explore any associations between data gathered in relation to the proposed risk and data gathered in relation to other risks and claims. Moreover, motor and other insurers have long had access to proprietary databases of historical, market-wide claims records. Using all this information, an AI can build, by

---

purposes. Infra-red satellite data is already available to check whether factories are, or were, being used for their stated business purposes.

7   There are however currently in development additional systems designed to understand, and express in terms comprehensible to humans, the essential features of the logic in a 'black box' system. These additional systems are called Explicable AI (or XAI). They do not replace the 'black box' system, but rather investigate its operations and report, at the cost of some simplification, on its main features and the key variables controlling a particular output. XAI may, in due course, provide an answer to the current objections to unsupervised systems in the underwriting context.

8   For example, Aviva's Ask It Never initiative was launched in order to substantially cut the number of questions the company posed to customers, but in reality there is a sophisticated system of third-party data collection running in the background.

9   In 2016, Admiral was forced to withdraw plans to use Facebook posts for this purpose. The intended use was said to be contrary to Facebook's platform policy. It also drew criticism from privacy campaigners. See www.theguardian.com/money/2016/nov/02/facebook-admiral-car-insurance-privacy-data. But social media remains a tempting resource for insurers: in many areas there is an now acknowledged correlation between the risk profiles of people you associate with and your own risk profile. The State of New York has permitted its use in risk assessment.

reference to its own perception of associations between its data, an individualised risk profile for the proposer – from which a base premium can be calculated (and from which adjusted premiums, based on optional extensions or exclusions of cover, can be derived).

An important aspect of this process is that an AI can, in principle, conduct its own research **16.014** into any data made available or accessible to it; can explore associations between data points and data sets; and can then self-adjust its own risk profile-building algorithms based on its own assessment of the significance of particular associations. Thus, the individualised risk profile will be built using not only 'provided data' (provided by a proposer of insurance) and 'observed data' (data found in other information made available to it), but also 'inferred data' – individual criteria or characteristics referable to the proposed risk which the AI infers from associations and correlations found between previously unrelated data.[10] One insurer is said to have developed more than 1,000 rating factors for its motor portfolio alone, including whether the proposer drinks tap or bottled water (although some of these data points – and particularly that one – may be related not to risk assessment but to price optimisation practices: see paragraph 16.016 below).

However, for reasons that will be discussed below, it is currently unlikely that risk-assessment **16.015** can be carried out by an unsupervised AI without running a significant risk of unlawful conduct by the insurer concerned.[11] Risk-rating performed by, or with the assistance of, an AI therefore will have to be subject to some human oversight and auditing, both in terms of the data sets made available to it and in terms of the risk-rating rules adopted and applied by the algorithm.

The individualised risk-profiles constructed by the AI will result in risk assessments that have **16.016** been described as 'granular' and 'hyper-personalised'. Indeed, depending on the quantity and accuracy of data available, those assessments can in theory begin to approach 'perfect personalisation', that is, assessing the risk represented by a particular proposer as well as all that available information and current knowledge would permit. One potential issue that may result from this new granularity is that newly discovered indicators of risk may show certain proposers/insureds to be effectively uninsurable on any affordable basis. (The converse is also possible: some of those previously considered uninsurable – for example, some young motorists – may be found to represent less of a risk than previously supposed.) If wide 'insurance deserts' – geographic or social – were to occur, it might in some circumstances prompt government action.[12]

Another consequence of AI assessment of proposers and their risks is that insurers may be able **16.017** to profile proposers in other ways, such as in terms of their price sensitivity, loyalty at renewal or willingness to consider additional protections at higher premium. This sort of profiling is called 'price optimisation' or 'price discrimination', a marketing practice that is widely adopted, not

---

10   The process is sometimes called 'correlation clustering'. For example, with home insurance, satellite data can be used to assess the reflectivity of surrounding surfaces: an indicator of their absorbency, correlating with flood risk.

11   Although XAI (referred to in footnote 7 above) may develop sufficiently to allow a risk-assessing AI to reject and re-work algorithmic rules that employ illegal considerations.

12   Cf. the UK's Flood Re scheme, under which home insurers can opt, for a fixed premium, to transfer the flood risk element of an insurance to a government-sponsored reinsurer supported by an industry-wide levy. This was a response to the perception that some homes were becoming uninsurable by their owners with commercial insurers. The perception was, or has become, true: some postcodes are now 'out of scope' for commercial flood insurance, and multi-variable pricing makes others effectively uninsurable, without the government scheme.

just across insurance markets. While it is controversial, in the UK at least it does not (yet) raise legal or regulatory issues.[13] However, since October 2018, the Financial Conduct Authority has been studying these practices as applied to general consumer insurance and in a recent report it recommended a requirement for retail and motor insurance products that any renewal price be no higher than the equivalent new business price for that customer through the same sales channel.[14]

16.018   From the legal perspective, a more troubling consequence of the autonomy of Deep Learning AI systems is that they can, spontaneously, discover associations and infer risk-relevant individual characteristics which it may be illegal for insurers to take into account when rating a risk. For example, in January 2018, *The Sun* reported[15] that motorists with the name of Mohamed were being charged substantially more than those with precisely the same characteristics but with the name John. Assuming (as must be very likely) that the pricing was AI-driven, it would appear that the AI systems concerned will have discovered an association between insureds with the name Mohamed and higher levels of claim. But, self-evidently, certain names may 'stand proxy for' other characteristics of the insured, on the basis of which it is unlawful to discriminate: in the case of the name Mohamed, for characteristics of race and religion.

D. UNLAWFUL DISCRIMINATION AND THE USE OF ILLEGITIMATE FACTORS IN THE ASSESSMENT OF RISK

1.   Discrimination

(a) The law

16.019   The Equality Act 2010 prohibits unlawful discrimination. Unlawful discrimination falls into two categories: direct discrimination and indirect discrimination.

16.020   Direct discrimination, prohibited by s. 13(1) of the Equality Act 2010, occurs where 'A person (A) discriminates against another (B) if, *because of a protected characteristic*, A treats B less favourably than A treats or would treat others'.

16.021   The protected characteristics for this purpose are those of age; disability; gender reassignment; marriage and civil partnership; pregnancy and maternity; race; religion or belief; sex; and sexual orientation.[16]

---

13   It is however reported that it has been banned by 20 US state insurance regulators: see https://nft.nu/sv/ethics-data-and -insurance-4-developments-worth-watching.
14   www.fca.org.uk/publications/market-studies/ms18–1-general-insurance-pricing-practices-market-study.
15   www.thesun.co.uk/motors/5393978/insurance-race-row-john-mohammed.
16   See Equality Act 2010, s. 4.

Indirect discrimination, contrary to s. 19 of the Act, occurs in the following circumstances: **16.022**

19 Indirect discrimination
(1) A person (A) discriminates against another (B) if A applies to B a provision, criterion or practice which is discriminatory in relation to a relevant protected characteristic of B's.
(2) For the purposes of subsection (1), a provision, criterion or practice is discriminatory in relation to a relevant protected characteristic of B's if—
   (a) A applies, or would apply, it to persons with whom B does not share the characteristic,
   (b) it puts, or would put, persons with whom B shares the characteristic at a particular disadvantage when compared with persons with whom B does not share it,
   (c) it puts, or would put, B at that disadvantage, and
   (d) A cannot show it to be a proportionate means of achieving a legitimate aim.

The protected characteristics for the purposes of s. 19 are the same as those applicable to s. 13, with the exception of pregnancy and maternity.   **16.023**

As can be seen, a person guilty of either form of unlawful discrimination is simply referred to in the Act as 'discriminating'.   **16.024**

Section 29 of the Act covers the provision of services (which includes the provision of insurance). In relation to discrimination, it provides in sub-sections (1) and (2) as follows: **16.025**

29 Provision of services, etc.
(1) A person (a 'service-provider') concerned with the provision of a service to the public or a section of the public (for payment or not) must not discriminate against a person requiring the service by not providing the person with the service.
(2) A service-provider (A) must not, in providing the service, discriminate against a person (B)—
   (a) as to the terms on which A provides the service to B;
   (b) by terminating the provision of the service to B;
   (c) by subjecting B to any other detriment.

But there are specific exemptions applicable to the provision of insurance and other financial services, in Schedule 3 Part 5 of the Act. There is a wholesale exemption in relation to insurance arranged by an employer,[17] and special provision is made for what would otherwise be discrimination on grounds of age and disability.[18]   **16.026**

So far as concerns age discrimination, Schedule 3 para 20A(1) specifies that nothing done in relation to the provision of a financial service can constitute age discrimination, provided however (in sub-para (2)) that: **16.027**

Where A conducts an assessment of risk for the purposes of providing the financial service to another person (B), A may rely on sub-paragraph (1) only if the assessment of risk, so far as it involves a consideration of B's age, is carried out by reference to information which is relevant to the assessment of risk and from a source on which it is reasonable to rely.

---

17   Sch. 3 para 20.
18   Sch. 3 paras 20A, 21. There is also a specific exemption for insurance policies entered into before the Act came into force, on 1 October 2010: Sch. 3 para 23.

16.028   As for discrimination on grounds of disability, Schedule 3 para 21(1) provides that:

> It is not a contravention of section 29, so far as relating to disability discrimination, to do anything in connection with insurance business if—
>
> (a)   that thing is done by reference to information that is both relevant to the assessment of the risk to be insured and from a source on which it is reasonable to rely, and
>
> (b)   it is reasonable to do that thing.

16.029   The Act provides for enforcement of obligations not to discriminate in a variety of ways. In s. 142(1) it provides that a term of a contact is unenforceable 'in so far as it constitutes, promotes or provides for treatment of that or another person that is of a description prohibited by this Act'.[19] But this is of little value in the insurance context: risk assessment will not be the subject of contractual terms. However, s. 114(1) gives the county court (or, in Scotland, a sheriff) the power to determine a claim relating to a contravention of (among other things) s. 29;[20] and available remedies include injunctions and claims for damages on a tortious basis, which may include compensation for injured feelings: s. 119(2).[21]

16.030   It is likely, however, that the greater consequences of a finding, or perception, of unlawful discrimination by an insurer will be in terms of reputational damage, with potential commercial impact.

(b) AI-assisted risk assessment; direct discrimination

16.031   It would clearly be unlawful for an insurer to allow an AI to discriminate directly, for example by applying higher risk ratings to any of the s. 13 protected characteristics. (The prohibition of discrimination on grounds of sex initially came as something of a surprise to many insurers, who had long rated women as representing a lower risk in relation to many forms of insurance. But that effect of the 2010 Act is clear.[22])

16.032   The implications of this for AI-assisted risk assessments for insurers (and more generally) would appear to be as follows:

(a)   The AI's risk assessment algorithms must be supervised to ensure that no weighting *at all* is given to any data (provided, observed or inferred) specifically on a person's gender

---

19   S. 143 provides for the removal or modification of such terms.

20   Subject to a six-month time-limit, starting with the date of the act to which the claim relates, or 'such other period as the county court or sheriff thinks just and equitable': s. 118(1).

21   But, so far as concerns indirect discrimination, where 'satisfied that the provision, criterion or practice was not applied with the intention of discriminating against the claimant or pursuer', the court (or sheriff) 'must not make an award of damages unless it first considers whether to make any other disposal': s. 119((5)(6).

22   It corresponds to the position previously established in EU law under the EU Equal Treatment Directive (2004/113/EC), Article 5 of which specifies that 'the use of sex as a factor in the calculation of premiums and benefits for the purposes of insurance shall not result in differences in individuals' premiums and benefits'. See Association Belge des Consommateurs Test-Achats & others (Case C-236/09), ruling that an exemption permitting 'proportionate differences in individuals' premiums and benefits where the use of sex is a determining factor in the assessment of risk based on relevant and accurate actuarial and statistical data' was invalid.

reassignment, marriage or civil partnership status; pregnancy or maternity status; race; religion or belief; sex; or sexual orientation.[23]

(b) So far as any weighting is given to factors of age or disability, the relevance of those factors where relied upon by an AI can be assumed, since it is the function of the AI to identify factors and associations bearing on the risk to be insured. But there will have to be some human supervision of the data used by the AI for this purpose, to ensure that it is from a source on which it is reasonable to rely (since that is the sort of judgement that an AI is may well not be able to form).

(c) AI-assisted risk assessment; indirect discrimination

The problems of monitoring and preventing *indirect* discrimination by AI systems are much greater. AI systems, in searching data sets and discovering associations between data, are highly likely, indeed almost bound, to develop within their algorithms risk-rating rules that will disproportionately affect, and put at 'particular disadvantage', those with protected characteristics as compared with others. **16.033**

The difficulties can be examined by considering the facts in the *Sun* newspaper report, referred to in paragraph 16.017 above. In that case, it appears that the AI systems had applied an increased risk-weighting to proposers named Mohamed, having discovered an association between insureds of that name and a higher claims record. There can be little doubt that the AI systems would have applied the same weighting to all those named Mohamed, regardless of race or religion[24] – but also that use of that criterion would put Muslims, or those of Middle Eastern race, 'at a particular disadvantage when compared with' others of different religion or race.[25] Put simply, use of the criterion would disadvantage far more Muslims and those of Middle Eastern race, compared with those of other religions and races, and would be *prima facie* discriminatory. **16.034**

The critical matter for judging the lawfulness of any indirect discrimination on the basis of the name Mohamed is therefore whether the insurers could show the use of that criterion to be 'a proportionate means of achieving a legitimate aim' within the meaning of s. 19(2)(c) of the Act. As to that, it is undoubtedly a legitimate aim to ensure that higher premiums are charged to those who represent a greater risk to an insurer. But, while there may be some correlation between insureds named Mohamed and a worse-than-average claims history, deciding whether name-checking of this kind represents a proportionate means of achieving that aim involves a careful judgement: one that AI systems are (as yet) ill equipped to make (or to predict that a court would make). In this particular example, the criterion applied could not be regarded as acceptable, both because its use obviously approximates very closely to direct discrimination on an illegitimate basis (that is, on the basis of race or religion) and because it is likely to be a blunt and, from the individual perspective, an unfair factor in the assessment of risk: some Mohameds may have had a very poor claims history, but many will not have done, and it is unfair to prejudice all Mohameds in the same way. **16.035**

---

23 This addresses *direct* discrimination by AI systems. But the machine will, almost inevitably, discover proxies for relevant but protected characteristics, achieving much the same effect as if it had used the protected characteristic itself. As will be seen, the real dificulties here lie in addressing what may be, even just barely, indirect discimination.

24 Cf. s. 19(2)(a) of the Act.

25 Cf. s. 19(2)(b) of the Act.

16.036   Similar difficulties can be seen in relation to discrimination on grounds of sex. It may be anticipated that certain job descriptions (for example, nurse) may correlate closely with that protected characteristic. If an AI were to apply a risk-rating discount on the basis that the proposed insured is a nurse, it might well be doing so effectively on the basis of sex. Unless it could be shown that female nurses represented a lower risk than, say, female teachers, and that the AI had applied a discount only *by that measure*, it is unlikely that the algorithmic rule applied could be considered a proportionate means of achieving the legitimate aim referred to in the preceding paragraph.

16.037   But not all criteria that correlate both with a worse-than-average claims history and with a protected characteristic will, when applied, necessarily represent illegitimate indirect discrimination. For example, it is known that an insured's postcode can correlate closely with that person's race or religion. Yet postcodes can also be strong indicators of risks of theft and criminal damage, and it is thought that, *to the extent that* they are used to weight such risks (of theft and criminal damage), their use would be proportionate, even if the result would be particularly disadvantageous to persons of certain races or religions: the risk-rating would be causally connected with the established risks of where they live, not with their race or religion. AI systems themselves cannot assess causation, otherwise than through the proxy of correlation. They cannot therefore discern the acceptability or unacceptability of assessing the risks of theft and criminal damage by postcode.

16.038   As can be seen, AI-assisted risk-assessment will require careful human supervision. Where an AI-developed algorithmic rule correlates, or is likely to correlate,[26] with a protected characteristic, human agency will be required to ensure that the AI is not recognising the particular criterion involved as relevant simply because it stands as a close proxy or surrogate for a protected characteristic. Even where a case can be made out that the criterion involved measures a risk factor which is independent of a protected characteristic, some oversight will be needed to ensure that any mark-up or discount applied to the risk-weighting is proportionate to the consequences of differences in that factor, and does not operate as a concealed rating of the protected characteristic.

16.039   How this can be done is a matter of some debate. Assessment of the impact of any change in an algorithm's rating rules, before they are approved for adoption, may have to be part of the process. It may be necessary to conduct periodic audits – perhaps akin to 'mystery-shopper' testing – of rating systems, to identify other hidden biases. But regular human review of, and judgement upon, the algorithm's rating rules is likely to be unavoidable, at least until technologies can develop sufficiently to monitor weighting factors that correlate, or are likely to correlate, with protected characteristics.

---

26   Data on most of the protected characteristics will not be available to the AI, so it may not be able to assess the extent of any correlation itself.

2.   Genetics and Genetic Testing

All insurers who are members of the Association of British Insurers have subscribed to **16.040** a Code,[27] agreed with the UK government, by which they have committed to:

(a)   not requiring or pressuring a proposer to have a predictive or diagnostic genetic test, under any circumstances; and

(b)   not asking for, and not taking into account of, the result of any predictive genetic test (the only exception at present being that if a proposer is applying for life insurance cover of more than £500,000, any predictive genetic test for Huntington's Disease must be disclosed, if asked for[28]).

Despite this Code, some results of genetic testing may become known to the insurer, for **16.041** example though erroneous disclosure of medical reports by a GP or because the proposer considers that the testing results are favourable to him (that is, they reduce his risk). At present, ABI insurers are bound to take account of any disclosed predictive testing results only where it is favourable to the proposer, and otherwise to ignore them.

Sophisticated AI systems are however increasingly likely to be employed by ABI insurers **16.042** in digesting medical reports, and, unless directed otherwise, they will employ their normal risk-profiling techniques in relation to all available data. They will therefore have to be specifically programmed/instructed to make use of supplied data on genetic testing *only* where this would in fact result in a lower risk rating; and otherwise to exclude that data from all further analysis.

There is however nothing wrong with an AI analysing family histories and other available data **16.043** (excluding predictive or diagnostic genetic test results) to identify potential genetic faults and conditions, and then using that data to build a risk profile based on its assessment of the probability of the proposer having such a fault or condition. A human underwriter would do likewise. It is possible that in time, AI systems may in this way – with access to vast data sets – profile genetic risks more accurately than human underwriters currently can.

For further reading on bias and discrimination, see Chapter 22.   **16.044**

E. DATA PROTECTION AND DATA RETENTION

1.   The Law

Regulation (EU) 2016/679 of the European Parliament and of the Council of the European **16.045** Union – the General Data Protection Regulation ('the GDPR') – was promulgated to harmo-

---

27   www.abi.org.uk/globalassets/files/publications/public/genetics/code-on-genetic-testing-and-insurance-final.pdf.   The current Code is the sixth iteration of a long-standing agreement – previously called the Concordat and Moratorium on Genetics and Insurance – originally launched in 2001.

28   The exception is recorded in Appendix I to the Code. The Code contemplates that the ABI may apply to amend that Appendix.

nise privacy and data protection laws across Europe, while protecting the rights of data subjects (that is individuals on whom personal data is held). Its scope extends to non-EU organisations that process European citizens' personal data.[29]

16.046　The operation of the GDPR in relation to AI systems generally is dealt with in Chapter 10. In this section, only a short survey can be attempted of some of the issues most likely to be of concern in connection with the use of AI in developing risk-rating algorithms, and in rating particular risks.[30]

(a) GDPR post-Brexit

16.047　Following the end of the Brexit transition period, on 31 December 2020 the European Regulation itself ceased to apply in the UK. But its provisions were directly incorporated into UK law – with some minor amendments[31] – as 'UK GDPR', by virtue of ss. 2 and 3 of the European Union (Withdrawal) Act 2018.[32]

16.048　If insurers operate in the UK, therefore, or if proposers or insureds are resident in the UK, the GDPR's provisions will therefore very largely continue to apply by virtue of UK GDPR. There has (as yet) been no change made by UK legislation to the core data protection principles, rights and obligations found in the GDPR, and little change to these core elements is expected in the foreseeable future. In what follows, therefore, reference will be made to the GDPR, without explicit reference to the UK version. But insurers need to be aware that it is 'UK GDPR' which now governs the position within the UK. (The text of UK GDPR may be found at www .legislation.gov.uk/eur/2016/679/contents.)

(b) Personal data

16.049　The GDPR controls processing[33] of personal data. It is concerned *only* with *personal* data, which means 'any information relating to an identified or identifiable living individual'.[34] An identifiable living individual means 'a living individual who can be identified, directly or indirectly, in particular by reference to – (a) an identifier such as a name, an identification number, location data or an online identifier, or (b) one or more factors specific to the physical, physiological, genetic, mental, economic, cultural or social identity of the individual'.[35]

29　The Data Protection Act 2018 (the DPA) enacts in English law some additional provisions supplementing the GDPR, and applies a broadly equivalent regime to certain types of processing to which the GDPR itself does not apply. But these details need not concern us here.

30　In particular, no consideration has been given to the restrictions on processing the 'special categories' of personal data, that is, those revealing racial or ethnic origin, political opinions, religious or philosophical beliefs, or trade union membership; or on processing genetic data, biometric data, data concerning health, or data concerning a natural person's sex life or sexual orientation. The reader is referred to Art. 9 GDPR.

31　Set out in the Data Protection, Privacy and Electronic Communications (Amendments etc) (EU Exit) Regulations 2019.

32　The Information Commissioner's Office (ICO) continues to be the independent authority responsible in the UK for upholding data protection rights and duties. The ICO has recently explained the status of GDPR post-Brexit in https:// ico.org.uk/for-organisations/dp-at-the-end-of-the-transition-period/transition-period-faqs/#gdpr.

33　"Processing" means any operation or set of operations which is performed on personal data or on sets of personal data, whether or not by automated means, such as collection, recording, organisation, structuring, storage, adaptation or alteration, retrieval, consultation, use, disclosure by transmission, dissemination or otherwise making available, alignment or combination, restriction, erasure or destruction': Art. 4(2) GDPR.

34　See Art. 4(1) GDPR and s. 3(2) of the DPA.

35　See Art. 4(1) GDPR and s. 3(3) of the DPA.

Under Article 5 GDPR, personal data processed should be only that which is 'adequate, rele- **16.050**
vant and limited to what is necessary in relation to the purposes of which it is being processed'.[36]
Further, the personal data must be kept in a form which permits identification of data subjects
for 'no longer than is necessary for the purposes for which the personal data are processed'.[37]
But there is no objection, thereafter, to stripping a database of all data that would permit identification of data subjects. Data thus anonymised can be used, transferred and sold, without
restriction.

Under Article 6.1 GDPR, processing of personal data is permissible only on one or more of six **16.051**
legal bases. For present purposes the following bases are potentially relevant:

(a)   the data subject has given consent to the processing of his or her personal data for one or more
specific purposes;
(b)   processing is necessary for the performance of a contract to which the data subject is party or in
order to take steps at the request of the data subject prior to entering into a contract;
[...]
(f)   processing is necessary for the purposes of the legitimate interests pursued by the controller or by
a third party, except where such interests are overridden by the interests or fundamental rights
and freedoms of the data subject which require protection of personal data, in particular where
the data subject is a child.

(c) Duties of the data controller, and the data subject's access rights

The data 'controller' is the person who determines the purposes and means of processing of **16.052**
personal data.[38] (For present purposes, the insurer can be considered the relevant controller.)
The controller is subject to various duties, including, under Art. 13 GDPR, a duty to provide
certain information to data subjects concerning the use of data *collected from the data subject*. The
data to be provided includes (under Art. 13.1):

(c)   the purposes of the processing for which the personal data are intended as well as the legal basis
for the processing;
(d)   where the processing is based on point (f) of Article 6(1), the legitimate interests pursued by the
controller or by a third party

and (under Art. 13.2):

(a)   the period for which the personal data will be stored, or if that is not possible, the criteria used
to determine that period;
(b)   the existence of the right to request from the controller access to and rectification or erasure of
personal data or restriction of processing concerning the data subject or to object to processing
as well as the right to data portability;
(c)   where the processing is based on point (a) of Article 6(1) or point (a) of Article 9(2), the existence of the right to withdraw consent at any time, without affecting the lawfulness of processing
based on consent before its withdrawal;
(d)   the right to lodge a complaint with a supervisory authority;
(e)   whether the provision of personal data is a statutory or contractual requirement, or a requirement necessary to enter into a contract, as well as whether the data subject is obliged to provide
the personal data and of the possible consequences of failure to provide such data;

---

36   See Art. 5(c) GDPR.
37   See Art. 5(e) GDPR.
38   Art. 4(7) GDPR.

(f)   the existence of automated decision-making, including profiling, referred to in Article 22(1) and (4) and, at least in those cases, meaningful information about the logic involved, as well as the significance and the envisaged consequences of such processing for the data subject.

16.053 Art. 14 GDPR creates a separate duty to provide data subjects with information about processing of any of their personal data *not obtained from them*, including (under Art. 14.1) information about:

(c)   the purposes of the processing for which the personal data are intended as well as the legal basis for the processing;

(d)   the categories of personal data concerned.

16.054 Art. 14.2 lists information to be provided covering the same matters as listed under Art. 13.2, and also:

(b)   where the processing is based on point (f) of Article 6(1), the legitimate interests pursued by the controller or by a third party;
        [...]

(f)   from which source the personal data originate, and if applicable, whether it came from publicly accessible sources;

16.055 A data controller is only relieved of its Art. 14 obligations in limited circumstances specified in Art. 14.5, including where and insofar as:

(b)   the provision of such information proves impossible or would involve a disproportionate effort, [...] or in so far as the obligation referred to in paragraph 1 of this Article is likely to render impossible or seriously impair the achievement of the objectives of that processing. In such cases the controller shall take appropriate measures to protect the data subject's rights and freedoms and legitimate interests, including making the information publicly available.

16.056 Under Art 15.1 GDPR a data subject has (subject to limited exceptions) *'the right to obtain from the controller confirmation as to whether or not personal data concerning him or her are being processed, and, where that is the case, access to the personal data'*, and also further information about the data and its (intended) processing.[39]

16.057 Further, Art. 30 GDPR specifies that the data controller must keep certain records of its processing of personal data, including:

(b)   the purposes of the processing;

(c)   a description of the categories of data subjects and of the categories of personal data;
        [...]

(f)   where possible, the envisaged time limits for erasure of the different categories of data.

(d) Automated decision-making

16.058 Art. 22 GDPR restricts decision-making based solely on automated processing:

---

39   This set of rights form a springboard to a data-subject's right to rectification of data (Art. 16); a right (in certain circumstances) to erasure of data – the 'right to be forgotten' – (Art. 17); a right (in certain circumstances) to restrict further processing (Art. 18); and (under Art. 21) a right to object to any processing legally based on Art. 6.1(f), that is, processing in the legitimate interests of the controller or another third party.

1. The data subject shall have the right not to be subject to a decision based solely on auto-mated processing [...] which produces legal effects concerning him or her or similarly significantly affects him or her.
2. Paragraph 1 shall not apply if the decision:
    (a) is necessary for entering into, or performance of, a contract between the data subject and a data controller;
    (b) is authorised by Union or Member State law to which the controller is subject and which also lays down suitable measures to safeguard the data subject's rights and freedoms and legitimate interests; or
    (c) is based on the data subject's explicit consent.
3. In the cases referred to in points (a) and (c) of paragraph 2, the data controller shall imple-ment suitable measures to safeguard the data subject's rights and freedoms and legitimate interests, at least the right to obtain human intervention on the part of the controller, to express his or her point of view and to contest the decision.

2.   Application to Insurers Employing Risk-rating AI Systems

There are three primary ways in which GDPR could impact the use of AI-based risk-assessment **16.059** systems, namely: (a) during data examination and collection, including the use of third-party data; (b) the use of AI in (automated) decision-making; and (c) the retention of personal data.

(a) Data examination and collection

An AI-assisted risk assessment process will involve accessing very large volumes of data, some **16.060** of it personal data, both (i) in order to train and educate its algorithms, and (ii) then (using the then-current algorithm) to assess individual risks.

These two separate uses of data require separate consideration.

Use of data to train and educate the AI's algorithms

Any collection of personal data from data subjects themselves triggers the information-provision **16.061** obligations in Art. 13 GDPR. If it is intended to use such collected personal data not just for rating the individual risk, but also for AI-training purposes, that intended purpose will there-fore have to be separately disclosed.[40] (Since this information should be provided to the data subject at the time of data collection, that also presents an opportunity to obtain consent to processing for that purpose, so as to permit such processing on the legal basis in Art. 6.1(a) ('consent'); although an insurer can choose to rely instead on other legal bases for this process-ing, such as the 'legitimate interests' basis (Art. 6.1(f)), if it wishes.)

There would, however, appear to be significant, though perhaps not insuperable, obstacles to **16.062** the use of personal data obtained *other than from the data subject* to train and educate an AI's algorithms:

(a) Only so much personal data as is 'adequate, relevant and limited to what is necessary' for that purpose should be used: Art. 5 GDPR. This may be a difficult test to satisfy here, because the use of data in this context is usually exploratory – seeking to discover

---

40   If it has not been communicated on collection but the insurer later wishes to use the data for this purpose, it will have to make a further communication of the new intended purpose before it embarks on that processing: Art. 13.3.

and establish relevant associations and correlations, to develop and test possible rules. It cannot be known in advance what (if anything) will be discovered. But, if a plausible possibility of discovering relevant correlations can be shown, it may be that this (somewhat transient) exploratory use of personal data specifically for the purpose of building and testing the AI's algorithms can be justified.[41] (If it cannot, the data sources used for this purpose may have to be restricted to anonymised data.)

As noted, any processing of personal data obtained other than from the data subject triggers, at least *prima facie*, the information-provision obligations in Art. 14 GDPR: that is, to provide the information there specified to those whose personal data it is intended to process.[42] But where such personal data is to be used in large volumes for AI-training purposes, the exception in Art. 14.5(b) might well apply, on the basis that having to comply with the Art. 14 obligations would render impossible or seriously impair the achievement of that purpose.[43] However, if that exception were inapplicable, compliance with the obligations under GDPR Art. 14 would be unlikely to be practical. (Again, the only solution would be to use anonymised data sets.)

16.063   Art. 30 also obliges the insurer to maintain records of at least the *categories* of data subjects and the *categories* of personal data processed for this purpose. But a suitably programmed AI should be able to create records of these categories, in relation to the data it consults to train itself and to develop its algorithms.

Use of personal data to rate the individual risk

16.064   As noted above in paragraph 16.013, insurers often only need to collect a handful of data points directly from proposers, the rest of the data relevant to the proposed risk being gathered elsewhere. But this can give proposers the false impression that insurers hold only such of their personal data as they have themselves provided, whereas the truth will be that the AI will have referenced and collected much other data (including personal data) from third-party sites and databases.[44] Mitigating this, the GDPR has created conditions for the use of *any* personal data so collected.

16.065   First, it is critical that an insurer *knows* what third-party data its AI system is using. As has been seen, Art. 14 obliges an insurer to give information about the personal data it will use, including 'the categories of personal data concerned'[45] and 'from which source the personal data originate, and if applicable, whether it came from publicly accessible sources'.[46] Where an AI will be employed in the risk-rating exercise, there ought not to be much difficulty in identifying what sorts of personal data it will use, and from where it will be sourced. This information ought to be disclosed (together with the other information specified in Art. 14) to the proposer when her

---

41   As 'necessary for the purposes of the legitimate interests pursued by the controller or by a third party' within Art. 6.1(f).

42   Unless they have already consented to processing for the intended purpose – perhaps an unlikely scenario.

43   It would probably have to be shown that use of personal data specifically was necessary to the achievement of the purpose of educating the AI adequately.

44   Centre for Data Ethics and Innovation, 'Snapshot Paper: AI and Personal Insurance', 12 September 2019, www.gov.uk/government/publications/cdei-publishes-its-first-series-of-three-snapshot-papers-ethical-issues-in-ai/snapshot-paper-ai-and-personal-insurance.

45   Art. 14.1(d).

46   Art. 14.2(f).

or she submits his or her own data. The AI will also need to be programmed to record all data sources consulted, and to copy and store all data points used in the rating exercise. Otherwise, the proposer will be unable to enforce his or her other rights under the GDPR, such as to obtain access to data an insurer holds about them, to challenge its accuracy, and so on.

Second, as set out above, under GDPR, the personal data gathered to rate the individual **16.066** risk should be 'adequate, relevant and limited to what is necessary'. As new sources of data become available, such as from wearable or telematic devices, insurers need to be careful that they are not collecting and storing more information about their customers than they need to rate. Unrequired data – not relevant to the AI's rating algorithms – should be rejected, not processed, and deleted.

None of this should however inhibit insurers from accessing and making use of the potentially **16.067** wide range of personal data that the AI's algorithm will have determined to be relevant to rating the risk. The more data, including personal data, an insurer collects on a proposer, the more accurate its risk assessments are likely to be, which in turn should mean that premiums will more accurately reflect individual risk.[47] Insurers also have a legitimate interest in collecting data in order to tackle fraud. If insurers are able to reduce instances of fraud and thus reduce the amount paid out in fraudulent claims, this should benefit all honest customers in the form of lower premiums.

As is clear from Art. 6(1), the GDPR does not oblige insurers to ask for explicit consent from **16.068** customers to collect and process their data: there are other bases on which the processing of personal data can be justified. But the GDPR does oblige insurers to act transparently, as indicated: perhaps to inform those whose personal data will be used to train and evolve their algorithms; certainly to advise proposers about the full range of their personal data, sourced elsewhere, that will be used in rating their risk. Customers should be under no illusions that the data they are providing is the only data which is being factored into insurers' decision making.

(b) Use of AI in (automated) decision making

Under Article 22.1 GDPR, a data subject has the right not to be subjected to a decision based **16.069** solely on automated processing, where the decision produces legal effects concerning him or her or similarly significantly affects him or her.

(a)   A decision based solely on automated processing is one that excludes any measure of active human assessment. Thus, if the relevant pattern were that a human underwriter would review an AI's risk-rating assessment (being in a position to understand how it was arrived at, and also able to reach his own assessment), before making the insurer's underwriting decision, it is unlikely that the case would fall within Art. 22.1. But the human involvement must be more than a token gesture.[48]

---

47   Centre for Data Ethics and Innovation, 'Snapshot Paper: AI and Personal Insurance', 12 September 2019, www.gov.uk/government/publications/cdei-publishes-its-first-series-of-three-snapshot-papers-ethical-issues-in-ai/snapshot-paper-ai-and-personal-insurance.
48   https://ico.org.uk/for-organisations/guide-to-data-protection/guide-to-the-general-data-protection-regulation-gdpr/automated-decision-making-and-profiling/what-does-the-gdpr-say-about-automated-decision-making-and-profiling/#id2.

(b) While perhaps open to some debate, it seems very likely indeed that a decision to refuse insurance cover, or to offer it only at a particular premium, *is* a decision that produces legal effects on, or is one similarly significantly affecting, a proposer.

16.070 Nonetheless, Art. 22.2 GDPR permits such automated decision-making (subject to Art. 22.3):

(a) where it is 'necessary for entering into, or performance of, a contract between the data subject and a data controller'.[49] This language cannot carry any implication of 'strict necessity': all decisions based on automated processing could be arrived at, though more onerously, with a measure of human assessment. Rather, the relevant test is probably one of reasonable necessity: in order for the insurer to rate the proposed risk with speed and accuracy and at acceptable cost, is a decision based solely on automated processing reasonably required? This appears to be the view of the ICO, which has referred in its Guidance to 'a targeted and reasonable way of meeting your contractual obligations'.[50]

(b) where it is 'based on the data subject's explicit consent'.[51] The ICO indicates that that means a 'freely given, specific, informed and unambiguous affirmative indication of the individual's wishes'[52] – such as ticking a positive 'opt-in' tick-box. Where the economics of an insurance scheme depend on underwriting decisions made solely on the basis of on automated processing of data, there does not appear to being any objection to a proposer being asked to give such consent, as a condition of consideration under the scheme.[53]

16.071 But any such permitted automated decision-making[54] requires, additionally, that the data controller implement 'suitable measures to safeguard the data subject's rights and freedoms and legitimate interests, at least the right to obtain human intervention on the part of the controller, to express his or her point of view and to contest the decision'. In part this is done through the information-provision obligations contained in Arts 13 and 14. But, explicitly, the data-subject (viz. the proposer) must also be given express notice of the fact that he or she will be subjected to automated decision-making, and that he or she will have the opportunity to challenge any decision reached in this way and to call for a human review of it.

16.072 What is not made clear by this provision is whether a data subject who has been subjected to automated decision-making has a right to an explanation of how the AI has reached its underwriting decision in the particular case. This question has been much debated.[55] Difficulty arises from the fact that while the GDPR's non-binding Recital 71 refers in terms to the desirability the data subject having the right 'to obtain an explanation of the decision reached', the effective legislative provision, Art. 22, conspicuously does not refer to such a right. ICO Guidance none-

---

49   Art. 22.2(a).

50   https://ico.org.uk/for-organisations/guide-to-data-protection/guide-to-the-general-data-protection-regulation-gdpr/automated-decision-making-and-profiling/when-can-we-carry-out-this-type-of-processing/. The language used is obviously inapposite in the context of a decision to *offer* contractual terms, but the relevant standard seems clear.

51   Art. 22.2(c).

52   https://ico.org.uk/for-organisations/guide-to-data-protection/guide-to-the-general-data-protection-regulation-gdpr/automated-decision-making-and-profiling/when-can-we-carry-out-this-type-of-processing/.

53   Note Art. 13.2.

54   Under Art. 22(2)(a) or (c).

55   Goodman and Flaxman, '*European Union Regulations on Algorithmic Decision-Making and a 'Right to Explanation'* 2017 AI Magazine **38**(3): 50–7; Wachter, Mittelstadt and Floridi, '*Why a Right to Explanation of Automated Decision-Making Does Not Exist in the General Data Protection Regulation*' 2016 International Data Privacy Law (28 December).

theless takes the view that the data controller must ensure that the data subject can 'obtain an explanation of the decision and challenge it'.[56] This is legally doubtful, at least. A better view is that where personal data is going be used in automated decision-making there is an obligation under Arts 13.2(f) and 14.2(g) to provide in advance 'meaningful information about the logic involved, as well as the significance and the envisaged consequences of such processing for the data subject', but that there is no corresponding obligation to explain the individual decision after the event.[57] If that is the true legal position, it may not be altogether surprising: while the broad logic of an AI's risk-rating and decision-making can usually be explained proleptically, the precise determinators, within the AI's algorithms, of the decision in the individual case may be near impossible to discern.

(c) Retention of personal data

The final way in which the GDPR impacts the use of AI risk-assessment systems is in the retention of personal data. Personal data is undoubtedly a valuable commodity to insurers, and there may be a temptation to keep it, perhaps in an unspecific hope that it might be capable of future use. But under Article 5 personal data should be held for 'no longer than is necessary'. That probably means that any personal data that has been used specifically to train and educate an AI should be deleted as soon as that purpose has been accomplished. So far as personal data used in the rating of individual risks is concerned, if cover is refused, or the insurer's offer rejected, all personal data supplied to rate the risk should be expunged promptly.[58] If cover is given and accepted, personal data can be retained for as long as a claim on the insurance remains a legal possibility (which in many cases will be at least six years after the end of any period of cover). During that period, great care must be taken to ensure the security of the personal data.[59] But, as mentioned at paragraph 16.049, there is no reason why the deletion or expunging of personal data should not take place in the context of the anonymising of other-wise useful databases, so that the anonymised database can be retained.

16.073

F. THE INSURER'S REMEDIES FOR MISREPRESENTATION AND UNFAIR PRESENTATION OF RISK

As a basic proposition, English law requires every material representation of fact made by or on behalf of the proposer to the insurer during negotiations for an insurance, and before conclusion of the contract, to be substantially true, and every material representation of expectation or belief to be made in good faith. In addition, both the proposer and his relevant agents (those who participate on behalf of the proposer in the process of procuring the insurance) must make

16.074

---

56   https://ico.org.uk/for-organisations/guide-to-data-protection/guide-to-the-general-data-protection-regulation-gdpr/individual-rights/rights-related-to-automated-decision-making-including-profiling/.

57   Burt, *'Is There a "Right to Explanation" for Machine Learning in the GDPR?'* IAPP Privacy Tech, 1 June, 2017.

58   Although if the insurer's decision is one based solely on automated processing, and the ICO is right that there is indeed a right to an explanation of the individual decision, not so promptly as to frustrate that right.

59   The Information Commissioner has power to impose swingeing fines on those whose data security is inadequate, up to up to 20 million euros or 4 per cent of annual global turnover (whichever is higher). On 16 October 2020 the ICO announced that it would, despite the economic impact of Covid-19, levy a record fine of £20 million on British Airways.

sufficient disclosure of material circumstances (which they know or ought to know) to constitute a fair presentation of the risk proposed for insurance.[60]

1. Consumer Insurance Contracts

(a) Misrepresentation; remedies

16.075 In relation to consumer insurance contracts, this basic position has been displaced by the Consumer Insurance (Disclosure and Representations) Act 2012. (A consumer in this context means an individual who enters into the contract wholly or mainly for purposes unrelated to the individual's trade, business or profession: s. 1(a).)

(a) Section 2(2) of the Act places a duty on consumers to take reasonable care not to make a misrepresentation.[61] In relation to consumer insurance contracts, any more general duty of disclosure of material circumstances has been abolished (s. 2(4)).[62]

(b) If a misrepresentation is made in breach of the duty, and the insurer shows that, without the misrepresentation, it would not have entered into the contract at all, or would have done so only on different terms, it is called a 'qualifying misrepresentation' (s. 4(1)).

(c) Where an insurer has been induced by a qualifying misrepresentation to enter into an insurance contract, the insurer's remedy will depend, firstly on the consumer's state of mind when making the representation in question.

    (i) If the misrepresentation was made deliberately or recklessly, the insurer may avoid the contract and refuse all claims (and will be able to retain the premium, except to the extent that it would be unfair to do so) (Sch. 1 para 2).

    (ii) If the misrepresentation was merely careless, then the remedy depends on what the insurer would have done if care had been taken by the consumer:

        (A) If the insurer would not have entered into the insurance contract on any terms, the insurer may avoid the contract and refuse all claims, but must return the premiums paid (Sch. 1 para 5).

        (B) If the insurer would have entered into the insurance contract, but on different terms (excluding terms relating to the premium), the contract is to be treated as if it had been entered into on those different terms, if the insurer so requires (Sch. 1 para 6).

        (C) In addition, if the insurer would have entered into the consumer insurance contract, but would have charged a higher premium, the insurer may reduce proportionately the amount to be paid on a claim (Sch. 1 para 7).

        (D) 'Proportionately' means in this context the proportion that the premium charged bears to the premium that would have been charged. For example, if the premium that would have been charged were to be double that which was charged, insurers can pay half of any claim made (Sch. 1 para 8).[63]

---

60   This known as the 'duty of fair presentation': set out in Insurance Act 2015 section 3, expanded in ss. 4–6.

61   The standard of care being that of a reasonable consumer (s. 3(2)).

62   Although a failure by the consumer to comply with the insurer's request to confirm or amend particulars previously given is capable of being a misrepresentation (s. 2(3)). It might previously have been analysed in terms of non-disclosure.

63   There are some complex provisions about the on-going status of a contract affected by a careless misrepresentation; about the effect of qualifying misrepresentations made in connection with variations of the contract; and about the effect of

As can be seen, in the case of a misrepresentation made carelessly[64] by a consumer, the remedy   **16.076**
of the insurer depends on what it would have done if care had been exercised. Where the risk
assessment has been substantially undertaken by an AI, it will be necessary to show how it
would have performed its task had different information been provided. But it is likely that the
issue of a remedy for the insurer will arise only some time after the risk assessment and underwriting has been carried out, by which time new or updated data sets may well have been made
available to the AI, and new algorithmic rules developed and adopted. Because, under Sch. 1
para 7 of the Act, the proportion of a claim that the insurer will have to pay depends on the
premium that would have been charged had care been exercised in the provision of information,
it seems that in principle the insurer will have to show how the AI would have assessed the risk,
with the data available then, using the rules it was applying then.

How easy it might be to 're-set' an AI to a former state, to show what the effect of a different   **16.077**
provision of information would have been then, is not known. But if a record has been kept of
the algorithm's rating rules as they stood at the earlier time,[65] and especially if the AI has stored,
for the risk in question, the 'value' of each data point used, in principle it should be possible to
show how the risk would have been assessed with a different provision of information and, with
sufficient accuracy, the premium likely to have been charged.[66]

2.   Non-consumer Insurance Contracts

'Non-consumer insurance contracts' refers here simply to insurance contracts not subject to the   **16.078**
2012 Act.[67] Such contracts will include insurances of larger or more complex commercial risks,
of the type described and discussed in paragraph 16.009 above. But the term also covers more
straightforward insurances entered into by small and medium-sized companies and partnerships, and by individuals for purposes related to their trade, business or profession. The degree
of involvement of AI systems in assessing the risks covered by these contracts will be very variable – ranging from full assessment, in which humans play no active part, to limited assessment
of specific aspects of the proposed risk, to no involvement at all. In what follows we discuss
those contacts where AI will have played at least some part in the risk-assessment process.

In relation to non-consumer insurance contracts, the duty of fair presentation, set out in ss. 3–6   **16.079**
of the Insurance Act 2015 and described in paragraph 16.075 above, applies.

(a) Knowledge of the insurer

So far as concerns disclosure of circumstances material to the risk, an insured need not disclose   **16.080**
matters that are already known to the insurer, or which ought to be known to it, or which can

---

a qualifying misrepresentations made in connection with group insurance. But these do not call for further consideration
here.
64   That is, not deliberately or recklessly.
65   In practice 'version-control' is likely to be exercised: the AI will update its rules and algorithms only periodically, and
will store the version of them (in effect the version of itself) in place prior to updating. This should permit, if necessary,
restoration to that prior state.
66   Plainly, that could not be achieved were an unsupervised AI to have been used in risk assessment.
67   And the term is used in that sense in the Insurance Act 2015: see s. 1.

be presumed to be known to it (s. 3(5)(b)(c)(d) of the 2015 Act). Section 5 of the 2015 Act expands that provision as follows:

(1) For the purposes of section 3(5)(b), an insurer knows something only if it is known to one or more of the individuals who participate on behalf of the insurer in the decision whether to take the risk, and if so on what terms (whether the individual does so as the insurer's employee or agent, as an employee of the insurer's agent or in any other capacity).

(2) For the purposes of section 3(5)(c), an insurer ought to know something only if—

    (a) an employee or agent of the insurer knows it, and ought reasonably to have passed on the relevant information to an individual mentioned in subsection (1), or

    (b) the relevant information is held by the insurer and is readily available to an individual mentioned in subsection (1).

(3) For the purposes of section 3(5)(d), an insurer is presumed to know—

    (a) things which are common knowledge, and

    (b) things which an insurer offering insurance of the class in question to insureds in the field of activity in question would reasonably be expected to know in the ordinary course of business.

16.081 'Knowledge of the insurer' raises some intriguing questions in relation to information which is available to an AI, or capable of inference by the AI, and which may (or may not) have been used by it to assess a risk but which are never within the actual knowledge of any human underwriter. The human underwriter will, it may be assumed, have used the AI-generated risk rating without examining all the data considered by it or used by it in applying its rating rules. Can an insurer complain of non-disclosure of circumstances, when the material information (not disclosed) was something that the AI could have 'known' or did 'know'?

16.082 The answer to that question should, instinctively, be 'no'. But it is not clear how that conclusion can be arrived at through s. 5. In that section, the references would appear to be to the knowledge of human actors. The vast arrays of data that an AI can have access to can hardly be described as 'common knowledge', within the meaning of s. 5(3)(a). Nor can every data point considered or used by an AI be considered something that an insurer should reasonably be expected to know in the ordinary course of its business, for the purposes of s. 5(3)(b) – although that description might well apply to some data, such as that which a human underwriter would have made use of had the risk-assessment exercise not been delegated to an AI. But an AI's trawl of data, under its risk-rating rules, is likely to be far wider than anything that a human underwriter would undertake. Perhaps the best approach to the question raised is through s. 5(2)(b), which refers to 'information [...] held by the insurer and [which] is readily available to' an individual who participates on behalf of the insurer in the underwriting. If the AI has stored, for each risk assessed, the 'value' of each data point used, and those values are readily accessible to such an individual (even if not routinely consulted by him or her), then that might serve to establish what information is held by the insurer and is available to its human underwriters; even if they themselves do not routinely access it as part of the underwriting process.

16.083 At the very least, in cases where non-disclosure of a material circumstance is alleged, insurers are likely to face calls for disclosure of the information held by the AI which would reveal what data it had had access to. Unless the AI has recorded all the databases it has consulted in rating the individual risk, it is likely that inferences will have to be drawn from the data points that it has recorded itself as actually using, in accordance with its own rating rules.

But such may be the complexity of its self-developed rules that the data points actually used may actually be proxies for others that it had access to and might have used. An AI may have 'known' far more than it records itself as knowing and using to rate a risk.

One thing at least is clear: that the presumed informational ignorance of insurers, on which **16.084** the duty of fair presentation is premised, may before long be wholly outdated. The 2015 Act is, at the time of writing, only six years old; but one wonders how long it may be before the formulation of that duty of fair presentation might require some reappraisal.

(b) Breach of the duty of fair presentation; remedies

A breach of that duty gives a remedy to the insured if the insurer shows that, but for the breach, **16.085** it would not have entered into the contract of insurance at all, or would have done so only on different terms: a 'qualifying breach' (see s. 8(1)(3) of the 2015 Act).

Again, as with consumer insurance contracts, the remedy available to the insurer in the event of **16.086** a qualifying breach depends, in the first instance, on the state of mind of the insured or relevant agent in committing the breach:

(a)   If the breach of the duty was committed deliberately or recklessly, the insurer may avoid the contract and refuse all claims (and need not return the premium) (Sch. 1 para 2 of the 2015 Act).

(b)   Otherwise, the remedy depends on what the insurer would have done if a fair presentation had been made. The regime is similar to that in Schedule 1 of the 2012 Act, and the problems and issues that this scheme of remedies raises for risks that have been assessed by or with the assistance of AI systems are the same as those arising in relation to consumer insurance contracts: see paragraphs 16.077 and 16.078 above.

G. CONCLUSION

Provided these legal issues can be negotiated successfully, the rating and underwriting of insur-   **16.087** ance risk with the assistance of AI represents a vast opportunity for insurers to improve the accuracy of their risk assessments while also making their processes more efficient. The streamlining of underwriting (and of other insurance processes) also has advantage for those seeking insurance: it should reduce the price of insurance generally. But improvements in the profiling of the individual risk will create both winners and losers. Some of those seeking insurance will discover that, with more personalised and/or granular assessment of their risk, their premiums will reduce. Others will discover that their risks have previously been under-rated, and costs of cover for them will rise.

The corollary of this, however, is that those insurers who invest successfully in AI to improve   **16.088** the risk assessment aspects of their underwriting will be better able than their competitors to identify both lower and higher risks. Such competitive advantage should allow them to cherry-pick the better risks, and refuse higher risks (or accept them only at enhanced prices). Those presenting a higher risk will therefore trend toward less well-informed insurers, willing to cover such risks at relatively lower cost. Those insurers who fail to invest in AI to improve their risk profiling will therefore be in danger of accumulating within their portfolios, for insufficient premium, more of the less attractive, higher risks. Over time, the consequences of that are inevitable.

17

RETAIL AND CONSUMER

Matthew Bennett

A. INTRODUCTION

Today, AI is not only a reality but an increasingly common feature of life for consumers. Using **17.001** voice and image recognition, natural language processing and machine learning, our smart phones and speakers are an integral part of our day-to-day.

While the development of AI may still only be in its infancy, the vast potential benefits are **17.002** already clear. This is nowhere more evident than in the world of retail and consumer products, which have already been through a period of significant technology-lead upheaval.

Many retailers learnt lessons from the failure to adapt quickly to the emerging '.com boom' the **17.003** first time round and have been early adopters of AI, from 'chatbots' to AI-assisted customer analytics. Or perhaps it is more the case that retailers are forever searching for new ways to improve the customer experience and boost sales, and have always looked to technology solutions to drive consumer spending and to reduce costs. From the pneumatic tube to the barcode, targeted coupons and data analysis, retailers have been early adopters; therefore it is no wonder that AI-enabled technology is the talk of the sector.

17.004 Section B of this chapter looks at practical use cases of AI-enabled technology in the retail sector. This is broken into the two perspectives of the retail sales journey: that of the retailer and that of the customer.

17.005 In Section C we look at the current and likely future legal and regulatory challenges to the use of AI-enabled technology. The key themes we discuss in this section are implications for data protection, the difficulty of ensuring transparency for consumers and issues around intellectual property rights.

B. RETAIL JOURNEY

17.006 A helpful structure for analysing the practical applications and implications of AI-enabled technology in the retail sector is to look at the five stages of the Retail Economics customer journey. The stages are shown in Table 17.1.

Table 17.1   *Practical applications and implications of AI-enabled technology in the retail sector*

Stage	Consumer	Retailer
1	Awareness	Influence
2	Research and consideration	Educate and channel
3	Purchase	Purchase
4	Fulfilment	Fulfilment
5	Service and support	Retention and loyalty

17.007 While this is not exhaustive, at each stage we look at the most prevalent or game-changing applications and examine how ready consumers and business really are to adopt AI-enabled technology in the retail sector. We then take a deeper look at how businesses plan to adopt AI technologies in their organisations, the areas they will target for investment and the key challenges they foresee.

1.   Stage 1: Awareness; Influence

17.008 Awareness is a primary battleground for any consumer brand or retailer in the hunt for sales and profits. There are various ways in which a customer can become aware of a brand, including TV or print advertising, personalised emails, recommendations from friends and family and targeted online advertising. Retailers, seeking any advantage they can gain in an increasingly competitive marketplace, are turning to AI technologies to help them create greater customer awareness. Two of the most dominant are personalisation and product recommendations. When combined, hyper-personalised omnichannel marketing strategies provide an opportunity to influence consumers in ways never seen before, for example using data to pull customers to purchase a product which may genuinely enhance their wellbeing. Other models provide products based on a customer's behaviour and do not require an active purchase.

(a) Personalisation

It is generally accepted that shoppers are more likely to purchase items in-store or online from retailers which send them relevant, personalised promotions and tailored offerings. **17.009**

In the past it has been possible to personalise experiences using simple rules, such as only displaying clothing available in a customer's size. However, machine learning means enormous and seemingly disconnected sets of data can be analysed deeply and quickly, allowing retailers to act in real time based on that analysis. We see that personalisation will continue to be a key tool for retailers, but the difficult balance will be in ensuring that such personalisation is effective and that shoppers' trust is not lost. There is a possibility that shoppers perceive too much data is held on them if ads are overly personalised, and there is a risk of damaging a customer's trust, even if the processes run by the retailer are within the bounds of the law. We are reminded of the retailer who was able to use specific purchasing habits of its customers to understand whether they were pregnant (and, within an impressive margin, their due date). The retailer, now famously, accidentally exposed the pregnancy of a high-school teenager to her parents by sending her coupons for baby clothes and cribs. Following concerns of over-personalisation the retailer changed its strategy, by dropping personalised pregnancy-related coupons among other seemingly random coupons which it sent out to its customers, and found an uptick in use of the pregnancy-related coupons. **17.010**

(b) Product recommendations

Similar to personalisation, one of the most recognised AI-powered applications used today is the automated suggestion of products and services to shoppers. These AI-powered recommendation engines vary greatly in sophistication but advanced algorithms can correlate disparate data such as purchasing habits, images viewed, social media content, location or weather in real time to customise the consumer's retail experience. Adding biometric data into the mix may allow bricks-and-mortar retailers to identify customers as they walk into a shop and inform real-time personalisation. **17.011**

More sophisticated personalisation requires more personal data; however, the extent to which consumers will be willing to provide personal data to enable companies to provide more targeted product recommendations is unclear. It may be that retailers will need to augment their approach based on the age of the consumer, as younger generations may be more accepting of hyper-personalisation. **17.012**

AI-enabled technologies have the ability to deliver multichannel marketing campaigns that seamlessly target consumers with personalised content and experiences across websites and mobile platforms and within physical stores. In the future this may include the use of AI-assisted facial recognition to register returning customers in a store, tracking data of a customer's journey through a shop to optimise store layout or optimising the functionality and design of a site based on a user's unique profile. **17.013**

2.   Stage 2: Research and Consideration; Awareness and Channel

17.014   Before making a purchase most consumers conduct research online or in-store, seeking out product information, online reviews or price comparisons. Companies can leverage AI to enhance the ways in which they educate consumers and provide information about their offering. We are already seeing human advice being replaced by intelligent virtual assistants and augmented and virtual reality to inform customers.

(a) Chatbots, virtual assistants, self-service kiosks and in-store robots

17.015   Perhaps the most established use of AI technology is chatbots that simulate human conversations in text or speech and often handle customer service enquiries, FAQs, delivery updates and product recommendations. Virtual assistants such as smart speakers perform tasks in response to verbal commands using natural language systems. They can be always-on, there is no need to visit a webpage and they are increasingly being integrated into other systems such as phones or smart homes.

17.016   Brands from Nestlé to Target have trialled in-store robots to perform functions including recognising faces, greeting customers, serving promotions, providing directions and recommending products. In the US, Amazon Go stores deploy AI technology to enable checkout-free shopping. Obviously, the performance of such technology will ultimately determine its success but, as referenced above, retailer and brands should be aware of the generational divide in deploying AI.

(b) Virtual reality and augmented reality

17.017   Virtual reality (VR) is an immersive, computer-generated experience that provides a fully simulated environment, such as a flight simulation with a headset. Augmented reality (AR) provides an interactive experience where real-world objects are enhanced, or augmented, with computer-generated information.

17.018   In this stage of the customer journey, AI offers consumer companies exciting possibilities including virtual stores, immersive marketing experiences and product visualisation. Advances in such technology, already used by furniture retailers to allow shoppers to see what a product might look like in their homes before they make a purchase, mean it is also possible to show the drape and texture of fabric, giving an online buyer a better appreciation of a garment. The prize for both of these technologies is not just increased sales but also lower levels of customer returns – one of the huge costs that affects the profitability of omnichannel retailers.

(c) AI-powered omnichannel

17.019   Omnichannel is a hotly used buzzword in the retail sector, referring to a business model encompassing a seamless experience for shoppers whether they are browsing online, on their phone or in a store. For example, a shopper in a store discovering that a product they want is out of stock should be able to buy it online either using their mobile or perhaps with the assistance of an in-store assistant equipped with an iPad.

17.020   AI-powered technology and 'smart' data analysis can greatly help retailers pursuing an omnichannel strategy, which is not an easy business model to perfect. Advanced data analytics identify patterns of shopper behaviour, making it easier to determine which marketing strategies are most effective within the various channels. Perhaps an advert on Facebook was better at driving footfall to stores while an Instagram promotion may have driven more online sales. Analysing customer dwell time in a shop or on a particular web page will help retailers identify the high-footfall areas where the highest-margin products should be placed. As with many AI applications used in retail, data is king.

(d) Remote stock checking

Increasingly retailers are integrating stores into their online offering, using them as micro warehouses for click-and-collect or local delivery. Timely stock accuracy is paramount to this approach and so some of the world's biggest grocery retailers are already using autonomous shelf-scanning robots. This also allows customers to check accurate and real-time stock availability in stores. Companies such as Bossa Nova are deploying robots on shop floors to scan shelves and report findings back to in-store staff and retailers' central stock and marketing systems. Even in a traditional model, stock availability is crucial. The use of robots to remotely check stock levels can also improve stock availability, improving the shopping experience.   **17.021**

3.   Stage 3: Purchase

In recent years we have changed the ways in which we pay for goods and services, with cash-based payments increasingly making way for frictionless, cashless, technologically secure payment systems. As payment methods change, so too does the system of checkouts in stores and online, with movement from cashier-free to checkout-free payment under way.   **17.022**

(a) Checkout-free payment

Retailers, particularly grocers, have been installing cashier-free payment systems in their shops for decades. The next phase is checkout-free payment, where retailers use embedded sensors, deep learning and computer vision to help automate the process so that shoppers can simply select their products and walk out of the store with minimal friction. However, despite the proliferation of cashier-free systems, in many cases consumers (particularly older customers) still tend to prefer staffed tills. Whether there will be any hesitation with respect to checkout-free systems remains to be seen.   **17.023**

(b) Dynamic pricing

Over the decades, a key focus for retailers has been how to effectively price their goods to win sales, particularly in the online sphere, where consumers can easily and quickly compare pricing for themselves.   **17.024**

Dynamic pricing refers to the practice of pricing an item according to a customer's perceived willingness to pay. The best known example of this is airlines setting flight costs which can vary according to the destination, time of day or time of year a passenger may be travelling. However, the next stage of dynamic pricing may involve determination of price based on the consumer's search history, other buying habits or the tone of their voice.   **17.025**

AI opens up possibilities for real-time and personalised price changes. The primary advantage for the consumer is that dynamic pricing should lead to more competitive pricing and better deals. While this concept is not new, what has changed with the use of AI is that the imple-   **17.026** mentation of dynamic pricing can be far more sophisticated and nuanced, responding not just to stock levels or general demand patterns but to an individual's unique profile, habits and needs. The benefits of dynamic pricing for retailers and brands can be enormous, including improved sales conversion, optimisation of margins and an ability to react to changing market trends. Therefore, dynamic pricing ostensibly has benefits for both the consumer and the retailer. However, organisations should be careful with personalised pricing, sometimes termed price discrimination, as it could lead to customers feeling frustrated by price changes, victimised, or unable to budget effectively. In the worst case, shoppers may feel that retailers have misused their data to devise a price discrimination strategy and may lose trust in the brand. In addition, dynamic pricing is not without legal considerations; see more in Section C below.

4. Stage 4: Fulfilment

17.027 One of the more difficult, and often expensive, challenges for brands and retailers is the fulfilment of orders generated online. Customers generally want parcels delivered as soon as possible, often to their front door, for the cheapest price possible. Companies have been deploying AI in this area, with providers such as Satalia assisting them to optimise all aspects of their logistics.

17.028 Retailers not only need to ensure that their current delivery and logistics systems are up to scratch but also need to ensure they have future capacity built into their systems, so they are not faced with expensive upgrades down the track – not least because the last mile of a delivery to a customer's home can often reach or exceed 50 per cent of the overall transportation costs. Companies are therefore enthusiastically talking about next-generation logistics systems such as drones and AI-powered in-home delivery. In an era of 'me-commerce' where instant gratification is paramount for most consumers, the importance of retailers and brands getting fulfilment right cannot be understated. The current AI-related applications being showcased within supply chains and logistics are likely to continue to yield significant levels of disruption in the immediate future, particularly around distribution and inventory management.

(a) Drones

17.029 While the saga of drone usage over airports will inevitably hasten greater regulation of the devices, drones powered by AI are considered to be a potentially exciting new development in online order fulfilment. The average commercial drone can hit speeds of 100 miles per hour and can safely carry a 2.2kg load with a deployment cost of just 78p per shipment, so it is easy to see why retailers and consumers alike are pursuing the potential of drone deliveries. However, this enthusiasm has yet to transfer over to the consumer, with many believing that drone deliveries will never become mainstream.

17.030 It is worth noting similar previous scepticism to other technologies, however. For instance, in 2007 Seth Porges predicted that 'a virtual keyboard will be about as useful for tapping out emails and text messages as a rotary phone'.[1]

---

1   TechCrunch piece titled 'We Predict the iPhone Will Bomb'.

(b) In-home delivery

While many consumers were previously horrified at the thought of letting a stranger into their   **17.031**
home, others have seen in-home delivery as a hugely convenient innovation and, in the future,
this may be a common occurrence. A key aspect of this will involve ensuring customer trust
through the use of advanced security, using AI technologies to identify faces, vehicles and
behaviours. It is no surprise that Amazon acquired Ring, a home security tech company, in
2018.

(c) Distribution

The world of distribution is on the cusp of a revolution. AI-powered autonomous vehicles   **17.032**
and optimised routing systems will deliver incredible cost reductions for many businesses by
removing inefficiencies from existing systems. When combined with AI-assisted distribution
analytics these new technologies can also help businesses improve forecasting and customer
service, mitigate risk and achieve faster delivery times.

There are already examples around the world of self-driving freight vehicles, such as the Uber   **17.033**
trucks currently operating in Arizona, as well as 'platooning', a concept where a single HGV
driver leads a convoy of several driverless vehicles. In some respects, autonomous vehicles may
be among the AI-enabled technologies set to have the greatest impact on the consumer and
retail industry in general.

(d) Inventory management

Mastering complex stock management issues is a crucial area for retailers to control. Fully   **17.034**
automated inventory management processes provide numerous advantages over systems that
rely partially or solely on human diligence. Next-generation inventory management systems
are using AI for image recognition and real-time data-sensing to more accurately manage stock
levels as well as predict future demand.

5.   Stage 5: Service and Support; Retention and Loyalty

Outstanding or poor customer service can be the difference between a customer for life or one   **17.035**
who never shops with a brand again. Many of the ingredients that make up good human service
and support, such as consistency, personalisation, accurate product information and clear communication, can now be replicated or enhanced through AI applications. As consumers become
increasingly acclimatised to non-human interaction for customer service issues, the use of AI
applications is only likely to increase.

From a retailer's perspective, retaining customers and instilling a sense of loyalty in them is the   **17.036**
Holy Grail. Retail and consumer brands have been at the forefront of using data to understand
and connect with their customers. Today, customer retention largely relies on brands possess-
ing large amounts of data on their customers around what they like and do not like, as well their
typical shopping behaviour. AI-driven technologies are making the amassing of vast amounts
of information – and, more importantly, understanding and acting on it – much easier.

This will usher in a new generation of customer service; for instance, delivering products   **17.037**
before a customer buys them and fixing issues before a customer realises they have a problem

(post-sales analysis). We predict that the success of these strategies is dependent on customer trust.

(a) Back to chatbots, virtual reality and augmented reality

17.038 In 2018 it was predicted that by 2020, 85 per cent of all customer service interactions would exclude human involvement.[2] Available every day of the year and every hour of the day, chatbots can help to reduce a retailer's issue-resolution time and increase customer satisfaction. For most consumers, use of messaging apps to interact with retail chatbots is now a familiar method to raise a product query, file a complaint, check an order, give feedback or troubleshoot a problem with a product.

17.039 The use of VR and AR also heralds interesting new possibilities, such as in-service centres, using technology to ensure that accurate product information is at a staff member's fingertips via a facility that allows two parties to see exactly what the other is looking at through a VR library of thousands of products, model variants, colours and sizes. This can help with swift issue resolution and help to increase customer retention through effective communication. A large majority of retailers and consumer brand companies feel that consumers would accept being served by AI-related technology but there is a generational divide in the acceptance of this technology by consumers.

(b) Next best action/post-sales analysis

17.040 Next best action marketing is also known as recommended action and refers to a customer-centric focus where retailers consider the different actions that can be taken for a customer and then decide on the best one.

17.041 Some of the next best actions that retailers might consider could include providing a personalised offer to an individual customer via social media to reward them for repeat custom, offering some advice on how to use a product recently purchased, texting or sending a catalogue in an attempt to sell associated products to an already loyal customer or delivering samples of a product that customer is likely to buy.

17.042 AI-powered data analytics will enable more sophisticated and personalised targeting of customers which will improve loyalty and lifetime value.

C. LEGAL CHALLENGES

1.   Customer Trust

17.043 Many of the technologies rely on vast amounts of customer personal data. Data is used to train neural networks and decision forests and then these AI systems use these networks to absorb more personal data provided by the customer. The adoption and overall success of AI tech-

---

2   www.gartner.com/en/newsroom/press-releases/2018–02–19-gartner-says-25-percent-of-customer-service-operations -will-use-virtual-customer-assistants-by-2020.

nology within retail and consumer products is dependent on customers' acceptance and trust. Customer acceptance and trust will drive the laws around AI and the technology it supports.

However, numerous surveys suggest that trust in retailers is low, and with AI acceptance hugely variable between technologies and age groups, consumer companies should not be over-confident in their ability to implement AI without alienating their customers. Consumers may be less willing to trust retailers and consumer companies to handle sensitive data properly as opposed to more traditional institutions such as banks and government bodies, which have been handling sensitive data for many years.   **17.044**

Retailers are only trusted slightly more than social networks – a rather scathing indictment given the scandals that have hit the headlines relating to the latter, although we would note that social networks hold huge amounts of personal data and have billions of active users despite consumers' stated low level of trust. This is perhaps why many organisations believe that customers will be accepting of AI-powered technologies.   **17.045**

2.   Data Protection

Data protection considerations in relation to AI are more fully discussed in Chapter 10 of this book. There are a number of challenges to consider with respect to data protection in a retail context. As referenced above, retailers need to ensure that they deal with consumers' personal information in a way that encourages trust and is as seamless as possible in the customer journey. Particular considerations arise with respect to data which in its own right may be sensitive (such as 'special category' data, as defined in the GDPR – meaning data relating to race or ethnic origin, health data or certain types of biometric data) and data which, in context, can be considered sensitive – see for example our earlier discussion around the retailer revealing a teen's pregnancy. Where customers trust the retailer, they are likely to be more willing to provide it with personal data. In turn, this will give the retailer the necessary tools to more effectively deploy AI within its business. With more (quality) personal information, the retailer may be able to better personalise the customer's purchasing experience.   **17.046**

One particular example of a key data protection consideration in the retail context is where AI-enabled technology involves automated decision making (ADM – making a decision about an individual solely by automated means) or profiling (automated processing of personal data to evaluate certain things about an individual). Where this occurs, there are regulatory hurdles to clear under GDPR. At a minimum, an organisation must inform the individual that this is happening.   **17.047**

AI processes are rarely transparent, though. If decisions cannot be explained, it makes them difficult to challenge and raises issues of liability for errors and harm. Organisations must find a way to meaningfully explain the rationale and consequences of decisions, and also implement some type of decision review process for when concerns are raised.   **17.048**

In addition, if the ADM produces legal effects (or effects that are similarly significant) then the organisation cannot utilise it unless an exemption applies (explicit consent of the individual, authorisation under law, or that the decision is necessary to perform the contract). More stringent exemptions apply if the personal data being used is 'special category' data (as referenced   **17.049** above). GDPR discourages using ADM that concerns children, and profiling of children must be done only subject to additional protections.

17.050 What constitutes a legal or similarly significant effect centres on the impact on the individual, in particular if the decision is likely to affect their rights or lead to discrimination or material prejudice. This may include decisions that have the effect of cancelling a contract or offering differential pricing based on personal details, such as if an individual is effectively barred from certain goods or services because prices are prohibitively high. Certain types of intrusive online advertising based on ADM or profiling may also have a 'similarly significant effect'.

17.051 If the AI technology does rely on this more restrictive category of ADM, the organisation either: (a) will be required to obtain an individual's explicit consent or find another basis for the ADM; or (b) will need to introduce some measure of human intervention (so that the processing is not 'solely' automated).

3. European Commission White Paper and Subsequent Reports

17.052 In February 2020, following public consultation, the European Commission published a White Paper on the European approach to AI. This White Paper describes the European Commission's intentions with respect to AI in the region, by setting out high-level principles for the EU's approach to research and development as well as proposing policy options for a common regulatory regime. The White Paper suggests that avoiding fragmentation in the market with respect to the legal framework supporting AI is important for supporting the EU's innovation capacity and speed of uptake of AI.

17.053 The retail industry has particular relevance here due to the Commission's desire to prevent harm to individuals, including consumers. In October 2020, the EU Parliament resolved to request the European Commission to submit a proposal for a regulation on liability for the operation of AI systems. This follows the European Parliament Committee's draft report in April 2020 which included recommendations on a civil liability regime for AI, which itself built on the proposals outlined in the White Paper. These recommendations are intended to address some of the issues raised by AI in context, namely:

(a) *Lack of transparency* – many AI systems are incredibly technical and in some cases 'black-boxed', therefore difficult for an average consumer to understand. In addition, allocating the burden of proof to the victim in this context may not be fair if the victim cannot access or understand the relevant AI system which caused the alleged harm (without costly investment in expert analysis).

(b) *'High-risk' AI systems* – a strict liability regime may apply to high-risk autonomous AI systems given that they can endanger the public to a higher degree. The resolution proposes that a high-risk system is a system which involves a significant potential to cause harm to one or more persons, in a manner that is random and goes beyond what can reasonably be expected. High-risk systems would be listed in an annex to the regulation. The 'operator' of a high-risk system could be liable to pay up to a maximum of €2 million compensation in the event of death or harm being caused to the health or physical integrity of an affected person. The earlier report released by the European Commission suggests that high-risk systems may include intrusive surveillance, systems which use biometrics, unmanned aircraft, and so on. Some of these are distinctly relevant to the retail industry. In addition, businesses facing individual consumers may be required, or may choose, to adapt the highest standards for non-high risk systems.

(c) *'Fault-based' law* – many legislative systems (including across the EU) have in place fault-based tort law (a retailer may be familiar with product liability regimes implemented across Member States), but there is difficulty allocating liability under these existing regimes in the context of AI. The proposed regulation suggests that liability will fall to the 'operator', which includes both the front-end and back-end operations. In many cases the back-end operator is the individual controlling the risk associated with the relevant AI system, so should not escape liability in high-risk settings.

Liability regimes in this area are clearly under review at the moment, and we expect to see **17.054** significant development in this area over the coming months and years. An EU-wide regulation may be beneficial in providing more of a 'known' legislative climate for operators to develop AI systems. However, if this is too restrictive, further advancements in AI may be discouraged. Ensuring appropriate protections for consumers while encouraging growth in AI will be a difficult balance for regulators to address.

4. Competition Law Issues

AI brings with it a number of competition law considerations, which are more specifically **17.055** discussed in Chapter 11. In particular, retailers should be aware of risks around implementing AI-enabled technologies including dynamic pricing and personalised pricing.

5. Dynamic Pricing

Dynamic pricing is a hot topic for competition regulators. The EU, the OECD and the CMA **17.056** have all recently looked at the effect of pricing algorithms on competition. They identified pro-competitive effects; for example, pricing algorithms can reduce transaction costs for firms, reduce friction in markets and give consumers greater information on which to base their decisions. However, there is concern around pricing algorithms leading to price collusion. This can lead to consumers paying higher prices and having less choice. Collusion may occur, for example, if competing sellers use the same independent algorithm to determine their prices, giving the algorithm an understanding of several suppliers' pricing policies. Concern may arise if this gives the algorithm an incentive to increase prices above the competitive level in order to maximise profits. Algorithms can also be used to monitor an existing agreement to fix prices, such as in the recent online posters cartel case where competitors used an algorithm to automatically match each other's price increases.

6. Personalised Pricing

The CMA considers that personalised pricing makes it less likely that algorithms could lead **17.057** to price collusion because, if pricing is truly personalised, there is no longer a single observable price that pricing algorithms can match. To date, there is no case law where personalised pricing has been established as an infringement of competition law. However, as these practices become more common, some competition authorities may decide to open investigations and tackle some forms of personalised pricing using existing competition law tools, such as finding it to be an abuse of dominance.

7. Intellectual Property

17.058 Retailers pay close attention to their brands and to their trade secrets. Trade secrets may protect IP but need to have appropriate protections in place to ensure that the standard of 'trade secret' under EU regulation is met. If the secret becomes generally known or readily accessible to persons who would normally deal with that type of information then it is no longer protected.

17.059 In April 2020 the European Parliament Committee on Legal Affairs published a draft report on IP rights, recommending a review and revision of IP policy and law in the region in light of recent developments in the AI sector.[3] There is concern that the current protections available to intellectual property (such as copyright, patent, design and trade secret) are not fit for purpose with respect to AI.

17.060 Outside of the above, a key issue for the retail sector in relation to intellectual property rights in respect of AI is ownership of data and algorithms. As is well accepted, the strength of an algorithm is strongly determined by the quality of data which underpins it. In many cases, data is used to 'teach' the algorithm so it can become self-learning. Developing an AI system which is able to provide real value to an organisation often takes significant investment and requires a large amount of data. Many retailers would not have the knowledge or resources to invest in a proprietary system. Some would argue that even if a retailer did possess such capabilities, they would be better placed to implement a system developed by a third party. This is because developers can leverage data sets across their customers to improve the quantity and quality of data, and therefore the AI system or algorithm they are providing.

17.061 IP considerations arise in this context, as there are obvious concerns around a retailer's data being used (even anonymously) in a system which ultimately benefits another retailer, potentially a competitor. For this reason, IP clauses in AI contracts should be carefully negotiated. Retailers should ensure that their competitors (or other third parties) are not able to access or derive their commercial information, or customer data, when using the provider's systems. A retailer should also seek to protect bespoke developments or integrations with systems to whatever extent necessary. On balance, provided that these risks are appropriately addressed in the relevant agreement, a retailer may be comfortable allowing its data to be indirectly used (that is, 'anonymously' within a data set which also pools data from other retailers), as a more comprehensive background data set can ultimately increase the benefit that the retailer is able to derive from the AI system.

17.062 Another intellectual property-related issue is around the use of 'copyleft' open source software when developing systems. Certain open source licences require those who use the licence to develop software to make that software available for public/general use (perpetuating the 'open' nature of the licence). While this may be acceptable in some instances, if the retailer is investing time, resources or data into an AI system it may be less likely to want that information, and any

---

3   www.europarl.europa.eu/doceo/document/JURI-PR-650527_EN.pdf.

developments associated with it, to be made public without charge. Therefore, understanding which, if any, open source software was utilised in developing an AI system procured from a service provider (or otherwise obtaining appropriate contractual protection) is an important consideration.

8.   Transparency/Consumer Protection Issues

- Issues of information asymmetry – algorithms/AI can be incredibly complex/difficult to understand – sometimes black boxed.
- Risk of inbuilt discrimination – unacceptable to, for example, target a certain race for a promotion and so on.
- Empower consumers to understand decision making made by AI.
- Transparency around use of data.

Artificial intelligence has its own key considerations in respect of consumer rights legislation, a subset of the law with which most retailers are familiar. Previously, consumer rights legislation at the EU level only applied to physical goods and services, but the recent Omnibus Directive[4] has broadened the scope of existing consumer rights directives so they now apply to digital content, goods and services. This Directive was required to be transposed by Member States into their national law by November 2021 and applied nationally from May 2022. The Directive requires businesses to let consumers know when prices of goods or services have been personalised to that individual on the basis of automated decision making or other form of automated profiling. Subject to certain exemptions, the Omnibus Directive also applies to transactions where personal data is used as consideration for the relevant digital good, content or service.   **17.063**

D. CONCLUSION

In this chapter we have considered AI-enabled technology in the retail sector by analysing legal and practical challenges at each stage of the consumer and retailer journey. The five stages outlined in this chapter provide a useful framework for understanding possible implications when deploying AI technology. From competition law, to data protection, to customer trust, it is clear that many 'hot topic' legal issues find a home in the retail space. The difficulty for retailers will be in balancing: (a) the (often legal-driven) need to undertake appropriate risk assessments across these topics prior to implementing AI-enabled technology, to ensure they understand the legal landscape; and (b) the commercial desire to continue to appeal to customers by utilising the latest technology, and to move in an agile way to keep up with developments in the market.   **17.064**

We expect to see regulatory changes in this area over the coming years and as the traditional 'high street' and the online marketplace continue to evolve, and it will be interesting to see whether legislation aims to match the pace at which AI-enabled technologies are deployed and develop in this sector.   **17.065**

---

4   eur-lex.europa.eu/eli/dir/2019/2161/oj#.

18

HEALTHCARE[1]

Roland Wiring

A. INTRODUCTION

18.001 Technologies based on AI and machine learning are widely considered to have the potential to transform healthcare by deriving new and important insights from the vast amount of data generated during the delivery of healthcare on a daily basis.[2] According to the US Federal Drug Agency (the FDA), one of the greatest benefits of AI in software lies in its ability to learn from real-world use and experience, and its capability to improve performance.[3] The FDA, the European Commission[4] and a number of other institutions, committees and stakeholders often express the view that AI/ML-based software will be able to deliver safe and effective software functionality. Such enhanced functionality would improve the quality of care that patients receive. The regulatory and legal framework is an important factor in the further development and application of AI solutions.

18.002 The strong development of AI in recent years has been driven by a number of factors. These are mainly technology-based, including the development of very sophisticated mathematical

---

1   This chapter is based upon an earlier chapter, 'Artificial Intelligence in Healthcare' in J Madir (ed) *Healthtech: Law and Regulation* (2020).

2   Federal Drug Agency, Proposed Regulatory Framework for Modifications to Artificial Intelligence/Machine Learning (AI/ML)-Based Software as Medical Device (SaMD) (2019), at 1.

3   Ibid.

4   The European Commission, Communication from the Commission – Artificial Intelligence for Europe, Brussels, COM(2018) 237 final (25.4.2018), at 1.

models. Increased processing power of computers and, in particular in the context of health-care, an unprecedented volume of data to examine have boosted the development of AI in the life sciences and healthcare industry beyond recognition.

Section B examines several use cases of AI in healthcare – from diagnostics to clinical trials **18.003** and surgery robotics. Section C analyses the main legal challenges surrounding the use of AI in healthcare and provides suggestions for overcoming them. These suggestions lead to the conclusions presented in Section D.

B. ARTIFICIAL INTELLIGENCE USE CASES IN HEALTHCARE

The following sections describe a few concrete examples of the impact and the potential of AI **18.004** in the healthcare sector. The focus is on the areas that are commonly identified as having the greatest potential to achieve the ultimate goal of applying AI in life sciences and healthcare – those related to improving people's health, increasing the quality of the healthcare system, relieving the burden on health professionals and giving them more time with patients. Broadly speaking, AI applications are intended to combat diseases and make therapies better and safer. Examples of high-value applications include earlier disease detection, more accurate diagnoses, identification of new observations or patterns on human physiology and development of per-sonalised diagnostics and therapeutics.

1.   Impact and Potential of AI in Healthcare

For some time now, nearly every industry has been exploring ways in which AI can improve **18.005** quality of service and reduce costs. The life sciences and healthcare sectors are no exception. One explanation for this development involves widespread governmental attempts to control the ever-increasing cost of healthcare. AI is perceived as having the potential to reduce the cost of drug discovery and delivery of healthcare services, as well as to improve the efficiency of product development and speed-to-market strategies.

Despite the significant opportunities to use AI to reduce healthcare costs and improve patient **18.006** outcomes, there are still significant obstacles to achieving success. Two of these in particular mean that the impact of AI on healthcare is likely to be rather slow.

First is the volume of data needed. The number of physiological interactions that (may) **18.007** have a role in any disease or health condition is high. There are also many ways in which this interaction actually takes place. For AI to develop further and address more complex interactions, computer processing power and capacity will need to increase even more. Only then can complex conditions be mapped and addressed. Second, the quality of data affects the quality of the outcome. A lot of healthcare and medical research data will be required and considerable curation will be necessary before it can be used to produce robust answers. That is a time-consuming and expensive process in itself.

These issues affect the economics of AI adoption in life sciences. First, the greater cost and **18.008** high risk of failure will affect return on investment for life sciences companies. It also makes the sector less attractive to the most talented AI developers, who are in very short supply and very high demand. A Deloitte report that analysed AI adoption in a range of industries placed life sciences and healthcare in the 'high AI investments/low returns' category (the only industry in that category).[5]

18.009 Notwithstanding these and other risks, there is a clear drive across the industry to develop AI solutions. The sections that follow describe some of the ways in which AI is being developed by, and is considered likely to have a material impact on, the life sciences businesses.

2. Diagnostics

18.010 Imaging techniques are among the most important examination methods for diagnosis in numerous fields. Use of image recognition (that is, the use of AI to examine medical images in order to identify disease) is already under way and is likely to be one of the early success stories in the use of AI in this sector. When it comes to mainstreaming, the key questions relate to how reliable and error-free AI systems are.

18.011 An example that received a lot of publicity recently was a programme jointly developed by Google DeepMind and Moorfields Eye Hospital in London. The programme was trained on approximately 15,000 images, after which it identified eye disease in approximately 1,000 images more accurately than a team of retinal specialists. The more images the programme reviews going forward, the more quickly and accurately will it be able to complete its analysis. What is more, the algorithm may even be adapted for purposes of reviewing radiotherapy and mammogram images.

18.012 Since intelligent systems have made significant progress in recent years, particularly in image recognition, they offer great potential for the early and reliable detection of cancer.[6] In relation to skin cancer, researchers have trained a neural network using a dataset of 129,450 clinical images consisting of 2,032 different diseases, and tested its performance against 21 board-certified dermatologists on biopsy-proven clinical images with two critical binary classification use cases: keratinocyte carcinomas versus benign seborrheic keratoses, and malignant melanomas versus benign nevi. The first case represents the identification of the most common cancers, while the second represents the identification of the deadliest skin cancer. The neural network achieved performance on par with all tested experts, demonstrating that AI was capable of classifying skin cancer at a level of accuracy comparable to that of dermatologists.[7]

18.013 Diagnostic accuracy can be optimised by using AI in combination with human medical expertise. For example, a computer-aided system developed by researchers for the automated detection of metastatic breast cancer in whole-slide images of sentinel lymph node biopsies was given an area under the receiver operating curve (AUC) of 0.925 for the task of whole slide image classification and a score of 0.7051 for the tumour localisation task. A pathologist who examined the same images received a whole slide image classification AUC of 0.966 and a score

---

5   Deloitte, *State of AI in the Enterprise,* 2nd edn (2018).
6   Christoph Auer et al., 'Artificial Intelligence in Healthcare', in Robin Haring, *Digital Health, Perspectives for Digitization in the Health Care System* (2019), at 42.
7   Andre Eseva et al., 'Dermatologist-level Classification of Skin Cancer with Deep Neural Networks', *Nature* 542 (2017), at 115–18.

of 0.733 for tumour localisation. By combining the predictions of the deep learning system with the diagnoses of the human pathologist, the AUC of the pathologist was increased to 0.995, which corresponds to a reduction of the human error rate by about 85 per cent.[8]

Comparable to the possibilities of image recognition for the early detection of cancer are speech recognition techniques used, for example, in the diagnosis of Alzheimer's disease. Through automated identification of small abnormalities in speech that are difficult for people to recognise, a diagnosis can be made at an earlier stage and with relatively little effort.[9] However, such early stage diagnoses of untreatable diseases always require special sensitivity on the part of physicians.   **18.014**

In another study using routine clinical data of 378,256 patients, ML significantly improved the accuracy of cardiovascular risk prediction, correctly predicting 355 (additional 7.6 per cent) more patients who developed cardiovascular disease compared with the established algorithm.[10]   **18.015**

AI is not only suitable for the diagnosis of physical diseases, but can also be used in psychological medicine and psychiatry. For example, researchers have built a predictive model based on ML using whole-brain functional magnetic resonance imaging (fMRI) to achieve a 74 per cent accuracy in identifying patients with more severe negative and positive symptoms in schizophrenia. This suggests that brain network analysis from the fMRI data can help diagnose schizophrenia and predict the severity of symptoms. However, the recognition of neuroimaging patterns requires large-scale analysis across multiple data sets.[11]   **18.016**

3.   Therapeutic Options

AI can be used not only to make a diagnosis but also to support healthcare professionals in choosing between different therapy options, often referred to as decision support software.   **18.017**

Currently the dosing of medicines is relatively generic, in that relatively little information about the individual patient is taken into account when choosing a therapy and setting dose sizes. To a large degree, these decisions are still a matter of trial and error. This will change when AI platforms are able to analyse a wide range of information about the patient and determine which drug has the greatest potential to successfully treat his/her condition and in what volumes. Also, by continually reviewing data the platform will, for example, be able to adjust dose size or, if the disease mutates, revise the decision and introduce a more effective alternative.   **18.018**

So far, a major problem with the selection of a patient-specific therapy has been the relatively low degree of standardisation of patient files, even if they are digitised. Consequently, it   **18.019**

---

8   Dayong Wang et al., 'Deep Learning for Identifying Metastatic Breast Cancer' (2016), available at: https://arxiv.org/abs/1606.05718.

9   Enquete Commission on Artificial Intelligence of the German Federal Parliament, Project Group, 'AI and Health': Summary of preliminary results, as of 18 December 2019, Commission printed paper 19(27)94 (2019), at 2.

10   Stephen F. Wenig et al., 'Can Machine-learning Improve Cardiovascular Risk Prediction Using Routine Clinical Data', *PLoS ONE* 12(4) (2017).

11   Mina Gheiratmand et al., 'Learning Stable and Predictive Network-based Patterns of Schizophrenia and its Clinical Symptoms, *npj Schizophrenia* 3, 22 (2017).

is difficult to extract relevant information or make connections that may allow meaningful insights into the underlying causes of ill health. AI can overcome some of these limitations. For example, natural language processing tools can ensure that information is captured in a more standardised way, making it more accessible to search tools. Other free text search programmes are able to extract key terms from less structured data. Diagnostic algorithms are helping predict (and therefore track and manage) the risk of future illness on the basis of historic health data.

18.020   Already today, these individual therapies tailored to individual patients (personalised therapies) are being carried out. Especially in the case of complex and costly therapies, such as cancer, it is extremely useful to compare individual circumstances with as many similar clinical pictures as possible in order to identify the best possible therapy.[12] An automated evaluation by an intelligent system makes such comparison much easier than manual work.[13] However, a prerequisite for the functionality of such system is the availability of the corresponding data registers which can be used for comparison.

18.021   In one study researchers trained a linguistic ML system, which demonstrated very good classification accuracy and was able to predict post-treatment symptom reductions within eight weeks with at least 88 per cent accuracy in training and 80 per cent accuracy in validation.[14] This shows that ML systems could help assign psychiatric treatments more efficiently, thereby optimising outcomes and limiting unnecessary treatment.

4.   Clinical Trials

18.022   With respect to the development of pharmaceuticals, clinical trials typically take a long time and are very costly. Speeding up this process and making it more cost-effective would have an enormous impact on today's healthcare and the way in which innovations reach everyday medicine.

18.023   An important application of AI in drug studies is drug candidate selection. Screening to identify molecules for drug development is a time-consuming, expensive and inexact process. It is subject to inherent biases that can cause inaccurate identification. At the same time, AI programmes are able to analyse large, complex data sets more quickly and precisely than before. They can also search scientific literature for relevant studies. It is anticipated that neural networks, which can cross-reference many different information streams and make connections that would otherwise be practically impossible, will increasingly provide a much more accurate shortlist of drug candidates more quickly and cheaply than existing processes, which will improve the economics of drug discovery immeasurably.

18.024   In this context, repurposing should also be mentioned. AI enhances the possibility of re-examining clinical and market data to determine whether existing drugs can be remodelled for other purposes. The incremental cost and the opportunity to repurpose will be economically attractive. There will also be an opportunity to explore data from failed historical clinical trials,

---

12   Ralf Huss, *Artificial Intelligence, Robotics and Big Data in Medicine* (2019), at 48 *et seq.*
13   Enquete Commission on Artificial Intelligence, *supra* note 9, at 3.
14   David E. Fleck et al., 'Prediction of Lithium Response in First-episode Mania using the LITHium Intelligent Agent (LITHIA): Pilot Data and Proof-of-concept', *Bipolar Disorders* (2017), at 259–72.

which may provide new insights into why the drug candidate failed and may also suggest alternative opportunities that were not obvious before.

For example, in 2014 Atomwise launched a virtual search for safe, existing medicines that could **18.025** be repurposed to treat the Ebola virus. Four months later, Atomwise's AI technology found evidence that two drugs had the ability to significantly reduce Ebola infectivity. These drugs were intended for unrelated illnesses and their potential to treat Ebola was previously unknown. This analysis, which would typically have taken months or years to perform, was completed in less than one day.[15] The COVID-19 pandemic has made the speed of drug development a mainstream concern.

5. Surgery Robotics

In recent years a large field of robotic surgery has emerged, which is mainly used in urology. **18.026** For example, standard procedures of urological oncology (for example, total removal of the prostate) are increasingly performed with the help of surgical robots. In the US, more than 90 per cent of all prostatectomies are now performed on a robotic-assisted basis; in Germany, the figure is more than 60 per cent.[16]

The idea of robotic surgery is to combine the advantages of minimally invasive techniques **18.027** with those of open surgery. The minimally invasive technique dispenses with large incisions and instead introduces an endoscopic camera and surgical instruments into the operating area through small incisions in order to operate.[17] This method offers advantages for the patient, such as less pain, risk of infection or blood loss. This, in turn, allows for a shorter hospital stay and faster return to everyday life. On the other hand, the use of long, rod-shaped surgical instruments without any degree of freedom and with a two-dimensional view poses new challenges for the surgeon, which can impair the treatment result and/or extend the operating time.[18] In response to these limitations, operating robots have been developed.

During the procedure, the operating robot is controlled by a surgeon sitting at a desk away **18.028** from the operating table. The operating robot provides the doctor with a three-dimensional and greatly enlarged view of the operating area. Further, the operating instruments can be controlled intuitively and offer significantly more degrees of freedom compared to conventional minimally invasive surgery.[19] Robotic surgery thus enables surgeons to perform procedures in otherwise inaccessible parts of the body.

Surgery robotics does not qualify as AI, however, because the surgeon has complete control **18.029** of the robot at all times. The system does not make any independent movements or decisions of its own. It is therefore not so much a robot in the classical sense of the word, but rather

---

15 Atomwise, 'Atomwise finds first evidence towards new Ebola treatments', press release of 25 March 2015, available at: www.atomwise.com/2015/03/24/atomwise-finds-first-evidence-towards-new-ebola-treatments/.

16 Karl-Friedrich Kowalewski et al., 'Collaborative Automation and Robotics in Medicine and Care – Processes in the Operating Room', *MedR* (2019), at 925.

17 Ibid.

18 Ibid.

19 Ibid.

a telemanipulator completely controlled by the operator.[20] The idea of autonomous and fully automated operation through technical systems has not yet become a practical reality.

18.030 Nevertheless, the vision of the self-operating robot still exists and has been pushing scientists and doctors to develop new concepts. Initially, partial steps of an operation are performed automatically. In one experiment, an autonomously operating robot outperformed human surgeons in suturing wounds in a pig model.[21] Currently a new robot-supported system is being tested in urology, which automatically ablates the tissue of the prostate – which has previously been defined by a doctor in ultrasound – with a water jet.[22] Initial studies have shown promising results in terms of shorter operation times and improved quality of life compared to conventional surgical methods.[23] However, further independent studies and long-term results are still needed to conclusively evaluate the superiority of this method in everyday clinical practice.[24]

18.031 Regardless of the autonomy of the technology system, the use of computer-aided surgical procedures generates huge amounts of data – for example, with respect to the lighting in the operating theatre, the ventilation setting of the anaesthesic devices, the positioning of the operating table and the operating instruments used.[25] This data can then be analysed, processed and interpreted in order to optimise surgical procedures. Once trained, a robot will be able to perform consistently and accurately no matter how long an operation takes, whereas human performance will inevitably decline with time. For example, an AI-based camera robot independently learns from videos of previous operations how to guide the camera during an operation.[26]

C. LEGAL CHALLENGES TO THE USE OF ARTIFICIAL INTELLIGENCE IN HEALTHCARE

18.032 The novel and distinctive characteristics of AI pose a number of regulatory and legal challenges. In many respects, the applicable legal frameworks have not yet been adapted to reflect the specifics of the use and further development of AI. Several institutions, commissions and associations, on the political and industry levels, have been working on identifying loopholes in the current legal and regulatory framework and possible solutions for closing them. Data protection liability, intellectual property and bias are all relevant, as covered in detail in other chapters.

---

20   Ibid.

21   Shademan et al., 'Supervised Autonomous Robotic Soft Tissue Surgery', *Science Translational Medicine* 8(337) (2016), at 337.

22   Peter Gilling et al., 'WATER: A Double-Blind, Randomized, Controlled Trial of Aquablation® vs Transurethral Resection of the Prostate in Benign Prostatic Hyperplasia', *The Journal of Urology* (2018), at 1252–61.

23   Ibid.

24   Ibid.

25   Kowalewski et al., *supra* note 16, at 926.

26   Martin Wagner et al., 'Cognitive Camera Robot for Cognition-Guided Laparoscopic Surgery', Proceedings of the Hamlyn Symposium on Medical Robotics (2015), at 23–4.

1.   Regulatory

A central issue in the development of software solutions based on AI is the regulatory classification of such software. The key question in this regard is whether software is to be classified as a medical device. This is of practical importance because medical devices may only be placed on the market if they bear a CE mark[27] and have been checked in a conformity assessment procedure. If a product qualifying as a medical device is distributed without a CE mark, competitors may request that its distribution is discontinued. Placing such a product on the market may even constitute an administrative offence or have criminal consequences, as, for instance, in Germany.   **18.033**

According to European Regulation (EU) 2017/745 concerning medical devices (the MDR), which became fully effective in May 2021, software solutions may qualify as medical devices. The qualification depends on the intended purpose of the software. Broadly speaking, if a software detects or helps to treat illnesses – for example, by supporting the diagnosis via image recognition or by calculating the dosage of medication – it will likely qualify as a medical device. If the software only provides knowledge or only saves data, the product will likely not have an intended medical purpose.   **18.034**

The MDR has brought about a number of challenges for industry players developing medical software involving AI. Namely, the MDR contains a new specific classification rule (Rule 11) for stand-alone software. According to this rule, most AI solutions will likely be upgraded from class I to at least class IIa under the MDR. This means the conformity assessment procedure may no longer be carried out in-house by the company itself, but must involve a notified body (that is, an external auditor). This will increase the administrative burden considerably. Some argue it may even discourage the development of such solutions within Europe. The UK's Medicines and Healthcare Products Regulatory Agency has developed a useful flowchart that can help ascertain the status of a piece of software. In any event, a company developing software solutions should consider this aspect very early on in the development process.   **18.035**

Medical devices involving AI that interact with healthcare professionals may blur the line between, on the one hand, providing a value-added service only to support clinicians and, on the other hand, providing a medical treatment service on its own. This can be in conflict with the current rules of the medical profession, which in most jurisdictions require that medical treatment be reserved to healthcare professionals, namely doctors. To avoid crossing this line and being exposed to legal and compliance risks, analysis of which AI functionalities could run afoul of this principle and how infringements can be avoided should take place early in the software development phase.   **18.036**

An example of this problem is surgery support software – surgery robotics. If software is designed to help a doctor during surgery, for instance by suggesting how concrete steps of a surgery are carried out, it becomes questionable to what extent the doctor is still carrying out his/her medical work. In this respect, the decisive factor will be whether the software and the robot carry out or at least significantly influence the course of the operation.   **18.037**

---

27   CE stands for *Conformité Européenne* (French for European Conformity).

18.038   As explained, the prerequisite for the functionality of any AI system is the availability of appropriate data registers that can be used for comparison. On the one hand, service providers therefore need a secure and efficient digital infrastructure for the storage and transmission of health data and the digitalisation of healthcare processes. On the other hand, an innovation-friendly and efficient legal framework for data protection is also needed, which will make health data usable in the research and development of AI solutions and preserve the digital sovereignty and data protection rights of patients.[28]

18.039   One issue that continues to attract considerable attention is the conflict between the fact that AI technologies rely on the availability of sensitive data and the legal requirements for the protection of personal data. Yet, central principles of data protection, such as transparency, purpose limitation and data minimisation, are opposed to the strategy of AI in some aspects, for instance because a large amount of data is required to feed AI systems and develop such systems further.

18.040   The above examples show that the regulatory framework places quite significant constraints on the development and use of AI applications in practice. Regulatory hurdles should be identified as early as possible in the development process of AI projects to avoid hiccups at a later stage. At the same time, uncertainties in the regulatory framework offer important opportunities. Using the regulatory leeway can help pave the way for unknown AI applications benefiting patients, industry players and healthcare providers alike.

18.041   The February 2020 European Commission White Paper on Artificial Intelligence (the White Paper)[29] is a pillar of the Commission's future digital strategy. It aims to promote the use of AI, while simultaneously reducing the risks associated with it. Healthcare is clearly one field where a risk–benefit analysis will have a heavy weighting to the risk side of the equation. Among the guiding principles of the White Paper, the creation of ecosystems for excellence and trust stand out in the context of healthcare.

18.042   The Commission posits that the existing European regulations should be adapted to AI and its effects. As core challenges it identifies changing functions of AI systems within their life cycle, uncertainties with respect to responsibilities within the supply chain and changes in security concepts. As a first step, the Commission intends to continue to apply the existing regulation in various sectors, such as health, including medical devices, product liability and data protection. The second step will entail the development of additional regulations that reflect the new challenges posed by AI, while at the same time ensuring that regulatory intervention is proportionate. To achieve this balance the Commission favours a risk-based approach, with new, extended rules applying primarily to high-risk AI applications.

18.043   A given AI application should generally be considered high-risk in light of 'what is at stake, considering whether both the sector and the intended use involve significant risks, in particular from the viewpoint of protection of safety, consumer rights and fundamental rights'. The White Paper includes health, as examples of sectors where 'given the characteristics of the

---

28   Enquete Commission on Artificial Intelligence, *supra* note 9, at 4.
29   European Commission, White Paper on Artificial Intelligence – A European approach to excellence and trust, COM (2020) 65 final (19 February 2020).

activities typically undertaken, significant risks can be expected to occur'. At the second stage, the question is whether the AI application is used in the sector concerned in such a way that significant risks are to be expected. According to the Commission, the reason for this criterion is that not every use of AI applications in the selected sectors necessarily involves significant risks.

With the White Paper and the accompanying report on the safety and liability framework,[30] the Commission has launched a broad consultation process on the AI concept in Europe. This includes not only political means but also, and above all, proposals for core elements of the future legal framework. It can be expected that the rapid spread of AI and its steadily increasing importance will entail further calls for effective regulation. **18.044**

2.   Liability for the Use of AI

The implementation of AI systems in healthcare and life sciences brings ever-growing benefits for patients. At the same time, however, it raises new questions regarding liability allocation in the case of damages caused by these systems. In addition to the physician, the technology manufacturer will be concerned about liability risks. A manufacturer can typically be found liable for its product causing harm under the product liability regime. The use of AI systems in the development of drugs, the diagnosis of patients and the design of individually tailored treatments will make it necessary to rethink liability principles, as well as the split of liability between manufacturers, physicians and patients. **18.045**

The law of tort of the EU Member States is largely non-harmonised, with the exception of product liability law under Directive 85/374/EEC (the Product Liability Directive). On a national level, it can generally be observed that the laws of the EU Member States do not (yet) contain liability rules specifically applicable to damages resulting from the use of emerging digital technologies such as AI.[31] Together with the White Paper, in February 2020 the European Commission published a report on the safety and liability implications of AI, the Internet of Things and robotics.[32] It contains a detailed analysis of the current legal framework, identifies a number of gaps and makes quite concrete proposals for adapting the legal framework. **18.046**

The strict liability of producers for defective products has been harmonised at the EU level by the Product Liability Directive. Article 1 of the Directive provides that the producer of a product is liable for damages caused by a defect in that product, irrespective of fault. However, the producer will not be liable if, among other things, he proves 'that the state of scientific and technical knowledge at the time when he put the product into circulation was not such as to enable the existence of the defect to be discovered'.[33] This can lead to the exclusion of liability, especially for autonomously acting robots. Constant progress in AI systems through deep **18.047**

---

30   Commission to the European Parliament, The Council and the European Economic and social Committee, 'Report on the safety and liability implications of Artificial Intelligence, the Internet of Things and robotics', COM(2020) 64 final (19 February 2020).

31   European Commission, Liability for Artificial Intelligence and other emerging digital technologies (2019), at 15.

32   Commission to the European Parliament, *supra* note 30.

33   Directive 85/347/EEC, Art 7(e).

learning makes it difficult to determine the state of play at the time of the product release, as well as to define a product defect in the first place.

18.048   Apart from the rules on product liability, damages suffered as a result of the operation of AI technologies can be claimed under the existing legislation on contractual and tortious liability in each EU Member State.[34] In general, these national liability regimes include fault-based liability and several specific rules which either modify the premises of fault-based liability (in particular the distribution of the burden of proof of fault) or establish strict liability.[35] There are some differences between the national legal systems with regard to the scope of these specific rules, the conditions of liability and the burden of proof. Most liability regimes also provide for the liability of others (vicarious liability).[36]

18.049   The sections that follow illustrate tortious and contractual liability for the use of AI using the example of the treatment error in the use of robots under German tort law.

18.050   As a starting point for liability in tort, the robot's manufacture or programming can be considered in addition to its use, because it is not only the person who operated the robot that is responsible for damages, but also the person who developed the robot-supported treatment method.[37]

18.051   If the malfunctions of the robot are not foreseeable to the person using it, fault-based liability will not apply. However, for reasons of patient protection, high demands will have to be placed on medical care when using robot-assisted treatment methods.

18.052   Namely, liability is excluded if the patient has consented to the use of the medical robot. However, the consent is only effective if the patient has been informed beforehand about all circumstances essential for the consent. This includes not only the course of treatment and the consequences and risks of the medical intervention, but also, and above all, the extent to which robotics is used and the specific risks associated with the use of robots.[38] According to case law of the German Federal Court of Justice, patients also need to be informed about alternative treatment measures which are equally apt at achieving the same treatment goal using manual technology.[39]

18.053   Under German tort law the injured party bears the burden of proving the conditions of liability. For treatment and product defects, however, case law has developed several simplifications of the burden of proof. For example, prima facie evidence can suffice if the health impairment at stake is the typical consequence of a violation of the medical standard of treatment. The burden may even be reversed in particular cases of significant violation of the standard of care.

18.054   While the tortious claim for damages is directed against the attending physician or the robot manufacturer, in the case of contractual liability only the physician or the hospital will be the

---

34   European Commission, *supra* note 31, at 15.
35   Ibid., at 16.
36   Ibid.
37   Oliver Brand, 'Liability and Insurance when Using Robotics in Medicine and Care, *MedR* (2019), at 945.
38   Ibid.
39   Federal Court of Justice (BGH), judgment of 13 June 2006, VI ZR 323/04.

defendant. The contractual claim has the advantage for the patient that the German Civil Code provides for a reversal of the burden of proof regarding fault. However, treating the robot as a vicarious agent, with the consequence that errors of the robot due to faulty programming would be attributable to the physician as culpable acts, is not possible, as robots are not legal entities and therefore cannot be accused of fault.[40]

For robots that do not make independent movements and do not make their own decisions but are completely controlled by the operator, there are no liability gaps under current law. In contrast, the question of liability for autonomously acting robots is much more complex. Through deep learning, these robots are able to make decisions that are usually unpredictable for both the manufacturer and the doctor. Attribution of treatment errors of the robot to either the doctor or the manufacturer is therefore regularly ruled out. In addition, the unpredictability of the autonomous system usually rules out the allegations of fault.[41] Since there is also no strict liability for the use of autonomous systems in German law, liability gaps may occur.   **18.055**

The implementation of new, unknown medical solutions based on AI naturally goes hand in hand with certain risks. The role of a product liability regime along with regulatory laws is to balance the benefits of new treatments and products with the potential risks for patients, while also splitting the remaining risks among the persons involved. The current legal framework in Germany follows that basic line, although there is debate as to whether those challenges can be solved with the existing product liability regime or if new specific regulations are needed.   **18.056**

The EU has reacted to those developments by setting up an expert commission, which has concluded that the liability regimes in force in the EU Member States ensure at least basic protection of victims whose damage is caused by the operation of AI technologies.[42] However, the specific characteristics of these technologies and their applications – including complexity, modification through updates or self-learning during operation, limited predictability and vulnerability to cybersecurity threats – would make it more difficult to offer these victims a claim for compensation in all cases where this seems justified.[43] It could also be the case that the allocation of liability is unfair or inefficient.[44] To rectify this, certain adjustments would have to be made to the EU and national liability regimes.[45]   **18.057**

There are two main approaches for the determination of liability with regard to AI systems. One could concentrate the risk with one party and determine it by reshaping prerequisites and definitions. Alternatively, one could try to create a system of shared risk among all participants. There are interesting arguments and solutions for both approaches, which range from implementing a system of mandatory insurances to more exotic ideas such as directing claims against the AI system itself by creating a new type of legal person to be held (financially) responsible.   **18.058**

---

40   Brand, *supra* note 37, at 946 *et seq.*
41   Ibid.
42   European Commission, *supra* note 31, at 3.
43   Ibid.
44   Ibid.
45   Ibid; see also Commission to the European Parliament, *supra* note 30.

18.059 Another solution might be to go one step back and define additional regulatory rules on testing requirements and risk analysis prior to the launch, as well as strict monitoring duties for AI systems on the market. The concomitant implementation of blockchain-based 'black boxes' – tools to track information on the use of AI systems based on blockchain technology – may make it easier to determine causality and at the same time help claimants to present the necessary evidence.

3. Intellectual Property

18.060 While man-made works have long been protected by copyright, the question of the protect-ability of works created by autonomous AIs – the so-called emergent works – remains largely unanswered. In this respect, it is a matter of constellations in which the AI service is provided without any human influence. One example is the autonomous development of drugs and therapies for the treatment of cancer.

18.061 In German copyright law, the protection gap results from the fact that only 'personal intellectual creations' are protected as 'works' within the meaning of the Copyright Act.[46] A human-creative activity is therefore required, which is why machines cannot create 'works'.[47]

18.062 Under European law, the limitation of copyright protection to human creations results from the fact that the relevant directives require the 'author's own intellectual creation'.[48] Moreover, the European Court of Justice has also ruled that copyright protection only applies to a subject matter which is original in the sense that it is the 'author's own intellectual creation'.[49]

18.063 In the UK, on the other hand, emergent works have been regulated by law. Thus, the Copyright, Designs and Patents Act 1988 states that '[i]n the case of a literary, dramatic, musical or artistic work which is computer-generated, the author shall be taken to be the person by whom the arrangements necessary for the creation of the work are undertaken'.[50] However, as discussed in detail in Chapter 12, it remains unclear what type and extent of human involvement is required in the creation of the arrangements for the production of the work for such an attribution of the rights ownership.[51]

18.064 In most European legal systems there is no copyright protection for emergent works because there is no human creator. Even the strongest AI could not currently apply for intellectual property rights, because it is not a legal entity. Attribution of the ownership of rights to a third party could help in this respect, but clear criteria are needed to determine the owner of the rights to the emergent work. In 2017 the Legal Affairs Committee of the European Parliament asked the European Commission to specify the criteria for determining under which conditions emergent works are to be regarded as 'own intellectual creations' – even if not actually devel-

---

46   German Copyright Act, s 2(2).
47   Tim W. Dornis, 'The Protection of Artificial Creativity in Intellectual Property Law', GRUR (2019), at 1255.
48   Computer Programs Directive 2009/24/EC, Art 1(3); Copyright Term Directive 2006/116/EV, Art 6; and Database Directive 96/9/EC, Art 3(1).
49   Judgement of the Court of Justice in Case C-5-5/08, ¶37.
50   UK Copyright, Designs and Patents Act 1988, s 9(3).
51   Dornis, *supra* note 47, at 1256.

oped by a person itself – eligible for copyright protection.[52] This is still a work in progress on the part of the EU Commission.

4.   Reimbursement

The AI-based collection and analysis of health data as a means of assessing performance of novel treatments and drugs in the real world brings a number of advantages, not least from the financial perspective. On the one hand, it enables the authorities to approve new therapies earlier, and thus more cost-effectively from the point of view of medical service providers, because they are constantly monitored for efficacy and side effects. On the other hand, AI can make a significant contribution to the early detection of diseases, precise diagnosis and the development of a patient-specific treatment strategy. Moreover, as AI will increasingly be included in the regular provision of health services, doctors will have to spend less of their time on diagnosis or on evaluating treatment options, impacting reimbursements.[53] As a result, it is estimated that health expenditure in Europe alone will be reduced by a triple-digit billion euro amount over the next ten years.[54]   **18.065**

Due to the increasing importance of AI in medical treatment, it will be important in the future to redefine the remuneration models. Current payer systems encourage doctors to provide as many services as possible, as remuneration is based on the volume of treatment and not on the value that the treatment has for the patient.[55] AI-supported processing of health data enables insurance companies to monitor patient care and analyse the success of treatment. This allows for a shift in healthcare financing towards value-based reimbursement.   **18.066**

In addition to changes in the remuneration structure, the increasing implementation of AI technologies sometimes calls into question the remuneration system as such. Traditionally, many remuneration systems (such as the German one) have been connected to a healthcare professional who, at least to some extent, plays a role in the diagnosis or treatment of a patient. For instance, a payment for a diagnosis is due if the healthcare professional carries out the diagnosis him/herself, possibly with the help of decision-support software. However, if in the future software were to carry out the diagnosis itself, without the need for a doctor, the question arises as to whether and how this would be reimbursed – even leaving aside issues related to the professional code of conduct. In other words, the question arises as to who will be entitled to remuneration for a medical intervention carried out by a robot acting completely autonomously, without a doctor's involvement.   **18.067**

---

52   European Parliament, Report with recommendations to the Commission on Civil Law Rules on Robotics, 2015/2103(INL) (27.1.2017), at 28.

53   PwC, Sherlock in Health – How Artificial Intelligence may Improve Quality and Efficiency, Whilst Reducing Healthcare Costs in Europe, available at: www.pwc.de/de/gesundheitswesen-und-pharma/studie-sherlock-in-health .pdf, at 21.

54   Ibid., at 2.

55   Ibid., at 21.

D. CONCLUSION

18.068   AI is widely regarded as one of the greatest hopes of our time. Especially in medicine, the number of people that AI will be able to help can only increase. In numerous fields of life sciences and healthcare there are already AI applications under development, existing as prototypes or already in use. The advantages of this technology, which at first glance appears rather abstract, have already been demonstrated by improvements in diagnosis, therapy and research. At present, AI technologies are still largely used as a support tool for physicians by providing diagnoses and therapy suggestions within a short period of time. The development of fully autonomous AI systems, such as surgery robots, will be followed with great interest.

18.069   As is often the case, progress in technology has been much faster than progress in law. So far, there is no specific legal framework for AI and its use. Instead, various use cases need to be fitted within the framework of the existing laws. However, existing laws are often incomplete – for example, with respect to the allocation of liability and protection of intellectual property. Naturally, this causes uncertainty, which is not atypical in new developments and progressive fields. Therefore it will be important to further develop the existing legislative framework(s) to address these uncertainties. In any event, developers, manufacturers and healthcare professionals will need to be aware of the applicable laws and regulations. These need to be taken into account sufficiently early in the development stage of a product using AI, as well as in the actual use of such product.

19

TELECOMS AND CONNECTIVITY

Suzanne Rab

A. INTRODUCTION

Developments in artificial intelligence (AI) and machine learning present a number of benefits, including improvements in economic outcomes, enhanced human decision-making, increased levels of productivity and potential solutions for complex and pressing economic and social problems. Yet challenges for law, regulation and policy remain. Not least, there is a challenge in ensuring that policy, laws and regulations governing systems enabled by AI are relevant, adequate, proportionate and targeted. **19.001**

This chapter seeks to understand (at a relatively high and exploratory level at this evolutionary stage) the key legal, regulatory and policy aspects of managing AI in the telecoms sector. In telecoms AI applications are transforming the ways in which providers operate, optimise and deliver service to their customers. At the same time, the sector has seen fewer sector-specific regulatory interventions in the area of AI and ML than have other sectors. The chapter anticipates how telecoms regulators may approach the topic by exploring how similar challenges have been dealt with in other relevant comparative sectors. **19.002**

19.003 Specifically, this analysis addresses the following areas. First, what is the overall legal, regulatory and policy framework for AI and is it adequate for an appraisal of AI in the telecoms sector? Second, to what extent are AI usage scenarios sensitive to the industry context? The analysis considers examples of how the risks and apparent or perceived regulatory gaps have been addressed in related sectors, and emerging policy lessons. The fintech, robotics and autonomous vehicles sectors are reliant on connectivity provided by the telecoms industry. The Internet of Things is a common point where devices and applications depend on or integrate with telecoms networks and services. AI challenges in the telecoms sector arise because most industries deploying AI depend on connectivity.

19.004 Alongside connectivity is data. Data can be 'pseudonymised'. Pseudonymised data is personal data that has been processed so that it can no longer be attributed to a specific data subject without the use of additional information such as a unique identifier which can make the data identifiable. An original dataset even without the identifier can still be personal data (in the hands of an organisation that holds both the dataset and the identifier) since it can be matched with the original database to make the data identifiable. In order to become pseudonymised data, the additional information must be kept separately and held subject to adequate technical and organisational measures. The data can then be considered as pseudonymised data even where the identifier is kept within the same organisation. Pseudonymised data remains personal data but pseudonymisation provides a security mechanism for reducing the level of risk exposure under the GDPR.

B. THE INTERNET OF THINGS

19.005 There is no universally accepted definition of the Internet of Things.

19.006 A convenient starting point is the OECD's reference to it as 'an ecosystem in which applications and services are driven by data collected from devices that sense and interface with the physical world'.[1] Specifically, according to the OECD, the IoT includes

> devices and objects whose state can be altered via the Internet, with or without the active involvement of individuals. This includes laptops, routers, servers, tablets and smartphones, often considered to be part of the 'traditional Internet'. However, these devices are integral to operating, reading and analysing the state of IoT devices and frequently constitute the heart and brains of the system. As such, it would not be correct to exclude them.[2]

19.007 The IoT has been further summarised as encompassing the following three elements:

- the 'sensors' that collect data about us and our environment (such as smart thermostats, street and highway sensors);

---

1 OECD (2016), The Internet of Things: Seizing the Benefits and Addressing the Challenges, OECD Digital Economy Papers, No. 252, OECD Publishing, Paris. Available at: http://dx.doi.org/10.1787/5jlwvzz8td0n-en.
2 OECD (2015), OECD Digital Economy Outlook 2015, OECD Publishing, Paris. Available at: http://dx.doi.org/10.1787/9789264232440-en.

- the 'smarts', which figure out what the data means and how to respond to it. This includes all the computer processors on the IoT devices and, increasingly, in the cloud, as well as the memory that stores all of this information; and
- the 'actuators' that affect the device and the environment. The point of a smart thermostat is, for example, not limited to recording the temperature; it is also to control other devices, such as an air conditioner.[3]

Telecoms usage scenarios that interact with the IoT are considered in section D.   **19.008**

C. THE LEGAL FRAMEWORK FOR AI

Our starting point for a discussion about the legal framework for AI in telecoms is to ask: what   **19.009**
is the nature of AI, and how does this inform the legal analysis of what rights and duties are or
should be attached to it?

In order to explore the interactions between AI and existing regulation it is necessary to under-   **19.010**
stand the multiplicity of existing legal rules and regimes that may be engaged in any telecoms
AI usage scenario. The debate around AI has been linked or conflated with debates around
access to (personal) data. While the issue is not confined to the telecoms sector, it has a particular significance there, because many of the AI usage scenarios in telecoms depend on access
to rich personal data. This includes personal data such as customer names and billing data as
well as data on usage and location.

Data or intelligence must be refined before it is useful; that is, it has to be turned into informa-   **19.011**
tion, knowledge or action. Data is a non-rivalrous good. A good is said to be rivalrous or rival if
its consumption by one consumer prevents simultaneous consumption by other consumers, or
if consumption by one party reduces the ability of another party to consume it. Most tangible
goods fall into this category. In contrast, a good is considered non-rivalrous or non-rival if, for
any level of production, the cost of providing it to a marginal (additional) individual is zero.
More generally, most intellectual property is non-rival.

In fact, this distinction is over-simplistic, as a good can be placed along a continuum ranging   **19.012**
from rivalrous to non-rivalrous. Data as expression and communication is limitless and it may
be said that subjecting data to legal rules about ownership would be inconsistent with its nature
as limitless. However, digital information is only available because of investment and creative
effort and therefore has some limits.

This equivocal position provides a starting point for legal analysis, which is that data or intelli-   **19.013**
gence so derived is a complex subject in legal terms. This is best explained by focusing attention
not on whether there are rights 'in' data or 'in' AI, but on the extensive rights and obligations 'in
relation to' such data and its outputs, including AI. In turn, this reframing of the legal analysis
raises a question of whether, and the extent to which, it may be excludable or partly excludable
(such as through intellectual property rights (IPR) or data protection/privacy regulation). As

---

3   B. Schneier (2017), Click Here to Kill Everyone with The Internet of Things. Available at: http://nymag.com/selectall/
     2017/01/the-internet-of-things-dangerous-future-bruce-schneier.html

a result, when discussing AI in legal terms it may be more correct to speak in terms of access to AI processes and outputs rather than ownership as such.

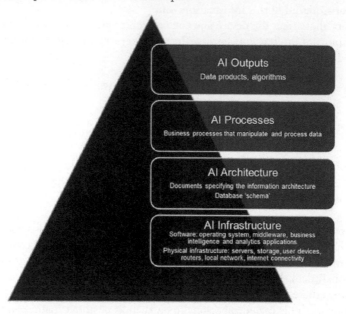

Figure 19.1 *AI topology*

19.014 The relevant rights and duties arise through different mechanisms including IPR, contract and regulation. These mechanisms operate across the following levels: AI infrastructure, AI information architecture and AI outputs (see Figure 19.1). Each of these is significant in assessing AI use cases in telecoms.

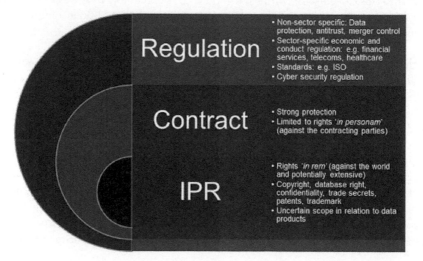

Figure 19.2 *Legal rights in relation to AI*

The legal framework accords positive rights (in the case of IPR and contract) which can, in   **19.015**
principle, be monetised. Breach of these rights can give rise to remedies including damages and
injunctions (in the case of IPR and contract), and other sanctions such as fines for breach of
a regulatory duty (see Figure 19.2).

Ongoing legal and regulatory developments in these areas mean that information rights law is   **19.016**
emerging as a new and sophisticated area of law and policy in its own right, revolving around
the intersection between these elements. Again, each of these is significant in assessing AI use
cases in telecoms.

D. AI REGULATION

1.   Lessons from Fintech

To illustrate the scale and breadth of changes that are taking place with AI, it is useful to examine   **19.017**
AI usage scenarios across different industry sectors. Given the limited telecoms-specific regulatory responses in the field of AI, relevant comparators from other analogous or related contexts
provide a useful guide to how the telecoms industry should consider these issues.

Fintech provides a use scenario in another regulated sector which has a dedicated sector regu-   **19.018**
lator and which is subject to technological change. An important issue in telecoms and other
network industries such as financial services is how the regulatory framework affects the incentives for investment in new infrastructure and applications, particularly infrastructure required
for the transition from legacy systems and environments. The issue raises new regulatory
challenges because regulation to date has tended to focus most heavily on networks that were
already built, and investments sunk. Now regulation has to be shaped to reflect the impact it
can have on the incentives for the development of new, innovative and potentially larger-scale
investments by a range of market participants. The dynamic nature of mobile technologies is
likely to present financial services companies with challenges and opportunities. First, 'mobile'
is less about a device or an application and more about how technologies can augment customer experience. Second, mobile is increasingly becoming the primary means through which
customers interact with their financial services provider.[4] (See, further, Chapter 15 on financial
services.)

AI in robotics provides a use scenario in a diverse sector where applications are regulated by   **19.019**
a variety of technical standards. The telecoms usage scenarios in an IoT environment which
deploy wearables, health monitors and implantable devices make AI in robotics a candidate
case for comparative assessment (see further section (2) below).

---

4   Deloitte (2014), Mobile financial services. Raising the bar on customer engagement. Available at: https://www2.deloitte
.com/content/dam/insights/us/articles/mobile-financial-services/DUP-693_FSI-Mobility_MASTER_kw.pdf.

19.020 AI in autonomous vehicles provides a use scenario which is connected closely with other sectors and which depends, in particular, on close integration with the communications network. AI user cases in Fintech that apply by analogy to telecoms include:

- internal controls (monitoring transactions for potential fraud and regulatory compliance);
- customer risk profiling (such as making decisions on lending and rates linked to lending and insurability criteria);
- customer service (automated call centres, online chat boxes);
- client advice (including advising financial services professionals and customers themselves).

BOX 19.1 TREATING CUSTOMERS FAIRLY

AI offers opportunities to provide more sales opportunities than can be offered via a website or human interaction. This brings with it a number of regulatory challenges.

Fairness: An AI customer service chatbot may decide to promote certain products, which raises a concern as to accountability for AI-based decisions.

Telecoms firms could be guided by the six consumer outcomes set by the FCA.

- Outcome 1: Consumers can be confident they are dealing with firms where the fair treatment of customers is central to the corporate culture.
- Outcome 2: Products and services marketed and sold in the retail market are designed to meet the needs of identified consumer groups and are targeted accordingly.
- Outcome 3: Consumers are provided with clear information and are kept appropriately informed before, during and after the point of sale.
- Outcome 4: Where consumers receive advice, the advice is suitable and takes account of their circumstances.
- Outcome 5: Consumers are provided with products that perform as firms have led them to expect, and the associated service is of an acceptable standard and as they have been led to expect.
- Outcome 6: Consumers do not face unreasonable post-sale barriers imposed by firms to change product, switch provider, submit a claim or make a complaint.

BOX 19.2   EXPLORING ALTERNATIVE REGULATORY TECHNOLOGY (REGTECH) APPROACHES AND SANDBOXES

The FCA explores how technology can make its regulations more efficient and reduce the regulatory burden on firms. One of the ways it does this is through 'TechSprints' that bring together financial services providers, technology companies and subject matter experts to develop solutions to regulatory challenges. In November 2017, the FCA and the Bank of England held a two-week TechSprint to examine how technology can make the current system of regulatory reporting more accurate, efficient and consistent. At the TechSprint, participants developed a 'proof of concept' which could make regulatory reporting requirements machine-readable and executable. In October 2018 the FCA published its Digital

Regulatory Reporting 'DRR' Feedback statement.[5] DRR has not to date been implemented successfully by any other regulator but the FCA believes it has the potential to fundamentally transform how the industry understands, interprets and then reports regulatory information. This could have compliance cost reducing benefits that could lower barriers to entry and promote competition.

These approaches could equally be applied by the telecoms regulator and industry participants in promoting technology innovation for the benefit of customers.

2.   Lessons from Robotics

A robot is defined by ISO Standard ISCO No.8373 as an 'actuated mechanism programmable in two or more axes [...] with a degree of autonomy [...] moving within its environment, to perform intended tasks'.[6]   **19.021**

Asimov's Three Laws of Robotics[7] provided the first rules to regulate the manufacturing of robots but these are not sufficient to take account of the full legal implications of robots and the multi-faceted areas of their deployment (including drones, medical devices, industrial applications, toys) and, now, their connectivity and communications capacity.   **19.022**

Boxes 19.3 to 19.5 present selected legal and policy areas for consideration based on AI use scenarios in robotics.   **19.023**

BOX 19.3   ENSURING THAT REGULATION IS FIT FOR PURPOSE

Toy robots take many forms (for example, humanoid, animals and games). They may be used for a variety of purposes, including educational and entertainment. The EU Directive on the Safety of Toys[8] defines toys as 'products designed or intended, whether or not exclusively, for use or play by children under 14 years of age' (Article 2(1)). This definition may capture products which were not originally intended as toys, raising a question as to whether a definitional approach based on function (as opposed to design or intention) may be more appropriate. Equally, there may be some arbitrariness in the selection of 14 years as a trigger for liability in the case of 'toys' which are designed for or targeted at a different age group but which may be used by children.

---

5   Financial Conduct Authority. FS18/2: Digital Regulatory Reporting Feedback Statement on Call for Inputs, Feedback Statement, October 2018.

6   ISO 8373:2012.

7   The Three Laws are: First Law – A robot may not injure a human being or, through inaction, allow a human being to come to harm. Second Law – A robot must obey the orders given it by human beings except where such orders would conflict with the First Law. Third Law – A robot must protect its own existence as long as such protection does not conflict with the First or Second Laws. I. Asimov (1950) Runaround. I, Robot (The Isaac Asimov Collection ed.). New York City: Doubleday.

8   Directive 2009/48/EC of the European Parliament and of the Council of 18 June 2009 on the safety of toys, O.J. L. 170, 30.6.2009, pp. 1–37.

BOX 19.4   ENSURING THAT REGULATION IS PROPORTIONATE AND
              PROVIDES LEGAL CERTAINTY

Industrial robots may qualify as 'machinery' under the EU Machinery Directive[9] as 'an assembly, fitted with or intended to be fitted with a drive system other than directly applied
human or animal effort, consisting of linked parts or components, at least one of which
moves, and which are joined together for a specific application' (as further defined in Article
2(1)(a)). It can be difficult to determine whether or not some types of robot, such as robots
used in service applications, qualify as machine robots. Where they do so qualify, this brings
with it stringent obligations, including health and safety.

BOX 19.5   ENSURING POLICY, LAW AND REGULATION REFLECTS THE
              PACE OF TECHNICAL DEVELOPMENT

Robots are increasingly used in the medical sector, with applications such as diagnostic robots, caregiver robots, surgeon robots or robotic prostheses. Such devices typically qualify
as medical devices and, as such, need to comply with specific regulation. EU regulation on
medical devices[10] imposes strict liability on importers and distributors of medical robots.
Medical robots also need to comply with strict security regulation, including ISO standard
No.13482.[11] Given the pace of technical development it is expected that these regulations
will likely become inadequate and out of step with the state of the (medical) art.

3.   Lessons from automated vehicles

19.024   Automotive and technology businesses use AI in the manufacture and deployment of autonomous vehicles, including driverless cars and trucks. AI and other technologies provide the
intelligence to assess a scenario, plan action and execute vehicle control decisions. Various
automated technologies are available, providing different levels of automation and a variety of
applications. All forms of automation rely on connectivity. For example:

- Automated cars use sensors to detect other vehicles and other situational aspects. AI technologies interpret the data to make decisions about vehicle speed and direction.
- AI can be used in commercial trucks to connect multiple self-driving trucks into platforms
  that reduce fuel consumption and labour costs.

---

9   Directive 2006/42/EC of the European Parliament and of the Council of 17 May 2006 on machinery, and amending
     Directive 95/16/EC, O.J. L 157, 9.6.2006, pp. 24–86.
10   Including Regulation (EU) 2017/745 of the European Parliament and of the Council of 5 April 2017 on medical devices,
     amending Directive 2001/83/EC, Regulation (EC) No 178/2002 and Regulation (EC) No 1223/2009 and repealing
     Council Directives 90/385/EEC and 93/42/EEC, O.J. L 117, 5.5.2017, pp. 1–175.
11   ISO 13482:2014 specifies requirements and guidelines for the inherently safe design, protective measures, and informa-
     tion for use of personal care robots, in particular the following three types of personal care robots: mobile servant robot;
     physical assistant robot; person carrier robot.

- Automated transit services (such as shuttles on defined routes within a closed user environment such as a university or airport) limit the complexity of the operating environment.
- AI may be available for home delivery performed by automated vehicles such as aerial drones or truck robots.

The following are selected legal and policy areas for consideration based on AI use scenarios in automated vehicles: **19.025**

BOX 19.6   ENSURING A CONSISTENT AND CONNECTED NATIONAL AND GLOBAL REGULATORY FRAMEWORK

AI vehicle solutions rely on connections in multiple spheres and industries, emphasising the importance of coordination across policy and legal and regulatory regimes. For example, automated vehicles embed communications devices (such as SIM cards), managed by mobile operators. They will also integrate automatic emergency calling, in-vehicle entertainment systems, telematics (machine-to-machine data transmission) and other communications and media technologies. Vehicle communication links and use of radar to avoid collisions place increasing demands on reliable spectrum resources. This requires careful planning and coordination of policy at national, regional and international (ITU) level.

While the availability and deployment of AI techniques is increasingly global, each country appears to be developing its own set of road and vehicles regulations. This has prompted reconsideration of international agreements such as the UN Conventions on Road Traffic. This is an evolving regulatory landscape where the end-point remains to be settled.

BOX 19.7   NAVIGATING IPR

In addition to AI, automated vehicles will incorporate a range of technologies and devices including antennas, touchscreens, cameras and lenses, onboard computers, applications and integrated mapping/GPS and mobile connectivity. These domains have been subject to patent litigation in the past decade involving claims against patent holders to grant access to their patent rights.

IPR is a further area which displays a lack of harmony globally and which compounds the complexities of navigating multiple legal regimes. For example, some countries operate copyright registration requirements while in others copyright arises by operation of law without a registration requirement (for example, in the UK there is no official registration regime for copyrights). Database rights in Europe do not apply to databases made outside the EU. The lack of harmony on IPR protection worldwide is not unique to the area of AI but this situation compounds the challenges in an IP-intensive environment.

AI and IP is considered in detail in Chapter 12.

BOX 19.8 RETHINKING LIABILITY

AI in automated vehicles requires a rethinking of traditional notions of liability. Most regulatory regimes and liability rules that impact vehicles are based on the assumption of a human driver. However, increasing attention is being given to evaluation of when humans and vehicles drive and where the boundaries of liability rest. University of Brighton researcher John Kingston put forward three legal theories of criminal liability that could apply to an entity controlled by AI. These are: (1) perpetrator via another – the programmer (software designer) or the user could be held liable for directly instructing the AI entity to commit the crime; (2) natural and probable consequence – the programmer or the user could be held liable for causing the AI entity to commit a crime as a consequence of its natural operation; and (3) direct liability – the AI system has demonstrated the criminal elements of a recognised theory of liability in criminal law.[12]

There are challenges in updating the approach to law enforcement and crash investigations for cases involving AI, which may necessitate an inquiry into where human error is involved or failures may relate to malfunctioning of AI technology.

A related issue affects the question of product liability and safety, where liability can be strict. Under the Consumer Protection Act 1987 (CPA) a manufacturer is strictly liable in respect of defective products and the injured party does not have to establish fault, only that a defective product caused the loss. A product is defective under the CPA if it is not as safe as persons are generally entitled to expect taking into account the purpose for which the product has been marketed, any instructions for use or warnings and what might reasonably be expected to be done with the product at the time when the product was supplied. The test is, therefore, one of consumer expectation. This will be more complex in the context of autonomous vehicles, where users are unlikely to have any significant understanding of the technology products used. Consumer expectations as to safety may even be higher or unrealistic in the case of autonomous vehicles.

AI and liability is considered in detail in Chapter 9.

E. TELECOMS

1. AI Usage Scenarios for the Telecoms Sector

19.026 AI applications are transforming the ways in which telecoms providers operate, optimise and deliver service to their customers.

---

12   See further, J.K.C. Kingston (2016) 'Artificial intelligence and legal liability' International Conference on Innovative Techniques and Applications of Artificial Intelligence (Springer, 2016).

(a) Network optimisation

AI underlies the build of self-optimising networks through algorithms that look for patterns **19.027**
within data, allowing telecoms operators to detect and predict network anomalies and proactively resolve problems before the customer is affected. For example, Nokia has launched its own ML-based platform to better manage capacity planning and to predict service degradations in advance.

(b) Predictive maintenance

AI algorithms and ML techniques are being used to improve service based on historic data. **19.028**
Telecoms companies can use the data insights to monitor equipment and predict failures and address hardware problems such as with power lines, data centres and even devices in customers' own homes. For example, AT&T reportedly uses AI to support its maintenance and has tested the use of drones to expand its long-term evolution (LTE) network coverage and use the analysis of video data to support maintenance of its cell towers. Predictive maintenance can also be deployed by the operator. KPN, a Dutch telecommunications company, has used call centre data and customers' behaviour in their home (such as switching channels on a modem) to proactively follow up to address any technical faults.

(c) Virtual assistants

Conversational AI – or 'virtual assistants' – can automate and scale person-to-person conversa- **19.029**
tions, drive efficiencies and reduce call centre costs in handling customer requests and dealing with troubleshooting. For example, Vodafone's chatbot – TOBI – handles a range of customer services questions at speed. DISH, a US television provider, has partnered with Amazon's Alexa to allow customers to search or purchase content using their natural voice.

(d) Robotics

Robotic Process Automation is a business process automation technology based on AI. This **19.030**
can drive efficiencies by allowing telecoms to more effectively manage back-office operations and repetitive functions (such as despatch of equipment, data entry, billing) and free up resources for greater value-added functions.

(e) Enhanced retention

AI can help telecoms companies improve customer retention and maximise profitability per **19.031**
user. AI use cases include personalised recommendations based on behavioural patterns and content preferences, making relevant cross-sell and upsell offers, assessing the best fit call and data package, detecting and addressing potential issues for customers before they are apparent and analysing social media to better understand what motivates customers to use the service provider and what might drive them to leave. For example, Comcast uses AI to process metadata and machine vision image recognition to make recommendations to customers on new content.

(f) AI and smartphones

As the quality of AI applications improves, due in part to better algorithms, datasets and AI **19.032**
hardware, telecoms users may be expected to make increasing use of AI functionality. According to research by Deloitte which asked respondents about their awareness and usage of a range of AI-enhanced applications, the most commonly used AI-enhanced application was predictive

text, followed by route suggestions.[13] For example, Deloitte found that in 2017 a quarter of smartphone owners used route suggestions. Deloitte expects this proportion to exceed 60 per cent by 2023, due in part to onboard AI chips which can learn, for example, the device owner's walking pace according to the time of day and offer more accurate recommendations.

2. The Internet of Things; AI and Telecoms

19.033 The significance of the IoT for the telecoms industry arises from its connectedness and from areas where devices and applications depend on or integrate with telecoms networks and services. A few examples will seek to illustrate these interactions.

19.034 *Wearables, health monitors and implantable devices* – A common IoT wearable is a smart watch. This is often used in conjunction with a smart phone as well as a basic fitness tracker. Health monitors may be built into those devices and applications and collect data not only on the functioning of the device itself but also on the individual it interacts with. Where wearables have a function that relates to the health and wellbeing of a consumer, they may be treated as medical devices. As such devices become higher-functioning and are able to detect and even monitor changes in a person's health and what treatment they may require to regulate that condition, the interface with medical device regulation will need to be addressed. AI in the healthcare sector is covered in detail in Chapter 18.

19.035 *Smart home applications* – IoT devices and applications in the home include smart thermostats that track energy usage; smart applications that regulate operations remotely, such as activation of home appliances before the homeowner arrives; smart locks and intruder security systems; sensors that can detect fire, flood or carbon dioxide; and home hubs that allow the owner to control operations remotely, such as a voice command to turn on lighting or appliances. The significance of the smart home from a safety perspective is most apparent in relation to appliances and security systems which are themselves a protective measure. Any interruption or failure in connection due to a network unavailability which interferes with performance or causes a delay in performance raises questions as to who or what should be held to account.

19.036 *Toys and childcare equipment* – This includes both devices used by children for play and devices used by parents to monitor safety and health. Some of these devices may include cameras and monitors that relay information about the child's location, body temperature and heart rate. Telefonica, for example, has profiled advanced toys including those used to entertain (such as by remembering answers given by a child, knowing what time it is or giving a weather forecast, and otherwise adapting to the child's responses); construction games permitting children to build programmable gadgets; and specially designed tablets that have various features permitting children to interact with their environment in different ways (including by uploading photos and documents to enhance personalisation).[14] Given the vulnerable nature of the user group, safety considerations can be expected to be at the forefront of regulatory policy concerns, in addition to concerns over security and data privacy. The usage scenario of toys also raises

---

13 Deloitte. Technology, Media and Telecommunications Predications 2018, p. 9.
14 Telefonica (2016), 5 amazing things made reality by IoT technology. Available at: https://iot.telefonica.com/blog/5 -amazing-things-made-reality-by-iot-technology-toys-edition.

questions about the suitability of instructions given on product updates, as these may require greater supervision by adults.

Connected automobiles – One of the most high-profile issues surrounding liability tor IoT **19.037** devices relates to driverless cars or applications that provide warnings to drivers about hazards. Increasing vehicle automation may reduce the rate of accidents by reducing the scope for errors due to human fallibility. However, this raises a question of who should be responsible where an automated vehicle causes an accident that injures another road user or causes damage to third party property. The range of possibilities for determining who may be held responsible is shown in Figure 19.3 later in the chapter; in principle, liability might extend to the ISP/ network operator. There is also technology being developed that allows a vehicle to be connected to other devices such as smart home devices, which are in turn linked to the owner's mobile phone. Issues of liability related to AI are covered in detail in Chapter 9.

3.   AI, e-Privacy and Telecoms

(a) Overview of EU privacy regulation

The volume and scope of data collected by AI systems, coupled with the complex and extensive **19.038** processing that the data undergoes in such applications, may present challenges with regard to laws and regulations on individual privacy and how such data is kept secure.

In parallel with its reform of EU data protection law and adoption of the GDPR, the European **19.039** Commission has developed a specific ePrivacy Regulation. This merits separate consideration here given that it affects the use of communications data, that is, both the content of the communication and the metadata around it, and it sets out very specific rules. It is beyond the scope of this analysis to provide an exhaustive examination of European e-privacy law. Instead, the focus is on the European Commission's proposed ePrivacy Regulation (the 'ePrivacy Regulation')[15] and its main impacts on AI usage by communications providers. The ePrivacy Regulation is intended to replace the ePrivacy Directive.[16] While the GDPR has been in force since 25 May 2018, the final text and precise timing of implementation of the ePrivacy Regulation is presently unclear. The latest revised proposal of the Regulation was submitted in February 2020, and discussions are still ongoing at the time of writing.

(b) How does e-privacy relate to data protection?

The GDPR is an umbrella or blanket piece of legislation that covers the collection and use **19.040** of all personal data, however the information is collected and whether it concerns consumers, employees or other identifiable individuals. The ePrivacy Regulation is a complementary piece of legislation which sits alongside and is supplementary to the GDPR, where it applies. It also sets out specific rules that apply to the collection and use of information over certain channels

---

15   Proposal for a Regulation of The European Parliament and of The Council concerning the respect for private life and the protection of personal data in electronic communications and repealing Directive 2002/58/EC (Regulation on Privacy and Electronic Communications), COM/2017/010 final – 2017/03 (COD).

16   Directive 2002/58/EC of the European Parliament and of the Council of 12 July 2002 concerning the processing of personal data and the protection of privacy in the electronic communications sector (Directive on privacy and electronic communications), O.J. L 201, 31.7.2002, pp. 37–47.

or through the use of tracking technologies. Table 19.1 lays out the relationship between the GDPR and the ePrivacy Regulation.

Table 19.1   Relationship between the GDPR and the ePrivacy Regulation

General Data Protection Regulation	ePrivacy Regulation
Protects personal data	Protects the confidentiality of electronic communications and the device
Covers all personal data independently of the means of transmission	Covers electronic communications and the integrity of the information on the device, independently of whether it is personal or non-personal data
Enshrines a right to protection of personal data	Enshrines a right to the privacy and confidentiality of communications
Introduces new and enhanced rights for individuals and obligations on organisations processing personal data	Aims to ensure that mobile communications, applications or internet services cannot be intercepted or interfered with
Applies from 25 May 2018	Timing of implementation unclear but not expected to be adopted before 2021
The ePrivacy Regulation complements the GDPR in the electronic communications sector	

(c) Main impacts of the ePrivacy Regulation on communications providers' use of AI

19.041   The ePrivacy Regulation will apply to the digital output of practically all organisations in their use of technology, including AI, and contains provisions on cookies and direct marketing communications. Communications providers are broadly in the scope of the current rules under the ePrivacy Directive. The ePrivacy Regulation will broaden the scope of existing EU e-privacy regulation with the aim to be reflective of the evolution in the kinds of communications services that are increasingly used.

19.042   The following are the main changes and enhancements:

(a)   *Application to new market participants* – The ePrivacy Regulation will apply to new market participants such as WhatsApp, Facebook Messenger and Skype, to ensure that they guarantee the same level of communications confidentiality as traditional telecoms providers.

(b)   *Communications content and metadata* – Privacy will be guaranteed for communications content and metadata, including information on the location and times of phone calls. Metadata should be anonymised or deleted if users do not give their consent (unless the data is needed for billing).

(c)   *Simplification of the rules on cookies* – The new rules aim to make it easier to accept or refuse tracking cookies and other identifiers.

(d)   *Protection against spam* – Strict rules concerning unsolicited electronic communications (by email, SMS and automated calling machines). It is possible that the final form of regulation could include a requirement to show the phone numbers of telemarketers or cite a prefix that indicates a marketing call.

(e)   *Sanctions* – The penalties under the ePrivacy Regulation are in line with the GDPR (up to €20,000,000, or in the case of a business, up to 4 per cent of worldwide annual turnover, whichever is higher).

(d) (Tele)communications content and metadata

As noted above, the ePrivacy Regulation distinguishes between two types of communications: **19.043** first, data, that is, the content of the communication (for example, what is said in a communication); second, the metadata (such as the location of the user).

The basic principle is that privacy is guaranteed for the communications content itself and **19.044** for the metadata of the content. Metadata needs to be anonymised or deleted in the event that there is no consent (with the exception of billing). For example, for billing purposes a communications provider might need to access the metadata to know how much to charge its customers. It might need to access the content and the metadata to ensure that it is resolving any technical issues with communication.

Communications providers can develop new services by leveraging content and/or metadata **19.045** (subject to anonymisation) or where consent is given. In principle, this could allow communications providers to develop new services through the use of AI technologies, but these limitations may present operational challenges where anonymisation or consent are not feasible. Whereas a communications provider might want to rely on its legitimate interests as a lawful basis for processing under the GDPR (Article 6(1)(f)), there is no such provision in the ePrivacy Regulation.

If a communications provider is proposing to use some of the content or metadata for the pur- **19.046** poses of marketing to specific customers, the expectation is that it would need to ask for both the sender's and the recipient's consent for that to occur.

Third parties may also be interested in such content and metadata to leverage the data, for **19.047** example to detect heatmaps and patterns showing the location and intensity of (mobile) users. It is not clear that anonymisation of such data would be possible or useful in all such deployments without compromising the rationale for seeking the data in the first place. For example, where the data is being sought by a researcher to identify trends in mobile usage then anonymisation may still deliver a useful output dataset. However, where the data is sought by a third party social media organisation to inform what services it may then provide to the user (such as suggestions of restaurants in the vicinity of the user), it appears that specific consent would need to be sought regardless of the communications providers' lawful basis for processing under the GDPR.

Where such data is shared with another communications provider (for example, to inform **19.048** better network optimisation), consideration will need to be given to the antitrust implications to the extent that such data sharing would involve sharing of competitively sensitive information with a competitor. Competition law and AI is covered in detail in Chapter 11.

4.   AI, Product Liability and Telecoms

The integration of AI and complementary technologies compounds the question of how lia- **19.049** bility for defects is to be identified and allocated across the supply chain. Connected devices will distinguish themselves in terms of their ability to self-learn over time and their ability to respond to consumer behaviour. The OECD notes in this context that

[a]t least in theory, this could mean that such products could come to detect patterns in consumer behaviour that may not have been fully anticipated by the designer of the product, and which may create a safety risk. In such cases the 'smart' product could adapt its own performance in order to reduce or minimise the risk, thereby creating higher levels of safety.[17]

19.050   IoT product liability risk for the telecoms sector was highlighted in a European Commission RAPEX notice[18] identifying a product as presenting a 'serious' risk to consumers. The European Commission notified a Europe-wide recall not because it believed that the product posed any physical risk to consumer safety but because it believed that the product did not adequately protect consumers' data and privacy and therefore posed a potential security concern for children.

19.051   The product in question is an internet-connected smartwatch which is intended to be worn by children. This gives parents the ability to track a child's location using a connected smartphone application and to make calls to the child through the application. The European Commission found that the device did not meet the requirements of the Radio Equipment Directive.[19]

19.052   The European Commission noted a number of concerns, including that 'the mobile application accompanying the watch has unencrypted communications with its backend server and the server enables unauthenticated access to data' and that 'as a consequence the data such as location history, phone numbers, and serial number can easily be retried and changed'. The notice states that a malicious user could 'send commands to any watch making it call another number of his choosing, can communicate with the child wearing the device or locate the child through GPS'.

19.053   This is believed to be the first time that a RAPEX notice has been used in relation to a product based on concerns over data privacy and security. As consumer demand for connected wearable devices grows, there is clearly a need for a more holistic approach to be taken to regulatory risk management. In that context product liability issues should not be considered in isolation from other areas of regulatory risk, where device manufacturers as well as network operators will increasingly need to be cognisant of the liability and reputation risks across their connected supply chains.

19.054   Some of the options that present themselves for managing liability for machines in these contexts include:

- extending or affirming strict liability to the owner of a machine whose self-learning algorithm causes damage;[20]

---

17   OECD (2018), Consumer Product Safety in the Internet of Things, OECD Digital Economy Papers, No. 267, OECD Publishing, Paris. Available at: https://www.oecd-ilibrary.org/docserver/7c45fa66-en.pdf?expires=1575826271&id=id& accname=guest&checksum=E8258D32B02A29540E1F64B5C8C87C0D.

18   European Commission (2019), Alert number: A12/0157/19. Available at: https://ec.europa.eu/consumers_safety/safety _products/rapex/alerts/?event=viewProduct&reference=A12/0157/19&ing=en (accessed 8 December 2019).

19   Directive 2014/53/EU of the European Parliament and of the Council of 16 April 2014 on the harmonisation of the laws of the Member States relating to the making available on the market of radio equipment and repealing Directive 1999/5/ EC.OJ L 153, 22.5.2014, pp. 62–106.

20   Swiss Re (2017), New Emerging Risks Insights 2017. Available at: www.swissre.com/library/expertisepublication/swiss _re_sonar_new_emerging_risks_insights_2017.html.

- a common enterprise liability system where each entity within a set of connected companies is held jointly and severally liable for the actions of other entities. There is no reason at least in principle why this notion of liability would necessarily be limited to entities in the same economic group that is conditioned on a relationship of control;
- granting legal personality to autonomous machines. This would seem to entail that the injured party sues the machine. As a result, the owner and other stakeholders would ultimately have to allocate responsibility between them or contribute to a self-insurance pool.[21] Insurers are increasingly underwriting the losses and costs of cyber events. As their models improve and they gain a better understanding of the risk profiles of digital technology – as well as the potential to mitigate risk – they will increasingly be able to estimate and insure against losses. This knowledge and evidence base may also have a role in informing assessment of traditional product liability claims by focusing on the costs that would be involved in preventing or mitigating the underlying risk (and therefore whether strict liability should be imposed for failing to take the relevant precautions).

5.   The Internet of Things, AI and Telecoms

The significance of the IoT for the telecoms industry arises from its connectedness and the areas where devices and applications depend on or integrate with telecoms networks and services. A few examples, expanding on details given above, will seek to illustrate these interactions.   **19.055**

(a)   *Wearables, health monitors and implantable devices* – A common IoT wearable is a smart watch. This is often used in conjunction with a smart phone as well as a basic fitness tracker. Health monitors may be built into those devices and applications and collect data not only on the functioning of the device itself but also the individual it interacts with. Where wearables have a function that relates to the health and wellbeing of a consumer they may be treated as medical devices. It is beyond the scope of this analysis to consider the potential crossover with medical device regulation but as such devices become higher functioning and are able to detect and even monitor changes in a person's health and what treatment they may require to regulate that condition, the interface with medical device regulation will need to be addressed.

(b)   *Smart home applications* – IoT devices and applications in the home include smart thermostats that track energy usage; smart applications that regulate operations remotely, such as activation of home appliances before the homeowner arrives; smart locks and intruder security systems; sensors that can detect fire, flood or carbon dioxide; and home hubs that allow the owner to control operations remotely, such as a voice command to turn on lighting or appliances. The significance of the smart home from a safety perspective is most apparent in relation to appliances and security systems, which are themselves a protective measure. Any interruption or failure in connection due to a network unavailability which interferes with performance or causes a delay in performance raises questions as to who or what should be held to account.

(c)   *Toys and childcare equipment* – This includes both devices used by children for play and devices used by parents to monitor safety and health. Some of these devices may include cameras and monitors that relay information about the child's location, body temperature

---

21   D. Kidman, and S. Turner (2017), Electronic persons: time for a new legal personality?, New Law Journal. Available at: www.newlawjournal.co.uk/content/electronic-persons-time-new-legalpersonality-0.

and heart rate. Telefonica, for example, has profiled advanced toys including those used to entertain (such as by remembering answers given by a child, knowing what time it is or giving a weather forecast and otherwise adapting to the child's responses); construction games permitting children to build programmable gadgets; and specially designed tablets that have various features permitting children to interact with their environment in different ways (including by uploading photos and documents to personalise).[22] Given the vulnerable nature of the user group, safety considerations can be expected to be at the forefront of regulatory policy concerns in addition to concerns over security and data privacy. The usage scenario of toys also raises questions about the suitability of instructions given on product updates, as these may require greater supervision by adults.

(d) *Connected automobiles* – One of the most high-profile issues surrounding liability for IoT devices relates to driverless cars or applications that provide warnings to drivers about hazards. Increasing vehicle automation may reduce the rate of accidents by reducing the scope for errors due to human fallibility. However, this raises a question of who should be responsible where an automated vehicle causes an accident that injures another road user or causes damage to third party property. The range of possibilities for determining who may be held responsible is shown in Figure 19.3, where, in principle, liability might extend to the ISP/network operator. There is also technology being developed that allows a vehicle to be connected to other devices, such as smart home devices, which are in turn linked to the owner's mobile phone.

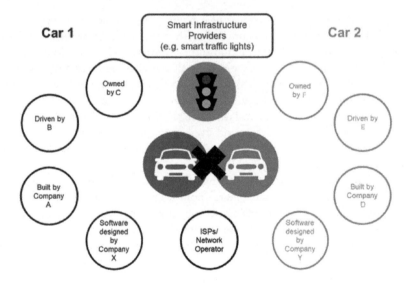

Figure 19.3   Multiple liability scenarios in connected automobile collision

---

22   Telefonica (2016), 5 amazing things made reality by IoT technology. Available at: https://iot.telefonica.com/blog/5 -amazing-things-made-reality-by-iot-technology-toys-edition.

6. Implications for the Sector

There is no question that AI has huge potential in the telecoms sector. Some of the key ques- **19.056**
tions that arise when considering readiness deployment of AI-powered systems and solutions
are as follows.

(a) *AI usage* – What are the key areas where the business would like to see improvement
(customer service and experiences, sales, service and product development network
operations)?
(b) *AI fitness for purpose* – Is AI the optimal solution to the real-world issues identified?
(c) *Data availability* – Does the business have the required data for the algorithms to learn
from or does it need to set up a data infrastructure or license or buy the data from third
parties?

Alongside the potential of AI to transform how telecoms providers operate and optimise their **19.057**
business, the following issues arise against a growing proliferation of data analytics and AI
usage in other sectors.

(a) *Network access* – The data and analytics in most AI applications will require access to
high-capacity communications network connections in addition to the sophisticated
hardware and software. The most immediate link to the user device will be a wireless link
where the device collecting, processing and storing the data will be moving it to. Most
AI users will have to rely on mobile connectivity provided by a third party because they
will not be in a position to build their own private networks. Providers offering reliable,
secure and ubiquitous high-capacity networks may include terrestrial as well as satellite
operators.
(b) *Sensitivity of AI application* – Although the requirements or sensitivity will depend on the
particular AI application, AI users will need to be satisfied that their applications will be
maintained according to their specific requirements and that an alternative is available
when a primary link is unavailable. Those operating in sensitive sectors and applications
(including financial services, defence, justice, healthcare, utilities and air transport) may
themselves be subject to additional requirements as to radio frequency limits, emissions
and other constraints.
(c) *Contracts* – Detailed consideration will be required to ensure that procurement contracts
undertaken to promote business goals contain appropriate contractual protections.
(d) *Customer experience and personalised offers* – Popular uses of AI in telecoms involve,
first, having an AI agent in the customer engagement process and second, matching
of customers with best-suiting data and call packages. From the customer perspective,
reducing call times to a call centre may be expected to lead to higher satisfaction but this
will depend on the complexity of the issue. Where algorithms are used to recommend the
best solutions to connectivity problems or new products or services, again the potential
benefits will depend on their relevance. The making of personalised pricing offers will
need to be examined from a data protection and antitrust perspective (see Chapter 11, by
the same author).
(e) *Regulation* – Regulation of the telecoms sector and related law will impact on all aspects
of the AI usage scenarios. Business will need to navigate communications law, spectrum
policy, IPR licensing, public procurement/State aid (where dealing with a public body),
data protection and privacy, competition law, cyber-security law and product liability,

among others. Where AI initiatives are at a more nascent stage of consideration at the national level, they will need to consider how they engage with relevant regulatory or government bodies to ensure that AI rollout is compatible with the national strategy (which is unlikely to be fully formed, if at all, in most jurisdictions).

7.   Regulatory Risk Management

19.058   It is evident that the challenges for regulatory risk management presented by AI are not unique to the telecoms sector. As noted in other chapters, this raises a question as to the optimal balance between general and specific regulation.

19.059   Regulation can be categorised, like any other law, according to the target audience. Regulation may be described as general, sector-specific or context-specific.

19.060   In the EU, for example, product liability regulation may be described as general, as it is applicable on a sector-neutral basis, albeit that it is supplemented by other more specific (vertical) regulation by sector, including in relation to product safety, as described in Chapter 9.

19.061   Sector-specific regulation is standalone regulation in a specific industry context, through a particular court or tribunal, via a group of individuals or by the appointment of a dedicated regulator for the sector.

19.062   This chapter has identified new technologies, and specifically the IoT, AI and virtual and augmented technologies, as areas meriting specific attention by a range of regulators in different industry settings. However, there is no universal acceptance on whether there is a case for dedicated regulation of these phenomena and it is not self-evident that there is a compelling need for regulation dedicated to a specific industry such as telecoms. Furthermore, such an approach would tend to go against the grain of EU policy in other areas of (generalist) consumer protection legislation, even if the resulting regulatory landscape might suggest otherwise.

19.063   Context-integrated regulation is similar to sector-specific regulation, but it is not standalone. Rather it is integrated into other forms of regulation and makes specific provision to deal with a crisis situation. The approach to product recalls in the telecoms sector (see section E(4) above) may be seen as an example of context-integrated regulation, albeit one where the underlying legal framework for action is established *ex ante* rather than as a response to a crisis event.

19.064   This consideration of the classification of regulation in terms of general, sector-specific and context-integrated may serve to highlight the focus of particular policy approaches. However, it is one where, in the specific context, there is scope for experimentation and the tensions presented by specific contexts and new technologies are becoming apparent.

19.065   Recognising the discrete focus of this chapter, Table 19.2 below highlights at a high level only the potential interfaces between developments in AI and different areas of regulatory risk management, and their significance for the telecoms sector and other sectors.

Table 19.2   *Potential interfaces between developments in AI and regulatory risk management*

Regulatory risk area	Telecoms-specific issues	Cross-sectoral perspectives
Consumer protection See further Chapter 17	IoT devices and applications will be able to initiate transactions with consumers in real-time using the consumer's mobile phone	EU consumer protection laws often require a form of written communication with consumers. This makes it challenging to pass on comprehensive safety information to customers in the context of IoT devices that are updated regularly
Data issues See further Chapter 10	IoT devices will generate higher volumes of real-time data (such as user/subscriber location) that will be shared with network providers	In addition to data protection and privacy law compliance, access to data about a person's location may pose a threat to health and safety if it is intercepted by a third party
Cyber security See further Chapter 10	Standards such as the European Telecommunications Standards Institute's standard on internet-connected devices[a] indicate that market player must build in strong cyber-security in IoT devices	Security-by-design may become a benchmark reducing the scope for 'state of art' and development defences to product liability claims
Network capacity	Increase in IoT devices will result in a need for increased bandwidth even within 5G networks (such as where smart home devices are connected to mobile devices)	Potential calls for 'net neutrality' rules in order to minimise potential for communications providers to vary levels and quality of service provision for different types of IoT devices and applications based on commercial considerations
Product expansion and development	The IoT relies on a range of connectivity technologies using different standards where telecoms providers compete[b]	The connected ecosystem of IoT presents challenges for allocating risk across the supply chain. Telecoms providers will need to factor in product liability risk in their pricing across an increasingly complex supply chain where connectivity is likely to be a driver of competition and product liability risk
Competition/ antitrust See further Chapter 11	Market power concerns arising out of concentration of valuable data within economic groups; standardisation between competitors; exchange of competitively sensitive information	Standards may be beneficial to minimise safety risks and stimulate an active insurance market for product liability risks
Intellectual property See further Chapter 12	Developers of sophisticated IoT solutions and standards will need strong IP protection and will need to consider Fair, Reasonable and Non-Discriminatory (FRAND) commitments for access to patents, among others	Open source and closed source software may be treated differently from a product liability perspective given that the former may be more open to industry and user co-development, including correction of defects after the product has been put on the market
Tax	The IoT blurs the line between products and services, which can affect the business risk allocation and trigger imposition of 'digital tax' liability in some jurisdictions in ways not anticipated	Tax implications should be considered in any IoT product development. There may not be alignment between the treatment of products/services under product liability and tax law Tax incentives for R&D, tax presence, withholding taxes, transfer tax and new digital taxes will need to be assessed

Notes:
[a] ETSI (2019), Technical Standard 103 645 v1.1.1 (2019–02); [b] Gartner forecasts that 5.8 billion enterprise and automotive IoT endpoints will be in use in 2020 (Gartner Tech Notes, Top 10 issues for the Internet of Things, 15 October 2019).

F. CONCLUSION

19.066   The development of AI has prompted a revisiting of the perennial policy and legal debate about whether existing legal tools are fit for purpose in addressing the challenges presented by new technologies. Almost every industry has been affected by these developments, inviting an inquiry as to the relevance, if any, of context and a sector-focused rather than generalist approach to regulation.

19.067   This telecoms sector-focused analysis looks at an industry which is experiencing a growing number of AI usage scenarios but which has yet to see dedicated sector-specific regulation. Clearly, AI and the IoT involve complex supply chains. This is not an area that telecoms operators have previously had to grapple with in detail. However, the special significance of AI for the sector cannot be ignored, as regulatory interest mounts and potential opportunities, harms and costs are becoming apparent.

19.068   This chapter has highlighted the trade-off between (fully) understanding the impact of a technology and the ease of controlling its impact. It is unclear at this stage how policy interventions can or should address all the concerns arising, not least because the development of AI is still in early stages, with a lot of potential yet to be realised. This is a very wide issue that covers not only anti-competitive behaviour but also issues such as privacy, IPR and ethics.

19.069   The following summarises the main themes emerging and the areas where additional research and evidence is needed to provide a more robust evidence base to inform appropriate regulatory and business responses in the telecoms sector, and potentially beyond.

19.070   In more general terms, this state of affairs (that is, regulating AI before the impact is fully understood) could hinder its positive impact as much as it may be an uncertain negative impact.

19.071   The overall conclusion is that as many regulators (including in the EU) remain in observational and diagnostic mode, robust evidence-based regulation requires more empirical studies.

19.072   The limited AI industry use scenarios considered in this analysis by way of benchmarking to inform the assessment of telecoms have shown that existing legal frameworks (including sector regulation, data protection, criminal law and consumer protection) can be applied or adapted. However, new paradigms and robust safeguards may be needed, particularly where AI disrupts traditional notions of liability based on a rational human agent. As AI and ML techniques continue to develop, organisations will need dynamic, sophisticated and joined-up compliance techniques.

19.073   Ways in which AI can be useful will depend on the characteristics of industries. For sectors like telecoms that rely on online distribution, there is a lot of scope for the use of AI to set prices and optimise inventory management.

19.074   The AI use scenarios presented in this analysis suggest a number of key themes for design of policy, including: (1) treating customers fairly, (2) navigating sector-specific regulation, (3) exploring alternative regulatory (regtech) approaches and sandboxes, (4) ensuring regulation is fit for purpose, (5) ensuring regulation is proportionate and provides legal certainty, (6) ensuring policy, law and regulation reflect the pace of technical development and (7) ensuring consistent and connected provision.

The analysis here in turn suggests that useful research could be conducted to better understand **19.075** AI developments and policy and legal developments in relation to at least the following, given their more direct and immediate interaction with the communications system: (1) drones, (2) smart homes and (3) space and satellite.

Other use scenarios with potential learnings for the telecoms sector include: (1) education (in **19.076** relation to the use of personal information from children in AI applications and collaborative research opportunities), (2) life sciences (in relation to compliance with sector-specific regulation) and (3) criminal justice (in relation to addressing liability, fairness and demographic concerns, privacy and civil rights concerns).

20

REAL ESTATE

Alastair Moore, Claudia Giannoni, Nick Kirby and Nick Doffman

A. INTRODUCTION

20.001 Land and property rights represent one the most important economic assets for millions of people globally. As an asset class land and property rights is larger than equities and debt securities, at a value of more than $250 trillion dollars.[1]

20.002 The asset class is a critical source of livelihood and private market activity, and is particularly important for the UK economy because of high levels of foreign direct investment.[2] Critical to the administration of land rights is information about assets and ownership and the flow of information between different parties to any transaction and beyond. Therefore, improvements to the technology and processes used to facilitate this information exchange will provide advantages not only to individual parties in terms of efficiency and cost savings, but to the market as a whole.[3]

20.003 During the past few decades we have witnessed a rapid expansion of artificial intelligence (AI) and machine learning technologies – the principal technologies used in transforming data and information from one form to another – used to solve an increasingly broad range of problems in real estate. This development is driven by the same factors driving AI in other sectors: the exponential growth of computational capacity that is available to a firm, either on premises

---

1   www.savills.com/impacts/market-trends/8-things-you-need-to-know-about-the-value-of-globalreal-estate.html.
2   Fuerst, F., Milcheva, S. Baum, A. (2013), Cross-Border Capital Flows into Real Estate.
3   Stiglitz, J.E. (2000), 'The Contributions of the Economics of Information to Twentieth Century Economics', The Quarterly Journal of Economics 115(4), 1441–78.

or consumed as a service; the industrialisation of software applications; and growth in both machine-readable and unstructured data within the market.

There have also been recent improvements in the state-of-the-art algorithms which enable AI and ML applications that were impractical 10 or 20 years ago. For example, automatic analysis of satellite data is combined with the use of Natural Language Processing to extract information from title deeds and documents. There is growing realisation across the industry that some real estate processes can be partially or fully automated via AI and ML, which in turn can expand commercial opportunities.

20.004

Although the market is large, the impact of technology in general in the real estate sector has been limited.[4] The main act of purchase and sale is still predominantly a manual and paper-based process. Land Registries have a limited degree of digitisation, and real estate markets are full of intermediaries and subject to high levels of fees, opacity and in general slow transaction completion times. For example, the registration of a property in the United Kingdom (UK) takes on average 22 days, and costs up to 5 per cent of the total property value.[5] The characteristics of the market, and its high heterogeneity and immobility, make it difficult to innovate and real estate transactions face the challenge of information inefficiencies and, consequentially, high transaction costs.[6]

20.005

In describing the applications of AI and ML to the real estate sector, and the particular relevance in this regard to law and regulation, we consider the lifecycle for real estate, starting with construction, then moving on to the processes of conveyancing and finally managing a real estate asset. An example of the different stages can be seen in Figure 20.1a, where we have illustrated a variety of different activities and processes.

20.006

Several domains, such as medical diagnosis and finance, have seen early adoption of AI and ML, and systems have been developed and successfully deployed in these areas. However, real estate is potentially different because information captured about an asset is often fragmented across different parts of the asset lifecycle. Moreover, the lifetime of the asset is often far greater than that of many of the actors involved in ownership and transactions, leading to many different dislocation points for data. In this regard, one broad trend to consider is that of the Internet of Things, as the omnipresence of low-cost, connected sensor networks is changing the way in which assets and buildings are instrumented. This means that information on buildings, servicing, plant and machinery, occupation and use levels is available for downstream processing in various AI and ML tasks.[7] In general, there are several different sets of technologies that may impact the sector and AI and ML may play a component part in the delivery of an end service, from valuation models,[8] to virtual reality (VR) and augmented reality (AR) for inspection

20.007

---

4   Spielman, A. (2016), Blockchain: Digitally Rebuilding the Real Estate Industry.
5   WorldBank (2018), Doing Business 2018: Reforming to Create Jobs. Report, World Bank. URL www.doingbusiness .org/en/data/exploretopics/registering-property
6   Agarwal R, Chandrasekaran S, Sridhar M. (2016), Imagining Construction's Digital Future. McKinsey, Capital Projects and Infrastructure.
7   For example, www.disruptive-technologies.com provides an IoT wireless micro-sensor developer able to detect temperature, movement and proximity.
8   Schulz, R., Wersing, M., Werwatz, A. (2014), Automated valuation modelling: a specification exercise. Journal of Property Research 31(2), 131–53.

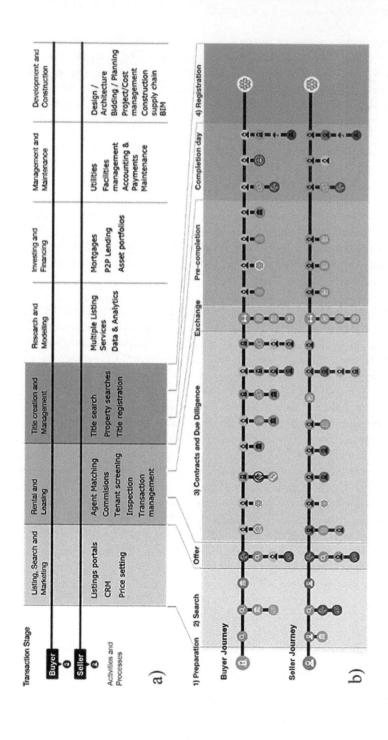

Notes:

a) Illustrating stages of the lifecycle of an asset, and selected activities and processes.

b) Residential conveyancing user journey highlighting a number of potential counter-parties (14 in this case) and different interactions that exchange information and assets across a transaction. Parties in the transaction include buyer, seller, agents, lawyers, banks, utility companies and so on. Further details of this simplified user journey are provided at https://github.com/LandRegistry/digital-street-community-dev-env/blob/master/docs/Buy-Sell-Journey.pdf. Note this is to be used in an advisory capacity only.

Figure 20.1   Real estate asset lifecycle

and marketing of an asset,[9] to transforming the data that goes into property passports, smart contracts and distributed ledger technologies. Each of these technologies in turn may also be supported by improvements in AI and ML. Ionascu and colleagues have analysed the relationship between real estate digitisation and transparency.[10] The authors explain that technology and innovation have led to the foundation of a new field, 'real estate technology', also called property technology or PropTech. The emergent PropTech industry has increased expectations of a significant improvement in transparency as PropTech generates large volumes of data that increases the information available on the property market and the assets that are traded. The efficient use of this data generally leads to higher returns on real estate investments. Consumers are now more cognisant of market information and this has a direct impact on helping consumers make more informed decisions.

One recurring theme, which is covered in more detail in Chapter 10 and elsewhere, is that when we consider the applicability of an AI or ML system it often comes down to how data is stored, in what format(s), whether any data standards have been used and how it can be accessed and by whom. For example, if the building information management (BIM) data is attached as a set of floor plans in a physical annex of a lease document it may well contain useful information for resolving a legal issue, but it will be humans rather than machines that have to extract and analyse that information. Broadly speaking, AI and ML technologies can help by supporting the capture, analysis and transformation of information across the real estate asset lifecycle.   **20.008**

At every stage in a property's lifecycle, data is central to facilitating transactions. For example, when purchasing an asset the investors need information about things like tenancy schedules, building operations, maintenance, capital expenses and cash flows, while also making an assessment of market assumptions and potential risk. All this information needs to be collated and transferred from the seller to various parties that facilitate it, from property managers to legal and financial advisors. An indication of the different parties and fragmentation of the existing transaction mechanisms is illustrated, for the case of residential conveyancing, in Figure 20.1b, which represents only a small section of the full asset lifecycle. With many different participants in any transaction, it is clear that the whole process is susceptible to inefficiencies and delays.   **20.009**

In this chapter we set out several different areas in which AI and ML is being applied across the real estate lifecycle. We give some examples of companies and technologies that are changing the practice of law in the sector and we highlight some of the areas of law that are being challenged or changed as a result. Issues related to data protection (see Chapter 10), competition for market share (see Chapter 11) and the commodification of data have become increasingly important in real estate. We conclude the chapter by discussing some of the strategic questions that require consideration before the technologies gain wider market adoption.   **20.010**

---

9   Farshid, M., Paschen, J., Eriksson, T., Kietzmann, J. (2018), Go boldly! Explore augmented reality (AR), virtual reality (VR), and mixed reality (MR) for business. Business Horizons 61(5), 657–63; Ionascu, E., Marilena, M., Anghel, I., Huian, M. (2020). The involvement of real estate companies in sustainable development: an analysis from the SDGs Reporting perspective. Sustainability 12, 798.

10   Ionascu, E., Marilena, M., Anghel, I., Huian, M. (2020), The involvement of real estate companies in sustainable development: an analysis from the SDGs Reporting perspective. Sustainability 12, 798.

B. DEVELOPMENT AND CONSTRUCTION

20.011   This chapter will focus on real estate applications, but it would be remiss to start without a discussion of the origination of information in the creation of the asset.

20.012   At the earliest stages of the real estate lifecycle, AI and ML are often used in tools to track and audit the various parts of a building as it is being constructed. This can help to ensure a better audit trail for any changes that are made during the design and build process. This might include automated audit of the construction site, using satellite or drone camera data, to assist with anything from recording the delivery of goods to checking what personnel are on site at any moment in time.

20.013   The information on what is actually built, contained in the Building Information Management (BIM) model, is a rich source of data. BIM includes the geometry of the building, its spatial relationships and geographic information, and also the quantities and properties of its components. BIM is a set of interacting policies, processes and technologies generating a 'methodology to manage the essential building design and project data in digital format throughout the building's lifecycle'.[11] BIM is an emerging technological and procedural shift within the Architecture, Engineering, Construction and Operations (AECO) industry. This intelligent 3D model-based process gives architecture, engineering and construction professionals the insight and tools to plan, design, construct and manage buildings and infrastructures in a more efficient way. It is a highly collaborative process that allows multiple stakeholders and AEC professionals to collaborate on the planning, design and construction of a building within one 3D model. The model contains information about size, location, relative spatial relationships and much more, while also working as an index which links to further information about material, such as quantity and cost to achieve goals of sustainable building design.[12] The BIM model is useful to track the various parts of a building as they are being constructed, to ensure components are going in the correct places and to provide information afterwards to facilitate building maintenance. Currently BIM processes are seldom linked to asset registries and are often siloed away from other property information. Companies such as 3DRepo[13] are changing this by facilitating online collaborative access to BIM models.

20.014   The construction industry has become increasingly litigious as projects have larger sums at stake and contractors and sub-contractors are forced to price their services more competitively.[14] Disputes arise in three main ways, the first being failure to properly administer the contract. Second, poorly drafted or incomplete/unsubstantiated claims are disputed. Third, parties fail to understand and/or comply with contractual obligations. Litigation can be lengthy and 82 per cent of disputes are usually resolved before trial via dispute resolution.[15]

---

11   Penttilä, H. (2006), Describing the changes in architectural information technology to understand design complexity and free-form architectural expression, ITcon 11, Special issue The Effects of CAD on Building Form and Design Quality, pp. 395–408.

12   Liu Z., Osmani, M., Demian, P., Baldwin, A. (2015), A BIM-aided construction waste minimisation framework, Automation in Construction 59, 1–23.

13   www.3drepo.com/.

14   Copper, R., Nelson-Williamsn, R., Kill, G., Recan, J., Torres, M. (2018), Global construction disputes report 2018 – does the construction industry learn from its mistakes?

15   Ibid.

Engineering and construction sector companies frequently litigate, with 80 per cent of companies filing at least one suit a year.[16] In 2017 the global average value of disputes was $43.4 million and the global average length of disputes was 14.8 months.[17] The number of disputes has largely remained the same year on year but both the time needed for dispute resolution and the disputes' value has increased. Time scales to resolve disputes average one month for adjudication, up to one year for arbitration and more than one year for litigation. The average payment time for construction companies and SMEs is 82 days, which can rise to up to 120 days, and even simple partial automation of reconciliation across supply chains will produce significant improvements. Various lenders and developers believe that monitoring and automation technologies will expedite the financing process and make them more confident in decision-making and quicker in disbursement of funds.[18] **20.015**

Due to the cost of legal disputes and the associated disruption to cash flows, it is important for investors to be confident in their procurement framework and contractual obligations and to have access to relevant information, as these elements are decisive factors for avoiding disputes. Here machine-assisted contract analysis can help,[19] and the construction sector has some significant advantages as a result of the standardisation of contract sets in the UK from the 1930s onwards.[20] With the improved clause risk analysis that is starting to appear,[21] the differences between standard clauses, commonly negotiated and litigated clauses and transaction-specific or deal-specific clauses offer the promise of reducing disagreement between parties. Companies with clause-level analysis products in the market include Leverton[22] and Kira;[23] some new start-up companies have exploited recent advances in transformer models[24] for contract analysis, including Casetext[25] and Della AI.[26] Contracts are discussed in more detail in Chapter 7 and dispute resolution is discussed at greater length in Chapter 14. **20.016**

C. TITLE AND TRANSFER

Once an asset, a property or a piece of land is in existence, we can then see what processes can be applied to ownership, transactions and management. This starts with the Title Register, which details full ownership information, rights, restrictions, encumbrances, leases and other **20.017**

---

16 Norton Rose Fulbright (2013), Litigation trends survey report, Dan McKenna.

17 ibid.

18 Maciel, A., Johnson, G., Campbell-Turner, B., E, P., Saxon, R. Garbutt, L. (2020), Blockchain Construction Cash Flow.

19 Burdick, D., Franklin, M., Issler, P., Krishnamurthy, R., Popa, L., Raschid, L., Stanton, R., Wallace, N. (2014), Data science challenges in real estate asset and capital markets. In: Proceedings of the international workshop on data science for macro-modeling. ACM, Snowbird, Utah, 1–5.

20 For example the Joint Contracts Tribunal (JCT), established in the 1930s by the Royal Institute of British Architects and the National Federation of Building Trades Employers, and the New Engineering Contract (NEC) contracts established in 1991.

21 Walters, E. (2018), Data-Driven Law: Data Analytics and the New Legal Services, 1st edn, CRC Press.

22 www.leverton.ai

23 www.kirasystems.com

24 Devlin, J., Chang, M.-W., Lee, K. Toutanova, K. (2019), BERT: Pre-training of deep bidirectional transformers for language understanding, Association for Computational Linguistics, pp. 4171–86.

25 www.casetext.com

26 www.dellalegal.com

information. Currently, in the UK, the process of tracking and checking changes to the Title Register requires significant manual input across multiple systems.

20.018 The term 'conveyance' refers to the legal process of transferring property from one owner to another. This process often includes the granting and redeeming of a mortgage. A property transaction broadly consists of five steps involving a host of actors, as shown in Figure 20.1b. Sellers and their agents are responsible for (1) the preparation and (2) the marketing required to establish an asking price of a property. Solicitors then organise the conveyance – the process by which rights of ownership and rights over land are transferred. This step includes all necessary legal work during (3) the due diligence period (such period often includes a number of other due diligence processes including technical review) and (4) the post-exchange period. Finally, a land registry collects fees and taxes (or evidence of payment of taxes) and records the change in legal ownership during the post-completion period.

20.019 Buying and selling a home is recognised to be one of the most stressful events a person will experience, often considered alongside other major life changes such as marriage or having a child. Problems have been identified by the UK Government's Ministry of Housing, Communities & Local Government,[27] which concludes that the conveyancing process is complex, lengthy, fragmented, opaque and multi-staged. Similar issues arise during the process of buying and selling commercial property or leasing it to occupiers. The Report recognised some key areas of concern such as (a) the time taken to complete a transaction, (b) transaction failures, (c) consumer inexperience, (d) lack of transparency, (e) weak regulation of estate agents and (f) lack of digitisation, all of which require urgent improvement.

20.020 Typically, the conveyance process consists of an exchange (that is, the exchange of contracts – the point at which the conveyance becomes legally binding on the transacting parties) and completion (that is, settlement and the date on which legal title to the real estate transfers). If the transaction involves the granting of a mortgage, it is almost certain that the lender will require that a solicitor be used for the conveyancing.

20.021 A typical residential conveyance involves, among other steps:

(a)   a price negotiation between transacting parties;

(b)   surveys, searches and pre-contract enquiries carried out by the buyer's solicitor or conveyancer;

(c)   the preparation of a draft contract by the seller's solicitor or conveyancer;

(d)   the disclosure of certain information by the seller's solicitor or conveyancer to the buyer's solicitor or conveyancer, in line with the Law Society of England and Wales' Conveyancing Protocol for residential conveyances; and

(e)   further due diligence questions by the buyer's solicitor or conveyancer of the seller's solicitor or conveyancer, based on the results of (b) and (d) above.

20.022 Due diligence involves reviewing several different documents along with the Title Register. The Title Plan, for example, is an official document proving the extent of the property and is

---

27   Improving the home buying and selling process in England. According to the House of Commons Briefing Paper n. 06980, published in 27 February 2019 ('The Report').

used by both professionals and non-professionals. It contains details of the extent of property owned, orientation, scale and property boundaries. One company that helps to check title documents is Orbital Witness,[28] which collects and digitises data sources such as the Land Registry and local authorities. The company applies rules-based and machine learning models to provide an instant view of issues that affect the valuation, liquidity or intended use of real estate. The models are trained by observing questions and processes lawyers use to perform due diligence. Machine learning is used to extract information from title documents using NLP but also for automatically estimating a measure of title risk by comparing the structure and information across multiple titles. A common problem that this approach can help resolve includes site access. For example, if a site was accessed by a private road spanning a large number of different properties it would be very tricky and time-consuming to piece together the access rights to the site by looking at the individual title plans for each property. Instead of reviewing multiple sets of Official Copy documents separately, you can search points of information in the register, have all the data in one place and visualise how the titles fit together and identify any area of unregistered land with a single view. This is one example of an area where automation can help to add new information and consolidate existing information to simplify the evaluation of legal risk.

Due diligence on the parties to the transaction involves activities such as anti-money laundering (AML) checks. As more aspects of the transaction are facilitated by digital platforms, the due diligence process can be initiated prior to the transaction process so that buyers and sellers are pre-approved. Companies are using AI and ML enabled services for Know Your Customer (KYC) and AML checks. These new approaches both aggregate different data sources and deploy specific technologies such as facial recognition for confirming a likeness. Companies that provide these services include Onfido,[29] Shield Pay[30] and Thirdfort.[31] The due diligence process can also include an assessment of the availability of financing, and this is often facilitated by ML-driven credit risk models. **20.023**

The due diligence process on the asset is initiated by solicitors, including the searches on the property discussed earlier. Due diligence remains slow and costly as manual interpretation of paper documents means 40 per cent of transactions are delayed and fees typically consume more than 1 per cent of overall transaction costs. As with the process of due diligence on the buyer and seller, it is likely that new ML models for assessing legal risk and for insuring against errors or gaps in information will emerge. **20.024**

Ultimately, when considering how ML may be used or the transaction process revised, the principle of *caveat emptor* makes a significant and protracted due diligence process essential for buyers and their lenders.[32] New models may appear where the risk of any gaps in automated due diligence can be passed on to a third party, for example with new insurance products. **20.025**

---

28   www.orbitalwitness.com
29   www.onfido.com
30   www.shieldpay.com
31   www.thirdfort.com
32   Johnson, H., 1985. 'Caveat Venditor' ('Let the Seller Beware'), Managerial Law 27(6), 1–19.

20.026 Another example document relating to title is the Deed Search, that provides a copy of all the conveyancing/transfer deeds available for a particular property. Invariably these different sources of information all feed into different parts of the due diligence discussed in more detail later. Dejaco and colleagues[33] argue that management of the urban environment is characterised by the presence of different actors asking for common needs in management and use of data. One proposed solution the authors explore is the use of the property logbooks as tools for collection, organisation and management of information, in a perspective of a streamlined real estate management process.[34]

20.027 'Building passport', 'Property logbook' and similar terms refer to a digital property register that is a common repository for all relevant property data. A well-maintained logbook should keep track of major events during a building's lifetime, such as change of ownership, searches, tenure or use, maintenance, refurbishment and other interventions in the fabric of the building. Copies of significant documentation and certification relating to these events should also be included, together with links to access those events on public and/or government repositories. Documentation could include administrative documents, plans, description of the land, the building and its surrounding, BIM, technical systems, traceability and characteristics of construction materials, performance data such as operational energy use, indoor environmental quality, smart building potential and lifecycle emissions, as well as links to building ratings and certificates.

20.028 There is growing interest around the property logbook. The Home Buying Selling Group (HBSG)[35] advising the UK government promotes the importance of having a dossier of information at an early stage in the process. Logbooks can be used in the verification of compliance with laws, authorisations and licences and the logbooks can be seen as a tool for risk management, given that these issues often have a bearing on disputes between the parties involved in a transaction. Companies offering logbook product offerings include Homeowners Passport[36] (which tries to predict completion timescales and provides a bespoke property passport report to speed up residential conveyancing), Faira[37] (with a brokerage model that combines a buyer's pack with insurance to protect sellers against abortive transactions) and Sprift[38] (which provides interactive reports).

20.029 In the UK, improvements to the registration system are limited by the availability of machine-readable data. The majority of service requests to Her Majesty's Land Registry (HMLR) that require information in a digitised format[39] are fulfilled as scanned digital copies of the original document, usually in the form of PDF documents. These records are difficult to parse automatically and therefore, notwithstanding services like Orbital Witness, often rely on manual interpretation to extract relevant information. This is where automation can make

---

33 Dejaco, M.C., Re Cecconi, F., Moretti, N., Mannino, A., Maltese, S. (2020) Building and District Data Organization to Improve Facility and Property Management.

34 Heidrich, O., Kamara, J., Maltese, S., Re Cecconi, F. and Dejaco, M.C. (2017), 'A critical review of the developments in building adaptability', International Journal of Building Pathology and Adaptation 35(4), 284–303.

35 HBSG is a stakeholder body of independent organisations across the property, legal and finance sectors.

36 www.homeownerspassport.com

37 www.faira.com

38 www.sprift.com

39 HMLR, 2017. Business Strategy 2017–2022. Report, HMLR, London.

a huge difference to time and cost efficiency. For example, the HMLR Digital Street project recently set out to explore how new technologies might improve the conveyancing process. On 6 March 2019 the sale of a refurbished, semi-detached house in Gillingham completed, taking a total of 22 weeks to complete against an initial estimate of six weeks. HMLR built a Distributed Ledger Technology (DLT)-based prototype that enabled a digital transfer of the property that automatically updated the Land Register and the deployed DLT-based proof of concept completed the conveyance, end to end, in less than ten minutes.[40] The Digital Street project continues to explore how a digital register might enable new business models to make conveyancing simpler, faster and cheaper. At the time of writing new projects include the 'Sign Your Mortgage Deed' service and the 'Find Property Information' service allowing citizens to download a summary of information about a property.[41]

The need to persist and reconcile information from multiple sources is the recurring theme, and **20.030** while AI and ML can be used to help support the review, measurement and automatic augmentation of data, DLTs offer the promise of creating trustworthy sources of data that can be relied upon by multiple parties. The term DLT refers to a broad umbrella of technologies that seek to store, synchronise and maintain digital records across a network of computing devices.

There is great potential for innovation by integrating BIM and distributed ledger technologies. **20.031** DLT-enhanced BIM implementation could potentially be beneficial to address the challenges in sustainable building design by effectively managing lifecycle information relating to real estate assets.[42]

One of the limitations to innovation in the transaction process is a continued requirement **20.032** that new technologies follow current regulation, for example that buyer and seller have to be represented by two separate solicitor firms.

Several companies are considering alternative iBuyer models, where a company uses technol- **20.033** ogy to automatically make an offer on a property. iBuyers represent a dramatic shift in the way people are buying and selling homes, offering in many cases a simpler, more convenient alternative to a traditional home sale. How iBuyers operate varies, but the underlying idea is that a company estimates the value of your home and makes an offer. Companies aim to make an offer in line with what a reasonable buyer would pay, commonly referred to as *fair market value*, and methods for estimating this are discussed in the following section. Companies that offer automated buying models include Nested,[43] which uses an AI and ML-powered iBuyer model to provide an instant offer for UK residential property, while Offerpad[44] and Opendoor[45] provide offers for US residential property.

---

40   www.mishcon.com/news/hm-land-registry-towards-a-distributed-ledger-of-residential-title-deedsin-the-uk
41   www.gov.uk/government/publications/hm-land-registry-business-strategy-2017-to-2022
42   Mathews, M., Robles, D. Bowe, B. (2017), BIM+Blockchain: A Solution to the Trust Problem in Collaboration? CITA BIM Gathering 2017.
43   www.nested.com
44   www.offerpad.com
45   www.opendoor.com

D. LEASING OF COMMERCIAL REAL ESTATE

20.034   The process of leasing commercial property to occupiers follows a similar structure to buying and selling property outlined in section C above (and suffers similar inefficiencies). However, there is additional complexity because the parties are required to produce and negotiate a commercial lease and other related documents. These documents are the building owner's source of income and the occupier's right to occupy the commercial property. In the UK there is little standardisation of commercial leases, notwithstanding multiple efforts across the sector to produce standard leases.[46] This lack of standardisation and digitisation leads to further inefficiency, significant transaction times and long periods where commercial property remains vacant.

20.035   As the leasing process remains largely manual, the leases generated are not machine readable. This means that the process of carrying out due diligence on leases on the purchase of commercial buildings leads to delays in transaction times and reduced liquidity for commercial real estate.

20.036   Multiple efforts have been made by a number of ML products (Leverton, Della AI, Kira, and others) to make commercial leases machine readable, but to date the majority of lease due diligence is still carried out by humans due to a lack of perceived progress in reliable output and the importance of the income generated by those leases. Just as there is a significant liquidity benefit to digitising the process of transferring real estate, leases which are completely machine readable (including a comprehensive record of the basic meaning of individual clauses) will reduce the time it takes to transact commercial real estate and increase liquidity. This will also likely build trust in AI (and therefore increase adoption) as the output becomes more reliable. This will drive standardisation and a better pool of structured data. This pool of data can be used by AI and ML tools to gain a better understanding of how and why leases are negotiated by counterparties.

20.037   In the absence of agreed structured data in the form of a logbook and standardised processes, several companies are trying to aggregate data from different parties to leasing transactions. For example, Least[47] offers a product to streamline the leasing process, capturing structured deal data and behavioural data around what, how and when decisions are made across the leasing lifecycle, in areas such as automating and streamlining the collection of important commercial and legal terms as the basis for constructing, drafting and completing a commercial lease. Structured data can be used to improve lease information extraction software using ML techniques.[48] Spacespot[49] is a digital platform in Norway that can similarly lead parties through

---

46   For example, the Model Commercial Lease (MCL) originally proposed by the British Property Federation's commercial committee launched and made freely available in 2014. Versions of the MCL that take account of landlord and tenant law in Scotland are likewise available free of charge from the Property Standardisation Group.

47   www.getleast.com

48   Burdick, D., Franklin, M., Issler, P., Krishnamurthy, R., Popa, L., Raschid, L., Stanton, R., Wallace, N. (2014), Data science challenges in real estate asset and capital markets. In: Proceedings of the International Workshop on Data Science for Macro-modeling. ACM, Snowbird, Utah, pp. 1–5.

49   www.spacespot.no

the process of identifying the best space option and negotiating lease agreements. Other companies, such as Openbox,[50] are using Robotic Process Automation for real estate due diligence.

Innovation in leasing models is also limited by regulatory considerations, for example limitations of the Landlord and Tenant Acts. A deed is a written document which is executed with the necessary formality (that is, more than a simple signature), and by which an interest, right or property passes or is confirmed. Any contract that must be executed as a deed[51] was until recently largely prohibited from using electronic signatures or fully automated transaction models.[52]   **20.038**

Several companies in the sharing economy[53] offer fractional use in order to better utilise commercial space and this allows for a greater degree of automation. To achieve this they use License to Occupy contracts, by which a licensor permits a licensee to use part of the licensor's building for commercial use on a temporary basis. Companies exploring fractional use in the retail space include AppearHere[54] and different occupier models such as Sook.[55] The best known examples, AirBnB[56] and WeWork,[57] have already substantially disrupted the hospitality and office markets and these sharing-economy models are likely to increase in importance.   **20.039**

E. PROPERTY LISTING, SEARCH AND MARKETING

At the beginning of a purchase transaction, a buyer needs to be able to identify a property of interest. In the 2000s many different online platforms started to facilitate real estate transactions. Companies such as Zillow,[58] Zoopla[59] and Rightmove[60] entered the market with listing models offering users significant choice and information to help make better informed buying decisions. Since the introduction of online listing platforms, 90 per cent of residential sales searches are now initiated by portals and only 5 per cent by high-street estate agents' shopfronts.[61] However, according to the UK's Department for Business, Energy & Industrial Strategy [62]and the Home Owner Alliance report,[63] the great majority of residential property   **20.040**

---

50   www.openboxsoftware.com
51   Execution of deeds. Practice guide 8. www.gov.uk/government/publications/execution-of-deeds
52   From 27 July 2020, HM Land Registry accepts 'witnessed electronic signatures': electronic signatures that enable an individual to sign legal documents, but which still require a witness who is present at the time to also sign the documents electronically.
53   Sundararajan, A. (2016). The Sharing Economy: The End of Employment and the Rise of Crowd-based Capitalism. MIT Press.
54   www.appearhere.co.uk
55   www.sook.space
56   www.airbnb.co.uk
57   www.wework.com
58   www.zillow.com
59   www.zoopla.co.uk
60   www.rightmove.co.uk
61   PropTech: Turning real estate into a data-driven market? 2020 Oxford Future of Real Estate Initiative Version 1.3 (Fabian Braesemann and Andrew Baum).
62   Research on buying and selling homes, Research paper, BIS/283.
63   A Home Owners Alliance Report, June 2017. Available at https://hoa.org.uk/wp-content/uploads/2021/02/HomeOwnersSurvey2018.pdf

buyers and sellers still use a traditional real estate agent to help with parts of the transaction process. Across the UK less than 10 per cent of sellers are using online-only agents.[64]

20.041 Online multi-sided marketplaces exhibit network effects[65] and this is a significant reason for competitive pressure in data-driven markets. Sellers have an incentive to use the platform with the largest user base, and similarly, buyers are keen to get the largest possible choice from a platform with many properties being offered. Non-digital markets used to have significant geographical barriers to entry;[66] however, online markets have economies of scale that follow from larger numbers of users, and this in turn encourages users to cluster on the platform that has the largest existing user-base.

20.042 Machine learning can be used in several ways on these marketplace models, including:

(a) creating, augmenting and curating inventory data;

(b) price estimation and auction modelling; and

(c) buyer and seller search, recommendation engines and inventory matching.

20.043 Pricing of property assets remains as much art as science. Real estate assessors face the challenging task of quantifying a realistic price that reflects what buyers are prepared to pay for both tangible and intangible qualities of an asset. For example, in residential house pricing the cost of a property depends not just upon the size of the property and the number of bedrooms and bathrooms – tangible assets – but also on its intangible assets, such as air quality or proximity to a school. Some of these aspects are measurable while others, such as the prestige or the visual impression of a neighbourhood, are difficult to quantify. Despite the well-known impacts that intangible qualities have on asset prices, measuring them has proved difficult and they often remain the sole judgement of the agent.

20.044 When it comes to curating inventory, machine learning is increasingly being used to systematically quantify these difficult-to-measure qualities, for example using street view images[67] and other imagery[68] to estimate the attractiveness of a road or automatically measuring distance and travel times to amenities like schools and shops, or estimating prices using sentiment-based models.[69]

20.045 Many large property companies are exploring the use of machine learning methods for customer management, primarily to target new customers and anticipate their consumption patterns. What information may be collected on customers and how it may be used is discussed further in the context of the General Data Protection Regulation in Chapter 10. Digital sales channels have led to the highly competitive and profitable area of digital marketing, where

---

64   Ibid.

65   Easley and Kleinberg (2010), Networks, Crowds, and Markets: Reasoning about a Highly Connected World.

66   Forman, C., Goldfarb, A., Greenstein, S. (2018). How Geography Shapes – and Is Shaped By – the Internet. Oxford University Press.

67   Law, S., Paige, B., Russell, C. (2018), Take a look around: using street view and satellite images to estimate house prices. arXiv preprint arXiv:1807.07155

68   Poursaeed O., Matera T., Belongie S. (2018), Vision-based Real Estate Price Estimation. arXiv preprint arXiv:1707 .05489 (2018)

69   Alexander-Dietzel, M., Braun, N., Schäfers, W. (2014), Sentiment-based commercial real estate forecasting with Google search volume data. Journal of Property Investment Finance 32(6), 540–69.

ML techniques are increasingly used for customer segmentation, alongside recommendation systems to maximise matching and marketplace volumes and to reduce the customer attrition rate.

F. REAL ESTATE MARKETS

In previous sections we have seen that the time taken to exchange and verify data and conclude a transaction has many consequences for the various parties involved in an individual transaction, but also influences market behaviour as a whole. **20.046**

The time taken to complete an investment sale and purchase is a key factor when talking about liquidity of real estate markets and investors see liquidity as a significant factor when choosing where to invest. The ability to enter and exit real estate markets is constrained by the time transactions take and the challenge of matching buyers and sellers with appropriate assets at appropriate prices. For buyers and sellers, this generates significant opportunity costs if investment or disinvestment is delayed. **20.047**

Most market participants would cite low liquidity as a (problematic) characteristic of commercial property as an asset class.[70] The time taken by a transaction, together with uncertain prices and changes to prices over the transaction period, constrains the ability to enter and exit property markets at specific times. Time to transact has important implications for risk and return. Delay in realising the capital value will result in reducing the total return, and uncertainty about timing of receipt of capital value adds to the volatility of expected returns. **20.048**

The lengthier the sale period, the more likely it is that market conditions will change or a buyer or seller may seek to withdraw from the transaction or change transaction terms and investors will become less certain about cash flow. Bond and Lizieri[71] identify a number of dimensions of liquidity, including: **20.049**

(a)   the rate of turnover/transactions and the time taken to transact;
(b)   the costs associated with transacting (both formal costs – buy or sell fees – and information costs);
(c)   the impact of the decision to transact on the price of the asset and the prices of similar assets; and
(d)   uncertainty as to achieved price or return at the time of the decision to transact.

Real estate market transparency and liquidity, bringing lower transaction costs, should positively impact the value of investment assets. Additionally, the financial crisis of 2007/8 has motivated regulators, central banks, foreign investors and real estate practitioners to contribute to increasing transparency by publishing data. This has led to significant improvements to transaction procedures and more efficient and close monitoring of lending. From this perspec- **20.050**

---

70   Crosby, N., McAllister, P. (2004), 'Liquidity In Commercial Property Markets: Deconstructing The Transaction Process', Real Estate Planning Working Papers
71   Bond, S., Lizieri, C. (2004) Defining Liquidity in Property, Working Paper 1, Investment Property Forum.

tive 'real estate data becomes a tradeable commodity, and that data might actually become the central resource of the digitalised real estate market'.[72]

20.051 Online listing sites such as Zoopla and Rightmove collect data on transactions as part of the listing process – incomplete as it may be, because the transactions do not complete on platform – but there are also many companies aggregating market data, including CoStar Group,[73] Datscha[74] and Realyse.[75] The processed information provided by these firms is essentially a service that adds value for users. While using the service users provide other valuable information to the firms, which can be the basis for novel products and services. High-dimensional and granular data provided by sellers and buyers of houses on platforms provides a unique source of market information for their owners.[76]

20.052 A study undertaken by Braesemann and Baum[77] shows significant evidence that PropTech is turning real estate into a data-driven market. It was also observed that data analytics, ML and related technologies are able to obtain substantially more venture capital funding in comparison to other sectors.

20.053 Traditional statistics can facilitate the process of understanding, modelling and forecasting the behaviour of real estate assets, but current developments of AI and ML algorithms provide novel approaches and perspectives, such as feature selection in high-dimensional data that mixes large structured and unstructured datasets and incorporates additional variables like the intangible qualities of visual appearance discussed earlier in section 20.43.

20.054 Applications of financial models in the real estate market could be used for investment, risk management or purchasing or trading decisions. There has been increased uptake of mass appraisal methodologies for price modelling, estimation and tribunal defence. Increased availability of and access to market data has spurred the development and application of Automated Valuation Models (AVMs), which can provide appraisals at low cost. AVMs are now well used in residential real estate,[78] but the state of the art is advancing rapidly.[79]

20.055 Developing better house price models is an important topic and conventional hedonic models have been criticised for specification error as a result of neglected non-linearities.[80] The impli-

---

72 Saull, A., Baum, A., Braesemann, F. (2020) Can digital technologies speed up real estate transactions? Journal of Property Investment and Finance, pre-print.

73 www.costar.com

74 www.datscha.com

75 www.realyse.com

76 Yanni Alexander Loukissas (2017), Taking Big Data apart: local readings of composite media collections, Information, Communication Society, 20(5), 651–64.

77 Braesemann, F. and Baum, A. (2020), PropTech: Turning real estate into a data-driven market? 2020 Oxford Future of Real Estate Initiative Version 1.3.

78 AVMs currently account for around a third of residential mortgage assessments in the UK.

79 Demirci, Onur (2021), Automated Valuation Models (AVMs): Machine Learning, namely Mass (Advanced) Valuation Methods and Algorithms.

80 Peterson, S., Flanagan, A.B. (2009). Neural network hedonic pricing models in mass real estate appraisal. Journal of Real Estate Research, 31, 147–64.

cation is that advances in ML models (such as neural networks) can be used to improve existing mass appraisal models which can be used in mortgage assessment.[81]

Property portfolios can provide an excellent opportunity for ML and AI practitioners to develop and test new models due to the availability of datasets and the persistent demand for novel solutions. However, there remain many issues, particularly within the areas of model explainability and defensibility of assessed values.[82] Other aspects of model explainability are discussed further in Chapter 29.   **20.056**

The central role that mortgage-backed securities (MBS)[83] as an asset class played in the financial crisis of 2007/8 has motivated regulators to tighten up the audit of these financial products. For example, the Securities and Exchange Commission (SEC) implemented revisions to Regulation AB and other rules regarding the offering process, disclosure and reporting for asset-backed securities,[84] altering credit ratings, references and eligibility criteria for asset-backed issuers.   **20.057**

Market participants are often in a position to trade off predictive accuracy for cost. For example, banks can use low-cost appraisals from AVM services when underwriting further loan advances, home equity withdrawals and re-mortgages.[85] Alternatively, risk managers may use an AVM as a cost-effective tool to monitor the collateral values underlying a portfolio of mortgage loans.[86]   **20.058**

It is difficult to estimate the true extent of the application of these methods in the industry, as publication of results has been sparse and limited in scope. Companies that offer products in this space include GeoPhy,[87] which uses supervised ML to create automated valuations for commercial real estate, and Hometrack,[88] which is used by 12 of the UK's 15 leading mortgage lenders and is behind Zillow's iBuyer 'instant offer' products.   **20.059**

G. PROPERTY MANAGEMENT, MAINTENANCE AND INSURANCE

Lastly, after a successful property transaction there is the ongoing issue of managing the property. This is especially true for residential short-term lettings and commercial property.   **20.060**

---

81   McCluskey, W., McCord, M., Davis, P., Haran, M., McIlhatton, D. (2013), Prediction accuracy in mass appraisal: a comparison of modern approaches. Journal of Property Research 30, 4.

82   Tulio Ribeiro, M., Singh, S. and Guestrin, C. (2016), 'Why should I trust you?': explaining the predictions of any classifier, arXiv:cs.LG/1602.04938.

83   MBS is a type of asset-backed security (an 'instrument') which is secured by a mortgage or collection of mortgages. The mortgages are aggregated and sold to a group of individuals that securitizes, or packages, the loans together into a security that investors can buy.

84   SECURITIES AND EXCHANGE COMMISSION 17 CFR Parts 200, 229, 230, 232, 239, 240, 243 and 249 Release Nos. 33–9117; 34–61858; File No. S7–08–10

85   Schulz, R., Wersing, M., Werwatz, A. (2014), Automated valuation modelling: a specification exercise. Journal of Property Research 31(2), 131–53.

86   Cajias, M. (2019), Understanding real estate investments through big data goggles: A granular approach on initial yields. International Journal of Housing Markets and Analysis 12(4), 661.

87   www.geophy.com

88   www.hometrack.com

20.061   In the context of the data cycle this means recording the ongoing changes to the asset, the management decisions and the building maintenance activities, so that the due diligence process can be expedited in any future sale. However, the primary use of data is to measure and record how an asset operates for the purposes of increasing efficiency. Increasingly, buildings equipped with myriad sensors and ML measurement devices can communicate with the owner's smartphone to optimise everything from energy efficiency, to occupancy, to predictive maintenance.

20.062   The success of solutions for aggregating real-world data from distributed systems also offer the opportunity for adaptive or data-dependent contracting.[89] For example, there are parametric flood insurance policies[90] that are triggered when water rises above a certain threshold and hits a sensor; the insurance policy becomes effective and pays compensation.

20.063   For industry to move towards automatic detection and settlement, there are three elements that need to be trusted in a transaction: the counterparty, the intermediary and the dispute resolution mechanism.[91] The data captured can also be used as a basis for online dispute resolution using platforms such as Jur.[92]

20.064   The variety and veracity of data sources can unlock hidden value in a range of domains that can benefit from efficient contract automation.[93] The overall cost and efficiency savings can be passed on by contracting parties to the data providers to ensure the integrity of the legal agreement, providing a new opportunity for a business around verified data sources.

20.065   Data processing in ML solutions is also moving closer to the measurement device as edge-side computing increases.[94] The roll-out of 5G technologies and low power networks such as NB IoT,[95] LTE-M[96] and LoRaWAN[97] has meant that the IoT devices can typically support high bandwidth or massive numbers of connected devices to send large amounts of captured data for central processing. The capabilities of mobile edge computing[98] also allows for complex processing at point of capture and pre-processing or aggregation before sending to a central server or cloud services. A practical example of this is use for footfall counting as provided by Hoxton Analytics,[99] which uses ML to provide proof of customers arriving in a shop or retail environment. This could be used in a retail contract for leasing arrangements to be determined by footfall, occupancy levels or other factors measured using a smart camera.

---

89   RICS, A critical review of distributed ledger technology and itsapplications in real estate. Technical report.
90   www.floodflash.co
91   Werbach, K. (2018), Trust, but verify: Why the blockchain needs the law. Berkeley Tech. L.J. 33, 489.
92   www.jur.io
93   Tasca, P., Vadgama, N., Xu, J. (2021), Enabling the Internet of Value: How Blockchain Connects Global Businesses Future of Business and Finance, 1st ed.
94   Agbo, B., Qin, Y., and Hill, G.. Research directions on big iot data processing using distributed ledger technology: A position paper. In Muthu Ramachandran, Robert Walters, Gary Wills, Victor Méndez Muñoz, and Victor Chang, editors, Proceedings of the 4th International Conference on Internet of Things, Big Data and Security, volume 1, pages 385–391, Portugal, May 2019. SciTePress. 4th International Conference on Internet of Things, Big Data and Security, IoTBDS 2019.
95   www.gsma.com/iot/narrow-band-internet-of-things-nb-iot/
96   www.gsma.com/iot/long-term-evolution-machine-type-communication-lte-mtc-cat-m1/
97   www.lora-alliance.org
98   www.etsi.org/technologies/multi-access-edge-computing
99   www.hoxtonanalytics.com

The increasing prevalence of sophisticated control systems means buildings are able to detect   **20.066**
and learn from owners' or occupiers' behaviour patterns to save energy and money, and simultaneously to make the building more comfortable.[100] The promise of this rich data environment is
that it can be linked to the title of the property to provide an exhaustive package of information
available to buyers and sellers, as well as to other real estate actors such as estate agents, occupiers, home insurance companies and mortgage brokers.

One of the limitations to wide adoption of these types of data-rich contracts is the availability   **20.067**
of standards. There is no clear universal legal lexicon to describe the details of these emerging
contractual relationships based on measuring changing properties of the world. Without
a formal definition and agreed data specifications, it is challenging from a contract perspective,
and it seems that this is likely to result in new regulation or industry standards similar to those
that have emerged for BIM, as discussed at the beginning of the chapter.

H. CONCLUSION

We have set out some areas of activity in the real estate sector and how they are being impacted   **20.068**
by AI and ML. We have given some examples of current processes and how data is used, and
of companies that are starting to apply these technologies to re-imagine how these activities
might work or operate in the future.

In the context of the use cases we have presented, it seems that a greater degree of the recorded   **20.069**
information related to a building's facilities and maintenance and an occupier's rent and other
terms will be aggregated or attached to the building's title (that is, via digital twins or digital
passbooks). With this, we can see the benefits of reduced costs, more efficient processes and
enriched data paving the way for new business models to be applied. Consider the example of
the HMRL conveyancing proof of concept discussed earlier – what would be possible if the
period of time taken for the purchase and sale of a building went from weeks and months to
mere minutes?

As well as verification of information, we have the transformation of market networks. Real   **20.070**
estate is often considered an asset class out of many people's reach, with significant barriers to
entry, particularly for the young. The possibilities for new shared ownership, partial ownership
and real estate access business models are emerging and are likely to challenge regulators.

Ultimately, as the largest asset class globally, real estate has surprisingly not seen anywhere   **20.071**
near the same levels of digital transformation that have occurred in many other industries. The
speed at which anything more than incremental shifts in the industry will occur in the future
is dependent on how far incumbent participants will accept these new technologies and where
regulation will adapt to it.

A key limitation for comparative research in the real estate industry is the geographical spec-   **20.072**
ificity of models and the lack of a common baseline dataset to test different methods against.

---

100   Li, Rita Yi Man, Li, Herru, Mak, Cho, Tang, Tony (2016), Sustainable smart home and home automation: Big Data
analytics approach. International Journal of Smart Home, 10(8), 177–87.

As a result, future research is needed within the community to develop a consistent, open, multi-modal and geographically diverse database.

20.073   The lack of an up-to-date, single pool of standardised property information in turn is one of the most critical causes for delay in real estate transactions. However, the most promising technologies to mitigate this problem, in particular digital property passports summarising all relevant building information, face substantial barriers to adoption and the current models make lengthy due diligence processes essential for buyers.

20.074   In conclusion, there are likely to be increasing returns to scale or scope in data acquisition as there is more learning to be had from the 'larger' datasets. We have given some examples of early stage companies that are re-imagining delivery of services. There is the possibility that early or aggressive entrants into an emerging area may be able to create a substantial and long-lasting competitive advantage over potential rivals merely through control over data, rather than through formal intellectual property or demand-side network effects.

20.075   Strong incentives to maintain data privately have the additional potential downside that data is not being shared across researchers and regulators, thus reducing benefits that arise from public aggregation. As the competitive advantage of incumbents is reinforced, the power of new entrants to drive technological change may be weakened.

20.076   Though this is an important possibility, it is also the case that, at least so far, there seems to be a significant amount of entry and experimentation across most key application sectors. With so much experimentation, the challenge for the regulator will be to try set standards to allow for the interoperability of various market-led approaches.[101]

---

101   For example, one approach to increasing data lead innovation in the banking sector was the CMA Retail Banking Market Investigation Order 2017 that led to the specification of the protocol and standards for Open Banking in the UK.

PART IV

HUMAN AI

21

ETHICS

Patricia Shaw

A. INTRODUCTION

21.001 According to UK government guidance[1] published in June 2019, 'AI ethics is a set of values, principles, and techniques that employ widely accepted standards to guide moral conduct in the development and use of AI systems'.

21.002 Ethics is framing. It underlies who we are, what we do and why we do it. It underpins our laws, our actions or inaction, our behaviour, our conduct, our culture, and ultimately our algorithmic, automated, artificial and intelligent systems (AI).[2]

---

1   www.gov.uk/guidance/understanding-artificial-intelligence-ethics-and-safety accessed 10 October 2020.
2   Although there is some divergence in definition of artificial intelligence, for the purposes of this chapter I am referring to the definitions presented by the OECD and AI HLEG. The recommendation on AI adopted by the Council of the Organization for Economic Co-operation and Development in 2019 ('OECD Recommendation') defines AI as 'a machine-based system that can, for a given set of human-defined objectives, make predictions, recommendations, or decisions influencing real or virtual environments'. The definition adds that AI systems are 'designed to operate with varying levels of autonomy'. The Independent High Level Expert Group on Artificial Intelligence appointed by the European Commission (AI HLEG) defines AI as 'software (and possibly also hardware) systems designed by humans that, given a complex goal, act in the physical or digital dimension by perceiving their environment through data acquisition, interpreting the collected structured or unstructured data, reasoning on the knowledge, or processing the information, derived from this data and deciding the best action(s) to take to achieve the given goal'. It adds that 'AI

Ethics affects the values and principles we hold to (or deviate from), how we apply them and **21.003** the result we are trying to achieve by their application. The application of ethics in humans (and most pertinently in human decision making) can be rational or irrational, utilitarian, individualistic or philanthropic, with a moral imperative,[3] consistent or inconsistent, reasonable or unreasonable; it may align with societal norms or be contrary to the perceived 'norm'.

There are multiple factors and variables at play within a given context that can affect the appli- **21.004** cation of ethics. These can include immediate or historic actual or perceived circumstances, control, economics, education, environment, societal influences and/or upbringing, among many other factors.

To put this into context, it is necessary to consider a few areas of application of ethics to AI. **21.005**

1.   AI as a Learning Machine

AI, unlike standard static rules-based software algorithms, is dynamic. It is trained on (often **21.006** historical) data, and continues to learn based on initial parameter rules set from its inputs and its environment. It adapts (whether in a supervised or unsupervised manner) to new situations and new application domains. Based on its 'learning', the AI can recognise patterns, make predictions, make recommendations and auto-label, helping to speed up processes, thus making them often faster and more efficient than human operations. This raises questions of whether such automatic labelling and/or AI-driven recommendations and predictions are accurate and fair.

The output from AI may correctly present the desired end goal, but it is unlikely to understand **21.007** the context in which that output is to be applied. This can lead to biased or domain-inappropriate results. Furthermore, the efficiencies of AI can also lead to fewer humans being employed in such tasks. This can lead to deskilling or a reduction in human capacity and capability. There are socio-economic effects of AI replacing humans in tasks, such as job losses or role changes, which also has implications for the future of work. This in turn has the potential to impact on how humans feel valued, feel significance and experience the fulfilment and joy of a 'job well done' that paid-for occupation can provide, which also can impact on income and ability to earn. A dim picture can be painted of a downward spiral of mankind if ethical and societal impacts even at smaller AI-task level are not taken seriously at an early stage.

2.   Anthropomorphised AI

Since AI can be summed up as an algorithmic system coded by programmers based on sta- **21.008** tistical mathematical models (or, as some would coin it, 'smart maths'), it is therefore neither intelligent (although it might fulfil some intelligent functions) nor truly able to compete with

---

systems can either use symbolic rules or learn a numeric model, and they can also adapt their behaviour by analysing how the environment is affected by their previous actions'.

3   Immanuel Kant's ethical theory of categorical imperative was that an action can only be good if the principle behind it was in fulfilment of a duty to the moral law, and that action arose from a sense of moral duty in the actor. Furthermore, his theories looked at the end outcomes and sought to imbue that all humans are due dignity and respect and must not be seen as a means to an end.

what humans can do and that of which they are capable. When AI is contained on hardware and in a plastic, metal, silicon or other material encasement, it is an artefact. Even embodied AI, which can now take on a human-like form and perform synthetic human functions such as communication and care, is still an artefact. When embodied AI is potentially being thought worthy of being granted rights of personality or citizenship, or could be conceived to be sentient and have a conscience, this raises other moral and ethical issues about what embodied AI is. For example, how do we treat embodied AI? How do we interact with embodied AI? What are the limits of what embodied AI ought to do for us in respect of function and task fulfilment, and when does it cross the line to affect our own feelings, emotions, hormones – how our own bodies function? How does embodied AI impact our ability to feel and have empathy for other humans? How does it impact on our wellbeing, our relationships, our ability to care for or to reciprocate emotions with other human being? How do reliable and predictable robots compete on the trust stakes with unreliable human beings? How do we ensure that human beings continue to be respected and valued over and above embodied AI? How can we ensure children can tell the difference? The list is endless.

3.   AI and Decision-making

21.009   Software algorithms and modelled data have been used to help inform decision-making with a human. The combination of AI and data means algorithmic systems can recognise patterns and process findings through decision trees to produce outcomes. Although technically the AI does not ever make a decision, AI is used for automated decision making without a 'human in the loop' or 'human over the loop', which has ethical implications.

21.010   For *fairness*, bias and direct and indirect unlawful discrimination produced in the inputs, the process, the outputs and the outcomes must be managed, but it is important to note that not all bias is unlawful. Some bias may even be useful or desirable for purposes of preventing negative outcomes.

21.011   For *accountability* and responsibility, decisions supported by AI must be identified. For *transparency* regarding the models used, the relative weight or importance ascribed to inputs (their characteristics, variables, attributes and vectors), and the processing by AI of the rules behind the decision-making process, must be capable of explanation. This is particularly tricky where certain AI systems are seen to be opaque and unexplainable.

21.012   For *agency and autonomy*, depending on the reliance placed on the outcome of the decision making and whether further human intervention is necessary, the architecture of AI systems must be capable of review. If humans leave unchecked automated decision-making systems and other AI which acts as an agent of any human decision or indecision, we may end up surprised as to what level of human and moral agency has been granted and delegated to AI, potentially undermining human autonomy. Knock-on effects might include lower levels of confidence in decisions made by humans without AI interventions, therefore potentially also limiting the scope of and predicating human choice.

4. AI and the iHuman

The processing power of AI used with neural interfaces or brain–computer interfaces could **21.013** blur the lines between the human cognitive mind and the machine. AI in this context has the potential, according to Royal Society research,[4] to aid humans by 'typing by brain' and use of a 'mental mouse' to control computers and devices; direct brain-to-brain communication, whether simple impulses or complex thoughts; wider medical applications, such as for Alzheimer's disease and mental health conditions; monitoring of brain activity to support health, safety and security; and augmentation of human memory, concentration and learning.

As a result of these technologies, there will be a great deal of benefit: advancement in acces- **21.014** sibility and improvements to quality of life. Ethics (whether strictly bioethics, data ethics or AI ethics) will be a concern to us all as a society. Evidence of accuracy, reliability, safety and security of this kind of AI will be required in order for people to put their trust in such new technologies if society is in any way to adopt them.

AI used in respect of or to replace pre-existent or non-existent bodily functions will necessitate **21.015** clear definition of ethical principles such as human dignity, human value and worth, respect, justice, fairness, privacy and personal security, both in their application and in the monitoring of these technologies. It will bring much challenge to how we apply ethical concepts of transparency and accountability, and what this means for personhood, personality and individual autonomy. Depending on the technology, it could have very profound impacts on reason, fairness, agency, freedom of conscience and from interference, and criminal responsibility. It will raise questions of ethical boundary lines concerning quality of life, and what constitutes necessary and reasonable human adaptation versus unnecessary human enhancement.

5. Education and Awareness

Some of the applications of AI highlighted above only serve to remind us that there needs to **21.016** be more awareness and education regarding ethics and its application to AI. AI (and the multiplicity of its components) provides both complexity and challenge to policy makers, legislators, regulators and legal advisors.

Focusing on the values considered in the origination of AI and the outcomes of AI provides **21.017** us with a starting point for applying ethics to AI, but it is not the whole story. It serves to aid us in the consideration of the risks and impacts of AI from an ethical and societal perspective, and demonstrates how a seemingly innocuous technology can and does impact on individuals, groups and wider society. For this reason, AI is not ethics-neutral.

In designing, developing, deploying, operating, maintaining, monitoring and decommissioning **21.018** AI, we need to be fully cognisant of accountability, autonomy, agency, bias, choice, controllability, data justice, equality, equity, exercise of personal authority, explainability, fairness, freedom, human dignity, independence, interdependence, loyalty, reliability, respect, safety,

---

4   iHuman: Blurring Lines between Mind and Machine Report (Issued September 2019) DES6094 ISBN: 978-1-78252–420–5, The Royal Society https://royalsociety.org/-/media/policy/projects/ihuman/report-neural -interfaces.pdf accessed 17 October 2020.

self-actualisation, transparency, trust, power and wellbeing. This is not an exhaustive list. It does however provide a useful checklist for what ought to be considered in a risk and impact assessment of AI, and helps to identify the kinds of harms we ought to be abating and mitigating in relation to the consequences (both intended and unintended) of AI.

B. FORMS OF PRACTICAL APPLICATION OF ETHICS IN AI

There is no lack of proposals for handling ethical aspects of AI. Many of these however do not adequately address the challenges…[5]

21.019 Applying ethics to AI practically *is* challenging, and complex, because generally it requires us to look at several moving parts and to apply multiple methods and ways of working with multi-layered, multi-faceted (internal and external to the organisation, depending on the multiple parties involved in an AI system), multi-disciplinary stakeholders and experts who are also in multiple jurisdictions. This section considers the challenge through lenses including frameworks, tools, principles, standards, regulation and certification.

21.020 The overall approach to applying AI ethics requires organisations handling AI (at whichever stage in the AI lifecycle is pertinent to their role in the ecosystem) to consider it in all its component parts (the data, the algorithmic intelligent system(s) and the outcomes); in all its application domains (including dual-use), because context matters; and in its short, medium and long-term impacts (assessing each of those component parts in terms of levels of risk to the rights and freedoms of the individual, the group and wider humanity and society).

21.021 To the degree that any element of the above is sourced externally to the organisation (whether that be an in-sourced component or outsourced service), due diligence is required. Digging deeper may include getting a greater understanding of:

- the project conceptualisation (and the original concept of operation and intended goal);
- what (if any) stakeholder analysis was undertaken;
- the diversity (and inclusivity) of the team(s);
- the interdisciplinarity of the team(s);
- how the concept of operation of the AI system is understood between teams;
- the cultural context in which these components or services are being designed and developed;
- the models used and why;
- how team decisions are made and evidenced, and what if any other factors (such as group dynamics) act as either a conflict or an influence in this process;
- what data was used to train, test and tune the AI, and where was it sourced;
- how representative was the data in relation to the end user audience, and how was that validated;

---

5   AI Ethics Impact Group in conjunction with Bertelsmann Stiftung, From Principles to Practice – An interdisciplinary framework to operationalise AI ethics (published April 2020) www.ai-ethics-impact.org/en#:~:text=bertelsmann %2Dstiftung.de-,AI%20Ethics%20Impact%20Group%3A%20From%20Principles%20to%20Practice,ethics%20from %20principles%20to%20practice accessed 17 October 2020.

- what training does the organisation have for its personnel in respect of identifying and mitigating ethical and societal impacts of AI;
- what technical and organisational security measures are in place both in respect of the development but also deployed operation; and
- what governance and human oversight is deployed in the AI systems to provide a safeguard against 'at rest' and 'in operation' harms.

This is not an exhaustive list of questions. Neither are these questions only applicable to out-sourced providers. This brief list is intentionally silent on matters of personal data or personally identifiable information usage in the context of AI, which would ultimately embroil us in discussion of adherence to the requirements and principles of the European Union's General Data Protection Regulation (GDPR) for those operating in a European environment or the US California Consumer Privacy Act of 2018 (CCPA) for those operating in a Californian context. The list is to note that these considerations need reflection in respect of all AI systems, whether anonymised data, synthetic data or no data is used. **21.022**

The use of such investigatory questioning serves to highlight both ethical and legal risks. Ethical risks can occur even with non-personal data, because data contains echoes of the person involved (whether they be the subject of the data or the organiser, categoriser or classifier of it), and may result in unconscious and inadvertent biased outcomes. Legal risks can be identified in that intellectual property such as copyright can subsist in databases of training data.[6] Training data not only has to trigger personal data rights, but it can also have much wider implications for equality and human rights. **21.023**

(a) Frameworks

There are a number of toolkits, canvases, checklists, ethics warning labs and consequence-scanning tools aiding governments and organisations alike to identify ethical issues.[7] Many are intended to help identify risks posed by AI and data-driven technologies, cognisant of the potential – intended and unintended – ethical and societal (and not just legal) impacts. **21.024**

While emerging practical tools to help assist in the application of ethics to AI are still nascent, most so far are based on risk and impact assessment and require an AI ethics governance framework for operationalisation. **21.025**

Before building any AI ethics governance framework, there are three key challenges to practically implementing AI ethics[8] which need to be addressed: (1) context dependence, in that the **21.026**

---

6   Benjamin Sobel, A Taxonomy of Training Data: Disentangling the Mismatched Rights, Remedies, and Rationales for Restricting Machine Learning (19 August 2020). Artificial Intelligence and Intellectual Property (Reto Hilty, Jyh-An Lee, Kung-Chung Liu, eds), Oxford University Press, available at SSRN: https://ssrn.com/abstract=3677548 or http://dx.doi.org/10.2139/ssrn.3677548 accessed 14 October 2020.

7   Such as the Open Data Institute's Data Ethics Canvas, DotEveryone's TechTransformed Project (now part of the Ada Lovelace Institute) and the Consequence Scanning Tool, UNBIAS Awareness Cards and UNBIAS AI for Decision Makers toolkit, and Ethical Explorer from the Omidyar Network.

8   AI Ethics Impact Group in conjunction with Bertelsmann Stiftung, From Principles to Practice – An interdisciplinary framework to operationalise AI ethics (published April 2020) www.ai-ethics-impact.org/en#:~:text=bertelsmann%2Dstiftung.de-,AI%20Ethics%20Impact%20Group%3A%20From%20Principles%20to%20Practice,ethics%20from%20principles%20to%20practice accessed 17 October 2020.

values depend of the application domain and cultural context; (2) socio-technical nature of AI, in that there are multiple factors and parties that can influence and have an impact on a AI's system design, development and implementation; and (3) the need for any AI ethics framework to be easy to use for a wide range of multiple stakeholders within the organisation and possibly also across AI ecosystem.

21.027 Constructing any AI ethics governance framework will require any organisation to identify:

(a)   its ethical principles in relation to AI, ensuring that there is clarity and consensus around the meaning of the ethical concepts and how they are to apply in specific situations;[9]

(b)   the governance structure and approach which will work with all the necessary stakeholders in the organisation and through which adherence to AI ethical principles will be monitored and measured. This may highlight the need for a separate governing body, such as an Ethics Advisory Board, with interdisciplinary expertise, or the need for more focused existing internal governance competence, capability and capacity;

(c)   the standards and documented processes and procedures (including any sector, industry or regulator-specific guidance) through which adherence to the AI ethical principles will be achieved. Processes and procedures should also include (a) mechanisms to assist with the identification of any tensions and trade-offs between practices and principles – non-compliance with the law is not negotiable; (b) mechanisms to assess technological capabilities and impacts; (c) mechanisms to assess data accuracies, capabilities and impacts; and (d) mechanisms to measure outcomes against the perspective of different people groups (often referred to as 'publics' when they concern different protected characteristics or are impacted by differing application domains) in the short, medium and long term.[10]

(d)   any certification requirements;

(e)   internal or external AI audit arrangements.

(b) Risk and impact assessment tools

21.028 Risk and impact assessment in A1 is not new. According to a McKinsey report,[11] traditional model risk management is insufficient for three main reasons: (1) AI poses unfamiliar and unknown risks and creates new territories for responsibility and potential liability; (2) AI use in many organisations is decentralised, making it difficult for risk managers to track; and (3) there is a lack of AI risk management capability. The same can be said for ethics competence and capability.

---

9   Nuffield Foundation and The Leverhulme Centre for The Future of Intelligence, Ethical and Societal Implications of Algorithms, Data, and Artificial Intelligence: a roadmap for research.

10   Supra.

11   Derisking AI by Design: How to build risk management into AI development, published August 2020 www.mckinsey .com/~/media/McKinsey/Business%20Functions/McKinsey%20Analytics/Our%20Insights/Derisking%20AI%20by %20design/derisking-ai-by-design-build-risk-management-into-ai-dev.pdf accessed 14 October 2020.

As a result, a few risk and impact assessment models are emerging to help organisations assess   **21.029**
their AI, ethical and societal risks. These include (this is not an exhaustive list):

- The Independent High Level Expert Group for AI, appointed by the European Commission (AI HLEG)'s Assessment List for Trustworthy AI (ALTAI), which, helpfully, is based on the AI HLEG's own seven requirements for trustworthy AI.
- The ECP Artificial Intelligence Impact Assessment (AIIA)[12] provides users with a roadmap for conducting the AIIA and a ready-made code of conduct. A useful tool for organisations wanting to start their ethical AI journey.
- ITechLaw's Multi-Risk Impact Assessment Tool[13] was devised for the assessment of Covid-19 tracking and tracing apps, tools and wearables, but the assessment calls out specific ethical and legal considerations based on iTechlaw's eight Responsible AI Principles.[14] Human agency, autonomy and privacy as well as wider societal impacts are considered. A Responsible Artificial Intelligence Impact Assessment (RAIIA) tool was published in May 2021, based on iTechlaw's eight Responsible AI Principles[15] set, to provide an in-depth risk and impact assessment purely in respect of AI and data.
- Not quite a risk and impact assessment tool, but equally not fitting squarely into the principles bracket either, is the Ledger of Harms produced by the Center for Humane Tech[16] This ledger focuses uniquely on harms which are posed through online technology platforms. Crucially, this risk assessment brings to the fore use of AI for attention and cognition deficit, for misleading and manipulative practices, for dissemination of mis- and dis-information and for systemic oppression of people groups based on protected characteristics or attributes. It also notes AI's use which impacts on social relationships, isolation and loneliness, ability to empathise, mental and physical wellbeing. All of these aspects are useful for ethical consideration beyond the realms of online harms.

Risk and impact assessment tools, although incredibly useful, do not (and cannot) provide   **21.030**
a holistic solution, nor tell of ways to mitigate the risks identified. This is where capability and
capacity for AI ethics risk identification, mitigation and resolution needs to be resourced with
budget as part of a wider AI ethics governance framework.

(c) Principles

According to the US government,[17]   **21.031**

> [p]ractical applications of AI are often brittle and the discipline of AI development is evolving, leaving
> the norms of AI use inchoate. Globally, the public sector, private industry, academia, and civil society
> are engaging in ongoing debates over the promise, peril, and appropriate uses of AI. [...] AI ethics

---

12   ECP Platform voor de InformatieSamenleving, Artificial Intelligence Impact Assessment https://ecp.nl/publicatie/artificial-intelligence-impact-assessment-english-version/ accessed 14 October 2020.

13   iTechlaw Multi-Risk Impact Assessment Tool www.itechlaw.org/sites/default/files/HTF%20Risk%20Assessment%20Tool_ENGLISH.pdf accessed 14 October 2020.

14   iTechlaw 8 Responsible AI Principles https://www.itechlaw.org/ResponsibleAI accessed 19 October 2020.

15   Supra.

16   Ledger of Harms https://ledger.humanetech.com/ accessed 14 October 2020.

17   AI Principles: Recommendations on the Ethical Use of Artificial Intelligence by the US Department of Defense, Defense Innovation Board, 31 October 2019 https://media.defense.gov/2019/Oct/31/2002204458/-1/-1/0/DIB_AI_PRINCIPLES_PRIMARY_DOCUMENT.PDF accessed 10 October 2020.

principles should therefore enrich discussions about how to advance the still-nascent field of AI in safe and responsible ways.

21.032 Before the application of ethics to AI can truly be considered, it is necessary to understand whose ethics is to be applied. Is it the business ethics of the organisation? Is it the personal ethics of the personnel within the organisation? Is it the ethics of the end user? Should it be considered from all these perspectives depending on whether it concerns the justification of the origination of the AI or the outcomes of the AI? Essentially, the question that must be asked is: what is the purpose of the ethical principles, and how are they to be applied in their relevant context?

21.033 There are multiple ethical principles applying to AI across the world[18] and at the time of writing this amounted to approximately 167 sets of principles globally. Although the majority seek to serve the same basic purpose (namely, to present a set of ethical values which provide scope for the governance of AI), the principles differ in a variety of ways.

21.034 Some commentators have argued for the use of human rights as a set of ethical principles, seeing as it already has an established terminology and a recognised legal framework.[19]

21.035 The principles differ in respect of their naming conventions (some are called principles, while others are presented as guidelines, frameworks and even national strategies). They differ in terms of their intended audience, composition, scope and depth.[20] As they are written by a variety of different authors, ranging from governments to inter-governmental organisations, companies, professional associations, civil society organisations, and multi-stakeholder advocacy groups, they vary culturally, contextually and with regard to their intended outcome or the sphere they are trying to engage.

21.036 While ethical principles may have some convergence in terminology, with some common themes appearing, such as accountability, fairness and non-discrimination, human control of technology, privacy, professional responsibility, promotion of human values, safety and security and transparency and explainability,[21] there appears to be divergence in definition.

21.037 First and foremost, there does not appear to be an agreed common definition of AI. Second, because of the variance in cultural, linguistic, geographical, organisational and professional discipline contexts, the definitions of the thematic topics themselves also vary. For example, a lawyer and a statistician will have different views of what fairness means. Third, terminology

---

18 AlgorithmWatch's Global AI Ethics Inventory monitors the ethical principles available globally, see their update: https://algorithmwatch.org/en/ai-ethics-guidelines-inventory-upgrade-2020/ and full inventory: https://inventory .algorithmwatch.org/ accessed 10 October 2020.

19 Filippo Raso, Hannah Hilligoss, Vivek Krishnamurthy, Christopher Bavitz and Levin Yerin Kim, Artificial Intelligence & Human Rights: Opportunities & Risks (25 September 2018). Berkman Klein Center Research Publication No. 2018–6, SSRN: https://ssrn.com/abstract=3259344 or http://dx.doi.org/10.2139/ssrn.3259344 accessed 15 October 2020.

20 Jessica Fjeld, Nele Achten, Hannah Hilligoss, Adam Nagy, and Madhulika Srikumar, 'Principled Artificial Intelligence: mapping consensus in ethical and rights-based approaches to principles for AI' Berkman Klein Center for Internet and Society (2020) http://nrs.harvard.edu/urn-3:HUL.InstRepos:42160420 accessed 10 October 2020.

21 Ibid.

is used interchangeably, such as in the case of interpretability and explainability.[22] This lack of common definition hinders the establishment of common principles.

Most published ethical AI principles lack legal force and effect and have no real teeth or conse-   **21.038**
quences to them for those who either authored them or seek to abide by them. Therefore, many principles lack genuine external accountability. While ethical AI principles act as a starting point for ethical governance, some have been perceived as a force of public appeasement or ethics washing and have induced a degree of ethics-shopping.[23]

While many principles in and of themselves offer afford self-regulation for the entity employ-   **21.039**
ing them, ethical principles also suffer from the global–local problem. For there to be a real impact on AI, ethical principles must have regard to the whole AI lifecycle and relate to each context in from which data is drawn and in which AI is designed, developed, deployed, main-tained and decommissioned.

Although there may be some synergies and commonality of purpose at a global level, much of   **21.040**
ethics' application at any point in its lifecycle is open to local interpretation within the local context. Different parts of the world hold to different values, prioritise them in varying ways and apply ethics appropriately and proportionately to the local context in any jurisdiction or continent.

To endeavour to regularise AI outcomes; to make them domain-specific; to ensure that the   **21.041**
outcomes are diverse and inclusive and not unlawfully discriminatory, that fair and unrea-sonable bias is mitigated; that outcomes are privacy-enhancing and respect human values and human rights and freedoms, ought to be a matter for transnational application and transna-tional enforceability.

Some hope for common ground may be found in the increasing adoption of both the AI Ethics   **21.042**
Principles of the Organisation for Economic Co-operation and Development (OECD) and those of the European Commission-appointed independent High Level Expert Group on Artificial Intelligence (AI HLEG).[24]

The OECD's five values-based AI Principles were agreed on 22 May 2019 and were set   **21.043**
out in their adopted Recommendation.[25] The OECD AI Principles were subsequently

---

22   Alejandro Barredo Arrieta, Natalia Díaz-Rodríguez, Javier Del Ser, Adrien Bennetot, Siham Tabik, Alberto Barbado, Salvador Garcia Sergio Gil Lopeza, Daniel Molina, Richard Benjamins, Raja Chatila and Francisco Herrera, Explainable Artificial Intelligence (XAI): concepts, taxonomies, opportunities and challenges toward responsible AI, Information Fusion 58 (2020) 82–115 https://doi.org/10.1016/j.inffus.2019.12.012 accessed 14 October 2020.

23   DatEthics.EU, Ethics Washing Is When Ethics Is a Substitute for Regulation (published 18 October 2018), https://dataethics.eu/ethics-washing-is-when-ethics-is-a-substitute-for-regulation/ accessed 19 October 2020.

24   Details of the EU HLEG and its expert members https://ec.europa.eu/digital-single-market/en/high-level-expert-group-artificial-intelligence accessed 17 October 2020.

25   The Recommendation of the OECD's Council on Artificial Intelligence adopted as a legal instrument in May 2019 by OECD's 36 member countries https://legalinstruments.oecd.org/en/instruments/OECD-LEGAL-0449 accessed 17 October 2020 identifies *five values-based principles* for the responsible stewardship of trustworthy AI: '(1) AI should benefit people and the planet by driving inclusive growth, sustainable development and well-being; (2) AI systems should be designed in a way that respects the rule of law, human rights, democratic values and diversity, and they should include appropriate safeguards – for example, enabling human intervention where necessary – to ensure a fair and just

adopted by 42 countries.[26] The OECD also has an AI Observatory[27] which provides data and multi-disciplinary analysis on artificial intelligence to facilitate global dialogue on AI.

21.044   The AI HLEG Ethics Guidelines for Trustworthy AI, which stipulate seven key require-ments[28] that AI systems should meet in order to be trustworthy, were finalised on 8 April 2019; although not mandated, it is likely that these guidelines will be applied by the 27 Member States of the European Union (EU).

21.045   What is clear is that simply replacing ethics with international human rights declarations[29] is not enough.[30] It should not be a choice that has to be made to use either ethical principles or a human rights basis; it should be the case that we use all tools available to us to identify and assess possible impacts. Both the OECD and AI HLEG appear to have taken on board fun-damental human rights as well as established ethical principles. It is however worth noting that there are differences between the Universal Declaration of Human Rights and the European Convention on Human Rights – not least in respect of their legally binding nature and ability to be enforced, but most pertinently in application to data privacy.[31]

(d) Standards

21.046   In the absence of international treaties concerning ethics in AI, standards frameworks are one way to bring about consistency of application to ethical principles and AI. Standardisation is where an industry recognising good practice seeks to translate these into repeatable outcomes through a series of normative and informative statements which help organisations put in place appropriate policies, processes and procedures, governance and oversight, consistent with the relevant standard.

21.047   There is currently no published consistent suite of standards in respect of AI[32] applicable globally. Internationally recognisable standards are currently being created by bodies such

---

society; (3) There should be transparency and responsible disclosure around AI systems to ensure that people understand AI-based outcomes and can challenge them; (4) AI systems must function in a robust, secure and safe way throughout their life cycles and potential risks should be continually assessed and managed; and (5) Organisations and individuals developing, deploying or operating AI systems should be held accountable for their proper functioning in line with the above principles.'

26   OECD announcement www.oecd.org/going-digital/forty-two-countries-adopt-new-oecd-principles-on-artificial -intelligence.htm (published 22 May 2019) accessed 17 October 2020.

27   OECD's AI Observatory https://oecd.ai/ accessed 17 October 2020.

28   The AI HLEG seven key requirements comprise: '(1) human agency and oversight; (2) technical robustness and safety; (3) privacy and data governance; (4) transparency; (5) diversity, non-discrimination and fairness; (6) environmental and societal well-being; and (7) accountability.' The full guidelines can be seen here: https://ec.europa.eu/futurium/en/ai -alliance-consultation/guidelines#Top accessed 17 October 2020.

29   Universal Declaration of Human Rights www.un.org/en/universal-declaration-human-rights/index.html and the European Convention on Human Rights www.echr.coe.int/documents/convention_eng.pdf accessed 15 October 2020.

30   Cansu Cansa, AI & Global Governance: Human Rights and AI Ethics – why ethics cannot be replaced by the UDHR, United Nations University Centre for Policy Research https://cpr.unu.edu/ai-global-governance-human-rights-and-ai -ethics-why-ethics-cannot-be-replaced-by-the-udhr.html accessed 16 September 2020.

31   Noteworthy is the violation of Article 8 of the ECHR highlighted by the dutch SyRI case: https://algorithmwatch.org/ en/story/syri-netherlands-algorithm/ accessed 17 October 2020.

32   For a full list of standards both published and in development, see the Global AI Standards Repository: https:// ethicsstandards.org/repository/ accessed 19 October 2020.

as the Institute of Electrical and Electronics Engineers (IEEE)[33] and the International Organisation for Standardization (ISO).[34] More localised efforts are recognised through the National Institute of Standards and Technology (NIST)[35] in the US and the British Standards Institution (BSI)[36] in the UK, as well as industry-specific standards in respect of healthcare. As standards, these are yet to be fully published, meaning that there is not one global standards framework to be applied.

Standards can be adapted to the relevant context and culture, can be updated following new   **21.048** understandings and revelations, and can flex relatively quickly to new situations, at what seems to be a faster rate than creation of new law. This makes standardisation an attractive tool to use in any ethical and/or regulatory framework.

Standards are a powerful tool. Although standards are usually completely voluntary, they serve   **21.049** to provide a demonstrable example of what 'good' or 'best industry practice' looks like. By virtue of an industry recognising standards as good practice, knowledgeable procurement teams often require adherence to such standards as part of purchasing agreements. Such business procurement practices make standards effectively enforceable through contract law. Standards can provide essential guidance to regulators when exercising powers of regulatory oversight, such that non-adherence to what is deemed as good industry practice is tantamount to a regulator holding behaviours as not in compliance with what ought to be expected of a regulated entity in those circumstances. A regulator can obviously go further and either require the adoption of standards as a mandatory requirement of regulation or adopt industry-created standards as the regulator's own standards.

In the sphere of ethical AI, some internationally recognisable standards are emerging, although   **21.050** many are still a work in progress.

IEEE

The IEEE, as part of its Ethically Aligned Design programme, has the P7000 series[37] of   **21.051** working groups and standards specifically looking at ethical considerations in the lifecycle of an autonomous and intelligent system for the benefit of humanity. These working groups cover aspects from the model process for addressing ethical concerns during system design (P7000) to transparency (P7001); data privacy (P7002); algorithmic bias (P7003); governance of child and student data (P7004); governance of employer data (P7005); use of personal data AI agents making decision without human input (P7006); ethically driven robotics and automation systems (P7007); nudging (P7008); fail-safe design of autonomous and semi-autonomous systems (P7009); wellbeing (P7010); process of identifying and rating the trustworthiness of

---

33   IEEE, with roots back to 1884 in New York, is the world's largest technical professional organization dedicated to advancing technology for the benefit of humanity: www.ieee.org/about/ieee-history.html accessed 17 October 2020.

34   ISO is an independent, non-governmental international organization with a membership of 165 national standards bodies, founded in 1946 in London: www.iso.org/about-us.html accessed 17 October 2020.

35   NIST was founded in 1901 and is now part of the US Department of Commerce.

36   BSI is the UK's national standards body founded in 1901: www.bsigroup.com/en-GB/about-bsi/our-history/ accessed 17 October 2020.

37   List of IEEE P7000 series of standards including in progress and completed works; https://ethicsinaction.ieee.org/p7000/ accessed 17 October 2020.

news sources (P7011); machine readable personal privacy terms (P7012); and ethical consideration in the emulation of empathy in autonomous and intelligent systems (P7014).

21.052 Out of all the IEEE ethical standards, P7010[38] 'Recommended Practice for Assessing the Impact of Autonomous and Intelligent Systems on Human Well-Being' is the only standard in this series that has completed its standardisation lifecycle[39] and been published so far at the time of writing.

21.053 In June 2020 the IEEE launched two new related initiatives: the IEEE Applied Artificial Intelligence Systems (AIS) Risk and Impact Framework Initiative and the IEEE Trusted Data and AIS Playbook for Finance Initiative.[40] It can be expected that more standardisation tools will follow.

ISO

21.054 The ISO, as part of its standardisation in AI programme, has the ISO/IEC JTC 1/SC 42 series of working groups. These working groups cover: AI Systems Engineering (ISO/IEC JTC 1/SC 42/AG 2); Dissemination and outreach (ISO/IEC JTC 1/SC 42/AHG 1); Governance implications of AI (ISO/IEC JTC 1/SC 42/JWG 1); Foundational standards (ISO/IEC JTC 1/SC 42/WG 1); Data (ISO/IEC JTC 1/SC 42/WG 2); Trustworthiness (ISO/IEC JTC 1/SC 42/WG 3); use cases and applications (ISO/IEC JTC 1/SC 42/WG 4); and Computational approaches and computational characteristics of AI systems (ISO/IEC JTC 1/SC 42/WG 5).

21.055 According to the ISO AI standards programme webpage,[41] six of the standards for this series have been published (which appear to be predominantly around 'Big data and reference architecture'[42]), and 21 are currently in progress.[43]

BSI

21.056 The BSI produced the first ethical design standard which was published in 2016 known as BS 8611:2016 'Robots and robotic devices: Guide to the ethical design and application of robots and robotic systems'.[44]

---

38 IEEE portal for P7010 standard https://standards.ieee.org/standard/7010–2020.html and https://ieeexplore.ieee.org/document/9084219 accessed 17 October 2020.

39 IEEE standards development lifecycle https://standards.ieee.org/develop/index.html?_ga=2.227803933.128388994.1 602936537–1643910293.1550070025 accessed 17 October 2020.

40 IEEE announcements about the two new initiatives https://ethicsstandards.org/ieee-standards-board-approves-new -artificial-intelligence-systems-initiatives/ accessed 17 October 2020.

41 ISO AI standard committee webpage www.iso.org/committee/6794475.html.

42 ISO published AI standards www.iso.org/committee/6794475/x/catalogue/p/1/u/0/w/0/d/0 accessed 17 October 2020.

43 ISO AI standards in progress www.iso.org/committee/6794475/x/catalogue/p/0/u/1/w/0/d/0 accessed 17 October 2020

44 BSI standard BS 8611:2016 Robots and robotic devices https://standardsdevelopment.bsigroup.com/projects/2015–00218#/section accessed 17 October 2020.

BSI formed its AI standards committee in 2017 to consider AI more broadly, taking into   **21.057**
account governance and bias, to help produce industry standards that would respect the public
interest.[45]

BSI has focused its international standards development efforts mostly in conjunction with the   **21.058**
ISO and International Electrotechnical Commission.[46]

In July 2018, the BSI and the IEEE (along with other standards bodies) set up the Open   **21.059**
Community for Ethics in Autonomous and Intelligent Systems (OCEANIS)[47] initiative with
the intention that there might be some harmonisation and cross-pollination of international
standards.

NIST

NIST, as part of the US Department of Commerce, has a slightly different AI standards   **21.060**
programme[48] which is designed to aid inter-agency collaborative efforts around AI. In August
2019, it released a 'plan for prioritizing federal agency engagement in the development of technical standards and related tools for AI'.[49] The plan recommended that the federal government
'commit to deeper, consistent, long-term engagement in AI standards development activities
to help the United States to speed the pace of reliable, robust, and trustworthy AI technology
development'.

Consolidated Standards of Reporting Trials – Artificial Intelligence (CONSORT-AI)

CONSORT-AI is a reporting guideline published in September 2020[50] (and is an extension of   **21.061**
the previous CONSORT reporting guidelines[51]) for clinical trials evaluating interventions with
an AI component. It was developed in parallel with its companion statement for clinical trial
protocols: Standard Protocol Items: Recommendations for Interventional Trials – Artificial
Intelligence (SPIRIT-AI). This is an example of a use case where standards (albeit that the key
output this work has produced is a checklist) have been created relatively rapidly for a specific
context.

---

45   BSI AI committee working groups and members https://standardsdevelopment.bsigroup.com/committees/50281655
     ?_ga=2.63443245.341286917.1602937682–778128081.1553783347 accessed 17 October 2020.
46   The IEC is the International standards and conformity assessment body for all electrical, electronic and related technol-
     ogies – basically all fields of electrotechnology. Founded in 1906 and based in Geneva, Switzerland, the IEC is one of
     three global sister organizations (IEC, ISO, ITU) that develop International Standards for the world.
47   OCEANIS initiative https://ethicsstandards.org/ accessed 17 October 2020.
48   NIST AI Programme www.nist.gov/topics/artificial-intelligence accessed 17 October 2020.
49   NIST plan for federal agency involvement in the creation of technical standards for AI (August 2019) www.nist.gov/
     system/files/documents/2019/08/10/ai_standards_fedengagement_plan_9aug2019.pdf accessed 17 October 2020.
50   Xiaoxuan Liu, Samantha Cruz Rivera, David Moher, Melanie J. Calvert, Alastair K. Denniston and The SPIRIT-AI
     and CONSORT-AI Working Group, 'Reporting guidelines for clinical trial reports for interventions involving artificial
     intelligence: the CONSORT-AI extension' (published 9 September 2020) Nat Med 26, 1364–1374 https://doi.org/10
     .1038/s41591–020–1034-x accessed 17 October 2020.
51   CONSORT www.consort-statement.org/.

21.062   AI in healthcare has applications which are wide-ranging and include AI systems for screening and triage, diagnosis, prognosis, decision support and treatment recommendation. Naturally, it would be reassuring for healthcare interventions involving AI to undergo rigorous and prospective evaluation to demonstrate impact on health outcomes, akin to that of other clinical trials. It would also introduce an added layer of transparency and provide an opportunity to address sources of potential bias and causes of potential harm or other unintended effects.

21.063   International ethical standards for AI are not being created fast enough. Despite the inherent need, much standard work relies on volunteer power. That being the case, standards making can also be dominated by representatives of larger organisations who have the capacity to dedicate resources and time to such initiatives. This fact can result in standards work being unduly influenced by self-interested parties. To expedite standards making, standards bodies would benefit from bringing in paid independent experts, from a variety of disciplines and jurisdictions, for even greater global coordination and collaboration. International standards bodies collaborating and not creating standards in siloes would enable standards to better complement each other and benefit from combining efforts and expertise (provided such expertise is not duplicated across these standards bodies) availed of during the standards-creation process.

21.064   Furthermore, standards would also benefit from not seeking to tackle the whole spectrum of AI head on, but being context-specific and so far as possible aligning with regulated and unregulated sectors, especially where existing guidance is available. What is clear is that AI standards are of interest to and impact both the private sector and the public sector. Future collaboration efforts regarding AI ethics standards ought to be international and intergovernmental.

(e) Regulatory Guidance

21.065   Many regulatory bodies have sought to create guidance and practical tools in respect of AI, trying to get governments and organisations to think beyond the mere application of law. These do not tend to be statutory documents or to be legally enforceable, but if not adhered to they provide strong evidence of a breach or of not following good practice in the area of that regulator's specific expertise.

21.066   A regulator which has been specifically active in trying to realise ethical principles in AI through its regulatory remit in providing guidance is the UK's Information Commissioner's Office (ICO). The ICO has produced a number of guidance documents to assist businesses and expert advisors concerning the processing of personal data by AI. Fundamentally, this calls for greater depth to existing risk and impact assessment through the more pervasive use of the Data Processing Impact Assessment (DPIA).

21.067   The list of guidance the ICO has created (either alone or in partnership with the UK's Alan Turing Institute) includes:

21.068   *Explaining decisions made with AI*,[52] which focuses on the ethical principle of transparency (including traceability, auditability, and explicability) and how this differs for those that need

---

52   The ICO Guidance on Explaining Decisions made with AI (published May 2020) https://ico.org.uk/for-organisations/guide-to-data-protection/key-data-protection-themes/explaining-decisions-made-with-ai/ accessed 17 October 2020.

to understand the process to achieving a given outcome and for those that need to understand the outcome.

The AI Auditing Framework,[53] which builds risk management and AI governance capability, **21.069** ultimately for accountability purposes. It helps organisations understand some of the tensions and trade-offs, including (but not limited to) fairness and transparency, profiling, accuracy, fully automated decision-making models, security and cyber, data minimisation and purpose limitation, exercise of data protection rights, impact on broader public rights within the scope of ICO investigation and audit.

Data protection and AI,[54] which acknowledges that where AI is involved, it is also likely to **21.070** require a DPIA. Risk does not just sit with the data controller so there is a real need to understand the AI and data supply chain and most of all remain in control.

The Accountability Framework,[55] which focuses on the ethical principle of accountability and **21.071** really bringing this to bear within internal governance and oversight teams.

The Age Appropriate Design Code[56] which received statutory status on 2 September 2020 and **21.072** thereafter a 12-month grace period before coming into full legal force and effect. This will be relevant in so far as it concerns online services and children, but there will be some transferred learning here. Key elements that this brings to ethical AI assessment are the use of geolocation data and tracking, parental and proxy user control, profiling, nudging techniques, wellbeing and empathy concerning use of connected toys and devices and overall greater accountability, governance and transparency.

The ICO itself proclaims that it 'does not provide generic ethical or design principles for the **21.073** use of AI. While there may be overlaps between "AI ethics" and data protection (with some proposed ethics principles already reflected in data protection law), [the Data Protection and AI] guidance is focused on data protection compliance.' The ICO's remit, like that of many domain-specific regulators, is therefore limited in this instance to data-informed or data-driven AI in so far as it processes and impacts personal data.

Until there is guidance from an overarching umbrella AI regulator, AI guidance from **21.074** a domain-specific regulator can only be truly reasoned and interpreted in the context of its regulatory scope. Furthermore, where guidance holds no statutory weight it is merely a pointer to what good practice ought to look like, until AI providers and their ethical practices are challenged in a court of law. Guidance is until then an opportunity for an organisation to improve competence and build capability and capacity.

---

53   The ICO AI Auditing Framework – draft guidance (published February 2020) https://ico.org.uk/media/about-the-ico/
consultations/2617219/guidance-on-the-ai-auditing-framework-draft-for-consultation.pdf accessed 17 October 2020.
54   The ICO Guidance on AI and Data Protection (published July 2020) https://ico.org.uk/for-organisations/guide-to-data
-protection/key-data-protection-themes/guidance-on-ai-and-data-protection/ accessed 10 October 2020.
55   The ICO Accountability Framework (published September 2020) https://ico.org.uk/for-organisations/accountability
-framework/ accessed 17 October 2020.
56   The ICO Age Appropriate Design Code (published September 2020) https://ico.org.uk/media/for-organisations/guide
-to-data-protection/key-data-protection-themes/age-appropriate-design-a-code-of-practice-for-online-services-2–1
.pdf accessed 17 October 2020.

(f) Certification

21.075 Certification is a useful tool to provide evidence of adherence to ethical AI standards, either for a regulator, for a party doing business with a certified organisation or for an end user. It helps raise awareness and provides a level of expectation with regard to the processes and procedures the organisation has in place, and often provides assurance of suitability, accuracy, reliability and/or the performance of a product or service.

21.076 The IEEE, through its Ethics Certification Program for Autonomous and Intelligent Systems (ECPAIS)[57] initiative, has been developing metrics and processes towards the implementation of a certification methodology addressing transparency, accountability, algorithmic bias and privacy.

21.077 In October 2020, the ECPAIS initiative produced first-of-a-kind recommendations for IEEE Certification Criteria to address the ethical challenges of Contact Tracing Apps and Contract Tracing and Tracking Technologies (CTA/CTT),[58] particularly where these technologies utilise AI.

21.078 GDPR provides for voluntary certification schemes to be able to be adopted. In February 2020 the ICO published guidance for organisations wanting to develop GDPR certification schemes.[59] Within the scope of the GDPR certification scheme would be the potential for an AI module of GDPR compliant certification, particularly if it concerned profiling or automated decision making and complied with recent ICO guidance.[60]

21.079 Ethical certification in respect of AI would be a useful and practical tool to provide assurance that an AI product or service had addressed key ethical concerns. Ethical certification, if conducted by a globally recognised body of experts, would be authoritative. If certification were to be coupled with a corresponding publicly recognisable series of ethical assurance marks or AI Ethics label[61] it would facilitate transparency and provide a quick-reference visual aid to communication with end users. The key to ensuring that the complexities of an AI system would not be overly simplified would be to ensure that the corresponding ethical assurance mark or AI Ethics Label was limited to the particular use case and not AI more generically. Certification would encourage organisations to have in place (and sustain) appropriate ethical practices, ethical culture and ethical governance and oversight. The commercial impetus to do this means that the cost of attaining certification would need to be commensurate with the

---

57 Details of the ECPAIS certification initiative, https://standards.ieee.org/industry-connections/ecpais.html accessed 17 October 2020.

58 IEEE ECPAIS report, Ethical Transparency, Accountability, and Privacy of CTA/CTT Use Case https://engagestandards.ieee.org/ECPAIS-CTA-TAPEFR-Report.html accessed 17 October 2020

59 ICO call for interest in developing Codes of Conduct and Certification schemes, February 2020, https://ico.org.uk/about-the-ico/news-and-events/news-and-blogs/2020/02/ico-codes-of-conduct-and-certification-schemes-open-for-business/ accessed 17 October 2020.

60 Supra.

61 AI Ethics Label was a concept proposed by the AI Ethics Impact Group in conjunction with Bertelsmann Stiftung, From Principles to Practice – An interdisciplinary framework to operationalise AI ethics (published April 2020) www.ai-ethics-impact.org/en#:~:text=bertelsmann%2Dstiftung.de-,AI%20Ethics%20Impact%20Group%3A%20From%20Principles%20to%20Practice,ethics%20from%20principles%20to%20practice accessed 17 October 2020.

expected increase in end user adoption of AI, so highly subject to commercial forces – that is, unless certification were mandated as part of a wider ecosystem of regulatory measures.

(g) Audit

An audit is essentially an independent examination of a state of affairs. Whether it is financial, **21.080** information technology, security, energy, performance, quality, forensics or data, the concept of auditing is not new.

In the UK, the ICO has used auditing with reference to AI since 2019. This has so far culmi- **21.081** nated in a draft AI Auditing Framework.[62]

In the US, the Algorithmic Accountability Act of 2019 was introduced to Congress into the **21.082** House of Representatives on 10 April 2019.[63] The bill 'requires specified commercial entities to conduct assessments of high-risk systems that involve personal information or make automated decisions, such as systems that use artificial intelligence or machine learning'. It also introduces the notion of audit: 'require each covered entity to conduct the impact assessments under subparagraphs (A) and (B), if reasonably possible, in consultation with external third parties, including independent auditors and independent technology experts.' It is currently uncertain if and when its passage will progress through the legislature, but not-for-profit organisations such as New York-based ForHumanity have already started to create an Independent Audit of AI and Autonomous Systems (IAAAS) to audit AI ethics, bias, privacy, trust and cybersecurity.[64]

Audit is traditionally something which provides a snapshot of a state of affairs over a given **21.083** period of time:

> Any notion of […] auditing without temporal dimensions misses seeing previous iterations, under-
> standing how they worked, why they changed, and how their interacting components actually con-
> stituted different systems. All of these limitations revolve around a central concern long studied by
> scholars of science and technology: how to understand seeing and insight as inseparably intertwined
> aspects of epistemology and knowledge production.[65]

If audit is to be applied to AI, which has a series of moving parts and is dynamic, then it is time to rethink not the fact that audit is a useful tool within a toolkit to apply to AI, but how AI audit might be conducted.

---

62   Ibid.
63   The text of the Algorithmic Accountability Act of 2019 can be found here: www.congress.gov/bill/116th-congress/
     house-bill/2231/text
64   Details of ForHumanity can be found here: www.forhumanity.center/what-we-do accessed 19 October 2020.
65   Mike Ananny and Kate Crawford, Seeing W.ithout Knowing: limitations of the transparency ideal and its application to
     algorithmic accountability (2016) New Media & Society 1–17: http://ananny.org/papers/anannyCrawford_seeingWith
     outKnowing_2016.pdf accessed 17 October 2020.

C. AI REGULATION TAKING ACCOUNT OF ETHICS AND POWER

Transparency and explainability as a way to control and mitigate possible biases producing discriminatory and/or harmful decisions/outcomes is very context-specific and should be considered in concrete and operational terms first, rather than being embedded into generalised and generic legal and regulatory prescriptions.[66]

21.084 AI ethics is powerless without law's effect and it is submitted by the author that this is currently lacking. It is necessary to design, develop, deploy, maintain and decommission for the best of humanity; it is necessary to protect, prevent, prohibit, safeguard and predict for the worst of humanity.

21.085 There is now a proven track record of the usefulness of voluntary schemes, unregulated principles and codes of conduct for raising awareness of ethical concerns relating to AI. Ultimately, these have been informative rather than normative, treated as 'nice to have' rather than as a 'must have', with few governments or organisations having had the existing capability or capacity – and not spending the necessary time, resources and budget – to bring ethical principles, standards, and ultimately governance to life, such that they can become truly effective and pervasive.

21.086 For this reason, government and organisations need a legislative imperative: ethical outcomes-based principles combined with normative standards mandated by an overarching law and context recognising sector-specific regulation, certification and audit.

21.087 Legislation does not have to mean stifling innovation. The European Union's Second Payment Services Directive, combined with the effects of the UK's Competition and Market's Authority Retail Banking Order, operated as a FinTech enabler.

21.088 The sceptic might say that it is to increase AI adoption and boost the economy, while the privacy conscious might see it is a genuine attempt to protect individual rights and their data – but either way, AI is a regulatory priority for the UK's ICO.[67] Whether or not the ICO is the appropriate regulator for AI is not within the remit of this chapter, but what is for certain is the ICO is well positioned when it comes to personal data-driven AI.

21.089 Innovation requires innovative approaches to measure demonstrable outcomes and to see dynamically counterfactual outcomes. 'A system needs to be understood to be governed – and in as many different ways as possible.'[68] A regulatory sandbox is one such innovative tool[69] and the ICO's 2020–21 focus in this regard was on 'Innovations related to data sharing, particu-

---

66 EiT Digital, A European Approach to Artificial Intelligence: A Policy Perspective www.eitdigital.eu/fileadmin/files/2020/publications/EIT-Digital-Artificial-Intelligence-Report.pdf accessed 14 October 2020.

67 https://ico.org.uk/about-the-ico/news-and-events/news-and-blogs/2020/05/new-priorities-for-uk-data-protection-during-covid-19-and-beyond/ accessed 28 September 2020 and https://ico.org.uk/for-organisations/guide-to-data-protection/key-data-protection-themes/guidance-on-ai-and-data-protection/about-this-guidance/ accessed 28 September 2020.

68 Mike Ananny and Kate Crawford, Seeing without knowing: Limitations of the transparency ideal and its application to algorithmic accountability (2016) New Media & Society 1–17 http://ananny.org/papers/anannyCrawford_seeingWithoutKnowing_2016.pdf accessed 17 October 2020.

69 The ICO Regulatory Sandbox https://ico.org.uk/sandbox accessed 17 October 2020.

larly in the areas of health, central government, finance, higher and further education or law enforcement', namely, areas of high risk.

Budgets within businesses are put where regulation requires it. GDPR in recent history itself **21.090** is proof of that.

Risk to reputation may be manageable (or, in some cases with large enough organisations, **21.091** self-insured) where AI products and services hold a large market position or fulfil a public utility role, such that no viable alternatives are available for end users. Furthermore, where no legal ramifications, consequences or liabilities prevail in respect of harms which are not unlawful, but are thought to be on the boundaries of what is ethically or societally beneficial, there is no accounting for the short, medium and/or long-term consequences or the opportunity costs of AI.

Without transparency, namely outcome explanation (or process transparency where necessary) **21.092** in language that is plain and clearly understood, how will end users or regulators respectively gain assurance of compliance with AI ethics principles and standards? Real and proportionate transparency is a hallmark of integrity and a precursor to genuine accountability, which in turn might aid consumer awareness and understanding and prove beneficial for AI adoption at the end of the day. Black boxes do not necessitate opaque or obfuscated end user journeys. Accountability to a regulator and feedback mechanisms to an independent redress body can in turn help redress unbalanced economic forces or data monopolies, bringing not only power plays but also privacy to the fore.

AI ethics (including making internal organisational provision for its governance and external **21.093** regulatory provision for its oversight) can be a competitive advantage, innovation-enabling and societally beneficial for all. Regulation of AI ethics would also prevent AI ethics itself being privatised and commoditised.[70]

The struggle may not be directly with AI itself; the focus of our legislative measures should **21.094** be on those with the ability to wield its power, recognising the powerful interplay between AI and the data that feeds it. As Norbert Wiener[71] wrote in 1954, 'machines, though helpless by themselves, may be used by a human being or a block of human beings to increase their control over the rest of the human race'. More recently, in 2018, Adrien Basdevant[72] devised the term 'Coup Data' to describe 'how data, the algorithms that process it and the platforms that concentrate it have taken on an immeasurable importance in our lives and economies, to the extent that they come into competition with traditional States power and influence the choice of their citizens, becoming a new tool of power',[73] proposing that no human should be reduced to the sum of their data.

---

70   Google offers AI Ethics Services, Wired (28 August 2020) www.wired.com/story/google-help-others-tricky-ethics-ai/ accessed 17 October 2020.
71   Norbert Wiener, The Human Use of Human Beings, Cybernetics and Society (first published 1950, Houghton Mifflin 1954, Published in Great Britain 1989 by Free Association Books).
72   Adrien Basdevant, L'empire des donnees (2018) www.lempiredesdonnees.com/ accessed 19 October 2020.
73   Coup Data, www.coupdata.fr/about accessed 19 October 2020.

D. BEST PRACTICE FOR REGULATORS

21.095   Imagine a world where all technology was fair, accountable, transparent and privacy-enhancing, and created responsibly; where algorithmic systems were used for good and were beneficial not only to individuals but to all citizens and groups of society, businesses, industries and the economy.

21.096   For this to happen requires a deliberate stock take of our existing legislative, regulatory, corporate governance and ethical frameworks. It necessitates that the potential benefits and risks are discussed openly, with positive and negative outcomes also considered in terms of opportunity cost. It requires the impact on the individual, on groups and on society as a whole to be front and centre in discussions, acknowledging the short, medium and long-term gains and consequences. The narrative has to be more than what AI can do 'for' humanity; it also ought to reflect on what AI is also doing 'to' humanity, in particular in terms of its second and third-order causal effects.

21.097   No longer can AI (in all its guises) operate in siloes: collaboration, drawing on interdisciplinary expertise, is vital to ensure we gain a holistic and pervasive view at every level.

21.098   All players must play their part, and for that reason there needs to be a top-down and bottom-up ethics and human rights-centric approach to the regulation and governance of AI and the data that feeds it. There are multiple types of algorithmic systems, multiple uses of AI and a myriad of application domains. It is clear that no one-size-fits-all approach can work.

21.099   In terms of a way forward to make AI more ethical, several AI policy makers and innovators are currently recommending the following.

- AI regulation[74]

  - For AI ethics practices, governance and oversight to be ascribed budget and fully deployed within public sector and organisations requires *enabling legislation* coupled with *empowering regulation*.
  - AI regulation, where implemented, should be *adaptable and flexible*, while minimising and mitigating risks and ensuring human rights and European values[75] are protected. The use of internationally agreed common ethical principles, ethical standards, ethical certification and ethical audit would aid that flexibility.
  - There should be *greater deployment of sandboxes* by regulators, not only to facilitate regulator learning and understanding of the potential benefits and risks of AI, but also to forge better lines of communication between bodies that are regulated and bodies doing the regulating, and to help filter out risks and potential issues earlier on in the process, prior to full operation deployment, much like that with clinical trials.

---

74   Commission President Ursula von der Leyen announced a coordinated European approach on the human and ethical implications of AI which culminated in the EU AI White Paper published in February 2020: https://ec.europa.eu/info/sites/info/files/commission-white-paper-artificial-intelligence-feb2020_en.pdf accessed 16 October 2020.

75   EiT Digital, A European Approach to Artificial Intelligence: A Policy Perspective (published 17 September 2020) www.eitdigital.eu/newsroom/news/article/a-european-approach-to-artificial-intelligence/ and www.eitdigital.eu/fileadmin/files/2020/publications/EIT-Digital-Artificial-Intelligence-Report.pdf accessed 14 October 2020.

- End users (whether individuals or businesses) must have a more effective mechanism to be able to identify, mitigate and *redress* harm caused to them by AI. This may not be sector-specific. The harm may not be identifiable uniquely to an individual but have a wider impact on certain publics/groups of society. The ensuing harm might not involve just one AI operators but an ecosystem of service providers. This is complex and would require a body, such as an ombudsman, to play a far more investigatory role.
- *Context matters*: When developing AI policy take in account the context of it application domain, whether that be a whole industry, a sector, and/or in respect of the end user audience, the whole public, or publics (groups sharing commonalities and/or communities of interest or place) within it – context matters. This should inform any regulation concerning AI.

- Risk and impact assessment

  - All AI should be risk assessed, involving a multidisciplinary team,[76] and with early and regular engagement with all relevant stakeholders.[77] The requirement to impact assess (whether that be for algorithmic, data protection, equality, ethical or other legal impact purposes) should not be left simply for so-called high risk AI.[78]
  - Not all data driven AI uses personal data, but anonymised aggregated data and meta/machine data (insofar as they are not re-identifiable to a person) are also powerful when used with AI, which can inadvertently produce unfair, unethical and biased outcomes and apply unreasonable inferences.[79]
  - Depending on the application domain and the potential riskiness of the outcomes, differentiation in legal and/or ethical requirement should be distinguishable between AI using personal data and AI using meta/machine data.[80]

- More effective human oversight

  - Building upon the foundations laid by the General Data Protection Regulation that all use of automated decision making be transparent and explainable, all decisions which utilise AI (not just those decisions which are fully automated) ought to be subject to the same level of scrutiny. Human decisions made following AI intervention can have a detrimental effect. A human reinforcing bias that the AI system already identified or introducing further bias into the AI lifecycle at given intervention points, can still result in negative outcomes undermining the benefits of human

---

76   EU High Level Expert Group on Artificial Intelligence, The Assessment List for Trustworthy Artificial Intelligence (ALTAI) published July 2020, https://ec.europa.eu/digital-single-market/en/news/assessment-list-trustworthy-artificial-intelligence-altai-self-assessment accessed 16 October 2020.

77   Ben Wagner, 'Ethics, an Escape from Regulation: from ethics-washing to ethics-shopping?' in Emre Bayamlioğlu, Irina Baraliuc, Liisa Janssens and Mireille Hildebrandt, 'Being Profiled: Cogitas Ergo Sum: 10 Years Of Profiling The European Citizen', 2018, Amsterdam University Press, doi:10.2307/j.ctvhrd092 and www.jstor.org/stable/j.ctvhrd092, accessed October 19, 2020.

78   EU AI White Paper, published February 2020 https://ec.europa.eu/info/sites/info/files/commission-white-paper-artificial-intelligence-feb2020_en.pdf accessed 16 October 2020.

79   Sandra Wachter and Brent Mittelstadt, Right to Reasonable Inferences – Rethinking data protection law in the age of big data and AI, published 2019.

80   EiT Digital, A European Approach to Artificial Intelligence: A Policy Perspective, *supra*.

oversight and causing it to be ineffective, known as 'human in the loop-hole'.

- Providing a mechanism for external multi-disciplinary independent oversight with (a) transparent decision-making procedures on how and why decisions were taken, (b) clear and plain language protocols where the selection of certain values, ethics and rights over others can be plausibly justified, (c) transparent details about if and how the decisions of external independent oversight mechanisms influence senior management and operations; and (d) clear and plain language protocols as to what happens when the relationship between an organisation's ethical principles or commitments conflict with existing legal or regulatory framework.[81]

- *Focused transparency*: Regulators will require a level of algorithmic transparency and explainability different from that of end users. AI processes ought to be presented to a regulatory body in such a way that they are interpretable, traceable and auditable and that AI outcomes can be justifiable, whereas end users might only require AI outcomes to be interpretable and justifiable.[82] AI outcomes may be explained to end users through the use of counterfactual analysis and tools to demonstrate the variance in AI outcomes dependent upon the AI inputs.[83]

21.100 Further practical steps that could help to apply ethical AI principles and underpin ethical accountability of AI arise through privacy management and data sharing. This means putting all the necessary infrastructure in place to ensure that no one loses control over their data and informational autonomy[84], including: (1) appropriate control over the use of all data (not just personally identifiable data), including for research, training, operational, testing, monitoring and improvement purposes; (2) empowerment of 'Data Trusts'[85] or other data sharing mechanisms both at industry and local level to steer what use is permissible and beneficial, or harmful and prohibited; (3) accurate and real-time permissions management; (4) the purpose (and re-purposing) of data within industries and sectors being consultative and aligning with that

---

81 Ben Wagner, 'Ethics, an Escape from Regulation: from ethics-washing to ethics-shopping?' in Emre Bayamlioğlu, Irina Baraliuc, Liisa Janssens and Mireille Hildebrandt, 'Being Profiled: Cogitas Ergo Sum: 10 Years Of Profiling The European Citizen', 2018, Amsterdam University Press, doi:10.2307/j.ctvhrd092 and www.jstor.org/stable/j.ctvhrd092, accessed October 19, 2020.

82 Concepts ascertained from David Leslie, Understanding Artificial Intelligence: implementation of AI systems in the public sector, The Alan Turing Institute (published 2019) https://doi.org/10.5281/zenodo.3240529 and www.turing.ac .uk/sites/default/files/2019–06/understanding_artificial_intelligence_ethics_and_safety.pdf

83 Sandra Wachter, Brent Mittelstadt and Chris Russell, Counterfactual Explanations, Without Opening the Black Box: Automated decisions and the GDPR, Harvard Journal of Law & Technology (2018) 31(2) https://jolt.law.harvard.edu/ assets/articlePDFs/v31/Counterfactual-Explanations-without-Opening-the-Black-Box-Sandra-Wachter-et-al.pdf accessed 16 October 2020.

84 Informational autonomy is defined as 'the control over one's personal information, that is to say the individuals' right to determine which information about themselves will be disclosed to whom and for what purpose': taken from the European Commission report 'The Right to be Forgotten and Informational autonomy in the Digital Environment' written by Cecile de Terwangne, published 2013.

85 Data Trust is a term originally coined by Dame Wendy Hall and Jerome Pesenti in an independent report to the UK Government on 'Growing the artificial intelligence industry in the UK' published 15 October 2017, www.gov .uk/government/publications/growing-the-artificial-intelligence-industry-in-the-uk accessed 19 October 2020. The concept, not intended to formulate a legal trust, has since been built upon by the UK's Open Data Institute, https:// theodi.org/article/data-trusts-in-2020/ accessed 19 October 2020, and by Sylvie Delacroix and Neil Lawrence, 'Bottom-Up Data Trusts: disturbing the 'one size fits all' approach to data governance', published 12 October 2018, International Data Privacy Law: Doi.org/10.1093/idpl/ipz014, SSRN https://ssrn.com/abstract=3265315 accessed 19 October 2020.

permissions management; (5) reliable and consistent data interoperability, with potential for industry and/or sector-specific open standards with regard to application programming interfaces or similar data-sharing enablers; (6) safe and secure data portability, and data mobility;[86] and (7) cyber security befitting of the environment where data is stored.

E. CONCLUSION

AI requires further ethical consideration. The *Awful AI list*[87] demonstrates the kinds of negative and unethical uses and outcomes that AI (with the help of humans) can produce. AI presents unchartered water. Each algorithmic intelligent system presents different opportunities, challenges and opportunity costs. It will require innovative regulatory and non-regulatory approaches to de-risk AI ethically, societally and legally. **21.101**

Fundamentally, pervasive self-regulation is unsustainable, as it has resulted in fragmented approaches and inconsistent definitions thus far. Cohesion, collaboration, coordination and most of all communication on the ethical issues impacted by AI as well as the consequences to human rights are needed at a global scale (with public sector, private sector and civil society stakeholders and representatives engaged) to ensure consistency of approach even where cultures and ethical contexts diverge. The work of the Council of Europe Ad Hoc Committee on Artificial Intelligence (CAHAI)[88] has been instrumental in bringing together existing and ongoing work on AI of many transnational initiatives and international organisations such as the European Commission, OECD, ITU, ISO and UNESCO to promote synergies, avoid duplication and share learning. **21.102**

We live in a global world and humanity is far from static. AI is dynamic and not bound by jurisdiction. To safeguard ethical and responsible AI which can be truly beneficial to humanity requires a globally recognised responsible and ethical AI response, one which is not devoid of law. **21.103**

---

86 A distinction can be made in that data portability rights under Article 20 of GDPR require processing to have been done on the basis of consent and to have proceeded by automated means in order to be leveraged. All other data processed by automated means, but on a basis other than consent, falls outside of the remit of the data portability right. As an individual might still benefit from sharing their data and requesting its transfer outside of the strict legal right to do so (particularly for use in connection with AI, privacy management or a data trust), the author has devised the term 'data mobility' to distinguish between the two kinds of processed data which are potentially transferable at an individual's request.

87 https://github.com/daviddao/awful-ai accessed 15 October 2020.

88 CAHAI's work is demonstrated through its update report of 23 September to the Committee of Ministers: www .coe.int/en/web/artificial-intelligence/-/publication-of-the-first-progress-report-of-the-ad-hoc-committee-on-artificial -intelligence-cahai- accessed 16 October 2020.

22

BIAS AND DISCRIMINATION

Minesh Tanna and William Dunning

A. INTRODUCTION

22.001 It is tempting to think that using AI is an objective and unbiased way to take decisions. However, while AI may have the potential to reduce bias in decision-making, it is becoming increasingly clear that there are numerous ways in which AI systems can be biased. Concerningly, this bias is capable of causing discrimination against individuals affected by such AI systems.

22.002 This is one of the key challenges posed by AI, and one of the predominant legal issues arising from its increasing prevalence. In many cases, legislative systems that were conceived prior to the rise of AI technology may be ill-equipped to deal with these new challenges. AI technology has unique characteristics (notably its lack of transparency) that make it difficult for pre-existing legal frameworks to adequately address the risk of bias and discrimination in AI systems.

In this chapter, we consider what bias and discrimination are (section B), how they occur in **22.003** AI systems (section C), how current law and regulation deals with bias and discrimination in AI systems (section D) and how law and regulation is likely to evolve to handle these new challenges (sections E and F).

B. WHAT ARE BIAS AND DISCRIMINATION?

1.   What Is Bias?

Bias is defined by the Oxford English Dictionary as: 'Inclination or prejudice for or against one **22.004** person or group, especially in a way considered to be unfair.'[1]

The easiest way to understand the potential impact of biases in the context of AI is by refer- **22.005** ence to cognitive biases that exist in humans, which have both beneficial and adverse effects. Although biases are typically understood to be morally bad, they are in fact central to the way that the human brain functions. They are, effectively, cognitive shortcuts that allow the brain to make decisions more quickly and efficiently than would otherwise be possible. Biases reflect the brain prioritising certain information – a shape that looks like a predator, for example – to make a quick decision. This can cut both ways: a bias may be the difference between life and death if it helps you to react quickly to an imminent threat, but may also lead you to leap to inappropriate conclusions, which can result in discrimination.

Biases can, broadly speaking, be grouped into five key categories:[2] **22.006**

(a)   *Pattern recognition biases* – These lead us to see patterns even when there are none. Identifying patterns is fundamental to how humans understand the world based on incomplete information. However, the tendency to identify patterns can also give rise to biases, such as confirmation bias (ignoring evidence that may disprove an existing hypothesis) and saliency bias (assigning excessive weight to memorable or recent events). AI operates by identifying patterns, so pattern recognition biases are particularly relevant to understanding bias in AI systems.

(b)   *Action-orientated biases* – These lead us to take action less thoughtfully than we should. Action-orientated biases reflect the human brain's preference for speed and efficiency. This is driven by humans' tendency towards overconfidence and excessive optimism in circumstances where information is considered imperfect, for example, because of availability bias (focus on information that is easily recalled).

(c)   *Stability bias* – This leads us to prefer the status quo in conditions of uncertainty. Stability bias reflects the human brain's preference for efficiency; when in doubt, mental energy tends not to be wasted. This includes biases such as loss aversion (tendency to feel losses more acutely than equivalent gains), anchoring (focusing on an initial value, leading to insufficient adjustment) and *status quo* bias (preference for the status quo unless there is pressure to change it).

---

1   Lexico Dictionaries, *Bias | Definition of Bias by Oxford Dictionary on Lexico.Com Also Meaning of Bias*, (*undated*) www .lexico.com/definition/bias, https://perma.cc/99KY-CT3X.
2   Dan Lovallo and Olivier Sibony, *The case for behavioural strategy*, McKinsey Quarterly, 2(1), 30–43, 2010.

(d)   *Social biases* – These arise from a preference for harmony over conflict. This can lead to groupthink (tendency to agree with the consensus of a group rather than realistically appraising a situation) and sunflower management (tendency of groups to align their views with those of their leaders).

(e)   *Interest biases* – These arise in the presence of conflicting incentives. Interest biases reflect the tendency of the human brain to consider individual interests alongside other issues, rather than considering those issues independently and more objectively.

22.007   These quirks in human decision-making are reflected in the way in which AI systems operate, as well as the context in which they are developed. By their nature, AI systems 'consider' only a limited range of factors in a predetermined way to reach often binary decisions: yes or no. Moreover, not only can biases arise as a result of such 'shortcuts' in AI-driven decision-making, but they can also arise because they are inherent in the data that AI systems use to reach decisions, or because they are introduced by those developing the AI system. This can happen in a number of ways, which are discussed further at in section C below.

2.   What Is Discrimination?

22.008   Discrimination is defined by the Oxford English Dictionary as: 'The unjust or prejudicial treatment of different categories of people, especially on the grounds of race, age, sex, or disability.'[3]

22.009   Whereas biases are fundamental features of the way that humans reach decisions, which are often reflected in the way AI systems behave, discrimination is specifically proscribed by law in most countries. It is, however, easy to see how biases in either human or AI decision-making can lead to discriminatory outcomes, and there are numerous examples of this happening in practice.

22.010   There are numerous other examples of serious discriminatory outcomes arising from bias in AI systems. In 2018, for example, a hiring algorithm used to sort résumés by Amazon was found to consistently prefer male candidates.[4] In 2019, a major US healthcare risk algorithm used on more than 200 million people in the US was found to systematically underestimate the healthcare needs of black patients.[5] Much recent attention has focused on the discriminatory performance of facial recognition systems, which have been found to perform to be worse at identifying women and people of colour than at classifying white, male faces.[6]

22.011   Quite aside from the obvious ethical issues surrounding discrimination, the possibility of AI-driven discrimination poses numerous material risks for companies. Depending on which part of the business it affects, AI-driven discrimination can lead to:

(a)   direct effects of an AI system incorrectly or inaccurately analysing data, leading to, for example, the loss of potential customers, the provision of inappropriate products to customers and flawed hiring decisions;

---

3   Lexico Dictionaries, *Discrimination | Definition of Discrimination by Oxford Dictionary on Lexico.Com Also Meaning of Discrimination*, (*undated*) www.lexico.com/definition/discrimination, https://perma.cc/Q2MU-GNNK.

4   Jeffrey Dastin, *Amazon scraps secret AI recruiting tool that showed bias against women*, Reuters, 11 October 2018.

5   Starre Vartan, *Racial bias found in a major health care risk algorithm*, Scientific American, 24 October 2019.

6   Davide Castelvecchi, *Is facial recognition too biased to be let loose?*, Nature, 18 November 2018.

(b) reputational damage resulting from the use of AI systems that are found to be discriminatory; and

(c) legal risks resulting from possible breaches of anti-discrimination and data protection law.

C. DIFFERENT TYPES OF AI BIAS

There are numerous ways in which bias may enter an AI system. In this section we discuss four of the key mechanisms by which bias arises in AI systems. Each of these types of bias has different characteristics, and some are more likely to lead to discriminatory outcomes than others. **22.012**

1. Biases Introduced by Data

Bias can be introduced by the training data which is used to 'teach' an AI system to take decisions. Where the data used is historical, AI systems are likely to repeat (and entrench) any bias or discrimination reflected in that data. An AI system can only be as good as the data used to train it, and often that data reflects real biases and inequities that influenced past human-made decisions.[7] The common maxim 'garbage in, garbage out' (meaning that poor input data will produce poor outputs) could be restated as 'discrimination in, discrimination out'. For example, if an AI system bases hiring decisions for an organisation on characteristics of successful past employees, that system is likely to identify the groups that were historically favoured in that organisation (whether gender, race, socio-economic or other), rather than accurately identifying desirable employee traits. **22.013**

Even with full awareness of this tendency of AI systems, it can be difficult to scrub the 'taint' of discrimination from historical data.[8] Some argue that there is no neutral way to merely transform historical data into an objective, non-discriminatory form; instead, 'methods of proof and corrective measures will often require an explicit commitment to substantive remediation rather than merely procedural remedies'.[9] Indeed, it can be so difficult to control for the unintended consequences of putting data into a system that it may be more productive to focus on the outputs and desired equity of results, rather than trying to ensure a perfectly neutral set of training data. **22.014**

The introduction of historical discrimination reflected in training data is likely to be particularly problematic in areas where discrimination has historically been a significant problem, such as policing or recruitment. The inclusion of historical biases in this way can happen even if the data does not contain characteristics such as age, gender or race, as other features of the training data may act as so-called proxy variables that reflect those characteristics. **22.015**

The data collection and selection process itself may also be biased. Data collection processes may introduce the subjective assessments of those collecting the data, or may result in the overrepresentation or underrepresentation of certain groups. This is particularly likely where groups **22.016**

---

7 Solon Barocas and Andrew D. Selbst, *Big Data's disparate impact*, California Law Review, June 2016.
8 Ibid, p. 672.
9 Ibid, p. 676.

live on the margins of big data[10] and may be less likely to use a smartphone, have internet access or register for online services, meaning that an AI system based on those datasets (people who use a particular app, check into certain locations or post on various social media networks, for example) will not capture them. If those populations intersect with particular socioeconomic, racial, gender or other groups, the AI system could produce biased decisions pertaining to those group members, despite the lack of any intentional discrimination.

22.017   If, for example, the dataset used to train an AI system that processes loan applications includes data on very few female borrowers, then the system will assign greater statistical significance to relationships that predict repayment rates for men than to any statistical patterns that only predict repayment rates for women. This could lead that system to systematically underestimate the repayment rates of women (even if they are in fact more likely on average to repay their loans), and therefore to be less likely to approve loan applications from women. Such issues may arise in relation to any group that is under-represented in training data.

22.018   Similar issues may arise in the development of facial recognition systems. If a facial recognition system has, for example, been trained on a disproportionate number of white, male faces, then it will naturally perform better at identifying individuals in that group.

2.   Biases Introduced by Developers

22.019   Bias may be introduced into an AI system when the developer of that system either consciously or unconsciously reflects their biases in the system's architecture. Although intentional inclusion of bias can occur when a developer purposefully encodes their own prejudicial preferences about certain groups of people or decision patterns with an algorithm, it has been argued that 'disproportionate attention' has been paid to this intentional and nefarious form of bias.[11] Developers of AI systems will make a very large number of decisions in the course of developing such a system, so there are numerous opportunities for an AI system to be compromised by its developers' biases.[12]

22.020   It is likely to be far more common that bias is introduced by developers following simple errors of judgement that have unintended consequences. As developers of AI systems are often creating systems that look to emulate or reproduce human thought, it is unsurprising that they may create systems that emulate or reproduce their own biases. Human biases, such as those discussed at paragraph 22.006 above can affect developers' work. Confirmation bias, for example, may lead the developer of an AI system to introduce bias. If the results produced by an AI system are in line with a developer's (biased) expectations, then that developer will be less likely to identify model design or sampling issues, and thus more likely to omit important data or other features. This could lead the model to reflect its developer's biases. Other biases could also play a role. For example, *status quo* bias may lead a developer to prefer commonly used data (regardless of how predictive it is, or whether better sources of data are available), while overconfidence may lead a developer to ignore red flags that a model is biased.

---

10   Ibid, p. 684.
11   Ibid, p. 693.
12   Tobias Baer, *Understand, Manage, and Prevent Algorithmic Bias*, 2019, p. 67.

3.   Stability Bias

Some forms of AI bias do not relate to bias for or against specific groups or outcomes, but **22.021** arise from broader characteristics of AI systems. One such trait is stability bias, or the tendency towards inertia, which is caused by algorithms discounting the possibility of significant change and assuming that things will generally continue as before.[13] This is a limitation of predictive models based heavily upon historical data, which struggle to recognise problems which are likely to arise at some point in the future but have not yet occurred.[14] Such models can ignore the possibility of significant new innovations, or struggle to adapt if rapid behaviour shifts occur. For example, some mortgage models in the United States which were designed before the 2008 financial crisis were mathematically unable to accept negative changes to home prices.[15]

Stability bias can also lead to users gaming the algorithm if it is unable to pick up on changing **22.022** behaviours. For example, if an AI system draws a link between high-risk customers and longer loan tenors such that the chance of approval for longer loans is reduced, salespeople may start to steer their customers towards shorter tenors to improve the odds of approval, and stability bias could stop the system from noticing the shift.[16] In the presence of stability bias, algorithms can also be led astray by data anomalies and unrepresentative events. In a recent example, AI hedge fund Voleon Group found its algorithms struggled to cope with the severe market volatility caused by the COVID-19 pandemic, an event with little historical precedent.[17]

Stability bias is a fundamental feature of AI systems: they develop rules about the world **22.023** based on the data on which they are trained, on history, and apply these rules going forward. Although stability bias itself may not introduce discriminatory bias into AI systems, it is part of the reason why developers struggle to remove historical discrimination from their algorithms, and a key reason why discriminatory bias in AI systems must be addressed proactively.

4.   Biases Introduced by AI Systems

It is also possible for algorithms themselves to introduce bias into an AI system. Predictions **22.024** produced by AI systems may be incorrect, particularly where the model has been trained on a relatively small dataset. Biases of this type are relatively unlikely to result in discriminatory outcomes, but the possibility that an AI system will itself discriminate as a result of biases it has developed should not be ignored.

5.   The Role of Human Users of AI Systems

Few AI systems yet operate entirely without human oversight, so the human users of AI **22.025** systems also have a role to play in facilitating the discriminatory effects of AI systems. At its

---

13   Tobia Baer and Vishnu Kamalnath, *Controlling machine-learning algorithms and their biases*, McKinsey & Company, 10 November 2017.
14   Ibid.
15   Ibid.
16   Ibid, 10.
17   Laurence Fletcher, *AI hedge fund Voleon suffers in choppy markets*, Financial Times, 07 September 2020, https://perma.cc/5E82–6DPZ.

extreme, people can be susceptible to so-called data fundamentalism, the notion that 'correlation always indicates causation, and that massive data sets and predictive analytics always reflect objective truth'.[18] Because AI systems often appear as a 'black box', users and decision-makers can have a tendency to trust their results as objective and not in need of further review. As a result, algorithmic decisions can face less scrutiny than those made by humans, even if the results demonstrate clear issues of bias and discrimination.

22.026   This effect is amplified by the lack of transparency of many processes (frequently, and of most concern, in the governmental sphere), which may be exacerbated by the lack of appropriate record-keeping to support the decisions that have been made.[19] This makes it even harder for a human decision-maker to review decisions independently and to check for any discriminatory biases. The use of AI systems may also encourage users to simplify their own processes and move away from nuanced approaches in order to more easily codify their data for use in an algorithm, even when this simplification can amplify bias or discrimination.[20]

D. THE CURRENT LEGAL POSITION ON AI BIAS AND DISCRIMINATION

22.027   The most important current areas of law relating to AI bias and discrimination are anti-discrimination law and data protection law. However, as will be seen below, the different focuses, goals and levels of sophistication of these laws mean that they provide, at best, a patchwork approach to dealing with AI-driven discrimination.

1.   Anti-discrimination Law

22.028   Most countries now have laws to address discrimination. Discrimination is prohibited in numerous treaties and constitutions, including the European Convention on Human Rights, the United Nations Declaration of Human Rights, the International Covenant on Civil and Political Rights and the Charter of Fundamental Rights of the European Union.

22.029   In the UK, the Equality Act 2010 (the Equality Act), which implements the EU's major Equal Treatment Directives, is the key source of anti-discrimination law. The protections offered by the Equality Act apply regardless of whether decisions are generated by humans or AI systems. In this chapter, we discuss two of the key protections provided by the Equality Act.

(a) Direct discrimination

22.030   Direct discrimination is prohibited by Section 13 of the Equality Act. Direct discrimination occurs where individuals are treated less favourably than others because of a protected characteristic.[21] More specifically, '[t]here must be a difference in the treatment of persons in analogous, or relatively similar, situations' that is based 'on an identifiable characteristic'.[22] The protected

---

18   Kate Crawford, *The hidden biases in big data*, Harvard Business Review, 01 April 2013.

19   D.K. Citron, *Technological Due Process*, Washington University Law Review, vol 85, 2008, p. 1249.

20   Ibid, p. 1262.

21   Section 4 of the Equality Act 2010.

22   ECtHR, *Biao v Denmark* (Grand Chamber), No 38590/10, 24 May 2016, para 89 and Article 2(2)(a) of the Racial Equality Directive 2000/42/EC cited on p. 19 of *Study on discrimination, artificial intelligence and algorithmic decision making*.

characteristics recognised by the Equality Act include age, disability, gender reassignment, marriage and civil partnership, pregnancy and maternity, race, religion or belief, sex and sexual orientation.[23] Neither the intention to act in a discriminatory manner nor even awareness of the discriminatory conduct are necessary for a person to be liable for direct discrimination.

Although it should be comparably straightforward for developers and users of AI systems to avoid discriminating against individuals directly on the basis of a protected characteristic, there are nevertheless examples of carelessly developed software discriminating in this manner. In 2015, for example, a paediatrician called Louise Selby found herself unable to access the changing rooms at her gym. This was found to be because the gym was using third party software that used a member's title (Ms, Mr, Mrs, and so on) to determine which changing room they could access, and the title 'Doctor' had been identified as male.[24] Quite aside from the negative publicity that resulted from this revelation, this act of discrimination could have formed the basis for a direct discrimination claim under the Equality Act.[25]   **22.031**

It is easy to imagine circumstances in which a similar oversight in the design of an AI system could have a great impact on an affected individual; for example, if such an error led to loan applications being refused, or to individuals from a protected group being charged more for insurance.   **22.032**

A person may also bring a direct discrimination claim under the Equality Act either where the protected characteristic belongs to someone with whom they are associated (direct discrimination by association) or because there is an incorrect perception that they have the protected characteristic.[26] The latter scenario is a particular risk in the context of AI systems, because AI systems may infer sensitive information about an individual by analysing their behaviour. If, for example, an individual is discriminated against because an AI system has drawn the incorrect inference that they are homosexual, then they may have a claim for direct discrimination under the Equality Act.[27]   **22.033**

(b) Indirect discrimination

Indirect discrimination can occur where a practice appears neutral but nevertheless results in discrimination against people of a protected characteristic. More particularly, indirect discrimination occurs where a person applies 'a provision, criterion or practice which is discriminatory in relation to a relevant protected characteristic'.[28] The 'difference in treatment may take the form of disproportionately prejudicial effects of general policy or measures which, though couched in neutral terms, discriminate against a group'.[29]   **22.034**

---

23   Section 4 of the Equality Act 2010.
24   Oliver Wheaton, *Gym's computer assumed this woman was a man because she is a doctor*, Metro, 18 March 2015.
25   Robin Allen QC and Dee Masters, *Algorithms, apps & Artificial Intelligence: The next frontier in discrimination law*, Cloisters, 16 October 2018.
26   Section 13 of the Equality Act 2010.
27   Robin Allen QC and Dee Masters, *Algorithms, apps & Artificial Intelligence: The next frontier in discrimination law*, Cloisters, 16 October 2018.
28   Section 19 of the Equality Act 2010.
29   ECtHR, *Biao v Denmark* (Grand Chamber), No 38590/10, 24 May 2016, para 103 and Article 2(2)(b) of the Racial Equality Directive 2000/42/EC cited on p. 19 of *Study on discrimination, artificial intelligence and algorithmic decision making*.

22.035   An objective justification can rebut suspected indirect discrimination if it can be shown that the provision, criterion or practice was 'a proportionate means of achieving a legitimate aim'.[30] This will be the case where it 'is objectively justified by a legitimate aim and the means of achieving that aim are appropriate and necessary'.[31]

22.036   There are numerous ways in which an AI system could lead to indirect discrimination. For example, if an AI system prioritises job applicants without gaps in their employment history, this could lead to discrimination against individuals with disabilities who may have had periods off work for health reasons. In order to avoid discriminating in this way, developers and users of AI systems should conduct extensive testing before deployment, as discriminatory effects may not be immediately obvious. In 2014, for example, Facebook was found to be using an algorithm that screened the names of individuals trying to sign up to use its service in an attempt to avoid the use of false names. This led to a member of the Kiowa tribe of Oklahoma being rejected as a user by Facebook's algorithm because his name, Shane Creepingbear, was not in accordance with Facebook's policy.[32]

22.037   It is also possible that the underlying dataset used to train an AI system could be a 'practice, criterion or provision' capable of leading to indirect discrimination.[33] If a dataset underrepresents a certain group leading to discriminatory outcomes, then this could amount to indirect discrimination. Such discrimination could have serious consequences. For example, failure to use a racially diverse dataset in the development of AI systems for the diagnosis of skin cancers may lead those systems to misdiagnose those in groups underrepresented in the dataset.[34]

22.038   For a detailed review of this legislation and its implications in a particular industry setting, see Section E of Chapter 14.

2.   Data Protection Law

22.039   As technology, and data in particular, play an increasing role in peoples' lives, countries are increasingly updating their data protection laws to reflect the increasing importance of data. In the EU, the chief source of data protection law is the General Data Protection Regulation (GDPR), which was implemented in the UK through the Data Protection Act (DPA). Data protection law aims to protect individuals' fundamental rights and, in particular, their rights to privacy and to non-discrimination.

22.040   Fairness and transparency in data processing are among the key principles of the GDPR.[35] The principle of fairness goes beyond discrimination and looks to ensure that individuals' data is only handled in a way that people would reasonably expect and is not used in ways that have unjustified adverse effects on them.[36] Transparency is fundamentally linked to fairness;

---

30   Section 19(2)(d) of the Equality Act 2010.

31   Article 2(2)(b) of the Racial Equality Directive 2000/43/EC.

32   Sara Wachter-Boettcher, *Technically Wrong: Sexist Apps, Biased Algorithms and other Threats of Toxic Tech*, pp. 54–5.

33   Robin Allen QC and Dee Masters, *Algorithms, apps & Artificial Intelligence: The next frontier in discrimination law*, Cloisters, 16 October 2018.

34   Angela Lashbrook, *AI-driven dermatology could leave dark-skinned patients behind*, The Atlantic, 16 August 2018.

35   Article 5(1) of the GDPR.

36   Information Commissioners Office, *Guide to the General Data Protection Regulation (GDPR)*, 22 May 2019, pp. 22–3.

without a clear understanding of how their data are being processed, individuals may be unable to identify breaches of their rights, both under the GDPR itself and under anti-discrimination law such as the Equality Act.

The GDPR and the DPA grant rights to individuals whose personal data are processed (data **22.041** subjects),[37] and impose obligations on parties that process personal data (data controllers).[38] Because of the fundamental importance of data to AI systems, numerous rights and obligations under the GDPR are potentially relevant to bias and discrimination of AI systems

The following paragraphs in this section consider how questions of bias and discrimination **22.042** interact with data protection laws.

An individual's right to be informed about the processing of their data is of particular impor- **22.043** tance.[39] All information and communication with the data subject must be in a 'concise, transparent, intelligible and easily accessible form'.[40] Users of AI systems should explain that they are using AI and the purposes for using AI.[41] Without adequate information about the data that are being collected on them and how those data are being used, it may be impossible for individuals to identify potentially discriminatory uses of their data in AI systems. Although the requirements of the GDPR intend to assist individuals in understanding their rights and when they may have been breached, this approach has serious shortcomings. All too often, GDPR-compliant information on these topics appears only in privacy notices that are, in reality, unlikely to come to users' attention.

The GDPR also includes specific rules in relation to automated individual decision-making **22.044** and profiling,[42] which were implemented with the aim, among others, of mitigating the risk of illegal discrimination from AI systems.[43] Specifically, Article 22 essentially prohibits fully automated decisions, including profiling, without human intervention where those decisions produce legal or similarly significant effects.[44] An example of a decision with 'legal effects' would be a court decision or a decision regarding a social benefit granted by law, such as pension payments.[45] An example of a 'similarly significant' effect includes where financial circumstances are affected, such as eligibility for credit or where there is an impact on access to health services.[46] Accordingly, the GDPR essentially prohibits the sole use of AI systems to make such decisions.

There are, however, several exceptions to the prohibition on automated decision-making, **22.045** which include where the decision:

---

37   Article 4(1) of the GDPR.
38   Article 4(7) of the GDPR.
39   Articles 13 and 14 of the GDPR.
40   Article 12 of the GDPR.
41   Information Commissioners Office, *Guide to the General Data Protection Regulation (GDPR)*, 22 May 2019, p. 98.
42   Article 22 of the GDPR.
43   Recital 71 of the GDPR.
44   Recital 71 of the GDPR.
45   Article 29 of Data Protection Working Party 2018 (WP251), p. 21.
46   Article 29 of Data Protection Working Party 2018 (WP251), p. 22.

(a)   is necessary for entering into the contract between the subject and controller;

(b)   is authorised by Union or Member State law to which the controller is subject; or

(c)   is based on the data subject's explicit consent.[47]

22.046   Where an exception applies, the controller must still implement suitable measures to safeguard individuals' rights and ensure that individuals have the right to obtain human intervention in relation to decisions, to express their point of view and contest decisions.[48]

22.047   As the prohibition on automated decision-making applies only to decisions with legal or similarly significant effects, it is doubtful whether it would capture all decisions by AI systems that are potentially discriminatory. Moreover, as this prohibition applies only to solely automated decision-making, it arguably does not fully address the role of human agents in the discriminatory actions of AI systems that are discussed at paragraphs 22.025 to 22.026 above. However, it does mean that developers of AI systems that take decisions with legal or similarly significant effects on individuals must implement suitable measures to ensure that those systems are not discriminatory.

22.048   Evidently, the GDPR imposes potentially onerous obligations on developers and users of AI systems that are relevant to bias and discrimination. Developers of AI systems will need to consider, among other things, whether they have provided individuals whose data are processed by AI systems that they develop with appropriate information about the way their data is used by the AI system, and whether the responsibility given to the AI system exceeds the limits placed on automated decision-making by the GDPR. Developers and users of AI systems that process individuals' personal data would be advised to complete a Data Protection Impact Assessment (DPIA) to ensure that the data protection risks of the project are appropriately identified and minimised.

22.049   More broadly, the data protection compliance of any AI system that processes individuals' personal data should be an important concern for any developer or user of such systems. Developers should be alive to the data protection risks associated with the use of AI, including the potential for prohibited discriminatory outcomes. These risks should be considered as early as possible in the course of any AI development, in order to avoid potentially costly retrospective steps to achieve compliance.

22.050   In principle, data protection regulators have the power to impose harsh sanctions for failure to comply with these and other provisions of the GDPR and the DPA. Infringement of the basic principles of data processing, the right to be informed or the right not to be subject to solely automated decision-making can carry a fine of up to the higher of 4 per cent of an undertaking's total worldwide annual turnover for the previous financial year or €20 million.[49] However, at the time of writing there have as yet, in the UK at least, been no fines that referred to any of these provisions. The key enforcement priority of the Information Commissioner's Office, the UK data protection regulator, appears to be requirements for data security under Article 32 of the GDPR.

---

47   Article 22(2) of the GDPR.
48   Article 22(3) Recital 71 of the GDPR.
49   Article 83(4) of the GDPR.

E. BIAS AND DISCRIMINATION IN THE CONTEXT OF ETHICAL/RESPONSIBLE AI

1. Understanding Ethical/Responsible AI

The concept of 'ethical AI' has only relatively recently gained prominence, mirroring the rise in AI adoption. Ethical AI has been said to encompass 'a set of values, principles, and techniques that employ widely accepted standards of right and wrong to guide moral conduct in the development and use of AI technologies'.[50] The concept has also been referred to as 'responsible AI' and, as suggested by this nomenclature, it is aimed at encouraging those involved in the development of AI systems to consider standards of right and wrong in that context. **22.051**

Despite the relative infancy of the concept of ethical/responsible AI, a number of organisations (including private enterprises, non-profit organisations and governmental or quasi-governmental bodies) have published principles or guidelines which address the subject. The organisation Algorithm Watch maintains an inventory of such documents and, at the time of writing, lists 167 'frameworks' relating to the development and implementation of AI or automated decision-making.[51] The vast majority of these frameworks were published in or since 2017. **22.052**

The perhaps surprising number of ethical/responsible AI frameworks reflects the increasing importance of this concept. It can also be explained by two other factors: first, the lack of binding regulation relating to the development of AI which is likely to have encouraged the introduction of non-binding instruments; second, the prevalence of AI adoption across many developed economies, which is reflected in ethical/responsible AI frameworks from organisations across numerous jurisdictions. **22.053**

The fact that these frameworks are non-binding does not diminish their importance. In particular, complying with the guidance contained in these frameworks is likely to engender numerous benefits for an organisation, ranging from protection from potential legal liability to commercial and reputational advantages. Furthermore, this guidance is likely to shape future AI regulation and so compliance with ethical/responsible AI principles is likely to facilitate better compliance with future binding regulation. **22.054**

The list of organisations that have published ethical/responsible AI frameworks includes prominent international bodies such as the United Nations, the European Commission, the Organisation for Economic Co-operation and Development (OECD) and the World Economic Forum. This chapter refers in particular to the OECD Principles on Artificial Intelligence (OECD Principles)[52] and the European Commission's High-Level Expert Group Guidelines for Trustworthy AI (HLEG Guidelines).[53] **22.055**

---

50   Leslie, D. (2019). *Understanding artificial intelligence ethics and safety: a guide for the responsible design and implementation of AI systems in the public sector*. The Alan Turing Institute, https://doi.org/10.5281/zenodo.3240529.

51   Algorithm Watch, *AI Ethics Guidelines Global Inventory*, https://inventory.algorithmwatch.org/, undated.

52   Council Recommendation, OECD/LEGAL/440, *Recommendation of the Council on Artificial Intelligence*, https://legalinstruments.oecd.org/en/instruments/OECD-LEGAL-0449, 22 May 2019.

53   High-Level Expert Group on Artificial Intelligence, *Ethics Guidelines for Trustworthy AI*, European Commission, https://ec.europa.eu/newsroom/dae/document.cfm?doc_id=60419, 8 April 2019.

2.   Bias and Discrimination in the Context of Ethical/Responsible AI

22.056   One of the key advantages which follows from the proliferation of ethical/responsible AI frameworks is the emergence of a consensus on the principles or themes which embody this concept. There are now a handful of principles which are recognised as being intrinsic to, or least forming an important part of, the ethical and responsible use of AI.

22.057   The elimination or avoidance of bias and discrimination is one of those principles. However, this principle is in some frameworks identifiable as a standalone principle in its own right while in other frameworks it is found in one or more other principles, including:

(a)   fairness
(b)   transparency and explainability
(c)   technical robustness and accuracy
(d)   accountability and oversight

22.058   These principles are discussed elsewhere in the book in a more general context. The following paragraphs address the principles from the direct perspective of bias and discrimination.

3.   Fairness

22.059   Bias and discrimination are closely associated with the principle of fairness, which is consistently found in ethical/responsible AI frameworks. The HLEG Guidelines refer to 'fairness' both in the context of foundational ethical principles for trustworthy AI and alongside diversity and non-discrimination in the context of more tangible principles for the achievement of trustworthy AI.[54]

22.060   Fairness is, however, a difficult concept. It is intrinsically imprecise, being capable of numerous meanings, and it is also a subjective concept. While the rationale for its inclusion in ethical/responsible AI frameworks may seem obvious, what it means in practice – particularly given likely differences in what constitutes 'fairness' across jurisdictions – is uncertain. This has not, however, precluded attempts to define what fairness means in this context.[55]

22.061   The HLEG Guidelines distinguish 'substantive' and 'procedural' fairness,[56] suggesting that the latter relates to the 'ability to contest and seek effective redress against decisions made by AI systems and by the humans operating them'. It is suggested that this relates more to accountability (discussed below) and regulation than to fairness, which is concerned more with the substantive decision-making of the AI system and its impact on humans.

22.062   Bias and discrimination – in terms of its societal context, rather than in the context of stability or algorithmic bias (as distinguished above) – is a core component of the fairness principle. In other words, it seems to be generally accepted that an AI system which treats a particular group less favourably than another on the basis of that's group's intrinsic characteristics is unfair.

---

54   Ibid, p. 8, Figure 1.
55   See, for example, a particular mathematical-based approach in *On the (im)possibility of fairness*. SA Friedler, C Scheidegger, S Venkatasubramanian. arXiv:1609.07236, 2016.
56   HLEG Guidelines, p. 12.

The *Loomis* case is a useful example. Mr Loomis – a defendant in the State of Wisconsin justice   **22.063**
system – was assessed to be at a high risk of recidivism based on an algorithmic tool (called
'COMPAS') and he was sentenced accordingly. He challenged the use of this tool, but the
Supreme Court of Wisconsin upheld the sentence.[57] Analysis has shown that the COMPAS
tool is biased – black defendants are predicted to have a higher risk of recidivism on the basis
of their skin colour alone.[58]

The presence of bias in the COMPAS tool, and its discriminatory assessment of the risk of   **22.064**
recidivism, is undoubtedly unfair and it is the use of AI in this way that ethical/responsible
AI frameworks are seeking to address. The fact that an unfair AI tool was (arguably) used to
deprive Mr Loomis of his fundamental right to liberty demonstrates the importance of the
principle of fairness.

4.   Transparency and Explainability

Mr Loomis apparently knew the type of information that the COMPAS tool was using to   **22.065**
assess his risk of recidivism, but not *how* it was using this information.[59] This is an example of
the 'black box' problem. This issue tends to arise because the developers of an AI system are
unable to explain how the AI system has reached a particular decision, rather than because they
are unwilling to disclose this information.

This issue has given rise to another fundamental component of ethical/responsible AI – trans-   **22.066**
parency or explainability. These two concepts have a slightly different emphasis, but they
closely interrelate and broadly relate to the same principle – the ability of humans to understand
and explain how AI systems operate.

As explained earlier in this chapter, bias and discrimination in AI is rarely intentional. Instead,   **22.067**
any bias in an AI system is likely to reflect the developers' own unconscious bias or, perhaps
more likely, a defect in the data used to train the AI system (perhaps a lack of representative
data). Transparency and explainability is an important concept in this context because it can be
an effective method of uncovering any bias in the system, ideally before it is capable of causing
discrimination to any users. In theory, the more transparent an AI system is, and the greater
the onus on the developers of an AI system to explain how it operates, the more apparent any
bias in the system should be.

Transparency and explainability are therefore important principles in the context of uncovering   **22.068**
any bias in an AI system. They are also fundamental principles more generally in the context of
ethical/responsible AI and, as such, are given prominence in both the OECD Principles[60] and
the HLEG Guidelines.[61]

---

57   *State v. Loomis*, 881 N.W.2d 749, 767 (Wis. 2016).
58   See Jeff Larson et al., *How we analyzed the COMPAS Recidivism Algorithm, ProPublica*, www.propublica.org/article/how
-we-analyzed-the-compas-recidivism-algorithm, 23 May 2016 , https://perma.cc/3V5S-W874.
59   See Rebecca Wexler, *When a computer program keeps you in jail*, N.Y. Times (13 June 2017), www.nytimes.com/2017/06/
13/opinion/how-computers-are-harming-criminal-justice.html , https://perma.cc/2WZG-LP77.
60   See Section 1, Principle 1.3.
61   See, for example, pp. 18 and 29.

5.   Technical Robustness or Accuracy

22.069   Technical robustness is another principle which is espoused in ethical/responsible AI frameworks. The Joint Research Centre of the European Commission published a paper in 2020 entitled *Robustness and Explainability of Artificial Intelligence*,[62] in which 'technical robustness' is referred to as the 'resilience, accuracy [and] reliability of AI systems'.[63] In that sense, robustness is another broad principle which can encompass various concepts (as is evident from its description in the OECD Principles[64]). In the context of bias and discrimination, robustness sits alongside accuracy in referring, in simple terms, to the ability of an AI system to achieve its intended purpose effectively.

22.070   Where the AI system is unable to do this, the issue might lie in the training data or in the training process itself. This issue could then manifest itself through the AI system's inability to make accurate decisions and/or to deal with new data or scenarios on which the system was not properly trained. Take, for example, an AI-based video interview tool which is used to film candidates during the recruitment process and provide feedback on their performance to the prospective employer. The AI system in this case may not have been trained to deal with all possible disabilities that a candidate might possess, in which case there is likely to be a question mark over the accuracy of its feedback.

22.071   This example demonstrates how the lack of technical robustness or accuracy in an AI system could easily cause bias and discrimination. As is rightly noted in the HLEG Guidelines, '[a] high level of accuracy is especially crucial in situations where the AI system directly affects human lives'.[65] This is particularly so where an AI system makes discriminatory decisions.

6.   Accountability and Oversight

22.072   Accountability and oversight are crucial principles in the context of ethical/responsible AI in light of AI's intrinsic ability to operate autonomously, with minimal human involvement. These important principles are reflected in both the HLEG Guidelines[66] and the OECD Principles.[67]

22.073   Accountability requires that a human or legal entity can be held responsible for the proper functioning of an AI system, which provides both an incentive mechanism on the organisations that develop and deploy the AI system to ensure that it functions properly and a mechanism for redress in case the AI system 'goes wrong' and causes harm.

22.074   Oversight requires that a human is involved in the development and deployment of an AI system, not only to facilitate accountability but also to provide an important human check on how the system has been developed and any issues which arise during its deployment. The

---

62   R. Hamon, H. Junklewitz and I. Sanchez, *Robustness and explainability of Artificial Intelligence – from technical to policy solutions*, EUR 30040, Publications Office of the European Union, Luxembourg, Luxembourg, 2020, ISBN 978–92–79–14660–5 (online), doi:10.2760/57493 (online), JRC119336.
63   Ibid p. 9.
64   OCED Principle 1.4.
65   HLEG Guidelines, p. 17.
66   HLEG Guidelines, pp. 16 and 19.
67   OCED, Principle 1.6.

idea of 'human-in-the-loop' AI, that is, AI which incorporates and works alongside human intelligence, is attracting more attention in the AI community.[68]

Accountability and oversight are therefore important principles in the prevention and cure of **22.075** bias and discrimination in AI. They facilitate human involvement and responsibility for the decision-making process of an AI system, which, if left unchecked, could result in discrimination (and which, worse still, may otherwise be undetectable).

F. HOW WILL BIAS AND DISCRIMINATION IN AI BE TACKLED IN THE FUTURE?

1.   Increased Focus on Bias and Discrimination through Ethical/Responsible AI

Ethical/responsible AI will continue to be an important subject and is expected to attract an **22.076** increasing level of attention in the short term. Once AI regulation starts to be introduced across jurisdictions – which is likely to be a trend in the coming years – ethical/responsible AI is understandably likely to become less of a focus for the AI community.

There is already, however, an increasing need for detail on *how* the generally accepted ethical/ **22.077** responsible AI principles discussed above are to be achieved. In other words, now that there seems to be a consensus on what those principles are, organisations need further guidance on how those principles ought to be implemented from a practical perspective. A notable (but perhaps rare) example of this sort of guidance is the UK Information Commissioner's Office work with the Alan Turing Institute on 'explainability', which resulted in a detailed report intended to provide practical advice on this important principle.[69]

The issue of bias and discrimination is separately attracting increasing attention, particularly in **22.078** more developed economies. This trend rightly reflects a growing awareness and acknowledgement of the need to recognise, and give effect to, the equal treatment of individuals. This trend, together with high-profile instances of AI being found to have caused bias and discrimination (the recent *South Wales Police* case, in which that police force was found to have used facial recognition technology unlawfully,[70] being a notable example) is likely to elevate the importance of this principle in the context of ethical/responsible AI. It is anticipated that the literature in this area will focus more on the avoidance of bias and discrimination, both as a goal to be achieved in its own right and through the other principles discussed above.

---

68   See, for example, Fabio Zanzotto, *Viewpoint: human-in-the-loop Artificial Intelligence*, Journal of Artificial Intelligence Research, February 2019, pp. 243–52.

69   ICO and Alan Turing Institute, *Explaining decisions made with AI*, Information Commissions Office, [https://ico.org .uk/for-organisations/guide-to-data-protection/key-data-protection-themes/explaining-decisions-made-with-ai/,   20 May 2020.]

70   *R (Bridges) v The Chief Constable of South Wales Police* [2020] EWCA Civ 1058, www.bailii.org/ew/cases/EWCA/Civ/ 2020/1058.html.

2.   Regulation of Facial Recognition Technology

22.079   The use of facial recognition technology understandably raises concerns about bias and discrimination, and these concerns are not without foundation. In 2018, MIT undertook a study which found that three commercially marketed facial recognition software systems failed to recognise darker-skinned complexions due, partly, to an issue with the data on which the systems were trained.[71]

22.080   Facial recognition technology is, by its nature, capable of causing manifest discrimination. Moreover, the technology appears thus far to have been adopted in areas in which the impact of discrimination can have profound implications for those affected by it – law enforcement and the justice system being the most obvious examples.

22.081   This has sparked a recent trend of regulation on facial recognition, particularly in the US. While the position at a federal level seems to be more liberal and light-touch when it comes to regulation, various US states and cities have legislated on facial recognition, whether in the form of an outright prohibition or of strict controls on its use.

22.082   For example:

(a)   In May 2019, the city of San Francisco introduced a ban on the use of facial recognition technology by city authorities, including the police.[72]

(b)   In January 2020, the state of California more widely commenced a three-year moratorium on the use of facial recognition technology in police body cameras.[73]

(c)   In September 2020, the city of Portland introduced a similar ban to that in San Francisco.[74]

22.083   This trend of regulating the use of facial recognition technology is likely to continue in the US.

22.084   Apart from in the EU (where an outright prohibition on the use of facial recognition technology has been discussed), there does not appear to be any significant momentum towards regulating the use of facial recognition technology in any other jurisdictions. This may reflect the fact that many jurisdictions are reluctant to introduce AI regulation more generally.

3.   Forthcoming AI Regulation which May Address Bias and Discrimination

22.085   As discussed earlier in this chapter, there are broader legislative instruments (such as the GDPR) which may indirectly regulate bias and discrimination in AI. Save for specific regula-

---

71   Larry Hardesty, *Study finds gender and skin-type bias in commercial Artificial-Intelligence systems*, MIT News, 11 February 2018, http://news.mit.edu/2018/study-finds-gender-skin-type-bias-artificial-intelligence-systems-0212.

72   San Francisco, Ordinance amending the Administrative Code – Acquisition of Surveillance Technology No. 190110, https://sfgov.legistar.com/View.ashx?M=F&ID=7206781&GUID=38D37061–4D87–4A94–9AB3-CB113656159A, 06 May 2019.

73   California, Law enforcement: facial recognition and other biometric surveillance Assembly Bill No. 125, Chapter 579, http://leginfo.legislature.ca.gov/faces/billNavClient.xhtml?bill_id=201920200AB1215, 09 October 2019.

74   Rachel Metz, *Portland passes broadest facial recognition ban in the US*, CNN Business, https://edition.cnn.com/2020/09/09/tech/portland-facial-recognition-ban/index.html, 10 September 2020.

tion which applies to facial recognition technology, however, there does not appear to be any regulation which is intended specifically to address bias and discrimination in AI.

This is unlikely to remain the case, however, and at the time of writing there are two pieces of legislation which may be introduced – in the EU and in the US – which could constitute the first examples of AI regulation directly addressing bias and discrimination. **22.086**

(a) EU

The EU's February 2020 White Paper entitled *On Artificial Intelligence – A European approach to excellence and trust*[75] set out various options as to how AI could be regulated in the EU and invited public feedback on these options. It thus provides an insight into the likely form and content of EU law on AI, which is expected to be introduced in the near future. **22.087**

The White Paper adopts a 'risk-based' approach to the regulation of AI, resulting in more onerous requirements of AI use which is considered to be 'high-risk'.[76] The White Paper suggests that AI should be considered as high-risk if it is used in a sector where, given the characteristics of the activities typically undertaken in that sector, significant risks can be expected to arise (the White Paper lists healthcare, transport, energy and parts of the public sector as examples of such sectors) and where AI is used in a manner which is likely to engender significant risks (for example, where it may have a significant effect on the rights of individuals or companies). While the White Paper does not provide further detail on this analysis, the risk of AI decision-making being discriminatory is surely likely to be considered a 'significant risk'. What is not clear, however, is why this use of AI (for example, through the use of AI-powered recruitment tools) should be considered as high-risk only when used in this way in certain sectors, not in others. **22.088**

Section D of the White Paper discusses legal requirements for AI uses which are considered to be high-risk and, in this context, directly addresses bias and discrimination. In the context of training data, for example, the White Paper suggests that developers will need to take 'reasonable measures' to ensure that the use of AI does not 'lead to outcomes entailing prohibited discrimination'.[77] The White Paper also suggests an auditability requirement, that is, retaining records of the AI system's training and testing, so as to '[avoid] bias that could lead to prohibited discrimination'.[78] **22.089**

(b) United States

In April 2019 the Algorithmic Accountability Act of 2019 (AAA) was proposed as a bill in the US.[79] The AAA has not yet been passed and there may be question marks about if, when and in what form it ever will be passed, particularly given that, at least at a federal level, the US is expected to adopt a more 'light-touch' approach to AI regulation. **22.090**

---

75 European Commission, *On Artificial Intelligence – a European approach to excellence and trust*, European Commission, 19 February 2020.
76 Ibid, p. 17.
77 Ibid, p. 19.
78 Ibid, 19 February 2020.
79 New York, House of Energy and Commerce, Algorithmic Accountability Act of 2019, H.R. 2231, www.congress.gov/bill/116th-congress/house-bill/2231/text, 10 April 2019.

22.091   In its current form, the AAA obliges the Federal Trade Commission (FTC) to regulate high-risk automated decision systems, which includes systems that use AI. A 'high-risk' system is defined as being one which poses a significant risk of resulting in or contributing to 'inaccurate, unfair, biased, or discriminatory decisions impacting consumers'.[80] In particular, the FTC would be required to introduce regulation requiring certain entities to conduct an 'automated decision system impact assessment',[81] which is defined as a study of the system's design, data and training process and its impact on 'accuracy, fairness, bias, discrimination, privacy and security'.[82]

4.   Challenges of Regulating Bias and Discrimination in AI

22.092   The issue of bias and discrimination in AI is likely to attract increasing attention as the use of AI technologies continues to rise. There will undoubtedly be technical solutions developed to detect, minimise and even eliminate bias and discrimination in AI systems. However, even with those solutions in place, there is likely to be increasing pressure to regulate bias and discrimination in AI, given the impact this can have on individuals' rights.

22.093   There is unlikely to be a uniform or even consistent approach on the regulation of bias and discrimination across jurisdictions, and lawmakers will face a number of challenges in responding to this pressure. For example:

(a)   Should bias and discrimination in AI be tackled using existing regulation which applies to bias and discrimination more generally (for example, the Equality Act 2010 in the UK) or new regulation intended specifically to address bias and discrimination in AI? The answer to this is likely to depend on the effectiveness and scope of existing regulation, particularly its ability to apply to a new and complex technology like AI.

(b)   Will new regulation prohibit bias and discrimination, or will it instead require or encourage behaviours designed to avoid bias and discrimination? Neither the EU White Paper nor the AAA suggests the former – the White Paper refers to organisations having to take 'reasonable measures' to avoid 'outcomes entailing prohibited discrimination' and the AAA refers to an 'impact assessment'. Given the importance of avoiding bias and discrimination, however, there is no obvious reason why lawmakers should not seek to prohibit this per se.

(c)   How will bias and discrimination be defined in any new regulation? This could be one reason why lawmakers may be reluctant to prohibit bias and discrimination per se, because this would require bias and discrimination to be clearly identified or defined. That said, there does not appear to be any reason why, conceptually, bias and discrimination in AI could not mirror existing definitions or understandings of bias and discrimination used in other areas or laws.

(d)   Should bias and discrimination be regulated in all uses of AI or only in certain areas or domains? As noted above, the reference in the EU White Paper to the use of AI being riskier in some sectors than others is surprising (after all, avoiding bias and discrimination in AI-based recruitment tools, for example, is surely equally important in all sectors).

---

80   Ibid, section 2(7).
81   Ibid, section 3(b)(1).
82   Ibid, section 2(2).

However, the context in which an AI system is used (including the purpose of the system and the impact on its users) is likely to be an important consideration in deciding upon appropriate regulation. For example, most people would agree that discrimination in a law enforcement context (which, as in the *Loomis* case discussed above, has the potential to deprive an individual of their liberty) is a particularly sensitive area.

A final question is: who will enforce the regulation? The proposed regime under the AAA, for **22.094** example, establishes a regulator with the power to introduce and enforce further regulation. An alternative would be to leave it to private actors to bring civil claims to enforce their rights under the regulation. In the context of bias and discrimination – which have the ability to have a profound impact on an individual's rights – the existence of a regulator (be that an existing or a new, dedicated regulator) is likely to be an attractive option. The effectiveness of a regulator, however, depends on it having the ability, willingness and resources to enforce the regulation effectively. Conversely, if reliance is placed on private actors, it may be a challenge to ensure that such actors are adequately equipped to enforce their rights.

G. CONCLUSION

Despite the relative infancy of AI, the issue of bias and discrimination in AI systems is attract- **22.095** ing an increasing level of attention. This is due, in part, to the intrinsic opaqueness of AI and already reported instances of AI having 'gone wrong', resulting in discrimination.

It is perhaps inevitable that bias and discrimination will become a focal point of AI, particularly **22.096** as AI models are entrusted with increasingly serious, potentially life-changing decisions, while also becoming increasingly complex and opaque. On a societal level, a heightened awareness of the need to treat all individuals equally (particularly in more developed economies) will also shine a spotlight on further instances of bias and discrimination caused by AI.

Bias and discrimination are already regulated in many jurisdictions. The *South Wales Police* **22.097** case in the UK demonstrates that existing regulation is capable of applying to AI. There is also a significant volume of literature on the ethical and responsible use of AI, and many ethical/responsible AI frameworks address bias and discrimination, either directly or through other important principles such as fairness, transparency, explainability, accuracy and accountability.

The importance of this subject is, however, likely to prompt further calls for regulation, **22.098** following the trend in the US of prohibiting the use of facial technology recognition, and as exemplified by the EU White Paper and AAA in the US. There will certainly be challenges for lawmakers in determining how best to regulate bias and discrimination in AI, but these challenges will no doubt be overcome.

23

PUBLIC POLICY AND GOVERNMENT

Birgitte Andersen

A. INTRODUCTION

23.001 This chapter is divided into three inter-related parts.

(a)   The first part considers how the AI revolution has caused a shift in policy-paradigms. It also reveals how contemporary AI policy processes are co-created – by the likes of think tanks, parliamentary groups (such as APPGs), committees and cross-government commissioned public consultations – through evidence-based research and engagement.

(b)   The second part addresses how AI policy has become a particularly important factor in economic recovery processes, which are exacerbated by current global health crises. Three key public purpose sectors are considered – education, national security and COVID-19. These sectors have each been affected and directly boosted by a strong technology policy overhaul, dating back to spring 2020.

(c)   The third part addresses how AI policy is designed around building innovation ecosystems, which connect science-based and commercial innovations with industry systems, investment, trade and improvements to our livelihood. Innovation ecosystems can be referred to as the glue that holds our economy and society together, while stimulating confidence and social capital regarding a technology. Without it, opportunities to create economic growth and wellbeing from AI innovation and implementation will be distorted.

23.002 Safeguarding AI use by the public and designing ethical utility is now at the heart of all AI regulation, adoption, or policy considerations in the UK.

B. SHIFTING POLICY PARADIGMS

Just as businesses and societies have finally adjusted to the economic landscape enabled by the **23.003** digital and internet revolution, the next technology revolution has come along to 'rock the boat' once more. But this time the revolution – namely Artificial Intelligence – looks very different from a policy perspective.

1.   Comparing Internet and AI Policy Paradigms

The early internet revolution, previously known as the 'New Economy', was framed by poli- **23.004** cymakers in relation to how it could facilitate a new digital infrastructure and directly support corporate innovation, competitiveness and financial revenue, and leverage network advantages. While the initial emphasis centred on the emergence of electronic commerce (or e-commerce) in the late 1990s, from about 2006 focus turned to the exponentially fast growth of the online social media industry.

During the early digital revolution governments also sought to address shortcomings, where **23.005** national performance measures were not capturing the productive role played by intangibles (data, software, business models, intellectual property, and so on). This is known as the pro- ductivity paradox, where investment in software and new electronic processes failed to manifest themselves through increased measures of productivity. This gap in valuation and understand- ing made decisions on budget allocation and investment maximisation, as well as other policy decisions, difficult.

However, the new economic measurement issue is that AI is a general-purpose technology, so **23.006** it is impossible to classify the AI sector for policy and the budgets using conventional meas- ures. Therefore, classifications are increasingly around technology, and where they are used or adopted.

For example, AI technologies can be classified into machine learning, data analytics, chatbots, **23.007** AI assistants, language processing and voice recognition, predictive analytics, face and emotion recognition and other technologies, and their industry adoption can be classified accordingly. Big Innovation Centre and Deep Knowledge Analytics have mapped how these technologies are adopted by different companies and industry sectors over time (2018 and 2021[1]). Such AI mapping also shows which AI technologies are the fastest growing, which sectors are the biggest AI adopters and which investors invest in which AI technologies and AI companies.

Regulation of intellectual property (IP) protection in the digital ecosystem has also been forced **23.008** to adjust. As the early internet revolution was user-driven, industry business models based on IP licensing and IP regulation on the internet were in a reactive, catch-up position. The biggest challenge of the early internet revolution was IP system design. Previously, IP was framed around an analogue system with centralised control on IP, which needed to be updated for interactive file-sharing systems and adjusted to suit new roles played by internet service provid- ers (ISPs). Today's challenges are not enforcement-related, but instead concern the rationales

---

1   Big Innovation Centre and Deep Knowledge Analytics (2018 and 2021) 'Artificial Intelligence Industry in the UK:
     Technologies, Companies, Inventors, Trends', Innovation Eye www.innovationeye.com/.

for the IP system – can machines or robots own IP when they develop new inventions through machine learning? How is an 'inventive step' defined in the AI world, where technology and machines (by their own accord) are constantly producing inventions?

Table 23.1   Towards policy frameworks

Policy context	The early internet revolution	The AI revolution
Core focus	Digital infrastructure: A digital infrastructure to support corporate innovation, competition, financial revenue, and leverage network advantages.	Data infrastructure and ethics: A new data infrastructure (as data is the 'fuel' for AI). Ethical considerations on the adoption and use of AI.
Key adopters	E-business sectors: E-business sectors as publishing, broadcasting and media companies, as well as Internet Service Providers (ISPs).	Public purpose sectors: Public purpose sectors such as education, health, national security, environmental services, combined with addressing social development goals. Businesses must become suppliers to solve public purpose goals.
Sector measurement issues for allocation of budgets, investment and policy decisions	The Productivity Paradox: National performance measures were not capturing the productive role played by intangibles.	AI classification: AI is not an industry but a 'general purpose' technology spanning industries, so how it is best classified for economic analytics to support decision making?
Intellectual property (IP) challenges	From analogue to digital: The IP system was designed around an analogue system.	Machines can 'think': Humans, companies, and governments can own IP, but can intelligent machines (or robots)? How is an inventive step defined in the AI world, where technology and machines (of their own accord) are constantly producing inventions?
Diffusion of adoption	End-user/consumer-driven: Demand-pull revolution (catch up by industry business models and policy).	Supplier/science-driven: Technology-push revolution (catch up by user-adoption by industry and end-users/consumers).

23.009 Digital policy creation for the internet was originally designed in relation to the private sector, which was considered the 'key adopter'. However, AI policy has first and foremost received attention with respect to public sector considerations, and the public sector's role in the innovation ecosystem. Key public sector adopters are addressing areas such as: (I) skills and education, (II) heath care, medicine, virology and COVID-19, and (III) national security and facial recognition. Hence, policy to support these segments of economic catalysts has shifted towards public purpose, support of sustainability development goals and AI as a social good.[2]

23.010 Furthermore, whereas the digital revolution was user-driven (or market-push, through user involvement in innovation processes), the AI revolution has been research and technology-driven (or tech-pull, wherein researcher involvement galvanises research and development).[3]

---

2   Vinuesa, Ricardo et al. (2020) 'The Role of Artificial Intelligence in Achieving the Sustainable Development Goals'. Nature Communications 11: 233.

3   (i) UK Research and Innovation (2021) 'Transforming Our World with AI: UKRI's Role in Embracing the Opportunity'. UK Research and Innovation; (ii) Parker, Lynne (March 2021) 'U.S. National Policies to Advance AI Research and Development'. National Artificial Intelligence Initiative Office.

Thus, AI policy is attempting to favourably frame the environment and to encourage industry and user adoption with a particular focus on ethics and data governance (personal, professional and societal), alongside other economic variables.   **23.011**

2.   Policy Processes and Co-creation: A New Modern Management System

The formation of digital policy for the early internet revolution was stakeholder-driven: key players representing the big publishing, broadcasting and media companies (moving from analogue to digital business models) faced off with internet service providers (ISPs), supplying new platforms which undermined the content providers' business models.   **23.012**

However, the formation of policy in the AI revolution happens in a very different way. It is co-created with the strengths of 'a new modern management system' – through research involvement, engagement with think-tanks, discussions with parliamentary groups (such as All-Party Parliamentary Groups in the UK parliament), select committee sessions, councils and cross-government commissioned public consultations.[4] This change in policy approach is possible due to the public purpose and ethical aspects of AI adoption.   **23.013**

Table 23.2   *Co-creators informing the direction of AI policy in the UK (an abridged listing)*

UK government and parliament	AI-related think-tanks and research hubs
(alphabetical listing)	*(alphabetical listing)*
● All-Party Parliamentary Group on AI (APPG AI)	● Ada Lovelace Institute
● Centre for Data Ethics and Innovation	● AI Policy Labs
● Competition and Markets Authority (CMA)	● Big Brother Watchdog
● Government Office for AI & The AI Council	● Big Innovation Centre
● House of Lords Liaison Committee on AI	● British Security Industry Association (BSIA)
● Information Commissioners Office	● Centre for the Study of Existential Risk
● Open Data Institute	● Future Advocacy
● Surveillance Camera Commissioner	● Future of Humanity Institute
● The Biometrics and Forensics Ethics Group	● Institute for the Future of Work
● The Committee on Standards in Public Life	● Leverhulme Centre for the Future of Intelligence
	● National Centre for Nuclear Robotics
Key government initiatives catalysing AI research and adoption include:	● Royal Academy of Engineering
	● Royal Society
● Centres for Doctoral Training (CDTs) and Turing Fellowships	● Society for the Study of Artificial Intelligence and Simulation of Behaviour
● Industrial Strategy Challenge Fund (ISCF): Artificial intelligence and data economy	● TechUK
● Innovate UK	● Teens in AI
● The Artificial Intelligence in Health and Care Award (AI Award)	● The Alan Turing Institute
● The Catapult network, incl. Digital Catapult	● The Institute for Ethics in AI
● The British Academy	● UCL Centre for Artificial intelligence
● UKRI – UK Research and Innovation	

---

4   (i) EU Council of Europe (17 December 2020) 'Ad Hoc Committee on Artificial Intelligence (CAHAI): Feasibility Study'. Strasbourg, Council of Europe; (ii) House of Lords Liaison Committee (2017) AI in the UK: 'AI in the UK: Ready, Willing and Able?' London, Report of Session 2017–19, House of Lords Liaison Committee; (iii) House of Lords Liaison Committee (2020) AI in the UK: 'No Room for Complacency'. London, 7th Report of Session 2019–21, House of Lords Liaison Committee; (iv) Leslie, D., Burr, C., Aitken, M., Cowls, J., Katell, M., and Briggs, M. (2021) Artificial Intelligence, Human Rights, Democracy, and the Rule of Law: A Primer. The Council of Europe; (v) OECD (2021) Recommendation of the Council on Artificial Intelligence – Legal Instruments (Trustworthy AI); (vi) The AI Council UK (January 2021) 'The UK AI Council: AI Roadmap'.

C. AI POLICY FOR PUBLIC PURPOSES

23.014   As of March 2020, three key public sectors – namely education, national security and COVID-19 – collectively received increased scrutiny and a technological policy review kick-off. This was at the time of the first UK nationwide lockdowns due to the COVID-19 pandemic, a period of prolonged home schooling, social distancing, travel restrictions and growing global health crisis.

23.015   These sectors are considered to be among most significant to the UK's economic recovery process and will now be addressed in turn.

1.   Towards AI Policy for Education

23.016   The shaping of AI policy in the education sector focuses mainly on children and youth-level institutions (primary and secondary schools), as well as the adoption of emerging technologies – artificial intelligence, blockchain, Internet of Things, virtual reality and augmented reality. These emerging technologies are not only changing jobs, but also disrupting the way future generations learn future skills.

23.017   The demand for future skills also poses a direct challenge to the education system. Of the children entering primary school today, 65 per cent will ultimately end up working in new professions that do not currently exist, so we can't educate children towards fitting the job market. This reactive inefficiency means future generations could be tasked with retraining mid-career; similar to the waves of adults currently retooling for careers in software development, engineering or coding. A report by Big Innovation Centre, the All-Party Parliamentary Group on Artificial Intelligence (APPG AI) and KPMG, entitled 'Learning to Learn', was the first to demonstrate how twenty-first-century citizens must be adaptable as lifelong learners.[5]

23.018   According to a 2020 presentation at the World Economic Forum, among the most valued soft skills currently are complex problem solving, critical thinking, creativity, people management, coordination with others, emotional intelligence, cognitive flexibility, judgement and decision making. The advent of new disruptive technologies (AI, VR, IoT and so forth) in tandem with a 'Learning to Learn' approach, can advance those skills.

23.019   At the December 2018 launch of the Digital Economy Strategy for the Arab League in Abu Dhabi (advised by the Big Innovation Centre executive team), presenters gave context as to how (i) classrooms are expected to become virtual in a real-time context, (ii) teachers must become designers and mentors, (iii) instruction becomes construction, (iv) subjects become phenomena, (v) teaching moves from reactive to interactive, (vi) standards become personalised frameworks, (vii) experts crowdsource information from peers, (viii) textbooks become 'the environment' as a living lab, (ix) learning becomes lifelong and (x) education has become fluid, adaptive and agile.

---

5   (i) Big Innovation Centre, APPG AI and KPMG (2018) 'Learning to Learn: The Future-Proof Skill'; (ii) DCMS Department of Education (January 2021): 'Skills for Jobs: Lifelong Learning for Opportunity and Growth'.

Policy must be designed to foster such transformation. The meetings of the All-Party **23.020** Parliamentary Group on Artificial Intelligence (APPG AI)[6] and a study facilitated by British Council Tunisia[7] discussed how best this could happen, as outlined below.

The adoption of AI into education can be an effective way to engage students at various levels **23.021** with disparate abilities, and an opportunity to use a variety of new learning styles. Nevertheless, success requires that learners, teachers, assessment and teaching material and the physical environment are futureproof.

Policies on the adoption of AI into education must ensure that all students have the same **23.022** foundation and equal opportunity from the start, irrespective of their background.

AI offers a new approach to learning methods, where inter-disciplinarity and problem-solving **23.023** is at the heart of learning environments. This will integrate soft skills (creative) and hard STEM (science, technology, engineering and mathematics) skills, and enhance the experience of and purpose in education. These AI-enhanced inter-disciplinarity and problem-solving skills are subject-agnostic, spanning across English, science, music, sports, art, drama, media, languages and geography.

Subjects and core competencies may need an update as well. For example, the introduction **23.024** of a new school module on the management of technology or innovation – even from a very young age – can stimulate the needs and development of future leaders, capable of managing technology and innovation. This update will complement the current 'hard' focus on STEM skills, which is only a part of future success. A new module in the information-centric society – data trust, critical analysis and information handling – is also relevant to learning at an early age. This skill can supplement the sourcing of information, inform youth on how to detect fake news and enlighten them as to how to manage personal data online.

Emerging technology can also offer a new approach to student assessment, feedback and perfor- **23.025** mance. AI has the capacity to improve each of these through the interactive nature of technology. This interaction provides an alternative to the 'studying for the exam' approach, which has a catalogue of drawbacks for long-term learning and the student experience. However, it will take time to implement new assessment methods. While digitally enabled home-schooling was imposed overnight globally due to governments' stay-at-home orders during the COVID-19 pandemic, more inroads and progress must be made regarding the educational performance toolkit. With the view that pandemics will become a recurrent issue, it is prudent to ensure that learning continues using new technology, regardless of assessment.

AI also offers opportunities for precision learning, and for each student to follow their interests **23.026** and skills. This can also free up time for teachers to foster class community. The taught edu-

---

6   (i) All Party Parliamentary Group on Artificial Intelligence (APPG AI) (October 2020) 'AI in Education: Embedding AI tools into teaching curricula'. Parliamentary Brief, Big Innovation Centre; (ii) All Party Parliamentary Group on Artificial Intelligence (APPG AI) (November 2020) 'AI in Education: Designing fair and robust AI-based assessments systems', Parliamentary Brief, Big Innovation Centre.

7   Big Innovation Centre and British Council Tunisia (December 2019) 'Education in Tunisia: Futureproofing Through Technology'.

cation curriculum must be revitalised with the adoption of AI and other emerging technology, both in how it is adopted into classroom operations for schools, and for the student experience. Additionally, protocols must be set regarding AI adoption in each education field, including purpose, ethics, impact and other criteria.

23.027 The alleged benefits of using AI in education should not be overstated for commercial interests. False statements concerning the current capabilities and reliability of using AI in education would risk a loss of public trust and could cause an overreliance on decisions generated by potentially flawed technologies. Deployment of AI education technologies in classrooms must happen with a nuanced consideration of these tools' suitability for serving the intended educational purpose. The technology must apply teaching methods that are adequate for the specific age group and abilities of the students.

23.028 To ensure that software is developed to fit their purpose, educators must be involved in the shaping of AI tools. However, for AI adoption into education to be successful, policy also must focus on 'training the trainers' to enhance a successful and speedy transformation of schools.

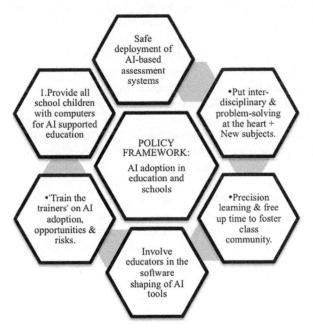

Source: Big Innovation Centre

Figure 23.1   Towards a policy framework for AI in education

23.029 Physical barriers to adoption, including access, physical infrastructure and costs, should be assessed and categorised, so an infrastructure investment plan can be prepared for policy. Naturally, schools must update equipment, but the home is equally important. Schoolchildren should be provided with the same computers and network accessibility set up by the school for school purposes, to facilitate AI and digitally supported education.

All of the above will help to unlock a vast and equitable society, but behavioural and ethical aspects of interacting with technology are also key for future welfare and society. **23.030**

2.   Towards AI Policy for Facial Recognition in National Security

A strategic imperative for national security is facial recognition. There are cameras every- **23.031**
where – street, transport, workplace and home, with the webcams built into our PCs and TVs.
Technology now allows cameras to recognise your face, your emotions and even your presumed
state of mind.

Facial recognition is indeed convenient for opening your mobile phone using its built-in **23.032**
camera, for sorting family photos on your phone or for digital games when children apply
face-filter technologies. But when surveillance cameras are applied for policing, at passport
control checkpoints and immigration, for security at football grounds or in shops for marking
purposes or in order to pay, we are in an entirely different situation, with new opportunities
and indeed challenges.

There are joint issues regarding the quality of the technology (how good is it?) and the ethics **23.033**
of its use (who controls our data, and for what are they used?)

Policy discussions have touched upon a variety of approaches, but it has become very clear that **23.034**
facial recognition deployment must guarantee data protection, not discriminate and be used
responsibly. A policy framework should: (i) ensure the quality and applicability of data sets used
for the training of facial recognition technologies; (ii) regulate audits and compliance checks;
and (iii) outline rules for the collection, processing and storage of citizens' biometric data for
public and commercial use.

Guidelines on the use of facial recognition technologies have been proposed by the APPG AI[8] **23.035**
(see below list as example), the British Security Industry Association,[9] the Surveillance Camera
Commissioner[10] and other groups.[11]

(a)   *Good quality for all groups and free of bias* – Face and emotion recognition technologies
must be representative and relevant for their specific purpose of use. This safeguards
and guarantees accurate results that do not replicate inherent biases and thus attempts to
prevent the reinforcement of societal prejudices and systematic discrimination of individuals and groups. In order to achieve this, collected data used to train facial recognition

---

8   All Party Parliamentary Group on Artificial Intelligence (APPG AI) (July 2020) 'Face and Emotion Recognition
Technologies: How Can Regulation Protect Citizens and Their Privacy?' Parliamentary Brief, Big Innovation Centre.

9   The British Security Industry Association (BSIA) (February 2021): 'Automated Facial Recognition: A Guide to Ethical
and Legal Use', The British Security Industry Association (BSIA).

10   The Surveillance Camera Commissioner (December 2020) 'Facing the Camera'. The guidance is for forces to follow
when considering the deployment of Live Facial Recognition (LFR) surveillance camera technology.

11   (i) Centre for Data Ethics and Innovation (CDEI) (November 2020) 'Review into Bias in Algorithmic Decision-Making';
(ii) Clement-Jones, Tim (March 2020) 'The Potential Role of Gov-Tech and Its Governance' (March 2020),
Provocation, APPG AI and Big Innovation Centre; (iii) Government Communications Headquarters (GCHQ)
(2021) 'Pioneering a New National Security: The Ethics of Artificial Intelligence', Artificial Intelligence at GCHQ;
(iv) National Security Commission on Artificial Intelligence (2021) 'Final Report', National Security Commission on
Artificial Intelligence.

technologies should be regularly revised and adjusted, and users should be 'in the loop' to ensure data is free of bias.

(b) *Protect privacy of citizens* – Technologies must be used in a way that protects citizens' privacy and must not reinforce societal prejudices or exploit vulnerable groups and individuals.

(c) *Must have a clear purpose of use* – Face and emotion recognition technologies must be regularly audited to guarantee their safety and to determine if they are still fulfilling the desired purpose.

(d) *Transparency of deployment and data handling* – Businesses, public and private institutions must be transparent about (i) where face and emotion recognition technologies are deployed, (ii) what kind of data they collect and (iii) how they are processed and stored.

(e) *Different 'types of facial recognition technologies' call for context when framing policy* – They each come with specific sets of risks that should be considered in the design of a national regulatory framework.

23.036 A meeting of the APPG AI (6 June 2020) proposed how a watchdog agency on technological application of facial recognition could ensure the above guidelines are enforced. Further, a public debate with citizens and stakeholders around the democratic implications of these technologies should be encouraged.

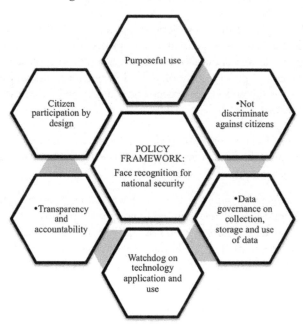

Source: Big Innovation Centre

Figure 23.2   Towards a policy framework for AI in national security and facial recognition

23.037 Figure 23.2 represents a clear regulatory framework to ensure fair and safe use of facial recognition technologies. This is especially important because developers or developers need to know the agreed standards, in order to secure their investment into our future infrastructure.

But this is the dilemma for the UK and many European countries.[12] Facial recognition is **23.038**
already being applied in major global regions which are now building accurate technologies
from collecting billions of gigabytes of data.

(a)   If we in the UK stop the use of facial recognition (while regulation is catching up), we
       are caught in a vicious circle, with no data (or R&D incentives) for our developers to
       innovate high-spec and safe solutions. The UK's entrepreneurs will fall behind and, once
       regulation is in place, our foreign competitors will already have superior solutions.

(b)   But if we use facial recognition now, our regulatory system is not in pace around safe-
       guarding its citizens – as we have not collected enough data to train our cameras for safe
       application.

To turn this vicious cycle into a virtuous circle, policymakers must work fast to be decisive on **23.039**
the 'purposeful use' and limits of facial recognition technologies, along with the underpinnings
of data governance.

3.   Towards AI Policy to Combat COVID-19 and Future Pandemics

AI can be applied in health care for diagnostic processes, treatment protocol development, **23.040**
drug development, the development of personalised medicine, patient monitoring services and
more. AI algorithms are used to analyse large amounts of data through digital health records
for disease prevention and diagnosis. Thus, AI applications in health care are used to analyse
relationships between prevention techniques and patient outcomes.

AI adoption has garnered special consideration in our efforts to combat COVID-19, assisting **23.041**
with preventative measures to slow the spread, through surveillance and contact tracing. AI
is used for analytics and, when combined with blockchain,[13] can improve the track-and-trace
technical infrastructure addressing the pandemic. AI can also be used for detecting and diagnosing the COVID-19 virus and predicting new variants, and for responding to the health
crisis through personalised information for precision healthcare. To combat COVID-19, AI
is also used in monitoring, recovery and improving early warning systems though symptom
analysis. Finally, AI is used in research seeking to understand the virus, which can accelerate
medical research on drugs and breakthrough treatments.

For this to happen effectively, policy needs to support two segments: (1) data policy, encour- **23.042**
aging ethical maintenance and availability of citizens' data; and (2) mechanisms such as mobile
applications, which can feed into and monitor citizens' data.

While it is clear that AI could be deployed to significant effect in the battle against viral diseases **23.043**
(not least of which in improvements to pandemic response measures), regulations around the
use of private citizens' data are essential to any further progress.

---

12   Big Innovation Centre (2020) 'Will Face and Emotion Recognition Change the UK?' Big Innovation Centre at the UK
      Political Party Conferences, Big Innovation Centre.
13   All Party Parliamentary Group on Blockchain (APPG AI) (June 2020) 'How Can Blockchain Help in the Time of
      Covid-19?' Parliamentary Brief, Big Innovation Centre.

23.044 Without rules, behavioural norms, and regulations in place to ensure the fair and responsible use of public health data – and the creation of a cross-border infrastructure that enables international and interdisciplinary collaboration on data information and epidemiological research – it is impossible for societies to move in the direction of the collective good. Public trust that data will be used fairly and anonymously is paramount.

23.045 One solution proposed by the UK parliament at the APPG AI[14] is the creation of an independent oversight body or watchdog, responsible for the fair and ethical application of any data-driven public health measures. Represented by multiple disciplines and vulnerable groups, it would oversee the quality and governance of data while ensuring that data-driven measures in the event of another pandemic would serve the public good. Transparency and responsiveness to the public must be prioritised and maintained throughout the entire process.

23.046 Second, COVID-19 has reshaped the possibility of 'mHealth' as a policy initiative. mHealth refers to personal health care over mobile phone applications (apps) or wearable technology.

23.047 A major study on the top 250 mHealth Apps globally, by Big Innovation Centre and Deep Knowledge Analytics, revealed the current trends.[15]

(a) *Penetration* – Today, delivering health services over mobile phone, tablet and wearable technology is a multi-billion dollar industry globally, exceeding $5 billion in global investment, with hundreds of millions of users. The market growth in both developing and developed countries is driven by widespread smartphone penetration.

(b) *Scope* – The scope of mHealth use cases is increasing at a commensurate rate through various channels: telehealth, mental health, fem-tech, sleep tech, diet and nutrition, diagnostics, symptom tracing and more.

(c) *Sophistication* – Technological sophistication is steadily rising for mHealth possibilities, with the adoption of AI. This has resulted in increased precision and personalisation of mHealth services over smartphone and wearable technology.

(d) *Diversification* – Following the increased diversification of mHeath applications covering a range of areas such as symptom tracing, health assistants and track-and-trace apps, government policies worldwide have turned towards mHealth applications to control the current pandemic. Most developed governments worldwide have adopted or launched their own 'official' mHealth applications to control COVID-19, and in countries such as China it has become mandatory for all citizens to allow for tracking at all times.

23.048 So why has COVID-19 been a major driver in the uptake of mHealth services? The constraints felt by health care systems in many developed economies have significantly impacted government attitudes towards mHealth. One can summarise this through five facts underpinning how COVID-19 is continuing to reshape the possibilities of mHealth:

(a) Fast growth in incidence of population with COVID-19.

(b) A high burden of COVID-19 disease prevalence.

---

14   All Party Parliamentary Group on Artificial Intelligence (APPG AI) (May 2020) 'Public Health: How Can AI Help in the Fight against COVID-19?' Parliamentary Brief, Big Innovation Centre.

15   Big Innovation Centre and Deep Knowledge Analytics (November 2020) 'Global mHealth Industry Landscape Overview', Innovation Eye www.innovationeye.com/.

(c)   Limited hospital capacity and healthcare workforce to tackle the pandemic.

(d)   Large cities with high concentration of people (easy to spread COVID-19).

(e)   Inadequate healthcare infrastructure and governmental health information systems to deal with the spread of COVID-19.

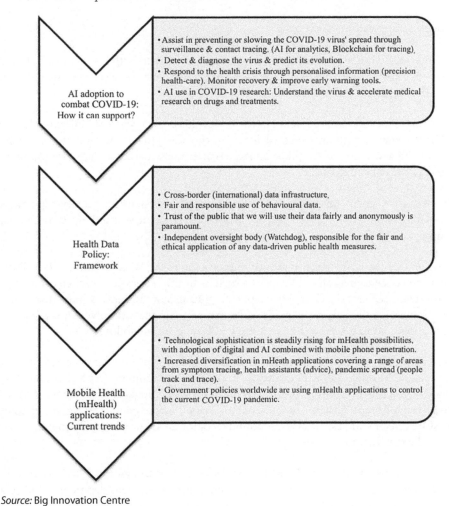

AI adoption to combat COVID-19: How it can support?

- Assist in preventing or slowing the COVID-19 virus' spread through surveillance & contact tracing. (AI for analytics, Blockchain for tracing).
- Detect & diagnose the virus & predict its evolution.
- Respond to the health crisis through personalised information (precision health-care). Monitor recovery & improve early warning tools.
- AI use in COVID-19 research: Understand the virus & accelerate medical research on drugs and treatments.

Health Data Policy: Framework

- Cross-border (international) data infrastructure.
- Fair and responsible use of behavioural data.
- Trust of the public that we will use their data fairly and anonymously is paramount.
- Independent oversight body (Watchdog), responsible for the fair and ethical application of any data-driven public health measures.

Mobile Health (mHealth) applications: Current trends

- Technological sophistication is steadily rising for mHealth possibilities, with adoption of digital and AI combined with mobile phone penetration.
- Increased diversification in mHeath applications covering a range of areas from symptom tracing, health assistants (advice), pandemic spread (people track and trace).
- Government policies worldwide are using mHealth applications to control the current COVID-19 pandemic.

Source: Big Innovation Centre

Figure 23.3   Towards a policy framework for AI to combat COVID-19 and future pandemics

Today, health and wellness are indicative of the economic viability of a given country. In the **23.049** wake of COVID-19 this is more true than ever before. Where there is poor health, there is a poor economy. As the global mHealth industry grows, our ability to assign weighting of economic stability by factoring in health will also become more sophisticated.

D. CONCLUSION

23.050 Industrial growth from AI innovation and investment is reaching astonishing levels, creating incredible opportunities within the global innovation ecosystem.

1. Innovation Ecosystems and Policy

23.051 National policies for innovation and growth are usually concerned with two factors: (i) building an industry of a critical size; and (ii) focusing on a healthy balance between current and emerging new industries, supply chain systems, investment and trade.

23.052 While still important, the real difference in the AI revolution has been the radical reassessment of thought leadership, with an increased focus on the strength of our modern management system with the assistance of AI think-tanks, research hubs, parliamentary groups, advisory boards and public consultations.

23.053 Furthermore, government investments to cultivate a talent system for AI development and adoption have promoted our universities as bastions of AI talent generation, for both science and creative skills.

23.054 Livelihood and wellbeing ecosystems are also succumbing to the AI revolution, as its utility has suddenly been concentrated on public sectors such as health, education, national security and the environment; see section C of this chapter for full review. Initiatives framed around 'AI for good' are successfully helping to guide leadership in their quest to solve our economic and existential crises, and to use AI to build ethical and lasting sustainability.

23.055 As we saw in section B, the AI revolution is supplier-led by a science base and R&D specialising in machine learning and data analytics. Acting as front runners and flag bearers for AI technology – in terms of industry concentration of company engagement – other AI sectors are quickly catching up, such as chatbots, AI assistants, language processing and predictive analytics. Of AI technologies, facial and emotion recognition are proving to be among the most complex and contextual to regulate.

23.056 Safeguarding the use of AI by public and private citizens, and designing ethical utility around AI, are two criteria now at the heart of AI adoption and policy considerations.[16] Policy and regulations aim to ensure that public and private institutions are transparent about how AI

---

16   (i) CMA Competition and Markets Authority (2021) 'Algorithms: How They Can Reduce Competition and Harm Consumers'; (ii) CMA Competition & Markets Authority (February 2021) 'The CMA's Digital Markets Strategy: February 2021 Refresh'; (iii) Rolls Royce (2020) The Aletheia Framework (a practical toolkit that helps organisations to consider the impacts on people of using artificial intelligence prior to deciding whether to proceed); (iv) ICO Information Commissioners Office (July 2020) 'Guidance on AI and Data Protection'; (v) Office for Artificial Intelligence (OAI), Government Digital Service (GDS) and Alan Turing Institute (2019): 'Understanding artificial intelligence ethics and safety: A guide for the responsible design and implementation of AI systems in the public sector', David Leslie, The Alan Turing Institute; (vi) UK Statistics Authority (2021) 'Centre for Applied Data Ethics Strategy: Enabling Ethically Appropriate Research and Statistics for the Public Good'; (vii) UN Secretary-General's High-level Panel on Digital Cooperation (June 2019): 'The Age of Digital Interdependence'.

technologies are deployed and for what purpose, including what kind of data they collect and how they are processed and stored.[17] Transparency is paramount.

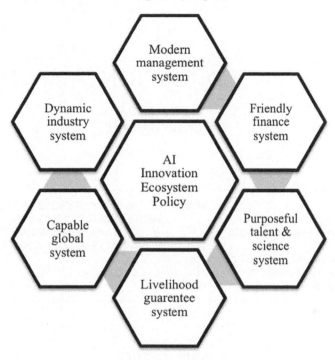

Source: Big Innovation Centre

Figure 23.4   AI innovation-ecosystem policy seeing the economy as an integrated 'whole'

Building AI innovation ecosystems for industry, investment, trade and livelihood has become **23.057** ingrained in policy. An innovation ecosystem approach recognises economy as a whole (see Figure 23.4), in which all nodes act as stimuli for each other's success. Innovation ecosystems can be referred to as the glue that holds our economy and society together, and which builds confidence and social capital around AI. Without it, economic growth or human wellbeing from AI innovation and implementation will be distorted.

The AI revolution has shown how (and why) national and international governments can (and **23.058** should) invest in the quality of our economic and political institutions and our innovation ecosystems.

---

17   (i) All Party Parliamentary Group on Artificial Intelligence (APPG AI) (April 2021) 'Data Governance in the Post-Brexit Era: Is the National Data Strategy Ambitious Enough?' Parliamentary Brief, Big Innovation Centre; (ii) Advisory Board Members of the APPG AI and APPG Blockchain Working Groups (November 2020): 'National Data Strategy Consultation Response', Big Innovation Centre; (iii) All Party Parliamentary Group on Artificial Intelligence (APPG AI) (June 2020) 'Data Governance: Beyond GDPR', Parliamentary Brief, Big Innovation Centre.

24

EDUCATION

Stefano Barazza

A. INTRODUCTION

24.001   The transformation of legal services, in particular through LegalTech, requires a parallel transformation of the ways in which legal education is provided to both future and current generations of lawyers. The extent of such transformation is currently the subject of intense debate[1] that hinges on the predicted role of LegalTech and legal technologists in the legal industry. Placing the emphasis on the disruptive potential of LegalTech justifies calls for the integration of LegalTech education into all stages of legal education and for new pedagogical principles that echo the more transformational aspirations of the LegalTech movement: the nurturing of computer science skills and abilities, of diffused entrepreneurial and leadership skills, of fast-paced inventiveness and creativity. A more conservative view of LegalTech suggests incremental addition to the educational offering of law schools and other legal education providers. The definition of pedagogical principles, however, can hardly depend upon the predicted

---

1   All websites cited in this chapter were last accessed on 1 September 2020. The educational debate invests many aspects of LegalTech, from the narrative adopted to support its pedagogy (K. Galloway et al., 'The Legal Academy's Engagements with Lawtech: Technology Narratives and Archetypes as Drivers of Change', (2019) 1(1) Law, Technology and Humans 27) to the need for legal technologists to acquire proficiency in coding (cf K. Grady, 'What "Teaching Legal Tech" Could Mean' (1 May 2018) Medium, available online at https://medium.com/the-algorithmic-society/what-teaching-legal -tech-could-mean-bf31cf0d4d10; M. Fenwick, 'Legal Education in a Digital Age: Why Coding Matters for the Lawyer of the Future' in M. Corrales Compagnucci et al. (eds), *Legal Tech and the New Sharing Economy* (Springer 2020) 103), to novel pedagogical approaches (e.g. D. Jackson, 'Human-centered Legal Tech: Integrating Design in Legal Education', (2016) 50(1) The Law Teacher 82; K. June Lee, 'A Call for Law Schools to Link the Curricular Trends of Legal Tech and Mindfulness', (2016–2017) 48 University of Toledo Law Review 55).

evolution of LegalTech: it seems more sensible to conceive a theoretical framework that aspires at supporting its transformational potential, while providing the flexibility necessary to adapt to the effective role that LegalTech, and legal technologists, will play in the industry.

The theoretical debate has not yet translated into concrete influence on the governmental policies implemented worldwide to stimulate the growth of LegalTech. Funding has primarily[2] been provided for the creation of legal laboratories and sandboxes,[3] for research into specific technologies and research projects,[4] for the commercial ideation of LegalTech solutions and their commercialisation,[5] for access to justice[6] and the advancement of digital justice. Efforts to support a LegalTech pedagogy have concentrated on the 'reskilling' of qualified lawyers, as well as on the creation of LegalTech hubs[7] providing central repositories of relevant information. Private consortia generally mirror this approach.[8]   **24.002**

Against the backdrop briefly sketched above, this chapter investigates the theoretical under-   **24.003** pinnings of LegalTech education, briefly overviews some early experiences and formulates some guidelines to deliver ambitious, transformative training that assumes, at its core, that LegalTech represents a fundamental shift in the way legal services are conceived. In doing so, this chapter approaches some key issues across the dimensions of interdisciplinarity, entrepreneurship, policy-making and ethics.

---

2   But not exclusively, as the recent LawTech Fund provided by the Hong Kong government to support, *inter alia*, LegalTech training demonstrates (see www.hkba.org/covid-19/lawtech-fund).

3   E.g. the recently announced Lawtech Sandbox in the United Kingdom, funded by the UK government and delivered in collaboration between Tech Nation, the Lawtech Delivery Panel and the Ministry of Justice (cf. A. Logan, 'Plans Announced for UK Lawtech R&D "Sandbox"' (21 May 2020) Tech Nation, available at https://technation.io/news/plans-for-lawtech-rd-sandbox/).

4   Singapore, for example, has recently committed to a $10.8m LegalTech research programme to digitise its legislation ('Singapore Government Commits $11m to Fund Legal Tech Research Programme' (11 March 2020) The Global Legal Post, available at https://www.globallegalpost.com/big-stories/singapore-government-commits-$11m-to-fund-legal-tech-research-programme-77990850/). The UK government has similarly funded research into the LawTech ecosystem at Oxford University ('University of Oxford Team to Study LawTech "Ecosystem"' (29 October 2019) Oxford University, available at www.law.ox.ac.uk/news/2019–10–29-university-oxford-team-study-lawtech-ecosystem).

5   Again, in a UK dimension, cf. the innovation competitions for 'Transforming accountancy, insurance and legal services with AI and data' launched by UK Research and Innovation in 2018 (https://apply-for-innovation-funding.service.gov.uk/competition/168/overview) and related Innovate UK funding rounds.

6   E.g., the Legal Access Challenge (https://legalaccesschallenge.org/), funded by the Regulators' Pioneer Fund launched by the Department for Business, Energy and Industrial Strategy (BEIS) of the UK government.

7   Tech Nation, for example, is building an online hub to provide '1) A go-to place to see and connect with the various activities in the legal sector, around technology [and] 2) A training environment through which all those interested (practitioners, students, specialists and others) can support their own learning and development' (https://technation.io/lawtechuk-vision/#our-vision).

8   See, *ex multis*, the LegalTech Hub Vienna (https://lthv.eu/), a private initiative supported by law firms, and the Nordic Legal Tech Hub (see www.nordiclegaltech.org/).

B. THE CURRENT LANDSCAPE OF LEGALTECH EDUCATION AND THE SWANSEA EXPERIENCE

24.004 The current LegalTech educational offering[9] in the higher education sector is in a state of rapid evolution and mostly consists of postgraduate degrees. Central to most of these programmes is an emphasis on key technologies seen as some of the main drivers behind LegalTech (big data, artificial intelligence, blockchain, smart contracts, and so on), accompanied by a focus on the entrepreneurial aspects related, in particular, to start-ups. The various programmes differ primarily in respect to the balancing of legal knowledge and computer science skills, with some programmes favouring courses aimed at contextualising key technologies and analysing the legal frameworks applicable to them and others proposing courses aimed at equipping students with practical knowledge in coding and data science. Another primary differentiator seems to be the existence of a supporting environment that is actively involved in LegalTech research, offering students the opportunity to further their learning in collaboration with institutional legal laboratories, hubs, or other practice- or commercialisation-focused initiatives.[10]

24.005 Beyond academic institutions, LegalTech training has been designed and provided both in-house, especially by major law firms[11] and international organisations, and through providers established by way of collaborations within the industry.[12] These courses, as will be discussed in this chapter, respond to clear industry needs and provide an immediacy and directness that is frequently absent from traditional university programmes. However, they provide a lower level of contextualisation and compress learning into a shorter period of time, sacrificing some of the mindset and skillset development that forms an integral part of many academic programmes.

24.006 Before continuing, we briefly describe the experience of the Hillary Rodham Clinton School of Law at Swansea University in providing LegalTech education, as it constitutes one of the first postgraduate programmes offered in Europe for LegalTech education – the LLM LegalTech,[13]

---

9   Some of the most well-known postgraduate programmes include the LLM LegalTech at Swansea University, the Master in Legal Tech at IE, the Master in Legal Tech at CEU, and the LLM in Law, Technology, and Entrepreneurship at Cornell Tech, but the list is growing and merely represents an exemplification of current offerings. Several postgraduate programmes in law and technology also offer LegalTech-relevant training, despite catering to a broader audience. Some well-known offerings exist also at undergraduate level, e.g. the Legal Informatics and Computational Law courses offered at Stanford Law School and supported by CodeX. For a more comprehensive list, see the 'Legal Tech Education Guide' compiled by Artificial Lawyer, available at www.artificiallawyer.com/legal-tech-courses/, reproduced in chapter [X] and 'The University Map of Legal Tech: Who Teaches It in the World' (18 March 2019) The Technolawgist, available at www.thetechnolawgist.com/2019/03/18/the-university-map-of-legal-tech-who-teaches-it-in-the-world/.

10   Relevant examples include the Legal Tech Lab at the University of Helsinki, the Legal Innovation Lab Wales at Swansea, the well-known CodeX Center for Legal Informatics at Stanford and several other laboratories at Copenhagen, Amsterdam, Frankfurt, Maastricht, Duke and other academic institutions.

11   Including in-house training programmes delivered by Eversheds (S. Lock, 'Eversheds Launches Legaltech Training For All Partners' (24 June 2019) Law.com, available at www.law.com/international-edition/2019/06/24/eversheds-launches -legal-tech-training-for-all-partners/) and Linklaters, which collaborated with Swansea University on its training programme (C. Dalla Bona, 'Linklaters Brings In Academics to School Trainees in Legal Tech' (3 March 2020) The Lawyer, available at www.thelawyer.com/linklaters-brings-in-academics-to-school-trainees-in-legal-tech/).

12   Such as Sweet Legal Tech (https://sweetlegaltech.com/) or the training materials and webinars produced by FORTE Markets in collaboration with industry partners (www.fortemarkets.com/legaltech-webinars).

13   See www.swansea.ac.uk/postgraduate/taught/law/llmlegaltech/.

launched in 2018.[14] The programme was designed from the start to respond to the industry need for legal technologists, with support from a variety of stakeholders in the legal services sector, with which the School has further developed research and training collaborations.

In this sense, Swansea has focused on the creation of a LegalTech environment in which   **24.007**
a community of students and academics from various disciplines can collaborate and grow together. The School of Law and the Department of Computer Science jointly provide expertise in standardisation, legal ontologies and natural language processing and the programme offers courses in computational thinking, principles and applications of artificial intelligence. This builds upon, and supports, interdisciplinary research and teaching within an open environment of legal and computer science academics. The 2020 opening of the Legal Innovation Lab Wales,[15] a LegalTech laboratory supported by a grant from the European Regional Development Fund, has provided the School with a space dedicated to academia–industry collaborations and to the development of disruptive LegalTech solutions in partnership with policy-makers, the legal sector in Wales and beyond and other relevant organisations. In parallel, the School has supported the creation of a LegalTech Wales network, organised events and summer schools in the field and incentivised academics from all areas of law to engage with LegalTech.

To give an example of the topics covered in such courses, the LLM LegalTech at Swansea   **24.008**
consists of six courses, roughly divided into three categories: first, a practical introduction to technological aspects (Computational Thinking, AI and the Law – Principles, AI and the Law – Applications), to teach the acquisition of a relevant mindset, of the skills needed for working in interdisciplinary teams and of competences in coding, development, management and the use of the AI tools most relevant to the industry; second, a discussion around the disruptive potential of LegalTech and its broader socio-economic significance, through courses in Digital Rights and Digital Intellectual Property, as well as a case study course in Blockchain and the Law; third, a LegalTech Entrepreneurship course, taught in partnership with other academics and with industry players (in particular from start-ups and law firms).

Swansea's experience, as that of other institutions around the world, provides a vantage   **24.009**
point through which educators can ignite a debate on the ideal LegalTech pedagogy. It also highlights, however, the challenges of designing suitably comprehensive and transformational programmes, suggesting that strong collaboration between academic institutions, law firms and other organisations is the only way in which existing and future programmes can provide excellence in LegalTech education.

---

14   The author of this chapter holds the position of Director of the LLM LegalTech at Swansea University and Academic
      Lead of the Legal Innovation Lab Wales.
15   See www.swansea.ac.uk/law/legal-innovation-lab-wales/. An overview of the developing LegalTech environment at
      Swansea University was provided by Chris Marshall, Director of Knowledge Economy at the Hillary Rodham Clinton
      School of Law, in his submission to the Commission on Justice in Wales in 2018, available at https://gov.wales/
      sites/default/files/publications/2018–12/Submission%20to%20the%20Justice%20Commission%20from%20Swansea
      %20Law%20School.pdf.

C. LEGALTECH AS AN ACADEMIC SUBJECT

24.010 Having reviewed, at least summarily, some of the current experiences of LegalTech education, it is now appropriate to reflect on its pedagogical underpinnings. The variety of approaches discussed above clearly suggests that LegalTech represents a fundamental challenge to the way in which legal education traditionally operates: it requires the mastering of knowledge and skills not normally included in the law school curriculum[16] (in particular, knowledge of a wide range of technologies and skills in coding, entrepreneurship, and so on) and prompts the development of a mindset that abstracts from specific legal cases to identify generic legal issues that can be solved through the application of technology, in a manner that is intended, at least in some cases, to be commercial in nature. The challenging nature of LegalTech education, in this sense, extends to the availability of staff with such a wide range of expertise; to the design of learning that supports the students in uncharted territory; to the flawless execution of interdisciplinary collaborations; to the availability of a suitable research and entrepreneurial environment; to the use of innovative teaching methodologies; to the formation of suitable collaborations with the industry; and to the inclusion of other subjects, such as ethics and intellectual property, that appear essential to complement entrepreneurial and technical skills.

24.011 The breadth of LegalTech, explored in detail elsewhere in this book, clearly suggests that it cannot be considered a traditional, self-contained, academic subject. It is not an area of law *per se*, nor a mere skillset: rather, it is an evolving amalgamation of skills and knowledge that is both applicative and notional in nature. The latter aspect, the notionality of LegalTech, comprises the knowledge that a legal technologist is expected to acquire, in particular in relation to the legal frameworks applicable to the relevant technologies, as well as to coding, leadership and management. The former aspect, the applicative nature of LegalTech pedagogy, focuses on learning opportunities that allow the student to develop prototype LegalTech solutions, investigate new technologies not currently subject to legal regulation and experiment with the ideation of commercial ventures in the LegalTech domain. Interestingly, these aspects do not correspond to the traditional view of law applied to technology and technology applied to law:[17] both areas need a notional and applicative approach. For example, students exploring the potential use of blockchain in LegalTech (technology applied to law) need to understand the technical foundations and principles of this technology (the notional aspect) and to be able to explore potential use cases and develop prototypes and proofs of concept (the applicative aspect). When approaching the legal regulation of blockchain (law applied to technology), students should familiarise themselves with the regulatory framework that is slowly coalescing around this technology (the notional aspect) and use this knowledge to predict and influence the evolution of this framework (the applicative aspect). Needless to say, all these distinctions

---

16   See, *ex multis*, W. Schäfke-Zell and I.H. Asmussen, 'The Legal Profession in the Age of Digitalisation', (2019) 15(1) Utrecht Law Review 65, proposing three pathways to determine the core competences of future lawyers; S. Canick, 'Infusing Technology Skills into the Law School Curriculum', (2014) 42 Capital University Law Review 663, revisiting the role of technological competences; M. Legg, 'New Skills for New Lawyers: Responding to Technology and Practice Developments' in *The Future of Australian Legal Education* (Thomson Reuters 2018) [2018] UNSWLRS 51, emphasising the soft skills required from new generations of lawyers, including resilience and emotional intelligence.

17   Cf. A Wyner, 'LegalTech Education – Considerations for Regulators', available at www.legalservicesboard.org.uk/wp-content/uploads/2020/05/Topic-5-Dr-Adam-Wyner-LegalTech-Education.pdf, footnote 3.

feel quite artificial: knowledge of regulations and technologies is of little relevance when devoid of application to new use cases and scenarios.[18]

Inspiration for a LegalTech pedagogy is more easily derived from the experience of law degrees than from individual courses. Law degrees seek to develop professionals from the ground up, ensuring that they possess not only the necessary academic knowledge or the relevant legal skills, but also a responsible and competent attitude.[19] Of course, whether this aspiration truly succeeds is another question. **24.012**

Much like a law degree, a LegalTech pedagogy requires educators to design a learning journey that is as comprehensive and learner-centred as possible.[20] In this sense, it becomes apparent that the first requirement for a LegalTech pedagogy is *time*: insights from educational theory[21] and neuroscience[22] suggest that the mastery of a complex array of theoretical and practical skills, across an interdisciplinary domain, requires a structured learning journey that develops over a substantial period of time. Current educational offerings are designed to fit predetermined time periods (for example, one year for a LLM programme, one or two semesters for a course, three years for a qualifying law degree) and offer a starting point to determine the appropriate length of time needed for an effective LegalTech tuition. However, a number of additional factors warrant more in-depth examination: **24.013**

(a)   The type of cohort and characteristics of learners.
(b)   The familiarity of the learners with (i) the subject-matter of the curriculum and (ii) the learning skills necessary to approach it.

---

18   B. Schneier discusses similar considerations in 'We Must Bridge the Gap between Technology and Policymaking. Our Future Depends on It' (12 November 2019) World Economic Forum, available at www.weforum.org/agenda/2019/11/we-must-bridge-the-gap-between-technology-and-policy-our-future-depends-on-it/. Recent developments, such as antitrust enquiries into the app stores provided by Apple and Google or inconsistent approaches to the validity and enforceability of smart contracts, suggest that more collaboration between policy-makers and technologists is needed (for a similar argument, see E. Dreyfuss, 'The US Government Isn't Just Tech-Illiterate. It's Tech-Incompetent' (5 November 2017) Wired, available at www.wired.com/2017/05/real-threat-government-tech-illiteracy/).

19   A broad corpus of research has explored these aspects, focusing, for example, on the grit and growth mindset (M. Bess, 'Grit, Growth Mindset, and the Path to Successful Lawyering', (forthcoming) 89 UMKC Law Review, available at https://papers.ssrn.com/sol3/papers.cfm?abstract_id=3458632), on experiential learning leading to professional responsibility (A. Thanaraj, 'Understanding How a Law Clinic Can Contribute towards Students' Development of Professional Responsibility', (2016) 23(4) International Journal of Clinical Education 89), on the acquisition of skills and values for responsible lawyering (R. MacCrate, 'Preparing Lawyers to Participate Effectively in the Legal Profession', (1994) 44(1) Journal of Legal Education 89; also R. Hyams, 'On Teaching Students to "Act Like a Lawyer": What Sort of Lawyer?', (2008) 13 Journal of Clinical Legal Education 21).

20   See M. Weimer, *Learner-Centered Teaching: Five Key Changes to Practice* (Jossey-Bass 2013, 2nd edition), who identified five aspects leading to learner-centred teaching, including the balance of power, the function of content, the role of teachers, the responsibility for learning and the process of evaluation. G.B. Wright reflected on these aspects in 'Student-Centered Learning in Higher Education', (2011) 23(3) International Journal of Teaching and Learning in Higher Education 92.

21   For example, in relation to the combination of theory and practice in the learning process, see J. Wrenn and B. Wrenn, 'Enhancing Learning by Integrating Theory and Practice', (2009) 21(2) International Journal of Teaching and Learning in Higher Education 258. The seminal work in the field, which detailed the learning process in depth, is Bloom's taxonomy: B. Bloom et al., *Taxonomy of Educational Objectives: The Cognitive Domain* (McKay 1956).

22   A valuable resource for readers interested in neuroscientific insights into learning is Efrat Furst's 'Teaching with learning in mind' blog (https://sites.google.com/view/efratfurst/teaching-with-learning-in-mind). As a starting point, see U. Goswami, 'Neuroscience and Education: From Research to Practice?', (2006) 7 Nature Reviews Neuroscience 406.

(c)   The availability of learning opportunities designed to enhance the acquisition of entre-preneurial skills (such as project assessments, groupwork, internships, and so on).

(d)   The personal development of the learner, insofar as a LegalTech pedagogy requires the formation of an ethical and responsible approach to the technology.

24.014 These are only some of the relevant factors, but they already pose challenging questions. The favoured approach, in higher education institutions, revolves around a one-year postgraduate degree (LLM or equivalent): is this length of time sufficient to fully develop a LegalTech professional? Is it possible to provide adequate learning opportunities for the development of entrepreneurial skills during this time? Does it allow a learner to master issues across the domains of ethics, policy-making and responsible use of technology? Does it cater to the needs of students with different backgrounds or at different stages of their careers?

24.015 A second factor that assumes primary importance in the construction of a LegalTech pedagogy is *breadth* – the breadth of the curriculum, but also the breadth of the teaching methodologies, of the experiences offered to students, of the skills created, of the diversity of learning opportunities, of the resources available and of other aspects of the educational offering. A full list is probably beside the point, as it is the principle that is of primary importance here: a suitable pedagogical approach should respect the complexity and richness of the academic subject it concerns. This book illustrates the complexity and richness of LegalTech, its connections with neighbouring subjects like computer science and management, its reflections on legal practice and policy-making, its entrepreneurial dimension and more – a suitable pedagogy needs to echo this breadth and help students assimilate it. Some of the key dimensions of this breadth include:

(a)   Introducing students to relevant computer science concepts and principles, including computational thinking, coding and management of the developmental process; providing suitable opportunities for the students to acquire terminological competence, practical experience and collaboration skills.

(b)   Providing a suitable introduction to data science and to technologies of primary importance in LegalTech, offering chances to reflect on their potential impact on legal practice.

(c)   Emphasising the acquisition of management and leadership skills, through groupwork, internships and other learning occasions that offer support and validation in a real-life context.

(d)   Exploring the regulatory frameworks with a comparative approach, encouraging active engagement with it and the acquisition of a policy-making attitude.

(e)   Keeping students updated on changes in the technological landscape as well as in the regulatory one; training them to react suitably to normative and technological change.

(f)   Raising awareness of the ethical issues involved in the use of technology in the legal sector; promoting a responsible attitude towards LegalTech.

(g)   Promoting interdisciplinary collaborations, academia-industry collaborations, entrepreneurial initiatives and involvement in research.

(h)   Adopting a wide range of teaching methodologies, such as flipped learning, scenario-based teaching, laboratory work, simulations and more, involving practitioners, professionals and policy-makers.

(i)   Providing a variety of assessment methods that give learners the opportunity to apply their newly acquired skills to a range of real-life situations.

Breadth, therefore, subsumes additional characteristics of a LegalTech pedagogy, including **24.016**
collaboration,[23] *interdisciplinarity* and *applicability*.

A reflection on LegalTech pedagogy cannot fail to acknowledge that the most crucial question **24.017**
concerns the *mindset* that learners should acquire throughout their studies. Some components of this mindset have already been discussed: the ability to cope with entrepreneurship,
interdisciplinarity and collaborations, for example. But there are some additional important
aspects, which include flexibility, openness, sharing, ingenuity, intellectual curiosity and sense
of responsibility.

A future legal technologist enters a field in which, contrary to expectations, questions are not **24.018**
only more readily available than answers, but also more valuable. Technologies evolve, disappear or suddenly come into play; in parallel, their use and regulation evolve at the same time.
Thus, flexibility means the ability to react suitably to such changes, but also to abstract from
technology-specific teaching to be able to autonomously apply relevant principles to new or
updated technologies in the future.

With some notable exceptions, openness does not readily describe the mindset of the legal **24.019**
industry, which has been portrayed as more conservative and protective, especially where much
of the value of the product (legal advice, for example) is intellectual in nature.[24] LegalTech,
however, challenges future legal technologists to embrace a more open and collaborative
approach. In part this is a factor imported from the technology sphere, which may require
openness as a condition for using certain tools and instruments that have been developed in
open source or academic environments, as a necessity for gaining access to complex, expensive
or unscalable technologies that no law firm or start-up can put to use individually, or even as
a technical requirement for a technology to be effectively deployed (such as a blockchain-based
platform, for which openness becomes synonymous with trust). But openness may also be
a market requirement, increasing accessibility and market opportunities (for example, the same
blockchain platform above may greatly benefit from becoming an industry standard, relying on
openness as a way to acquire *de facto* prominence in the market), may be required as a condition for operating in the legal space (for example, in the fields of digital justice or distributed
autonomous organisations operating as online courts) or may be mandated as a consequence of
dominance in the market, under competition law. Perhaps even more importantly, openness
can be an ethical imperative, for improving access to justice, protecting human rights or preventing abusive or criminal conduct.

In this perspective, sharing acquires multiple meanings. It is a reflection of openness, in terms **24.020**
of sharing source code, solutions, approaches, if not final products in some of the cases highlighted above – with the caveat, of course, that openness and sharing need to be reconciled with
intellectual property law and other frameworks protecting trade secrets and confidential infor-

---

23   Collaboration has long been recognised as a key feature of a suitable legal pedagogy: S. Bryant, 'Collaborating in Law
     Practice: A Satisfying and Productive Process for a Diverse Profession', (1993) 17 Vermont Law Review 459.
24   Despite its pedagogical importance, the legal sector has traditionally lagged in embracing collaboration. According to
     M.A. Cohen, 'The Legal Industry Is Starting to Collaborate – Why Now and Why It Matters' (22 July 2019) Forbes,
     available at www.forbes.com/sites/markcohen1/2019/07/22/the-legal-industry-is-starting-to-collaborate-why-now-and
     -why-it-matters/#6d8174ae343d, however, the tide is finally turning.

mation. However, sharing may also refer to knowledge, skills and experiences – in other terms, to the intangible heritage that will progressively form as LegalTech evolves. A willingness to partake in the formation, sharing and transmission of this heritage is a commitment not only to the development of LegalTech, but also to the development of future generations of legal technologists; thus, it is among the chief characteristics that an ideal pedagogy should seek to foster in a learner.

24.021　Ingenuity and intellectual curiosity echo both the entrepreneurial, applicative, empirical dimension of LegalTech and its current state as a fast-evolving field. They suggest that legal technologists should not be passive recipients of information, but seekers of knowledge, experimenters, pioneers and, to an extent, also failers, questioners and critics. From a pedagogical point of view, LegalTech learners should develop autonomy, independence and a level of practical ingenuity that is more common in other academic domains than in law. Failure is also a natural consequence of ingenuity and intellectual curiosity, and one that learners typically struggle with: an ideal LegalTech pedagogy needs to acknowledge the risk of failing and accustom learners to failure as part of the development of a legal technologist.

24.022　Finally, the acquisition of a sense of responsibility is, perhaps, one of the most important aspects in the construction of a suitable pedagogy. This concept goes beyond, and incorporates, the ethical concerns arising, *inter alia*, from the use of technology and data. It stretches to comprise an understanding of the effects of the LegalTech solutions developed, of their impact on different categories of stakeholders, of their socio-economic relevance, of their potential for enhancing justice and human rights, of the risk of misuse or abuse, of their predicted lifecycle and obsolescence, of their market dynamics and more. This sense of responsibility should also be towards the legal technologist herself, as the transformative, powerful, potential of LegalTech may subject her to undue pressures or influences.

24.023　In summary, the prospect of a pedagogical approach that provides sufficient *time* to experience the full *breadth* of LegalTech, in terms of knowledge and skills but also of *collaboration, interdisciplinarity* and *applicability*, seems to be a sensible way to foster the development of legal technologists with a *mindset* that is as open, ingenious and responsible as possible.

24.024　The following sections propose some thematic considerations across four dimensions: interdisciplinarity, entrepreneurship, policy-making and ethics.

D. THE INTERDISCIPLINARY DIMENSION

24.025　Since the inception of the LegalTech movement, interdisciplinarity has been a keyword closely associated to it, with different connotations.[25] At one end of the spectrum, it has raised ques-

---

25　The literature on collaborations is extensive. Some recommended readings include J.C. Gooch, 'The Dynamics and Challenges of Interdisciplinary Collaboration', (2005) 48(2) IEEE Transactions on Professional Communication 177; V. Boix Mansilla, M. Lamont and K. Sato, 'The Contributions of Shared Socio-emotional-cognitive Platforms to Interdisciplinary Synthesis', paper presented at 4S Annual Meeting, Vancouver, Canada, 16–20 February 2012, available at http://nrs.harvard.edu/urn-3:HUL.InstRepos:10496300; M. MacLeod, 'What Makes Interdisciplinarity Difficult? Some Consequences of Domain Specificity in Interdisciplinary Practice', (2018) 195 Synthese 697. On collaborations between

tions as to the availability of qualified resources, the extent of the investments required to gain expertise in non-legal domains, the effectiveness of collaborations and leadership, the potential informational asymmetry and communication barriers. At the other end, it has raised the prospect of a renewed approach to legal thinking, of previously unavailable commercial opportunities, of increased service integration and administrative efficiencies, of cost savings and of a wide-scale enablement of next generation legal services. But what about interdisciplinarity in an educational context?

Taking collaborations between law and computer science as the reference point, the main **24.026** challenge of interdisciplinarity appears to be a communicative one. A first hurdle is the different approach of lawyers and computer scientists towards problems requiring a solution: it is probably common experience that, while lawyers generally focus on unbundling the complexity of the problem and appreciating all of its meanders, computer scientists more easily concentrate their attention on the solutions and exhibit more immediate decision-making skills. Of course, neither of them ignores the solution or the problem, but places a different emphasis on each, at different stages of the thinking process.

A second communicative hurdle is to be found in the self-referential nature of the legal dis- **24.027** course.[26] In fact, while lawyering has traditionally limited its reliance on other subjects (but not completely eschewed it, relying, for example, on economists for calculating damages or royalties, on various professionals as expert witnesses, and so on), computer science has an inherent enabling role that requires a constant joining up of disciplines and expertise. In the field of LegalTech, this may result in misunderstandings as to the role of lawyers and computer scientists and may hinder effective collaboration where one crosses excessively into the domain of the other, or refuses to cross that boundary at all. For example, tensions may arise where a lawyer interferes with technological choices to the extent of ignoring or distorting the advice received, or where a computer scientist refuses any engagement with the legal issue to be addressed, providing a mere technical competence that does not allow a lawyer to comprehend the benefits of the proposed solution.

A third hurdle relates to the nature of the communication, which appears more nuanced **24.028** and indirect among lawyers[27] and more clear and direct among computer scientists.[28] In an

---

humanities and science, see M. Willis et al., 'Humanities and Science Collaboration Isn't Well Understood, but Letting Off STEAM Is Not the Answer' (26 March 2018) The Conversation, available at https://theconversation.com/humanities-and -science-collaboration-isnt-well-understood-but-letting-off-steam-is-not-the-answer-92146; R.A. Blythe and W. Croft, 'Can a Science–Humanities Collaboration Be Successful?', (2010) 18(1) Adaptive Behavior 12.

26 A partly similar line of reasoning, in relation to social sciences more generally, is found in J.M. Lewis, 'Barriers to Research Collaboration: Are Social Scientists Constrained by their Desire for Autonomy?' (17 October 2017) LSE Blog, available at https://blogs.lse.ac.uk/impactofsocialsciences/2017/10/17/barriers-to-research-collaboration-are-social-scientists-constrained -by-their-desire-for-autonomy/.

27 Some reasons for this stem from the development of linguistic conventions and rules, for lawyers, meant to be used for the purpose of persuasion. In the words of W. Probert ('Law and persuasion: the language-behavior of lawyers', (1959) 108 University of Pennsylvania Law Review 35): 'legal language becomes something other than a matter of logic, yet something more than oratory'. To the extent that legal language becomes the default linguistic approach of lawyers, these words explain the anecdotal complexity suggested here.

28 An example to illustrate this point is provided by L. Blume et al., 'A "Communication Skills for Computer Scientists" Course' (August 2009) ACM SIGCSE Bulletin, DOI: 10.1145/1562877.1562903, available at www.researchgate.net/

interdisciplinary environment,[29] unless there is an appropriate understanding of this different communicative approach, it is possible that computer scientists may perceive communication in the legal domain as complex, inefficient or inconclusive, and that lawyers may perceive communication in the computer science domain as impersonal, inopportune or insensitive. More importantly, both may read implicit meaning in each other's communicative style, leading to misunderstandings and potentially conflicting or inefficient work relationships.

24.029 These dynamics affect educators, learners and professionals in similar ways. A law student may struggle to cope with the fast, seemingly simplified or direct teaching style of a computer scientist educator; a computer science student may find a law-focused LegalTech class daunting, confusing or devoid of clear answers and directions. Similarly, a law student may perceive the directness of a computer science instructor as a lack of interest in her work or in her development as a student; a computer science student may take a complex answer from a legal educator as an attempt to evade a challenging question.

24.030 From a pedagogical point of view, the establishment of a common understanding surrounding any interdisciplinary work is of the essence. The integration of staff with different expertise on a level of parity, the balancing of different approaches within the curriculum, the introduction of the whole teaching team to students as a coherent ensemble can help foster better interdisciplinary collaboration at programme level. Another extremely effective instrument is co-teaching,[30] which breaches communicative barriers in the classroom. Rendering the communicative asymmetries explicit, and providing an explanation of the reasons behind them, is also of great importance.

24.031 The communicative hurdles are, generally, more impactful than the knowledge-based ones. However, it is indisputable that the lack of a minimum level of subject expertise in an unrelated discipline, such as law or computer science, constitutes a substantial barrier to entry in the learning journey. In this sense, once the communicative issue has been properly addressed it becomes essential to support the learning journey with a variety of means, including co-teaching, use of examples and scenarios that are already familiar to the students, introductions to subject-specific terminology, flipped-classroom experiments, mixed group seminars (involving students from different disciplines), empirical learning and a constant effort to explain the thinking and rationale behind discipline-specific approaches, as suggested above.

24.032 A final consideration on the interdisciplinary dimension concerns a frequently neglected aspect, that of employability skills and career development prospects. The pedagogical approach sketched above aims at forming professional figures that have unique interdisciplinary competences and abilities. Such figures are relatively rare on the current job market, although their

---

publication/220808176_A_Communication_Skills_for_Computer_Scientists_Course. The authors describe their experience of the communicative skills of computer science students and propose training that emphasises clarity and directness.

29 Cf. M. Monteiro, E. Keating, 'Managing Misunderstandings: The Role of Language in Interdisciplinary Scientific Collaboration', (2009) 31(1) Science Communication 6.

30 Some interesting reflections on the topic can be found in E.M. Henley and S.E. Cook, 'Lessons from Designing a Co-taught Interdisciplinary Course', available at http://sites.bu.edu/impact/previous-issues/impact-winter-2018/lessons-from-designing-a-co-taught-interdisciplinary-course/. See also, with a focus on the beneficial effects of co-teaching for students, A. Little and A. Hoel, 'Interdisciplinary Team Teaching: An Effective Method to Transform Student Attitudes', (2011) 11(1) The Journal of Effective Teaching 36.

presence is constantly increasing, and the employability skills that they need to possess should be accurately evaluated to allow learners to maximise their employment opportunities. This is, of course, not only an educational concern; rather, it is a reflection that the whole LegalTech industry needs to openly make, in order to recognise the specific skillset that these new professional figures possess and to value it appropriately.[31]

E. THE ENTREPRENEURIAL DIMENSION

The pedagogical questions on the teaching of entrepreneurial skills have been the subject of ample academic debate.[32] However, the LegalTech industry exhibits a number of peculiarities that warrant some further discussion.   **24.033**

The prevalence of start-ups and the disruptive potential of LegalTech in terms of automatisation and digitalisation emphasise the need to approach the subject with commercial awareness and with an inventive, entrepreneurial spirit. Entrepreneurship, in this sense, comprises not only the more structural aspects, such as costs, resources, predicted revenues, business structure, shares and so on, but also all those acts which are merely propaedeutic to commercialisation, including pitching an idea, prototyping, conducting investment rounds, securing and allocating intellectual property rights, branding, pricing and market penetration strategies, market studies and analysis. LegalTech programmes should adopt a wide range of teaching methodologies to cover the breadth of this notion of entrepreneurship, creating learning opportunities that offer ample chances to practice newly acquired skills. Arguably, the importance of the second category of skills outweighs that of the structural aspects: would a legal technologist be better served by soft skills that allow her to confidently and effectively pitch an idea with commercial acumen and awareness or by hard skills that parallel those of accountants and advisors? The question, of course, remains valid if the viewpoint changes: what skills would better serve the development of LegalTech?   **24.034**

It is important to note, however, that start-ups do not exhaust the entire landscape of LegalTech. In-house LegalTech solutions are increasingly being developed,[33] either as standalone ventures or as internal projects within law firms and other organisations: it is therefore   **24.035**

---

31   To gain an immediate understanding of this point, it is sufficient to carry out a search for LegalTech jobs on common search engines and job platforms. A search carried out at the time of writing, in September 2020, returned a list of job titles including data scientist, legal solutions specialist, legal engineer, legal operations manager, data analyst, legal solutions architect and technology advisor. All these job advertisements required a degree in computer science or related fields, making no explicit allowance for legal technologists who may have a different background.

32   Some introductory readings include G. Linton and M. Klinton, 'University Entrepreneurship Education: A Design Thinking Approach to Learning', (2019) 8(3) Journal of Innovation and Entrepreneurship; C. Mason and N. Arshed, 'Teaching Entrepreneurship to University Students through Experiential Learning: A Case Study', (2013) 27(6) Industry and Higher Education 449; C. Carrier, 'Strategies for Teaching Entrepreneurship: What Else beyond Lectures, Case Studies and Business Plans?' in A. Fayolle (ed.), *Handbook of Research in Entrepreneurship Education*, vol. 1 (Edward Elgar Publishing 2007).

33   Linklaters, to borrow an example already made above, created an internal LegalTech team tasked not only with the provision of LegalTech training within the firm, but also with the development of LegalTech solutions responding to needs arising from Linklaters' legal services (www.linklaters.com/en/about-us/innovation). Other law firms have complemented in-house teams with acquisitions, as did Simmons & Simmons with the acquisition of Wavelength (www .wavelength.law/blog/someexcitingnews).

essential that future legal technologists learn about entrepreneurship also in these contexts. Here entrepreneurship means, first of all, the adoption of a propositive, active, engaged attitude, accompanied by the ability to work in teams, to collaborate with colleagues from other areas and departments and to develop a more rigidly structured programme of work. Further, entrepreneurship in this context requires an appreciation of the cost–benefit balance, of available resources and future development plans, of internal efficiencies and externalities – in short, of all those pre-existing conditions that inevitably influence more commercially minded developments.

24.036   Acquiring and training entrepreneurship skills across these two complementary, but partly divergent, definitions requires suitable learning opportunities, which can take the form of projects, supported by legal laboratories, internal competitions or funded entrepreneurship prizes and incentives, for the start-up entrepreneurship, as well as of internships and placements within existing LegalTech teams in law firms and other organisations for in-house entrepreneurship.

24.037   Some space within the entrepreneurship discourse should also be dedicated to the concepts of corporate social responsibility, protection of the environment, employee rights, consumer rights and other categories of rights and responsibilities. Incorporating these concepts within entrepreneurship training in LegalTech ensures a harmonic and responsive development of the industry, right from its inception.

F. THE POLICY-MAKING DIMENSION

24.038   More neglected, but of great importance, is the issue of policy-making.[34] Contrary to other areas of law, where the regulation has reached a level of maturity and stability, LegalTech has a more tentative, developing and scattered normative background. Furthermore, such background is naturally destined to experience significant changes and adjustments as new technologies become available. In this context, a LegalTech pedagogy should take the policy-making dimension into account, offering learners a chance to acquire the skills needed to influence, and participate in, the policy-making processes.

24.039   Inspiration to achieve this objective is offered by the traditional teaching approach of civil law jurisdictions,[35] which places strong emphasis on the theoretical underpinnings of legal regulations, analysed in terms of general principles and structural role within a corpus of law. In fact, discussing the background that has led legislators to adopt a specific normative position,

---

34   Research on teaching policy-making skills to law students is mostly focused on classroom experiences: in this sense, the experience of B.E. Berkman and K.H. Rothenberg, discussed in 'Teaching Law Students to Be Policymakers: The Health and Science Policy Workshop on Genomic Research', (2012) 40(1) Journal of Law and Medical Ethics 147, is an excellent starting point.

35   Some of these differences are illustrated, from an academic point of view, in J.H. Merryman, 'Legal Education There and Here: A Comparison', (1975) 27(3) Stanford Law Review 859 and in H. Whalen-Bridge, 'The Reluctant Comparativist: Teaching Common Law Reasoning to Civil Law Students and the Future of Comparative Legal Skills', (2008) 58(3) Journal of Legal Education 364; for a student perspective, see D. Becker, 'Studying Law Without the Socratic Method' (21 May 2013) Marquette University Law School Faculty Blog, available at https://law.marquette.edu/facultyblog/2013/05/studying-law-without-the-socratic-method/.

the pros and cons of such a decision and the potential alternatives already offers students the opportunity to reflect upon the policy-making process and to abstract principles and processes that can be applied to future policy-making.

The interdisciplinarity of LegalTech programmes also offers a particularly valuable vantage point through which learners can assess the best forms of regulation for specific types of technology, exploiting the expertise gained in both the legal and the technological domains. Similarly, the entrepreneurial skills acquired allow that assessment to also take into account the impact of existing or potential regulations on actual use cases and on the LegalTech market. While all of these perspectives are represented, in various ways, within policy-making processes, legal technologists find themselves in a fairly unique position to provide a wide-ranging contribution to the development of regulatory frameworks for LegalTech.   **24.040**

To this aim, the involvement of policy-makers as guest lecturers, visiting staff or speakers at conferences and seminars should be a routine experience in LegalTech programmes. Practical policy-making exercises, which may include mock committee work and drafting attempts (in relation to legislation as well as supporting documents, such as reports and policy recommendations), should play an equally important role. Comparative exercises, simulations and guided debates could offer additional chances for the students to understand the intricacies of policy-making and to investigate alternative forms and means of regulation.   **24.041**

Policy-making institutions should also be incentivised to offer internships and other opportunities to allow LegalTech learners to familiarise with, and support, the policy-making process.   **24.042**

G. THE ETHICAL DIMENSION

The final mention, and substantial reflection, should be given to the ethical dimension. Ethics, in law and technology, may have plural meanings, referring to standards of professional conduct, to auto- or etero-determined rules of morality or to a more generic sense of responsibility. At its core, ethics calls into play the concept of justice,[36] which is inextricably linked with a wide range of questions concerning morality, fairness, fundamental rights and personal responsibility.   **24.043**

In the technology space ethical debates abound, especially in relation to the deployment of technologies that may have a substantial impact on the way we live, work or behave. LegalTech makes no exception and presents key ethical debates right at the outset. The analysis of judicial decisions may lead to forum shopping,[37] but unearth hidden bias and lead to more pondered, and better justified, decisions. The application of machine learning to big data repositories may increase efficiency and lower the cost of legal services, but it may limit access to tailored legal   **24.044**

---

36   Indeed, the two concepts are closely interwoven in Aristotle's *Nicomachean Ethics*, which conceived justice as a virtue of character and distinguished 'general' from 'particular' justice.

37   This is the view taken in some jurisdictions, like France, which recently introduced legislation that prevents analytics that takes into account the identity of magistrates and members of the judiciary (see 'France Bans Judge Analytics, 5 Years In Prison For Rule Breakers' (4 June 2019) Artificial Lawyer, available at www.artificiallawyer.com/2019/06/04/france -bans-judge-analytics-5-years-in-prison-for-rule-breakers/).

advice, adversely affect the assertion of rights, or misuse or misidentify personal information. The use of automatic systems to review massive amounts of digital evidence may render trials more efficient and cost-effective, but may increase the risk of injustice or mistrial, especially for clients from disadvantaged backgrounds.

24.045 In other disciplines, notably medicine,[38] ethical debates form a routine part of the pedagogical model. A similar approach is needed in LegalTech, to ensure that an assessment of ethical concerns becomes a natural step in the legal technologist's routine. In parallel, learners should be encouraged to play an active role in the formation of standards of professional conducts in the field: the application of standards designed for related disciplines appears unsatisfactory and may lead to complacency and disengagement.

24.046 It is worth remembering that the transformative potential of LegalTech is not just commercial in nature: its impact on access to justice, for example, can be extremely disruptive and beneficial.[39] In this perspective ethical considerations do not merely focus on the use or regulation of technology, but extend to the use or regulation of products and services, as well as to the conditions at which they are made available to the public. Thus, any entrepreneurial consideration needs to be tempered with an ethical assessment, which may influence strategic market decisions.

24.047 Finally, ethics applies also to the choice of, and organisational approach to, technologies, calling for an introduction to concepts such as responsible artificial intelligence[40] and ethical tech.

H. CONTINUING PROFESSIONAL DEVELOPMENT AND THE DESIGN OF TRAINING FOR LAWYERS

24.048 The point of view taken in the previous sections has focused on higher education, although the pedagogical approach outlined is equally applicable to training programmes provided by other organisations or in-house within law firms. A few differences, however, should be examined with more attention.[41]

24.049 Universities provide a unique expertise in the research domain, accompanied by a focus on pedagogy, teaching methodologies, learning skills and academic support. Other organisations, including law firms, present different strengths, which normally include a more practical approach to learning, real-life experience, stronger industry links, increased resources and organisational support, and others. It appears evident that the most appropriate course of action is cooperation between the two types of organisations, to ensure that LegalTech training is as

---

38   L. Doyal and R. Gillon, 'Medical Ethics and Law as a Core Subject in Medical Education', (1998) 316(7145) BMJ 1623.

39   A comprehensive review of this point is provided by J.E. Cabral et al., 'Using Technology to Enhance Access to Justice', (2012) 26(1) Harvard Journal of Law & Technology 243.

40   Cf. V. Dignum, *Responsible Artificial Intelligence* (Springer 2009).

41   Some interesting perspectives can be found in L.L. Lorenzo and M. Roellig, 'Training the Modern In-house Lawyer', (November 2015) PD Quarterly 30, available at www.lcldnet.org/media/uploads/resource/PDQ_Lorenzo_Roellig.pdf, and J. Wood, 'Education, Education, Education', (Autumn 2017) IHL, available at www.inhouselawyer.co.uk/feature/education-education-education/.

comprehensive and varied as possible. Some experiences, such as the collaboration between Swansea University and Linklaters for the design of LegalTech in-house training, have already followed this approach.

A first consideration should focus, once again, on time and breadth. The temptation to con-   **24.050**
dense LegalTech training into fast-paced, short-term, educational experiences, and to reduce its breadth to fit it within busy schedules and tailor it to existing client needs, is understandable. But the trade-off may not be worth it: rolling out a basic level of LegalTech training may achieve the objective of raising awareness of new technologies and of their impact on the legal services offered by an organisation, but inevitably fails in developing legal technologists with the appropriate mindset and skillset. A more suitable approach, at least for a subset of personnel, would be the identification of alternative arrangements or educational paths that do not sacrifice either the time needed for, or the breadth of, pedagogically appropriate LegalTech training.

A second consideration revolves around the career significance of LegalTech training. For   **24.051**
a professional, access to LegalTech education may pose a threat to their existing expertise and role, due to the toll taken on time, career progression and focus. The LegalTech pedagogy envisioned in this chapter suggests that the learner should be committed to a significant investment, in terms of engagement, attitude and learning, in the field. This requires a careful assessment of the motivations of professionals undertaking LegalTech training and, inevitably, the availability of suitable organisational support for the learners. Thus, two learning paths should be delineated: one that offers LegalTech orientation and basic awareness training, with the recognition that such an approach does not equate to the formation of legal technologists, and another that offers a pedagogically compliant educative path, with the aim of forming legal technologists who will transition their careers towards this domain.

Other considerations concern the risk that certain forms of learning opportunities may be   **24.052**
lacking within these organisations, such as research-based teaching and interdisciplinary collaborations. Once again, a suitable solution would be the development of collaborations between industry organisation and academic institutions.[42] This approach allows useful cross-fertilisation between research and practice, exploits the interdisciplinary environment of higher education institutions and the highly specialised, experienced environment of industry organisations, confers efficiency and structure to learning programmes without sacrificing mindset-focused learning opportunities, embraces transformative assessment and teaching methodologies, and allows space for policy-making, entrepreneurship and ethical considerations that industry organisations may view, in the short term, as having secondary importance.

---

42   A good reference point, albeit in the field of intellectual property law, is offered by the Postgraduate Diploma in Intellectual Property Law and Practice offered in collaboration between the University of Oxford and the Intellectual Property Lawyers' Association (see www.law.ox.ac.uk/programme/postgraduate-diploma-intellectual-property-law-and -practice). The programme is designed to fit professional needs, in terms of time constraints, involvement of practitioners and academics as teachers, choice of content and mode of delivery.

I. CONCLUSION

24.053   This chapter has provided a series of questions, recommendations and guidelines that aim to establish the foundations of a LegalTech pedagogy capable of forming competent, skilled, creative and responsible legal technologists. It has embraced the transformative potential of LegalTech and emphasised the need to translate this potential into a suitably comprehensive, ambitious and cutting-edge training programme. In doing so, it has taken a view that may partly conflict with the existing academic and industry offering, which is challenged by resources, time constraints and the need to pursue short-term objectives.

24.054   A pedagogy, in terms of its content and method, plays a crucial role in influencing the development of a domain of knowledge: the students of today are the professionals of tomorrow – in this case, the creators of future LegalTech solutions, the funders of future start-ups, the drafters of future regulations and the future partners of law firms that will, most likely, provide legal services profoundly transformed by LegalTech. This is the reason why the pedagogical view offered in this chapter has embraced a comprehensive and ambitious approach: to ensure that LegalTech realises its transformational potential, we need an educational environment that embraces the same values and approach.

24.055   The next few years will be a defining period for the development of LegalTech education: success in this field will be measured by our ability, as academics and professionals, to design together a series of complementary educational programmes that put interdisciplinarity and collaboration in the spotlight, that cultivate values of openness and responsibility and that foster an entrepreneurial spirit that never loses sight of the implications of LegalTech for society, economy and, above all, justice.

PART V

TECHNICAL AND CONSULTING

25

TAXONOMY OF AI

Tirath Virdee, Doug Brown, Scott Stainton and Shaun Barney

A. INTRODUCTION

25.001 Data (through measurements and estimations) has always been crucial in calculating and predicting things. In the past, data was sparse, and one would use mathematical formulae and/or statistical techniques to make predictions. With the rise of big data, data alone is sufficient to enable appropriate predictions and estimations to be made. This, in combination with an exponential rise in computational power, has brought together the possibilities of consuming big data at scale, at speed and in a way that enables contextualisation and personalisation. In addition, it has allowed data to be collected, harvested and repurposed for collective insights. Big data enables a type of intelligence that, in the past, was only possible with biological brains. Now it is possible in digital machines and it is a subdomain of a field of computer science called AI.

This chapter will cover the taxonomy of AI (by looking at various paradigms and abstractions) **25.002** and the components of intelligent systems (through an innovative AI Periodic Table), and hopefully remove some of the confusion related to the relevant terminology.

To understand the taxonomy of AI and the lexicons, one needs to visit the basics. AI, Machine **25.003** Learning (ML) and Deep Learning Neural Networks (DNN) are used by different people in different ways. The terms are used improperly and in many cases without any reference to what they mean. The purpose of this chapter is to give the reader some of the basic foundations so that the terms can be used in the intended ways.

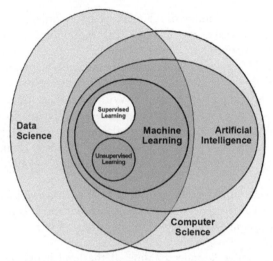

Source: This chart is so popular that it is hard to trace its source. Credit at this stage will be given to A. Wahid (gleetech) with recolouring by SMU.

Figure 25.1   Relationship between AI, computer science and data science

The problem with many technical terms is that they keep evolving and they keep on being over- **25.004** loaded. AI is constantly redefined as if to confine the concept to the leading edge of technology or beyond, in uncharted or unproven territories – in other words, to what has not been solved yet or what is coming into vogue. With greater understanding of the human cognitive function and the realisation of the distinction between edge sensory perception and the transfer of that information to the neural cortex, similes are drawn with natural intelligence in the implementation of connected devices and their connection to a cognitive centre. Edge computing, edge intelligence, digital twins, data security and data provenance, as well as decentralisation, begin to feature in the way intelligence works. What was deemed AI yesterday may not be today if it has become a household name or a common application. Previously seemingly complicated intelligence is just seen as an off-the-shelf technology and no longer as AI. Consider, for example, facial recognition on your mobile phone, or a chess app that just about wins every time unless one sets it to a sufficiently simple setting.

Another reason for the misuse of the term AI is that it is a victim of its own success. The number **25.005** of people talking about AI outgrows their education on the topic. AI and particular deep neural net topologies are labelled with misconceptions and unrealistic expectations. Judgements on AI are plentiful and seldom balanced. AI is alternatively hailed as the cure to all our woes, or the beginning of human downfall. Understanding starts by looking at the taxonomies, lexicons and ontologies. It starts with naming and defining things and their relationships, and it allows for an evolving understanding of the definitions as the technology changes.

25.006 There are numerous glossaries of AI. The most comprehensive, researched and up to date is possibly that of Wikipedia. We will use it as a reference and link many of the technical terms we use below. In a section below we cover the basics of the taxonomy of AI.

25.007 We give a basic and enduring definition of AI in Chapter 3. In order to solidify the concepts, we cover a range of use cases as well as the landscape in terms of governance and ethics. Artificial Intelligence, presently, is a method in digital computer science that enables such machines to learn from digital data. This learning then enables new data to be presented and outputs to be generated in a manner that resembles the way human cognition works. Currently, the most popular AI technique is called Deep Learning. With Deep Learning, interlinked nodes are loosely modelled after the human neural network paradigm. These can then be trained to do things such as detect financial fraud or cancers, understand speech and natural language, drive a car or other modes of transport, recommend similar products, optimise logistics, predict demand, detect anomalies in a multitude of scenarios, optimise logistics, and so on.

25.008 Key to any intelligence are the data, the data context and environment and the desired actions. To understand Artificial Intelligence, one needs to understand the way natural intelligence works, as this gives a better understanding of the taxonomy of AI.

25.009 Crucial to the entire narrative is understanding of the legal issues related to data (privacy, security, ethics, governance in general). In addition, it is important to understand how much we want to limit the scope of Artificial Intelligence. If we extend the scope of AI to that of natural intelligence, then we introduce a set of complexities that will give us a number of significant ethical and legal problems.

25.010 In 2021, two of the authors of this chapter (Virdee and Brown) introduced the AI Periodic Table to enable a diverse audience to understand the multitude of concepts around Artificial Intelligence. In particular, we highlighted the crucial concepts around data democratisation and AI democratisation, as well as the frameworks in which any intelligence needs to sit for it to be effective.

25.011 The AI Periodic Table is used in this chapter as it enables us to put together various elements from different groups and create end-to-end processes to describe intelligent systems. The purpose of this chapter is to describe the various concepts around intelligence and to relate them to things that one may want to hold up as tangible. This enables a discourse when discussing technologies, frameworks, intelligence and legal issues.

25.012 Over and above this, one of the emergent issues is the change in human culture where sensory intelligence and sensory enhancement devices pull us into a more virtual world which is more fulfilling and experience enhancing. So increasingly, sensory AI and data will enable us to learn, experience and live in the virtual environment, where the escape to reality is merely to fulfil our natural sustenance requirements and decreasingly important social obligations.

So the importance of data as well as the monetisation of the virtual worlds will surpass that **25.013** of the real world as there may be a time when the physical processes (production, harvesting, distribution, consumption, and so on) are increasingly mechanised and automated in a way that diminishes the human in the natural environment.

B. DIMENSIONS OF AI TAXONOMY

From any perspective that requires a forensic analysis and discourse of data intelligence **25.014** algorithms and their lineage and creation, it is possible to consider a number of dimensions. Bernard Golstein (www.sharper.ai/taxonomy-ai/) gives a good set of dimensions:

(a)   the segmentation of AI per:
    (i)   breadth of intelligence (narrow, general),
    (ii)   historical progress (waves),
    (iii)   learning ability (symbolic learning, machine learning);
(b)   the segmentation of Machine Learning per:
    (i)   type of application (classification, estimation, clustering, skill acquisition...),
    (ii)   learning paradigm and usage of data (supervised, unsupervised, reinforcement, transfer),
    (iii)   algorithmic paradigm (connectionist, evolutionary, by analogy...);
(c)   the segmentation of Artificial Neural Networks per:
    (i)   depth (deep, simple),
    (ii)   type of algorithm (feedforward, CNN, RNN, GAN, spiking, ...);

and finally, the segmentation of Artificial Intelligence per modernity (traditional, advanced).

The main issues that we see emerging are along the lines of intelligence abstraction that enables **25.015** the emergence of general and multi-purpose utility. Consequently, the key features will include a refined narrative around the breadth of intelligence (such as emergence, manifold mapping, hypotheses and synthetic data generators and edge data cognition).

C. SEGMENTATION OF AI

1.   Per Breadth of Intelligence : Narrow vs General

AI now outperforms humans at a number of cognitive tasks, for instance converting speech to **25.016** text or lipreading; recognising faces or malignant tumours; predicting the right price to charge or the next film to recommend. The list gets longer with each passing day: autonomous driving, inventory taking by drone, accelerated drug discovery, predictive maintenance on airplane engines or tunnel-boring machines, customer relationship management by cognitive agents. However, while AI is used as a collective term, it is each time a different system which excels at a given task. Consequently AI is said to exhibit Narrow Artificial Intelligence (or weak AI): it operates on a very narrow scope.

25.017   In contrast, the hope for AI is that of Artificial General Intelligence (AGI) or strong AI. AGI is the ability to demonstrate human-level intelligence across the range of cognitive tasks that humans perform in their lives. The AGI will be able to jump from one topic to another with equal ease and, more importantly, establish links between them. There is no identified, straightforward path to achieve AGI from today's algorithms. This is why forecasting when, if at all, that moment will take place is anyone's guess. We predict it will take a few decades, perhaps towards 2050 or 2060; a very small number say ten years or so and an equally small number say several hundred years, at best. If that level is achieved then the Singularity, with Superhuman Intelligence or Artificial Super Intelligence (ASI), will perhaps be around the corner. There is no doubt that machines can consume much more data and make decisions faster. What is in doubt at the moment is the ability of cognitive frameworks to make sense of the data objects that enable iterative, progressive and human-centric proactive intelligence. Then come the problems around intentionality for ASI.[1]

2.   Historical Progress

25.018   The First Wave of AI, until the late 1990s, was good at reasoning in the exact way it had been programmed to, typically by following a set of 'if … then…' rules. It could not learn and evolve. We are currently in the Second Wave, which started in the early 2000s. It boasts a dramatically increased capacity to perceive and learn on a narrow scope. The Third Wave, expected in the 2020s or 2030s, will add to its perceptual capabilities the power to generalise from its narrow scope to a broader one, with an ability for contextual adaptation. The Fourth Wave, if it is ever to see the light of day, would usher in Artificial General Intelligence.

3.   The Four Waves of AI (credit: DARPA then Scott Jones)

(a)   Segmentation of AI per learning ability: Symbolic AI vs Machine Learning

25.019   The initial attempts to have a machine mimic human intelligence in order to solve problems and make decisions resorted to symbolic AI. The path taken, characteristic of the First Wave, was focused on humans imparting knowledge and rules to the system. The system in turn would methodically execute instructions and follow the rules. The approach had some successes. One of them was expert systems. Another one, to some extent, was robotics and automation minutely and thoroughly programming instructions of movement. But by and large, describing the rules that govern a specific complex system proved much too tall an order. In language translation, for instance, the rule-based models that started in the 1970s and survived until the turn of the century were extremely limited and ineffective aside from structured and constrained communication.

25.020   A different approach was explored in parallel – non-symbolic or sub-symbolic, without a specific representation of knowledge. It led to Machine Learning. Machine Learning

---

1   In May 2017, 352 AI experts who published at the 2015 NIPS and ICML conferences were surveyed. Based on survey results, experts estimate a 50 per cent chance that AGI will occur until 2060.

grants a system the ability to execute a task without being explicitly programmed to do so (for instance, an autonomous car can drive on a road it has never seen before); it is also defined as a process where performance increases with experience. In other words, the machine learns. It is taught by humans how to learn, but not what the output should be. This logic is sometimes referred to as statistical or biological.

The modern techniques of Machine Learning drastically outperform Symbolic AI on most **25.021** descriptive, predictive and prescriptive tasks. But Deep Learning, one of its most effective and popular approaches, has one major weakness: it is a black box. In other words, its outcome cannot be logically explained because the data representation is much too complex to be interpretable. If an individual is denied a loan or a suspect is convicted, the lack of explainability is an issue. In contrast, Symbolic AI does not suffer from this shortcoming. The best of both approaches may have a common hybrid future.

4.   Possible Symbolic and Statistic AI interactions

(a) Segmentation of Machine Learning per type of application: Classification, Continuous estimation, Clustering, Skill acquisition…

The tasks performed by Machine Learning can be grouped into typical applications; here we **25.022** will list the most popular of them.

Topping the list of usage is classification. In the late 1990s postal code recognition was auto- **25.023** mated when digits were correctly identified (pictures were classified in the right digit category). Most image processing or computer vision is based on classification, from automatic friend tagging on Facebook to tumour detection on an MRI; from quality control on a manufacturing line to obstacle identification by autonomous vehicles.

The second most popular application is continuous estimation. This application is also known **25.024** by the class of algorithm that it implements: regression. Determining the likely price of a house or the yearly sales for a product and forecasting demand for electricity or the number of years that an employee might stay in a given position are all continuous estimation problems. They usually benefit from tapping a large number of input variables ('features').

A third application is clustering. Typically, a population must be sorted and grouped based **25.025** on common characteristics. One can identify market segments for consumers, or students with similar strengths and challenges, or words that belong to similar semantic groups. In its broadest sense, clustering also includes recommender systems, prescribing the next product to offer to a customer.

Another important application of Machine Learning is skill acquisition. DeepMind first rose **25.026** to public fame by having an AI play Atari arcade games. The AI quickly reached superhuman performance and in passing devised winning strategies that the developers had no knowledge of. A robot can learn to fold and unfold laundry, to catch a ball or to climb a wall. A car might improve its navigation and trucks could optimise their delivery sequence. Traffic lights in a neighbourhood may be coordinated to avoid congestion.

D. SEGMENTATION OF MACHINE LEARNING PER LEARNING PARADIGM AND USAGE OF DATA

1. Supervised, Unsupervised, Reinforcement Learning, etc

25.027 There are different paradigms to train algorithms (also see Chapter 3). In Supervised Learning, data is labelled by humans and fed into the algorithm. For instance, in a famous initial application of supervised learning in the late 1980s Yann Lecun trained an AI by showing it tens of thousands of pictures of digits labelled 1 to 10. Thereafter, the system was able to correctly categorise new, unlabelled digits it was presented with. Recent applications of supervised learning on images, video or sound are innumerable: from detecting heart disease on eye scans to sorting ripe vegetables; from checking presence at school to adjusting course content based on engagement; from analysing mood on a tourist site to enforcing law and order; from detecting sentiment in customers' voices at a call centre to relieving patients in psychological distress.

25.028 Unsupervised Learning uses data that the system is typically tasked with clustering or reducing dimensionally. The process is said to be unsupervised because it determines by itself the proper categories (if told how many there should be, or even by letting the algorithms come out with clusters automatically). For instance, if retail data is fed into an unsupervised system required to extract four customer segments, it will be able to do so without additional help. In multi-dimensional problems it can also figure out which dimensions are the most meaningful, that is, would not distort the information too much if the other dimensions were discarded. This is how compression works on data files: less data leads to smaller files while not losing too much information.

25.029 In Reinforcement Learning, the system is simply given an objective but not shown how to achieve it. After completing the task it receives feedback (the 'reward'): was the objective achieved, or not? By repeating the process thousands or millions of times, the system develops strategies to execute the task correctly. Reinforcement Learning was famously used by DeepMind's AlphaGo Zero when this AI beat Li Ke Jie, the world champion at the game of Go. AlphaGo Zero was merely given the rules of the game and repeatedly played against older versions of itself, until it became unbeatable even by the world champion.

2. Machine Learning Segmentation

25.030 These different learning paradigms denote very different usage of data. By essence, unsupervised learning requires data that it must categorise. Supervised learning, the most used learning paradigm in today's applications, also needs large quantities of data to be trained effectively. This causes data to be dubbed 'the new oil', and numerous concerns to be voiced about data availability, privacy, ownership and so on. But implying in a blanket statement that massive data is indispensable for AI is a fallacy. Reinforcement learning, for example, does not require data at all.

25.031 Adding to this, recent approaches have attempted to accommodate scarcity of data (although it requires an environment to interact with, from which it derives data, inputs, outputs and so on). In Transfer Learning, for instance, a previously trained system learns to apply its skills to new situations for which it was not specifically trained. AlphaGo Zero, for instance, became

Alpha Zero after Transfer Learning and beat the best chess software in the world after a mere four-hour training session. In Deep Neural Machine Translation, independent language models are developed for source and target languages; a very small bilingual dictionary is then sufficient to translate any content from one language to the other. More generally, Small Data is becoming as coveted a field of study as Big Data once was. Once again we have reached a point in time at which we are limited by our technology and resources: GPT3 cost around $5M to train; this state of the art is now again reserved for big players and potentially nation states. This is a way of trying to rein in that gap.

Indeed, there are many ways to segment Machine Learning per algorithmic paradigm. In a 2015 'Talk at Google', Pedro Domingos of the University of Washington proposed what he called five approaches or tribes, all pertaining to schools of thought in Computer Science.   **25.032**

A first paradigm is connectionist. Data is represented on units connected to each other. Sound familiar? This is none other than Artificial Neural Networks (ANN), which became popular with the increase of computing power and of data. They are designed to loosely mimic the way the brain functions, where neurons are fired (or not) by upstream neurons based on the strength of their synaptic connection. In an ANN, data is decomposed on a 'neural' system with multiple layers of representation and abstraction. An input layer contains the features of the population in the initial dataset; an output layer provides the final description (for instance, the category in a classification problem); hidden layers contain intermediary calculations on so-called neurons, each neuron being activated or not by weighted signals from previous neurons.   **25.033**

A second paradigm is evolutionary. So-called genetic algorithms are left to evolve like living organisms: if they are fit enough they reproduce, subject to crossover and mutations. At the next generation natural selection once again picks the strongest for another cycle. The concept of genetic programming is so promising that it has been extended to physical robots – initially a bunch of almost random parts, turning into pretty efficient machines through 'evolution'.   **25.034**

A third paradigm is Bayesian. With this statistical and probabilistic school of thought, a prior hypothesis gets reinforced or weakened based on the evidence that is progressively collected. Spam filtering was one initial success story of Bayesian Learning; today's autonomous vehicles also carry some Bayesian Learning algorithms.   **25.035**

A fourth paradigm is by analogy. The principle is that whatever is similar can be grouped together. This is used in clustering algorithms such as K-Nearest Neighbour (KNN) or classification algorithms such as Support Vector Machines (SVM), aka kernel machines. SVMs were among the most powerful ML tools before ANNs made a breakthrough. Recommender systems are the most common application of learning by analogy.   **25.036**

The fifth paradigm is inductive logic programming, which Domingos calls symbolist (because this branch of Machine Learning is also a subfield of Symbolic AI). With given background knowledge, positive examples and negative examples, the system makes hypotheses (and thus 'learns').   **25.037**

E. FIVE TRIBES OF ML AND UNIFICATION

25.038 The reader may ask whether there are paradigms of Machine Learning that are mutually exclusive and incompatible. Today, they seem to solve very different problems. This is not a unique case. Physics has four known fundamental forces and has tried to unify them; so far, the Standard Model has managed to do so in the case of three of them. The human brain is one brain, but it computes to specific areas with some degree of specialisation for given cognitive functions. Similarly, experts such as DeepMind's Demis Hassabis are of the opinion that future, more sophisticated AIs might resort to a portfolio of different algorithmic approaches depending on the tasks at hand; Pedros Domingos suggests they will turn to one Master Algorithm.

25.039 An Artificial Neural Network is usually considered a Deep Neural Network (DNN) when there is more than one hidden layer, that is, more than three layers in the total network (counting the input layer and the output layer). All else being equal, increasing the depth of the network usually increases the performance of the algorithm provided there is sufficient computing power to train it. The type of non-linearities used for each 'neural cell' further differentiate these architectures.

25.040 As the technology develops, so does the terminology. Deep Learning most often refers to the use of Deep Neural Networks, although there are other cases as well, such as Deep Belief Networks and more natural types of network that allow for appropriate neuroplasticity and memory curves.

F. SIMPLE VERSUS DEEP NEURAL NETWORKS

25.041 The basic ANN algorithm is said to be simple feedforward. The algorithm 'travels' along the neural network in a single direction, from the input layer to the output layer without ever coming back or looping. However, the training of the network, in order to determine the proper weights associated with each neuron, resorts to a backpropagation calculation flowing in the other direction.

25.042 There are variations of the simple feedforward algorithm. In Convolutional Neural Networks (CNNs), the connectivity patterns between neurons resemble that of animals' visual cortex. CNNs are particularly well suited for image recognition. Recurrent Neural Networks (RNN) capture the notion of sequence. They power many Natural Language Processing applications. Generative Adversarial Networks (GANs) have two concurrent networks working in conjunction or in opposition, one often testing the work of the other. They are efficient in generating data when the original is scarce … or when people want to fake it.

25.043 By its very nature, this segmentation is a moving target. Today's 'traditional' is probably yesterday's 'advanced'" In the case of AI, 'advanced AI' usually refers to Deep Learning techniques. All the rest is deemed traditional or classical AI, including the non-Deep Learning parts of Machine Learning.

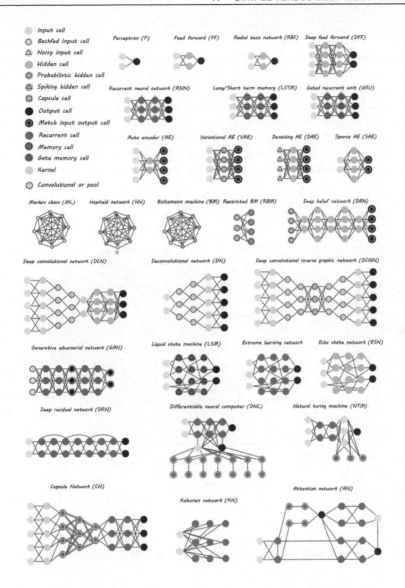

Figure 25.2   Segmentation of AI per modernity: traditional vs advanced

This segmentation remains fuzzy. To counter the ambiguity, one must clearly explain the **25.044**
conventions applied. McKinsey, for instance, does an excellent job in a recent report by stating
upfront, and several times, its definitions: 'As artificial intelligence technologies advance, so
does the definition of which techniques constitute AI. For the purposes of this paper, we use AI
as shorthand specifically to refer to deep learning techniques that use artificial neural networks.'

G. THE AI PERIODIC TABLE

25.045   The AI Periodic Table is a collection of the basic elemental groups required for intelligence. It is primarily derived from the workings of intelligence in nature in general and the human brain in particular (see Figures 25.3 and 25.4). The AI Periodic Table relates to the digitalised world. It includes data, data security and provenance, neural nets, languages and libraries. All of these are necessary for constructing cognitive sciences, elements to enable evolution of cognitive intelligence and a large group of elements that represent cognitive functions. The AI Periodic Table connects through to another framework of full-stack DevOps, so that it ends up completing the motor and real-world feedback mechanisms, functions and manifestation.

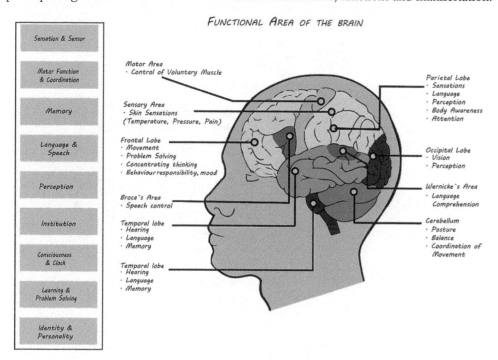

Figure 25.3   *The functional areas of the human brain and their main functions*

25.046   The purpose of the Periodic Table is to educate, inform and engage those involved in trying to get value from ML and AI. It enables a forward-looking narrative for business value (rather than the oft-used regressive one). It also enables us to make data alchemy a reality as opposed to conceptual magic.

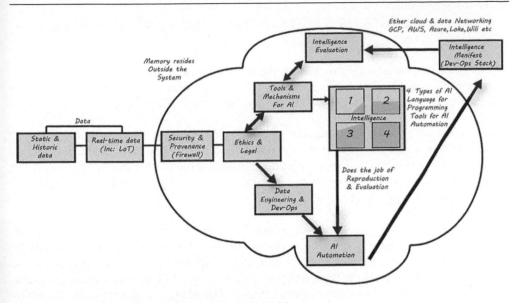

Figure 25.4   The 14 groups of the AI Periodic Table

The groups have been constructed with special reference to the human cognitive functions   **25.047**
and the way they are connected to the world. The human brain essentially has the following
components:

(a)   Sensations and sensors – data group and connections (partly the Cloud).
(b)   Motor functions and coordination – represented in the DevOps stack.
(c)   Memory – represented as Cloud (Cloud and third+ wave – some bits in second wave).
(d)   Language and speech – AI stack (second+ wave).
(e)   Perception – AI stack (second+ wave).
(f)   Intuition – AI stack (third and fourth waves).
(g)   Consciousness and clock – AI stack (fourth wave AI).
(h)   Learning and problem solving – AI stack (all groups of AI).
(i)   Identity and personality – AI stack (all groups of AI).
(j)   Evolutionary aspects through genetic natural selection (evolutionary aspects such as
      genetic algorithms, synthetic data and hypothesis generators, and adaptive hypermeter
      optimisation).

There are many aspects that are going to be unknowns in our Periodic Table. These will be   **25.048**
components that recognise and articulate aspects such as contextual adaptation (already emerging in some spheres through, for example, GPT-3 and Turing-NLP) and awareness (through
hyper-data fabric that enables the use of humans for construction of new forms of consciousness – connected sensors and emergent organs of a smart mega-city – if you can entertain the
idea; the human is the new neuron in a manifest creature that has edge-cognitive functions for
them).

For AI analysis we need to concentrate on the various topologies, such as Feed Forward,   **25.049**
Recurrent Neural Nets, Convolution Neural Nets, Boltzmann Machine, Deep Belief Network,

Generative Adversarial Network, Liquid State Machine, Spiking Neural Net, Neural Turing Machine, and so on.

25.050 A project requires tools to develop and to manage the project financially, such as timescales, budgets and reporting. Technically speaking, languages, source control, DevOps stack, data engineering and analysis, containerisation and productisation are needed.

25.051 A sense could be a physiological capacity of living beings that gives information for discernment. The senses and their operation, classification and hypothesis are intersecting themes considered by an assortment of areas, most notably neuroscience, cognitive mind research and philosophy of perception. The nervous framework includes a tactile nervous framework and a sense organ, or sensor, devoted to each sense.

25.052 Humans are traditionally recognised as having five types of sensors: visual, auditory, gustatory (taste), olfactory (smell) and somatosensory (touch). However, other stimuli can also be detected, and these sensory modalities include thermoception (temperature), proprioception (kinaesthetic), sense (proprioception), nociception (pain), equilibrioception (balance), mechanoreception (vibration) and numerous internal stimuli. The sensors in other creatures are different and of different sensitivities. For example, some animals can sense electrical and magnetic fields; some can detect currents and pressures. In any case, what is inclusive of a sense could be a matter of discussion, which raises the problem of characterising precisely what a sense is and where the limits lie between reactions to related stimuli.

25.053 The point above explains that the ways and means by which information is collected are as crucial as the information one collects for understanding the extent of AI. And yet there are obvious difficulties in the analogy. Can one really separate out genomics and reproductive systems? What will the Periodic Table cover in the human analogy context? It must obviously cover the brain, the sensory perceptrons and perhaps a mechanism for enabling improvements in the brain in a machine context. It is the limit; beyond this we are into the respiratory, lymphatic, urinary, reproductive systems. The reproductive system gives pause for thought as the context of an evolutionary aspect of AI (whether it is hyperparameter optimisation using evolutionary approach to data, or whether it is genuinely an evolving neural net).

25.054 The security and integrity aspect of the brain also gives pause for thought. Until recently the issue did not even arise, in that it was believed that one could not know what someone was thinking. To be able to hack a brain is to fundamentally affect its purpose. We now know that we are vulnerable to hackers. Technology is already allowing scientists and devices to read people's thoughts and even plant new ones in the brain. Intelligent systems require protection and AI systems can be made more secure than the human brain. This must be a key part of the AI Periodic Table. The Periodic Table must cover AI (and all that term implies), data, security (blockchain and neural quantum cryptography, and whatever succeeds it) and a mechanism for evolution/iterative refinement.

1.   The 14 Groups in the AI Periodic Table

25.055 The Periodic Table is organised as a set of groups with different properties. There are 14 groups:

(a)   Two groups related to data (broken down into real time, including IoT, and non-real time). This is to represent the central nature of data in any intelligence and models. There are endless data sources and for the moment we will include about 20 of the most familiar sources.

(b)   Four groups representing the four waves of AI and ML – this covers the evolution of data science from simple univariate linear regression to self-aware cognition. It includes aspects such as cognition, problem solving, language and speech. Aspects that we have no handle on can just be represented as missing elements in the Periodic Table and can be added when discovered (Mendeleev used the Sanskrit prefixes *eka- dvi-* and *tri-* to provisionally name elements that he knew to be missing from his table. We shall use the prefix *teen-AI* and *char-AI* to represent the third and fourth waves of AI elemental groups).

(c)   The four types of AI are broken down into elemental entities – probably 50 discovered and about 20 undiscovered ones. Aspects related to supervised, unsupervised and reinforcement are covered, as well as some elements alluded to during the discussions above related to intelligence, consciousness and problem-solving. What is clear from the discussions around the types of natural neurons and their density and location is that we perhaps ought to consider a topological model of collection of neurons and interfaces to data from other collections to start building up levels of abstractions of cognition. Some hardwiring is important to enable aspects such as generalised intelligence to be expressed in the table;

(d)   One group that deals with data provenance and security (we want the un-hackability of data and its provenance for digital intelligence. While the non-linear human mind does not really have a safeguard against being hacked, it deals with internal data with jealousy and prejudice).

(e)   One group that enables tools for AI automation.

(f)   One group that deals with ethical and legal issues.

(g)   One group for data engineering and data DevOps.

(h)   One group for languages and libraries for programming AI.

(i)   One group that represents the electricity between the neurons – currently provided by Cloud technologies.

(j)   One group for UX DevOps.

(k)   One group that enables evolution and improvements of cognitive functions: there are mechanisms for enabling the beast to become alive and useful (model validation, parameter tuning, model evolution – ten elements perhaps, and manifest elements of that intelligence by affecting experience and interaction – whether it is with other intelligent entities or whether it is with various bits of data to improve the basic elements of the prime directive: survival, exploration, discovery, change and expression).

Once we have the basic building blocks of intelligence (as groups) that are invariant, it is possible to begin to populate the actual elements: **25.056**

(a)   Real-time and IoT data: Reddit, Twitter, Pinterest, TikTok, Facebook, and so on;

(b)   Static and historic data: data.gov.uk; data.gov;

(c)   Traditional Statistics: Q-Learning, Decision trees, Naive Bayesian, Regression, Support Vector Machine, Nearest Neighbours, k-means Clustering, Time-series predictions;

(d)   Deep Learning and ML: Feed forward neural network (FFNN); Radial bias function (RBF) network; Recurrent neural network (RNN); Long and short-term memory network (LSTM); Gated recurrent unit (GRU); Autoencoders (AE) and Variational autoencoders (VAE); Denoising encoder (DE) and Sparse encoder (SAE); Markov chains (MC), Hopfield network (HN); Boltzmann machines (BM) and Restricted Boltzmann machines (RBM); Deep belief networks (DBN); Convolutional neural network (CNN) and deep convolutional neural network (DCNN); Deconvolutional network (DN); Generative adversarial network (GAN); Liquid state machine (LSM); Extreme learning machine (ELM); Eco state network (ESN); Neural Turing machine (NTM);

(e) AGI: Manifold Learning, GPT-3, Turing NLG;

(f) ASI: No elements discovered or invented yet;

(g) Governance: Blockchain, HyperLedger, Azure AD;

(h) AI and ML DevOps automation and democratisation: DataRobot, MindFoundry, H2O, Algorithmica, SI, AutoML, Azure Services, IBM Watson Studio DL, Deep Cognition – DL Studio, AWS – SageMaker and DeepLens;

(i) Ethical and legal issue toolkits and frameworks;

(j) Data engineering, data DevOps and data democratisation, Dawex, Dataex, AWS Data Exchange, Denado, Azure Purview, DataBricks, SnowFlake, Matillion;

(k) Languages and libraries for programming AI: R, Python, Scikit Learn, PyTorch, TensorFlow, Keras, Julia, C++, MXNet, Caffee, Azure Cognitive Services, AWS AMIs;

(l) Clouds: Azure, GCP, AWS, IBM Cloud, Digital Ocean;

(m) Intelligence Operations; and

(n) Environmental Adaptation: Seldon.io.

25.057 It is worth noting that these elements are prone to change as technology and frameworks change. However, the groups of the Periodic Table are invariant as they are based on similes to natural abstractions.

H. ETHICS, GOVERNANCE – DIFFERENCES AND SIMILARITIES BETWEEN NATURAL AND ARTIFICIAL INTELLIGENCE

25.058 If we look at nature and consider the way natural intelligence consumes data, the processes that are hardwired into the senses, the filtering that goes on and the way the neural pathways connect to different cognitive structures to enable decisions and reactions based on learned experiences, memory and evolutionary and purposeful tuning, it is clear that we face similar decisions about the data we need to sense and consume within businesses. In the natural context, the senses and sensors have only changed gradually and are tuned to the prime directives. In the case of machine learning, the senses and data have changed an enormous amount – the advent of mobile and connected devices, the generation of diverse business data that is sometimes for one-off use in a rapidly evolving business eco-system, the ability to consume all sorts of data, some of which is not even related to the problems we need to solve in specific cases, and so on. It is crucial we think deeply about data, its lineage, its provenance, and what it represents. When we divorce the data from its context, we run into problems of trying to determine its taxonomy and its relationship to business objects that will not become extinct. Contextualising and objectifying data in nature is easy; in business it can be difficult, as it depends on the engineers being able to make and preserve that connection and ensuring that those objects still exist. It is why many people and businesses get confused about the taxonomy, ontology and lineage of data, especially when all the senses are flooded, and most people end up sitting in data swamps where everything is as clear as mud.

In order to deal with governance issues around AI, we have to home in on governance issues **25.059** around data: data and types of data including big data and IoT data; the taxonomy, the topology and the characterisation of data; the mining, the transportation and its polishing; the creation of synthetic data and its usage; privacy and issues around the ethical and legal issues necessary to make sure that the societal transmutations are in keeping with our collective and democratised prejudices; the usage of social capital; the automated gold-panning of data swamps and data lakes for the nuggets that can add transformative value at so many levels; and then finally on to the processes that we need to go through to make that data useful in our increasingly digital and virtual society and eco-systems. It is, in my view, wrong to talk about AI ethics, as it is the data that is the genesis of ethics. The truth is in the data and if we want to engineer a solution for society in a certain ethical way, we have to ensure that we look at our data objects and how they are consumed. We cover issues around ethics and governance in some detail in Chapter 3.

I. THE ROAD TO DEMOCRATISATION

The road to democratisation for data and AI is crucial, as is that of the pipelines that transform **25.060** sensor data to effector data.

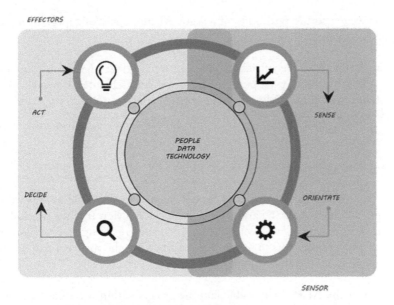

Figure 25.5   Generalised intelligent system architecture

The purpose of democratisation is to make use of tools that empower the transformation of **25.061** sensor data to effector data. It involves toolsets to:

(a)   democratise data through parameterisation, through the use of secure data exchanges that enable appropriate monetisation for data providers. In addition, the purpose of such tools (such as AWS data exchange, Dataex) is to reduce the ceiling for engagement in the use of data; and

(b)   democratise AI through the use of tools (such as H2O, Data Robot, MindFoundry, AutoML, and so on) that enable supervised, unsupervised, semi-supervised, and transfer-learning.

J. OTHER ISSUES AROUND AI

25.062   The very nature of ground-breaking innovation and technology is that it leads any legislative framework. Consequently, issues around AI law and regulation are usually far behind the curve. An easy example here is that of autonomous driving. Teslas have more autonomous features in the US than they do in the UK, for example (see www.which.co.uk/news/2019/05/tesla-model -3-dont-be-fooled-by-full-self-driving-claims/).[2]

25.063   Legal issues around data are now mainstream but legal issues around AI, algorithms and use of algorithms so far are not. This book aims to start changing that.

25.064   There are not yet many press reports on these legal issues playing out on a global scale. China is ahead of the rest of the world in areas like facial, behaviour, and social analysis because it has sufficient resources and infrastructure to play 'fast and loose' with algorithmic ethics.

25.065   There is a concerning future possibility of a giant AI monopoly/oligopoly with patents over algorithms and architectures.

25.066   The argument is that it is beneficial to pre-emptively patent algorithms and make them available to all for free. But at what point in the future does self-interest prevail? A staggering percentage of deep neural networks will use Dropout: at some point in the future, will we all have to pay Google for that privilege?

K. CONCLUSION

25.067   This chapter has tackled the fundamental aspects related to the building blocks of artificial intelligence and their analogues in nature and as such offers a view into the possibilities of artificial intelligence. In addition, we have looked at the various paradigms for classifying various types of algorithms and concepts to enable the reader to see the progress that has been made and the research that has enabled us to get to the current state.

25.068   The importance of the AI Periodic Table and the groups within it cannot be overstressed in terms of the education of all communities. It is necessary that the possibilities of AI should be made accessible to all so that AI is not seen as a stranger or inaccessible. This is important as there will be growing debates about limiting the possibilities of AI. Informed debate is predicated on education. This chapter is to be seen very much in that vein.

---

2   See www.which.co.uk news/2019/05/tesla-model-3-dont-be-fooled-by-full-self-driving-claims/.

L. REFERENCES

Developments are moving quickly in the technical context. One important cultural development is the increase of interdisciplinary work. Technologists and lawyers must collaborate to enable AI to reach its best potential. The following references will assist lawyers who want to know more.

25.069

Domingos, P., The Master Algorithm, Penguin, 2015.
Golstein B., A Brief Taxonomy of AI, www.sharper.ai/taxonomy-ai/, October 2018.
Kojouharov, S., Cheat Sheets for AI, Neural Networks, Machine Learning, Deep Learning & Big Data – The Most Complete List of Best AI Cheat Sheets, https://becominghuman.ai/cheat-sheets-for-ai -neural-networks-machine-learning-deep-learning-big-data-678c51b4b463.
McKinsey, Notes from the AI Frontier, McKinsey Discussion Paper (April 2018).
Virdee, T.S., and Brown, D., Data Alchemy – The Genesis of Business Value, LID Publishing, 2021.

26

AUTOMATION AND FAIRNESS

Emre Kazim, Adriano Koshiyama, Jeremy Barnett and Charles Kerrigan

A. INTRODUCTION

26.001　This chapter questions whether the automation of fairness is in itself inherently unfair; that is, whether that the very attempt to automate a particular process that involves issues of justice will necessarily be unfair. It does this by first explaining fairness and then discussing the notion of discernment, that is, deciding what kinds of fairness to choose between in cases of reasonable pluralism. Following this it outlines the difference between *automating implementation and automating fairness* in terms of discernment, that is, the making of a fairness judgement, and the legitimacy of the judgement made. It discusses the benchmarking of performance of automated systems and the comparative legitimacy of the fairness judgements of human reasoning and black box systems. It concludes with a note on the challenge that questions of fairness and automation pose in a world of increasing automated decision making.

B. FAIRNESS

26.002　Within the literature and popular discourse concerning the ethics of autonomous systems (commonly understood as referring to artificial intelligence), questions of how fair and just these systems are, and of the social consequences of using such systems, have risen to the surface.[1]

Broadly, we assert that the problem of fairness can be divided as follows: **26.003**

1.   Unfairness in Systems

Here a system can be thought of as unfair towards particular individuals and/or groups. This **26.004**
unfairness is often reduced to a bias in the dataset used to train a system (dataset unfairness) or
to the way the system is created in itself (program and parameter unfairness).[2]

2.   Automation is Unfair

Here there is a stronger claim, namely that the attempt to automate a particular process that **26.005**
involves legal issues will necessarily be unfair.[3]

The first can be thought of as an engineering problem, where the problem of unfairness can **26.006**
be addressed through an intervention in the dataset and/or the system. In other words, this
problem is at the very least theoretically solvable. The second of these two can be thought of as
expressing the proposition that no engineering solution can be found to de-bias a system; that
is, it is the claim that *automation is unfairness*.

The second proposition is the one we will primarily address in this chapter, because the first **26.007**
proposition is contingent upon the second being dissolved.

We do this by first conceptualising and outlining the fairness problem by explaining what we **26.008**
mean by fairness, and then discussing the notion of discernment, that is, deciding what kind of
fairness to choose between in cases of reasonable pluralism and outlining how to legitimise that
choice. Following this we outline that the point at which the 'fairness choice' is made – that is,
if the choice is made prior to automation (*automating implementation*) or through automation
(*automating fairness*) – changes the nature of the ethical question with respect to automation
and fairness. We discuss the latter in terms of discernment, that is, the making of a fairness
judgement, and the legitimacy of the judgment made.

C. WHAT IS FAIRNESS

In order to unpack the claim that automation must be unfair, we will first need to understand **26.009**
what exactly is meant by 'fairness'. Within the philosophical literature there are a myriad of
definitions concerning what is and what is not fair, and they are typically covered by theories of
justice. The two dominant notions within the discussion are *outcome* and *procedural*.

---

1   Kazim, E. and Koshiyama, A. (2020). A High-Level Overview of AI Ethics.
2   See Oneto, L., et al. (2019). General Fair Empirical Risk Minimization, and Chouldechova, A. and Roth, A. (2018).
     The Frontiers of Fairness in Machine Learning.
3   Wachter, S., et al. (2020). Why Fairness Cannot Be Automated: Bridging the Gap between EU Non-discrimination
     Law and AI.

1. Outcome

26.010 Fairness within the context of resource allocation (socio-economic parity in outcomes for people regardless of their starting point: socio-economic, gender, racial origin, age and so on).

2. Procedural

26.011 Fairness within the context of systems or rules or procedures (parity in how people are treated irrespective of who a person is or what their starting point may be: socio-economic, gender, racial origin, age and so on).

26.012 However, there are other notions of fairness and justice that prioritise a particular group or concern, often due to historical reasons; for example, if a demographic has been historically subject to injustice, it may be the concern of justice to address this with a notion of fairness that targets that particular demographic. Importantly, this point can be cashed out in terms of both outcome and procedural notions of fairness.

3. Mutual exclusivity of fairness definitions

26.013 As such, we can note that there are competing notions of fairness. Importantly, *these notions are understood as mutually exclusive, that is, each notion of fairness stands alone and is at the exclusion of another, competing, notion of fairness.* This presents a question regarding what the notion of fairness should be: in other words, we can treat these as competing claims which we need to discern.

26.014 In response to this we can think of a number of strategies.

4. Pick One(!)

26.015 Here one bites the bullet and commits to a particular notion of justice. Equality of outcome is fairness; procedural equity is fairness; and so on.

5. Prioritise Notions of Fairness

26.016 Here one takes a pluralistic position and asserts that differing notions of fairness can be maintained, and that what kind of notion of fairness is enacted depends upon a particular context.

26.017 In either case the mutually exclusive nature of fairness conceptions is maintained.

26.018 The second option is appealing because within a liberal democratic community, a reasonable amount of plurality is not only accommodated but indeed celebrated – a pluralistic approach to fairness and justice is to recognise competing claims and maintain the possibility of *challenge*. In other words, both the 'liberal' and the 'democratic' are premised on this pluralism and possibility of change.

26.019 Consequently, and somewhat paradoxically, it appears as though a society that is self-defined as liberal and democratic – that is, just and fair – rests upon an open (contentless) notion of fairness. The question becomes: how is fairness possible when in fact there is no shared and stable notion of fairness, and, in the context of automation, if there is no shared and stable notion of fairness, then must it (necessarily) be the case that fairness cannot be automated?

6.   Fairness and Discernment

A reply to this characterisation would be to state that although there is no one single shared **26.020** and stable notion of fairness, definitions of fairness are conditioned and indeed underpinned by the shared notion of human dignity, that is, that each and every human is equal and has an inviolable value.

As such, in each case of fairness the *prima facie* mutual exclusivity/competing nature of each **26.021** definition is dissolved by the introduction of context. The claim that a particular demographic should be prioritised, or that a particular procedure should be equal, or that outcomes should be equal, and so on is conjoined by the contextual reality that gives a fairness claim its potency. That fairness notion X is the notion of fairness that is appropriate depends on the circumstances within which justice and fairness is sought. As such, fairness requires discernment informed and directed by context.

Additionally, it is important to note that the shared notion of human dignity excludes various **26.022** claims to fairness. Indeed, reasonable accommodation within the milieu of liberal–democratic communities demands that fairness notions which respect human dignity be respected, whereas those that do not, be excluded. For example, a claim of fairness that prioritises a particular demographic that has been historically excluded is to be respected (consider cases of historical racial group discrimination), whereas a claim of fairness that prioritises a particular racial demographic simply by virtue of being from that demographic is not respected (consider cases of fascism). Whereas the former fairness claim is premised upon the equality and dignity of all humans, the latter is premised upon the inequality of all humans.

As such, fairness notions are pluralistic insofar as they represent a reasonable accommodation **26.023** of various claims premised upon the shared notion of human equality and dignity. In other words, reasonable pluralism is not premised on relativism; that is, not all claims of fairness are to be accommodated and respected. Another way of articulating this is to assert that *respect for human equality and dignity can be thought of as the boundary condition of reasonable pluralism.*

Fairness is hence a discernment between reasonable notions of fairness (with 'reasonable' understood **26.024** as any notion of fairness that is at the very least premised upon the equality and dignity of all humans). Such discernment is limited with this boundary condition and is *context dependent,* where context is the empirical reality (social, economic, political, and so on) of a particular place at a particular time.

7.   Who Discerns?

In the above, the remit of reasonable notions of fairness has been demarcated and the need **26.025** to discern between such notions in a particular context has been asserted. The questions then become: who and how?

26.026 In the current social democratic context the broad notions of fairness are delimited by the legislature through democratic processes and law making. Here the boundary conditions and 'options' as to what falls under the remit of acceptable, that is, reasonable, are determined. The law can be thought of as a codification of notions of fairness that reflect the liberal and democratic nature of the political process and (ideal) governance.

26.027 Within this context two dimensions can be thought out, the first being whether a particular notion of fairness falls within the law and thereby the notions of fairness considered reasonable/legal, the second concerning cases where a choice has been made between different (reasonable) notions of fairness.

26.028 The UK's Equality Act 2010 serves as an example to explicate this point. The following nine protected characteristics are identified: age, disability, gender reassignment, marriage and civil partnership, pregnancy and maternity, race, religion or belief, sex, and sexual orientation. The list of protected characteristics can be thought of as the boundary conditions, that is, reasonable plurality, thereby illustrating the first dimension of fairness. With respect to the second dimension – namely, choosing between the different notions, based upon the assumption that all characteristics cannot be protected simultaneously[4] (see Appendix) – here discernment is required. A straightforward approach to discerning what is appropriate is via a contextual argument, which outlines the logic and appropriateness of the choice to prioritise particular characteristics over others.

26.029 With respect to such contextual arguments, the question becomes what in itself is considered a legitimate/reasonable contextual argument. There are two ways this can be resolved: the first is by presenting a scheme or framework within which reasonableness is determined, that is, a set of conditions that would have to be met when presenting a context-dependent justification of a particular fairness choice; the second is by deferment to an authority. Here various approaches to authority can be postulated, such as 'fairness' standards or regulatory bodies (see for example the Information Commissioner's Office with respect to data) or, as is already the case, deferment to a judicial process in the form of a judge.

D. WHEN AND WHAT TO AUTOMATE

1. Automating Implementation

26.030 Indeed, deferment to a judge, who will discern with respect to the appropriateness of a fairness choice made between competing notions of reasonable fairness, is a clear example of lawfulness and justification of the respective value judgement that has been made. With respect to automation, this can be thought of as a fairness choice which occurs before something is automated. In other words, fairness is not automated with respect to fairness choices; rather, fairness is automated with respect to implementation.

---

4   It is relatively straightforward to show mathematically that if compliance depended upon protecting all nine characteristics in parallel it will be very unlikely that we will find an algorithm compliant. Indeed, even satisfying two or three characteristics in parallel is extremely difficult.

2.   Amplification of Unfairness

One principal ethical concern with automation of implementation is the problem of amplifica-   **26.031**
tion of unfairness. Here we can think of cases where a fairness choice is considered problematic,
and due to the nature of automation that problematic fairness choice is amplified through the
efficiency of computer systems. Although the ethical concern that automation presents with
respect to amplification of wrong choices is an acute problem to address, it nonetheless is a different kind of problem and one that can be stated as agnostic with respect to fairness itself. In
other words, amplification of harm through automation is a problem that can be presented in
cases of other harms, most clearly in the case of safety.

3.   Automating Fairness

An alternative scheme is one where the automation occurs in the fairness judgment itself.   **26.032**
Here, discernment between different notions of fairness occurs via processes in the algorithmic
system itself. In this scheme a system will produce a series of outcomes regarding what is
optimal and these outcomes will involve the preferential weighing and prioritising of particular
data over others. Here an automated system can be thought of as solving a problem (which has
been specified by the developer and deployer of the automated system) and by virtue of this,
in a context where 'fairness' issues are relevant, the system will *de facto* be making a fairness
'judgement'.

4.   Automated Intentionality

We have placed 'judgement' in quotation marks because in the context of an automated system,   **26.033**
the system cannot be said to have discerned/judged in the manner that a human being (for
example, a judge) can be said to have discerned/judged. Here we veer into the problem of the
legal status of an algorithm and the question of intentionality, where notions of responsibility
and accountability for judgements and choices that are made are premised on notions of
personhood which themselves are rooted in viewing persons as *intentional* (capable of making
a choice), that is, *compos mentis*, and having exercised such intentionality, that is, chose one
course of action over another. At present algorithms are not granted legal personhood status
and as such cannot be said to have made intention fairness judgements; hence our statement
that *de facto* (rather than *de jure*) the system is making a fairness judgment.

We will return to the discussions that touch upon the issue of intentionality when discuss-   **26.034**
ing the problem of automating fairness in the context of opacity, that is, black box systems
and human cognition (section 5). Before doing so, in the following section we explore and
address an argument in the literature that calls for consistent assessment procedures that
define a common standard for statistical evidence to detect and assess *prima facie* automated
discrimination – in terms of the above discussion this would fall into an attempt to standardise
and create a framework whereby automated systems, which make decisions which touch upon
issues of discrimination, are deemed fair or not.

E. BENCHMARKING OR DETECTION AND ASSESSMENT OF DISCRIMINATION

26.035   In 2020, Wachter and colleagues called for consistent assessment procedures that define a common standard for statistical evidence to detect and assess *prima facie* automated discrimination which are urgently needed to support judges, regulators, system controllers and developers and claimants. In this section we will argue that there is a risk that if this proposal is adopted, the automation of judicial reasoning rather than judicial support will result.

26.036   Although consistency is a laudable objective, primary and secondary EU legislation exists to protect the interest of minorities which judges can use to decide the facts of the cases before them. What is required is a framework to ensure that the algorithms that are placed on the market are 'safe', akin to the UK's General Product Safety Regulations (2005) which ensure that all products intended for or likely to be used by consumers under normal or reasonably foreseeable conditions are safe.[5]

26.037   Wachter uses the phrase 'automated fairness' as shorthand to refer to the plethora of interdisciplinary work meant to embed considerations of fairness into the design and governance of automated systems, including statistical metrics for fairness, bias testing using sensitive data, due process rules for algorithms, and developer and institutional codes of conduct. Complementary duties have been proposed for system controllers and developers, including a duty of care for online harms and fiduciary duties for technology companies.[6]

26.038   Here, the draft UK Information Commissioner's Office *Guidance for an AI Auditing Framework* (2020) is relevant and has to be considered in context. It is a comprehensive report on governance and risk management for AI systems but is primarily concerned with the limited issue of data protection, rather than the wider issues of the regulation and governance of AI systems.[7] The approach of the guidance, in separate consideration of the development training and deployment phases, together with identification of roles and responsibilities of various stakeholders, is to be encouraged.

26.039   In contrast, Wachter proposes Conditional Demographic Disparity (CDD) as a standard for statistical evidence that is harmonious with the aims of EU non-discrimination legislation as well as the gold standard for statistical evidence previously set by the ECJ. If adopted as an evidential standard, CDD will help answer the two key questions concerning fairness in automated systems *that can be justifiably delegated to the machine learning community*. Specifically, in any given case of *prima facie* discrimination caused by an automated system, these questions are:

(a)   Across the entire affected population, which protected groups could I compare to identify potential discrimination?

(b)   How do those protected groups compare to another in terms of disparity of outcome?

---

5   Cartwright, P. (2018). The General Product Safety Regulations 2005: Implementing Directive 2001/95–EC in the UK. In The Yearbook of Consumer Law 2007 (pp. 309–325). Routledge.

6   Woods, L. and Perrin, W. (2019) Internet Harm Reduction: A Proposal. www.carnegieuktrust.org.uk/blog/internet-harm-reduction-a-proposal/

7   Treleaven, P., Barnett, J. and Koshiyama, A. (2019). Algorithms and the Law. Algorithms: Law and Regulations. Computer, 52(2) 32–40.

CDD answers both of those questions by providing measurements for making comparisons **26.040**
across protected groups in terms of the distribution of outcomes.

We argue that this fundamentally misunderstands the rationale of judicial decision making. **26.041**
It is essential for the administration of justice that the decision is made by a human being,
not a machine – that a human being is appointed by a process that has the trust of the public,
and involves above all an ability to listen to convincing arguments, weigh up the points made,
decide on the facts and apply the relevant law. Any attempt to fetter that independence undermines the rule of law.

The points made in Wachter's paper may be well considered and reasoned, but they need to **26.042**
be considered in context. The judicial decision-making process accommodates a disparity of
views among experts. In an adversarial system, either side can make a point by calling expert
evidence, and provided the evidence is fair and relevant, the judge can listen to the views of the
expert. The opposing side can contradict that view by cross examination to demonstrate the
flaws in the methodology or application of theory to the facts, and then call its own expert to
offer the opposing view. The judge weighs up the evidence and argument, reaches his or her
own decision on the facts of the particular case and interprets the law accordingly.

The decision has to be made in accordance with legal principles and has to be transparent. Any deci- **26.043**
sion is subject to an appeal to a senior court, where the decision making process and content is
subject to detailed review. If it transpires that the legal framework is unclear, then the law can
be clarified in further appeals (in the UK to the Court of Appeal, Supreme Court and ECJ in
certain circumstances). Any attempt to fetter that ability to decide the case subverts the entire
basis of the legal system.

The role of the 'machine learning community' is to investigate and report upon the issues that are **26.044**
covered in this chapter and, if called upon to do so by either party, give expert evidence on a given set
of facts that can be tested in trial. Setting out standards and accepted protocols and 'best practice'
is part of that process, so that individual cases can be benchmarked against the consensus view
of a given issue. But this approach should never be allowed to usurp the role of the judicial
decision maker, and should be limited to the provision of judicial support tools which the judge
can decide whether or not to utilise given the issues that arise in the instant case.

In 1977, Anthony D'Amato asked the question: 'Can/Should Computers Replace Judges?'[8] He **26.045**
asked what would be gained and what would be lost, and quickly concluded that decisions on
facts must be the province of humans. He pointed to aspects of human judgement that cannot
be reduced to algorithms, and concluded that such systems should not be encouraged.

The use of algorithms by judges has been the subject of research for many years. Judicial support **26.046**
systems were considered in 2000[9] and were extensively reviewed by Professor John Zeleznikow
in his 2017 paper which draws the distinction between judicial support and judicial making
systems. He concludes that online dispute resolution should not be fully automated, a view that
has prevailed in France since 1978: Law 78–17 of 6 January 1978 as amended states that

---

8   D'Amato, A. (1977). Can/Should Computers Replace Judges? Georgia Law Review, 11, 11–36.
9   Scholberg, S. (2000). Foreword. International Review of Law, Computers & Technology, 14(3): 277–8.

No judicial decision involving an assessment of a person's conduct may be based on an automated processing of personal data intended to evaluate certain aspects of his personality.

No other decision which has legal effects on a person can be taken solely on the basis of an automated processing of data intended to define the profile of the person concerned or to assess certain aspects of his personality.

26.047   It is contended, however, that the objectives of achieving consistency in judicial decision making – speed and efficiency – will slowly erode this 'hardline' position. An often quoted example is the Alabama Sentencing Commission, which had as one of its objectives 'prevention of prison overcrowding as a governing purpose', thus affecting tariff sentencing based on availability of prison places. Sentences were calculated using worksheets to score offence based and aggravating/mitigating features. Sentences were 'presumptive', giving the judge limited discretion to vary the proposed tariff. It is understood that this project was quietly shelved following criticism from various parties.[10]

26.048   A more comprehensive approach is set out in Dupont and colleagues' 2020 discussion document 'The Governance of Artificial Intelligence in Finance', which sets out detailed independent criteria for evaluating AI algorithms and tools in finance, together with a focus on integration into the business process and human/algorithm interactions in the algorithm's design phase. The important criteria are performance, stability and explainability, as well as issues of consent and bias in data management.

26.049   Care has to be taken in designing prescriptive measures to import concepts such as 'preventative, corrective and detective' tools to detect bias and discrimination, not to subvert the role of the judicial process and bring about the oft cited phrase 'code is law' by a process of stealth.

F. OPACITY AND THE LEGITIMACY OF PUBLIC REASONING

26.050   We can summarise our argument in the previous section in terms of an erosion of the judicial process if a benchmarking of performance of automated systems is implemented. Note that this is not a critique of the concern for automating implementation; rather, it is a critique of automating fairness with respect to standardising the discernment phase of fairness determination. Notwithstanding this, the call for benchmarking appeals to the intuition that discernment itself needs to be fair; another way of stating this is that procedural fairness is sought.

26.051   With this in mind, and moving beyond the case of judicial reasoning, we can state the problem of fairness discernment in terms of legitimacy: in the current social contract the processes that appeal to (public) human reasoning are the *standards* of a (legitimate) fairness judgment; the developers and deployers of automated systems are not.

26.052   Granting this, an additional issue of concern within the fairness and automation debate is that automated systems that fall under the umbrella of machine learning/artificial intelligence are thought of in terms of opacity. By opacity we are referring to cases where the operation of an

---

10   Ala. Acts 596, p. 1192, § 1. (2000). https://sentencing.umn.edu/sites/sentencing.umn.edu/files/Alabama%20Profile .2015.v1.pdf.

automated system is not transparent to the users of that system. This is a reference to systems that lack *transparency* and as such cannot be probed or explained. Transparency is important for a number of reasons, one of which is accountability.

Let us state this problem in terms of a contrast between the public reasoning and opaque auto-   26.053
mated systems. The public reasoning is said to be legitimate (in part) because it is transparent, whereas opacity in an automated system renders it illegitimate.

One speculative concern with the above conjunction of transparency and legitimacy is that the   26.054
transparency of the public reason can be presented in two ways. The first is a straightforward step from transparency in the processes of public reasoning (through the publishing of the arguments, judgments and reasoning) to legitimacy. The second way is to challenge the 'trans-parency' of the published reasoning. Here the argument is presented that in cases of fairness and justice, there are reasons to believe that notwithstanding the public nature of human rea-soning processes, there is unfairness. The challenge is two-pronged, the first being to point to the irony that much of the bias in automated systems can be found in biases in the (historical) dataset being translated into system output bias. A particularly acute example of this is found in the automated criminal sentencing systems – where training data is drawn from historical prec-edents and such data has been shown to be biased (shown clearly in the bias of the automated recommendations and recommendation tools).

Second, an argument can be made that published arguments – that is, reasons for judgements   26.055
and decisions made by humans – do not reveal the 'reason' why particular judgements are made. Maintaining the honesty of the human reasoner (the agent), it is still possible to argue that an unconscious bias is unwittingly translated into the rationale; this argument draws from the historical data, where one reason for bias in the historical data is the presence of this very bias: a bias that may not be revealed by readings of individual cases of human reasoning (that is, the specific data point), but is revealed through statistical correlation presented in the larger dataset.

We note that this argument relies on a number of assumptions about human reasoning. One   26.056
such assumption is that there is a disconnect between a person's avowal of what they believe and/or why they have acted and the 'truth' of what they actually believe and why they have acted. This is a well-known psychological phenomena. Another, more fundamental, assump-tion is that *human reasoning is opaque*. There are a number of ways in which this claim can be fleshed out; however, for the current purpose, opacity is a reference to knowledge of a person's reasoning, which we read both in terms of the inability of a person to have privileged and trans-parent access to their reasoning and the inability of a third party to access (transparently) this reasoning. Note that this is a strong claim: the claim is not that it is difficult to access the 'truth' of a person's reasoning, but rather that it is impossible (we can call this the 'opacity thesis').

If the opacity thesis is true then it presents public reasoning, indeed human reasoning writ   26.057
large, as analogous to descriptions of some automated systems as 'black box'. Given that an important, indeed foundational, aspect of responsibility and accountability is transparency, this speculative argument would place the same problem of explainability on human reasoning as it does on black box systems.

26.058   Although there is a growing body of computer science literature on 'opening up the black box' – also referred to in terms of explainability – techniques used to 'explain' automated decisions in complex algorithmic systems cannot be said to be 100 per cent valid; that is, such systems cannot be made 100 per cent transparent (similar to the strong claim made in the opacity thesis). As such, the opacity thesis can be thought of as applying both to human reasoning and to automated decisions in complex algorithmic systems. If the problem of transparency is present in both, it may be argued that public reasoning loses some of its legitimacy.

26.059   The speculative argument we have presented can be read in terms of placing a strain on the current social contract with respect to the ultimate legitimacy of public reasoning. However, the argument that human reasoning is opaque and thereby falls foul of the same critique of black box systems – that they lack transparency and thereby legitimacy – is itself problematic. There are a number of reasons for this, the first of which is that the opacity thesis relies on a bevy of assumptions, each of which would be considered contestable. Second, even if the opacity thesis was true, all it would establish is that an individual's (human) judgment is opaque; it is already the case that public judgements can be contested, which is a possibility because the fallibility of human judgements is always considered. Third, a host of structures and procedures underpin public human judgement, such as institutions and democratic processes. However flawed these may be, there is considerable public and collective engagement (and thereby trust); this can be compared with the much smaller community of AI engineers (researchers in a university, developers in a company, and so on). Finally, a core argument underpinning the legitimacy of public reasoning is that responsibility is explicitly human. Although there are debates regarding the legal status of algorithms and even conferring legal personhood in particular instances, locating the 'human' in the system is critical to understanding why and how systems operate in the world (particularly in attributing responsibility, facilitating redress and intervention). Automating fairness – via a claim that humans are just as black box as some automated systems – creates the impression that systems are biased in themselves, rather than through human decisions that have been made in developing and deploying automated systems.

G. CONCLUSION

26.060   In this chapter we have probed whether automation of fairness is inherently unfair by first exploring what is meant by fairness and then discussing the problem of discernment, that is, legitimacy of judgements of fairness. Notwithstanding the opacity of human psychology, processes that appeal to public reason sit within a cluster of accountable and public/democratic institutions (something that the developers and deployers of automated systems lack).

26.061   In a world of rapid adoption of automated decision systems, the question of fairness and automation is pressing. In this chapter we asserted both the primacy of human responsibility and the importance of ensuring that fairness judgements remain within the remit of human judgements built on processes of democratic trust and accountability. In order to automate fairness in any way it is paramount that public discourse, legislators and regulators clearly articulate the standards and framework within which automation implementation can take place – that is, explicit human judgment, in the context of fairness choices, is to take place before automation. Even regardless of this, it is paramount that businesses and legal practitioners working with them take account of these points and are able to articulate and evidence them in system design and implementation.

The chapters in this book on ethics, discrimination, explainability and others are of course closely related to much of the analysis in this chapter.

27

RISK MANAGEMENT

Stephen Ashurst

A. INTRODUCTION

27.001 This chapter is an introduction to its subject, giving context to the interrelationships between law, modern risk management, artificial intelligence and data science. In this new world AI, and specifically machine learning, are changing both technology and outcomes for professional risk managers in industry and government. But there are questions: what about discretion – the ability and requirement for a risk manager to be able to make responsible decisions – and who sets risk boundaries and appetites? If a risk is an opportunity *and* a threat then does overly zealous risk management, and the inherent biases of risk software programmers, create too much threat mitigation but digital scarcity for opportunity, for example?

27.002 The chapter looks at professional risk management in practice and discusses the pros and cons of augmented (as opposed to automated) machine-learning risk management, a hybrid approach to AI and risk.

27.003 On the face of it, artificial intelligence and risk management are well-matched.

27.004 Markets and societies operate using risk management as a system of identifying and mitigating risk. With a basis in mathematics, probability, game theory, statistics and law, risk management is an advanced, scientific approach to the identification and mitigation of risks, where risk is defined as both an opportunity and a threat.

Artificial intelligence (and especially machine learning) makes it possible for machines, **27.005** powered by software, to learn from experience by adjusting to new data inputs and to perform human-type tasks or processes based on accumulated data. Machine learning relies on large sets of data, deep learning capabilities and natural language analysis.

Until recently, risk management was carried out by humans assisted by pre-programmed, **27.006** specialised (but constrained) software. The unintended consequence of this was that human biases were the predominant form of risk management, albeit based on the best available data.

AI can alleviate some of the constraints of traditional risk management by using machine **27.007** learning to widely analyse far greater data and to make mitigations based less on biases and more on the facts – or at least, that's the theory. The purpose of AI-driven risk management is to attempt to rigorously predict patterns based on clusters in large and dynamic data sets. The outcome of this risk analysis is to recommend targeted mitigation to decision-makers in order to achieve better outcomes than would otherwise have been available.

In possession of sound risk predictions and effective mitigations, the theory runs, professional **27.008** and commercial risk-takers stand to benefit financially, physically and reputationally from the potential of AI and machine learning, as do we, in our roles as consumers and citizens. Risk management is part of our community and economy, and better risk management tools and capabilities offer benefits to private and social entrepreneurs, institutional investors, asset managers, insurers, state countersecurity organisations and project managers delivering large-scale information technology, public health or infrastructure projects, to name only a few.

The advantages that AI can bring to the practice and theory of risk management are many. But **27.009** what is the reality?

It is a fact that risk management and AI have issues that need to be overcome in order to **27.010** truly interoperate. There are the known technical constraints of AI where, for example, a lack of wide and unbiased data points or language makes it hard for true patterns to be detected, regardless of the specific source or the technology used.

And contrary to the hype, perhaps, machine learning – AI's most prominent articulation – still **27.011** follows the old computer science rule of GIGO more closely than we might care to admit: garbage in, garbage out.

In almost all cases, and lacking real discretion, machine learning plays the hand it has been **27.012** dealt and delivers an outcome – quite reasonably – that is the best that could have been achieved *under the circumstances*. Is this enough to make a material difference?

This chapter will take a look at some of the current legal and practical challenges facing risk **27.013** management's adoption of AI and will pose further questions as to how these two major disciplines might work better together.

B. A CASE STUDY IN AI AND MACHINE LEARNING

27.014   A few years ago, a highly qualified data scientist recounted to me an example of the practical origins of machine learning.

27.015   At the request of the local security services, huge pools of mobile phone calling data was being sifted by data scientists to identify the ringleaders of potential terrorist cells. Not the *content* of the calls or texts – that was not admissible in court – but the *pattern* of calls, that is, who was calling whom, and when.

27.016   Now, from the outside looking in, the terrorist cell appeared to a have a visible leader. But it was also known that cell members had been trained, by way of decoy, to act as if a proxy person were the leader of the cell, making it harder for their enemies (in this case, law enforcement agencies) to be sure who was their true boss.

27.017   In public, and even in private gatherings, the *de facto* proxy leader was treated as if they were the officer in command.

27.018   But the data scientists could see a different *pattern* in the call data versus the social façade presented by the cell. The pattern of calls allowed data scientists to better assess, monitor and mitigate the terrorist risk.

27.019   Following the data analysis it was clear that there was in fact potentially a different leader, or at least co-leader, of the terrorist cell than the obvious candidate. This shadowy figure was the person to whom almost all the mobile phone calls were made and from whom a constant stream of short, sharp calls were sent. This hidden figure was not, it turned out, the person who looked like they were running the operation.

27.020   When the calls were clustered further based on the same pattern-matching logic it became obvious how the rest of the cell was organised, based on the location, frequency, direction and timing of the follow-on calls to and from the leader.

27.021   Before long, data science had predicted the organisational structure of the entire cell.

27.022   Following this, the data scientists' employer moved to monetise this new expertise for its own commercial customers: the mobile phone companies themselves. A new 'data science' professional service was devised, offering the same clustering and prediction identification techniques as used in the terrorist case, but this time to enable the mobile phone companies to identify those of their clients who might be dissatisfied with their current phone services and who would be negatively and effectively spreading their discontent about the phone company to all the other human beings ('nodes') in their social networks.

27.023   The data scientists deployed the same influencer/leader pattern analysis techniques to identify and then target (with discounts, offers and free handset upgrades rather than arrest) those phone customers who were the cluster nodes of disaffection.

As a result, the mobile phone companies were able to dramatically reduce their risk of customer   **27.024**
churn, and the data scientists were rewarded accordingly.

C. THE BOUNDARIES AND RULES OF RISK MANAGEMENT

Not all of us think and act defensively in terms of the data exhaust we trail behind us constantly.   **27.025**
If we did, we would probably quickly thwart the best efforts of pattern-spotting by marketing
algorithms and law enforcement agencies alike. But such pre-meditated personal behaviour
would be almost impossible to sustain for long periods.

Where is the boundary between 'fair' risk management by third parties using our data versus   **27.026**
our privacy, for example? Which actors can cross that boundary and why, and what might
a reasonable government or business be expected to offer us in terms of risk management when
using our own data? Is there a duty of care and what might be legally construed as intrusive or
invasive risk management? Are there specific legal duties and obligations to consider?

Equally important is: who decides and sets the boundaries of AI for risk? Is it us, the software   **27.027**
programmers or even the machine itself? And what role does the law play?

Risk management works when the mitigations it deploys save lives, money and effort that could   **27.028**
be better spent, public or privately, elsewhere. Current theory runs that better risk management
can be delivered by artificial intelligence and in particular, machine learning.

And this is certainly true in most real-world risk management practical instances.   **27.029**

D. HOW RISK MANAGEMENT CAN HELP AND HINDER

Let's take a common example of machine-learning risk management in the everyday: retail   **27.030**
banking. All of my online and card transactions are logged in my bank's central database continually, where they are examined for patterns and habits – specifically, for outliers and edge
cases that predict that my bank account or card may have been cloned or somehow accessed
and compromised by a thief.

One day, out of the blue, in a place I've never been before (based on the roaming location or   **27.031**
IP address used), I apparently transfer a large sum from my bank account to another account
in a different name.

At this point as consumers we'd usually be relieved to get a text message or call from our bank   **27.032**
advising that the suspect transaction had been frozen and the card locked, pending our call to
customer services to discuss the details further.

But we'd probably be less relieved if it was a genuine transaction to pay for – say – emergency   **27.033**
medical treatment for my family *en route* to a holiday destination.

27.034   And we might be less than amused if we'd already advised the bank that we were travelling in any case, only for the payment to still be blocked in apparent error.

27.035   Risk managers see inconvenience on a scale of damage caused versus liability and, therefore, when one scale exceeds the other mitigation happens regardless. This matters because it is risk managers who are programming machine learning software AI tools, and so it is *their* risk appetite metrics, biases and ambitions that the software initially uses and then learns from to deploy as risk mitigations. The apple doesn't fall far from the tree.

E. PHILOSOPHICAL LOGIC AND A LACK OF REASONABLENESS

27.036   In risk management terms, AI and machine learning can negate some of their benefits by lacking a most important human ability: discretion.

27.037   Machine learning doesn't necessarily have the concept of a 'reasonable' man or woman programmed in. That may not matter where we accept the premise that machine learning can learn reasonableness – but can that happen? In fact, logic itself doesn't consider reasonableness as a valid state: true or false; one or zero, okay – but maybe? No.

27.038   Syllogism is the method that is part of the foundation of modern computer programming logic.

27.039   In a syllogism, two or more propositions (*all men are mortal, Socrates is a man* and so on) that are asserted to be true drive deductive reasoning to arrive at a conclusion (*Socrates is mortal*).

27.040   There is no discretion in this decision tree. In this syllogism, it is not reasonable to assert that Socrates is immortal or some other gender (even though we have no actual proof that Socrates ever existed or, if he did, whether he was in fact a man – maybe 'he' was a syndicate of writers, or a child?)

27.041   There is no discretion either, for example, in smart contracts: hard-coded business rules that determine and execute legal contract enforcement in transaction operating on a decentralised ledger or blockchain.

27.042   Software – and especially modern software such as machine learning and smart contracts – has no capacity for reasonable discretion and cannot be expected, on current capabilities, to provide it.

27.043   AI software is no different. It descends from the same rigorous logical tradition of the ancient Greeks. Patterns can be found by machines in data and especially via language analysis. There is no denying the usefulness of cognitive speed in a busy and complicated world of technology where humans are distracted and slow by comparison.

27.044   But do we always want to tightly couple risk mitigations to this risk pattern analysis – or should we reserve the discretion to decide on how to mitigate risks for ourselves?

This is not a criticism but an observation. Is machine learning the wrong tool to deploy in risk   **27.045**
management, where discretion can be key?

F. THE VALUE OF DISCRETION

There are good examples of useful discretion in risk management that have provided life-saving   **27.046**
mitigations, but perhaps none more so than the strange story of Stanislav Petrov and the
world's escape from nuclear destruction in the Cold War. This close shave was apparently due
to the instinct and cool-headed thinking of one specific risk manager…

Stanislav Yevgrafovich Petrov (Russian: Станислáв Евгрáфович Петрóв; *7 September 1939–19*   **27.047**
May 2017) was a lieutenant colonel of the Soviet Air Defence Forces who played a key role in the 1983
Soviet nuclear false alarm incident.

On 26 September 1983, three weeks after the Soviet military had shot down Korean Air Lines Flight   **27.048**
007, Petrov was the duty officer at the command center for the Oko nuclear early-warning system
when the system reported that a missile had been launched from the United States, followed by up to
five more.

Petrov judged the reports to be a false alarm, and his decision to disobey orders, against Soviet military   **27.049**
protocol, is credited with having prevented an erroneous retaliatory nuclear attack on the United
States and its NATO allies that could have resulted in a large-scale nuclear war.

An investigation later confirmed that the Soviet satellite warning system had indeed malfunctioned.   **27.050**

Would machine learning have had the *sang-froid* displayed by Petrov? Perhaps, although none   **27.051**
of us would want to find out in reality. Left unattended, or unmonitored, machine learning
(the part of AI that really matters in risk management) would not deploy any discretion at all.

G. CREATIVITY AND INSIGHT

The risk management shortcomings of AI and machine learning exist as a direct result of AI's   **27.052**
binary DNA – hard-coded logic – inherited from AI's computer programmer creators and their
forebears. And for as long as machine learning is just that ('machine learning'), then the same
constraint will surely apply.

Can machine learning pick up on sarcasm or humour? This is important because, on that   **27.053**
basis, it would be likely, for example, that AI could repeat the rumoured breakthrough by the
(human) code-breakers at Bletchley Park during the Second World War who began to crack
open the German military cyphers when the enemy frequently signed off encrypted messages
with the simple phrase '*auf wiedersehen*'. This habit provided the code breakers with a window
of opportunity to analyse exactly the same patterns in speech in similar messages – eventually
breaking the code.

27.054 'Discretion' is part of the risk management process and is a legal and practical requirement currently and for the foreseeable future. Common law systems involve some judicial discretion in decision-making. Consequently, practising lawyers must anticipate when giving advice how this may be exercised. Without discretion and without legally responsible humans assisting and intervening, risk management becomes simply a sliding scale of automated risk calculations, picking the least worst mitigation option in each case, and then enforcing it mercilessly.

27.055 Consider the (now infamous) scenario that could be faced by the risk management module of a self-driving car as it is presented with a split-second demand for the judgement of Solomon: to save the life of its pregnant passenger, the car must choose to swerve and surely kill either the motorcyclist in the escape lane next to it or plough into the frozen-in-terror schoolchild rooted in the car's path.

27.056 This is risk mitigation at its most brutal and logical – and without the bravery, creativity and discretion that a human might bring to the situation at the critical moment.

27.057 But can or could human discretion create a different outcome, or is this a vain hope when hard choices need to be taken, and quickly?

27.058 In the self-driving car scenario, where judgement is allowed, there are human variables at play that would make on-the-spot discretion useful, if not transformative. Is the schoolchild known to people as the neighbour's gymnastics champion kid, who could potentially vault out of the car's way? Is the motorbike rider on a visibly powerful enough machine to accelerate out of trouble? Is the pregnant passenger trained cabin crew who is already braced for the crash and ready – as much as she ever could be – for impact?

27.059 Humans could and can potentially ace machine learning and use discretion to mitigate better.

H. DESCRIPTION OF THE RISK MANAGEMENT INDUSTRY AND PROCESS

27.060 Risk management doesn't operate in a vacuum. It actively monitors and assesses the world around it – importing and analysing metrics, natural language, data, statistics, sentiment and more into its calculations. Risk management is a practice founded on scepticism: like lawyers, risk managers frequently advise caution as a default position.

27.061 This is, in general risk management terms, a good thing. Who'd want a risky risk manager? But the naturally conservative and cautious approach of the majority of professional risk managers creates a distinct bias in the artificial intelligence and machine learning fostered by them.

27.062 Risk thresholds are set according to risk appetite: staying the preferred side of a risk threshold is the approach to risk an enterprise or organisation feels it is comfortable taking in a given situation, real or imagined. When challenged, most enterprises will state that they are 'risk averse', meaning that when presented with a risk, they'd rather not proceed at *all* with an activity that might exceed their threshold and thereby simply remain as they are.

Lawyers will be familiar with this in many contexts. It is possible to take conservative or aggressive positions in relation to financial regulation or data protection rules, for example. The challenge for lawyers is often that it is possible to understand a client's position on risk but hard to quantify comparisons. This may be an area where AI can help.   **27.063**

Leaving aside the question as to whether this is a viable long-term position for a commercial (and therefore, entrepreneurial) organisation like a business to take where the greater the risk the greater the return (or loss), there are issues with this approach as it entirely excludes the 'risk upside' – the opportunity.   **27.064**

That risk boundary – the threshold between the risks an enterprise wants to take and those it prefers to shun – is the first parameter to be configured by a human into any machine learning deployed for risk management.   **27.065**

Risk appetite is a good example of the almost invisible 'bias' guardrails that are imposed by humans on machine learning from the start. Faced with a restrictive risk appetite and a very low threshold for risk-taking, machine learning will constantly deal down on opportunities, making other vectors of risk (the risk of failing to win new business, the risk of losing customers bored by lack of innovation, and so on) more salient by comparison.   **27.066**

Are machine learning capabilities cognisant of the downsides of low risk appetite, in this example? It seems unlikely that a machine taught to avoid risk will have awareness of the constraints it is causing in the opportunities denied. No risk manager would think like that, so why would her mechanical apprentice?   **27.067**

I. A PRACTICAL INTRODUCTION TO RISK MANAGEMENT IN THE REAL WORLD

Let's consider some of the risk management processes used in the software development industry as an example of some of the inherent biases and parameters that may be encountered by machine learning in this space.   **27.068**

Delivering a large IT project is fraught with risk. There are direct risks (failure of integration software to work, the risk of software build requirements being missed, the risk of poor stakeholder management affecting decisions being made late or scope reduced, and so on) and indirect risks (key supplier insolvency, legal and contract risks, regulatory risks, a public health emergency such as the COVID-19 global pandemic, a sudden and catastrophic change in regulations, and so on).   **27.069**

From a lawyer's perspective, these points are currently dealt with by vague or ambiguous clauses. The ability to use AI reporting and tracking systems to assist in determining compliance would be valuable and make its contracts more useful for the businesses subject to them.   **27.070**

A professional risk manager working on a major IT project will capture and categorise these risks at the outset of the programme of work in a dedicated risk plan. The risk plan will be a shared document (that is, with open access to colleagues) complete with a schedule of risks (a risk log), RAG (red, amber, green) statuses for reporting risks on a frequent basis, a series of   **27.071** risk mitigation plans and effectiveness calculations for each (some risks are simply unavoidable regardless of the mitigation available, others can be avoided altogether) and a governance structure for risks in general: who is told, who decides, and so on.

27.072 In the evolution of the events of the IT project it is the risk manager's task to constantly assess, report, govern and mitigate the risks as and when they occur. No two risks or indeed projects are the same, but as the project nears delivery (assuming it does deliver), the IT risk manager's risk log and other collateral become less and less relevant and useful until – based on events – the work is complete.

27.073 In the real world, it's not quite so straightforward. For the experienced risk manager, it is true that IT project risks tend to emerge from similar hotspots, time after time. For example, integration is a common area for IT project risks to be encountered: plumbing together two entirely different software systems is fraught with complexity and 'discovery' of the to-be-integrated systems only usually starts in detail once a project has commenced. Not only that, but some fruitful risk areas in IT projects are usually not in the sphere of software at all: legal, risk and compliance can cause a hard stop to an IT project, and frequently do at the very last minute.

27.074 Digital transformation projects involve lawyers from various fields: outsourcing, commercial contracts, IP, data, and so on. The legal teams on these projects require close management and project plans as much as the technology teams. It is often the case that the edges where the teams connect pose particular risk challenges, and these must be managed suitably.

J. APPLIED AI IN THE REAL WORLD

27.075 How would artificial intelligence, and machine learning in particular, cope in this challenging environment? Let's assume, in the example of the IT delivery project, that first, the parameters of the machine learning risk management tool are established in the risk/AI tool by a human. Key configurations would be the types and kinds of metrics available for the risk/AI tool to use, for example, risk language key phrases and words – as well as their meanings; data feeds or file uploads; management information reports; external data, such as a key supplier's share price, for example; and macro indicators such as the rate of inflation and interest rates.

27.076 At a lower project level, the risk management AI tool will need custom settings configured for risk thresholds derived from the sponsor's risk appetite – standard and specialised mitigations depending on each risk that can be predicted on a case-by-case basis, and a library of data points and language from other projects. An AI tool should also hold a cache or data store in order to contribute its own data sets created in this specific IT project.

27.077 Armed with all this data, the risk management AI tool in this example is ready to work. With the human-defined risk guardrails established and the overall risk appetite set, how would the AI tool learn to dynamically traverse the IT project, analysing data points, looking at language and making discretionary decisions based on its vast library of previous IT project outcomes?

27.078 A human being would risk manage an IT project with extra information when compared to the AI or machine learning software: for example, in a global health emergency such as the

COVID19 pandemic, humans might prioritise the health and wellbeing of the remote-working IT project team that are also home schooling their children over, say, productivity or specific timekeeping. Measuring the mental health of colleagues is tricky enough for face- and body-language reading humans on Zoom calls and on that basis likely impossible for a machine learning to adduce, if at all. An AI risk management algorithm would probably have shut the project down as the only realistic option left in a crisis… or push the team too hard to try to realise ever greater productivity, to offset the risk of non-delivery.

Let's consider another variable in the risk management example of this fictional IT project: the **27.079** pivot. In many IT deliveries, and because IT domains such as data, applications and so on can change rapidly due to impacts from external factors, there is a constant risk that a nimbler competitor emerges mid-delivery or, and perhaps even more likely, the risk of the scope of delivery being too wide, meaning a material and un-expected de-scoping has to take place in order to reach an already tough delivery landing strip.

In classic risk management terms, an IT project delivery can be put under threat by having to **27.080** deliver too much with too few resources, budget or capacity as go-live approaches. The mitigation is almost always the same: de-scope to deliver a *minimum viable product* (MVP) and push the undelivered items to a second phase, the infamous IT 'Phase 2'.

This de-scoping is a focusing of minds and almost always reveals what were the core compo- **27.081** nents of the IT project that had to be delivered (typically the functionality dealing with the flow, management and reconciliation of cash).

But there is an opportunity to pivot here too: shorn of the 'full' delivery scope it usually tran- **27.082** spires that the core functionality usually works surprisingly well and allows product owners and sponsors to reflect on what actually needs to be delivered in 'Phase 2' after all. Is there an *opportunity* in the risk mitigation that's sometimes greater than the perceived *threat* to the original delivery?

Machine learning would presumably not struggle with de-scoping, but almost certainly would **27.083** not flag up the MVP-based pivot opportunity (Why would it? A machine cannot read minds, or body language, let alone be aware of the market and other macro factors).

To recap this section, while machine learning has a significant role to play in the example given **27.084** – that of a major IT delivery project – machine learning has a somewhat blinkered view of the positive options available to the human sponsors and is almost certainly not alive to the threats and opportunities possible in pivoted or de-scoped deliveries.

This should make lawyers and practitioners pause for thought and consider a less fashionable **27.085** but practical possible evolution of the concept of AI in risk management: not *automated* risk management but *augmented* risk management, where the best of human and artificial intelligences work together to minimise threats but maximise opportunities.

There is a legal consideration here too. Clauses in IT project agreements, as in this example, **27.086** often describe the negative *threat* elements in risks and set out mitigations expected and penalties to be levied if and when such events are triggered. But is there scope for lawyers to consider drafting clauses in project agreements that provide a mechanism for the sharing of possible rewards from opportunities that may be discovered by machine-learning risk management mid-project? Does this matter – and is it even what parties typically want or look for in risk management?

K. A POSSIBLE FUTURE FOR AI IN RISK MANAGEMENT

27.087   It took some 20 to 30 years after its invention for the use of electricity to become ubiquitous.

27.088   Now, electric motors large and small surround us, providing labour-saving help (washing machines, hairdryers, electric razors, dishwashers, tumble driers), propulsion (electric trains, scooters, cars), cooling (fans, air-conditions, refrigerators) and countless sundry applications such as car windows, pencil sharpeners, blenders and lawnmowers.

27.089   It is likely that AI and machine learning will follow the same trajectory of adoption. Car driver assistive technology, such as lane direction, adaptive cruise control and blind-spot monitoring, has not hastened the advent of *automated* driving but something resembling *augmented* driving.

L. CONCLUSION

27.090   In risk management terms it is likely that machine learning, tightly coupled with human discretion, will prove to be the optimal solution for risk managers in professional environments.

27.091   There's no doubting the ability and superiority of AI and machine learning when it comes to pattern identification, traversing vast data and language sets, deep learning and clustering of likely nodes. This is an extraordinary breakthrough that will greatly enhance the risk mitigations available to humans.

27.092   But left to its own devices, machine learning risk management is not an optimal solution. Humans, with our ability to understand reasonableness, discretion, empathy and strategy, are and must remain the ethical and legal controllers of serious risk management mitigation decisions.

27.093   The role for lawyers in all of this is not simply to advise on questions of law but to be proactive team members in the delivery of large and complex projects, with knowledge of how to approach the management of risks in the project.

28

BUSINESS MODELS AND PROCUREMENT

Petko Karamotchev

A. INTRODUCTION

Acquiring AI for use in a business is not straightforward: deep technology software vendors are dealing with customers with business models facing extraordinary challenges. These challenges come primarily from artificial intelligence systems and automation driven by machine learning and deep learning. The technology is leading to pervasive changes as it restructures the economy and gives rise to the business models of the companies of the future.[1,2]   **28.001**

---

1   '(AI) is the runtime that is going to shape all of what we do going forward in terms of the applications as well as the platform advances.'

2   AI Business. 2020. Satya Nadella: AI Is Going To Shape All Of What We Do. [online] Available at: https://aibusiness .com/document.asp?doc_id=760599.

B. BUSINESS MODELS

28.002 Even with basic artificial intelligence, we are already witnessing unprecedented changes in the ways that businesses operate. We do not need to reason with the computer; we expect that through AI we will be able to get rid of the repetitive tasks of the past and focus on more creative and interesting work. AI will replace jobs, as happened before with other technology revolutions. At the same time, AI will help humanity create new jobs. People should not be thinking about competing with machines for jobs that do not require human traits.

1. Areas of AI Application

28.003 In July 2020 the Financial Times Future Forum think-tank convened a panel of experts to discuss the realities of AI. The panel was entitled 'The Impact of Artificial Intelligence on Business and Society' and for the discussion, it defined AI as 'any machine that does things a brain can do'.[3] As such, AI will not simply replace human activities; AI and ML are about dealing with the complexity of data and extracting (via learning algorithms) the value from it. In other words, growth will mean collecting more intelligence data from different connected devices, social and professional media and industry data, and then automating corporate decisions or actions based on this data. Over the years digital data has been growing at a staggering pace across enterprises. Artificial intelligence and machine learning can be applied in various industries and sectors; when considering a mandate to build AI systems for a customer, a vendor starts with a consideration for that customer of which business scenarios can be automated. After identifying and characterising the business scenarios we next typically work through the type of AI that can be used. In so doing we use the two high-level categories that have been discussed elsewhere in the book to help the client understand how the systems can operate.

2. Narrow (also called Weak) AI

28.004 It is important to understand that narrow AI systems are optimised for the execution of a single task. The task can be very complex but AI systems are trained to become proficient in solving it. The specific training of an AI system is designed to solve only this complex task and nothing else. A typical example of a narrow AI is facial recognition. A well-trained AI system is capable of recognising a particular face among a big dataset including millions of other faces, but would not be able to recognise the difference between a cat and a dog.

3. Broad (also called Strong) AI; General Artificial Intelligence

28.005 Such systems are capable of displaying intelligent behaviour like answering a philosophical question. However, even a strong AI system 'merely mimics opinions', which means it will sometimes produce conflicting responses to identical questions.[4] Strong AI aims to replicate

---

3   Colback, L. 2020. The Impact of AI on Business and Society. [online] Ft.com. Available at: www.ft.com/content/e082b01d-fbd6–4ea5-a0d2–05bc5ad7176c.

4   Macaulay, T. 2020. This Philosopher AI Has Its Own Existential Questions to Answer. [online] Neural | The Next Web. Available at: https://thenextweb.com/neural/2020/08/24/this-philosopher-ai-has-its-own-existential-questions-to-answer/.

capacities of human intelligence. It is considered experimental, although there are companies (most notably OpenAI) that examine the implementation of General Artificial Intelligence.

The line between narrow and strong AI is blurred. There are complex AI systems that combine **28.006** several narrow systems (self-driving vehicles; voice assistants such as Siri and Alexa). Their application is wide and beneficial for end-users; however, they do not represent a broad AI in themselves.

Before answering the question for the customer: 'What is the area of AI Application?', we first **28.007** have to answer the question 'What is the technology capable of?' Depending on the customer's intended use case, an AI system has the potential of doing some but not all human tasks to achieve the business objective.

Table 28.1   Technological capabilities of AI

Classification	You can ask a learning algorithm to help you separate the spoons and forks in the drawer by asking it to make a selection of different products, either based on their barcodes or simply judging by the way they look
Prediction	You can ask a learning algorithm to monitor how much stock a company needs to keep in its warehouse, but you need to decide if this is to be based on the weather forecast, stock prices, temperatures, etc.
Control	You can ask a learning algorithm to handle more complex scenarios that involve managing whole systems autonomous machines
Generation	You can ask a learning algorithm to generate synthetic data: a common current example is voice data, for example Siri, Cortana and Alexa and customer chatbots that interact out of the system

Most of these activities are currently executed by humans. Compared to the traditional execu- **28.008** tion of these processes, AI excels because of its scalability. Machines deal with a wider scope of activities and are connected to many different digital services, applications or systems. This takes the performance of the system beyond the scope of the human. It can be demonstrated to the customer that it will lead to more consistent, accurate, complex and sophisticated results. Removing unnecessary repetition will reshape the way companies operate; it will fundamentally make people more creative. Currently most use cases do not use Strong AI. Weak AI applications are now common, helping us with repetitive activities. The technology industry is transforming the environment that firms operate in.

4.   Industry and Areas of (Weak) AI Integration

Many of our projects use AI technology to meet specific targets for customers. Common targets **28.009** are: (a) to boost efficiency; (b) to achieve operational excellence; or (c) to grow a customer's base. The following types of project are now mainstream for vendors of AI systems.

(a)   Healthcare (detection of diseases such as malaria, cancer diagnostics, studying heart diseases, drug discovery, biomedical intelligence).
(b)   Transport (autonomous vehicles, professional drivers and trucks, public transportation).
(c)   Finance (insurance, algorithmic trading, KYC/AML/CFT, credit decisions, managing risk, personalised banking and finance management, and fraud detection).

(d)   Marketing (social media, PPC advertising, highly personalised website experience, recommendation engines, content creation, intelligent email content curation, chatbots, smart customer engagement, customer insights).

(e)   Science automation (image processing, text analysis, chemistry, electromagnetism, materials science, fundamental physics, neuroscience and medicine).

(f)   Cybersecurity (threat exposure, fighting spam and malware, anti-phishing, improving IoT security, fighting deep fakes).

(g)   Automation of knowledge work (grammar checking, electronic discovery, recruitment, improving knowledge databases, venture capital investment).

(h)   Law (document review, contract analysis, litigation prediction, legal research, predicting results).

5.   Strong AI and Implications for Business

28.010   The most cutting-edge business projects now relate to the language model known as GPT-3, developed by OpenAI. It enables products created by R&D AI firms' end customers and businesses. In September 2020, only three months after the release of the research paper describing the GPT-3 technology, Microsoft received an exclusive licence to make it available to the general public. This rapid development displays the potential of AGI.

28.011   The most important feature of GPT-3 is the fact that it uses a relatively small number of examples to derive underlying rules. This includes basic grammatical principles, tackling maths problems and even simple coding. There are clear limitations of this application: the lack of context with no general model of the world to draw on means that its value is in specific terms. But this makes it suitable to display in existing use cases, and GPT-3 shows remarkable success in generating usable results and could be commercialised before other AGI technologies.

28.012   GPT-3 generates unique content. In commercial prototype it found useful information in large quantities of legal prose, research material, documentation and legislation. It has been used to produce financial information from a piece of text and enter it into a spreadsheet, turning it into a form of an automated accountant.

6.   GPT-3 and the Emergence of the AI as a Service

28.013   GPT-3 is the third version of the 'Generative Pre-trained Transformer' developed by the research company OpenAI (co-founded by Elon Musk). It uses 570GB (half a trillion words) of text information gathered by crawling the internet to learn through immersion and expand and speeds up new products.

28.014   GPT-3 could use natural language processing AI algorithms to answer questions, write essays, do 'fill in the blank' tasks, translate, summarise long texts and even do simple arithmetic calculations. This is the most important advancement towards Artificial General Intelligence by far, and the 'most powerful language model ever'.[5]

---

5   Heaven, W. 2020. Openai's New Language Generator GPT-3 Is Shockingly Good – and Completely Mindless. [online] MIT Technology Review. Available at: www.technologyreview.com/2020/07/20/1005454/openai-machine-learning -language-generator-gpt-3-nlp/.

GPT-3 is based on a transformer architecture for deep learning neural networks that was **28.015** originally developed by Google. This architecture is different from the convolutional neural networks used for image recognition or recurring neural networks used for simple language processing. GPT-3 is designed to allow computation on very long sentences and to do it concurrently instead of sequentially.

Today, high-quality natural language processing applications use bespoke models and custom **28.016** architecture and must be fed large quantities of data to train them on every single task. This makes procurement timetables long and dependent on substantial customer input. Procurement models must take into account that requirements change, which can mean you have to retrain the model. OpenAI trained GPT-3 completes complex tasks without retraining and without sacrificing the quality of the results compared to the fine-tuned bespoke models.

7.   Components of GPT-3

Business models and procurement specifications are being updated to take account of features **28.017** of AI:

(a)   Pretrained autoregressive language model optimised for a variety of natural language processing tasks.
(b)   An API bridge allowing developers to ask questions of this model. Developers are not given access to the model.

GPT-3 solves the problem most developers experience with the lack of the infrastructure to **28.018** train the model. It has been estimated that to develop and test GPT-3 from scratch would cost $5–10M in cloud computing time. In this way OpenAI lowers the barrier to entry for developers by providing the already trained model 'as a service' via an API bridge to end users.

OpenAI built an API bridge to the model instead of providing direct access for developers as an **28.019** ethical choice. As stated in their business model, they will not release their model to the public so it cannot be used for criminal purposes such as generating fake news articles. Through the API bridge OpenAI can monitor who is using the model and for what purposes.

The achievement of learning on the scale of GPT-3 has always been a dream of technologists, **28.020** visioners and artists. In the 1997 film The Fifth Element, one of the main characters is Leeloo – one of the Supreme Beings of the Universe. Leeloo (portrayed in the movie by the actress Milla Jovovich) was able to learn English and 5,000 years of human history in just a few days.

Exactly what's going on inside GPT-3 isn't clear. But it is good at synthesising text on the **28.021** internet, making a kind of vast, eclectic scrapbook created from millions of snippets of text that it then glues together on demand.[6] This is the most sophisticated natural language process of its kind and in the long term it will help vendors solve many existing problems, such as building modern chatbots that provide customer support, by analysing huge amounts of text.

---

6   Heaven, W. 2020. Openai's New Language Generator GPT-3 Is Shockingly Good – and Completely Mindless. [online] MIT Technology Review. Available at: www.technologyreview.com/2020/07/20/1005454/openai-machine-learning -language-generator-gpt-3-nlp/.

28.022   Instead of building bespoke models, many companies will turn to providers such as OpenAI and use their pre-trained models 'as a service' to save the time, effort and money currently required in cloud computing. Developers will be able to show several examples of problems to the next generation of GPT-3 and the model will be able to solve those problems with great accuracy, without the need to be retrained. Ethical usage of the model will be monitored through the API. As a developer I argue that this is the beginning of 'AI as a Service'.

8.   Wolfram Alpha: Computational Knowledge on Demand

28.023   A similar 'AI as a Service' business model has been developed by Wolfram Alpha. In this case, we should call it 'Computation as a Service'. Wolfram provides a unique engine for computing answers and providing knowledge, working with a vast store of expert-level (that is, not simply information appearing on the internet) knowledge and algorithms to automatically answer questions, do analysis and generate reports. It works by breaking down the pieces of a question, whether a mathematical problem or something like 'What is the centre of the United States?', and then cross-referencing those pieces against an library of datasets that are constantly expanded. These datasets include information on geodesic schemes, chemical compounds, human genes, historical weather measurements and thousands of other topics that, when brought together, can be used to provide answers.[7]

28.024   Wolfram Alpha is a powerful system but unlike GPT-3 it is constrained by the limits of its data library and unable to interpret every question. It is similar to a search engine, but delivers very specific answers instead of pages of potentially relevant results.[8] It cannot, unfortunately, interpret every question and it cannot respond in natural language, or what a human would recognise as conversational speech. However, taking into account that Siri relies on Mathematica, another Wolfram Research product and the engine behind Alpha, we can see the future and the potential of the 'Computation as a Service' model.

C. CAN WE HAVE AN 'AI ONLY' BUSINESS MODEL? THE DIFFERENCE BETWEEN TRADITIONAL SOFTWARE DEVELOPMENT AND AI

28.025   Is traditional software moving towards data and ML? The question is important in the procurement context because it may mean that businesses will now purchase products with different characteristics from traditional software from vendors that themselves have different characteristics from a traditional software firm. To answer this question, we need to go back to the roots of the issue. The starting point is the question: what is an 'Information System'? The classical theory says that it is a group of components that interact with each other to produce information. A typical information system comprises a five-component framework: Hardware, Software, Data, Procedures and People.

---

7   Biddle, P. 2020. AI Is Making It Extremely Easy for Students to Cheat | Backchannel. [online] Wired. Available at: www.wired.com/story/ai-is-making-it-extremely-easy-for-students-to-cheat/.

8   Biddle, P. 2020. AI Is Making It Extremely Easy for Students to Cheat | Backchannel. [online] Wired. Available at: www.wired.com/story/ai-is-making-it-extremely-easy-for-students-to-cheat/.

These elements are divided into two sides: hardware and software on the computer side; proce- **28.026**
dures and people on the human side. Data is considered to be the bridge.

Machine learning and AI are based on data and therefore we can expect differences in the ways **28.027**
in which the typical SaaS (software as a service) companies operate. AI/ML companies differ
significantly from traditional software business.

A typical software development company (a SaaS company, for example) runs with a relatively **28.028**
high profit margin of 70–80 per cent. The reason for this is economy of scale: you can sell
more software without producing more; the team that builds the software remains same even
when the software is adopted by many different customers. Software companies also have the
potential to build strong defensive moats because they own the intellectual property (typically
the code) generated by their work.[9]

Data is complex. To extract value from it, more people are required to analyse and process it. **28.029**
The business model requires an increasing number of people working on data: labelling it,
cleaning it, improving it. Software is being commoditised. AI work is more like a service, and
service businesses are different to software businesses. In an AI service business the data and
ML scientists work within the firm and all the value remains within your organisation. There
are several types of AI business model.

1. Company A: The Cloud SaaS Provider

This is a company developing the tools and the software necessary for AI models and algo- **28.030**
rithms. These are infrastructure companies that build tools for data science and AI/ML.
These companies usually sell to customers' IT departments. They charge high costs: the more
demanding the software, the higher the bill. *Training a single AI model on cloud infrastructure
could cost hundreds of thousands of dollars.*

2. Company B: The AI Service Company

This is a company that applies AI algorithms to an industry or customer. It is far more complex **28.031**
than company A. It deals with new problems. It is a relatively new type of company that
processes data rather than writing software. The margins come not from how well it creates
software, but freom how well it processes data. Success comes from building models, refining
models and executing services on top of them. The companies do not sell to the typical IT
department. They sell directly to business. This represents a new type of business because it is
more of a professional service than a software company. Each customer will have its problems
to be solved and its own dataset and structure. Part of the work can be uploaded to the customer
(such as data cleansing: see Company C). Part of the work can be automated by implementing
bespoke frameworks and proprietary reference models. The companies' market exists because
organisations that own its customers do not contain their own educated professionals and lack
understanding of AI.

---

9   Andreessen Horowitz. 2020. The New Business of AI (and How It's Different from Traditional Software). [online]
     Available at: https://a16z.com/2020/02/16/the-new-business-of-ai-and-how-its-different-from-traditional-software/.

28.032 Companies such as QuantumBlack and INDUSTRIA[10] supply these services, helping businesses harness their data, analytics and design to improve performance.

28.033 The roles of software engineering and data science have different perspectives. With software you know what the inputs are and the goal is to build a system that uses these inputs to create outputs, so you have nice definitions of correctness. Data/ML/AI scientists cannot rely on such definitions. For some sets of values you will be correct, but for others your predictions will be wrong. Your system is dependent on values and this is the key difference between machine learning and classical software engineering. The correctness of a function is value and performance-dependent.

3. Company C: Cleaning Data, Data Labelling as a Service, Generation of Synthetic Data

28.034 This company addresses the need for data labelling tools that put together datasets and ensure high-quality data production. Companies such as Amazon Mechanical Turk, Lionbridge and Edgecase provide tools that are simple to use, require minimal human involvement and maximise efficiency while keeping quality consistent. Data labelling can be done in-house, outsourced to a vendor or provided as a crowdsourcing service.

28.035 Training AI systems also requires synthetic data. Synthetic (also called simulated) data includes images and videos created to mirror the real world. In a picture the weather, background, camera placement and objects can be changed, allowing for the automatic creation of millions of training images that quickly become a dataset for your training algorithms. Vendors provide easy-to-use SaaS platforms for creating the necessary synthetic datasets.

28.036 Clients can bring in vendors to clean or label (or both) data. Vendors will also advise on the best approach to data labelling for a customer. The best approach depends on the complexity of the use case, the training data, the size of the company and data science team, the budget and the deadline.[11]

4. Company D: AI as a Service

28.037 This type of company aims to place as much of the power of AI in the hands of the customer as is possible. For example, Twilio is a company that allows software developers to programmatically make and receive phone calls, send and receive text messages and perform other communication functions using its web service APIs.

28.038 AI cloud offerings including Amazon Machine Learning, Microsoft Cognitive Services and Google Cloud Machine Learning help organisations build their own intelligent apps without machine learning knowledge and experience. They provide a trade-off between unsuitability and sophistication. Microsoft's $1 billion investment in OpenAI is perhaps the first step towards making the next generation of very large AI models and the infrastructure needed to train them available as a platform for other organisations and developers to build upon. This is

---

10   Note: the author of this chapter is a director of INDUSTRIA.
11   Lionbridge AI. 2020. 5 Approaches to Data Labeling for Machine Learning Projects. [online] Available at: https://lionbridge.ai/articles/5-approaches-to-data-labeling-for-machine-learning-projects/.

a big step towards the 'AI as a Service' concept. Microsoft has built one of the top five publicly disclosed supercomputers in the world, making new infrastructure available in Azure to train extremely large artificial intelligence models.

The supercomputer hosted in Azure was built in collaboration with and exclusively for OpenAI   **28.039**
and designed specifically to train that company's AI models. It represents a key milestone in a partnership announced in 2019 to jointly create new supercomputing technologies in Azure.[12]

D. AI AND IT JOBS

Big data and analytics will be at the root of AI success. AI is transforming many companies and   **28.040**
creating new ones. Existing positions at IT companies (designer, product manager, engineer) are changing and new positions are emerging.

The product manager role will change drastically because managing AI projects involves more   **28.041**
unknowns, non-deterministic outcomes, new infrastructures, new processes and new tools – a lot to learn, but worthwhile to access the unique and special value AI creates in the product space.[13] In procurement terms, the job descriptions of the vendor and the customer change.

E. AI AND COMPETITION

We have unprecedented competition between AI-enabled companies. Winners in AI will build   **28.042**
predictive modelling on data that exists not only within their organisations but also across the wider business network(s) in which they operate. AI's potential to augment the abilities of human workers will give rise to new 'AI Companies' utilising the technology in a way that we cannot currently imagine.

1.   Streamlining Business Operations and Replacing Human Labour

The general expectation that the most repetitive jobs will be replaced by AI ignores studies   **28.043**
finding that just because a job is automatable, this does not mean it will be automated. Both theoretical models and historical evidence show that even when most of the labour of an industry is automated, employment can grow rapidly.[14] A computer that digitally represents human activity can improve itself over time at a pace and scale impossible for humans. The benefits of current commercial AI applications are much more often about enhancing human capabilities rather than reducing labour costs. AI will make companies more competitive not by eliminating human labour but through augmenting human abilities.

---

12   The AI Blog. 2020. Microsoft Announces New Supercomputer, Lays Out Vision for Future AI Work – The AI Blog. [online] Available at: https://blogs.microsoft.com/ai/openai-azure-supercomputer/.

13   Peter Skomoroch, M. 2020. What You Need to Know about Product Management for AI. [online] O'Reilly Media. Available at: www.oreilly.com/radar/what-you-need-to-know-about-product-management-for-ai/.

14   Bessen, J., Impink, S., Seamans, R. and Reichensperger, L. 2018. The Business of AI Startups. SSRN Electronic Journal.

2. Quantity and Quality of Data; Network Analysis

28.044 To get something from AI a business needs to understand its data. Data is numeric (sales, number of clients or employees, loan amounts, customer retention rate), categorical (customer groups, product types, product sizes), free text (reports and emails, comments on the opportunity details in Salesforce), pictures, sound and video.

28.045 To develop practical AI and machine learning solutions, data collection processes need to be established. Data is the lifeblood of AI. It must be collected, stored and cleared (that is, checked for errors and relevance) to make it ready for predictive modelling. Google constantly experiments with its search engine to improve its results rather than simply relying on its volume of search data. Amazon has found that the accuracy of its predictions in e-commerce does not continue to improve by simply adding more products.[15]

28.046 It is of paramount importance to understand that data rarely exists only in silos inside the business. While traditional industry analysis focuses on specific, isolated industry segments, network analysis involves understanding the open and distributed connections across many firms, each of which is connected to a large number of networks across disparate industries.[16]

3. Unique AI Companies

28.047 Some businesses seek to implement AI to simply replicate their existing processes. But advanced firms will use vastly different operating models to deliver value to customers. Grammarly, a grammar-checking tool using AI and natural language processing to find and fix grammatical errors, changed its sales model from universities to the private consumer market.[17]

28.048 The company is seen as one of the best in the industry, providing state of the art NLP software (no precise information regarding its technical architecture is available to the public because the software is not open source) and augmenting its AI services by providing human proofreading services. This is an example of the sort of 'AI Company' we will see more of in the future.

F. PROCUREMENT

28.049 Traditional procurement using the 'three quote approach' does not work for acquiring AI services. There may be two specialist suppliers or just one. It may not be possible for anyone to compete with OpenAI and GPT-3. The procurement department may now know the size of the system that has to be deployed, the necessary resources and the steps of the timeline for the right AI project to be successful (planning, inputting, computation and interpretation).

28.050 Some of the key points for procurement in AI are:

---

15 Harvard Business Review. 2020. The Competitive Landscape of AI Startups. [online] Available at: https://hbr.org/2018/12/the-competitive-landscape-of-ai-startups.

16 Iansiti, M. and Lakhani, K. 2020. Competing in the Age of AI.

17 productmint. 2020. The Grammarly Business Model – How Does Grammarly Work & Make Money? [online] Available at: https://productmint.com/the-grammarly-business-model-how-does-grammarly-work-make-money/.

1.   Lack of Understanding

What is AI, beyond the learning algorithms? Before evaluating a project with an AI company   **28.051**
a buyer must define AI as a system of relevant tools (data, sources planning, storage and computation). These build and design; they don't work 'out of the box'. The output must be defined
in testable ways and must reflect the values of the organisation and society.

2.   Focusing on Exact Specification

This is not likely to be possible for something that has never been purchased before, especially if   **28.052**
the solution is not finished yet. You need to build a mission statement. 'What problem are you
trying to solve?' You cannot automate what you cannot articulate. You need to be formal and
pedantic about numbering every step of the job that needs to be automated.

3.   Access to High-value Data

Models and algorithms suitable for the specific industry and process domain are crucial. The   **28.053**
history of AI services includes many ambitious projects that fail because of issues with data
collection and cleaning.[18]

4.   Cooperation

You need to work shoulder to shoulder with the vendor and understand the ontology of the   **28.054**
task. Projects must be designed and built in an unprecedented collaboration. Merging datasets
and applying algorithms is a non-trivial task. Understanding of the datasets cannot be simply
'given to the IT company'; it needs to be instilled with collaboration with the client. Within the
client, corporate silos of data and lack of cross-departmental collaboration can be fatal. Building
AI is about teamwork.

5.   AI as a Threat and Fear of Displacement

Since team buy-in is critical, everyone must be on the same page and share the same under-   **28.055**
standing of the task. Where groups feel threatened their resistance will sink the project. It is up
to the senior team to be engaged to explain the opportunity to augment jobs rather than replace
them, and to understand the new creative jobs in AI.

G. CONCLUSION

Businesses should know that to make a significant change, implementation of AI might   **28.056**
require more than a simple replacement of existing business processes with technology. Quite
often such a transition might require a complete organisational redesign and this could lead to

---

18   Brightwork Research & Analysis. 2020. How Many IBM and Other AI Projects Will Fail Due to a Lack of Data? –
Brightwork Research & Analysis. [online] Available at: www.brightworkresearch.com/how-many-ai-projects-will-fail
-due-to-a-lack-of-data/.

machines replacing many of the boring and tedious tasks, but this doesn't mean that we need to start worrying about the jobs being lost. Both theoretical models and historical evidence show that even when most of the labour of an industry is automated, employment can grow rapidly. Ultimately AI will make companies more competitive but procuring AI will be a challenge because of the innovativeness of the area. For maximum effect, businesses should work with AI companies similarly to how they work with their external legal or marketing teams.

29

EXPLAINABLE AI AND RESPONSIBLE AI

Charles Kerrigan and Oliver Vercoe

A. INTRODUCTION

Artificial Intelligence (AI), reaching a point where its capabilities can outperform humans at **29.001** certain tasks and, as a technical matter, operate with almost no human intervention,[1] has deep implications for developers and users. Unlike the original rudimentary AI systems, which could be understood relatively easily, new systems have become opaque and difficult. These are the infamous 'black-box models', lacking transparency and interpretability.[2] Policy debates across the world call for some form of AI explainability and a shift towards 'responsible AI', that is, technologies predicated on transparent models that offer identifiable patterns and trace how decisions have been reached. Public awareness of AI integration, and concerns over the role that regulators should be playing in safeguarding consumers against technology, elevate this topic. Although trade-offs may be involved, fundamentally AI systems do not need to be opaque.

The debate centres on concerns over machine learning, as opposed to human-managed AI **29.002** systems, and how this relates to ethics and codified values. Human systems management has been perceived in technical terms to come at the cost of advancement. As this chapter will set out, some conflicts in terminology and in motives for developing AI systems can highlight preferences among stakeholders for one approach over the other. The variety of terminology, though problematic in defining the issues, highlights the broad range of views and literature on

---

1   Arrieta, A.B., Diaz-Rodriguez, N., Del Sar, J., Bennetot, S., Tabik, S., Barbado, A., Garcia, S., Gil-Lopez, S., Molina, D., Benjamins, R., Chatila, R. and Herrera, F. (2020) 'Explainable Artificial Intelligence (XAI): Concepts, Taxonomies, Opportunities and Challenges towards Responsible AI', Information Fusion 58: 83.
2   Arrieta, A.B., Diaz-Rodriguez, N., Del Sar, J., Bennetot, S., Tabik, S., Barbado, A., Garcia, S., Gil-Lopez, S., Molina, D., Benjamins, R., Chatila, R. and Herrera, F. (2020) 'Explainable Artificial Intelligence (XAI): Concepts, Taxonomies, Opportunities and Challenges towards Responsible AI', Information Fusion 58: 83.

the topic. At the time of writing, however, there is now a consistent focus on the importance of some form of 'responsible AI'. This is both the philosophy of developing AI in a responsible and ethical manner and the desire to comprehensively understand AI solutions and their underlying processes and pathways.

29.003   This chapter first considers the current definitions associated with understandable AI and the contrasting terminology, highlighting the lack of common ground and the effect that this has on the development of a unified development goal. This is then contextualised within the current map of understandable AI and its means of use, where the approaches are also considered. Later sections should be read in conjunction with previous chapters that discuss why transparency is necessary and the challenges in procuring it.

B. DEFINITIONS AND USE

29.004   The best known early discussion of explainable AI ('XAI') was put forward by Van Lent et al. in 2004, describing the ability of the system that they had developed to explain the behaviour of AI controlled entities in simulation games.[3] After this the field received relatively less interest until a renewed resurgence in the past few years, as illustrated by Figure 29.1,[4] resulting from the widespread permeation of AI technologies into everyday life.[5] This has consequently seen a corresponding rise in the total number of publications with a focus on XAI. In 2012, there were fewer than 50 contributed works in the literature, with the vast majority referring to 'Interpretable AI'; by 2019, the total number of publications was more than 300, with 'Explainable AI' the dominant term. Despite the renewed interest, a categorical definition of XAI remains elusive; as a starting point, the US Defense Advanced Research Projects Agency (DARPA), which is active in the XAI research field, defines XAI development as the aim to 'produce more explainable models, while maintaining a high level of learning performance; and enable human users to understand, appropriately trust and effectively manage the emerging generation of intelligent partners'.[6] A prevailing issue with appropriately addressing XAI, however, is the broad range of definitions and usage terms that are applied to the topic. The interchangeable use of 'interpretability' and 'explainability' in the literature hinders finding common ground due to differences among these concepts.[7]

---

3   Van Lent, M., Fisher, W. and Mancuso, M. (2004) 'An Explainable Artificial Intelligence System for Small-unit Tactical Behavior, Proceedings of the 16th Conference on Innovative Applications of Artificial Intelligence.

4   Adadi, A. and Berrada, M. (2018) 'Peeking Inside the Black-Box: A Survey on Explainable Artificial Intelligence (XAI)', IEEE Access 6. Available at: https://ieeexplore.ieee.org/document/8466590.

5   Adadi, A. and Berrada, M. (2018) 'Peeking Inside the Black-Box: A Survey on Explainable Artificial Intelligence (XAI)', IEEE Access 6. Available at: https://ieeexplore.ieee.org/document/8466590.

6   Turek, M. (2018) 'Explainable Artificial Intelligence (XAI)' Defense Advanced Research Projects Agency (DARPA). Available at: www.darpa.mil/program/explainable-artificial-intelligence.

7   Arrieta, A.B., Diaz-Rodriguez, N., Del Sar, J., Bennetot, S., Tabik, S., Barbado, A., Garcia, S., Gil-Lopez, S., Molina, D., Benjamins, R., Chatila, R. and Herrera, F. (2020) 'Explainable Artificial Intelligence (XAI): Concepts, Taxonomies, Opportunities and Challenges towards Responsible AI', Information Fusion 58: 113.

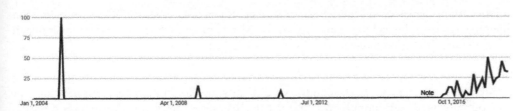

Figure 29.1   Interest over time for 'Explainable Artificial Intelligence' term

Interpretability is used to define the 'passive characteristics' of a model, that is, how much sense **29.005**
the model makes to a human in its own right.[8] This concerns the model's own way of displaying
and outputting data.

Though interpretability is regarded by some as the more holistic definition, because a model **29.006**
being interpreted is characterised by reference to its definitive processes and how much
a human can interpret those processes in that form, it relies on the understanding of the human
interpreter. The better the understanding of AI processes and machine learning that the human
interpreter has, the more interpretable the model will be to them. While the process may be
transparent, human characteristics, education and perspectives may all lead to different inter-
pretations and interpretability, thus reducing the reliability of the concept.

Conversely, explainability relates to the 'active characteristics' of a model, a more general **29.007**
term used to denote any further steps or actions taken by the model to give contextual clarity
or information about the machine learning and AI processes.[9] This still relies on interaction
between a model and a human interpreter, but here understanding is dependent on the machine
explaining its processes rather than a human interpreting the model on its own terms.[10]

Though this, to an extent, negates the disadvantage of interpretability as a tool described in **29.008**
paragraph 29.006, the increased reliance on the machine leads to questions over the understandability of the additional processes involved. While making AI more explainable to
a human interpreter, the processes behind this require a high degree of transparency and trust
in the model's design.

Transparency is often used synonymously with interpretability and refers to the characteristics **29.009**
of a model that make it understandable to humans.

Understandability refers to the degree to which a human can follow the steps in a decision **29.010**
made by a model. It is therefore of use as a general concept for a wide audience of AI stake-

---

8   Arrieta, A.B., Diaz-Rodriguez, N., Del Sar, J., Bennetot, S., Tabik, S., Barbado, A., Garcia, S., Gil-Lopez, S., Molina,
     D., Benjamins, R., Chatila, R. and Herrera, F. (2020) 'Explainable Artificial Intelligence (XAI): Concepts, Taxonomies,
     Opportunities and Challenges towards Responsible AI', Information Fusion 58: 86.
9   Arrieta, A.B., Diaz-Rodriguez, N., Del Sar, J., Bennetot, S., Tabik, S., Barbado, A., Garcia, S., Gil-Lopez, S., Molina,
     D., Benjamins, R., Chatila, R. and Herrera, F. (2020) 'Explainable Artificial Intelligence (XAI): Concepts, Taxonomies,
     Opportunities and Challenges towards Responsible AI', Information Fusion 58: 87.
10   Guidotti, R., Monreale, M., Ruggiere, S., Turini, F., Giannotti, F. and Pedreschi, D. (2018) 'A Survey of Methods for
     Explaining Black Box Models', ACM Computing Surveys 51(5): 93.

holders, from businesses and consumers, to developers and policymakers.[11] The 'approximation dilemma' refers to the fact that explanations for AI and machine learning models must match the understandability requirements of the relevant audience.[12]

29.011   In science and computing, the term 'black-box' is used to describe an opaque system operating with closed components.[13] In relation to AI, difficulty in providing adequate explanations for how outputs have been formulated is termed the 'black-box problem'. The literature on the problem is extensive. A view among researchers is that transparency is inversely proportional to effectiveness: 'deep learning algorithms' sacrifice transparency and interpretability for prediction accuracy.[14] On this view 'black-box models' are perceived to be able to process larger quantities of data, applying more complex algorithms. The goal of XAI is to transform these black-box models into 'glass-box models'.[15]

29.012   For reasons explained in other chapters, for example relating to safety, ethics and the views of regulators and users, XAI is now an important independent field of study aiming, according to one commentator, to 'create [...] machine learning techniques that enable humans to understand, appropriately trust and effectively manage the emerging generation of artificially intelligent partners, without sacrificing complexity'.[16]

C. CURRENT STATUS OF EXPLAINABLE AI

29.013   XAI relies on developers and users knowing why they want to achieve transparency and explainability. All AI models are judged on 'results' and 'effectiveness', but varying definitions of these terms, and variations in the audience and the person using the terms, lead to different measures being applied to them. An AI software engineer may apply the highest value to accuracy in judging a voice recognition tool; a consumer may conversely apply the highest value to data privacy in judging the same tool.

29.014   This was evidenced in 2019 by a comprehensive review of XAI-focused literature to consider the goal of XAI.[17] The study found that the most common goal discussed in this context was 'informativeness'. Informativeness combines elements of data, context and clarity about a problem being addressed to avoid 'misconception pitfalls'. The study found that, to be most

---

11   Arrieta, A.B., Diaz-Rodriguez, N., Del Sar, J., Bennetot, S., Tabik, S., Barbado, A., Garcia, S., Gil-Lopez, S., Molina, D., Benjamins, R., Chatila, R. and Herrera, F. (2020) 'Explainable Artificial Intelligence (XAI): Concepts, Taxonomies, Opportunities and Challenges towards Responsible AI', Information Fusion 58: 87.

12   Theodorou, A., Wortham, R. H. and Bryson, J.J. (2017). 'Designing and Implementing Transparency for Real Time Inspection of Autonomous Robots', Connection Science 29(3): 230–41.

13   Adadi, A. and Berrada, M. (2018) 'Peeking Inside the Black-Box: A Survey on Explainable Artificial Intelligence (XAI)', IEEE Access 6. Available at: https://ieeexplore.ieee.org/document/8466590.

14   Rai, A. (2020) 'Explainable AI: From Black Box to Glass Box', Journal of Academy of Marketing Science 48: 137.

15   Rai, A. (2020) 'Explainable AI: From Black Box to Glass Box', Journal of Academy of Marketing Science 48: 137.

16   Turek, M. (2018) 'Explainable artificial intelligence (XAI)' Defense Advanced Research Projects Agency (DARPA). Available at: www.darpa.mil/program/explainable-artificial-intelligence.

17   Arrieta, A.B., Diaz-Rodriguez, N., Del Sar, J., Bennetot, S., Tabik, S., Barbado, A., Garcia, S., Gil-Lopez, S., Molina, D., Benjamins, R., Chatila, R. and Herrera, F. (2020) 'Explainable Artificial Intelligence (XAI): Concepts, Taxonomies, Opportunities and Challenges towards Responsible AI', Information Fusion 58: 90.

useful in view of the need for explainability, AI models 'should provide more information about the problem being tackled'.[18]

Other goals included trustworthiness, confidence, fairness, accessibility and privacy awareness, but these ranked lower and featured in only a handful of papers (only one paper cited privacy awareness as a goal of explainable AI). This is indicative of reasons for the inconsistent development of XAI. On the other hand, if software engineers and XAI scholars prioritise informativeness, they must take care that this does not come at the cost of ethical transparency, privacy and fairness.

29.015

Current approaches to XAI development can mostly be differentiated between those that are human-centric and those that are machine-centric. Human-centric approaches use analyses of logic and inference to transform AI issues into human problems that then receive human input. Machine-centric approaches use statistical methods.

29.016

Human-centric or 'symbolic' AI is generally regarded as more explainable because it uses interpretable outputs. Datasets codify human knowledge and behaviour to automate decision-making while attempting to recreate and show the type of pathway thinking that is familiar to a human. This approach naturally lends itself to explainability, with the ideal outcome providing identifiable steps along a process that formulates a decision. The qualitative nature of this approach fits well with explainability. The very large-scale datasets involved mean that qualitative approaches are limited, however, as some level of abstraction is required in almost all use cases.[19]

29.017

Data-centric approaches apply statistical techniques to analyse data to find patterns and causation. Their effectiveness depends on large amounts of data and the use of deep learning, both of which test the limits of explainability. As the market and policy requirement for explainability has become clearer, however, programmers have addressed this by adding code at each step of a model to display the step and the input or output values of that step. The code can display, on a screen or in a file, each processing step so that explainability becomes a design feature of the code.

29.018

D. NEED FOR RESPONSIBLE AI

This section supplements Chapter 18 (Healthcare), Chapter 21 (Ethics) and Chapter 22 (Bias and Discrimination), among others, focusing on how incorporating transparency and explainability into AI bolsters the effectiveness and serviceability of the technology and, in particular, embeds ethical considerations into AI.

29.019

---

18   Arrieta, A.B., Diaz-Rodriguez, N., Del Sar, J., Bennetot, S., Tabik, S., Barbado, A., Garcia, S., Gil-Lopez, S., Molina, D., Benjamins, R., Chatila, R. and Herrera, F. (2020) 'Explainable Artificial Intelligence (XAI): Concepts, Taxonomies, Opportunities and Challenges towards Responsible AI', Information Fusion 58: 90.
19   The Royal Society (2019) 'Explainable AI: The Basics', Policy Briefing.

29.020   AI development in highly sensitive policy areas such as facial recognition and data collection has increased demand for transparency across stakeholder groups.[20] As the range of AI-operative tasks grows, the potential for accidents and misuse also grows, raising safety and security concerns.[21] Increased regulatory attention, for example resulting from the implications of GDPR-type regulations, affects the way that data can be handled.

29.021   Interpretability is necessary as a tool to recognise and rectify errors produced by AI systems. It therefore has significant safety applications. In the case of autonomous vehicles, for example, it is important to be able to understand even minor system malfunctions. In this respect, interpretability is crucial in tracking the use of data and identifying any error to prevent duplication across a wider system.

29.022   In medicine,[22] healthcare professionals require more transparency than a simple binary prediction for AI systems to be useful to support diagnoses. Outputs from AI systems require a high threshold.

E. CHALLENGES

29.023   While there is now a consensus among researchers and developers that AI requires a degree of explainability, challenges remain in enacting full-scale transformation of AI to XAI.

29.024   Part of the case for XAI comes from the fact that humans are naturally reticent about adopting systems where there is a lack of transparency and difficulties in interpretation.[23] If transparency comes at the expense of effectiveness,[24] however, designers and users will need to make trade-offs, taking into account their respective motives. Therefore, learning to identify and define motives is becoming a valued skill. Researchers may face less pressure to sacrifice performance for explainability in the lab, but customers and policymakers require the trade-offs to be made at some point before implementation.

29.025   As discussed in Chapter 22, there are concerns over discrimination and bias in the use of AI. Black-box models cause doubt about their potential to unfairly consider discriminatory factors such as gender, age or race and incorporate these into a decision-making process in a way that a human would not.[25] Machine learning AI models require vast amounts of data to learn and develop, and the challenge arises in providing representative data and mitigating consequent bias favouring certain groups over others in unrepresentative data. While 'explainable AI'

---

20   Preece, D., Harborne, D., Braines, D., Tomsett, R. and Chakraborty, S. (2018) 'Stakeholders in Explainable AI', *Artificial Intelligence in Government and Public Sector*. Available at: https://arxiv.org/abs/1810.00184.

21   Amodei, D., Olah, C. et al. (2016) 'Concrete Problems in AI Safety', arXiv. Available at: https://arxiv.org/abs/1606.06565.

22   Varshney, K.R. and Alemzadeh, H. (2017) 'On the Safety of Machine Learning: Cyber-Physical Systems, Decision Sciences, and Data Products', *Big Data* 5(3): 246.

23   Goodman, B. and Flaxman, S. (2017) 'European Union Regulations on Algorithmic Decision-Making and a Right to Explanation', *AI Magazine* 38(3): 50.

24   Dosilovi, F.K., Brci, M and Hlupi, N. (2018) 'Explainable Artificial Intelligence: A Survey', MIPRO: 21.

25   D'Alessandro, B. O'Neil, C. and LaGatta, T. (2017) 'Conscientious Classification: A Data Scientist's Guide to Discrimination-Aware Classification', *Big Data* 5(2): 120.

implies a transparent process, 'responsible AI' incorporates a layer of ethical considerations that is now the goal in developing many AI systems.

Issues around terminology present a further challenge in the adoption of XAI. XAI is impor- **29.026** tant for researchers and developers in relation to the informativeness of AI systems, but it may not be sufficient for users. For them AI must be explainable, responsible and ethical. Each of these in their own way requires transparency of process. AI can leverage financial gains, but businesses are also judged on corporate responsibility and sustainability goals that may not be traded off. From a user perspective, the use of AI must be fair and shown to be so through glass-box processes, for example to correspond to diversity and inclusion initiatives.[26]

A challenge remains in encouraging businesses to adopt AI in business-as-usual functions. AI **29.027** systems create value for businesses and customers but incorporation of AI without responsi- bility is problematic.[27] Using AI responsibly provides both competitive advantage in business terms and accountability for outputs – the type of balance that takes into account motives, as described above.

F. CONCLUSION

Issues remain with XAI and the 'black-box problem'. Trade-offs and a lack of common ground **29.028** hinder movement to a unified and cohesive strategy for implementation. This partly stems from the discrepancies highlighted in the reasons for wanting XAI. The cited literature evi- dences the value of transparency of informativeness; whereas social concerns such as privacy and discrimination should weigh equally in the balance.

Developing AI responsibly may mean that financial benefits are not immediately obvious **29.029** or forthcoming.[28] The incentives to develop responsible AI technology come not only from consumer demand, however, but also from laws relating to liability and regulation relating to consumer protection. The combination is likely to have great impact.[29]

Consumer and stakeholder values requiring digital products and services that use data in an **29.030** ethical and transparent way now influence the development of AI system implementation. XAI is also part of what will ensure that AI develops among a diverse and representative audience.[30] In this case, improved technology should be tasked to help improve society.

26 Benjamins, R., Barbado, A. and Sierra, D. (2019) 'Responsible AI by Design in Practice', arXiv. Available at: https://arxiv.org/abs/1909.12838.
27 Askell, A., Brundage, M. and Hadfield, G. 'The Role of Cooperation in Responsible AI Development', arXiv. Available at: https://arxiv.org/abs/1907.04534.
28 Askell, A., Brundage, M. and Hadfield, G. "The Role of Cooperation in Responsible AI Development" arXiv. Available at: https://arxiv.org/abs/1907.04534.
29 Arrieta, A.B., Diaz-Rodriguez, N., Del Sar, J., Bennetot, S., Tabik, S., Barbado, A., Garcia, S., Gil-Lopez, S., Molina, D., Benjamins, R., Chatila, R. and Herrera, F. (2020) 'Explainable Artificial Intelligence (XAI): Concepts, Taxonomies, Opportunities and Challenges towards Responsible AI', Information Fusion 58: 115.
30 Howard, A., Zhang, C. and Horvitz, E. (2017) 'Addressing Bias in Machine Learning Algorithms: A Pilot Study on Emotion Recognition for Intelligent Systems', Proc. Adv. Robot. Social Impacts (ARSO): 1.

30

LEGALTECH

Richard Tromans

A. INTRODUCTION

30.001 AI is a term we have heard so often in the legal field that it is understandable that people get confused about what it means in practice today, or lose sight of where it is actually used by practising lawyers.

30.002 The reality is that 'legal AI' in the majority of cases refers to NLP (software that has been 'trained' via machine learning). Again, in most cases its primary function is to examine text that is unstructured rather than structured data, and to find and retrieve what is searched for and what is relevant to the matter in hand.

30.003 Aside from the underlying language models and various machine learning techniques – which we will not get into here because we are focused on legal sector outputs not technology patents – the world of legal AI is surprisingly simple.

30.004 What holds people back is perhaps just how many ways this approach can be used, as well as confusion over what we might call visible AI and invisible AI.

B. AI IN LEGALTECH

30.005 In many cases the AI component – that is, the NLP and machine learning – is not explicitly visible to the user of a piece of software, nor are they expected to knowingly engage in its training – no more than Google ever asks you to help to deliberately improve its own NLP software. You use their platform and it learns as you use it; that is, it's invisible AI.

The same can be seen with some legal research systems that may have received huge amounts   **30.006**
of supervised and unsupervised machine learning input and an equally enormous amount of
expert input on how a system should rank returns from a digital law library to make them most
relevant to a search query posed in a natural language sentence, as opposed to a simple key word
search.

Again, the user does not consciously get involved in the training of the research system,   **30.007**
although it may learn from their search behaviour.

In other cases, especially around large-scale document review exercises, active and very visible   **30.008**
training is needed. The challenge there is primarily around a law firm understanding that it
will need its lawyers to work on that training, as pre-set NLP solutions for a particular set of
commercial documents may need to be fine-tuned, or even trained up from a very early stage.
This is more akin to Ikea furniture that comes 70 per cent assembled but then demands several
hours of your time to actually make it useable.

That is probably the largest speed bump, but once it has been passed you are free to explore   **30.009**
what is a broad world of use cases, along with associated use cases that connect to natural
language generation, audio-based language processing and – a very niche use case – visual cue
processing based on human reactions. Figure 30.1 shows some of the main use cases and where
they've got to so far.

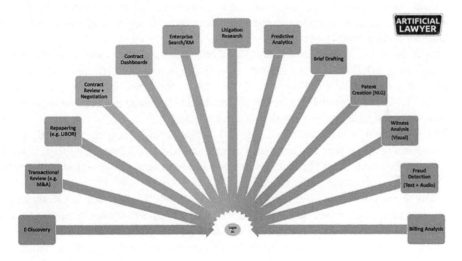

Source: Artificial Lawyer, 2021

Figure 30.1   Main use cases of AI

As the figure shows, there is a mass of use cases, all with their own quirks and particular ways   **30.010**
of working:

(a)   EDiscovery – this is very different to document review in that you are trying to exclude
       documents from often gigantic stacks, rather than finding specific clause data. However,

NLP and ML can play a big role here, especially in finding linked concepts or for building a taxonomy for a large doc stack.

(b) Transactional review – this is the classic legal AI use case, that is, NLP/ML for finding key clauses in docs so that a human can then review them in detail. Uptake is fairly healthy among large commercial firms, but smaller firms still struggle as they cannot see the economic benefits, nor do clients push them to use technology for smaller deals.

(c) Repapering – this has come into its own with the LIBOR/IBOR changes, needing hundreds of thousands of documents to be analysed and key clauses rewritten to meet new interbank rates regulation. This has often been done hand-in-hand with process groups and the Big Four.

(d) Contract review and negotiation – this is an area ripe for change using NLP/ML. What happens is a third party paper is analysed by a system that has been pre-set with a company's or firm's playbook for that type of contract. The system highlights language and terms that don't fit the playbook and suggests new language – this can then massively accelerate contract review, at least for more basic contracts.

(e) Contact dashboards – these can be built using NLP to show not just legal factors but also pure commercial data, for example when sales contracts expire, or the value of contracts across a business. In effect, this is turning doc review into a business intelligence tool.

(f) Enterprise search/Knowledge Management (KM) – a lot of KM tools are fairly basic but, working with a business NLP, companies can train up their Knowledge Management system to not just recognise single documents but find groups of documents that contain related clause information, or operate on any 'meaning taxonomy' you wish. The challenge here is that such projects need a lot of investment to work across a firm. But the long-term value could be immense.

(g) Litigation research, predictive analysis and brief drafting – all doing basically the same thing: using NLP to analyse case law and related documents, then help the user to find what they want, and/or to show what is relevant to their case, or to provide a data foundation for creating models for how a future similar case may unfold, mostly around key aspects of that case, rather than the case as a whole.

(h) Patent creation – now we move into NLG, or natural language generation, where long-form text of a patent is analysed and then turned into a brief patent application, or at least a first draft of it. This is a rare use case and has not really gone that far yet in terms of uptake or companies doing this.

(i) Witness analysis – this is another novel use case, which uses facial analysis to gauge emotions in people when they listen to a witness or expert witness before a case comes to court. This allows lawyers to get a steer on how a jury may respond to that witness or how they express their evidence. In effect, this is an emotional response system based on visual machine learning analysis. Again, this is niche and not widespread.

(j) Fraud detection – systems that both listen to staff, for example in an investment bank, and read emails and company messages are trained to indicate if a fraud is about to be committed. ML software learns potential signals and then alerts the risk and compliance team. There are of course some serious ethical issues here.

(k) And, back to a more mundane area, billing analysis – this uses NLP to read the narratives in law firm bills which allow clients to get a better understanding of what has been done; this can be linked to billing rules that can immediately raise a red flag if a bill contains disallowed items, such as billing out multiple junior lawyers for listening to a conference call.

So, there you go. And there are more and new use cases coming to market every day. **30.011**

Also, even in areas where the tech is established, such as M&A due diligence, companies are **30.012** developing new approaches, such as developing Q&A systems that allow a lawyer to simply type in a natural language question about a document stack and get back relatively clear and simple answers.

C. BARRIERS TO THE LEGAL AI USE

Of course, all of this is academic if people don't use the above legal AI tools. To paraphrase an **30.013** old adage about trees and forests, if a legal tech solution is launched but few use it, did it ever really happen...?

The challenge is that, depending on which data you look at, the legal market is worth around **30.014** $700 billion or more per year globally. If we consider the huge unmet need then it is likely potentially a lot larger. For example, a survey in the UK found that many SMEs that have a clear legal need do not use a lawyer for fear of getting stuck with a large bill. Other surveys on access to justice in the US and UK also repeatedly state that the majority of people also have legal needs that go unaddressed due to cost issues.

For the 'small law' segment of the market, simply operating a basic practice management **30.015** system and keeping track of bills electronically would be a big step forward. We cannot expect much change to happen there – even if the market has a need for better methods of delivering services.

Commercial law firms also have a serious challenge. Greater speed and efficiency not only **30.016** delivers additional value to the clients in terms of economic returns; it also allows work to be done that may have been impossible before, and can allow deeper insights into data that benefits the client.

However, in some cases this 'work' by the software could be seen as billable time that lawyers **30.017** could profit from and in some cases not. For example, a law firm that has been asked to review 10,000 documents may need to agree with its client how to charge for using technology.

For other aspects – for example legal research, which likely may not be billable in any form no **30.018** matter how it is done – the faster a firm can access its KM stores and leverage external case law systems, the better.

However, any barrier to new technology is one barrier too many. **30.019**

Then there are the ethicists who worry about the impact of legal AI. Luckily, the use of NLP **30.020** tools for commercial legal needs doesn't raise too many ethical issues. The ethicists are mainly worried about bias and areas such as the use of algorithms to make decisions about things such as with job candidate filtering systems, or when judges use decision systems to make a ruling on whether a prisoner can be let out on remand.

30.021 However, in most cases there are no 'AI' tools to start with, as they rarely are machine learning tools. Mostly they are very 'clunky' manmade algorithms using a variety of very explicit and simple factors to come to their conclusions. These do indeed raise many ethical issues, but they are not in most cases related to the use of AI.

30.022 AI issues certainly arise with machine learning and facial recognition systems that 'spot suspects' and automatically trigger a response from law enforcement, or perhaps building security on private commercial land. These have been known to mis-identify people, causing distress to those labelled by the system. But, again, of deeper worry is the way that an algorithm – pre-made to make decisions – could be used to make decisions about someone and that decision then find its way into some kind of national database. We see such actions in China today with its Social Rewards programme.

D. CONCLUSION

30.023 To conclude, the future of legal AI is in the hands of the clients. The law firms are already very aware of what is possible – at least, the larger firms are. Real change and adoption at scale will come from the law firms driving change by demanding change in how work is done and explicitly refusing to pay for certain types of activity, or refusing to allow a time-based model to cover part of that work.

30.024 Economics is what will drive real change. The tech is here, we just need people to use it.

INDEX